Common dialogs

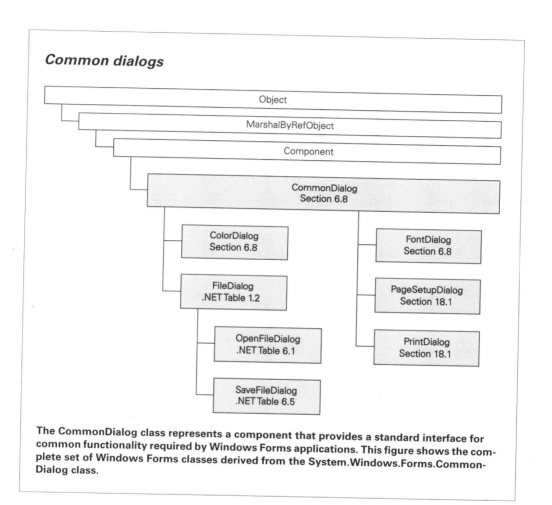

The CommonDialog class represents a component that provides a standard interface for common functionality required by Windows Forms applications. This figure shows the complete set of Windows Forms classes derived from the System.Windows.Forms.CommonDialog class.

Windows Forms
Programming with C#

ERIK BROWN

MANNING

Greenwich
(74° w. long.)

For online information and ordering of this and other Manning books,
go to www.manning.com. The publisher offers discounts on this book
when ordered in quantity. For more information, please contact:

Special Sales Department
Manning Publications Co.
209 Bruce Park Avenue   Fax: (203) 661-9018
Greenwich, CT 06830   email: orders@manning.com

Manning Publications Co.   Copyeditor: Lois Patterson
209 Bruce Park Avenue   Typesetter: Syd Brown
Greenwich, CT 06830   Cover designer: Leslie Haimes

ISBN 1930110-28-6
Printed in the United States of America
2 3 4 5 6 7 8 9 10 – VHG – 06 05 04 03

In memory of Thelma Rose Wilson,
and for her beautiful daughter whom I love

brief contents

Part 1 Hello Windows Forms 1

   1 Getting started with Windows Forms 3

   2 Getting started with Visual Studio .NET 34

Part 2 Basic Windows Forms 67

   3 Menus 69

   4 Status bars 102

   5 Reusable libraries 126

   6 Common file dialogs 161

   7 Drawing and scrolling 194

   8 Dialog boxes 224

   9 Basic controls 263

  10 List controls 314

  11 More controls 353

  12 A .NET assortment 383

  13 Toolbars and tips 410

Part 3 Advanced Windows Forms 437

  14 List views 439

  15 Tree views 485

  16 Multiple document interfaces 525

  17 Data binding 564

  18 Odds and ends .NET 603

contents

brief contents *vii*

contents *ix*

preface *xix*

about this book *xxi*

acknowledgments *xxviii*

about .NET *xxx*

about the cover illustration *xxxiv*

Part 1   Hello Windows Forms 1

1   *Getting started with Windows Forms   3*

   1.1 Programming in C#   4
   Namespaces and classes   6 ✦ Constructors and
   methods   8 ✦ C# types   9 ✦ The entry point   11
   The Application class   11 ✦ Program execution   13

   1.2 Adding controls   13
   Shortcuts and fully qualified names   15
   Fields and properties   16 ✦ The Controls property   18

   1.3 Loading files   18
   Events   20 ✦ The OpenFileDialog class   22
   Bitmap images   24

   1.4 Resizing forms   26
   Desktop layout properties   28 ✦ The Anchor
   property   29 ✦ The Dock property   31

   1.5 Recap   33

2   Getting started with Visual Studio .NET   34

2.1   Programming with Visual Studio .NET   35
Creating a project   36   ✦   Executing a program   39
Viewing the source code   39

2.2   Adding controls   43
The AssemblyInfo file   43   ✦   Renaming a form   46
The Toolbox window   48

2.3   Loading files   54
Event handlers in Visual Studio .NET   54
Exception handling   58

2.4   Resizing forms   61
Assign the Anchor property   63
Assign the MinimumSize property   64

2.5   Recap   65

Part 2   Basic Windows Forms   67

3   Menus   69

3.1   The nature of menus   70
The Menu class   71   ✦   The Menu class hierarchy   71
Derived classes   73

3.2   Menu bars   74
Adding the Main menu   74   ✦   Adding the File menu   77
Adding the dropdown menu   79   ✦   Adding a View menu   83

3.3   Click events   85
Adding handlers via the designer window   85
Adding handlers via the properties window   86

3.4   Popup events and shared handlers   88
Defining a shared handler   89   ✦   Handling Popup events   93

3.5   Context menus   97
Creating a context menu   98   ✦   Adding menu items   100

3.6   Recap   101

4   Status bars   102

4.1   The Control class   103

4.2   The StatusBar class   105
Adding a status bar   106   ✦   Assigning status bar text   109

4.3   Status bar panels   110
Adding panels to a status bar   111   ✦   Assigning panel text   116

4.4 Owner-drawn panels   118
    The DrawItem event   118 ✦ Drawing a panel   121

4.5 Recap   125

5   *Reusable libraries   126*

5.1 C# classes and interfaces   127
    Interfaces   128 ✦ Data collection classes   129

5.2 Class libraries   133
    Creating the class library   134 ✦ Using the command-line
    tools   138 ✦ Creating the PhotoAlbum class   139
    Creating the Photograph class   141

5.3 Interfaces revisited   145
    Supporting the ICollection interface   146
    Supporting the IList interface   146
    Implementing album position operations   148

5.4 Robustness issues   151
    Handling an invalid bitmap   151 ✦ Overriding methods in
    the Object class   154 ✦ Disposing of resources   157
    Associating a file name with an album   159

5.5 Recap   160

6   *Common file dialogs   161*

6.1 Design issues   162
    Changing the menu bar   162 ✦ Adding class variables   165

6.2 Multiple file selection   166
    Adding images to an album   166
    Removing images from an album   169

6.3 Paint events   169
    Drawing the current photograph   170
    Displaying the current position   171

6.4 Context menus revisited   173
    Displaying the next photograph   174
    Displaying the previous photograph   174

6.5 Files and paths   175
    Creating a default album directory   175
    Setting the title bar   179 ✦ Handling the New menu   180

6.6 Save file dialogs   181
    Writing album data   182 ✦ Saving an album as a new file   186
    Saving an existing album   188

6.7 Open file dialogs   189
    Reading album data   190 ✦ Opening an album file   191

6.8 Recap   193

7   *Drawing and scrolling*   194

  7.1   Form class hierarchy   195
      The ScrollableControl class   196   ✦   The Form class   196

  7.2   Image drawing   198
      Deleting the PictureBox control   198   ✦   Handling the
      Image menu   199   ✦   Implementing the Stretch to
      Fit option   202   ✦   Implementing a Scale to Fit option   205
      Repainting when the form is resized   210

  7.3   Automated scrolling   212
      Properties for scrolling   213
      Implementing automated scrolling   213

  7.4   Panels   215
      Adding a panel   217   ✦   Updating the menu handlers   218
      Drawing the status bar panel   219   ✦   Drawing the image   220

  7.5   Recap   222

8   *Dialog boxes*   224

  8.1   Message boxes   225
      The MessageBox.Show method   227   ✦   Creating an
      OK dialog   227   ✦   Creating a YesNo dialog   229
      Creating A YesNoCancel dialog   230

  8.2   The Form.Close method   233
      The relationship between Close and Dispose   233
      Intercepting the Form.Close method   235

  8.3   Modal dialog boxes   237
      Adding captions to photos   238   ✦   Preserving caption values   239
      Creating the CaptionDlg form   240   ✦   Adding properties to the
      CaptionDlg form   247   ✦   Displaying the dialog in the
      MainForm class   249

  8.4   Modeless dialogs   252
      Creating the PixelDlg form   253   ✦   Adding class members to
      PixelDlg   255   ✦   Displaying the modeless PixelDlg form   256
      Updating the PixelDlg form   259
      Updating PixelDlg as the mouse moves   260

  8.5   Recap   262

9   *Basic controls*   263

  9.1   Form inheritance   264
      Creating a base form   265   ✦   Creating a derived form   269

  9.2   Labels and text boxes   271
      Expanding the Photograph class   272

Creating the PhotoEditDlg panel area   277
Creating the multiline text box   281   ✦   Adding PhotoEditDlg
to our main form   285   ✦   Using TextBox controls   287

9.3   Button classes   290
Expanding the PhotoAlbum class   293   ✦   Using the new album
settings   296   ✦   Creating the AlbumEditDlg panel area   298
Using radio buttons   300   ✦   Using check box buttons   304
Adding AlbumEditDlg to our main form   310

9.4   Recap   313

10   List controls   314

10.1   List boxes   315
Creating a list box   315   ✦   Handling selected items   322

10.2   Multiselection list boxes   325
Enabling multiple selection   325   ✦   Handling the Move Up and
Move Down buttons   328   ✦   Handling the Remove button   331

10.3   Combo boxes   333
Creating a combo box   333   ✦   Handling the selected item   336

10.4   Combo box edits   339
Replacing the photographer control   340
Updating the combo box dynamically   341

10.5   Owner-drawn lists   343
Adding a context menu   344   ✦   Setting the item height   346
Drawing the list items   348

10.6   Recap   352

11   More controls   353

11.1   Tab controls   354
The TabControl class   355   ✦   Creating a tab control   356

11.2   Tab pages   359
Creating tab pages dynamically   360
Creating tab pages in Visual Studio   363

11.3   Dates and Times   366
Dates and times   367
Customizing a DateTimePicker control   369

11.4   Calendars   372
Adding a MonthCalendar control   372
Initializing a calendar   374
Handling mouse clicks in a calendar control   376

11.5   Recap   381

12 A .NET assortment 383

 12.1 Keyboard events 384
  Handling the KeyPress event 384
  Handling other keyboard events 386

 12.2 Mouse events 387
  The MouseEventArgs class 388 ✦ Handling mouse events 388

 12.3 Image buttons 393
  Implementing Next and Prev buttons 393 ✦ Drawing bitmaps for
  our buttons 399 ✦ Placing images on our buttons 402

 12.4 Icons 405
  Replacing the icon on a form 406
  Replacing the application icon 408

 12.5 Recap 409

13 Toolbars and tips 410

 13.1 Toolbars 411
  The ToolBar class 411 ✦ Adding a toolbar 412
  The ToolBarButton class 413

 13.2 Image lists 416
  The ImageList class 416 ✦ Creating an image list 417

 13.3 Toolbar buttons 420
  Adding a push button 420 ✦ Adding a dropdown button 424
  Adding a toggle button 426

 13.4 Tool tips 430
  The ToolTip class 431 ✦ Creating tool tips 431

 13.5 Recap 434

Part 3 Advanced Windows Forms 437

14 List views 439

 14.1 The nature of list views 440

 14.2 The ListView class 443
  Creating the MyAlbumExplorer project 443
  Creating a list view 445 ✦ Populating a ListView 448

 14.3 ListView columns 453
  Creating the columns 454 ✦ Populating the columns 456
  Sorting a column 458

 14.4 Selection and editing 464
  Supporting item selection 464 ✦ Supporting label edits 468

14.5 Item activation   472
Handling item activation   473 ✦ Defining new columns   474
Populating the ListView   476 ✦ Sorting a column (again)   477
Updating the properties menu   480 ✦ Updating label
editing   481 ✦ Redisplaying the albums   483

14.6 Recap   483

15   *Tree views*   *485*

15.1 Tree view basics   486

15.2 The TreeView class   486
Creating a tree view   488 ✦ Using the Splitter class   489
Using the TreeNode class   492

15.3 Dynamic tree nodes   497
Assigning index constants   497 ✦ Creating the album nodes   498
Creating the photograph nodes   501

15.4 Node selection   505
Supporting node selection   506 ✦ Revisiting the list view   509

15.5 Fun with tree views   513
Displaying the photograph   514 ✦ Supporting label edits   516
Updating the properties menu   520

15.6 Recap   524

16   *Multiple document interfaces*   *525*

16.1 Interface styles   526
Single document interfaces   526 ✦ Explorer interfaces   526
Multiple document interfaces   527
Support in Windows Forms   529

16.2 MDI forms   530
Creating an MDI container form   531 ✦ Creating an MDI
child form   532 ✦ Adding a new entry point   533

16.3 Merged menus   535
Assigning merge types   535 ✦ Assigning merge order   537
Opening a child form   541

16.4 MDI children   543
Replacing the toolbar   543 ✦ Displaying pixel data   548
Opening an album twice   551 ✦ Updating the title bar   553
Revisiting the activation events   556

16.5 MDI child window management   557
Arranging MDI forms   558 ✦ Creating an MDI child list   561

16.6 Recap   563

17   *Data binding   564*

17.1 Data grids   565
Creating the MyAlbumData project   568
Displaying data in a data grid   569

17.2 Data grid customization   573
Customizing table styles   574   ✦   Customizing column styles   576

17.3 Editable objects   580
The IEditableObject interface   580   ✦   Supporting the
IEditableObject interface   582   ✦   Using editable objects   584

17.4 Simple data binding   586
Altering the MyAlbumData application   587
Performing simple binding   590   ✦   Updating data bound
controls   594   ✦   Displaying the image   599
Saving changes to bound controls   601

17.5 Recap   602

18   *Odds and ends .NET   603*

18.1 Printing   604
Using the print classes   605   ✦   Drawing a print page   607

18.2 Timers   611
Creating a slide show form   612
Implementing the slide show behavior   615

18.3 Drag and drop   618
Initiating drag and drop   620   ✦   Receiving drag and drop   622

18.4 ActiveX controls   625
Creating the About box   626   ✦   Wrapping the web browser
control   629   ✦   Using the web browser control   631

18.5 Recap   635

A   *C# primer   637*

B   *.NET namespaces   674*

C   *Visual index   680*

D   *For more information   690*

bibliography   692
index   695

preface

In early 2001 I began using Microsoft's .NET Framework for a project I was working on with a small startup company. Unfortunately, the winds changed and I found myself with more free time than I would normally hope for. So when Manning Publications asked me if I would contribute to a book on programming with the .NET Framework, I welcomed the idea.

As events unfolded, I found myself with some fairly strong opinions about how such a book should be organized, and offered up a proposal to write a solo book on programming Windows Forms applications. I have always enjoyed the book *Programming Windows 95 with MFC* by Jeff Prosise, so a book about developing Windows-based applications with the .NET Framework seemed like an obvious subject.

The core idea behind my proposal was to build a single application over the course of the book. The application would evolve to introduce each topic, so that by the end of the manuscript readers would have a robust application they had built from scratch. Manning Publications seemed to like the idea as well, and thus I suddenly found myself writing this book.

In approaching the task, I set out to achieve two objectives. The first was to provide ample coverage of most of the classes in the namespace. I have been frustrated by many books that do not provide robust examples for a topic. So I try to provide detailed examples that demonstrate how Windows Forms classes can be used and manipulated in real applications.

A second objective was to present advanced user interface topics such as tree views and drag and drop. While the book spends a good deal of time on fundamental classes, such as menus and buttons, more than a cursory glance is given to some of the more complex controls available for Windows-based programming.

The result of my proposal, these objectives, and a number of late nights is the book you see before you. I take a tutorial approach to application development by creating a common application throughout the book, and provide summaries of relevant classes and other topics that might be of further interest. Hopefully, this approach provides enough detail to demonstrate how Windows-based applications are put together with the .NET Framework, and yet offers additional information that should prove helpful as you develop and expand your own .NET projects.

While the book is not specifically about C# and Visual Studio .NET, the text does attempt to introduce and explain the syntax and usage of C# as well as the features and functionality of Visual Studio .NET. These topics are presented "along-the-way" by introducing relevant concepts and features as they are used in the examples. An overview of C# is also provided in appendix A at the back of the book.

about this book

The .NET Framework contains such a large selection of topics that it is impossible to cover all of them in a single book of any depth. This section introduces the focus of this book, and provides an overview of the contents and conventions used in the text. The end of this section describes the online forum available for any questions or comments on the book, and explains how the source code used in the book can be downloaded from the Internet.

Before we discuss the book specifically, we should introduce the concept of *namespaces*. A namespace defines a group, or *scope*, of related classes, structures, and other types. A namespace is a bit like a family: it defines a group of distinct members with a common name and some shared sense of purpose.

All objects in the .NET Framework, and indeed in C# itself, are organized into namespaces. The System namespace, for example, includes objects related to the framework itself, and most namespaces defined by .NET are nested within the System namespace. The System.Windows namespace defines types and namespaces related to the Windows operating system, while the System.Web namespace defines types and namespaces related to web pages and servers.

This organization into namespaces permits two objects with the same base name to be distinct, much like two people can both share the same first name. For example, the Button class in the System.Web.UI.WebControls namespace represents a button on a web page, while the Button class in the System.Windows.Forms namespace represents a button in an application window. Other namespaces in .NET include the System.IO namespace for file and directory related objects, the System.Data namespace for database-related objects, the System.Drawing namespace for graphical objects, and the System.Security namespace for security objects. An overview of the more commonly used namespaces in .NET is provided in appendix B.

THE WINDOWS FORMS NAMESPACE

In addition to imposing structure on the vast collection of objects supported by the .NET Framework, the namespace concept also provides some direction and focus for writing a book. This book focuses on the System.Windows.Forms namespace, affectionately known as *Windows Forms*. Windows Forms applications are programs that are executed by the Windows operating system, and that employ the user interface features familiar to Windows desktop users everywhere.

The book attempts to provide a somewhat methodical approach to the Windows Forms namespace. Most of the types defined by this namespace are covered in the book. Appendix C provides a class diagram of the Windows Forms namespace, and includes a reference to the location in the book where each class or other type is discussed.

The book contains 18 chapters organized into three parts.

PART 1: HELLO WINDOWS FORMS

The first part of the book introduces fundamental concepts behind C# in general and Windows Forms specifically. Chapter 1 creates the application shown in figure 1 using a text editor. We discuss how a Windows Forms application is executed by the .NET Framework, and how a Windows Forms program is structured in C#.

In chapter 2 we begin using Visual Studio .NET, the graphical development environment from Microsoft for creating applications in the .NET Framework. This chapter recreates the application constructed manually in chapter 1. We will call this application MyPhotos.

Figure 1
The MyPhotos application as it appears in part 1.

PART 2: BASIC WINDOWS FORMS

In part 2 we begin a systematic approach to the classes in the Windows Forms namespace. This part continues the development of our MyPhotos application, shown in figure 2 as it appears in chapter 13. As you can see, part 2 covers the core user interface components required to build Windows Forms applications, including menus, status bars, dialog windows, text boxes, and combo boxes.

The MyPhotos application will display the contents of a photo album consisting of one or more image files, or photographs. The application stores each photo album in a file, and permits the user to view the images one at a time and edit the properties of both albums and photographs.

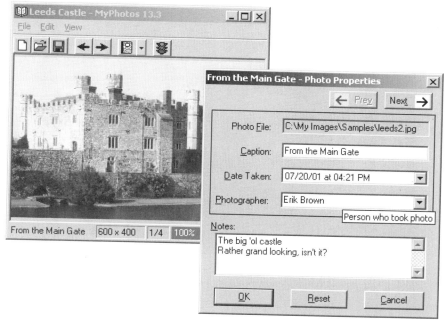

Figure 2 The MyPhotos application from chapter 13. This figure shows the main window along with a dialog box for editing the properties of a specific photograph.

PART 3: ADVANCED WINDOWS FORMS

More advanced topics such as list views and drag and drop are covered in part 3 of the book. Part 3 builds a few different applications using the photo album concept, including an application similar to Windows Explorer for browsing photo albums, and a data-driven application that shows how to bind the contents of Windows Forms controls to values taken from a data source.

Figure 3 shows the main window for our MyPhotos application as it appears in chapter 18. The application is converted into a multiple document interface that can display multiple albums. A number of additional features are added here as well, such as dragging photos between albums and displaying the book's web site from within the application.

Figure 3   The MyPhotos application from chapter 18. A parent window now exists within which the MyPhotos window from part 2 of the book is displayed.

WHO SHOULD READ THIS BOOK?

Like any author, I would like everyone to read this book. The more the merrier! In the interest of full disclosure, however, I wrote *Windows Forms Programming with C#* with three kinds of people in mind:

- Windows programmers interested in developing desktop applications with .NET.
- Developers familiar with .NET or C# interested in learning more about Windows Forms classes and programming.
- C++ programmers with little or no experience creating Windows applications.

Once again, I should point out that this book examines one portion of the .NET Framework, namely the classes contained in the System.Windows.Forms namespace. The book also provides a great deal of information about C# and Visual Studio .NET, and in particular it will guide you through the steps necessary to build each sample application using Visual Studio .NET. For additional information, appendix D provides a list of additional resources for C# and .NET, and the bibliography at the back of the book references a number of other books that cover various aspects of C# and the .NET Framework.

For a broad approach to the .NET Framework in general, check out *Microsoft .NET for Programmers* by Fergal Grimes, also available from Manning Publications.

CONVENTIONS

The following typographical conventions appear throughout the book:

- Technical terms are introduced in *italics*.
- Code examples and fragments appear in a `fixed-width` font.
- Namespaces and types, as well as members of these types, also appear in a `fixed-width` font.
- Sections of code that are of special significance appear in a **`bold fixed-width`** font. Typically, these sections highlight changes made to code when compared with a previous example.
- Many sections of code have numbered annotations which appear in the right margin. These numbered annotations are then discussed more fully in a subsequent numbered list following the code.

In addition, a number of graphical conventions are used to present the information in the text. Starting in chapter 2, all modifications made to example applications are illustrated with an Action-Result table showing step-by-step instructions for making the change in Visual Studio .NET. An example of this is shown here.

	DESCRIPTION OF THE TASK DESCRIBED BY THIS TABLE	
	Action	**Result**
1	Description of the action to perform.	Description of the result of this action. This is a textual description, a graphic, or the resulting code.
2	The second action to perform. **How-to** a. Detailed steps required to perform the described action. b. More steps if necessary.	The second result. **Note:** A comment about or explanation of the result.

In addition to these tables, a number of classes and other types found in .NET are summarized using a *.NET Table*. These tables provide an overview of a .NET Framework class or other type discussed in a nearby section, and serve as a quick reference when referring back to these pages at a later time. Full details on these and any other members of the .NET Framework are available in the online documentation. For example, in Visual Studio .NET, bring up the Index window and enter the name of the class or member in which you are interested.

Of course, most of these .NET Tables describe members of the Windows Forms namespace. An example of this format is shown here as .NET Table 1 using the `PictureBox` class.

.NET Table 1 PictureBox class

The `PictureBox` class represents a control that can display an image. Scroll bars are not supported when the image is larger that the client area, so care must be taken to ensure that the image appears properly within the control. This class is part of the `System.Windows.Forms` namespace, and inherits from the `Control` class. See .NET Table 4.1 on page 104 for more information on the `Control` class.

Public Properties	BorderStyle	Gets or sets the style of border to display for the control.
	Image	Gets or sets the image to display in the picture box.
	SizeMode	Gets or sets the `PictureBoxSizeMode` enumeration value indicating how the image is displayed. The default is `Normal`.
Public Events	SizeModeChanged	Occurs when the value of the `SizeMode` property changes.

Note the following features of these tables:

- An initial paragraph defines the purpose of the class, the namespace that contains the class, and the base class. If the namespace containing the base class is not indicated, then it can be found in the same namespace containing the described class. If the base class is not indicated, then the class is derived from the `System.Object` class.

- A table shows the public members of the class, namely the properties, methods, and events specific to this class.[1] The members inherited from base classes are not shown in these tables. In .NET Table 1, there are four members shown, namely three properties, no methods, and one event.

A final convention in the book is the use of special paragraphs to highlight topics for further exploration of Windows Forms and the .NET Framework. These are either TRY IT! sections or More .NET sections.

TRY IT! These paragraphs provide suggestions or discussions of further changes that can be made to the sample application using the material discussed in the prior sections. TRY IT! paragraphs provide an opportunity to further your understanding of the related topic. The code for these sections is not provided in the book, but is available on the book's web site.

The TRY IT! paragraphs appear throughout the text, and occasionally discuss class members that were not directly used in the sample code. The More .NET paragraphs,

---

[1] We define exactly what these terms mean in part 1 of the book.

an example of which follows, also appear throughout the text, although they more often occur at the end of a chapter.

More .NET   These paragraphs provide additional details about the .NET Framework or sources of additional information accessible from the Internet. The URL addresses shown in these paragraphs were valid as of January 1, 2002.

SOURCE CODE DOWNLOADS

All source code for the programs presented in *Windows Forms Programing with C#* is available to purchasers of the book from the Manning web site. Visit the site at www.manning.com/eebrown for instructions on downloading this source code.

AUTHOR ONLINE

Free access to a private Internet forum, Author Online, is included with the purchase of this book. Visit the web site for detailed rules about the forum, to subscribe to and access the forum, to retrieve the code for each chapter and section, and to view updates and corrections to the material in the book. Make comments, good or bad, about the book; ask technical questions, and receive help from the author and other Windows Forms programmers. The forum is available at the book's web site at www.manning.com/eebrown.

Manning's commitment to readers is to provide a venue where a meaningful dialog among individual readers and among readers and the author can take place. It is not a commitment to any specific amount of participation on the part of the author, whose contribution remains voluntary (and unpaid).

Erik can be contacted directly at eebrown@eebrown.com or through his web site at www.eebrown.com.

acknowledgments

It never ceases to amaze me how the tangled threads of our lives come together to produce a tangible result, in this case the book you are reading. While the front of this book bears my name, a number of people knowingly or unknowingly contributed to its conception and development.

Special thanks go to my family: to my wife Bridgett for her patience and love; to Katie and Sydney for their regular office visits and unconditional acceptance; and to Bianca, my faithful companion, who curls up on the other chair in my office on a daily basis.

I am also grateful for my parents, David and Janet, and teachers and others who have supported me throughout my life. Special recognition goes to Steve Cox and David Cobb, who first interested me in computer programming so long ago.

Thanks also go to my many friends who provided support and encouragement in ways that only friends can do, most notably Jean Siegel, Janet Heffernan, Tony Mason, and Marc Zapf. I would also thank my soccer team, the Haymarket Outer Limits, for putting up with numerous impromptu practices while I was working on the manuscript, and yet still producing a fun and productive season.

I am also indebted to the many reviewers from all corners of the globe who dedicated their time and energy to reading early versions of various chapters. This book would not be the same without their assistance and efforts. This includes Marc Zapf for his technical review of the final manuscript; Javier Jarava for his exhaustive reviews of the code and text in each chapter; Josh Mitts for his thoughtful and encouraging comments; Andreas Häber for finding various important technical points (I apologize, Andreas, that I never did cover the PropertyGrid control); Craig Fullerton for his meticulous review of the first half of the book; Mark Boulter for his detailed comments on the original chapters; Sam Raisanen for his thorough review of chapters 1, 3, and 16; and others who provided insightful comments and criticisms, including Dharmesh Chauhan, Chris Muench, Tomas Restrepo, and Vijay Upadya.

I would also like to recognize the reviewers of my original outline, namely Steve Binney, Mark Boulter, Drew Marsh, Josh Mitts, and Kunle Odutola. Their suggestions were critical to starting the book on the right note and producing the final manuscript.

Finally, I would like to acknowledge the many people I worked with from and through Manning Publications whom I have never met and yet provided critical support throughout the writing process. This especially includes Susan Capparelle for seeing some merit in my original proposal; Marjan Bace for his perceptive comments and suggestions over numerous phone discussions; Ted Kennedy for coordinating all the reviewers and their feedback; Syd Brown for reformatting my tables so many times and for the final typesetting of the book itself; Leslie Haimes for redesigning the cover after I had approved an earlier version; Mary Piergies for overseeing the production staff and answering my many questions; Rebecca Pepper and Lianna Wlasiuk for encouraging me to change numerous structural elements of the book; Lois Patterson for her detailed wordsmithing of the final manuscript; and finally Lee Fitzpatrick for signing my royalty advance checks.

AUTHOR ONLINE

about .NET

The history of .NET is both long and brief. While the .NET Framework is based on programming languages and development environments that came years before, it is relatively new and its success in the marketplace is yet to be proven. This section provides an abbreviated history of the C# programming language, pronounced *see-sharp*, and the .NET Windows Forms functionality.

The C programming language was originally developed in the early 1970s at Bell Telephone Laboratories in conjunction with the UNIX operating system. It evolved from a previous language called "B" which itself derived from a language called "BPCL." The language became popular throughout the 1970s and was eventually standardized by the American National Standards Institute (ANSI) in the mid-1980s. One of the more definitive books on C, first published in 1978, was and still is *The C Programming Language* by Brian W. Kernighan and Dennis M. Ritchie.

The C++ language was designed by Bjarne Stroustrup, who originally published his well-known book *The C++ Programming Language* in 1986. This language was also standardized by ANSI and other organizations, and has grown in popularity to its rather ubiquitous use today.

The C language was used with the Windows operating system early on, beginning with Windows 1.0 in the mid 1980s. One of Microsoft's first attempts at an interactive development environment (IDE) occurred around 1990 with Microsoft C 1.0. This environment grew to include C++ and eventually became the basis for Visual C++ in the mid 1990's and later Visual Studio 6.0 supporting C++, Visual Basic, and a nonstandard variant of Java. The Windows operating system and Win32 API formed the foundation on which these products were built and extended.

Also worth mentioning are two competitive products for Microsoft Visual Studio, namely Borland C++Builder and Borland Delphi. Both products are highly successful visual development tools and have likely influenced the design and development of the .NET Framework. In fact, the Chief C# Language Architect at Microsoft, Anders Hejlsberg, was one of the original designers of Borland Delphi.

Other products swirled through this history as well: dynamic link libraries, the advent of OLE and COM, database technologies such as ODBC and ADO, the growth of the Internet, and the redesign of the DOS-based Windows into Windows NT and Windows XP.

CASTING THE .NET

Against this backdrop of technologies and products, the Internet has been redefining the way we as programmers think about user interfaces and application development. With the success of the Internet and companies such as Netscape and Amazon.com, a product or interface may now appear in a web browser rather than a more traditional Windows application. The Java programming language has had much success in UNIX and web server environments, and is the language of choice for many large-scale web applications at present.

Perhaps in response to these changes, or perhaps because it became clear that the line between a user's desktop and the Internet was starting to blur, Microsoft set out to revolutionize the way we think about and develop applications. The result of their work is the .NET Framework and the C# programming language.[2]

The easiest way to understand C# might be to imagine someone writing down all the annoying aspects of C++ and then designing a language to do away with each item on this list. In C++, for example, dealing with pointers can be painful; a number of coding errors are not caught by the compiler (such as if (x = 5)); manipulating strings can be difficult; and there is no good way to safely "downcast" an object to a derived type. The predecessors of C and C++, the B and BPCL languages, did not define a formal type system, which may well account for the free-wheeling nature of integers, pointers, and characters in these languages.

The C# language was redesigned from the ground up with the idea of retaining the flexibility of C and C++ while formalizing the type system and language syntax. Many common runtime errors in C++ are compiler errors in C#. Other distinct features include a built-in string type, lack of global variables, and integration of critical system and application errors into a common exception model. Appendix A of this book provides an overview of the syntax, keywords, and features of the C# language.

While not strictly required from a design perspective, the C# language and .NET Framework will likely remain tightly intertwined for some time. The .NET Framework is a programming interface and execution environment for Windows operating systems, and large parts of the framework itself were written in C#.

The .NET Framework includes almost all of Microsoft's development technologies and environments that have evolved over time, from COM to XML and ASP to Visual Studio. These technologies are recreated and reinvented under a single umbrella. While backward compatibility has not been totally lost, the .NET Framework redefines the classes and methods for these technologies and the products that use them. In particular,

---

[2] The Visual Basic language was also redesigned, and numerous Microsoft products have been affected. Visit the site www.microsoft.com/net for detailed information about the history and scope of .NET.

the framework includes new support for Windows application development, web site access and deployment, remote program communication, database interaction, security, local and remote installation, and other technologies as well.

My goal is not to enumerate all of the technologies to be found in .NET, nor try to convince you of its advantages or disadvantages. There are a number books and articles that provide this information, and you would probably not be reading this introduction if you were not aware of at least some of them. My point is only to indicate that Microsoft has taken a fresh approach to its many technologies and products, and endeavored to integrate these various initiatives under a single offering called the .NET Framework.

WINDOWS FORMS OVERVIEW

As we mentioned in the *About this book* section, all objects in the .NET Framework, and indeed in C# itself, are organized into namespaces. Appendix B provides an overview of the more commonly-used namespaces defined by the .NET Framework.

This book focuses on the `System.Windows.Forms` namespace used to build Windows-based applications. This section provides a summary of the classes defined by this namespace. A graphical index of the Windows Forms namespace in given in appendix C.

Before we discuss specific classes, there are three terms that are critical to understanding the .NET Framework in general and the Windows Forms namespace specifically, namely components, containers, and controls. The book covers these terms in detail, so this section will provide only a brief introduction and a few examples.

A *component* is an object that permits sharing between applications. The `Component` class encapsulates this notion, and is the basis for most of the members of the Windows Forms namespace. Also of note is the `IComponent` interface, which defines the members supported by all components. We discuss interfaces in chapter 5, and the `Component` class in chapter 3.

A *container* is an object that can hold zero or more components. A container is simply a grouping mechanism, and ensures that sets of components are encapsulated and manipulated in similar ways. Containers are used throughout the Windows Forms namespace whenever a group of objects is required. The `Container` class encapsulates the container concept, with the `IContainer` interface defining the members required by all containers.

A *control* is a component with a visual aspect. In the Windows Forms namespace, a control is a component that presents a graphical interface on the Windows desktop. The Windows Forms `Control` class, discussed in chapter 4, is the basis for all Windows Forms controls. It is worth noting that the `System.Web.UI` namespace defines a `Control` class as well to represent graphical objects that appear on web pages.

Generally speaking, any visual interface you see on the Windows desktop is a control, and any behind-the-scenes object is a component. For example, a status bar panel is represented by the `StatusBarPanel` class, which is a component. The actual status bar you see in an interface is represented by the `StatusBar` class, which is a control. Status bars are the subject of chapter 4.

Controls may also be containers in that they may contain a set of controls or components. The `StatusBar` class is a container for zero or more `StatusBarPanel` components. One of the more important container controls is the `Form` class, which represents an application window for display on the Windows desktop. The `Form` class is introduced in chapter 1 and discussed throughout the book, most notably in chapter 7, "Drawing and scrolling," chapter 8, "Dialog boxes," and chapter 16, "Multiple document interfaces."

Most visual elements of graphical interfaces such as buttons, text boxes, trees, and dialog boxes are all represented by control classes. The one exception is menus, which are the subject of chapter 3 and revisited again in chapter 16. Menu objects are all components, and are treated in a special manner by the `Form` class itself.

The controls in the Windows Forms namespace are discussed throughout the book. Many of the more common controls appear in chapter 9, "Basic controls," chapter 10, "List controls," chapter 11, "More controls," and chapter 13, "Tool bars and tips." Advanced controls such as list views, tree views, and data grids are covered in part 3 of the book.

In addition to the controls, containers, and components found in the Windows Forms namespace, there are a number of other objects provided to support the development of Windows-based applications. Some of these are presented in chapter 12, "A .NET assortment," and chapter 18, "Odds and ends .NET." Of specific importance is the concept of data binding, covered in chapter 17.

A book on creating Windows Forms programs would be remiss if it did not also discuss the creation of reusable libraries. Chapter 5 discusses this concept by building a photo album library that is then reused throughout the remainder of the book. In particular, chapter 6, "Common dialogs," makes use of this library.

about the cover illustration

The figure on the cover of Windows Forms Programming with C# is a "Pescador del Cabo de buena Esperanza," a fisherman from the Cape of Good Hope in Africa. This fisherman is especially appropriate here, since the author, Erik Brown, worked with the U.S. Peace Corps in Botswana, which is not too far from the Cape of Good Hope. The illustration is taken from a Spanish compendium of regional dress customs first published in Madrid in 1799. The book's title page states:

> *Coleccion general de los Trages que usan actualmente todas las Nacionas del Mundo desubierto, dibujados y grabados con la mayor exactitud por R.M.V.A.R. Obra muy util y en special para los que tienen la del viajero universal*

which we translate, as literally as possible, thus:

> *General collection of costumes currently used in the nations of the known world, designed and printed with great exactitude by R.M.V.A.R. This work is very useful especially for those who hold themselves to be universal travelers.*

Although nothing is known of the designers, engravers, and workers who colored this illustration by hand, the "exactitude" of their execution is evident in this drawing. The "Pescador del Cabo de buena Esperanza" is of course just one of many figures in this colorful collection. Their diversity speaks vividly of the uniqueness and individuality of the world's towns and regions just 200 years ago. This was a time when the dress codes of two towns, separated by a few dozen miles, identified people uniquely as belonging to one or the other. The collection brings to life a sense of isolation and distance of that period and of every other historic period except our own hyperkinetic present.

Dress codes have changed since then and the diversity by region, so rich at the time, has faded away. It is now often hard to tell the inhabitant of one continent from another. Perhaps, trying to view it optimistically, we have traded a cultural and visual richness for a more varied personal life. Or a more varied and interesting intellectual and technical life.

We at Manning celebrate the inventiveness, the initiative, and the fun of the computer business with book covers based on the colorful tapestry of regional life of two centuries ago brought back to life by the pictures from this collection.

Hello Windows Forms

It is common practice to write some sort of "Hello" program at the beginning of a book. This book is no different, and we begin our discussion on Windows Forms with the most basic of forms: an empty window. While this book is all about Windows Forms, Microsoft's new interactive development environment Visual Studio .NET is an important part of creating .NET applications. To introduce both Windows Forms and Visual Studio .NET, we will create the same program in two subsequent chapters.

Chapter 1 is titled "Getting started with Windows Forms." This chapter introduces Windows Forms programming and covers some fundamentals of the C# language and the .NET Framework. Here we use the C# command-line compiler in order to focus on a sample program and not get distracted by the graphical environment. While the remainder of the book will use Visual Studio .NET for the examples, enough detail about the command-line tools is provided in case you want to follow along using an alternate editor.

Chapter 2 covers "Getting started with Visual Studio .NET." Here we rebuild the example from Chapter 1 within the Visual Studio .NET interactive development environment. This will give us a chance to cover additional subtleties of .NET and C#, and give you the reader a second go at understanding any code you missed in chapter 1.

Part 2 of this book will extend the program built in chapter 2 as it continues our investigation of the new world order for Windows application development.

C H A P T E R   1

Getting started with Windows Forms

1.1   Programming in C# 4
1.2   Adding controls 13
1.3   Loading files 18
1.4   Resizing forms 26
1.5   Recap 33

With the introduction behind us, we can get down to business. We will start with a basic application of the "Hello World" variety, adding some functionality to introduce some key features and concepts. We will take a quick look at the following aspects of Windows Forms programming:

- The Form class: creating a blank form.

- Program execution: how the Microsoft .NET Framework executes a program.

- Controls: how each control is a distinct class, and how controls are added to a form.

- C# classes: different kinds of class members, and how to use them in our program.

- Files: opening an image file in C#.

- Events: using C# events to process user actions.

As you likely know, part of the .NET experience is a new interactive development environment called Visual Studio .NET. Within this environment, a set of command-

3

line programs does the real work of compiling and linking programs. In this chapter, we will use the same command-line tools employed by Visual Studio .NET internally. This will allow us to focus on C# and Windows Forms concepts, and not discuss Visual Studio .NET until the next chapter.

If you have prior experience with Windows programming, you will see many similarities in the names of the .NET controls. This chapter will show some of these names, and introduce some new terms and features as well. If you are new to Windows programming, you'll find this chapter a good foundation for the remainder of the book.

This chapter is a bit of a wild ride through .NET, so don't worry too much about the details here. The concepts and topics in this chapter should become clearer as we progress through the book.

This chapter assumes you have successfully installed the Microsoft .NET Framework SDK on your computer.

1.1   *Programming in C#*

Let's create a blank form in C# to see how a program compiles and runs in the .NET Framework. Such a form is shown in figure 1.1. This is the most basic of Windows applications that can be created in .NET. You may be tempted to skip this section, but don't: the remainder of this chapter builds on this most basic of forms, so you'll want to have it ready.

Figure 1.1
Our first Windows Forms program produces this skeleton form. We'll build on this program throughout the rest of this chapter.

Crank up your favorite editor and type in the code shown in listing 1.1. If you're not sure which editor to use, type this code into Notepad here and throughout the chapter. Save this file as "MyForm.cs" in a convenient directory. Note that "cs" is the standard extension used for C# files.

Listing 1.1 Your first form

```
[assembly: System.Reflection.AssemblyVersion("1.1")]
namespace MyNamespace
{
  public class MyForm : System.Windows.Forms.Form
  {
    public MyForm()
    {
      this.Text = "Hello Form";
    }

    public static void Main()
    {
      System.Windows.Forms.Application.Run(new MyForm());
    }
  }
}
```

To compile this program, we will use the C# compiler, called csc, for C sharp compiler. You will need a command prompt with the PATH environment set to access the .NET Framework programs and libraries. You can define these settings by hand or via a batch program, or use the shortcut Microsoft provides to do this for you. We will employ the shortcut, which is available via the Start menu.

To reach this shortcut, click the Start menu, then Programs, then Microsoft Visual Studio .NET, then Visual Studio .NET Tools, then Visual Studio .NET Command Prompt. This item opens a command window and executes a batch file that sets the appropriate environment variables. With the default installation directories, this menu item executes the following command:

```
cmd /k "C:\Program Files\Microsoft Visual Studio .NET\
        Common7\Tools\vsvars32.bat"
```

Open a Visual Studio .NET command prompt as previously described and compile the program using the following command.

```
> csc MyForm.cs /reference:System.dll
/reference:System.Windows.Forms.dll
```

The /reference switch specifies a library containing additional functionality for the program. In .NET, libraries as well as programs are referred to as *assemblies*. For our application, we reference the System assembly (System.dll) and the Windows Forms assembly (System.Windows.Forms.dll).[1]

---

[1] Strictly speaking, the csc compiler automatically references all major System DLLs. As a result, the /reference switches here are not really needed. We use them here and throughout the chapter to be explicit about the libraries required by our program.

Once this command completes, you should see a MyForm.exe file in your directory. Run the program using the `myform` command to see the result. You should see a window similar to figure 1.1.

```
> myform²
```

While our program is not very useful yet, it only took us a few lines of code to create a fully functional Windows application. Most of the work is done internally by the .NET Framework and Windows. This includes drawing the outer portion of the window such as the title bar and frame; handling the taskbar and standard windows interactions such as minimize, maximize, move, resize, and close; and redrawing the window when the application is behind, in front of, or obscured by other windows.

Stand up, stretch, stifle a yawn, and go tell your neighbor that you just wrote your first .NET Windows Forms application.

We will add bells and whistles to this application, of course. But before we do, our fully functional program warrants some discussion. Let's break down the parts of our code to examine how the .NET Framework executes our program.

The first line of the program simply sets the version number for the program to 1.1, matching the section number of the book.

```
[assembly: System.Reflection.AssemblyVersion("1.1")]
```

You can verify this by right-clicking the myform.exe file, selecting the Properties item, and then clicking the Version tab. We'll look at version numbers more closely in chapter 2, so we will not discuss this line any further at this point.

1.1.1   Namespaces and classes

The introduction discussed the use of *namespaces* in .NET to define a scope for a set of classes and other types. In our program we use the `namespace` keyword to declare a new namespace called `MyNameSpace`.

```
namespace MyNamespace
{
    . . .
}
```

A namespace contains one or more types, such as the class `MyForm` in our program. A *class* defines a new data abstraction, in that it defines a class name and a collection of members for representing and operating on the class. A class is just one of the types possible in a namespace. We will discuss additional types further along in the book, or you can visit appendix A for a complete listing of the possible types.

Classes in C# support *single inheritance*, in that each class inherits from at most one other class. As a quick description of inheritance, suppose you wanted to design

---

² When you run this program, you will note that the console waits for the application to exit. This is because the compiler creates a console application by default. We will see how to create a Windows-based application using the `/target` switch in chapter 5.

CHAPTER 1   GETTING STARTED WITH WINDOWS FORMS

a program to track the traffic patterns in a city. You might want to differentiate between cars, trucks, delivery vehicles, buses, and other types of vehicles. It would be beneficial to define a core set of functions that all types of vehicles would employ, and then define additional functions for each type of vehicle as required. With inheritance, a Vehicle class could define this base functionality, and subsequent classes, called *derived classes*, would define additional functions for each vehicle type. For example, you might have the following:

```
namespace Traffic
{
  // The base Vehicle class
  class Vehicle
  {
    . . .
  }

  // The Car class is derived from the Vehicle class
  class Car : Vehicle
  {
    . . .
  }

  // The Bus class is derived from the Vehicle class
  class Bus : Vehicle
  {
    . . .
  }
}
```

Back to our program, we define a class called MyForm that inherits from the Form class, which is found in the System.Windows.Forms namespace. The period notation is used to separate namespaces and classes, so that the complete, or *fully qualified*, name for the class is System.Windows.Forms.Form. We will see how to abbreviate this name later in the chapter.

```
namespace MyNamespace
{
  public class MyForm : System.Windows.Forms.Form
  {
    . . .
  }
}
```

The Form class is the cornerstone of Windows-based applications in .NET. It represents any type of window in an application, from dialog boxes to MDI (Multiple Document Interface) client windows. The Form class provides the ability to display, place controls within, and interact with an application window. We will discuss this class in detail in chapter 7, and dialog boxes and MDI applications in chapters 8 and 16, respectively. For now, simply understand that the Form class represents the application's main window.

Classes in .NET contain one or more *members* that define the behavior and features of the class. We will discuss the members of our `MyForm` class next. Class members may be constants, fields, methods, properties, events, indexers, operators, constructors, and nested type declarations. Each of these members is discussed in subsequent chapters. For now, let's take a quick look at the two members employed by our program.

1.1.2 Constructors and methods

Take another look at the declaration of our `MyForm` class. Note how two members of this class are defined, namely the `MyForm` constructor and the `Main` method.

Both members are declared as `public`, as is the class `MyForm`. C# provides the accessibility levels `public`, `protected`, and `private` that C++ programmers should be familiar with. These are discussed in appendix A, as are the additional access levels provided by C#, namely `internal` and `protected internal`.

```
public class MyForm : System.Windows.Forms.Form
{
  public MyForm()
  {
    this.Text = "Hello Form";
  }

  public static void Main()
  {
    System.Windows.Forms.Application.Run(new MyForm());
  }
}
```

The first member is called a *constructor*, and works much like a constructor in C++. This is an *instance constructor* since it initializes new instances of the `MyForm` class. An instance constructor with no parameters, such as our constructor here, is called the *default constructor*. C# also supports *static constructors* to initialize the class itself. Appendix A contains more information on both kinds of constructors.

In the constructor for our `MyForm` class, a single statement sets the `Text` property of the form to the string `"Hello Form"`. We will discuss exactly what a *property* is shortly. It is enough for now to know that this line simply places the string `Hello Form` on the title bar of the application window. As in C++, the `this` keyword refers to the current object.

The second member of our class is a *method*. A method is a member that performs an operation for the class. An *instance method* operates on a class instance, while a *static method* operates on the type itself. Methods in C# work much like their C++ counterparts.

An instance constructor for a class is invoked when an object of that class is first created. Typically, objects of any type are initialized using the `new` keyword, which we discuss next. A method must be invoked explicitly within a program. The `Main` method used here is the *entry point* for our program and is invoked by the .NET Framework itself, a topic we will return to in a moment.

1.1.3   C# types

The new keyword is used to initialize any type in C#. This includes classes and structures as well as simple types such as int and enumerations. In fact, it is a compiler error to use an object before it has been initialized. Any instance constructor provided for a given type, in our code the Main constructor, is invoked during initialization. In our case, we initialize the MyForm class with the following code.

```
public static void Main()
{
    System.Windows.Forms.Application.Run(new MyForm());
}
```

There are two classifications of types in C#, with different initialization behavior for each. *Value types* contain the actual data for the type. These include built-in types such as int, char, and bool as well as all structures created with the struct keyword. Value types are typically small or short-lived, making it useful to have their value stored in place, either on the stack or within the object containing them, such as an integer declared as a member of a class.

Reference types contain a reference to the actual data for the type. This is a bit like a pointer in C++, except that the reference is implicit in C#. All classes in C# are reference types, as are the built-in object and string types. The compiler automatically converts value types into reference types as required, using a process called *boxing*. We will discuss boxing later in the book.

As an example, consider the following code:

```
int x = new int();
x = 54;
string s = new string();
s = "Fifty-Four";
```

As you might guess, this can be abbreviated as:

```
int x = 54;
string s = "Fifty-Four";
```

The storage allocated as a result of this code is illustrated in figure 1.2. The variable x is a value type and contains the integer 54. The variable s is a reference type, so that the string "Fifty-Four" exists somewhere else in memory. The variable s simply contains a reference to this memory.

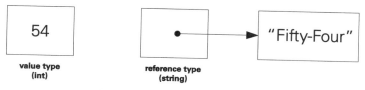

value type
(int)

reference type
(string)

Figure 1.2   This graphic illustrates the two kinds of types in C#. The integer type, a value type, contains the value 54, while the string type, a reference type, refers to the value "Fifty-Four."

The area of memory reserved for reference data is called the *heap*. Memory allocated on the heap, such as the string in figure 1.2, is reclaimed using *garbage collection*. The *garbage collector*, as it is called, automatically identifies blocks of memory that are no longer accessible and reclaims it when the program has extra processing time or requires more memory. Rather than the constant memory management required by C++ programmers using the new and delete keywords, garbage collection manages memory behind the scenes so you can concentrate on writing your program. Of course, from a performance perspective, you have to pay the piper sooner or later, but delaying such reclamation may allow an idle CPU cycle or two to be discovered and provide better overall performance.

No need to get knee-deep in this topic. For our purposes, garbage collection means no more pointers lying around leaking memory and resources. Of course, there are other ways to mismanage your memory and resources, and garbage collection creates its own set of problems, but more on that as we go along.

We know from this discussion that classes are reference types, and an instance of a class cannot be used until it is assigned to an actual object using the new keyword or an existing object. In the case where one reference type is assigned to an existing reference type, both objects refer, or point, to the same block of data on the heap, and both variables must be destroyed before the object can be reclaimed by the garbage collector.

Back in our application, the MyForm class is a reference type, so we create a MyForm object using the new keyword.

TRY IT!   Go ahead, break your code. Change your Main function to the following:

```
public static void Main()
{
  MyForm badForm;
  System.Windows.Forms.Application.Run(badForm);
}
```

If you compile this change, you should receive an error as follows:

Error   Use of unassigned local variable 'badForm.'

We could have implemented our Main function with a variable to represent the form.

```
public static void Main()
{
  MyForm goodForm = new MyForm();
  System.Windows.Forms.Application.Run(goodForm);
}
```

However, this variable is not needed, so we wrote the Main function without it.

```
public static void Main()
{
  System.Windows.Forms.Application.Run(new MyForm());
}
```

Let's talk about the Main function next.

1.1.4   The entry point

Every C# program starts execution in a `Main` function, just like it does in C, C++, and Java (although in C# it must begin with a capital M). This function is the starting point, or *entry point*, for our application. After the Windows operating system creates a new process, initializes various internal data structures, and loads the executable program into memory, our program is invoked by calling this entry point, optionally providing the command-line arguments specified by the user.

The entry point in C# is similar to the `main` function found in C and C++, except that in C# it must be a static member of a class. The `Main` function can be `void` or return an `int`, and it can optionally receive the command-line parameters as an array of strings. The four possible forms for this function are shown below.

```
public static void Main();
public static int Main();
public static void Main(string[] args);
public static int Main(string[] args);
```

The expression `string[]` specifies an array of `string` objects. Arrays in C# are zero-based, so the array `args` shown here has `string` values `args[0]`, `args[1]`, and so forth. Unlike C++, the first element in the array here, namely `args[0]`, is the first parameter for the program, and not the name of the executable.

The C# compiler uses the first instance of `Main` it locates as the entry point for the program. In our case there is only one. If there are multiple `Main` functions, the `/main` switch can be used to specify which instance should be used.

```
public static void Main()
{
    System.Windows.Forms.Application.Run(new MyForm());
}
```

Our `Main` function is `void` and accepts no arguments. It contains a single statement, which we will discuss next.

1.1.5   The Application class

The `Application` class is used to manage applications, threads, and Windows messages. A summary of this class for future reference appears in .NET Table 1.1. This class is commonly used to display the initial form in an application and to wait for user actions to occur within this form, which is exactly how we use this class here.

```
public static void Main()
{
    System.Windows.Forms.Application.Run(new MyForm());
}
```

The `Run` method begins a message loop in the current thread to wait for operating system messages. If a `Form` object is provided, as is done in our program, then this form is displayed on the desktop and starts interacting with the user.

The `Application` class is an object that encapsulates the static members necessary to manage and process forms, threads, and Windows messages on behalf of a program. This class is *sealed*, meaning that the class cannot be inherited. The `Application` class is part of the `System.Windows.Forms` namespace. You cannot create an instance of this class, as no accessible instance constructor is provided

Public Static Properties	CommonAppDataRegistry	Gets the `RegistryKey` for application data shared among all users.
	CurrentCulture	Gets or sets the locale (for internationalization) for the current thread.
	ProductName	Gets the product name associated with the application.
	ProductVersion	Gets the product version associated with the application.
	StartupPath	Gets the path for the executable file that started the application.
	UserAppDataRegistry	Gets the `RegistryKey` for application data specific to the current user.
Public Static Methods	AddMessageFilter	Installs an `IMessageFilter` interface to monitor routing of Windows messages on the current thread. Such a monitor can be used to intercept incoming messages to a form.
	DoEvents	Processes any Windows messages currently in the message queue.
	Exit	Stops all running message loops and closes all windows in the application. Note that this may not force the application to exit.
	ExitThread	Stops the message loop and closes all windows on the current thread only.
	Run	Starts a standard message loop on the current thread. If a `Form` is given, also makes that form visible.
Public Static Events	ApplicationExit	Occurs when the application is about to shut down.
	Idle	Occurs when the application is about to enter the idle state.
	ThreadException	Occurs when an uncaught `ThreadException` occurs.
	ThreadExit	Occurs when a thread is about to shut down.

1.1.6 Program execution

Before we leave this section, let's review what we've learned about how our program executes within the operating system. Run the MyForm.exe program again to see this in action. When you execute this program, the Windows operating system creates and initializes a process that:

1. Uses the `Main` method as the entry point for execution, which:

   a. Instantiates an instance of the class `MyForm` using the `new` keyword, which
   b. Invokes the instance constructor for `MyForm`, which
   c. Assigns the string "Hello Form" to the title bar.

2. Back in our `Main` method, the `Application.Run` method is called with the newly created `MyForm` object as a parameter, and:

   a. Displays `MyForm` as the application window, and
   b. Waits for and processes any messages or user interactions that occur.

3. When the application window closes:

   a. The `Application.Run` method returns, and
   b. The `Main` method returns, and
   c. The program exits.

And that is how it is done in the world of .NET.

1.2 Adding controls

Let's make our program a little more interesting by adding some controls. Throughout the course of the book, we will be building a photo viewing application, so let's add a button for loading an image file, and a box where the image can be displayed. When we are done, our form will look like figure 1.3.

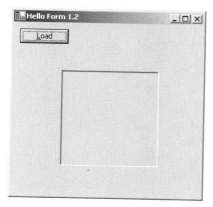

Figure 1.3
The main window shown here contains a Load button and a picture box control.

Revise your code as shown in listing 1.2. Changes from our previous code listing are shown in bold. Note that we have changed the version number of our program to 1.2

to distinguish it from our original code and to match the current section. This new version number is also displayed on the title bar. In chapter 2 we will see how to obtain the application's version number programmatically. For now, changing it by hand will do just fine.

Listing 1.2   A Button and PictureBox control are added to the form

```
[assembly: System.Reflection.AssemblyVersion("1.2")]

namespace MyNamespace
{
  using System;
  using System.Windows.Forms;

  public class MyForm : Form
  {
    private Button btnLoad;
    private PictureBox pboxPhoto;

    public MyForm()
    {
      this.Text = "Hello Form 1.2";

      // Create and configure the Button
      btnLoad = new Button();
      btnLoad.Text = "&Load";
      btnLoad.Left = 10;
      btnLoad.Top = 10;

      // Create and configure the PictureBox
      pboxPhoto = new PictureBox();
      pboxPhoto.BorderStyle =
      System.Windows.Forms.BorderStyle.Fixed3D;
      pboxPhoto.Width = this.Width / 2;
      pboxPhoto.Height = this.Height / 2;
      pboxPhoto.Left = (this.Width - pboxPhoto.Width) / 2;
      pboxPhoto.Top = (this.Height - pboxPhoto.Height) / 2;

      // Add our new controls to the Form
      this.Controls.Add(btnLoad);
      this.Controls.Add(pboxPhoto);
    }

    public static void Main()
    {
      Application.Run(new MyForm());
    }
  }
}
```

Compile this program as before and run it to see our changes. We will walk through these changes one at a time.

CHAPTER 1   GETTING STARTED WITH WINDOWS FORMS

1.2.1 Shortcuts and fully qualified names

The first change you may notice in our new code is the using keyword at the beginning of the program.

```
using System;
using System.Windows.Forms;
```

Programmers are always looking for shortcuts; and older programmers, some would say more experienced programmers, often worry that their lines may be too long for the compiler or printer to handle. The programmers at Microsoft are no exception, so while one team probably agreed that fully-qualified names are a good idea, another team probably sought a way to avoid typing them. The result is the using keyword.

The using keyword actually plays two roles in C#. The first is as a directive for specifying a shortcut, as we are about to discuss. The second is as a statement for ensuring that non-memory resources are properly disposed of. We will discuss the using keyword as a statement in chapter 6.

As a directive, using declares a namespace or alias that will be used in the current file. Do not confuse this with include files found in C and C++. Include files are not needed in C# since the assembly incorporates all of this information, making the /reference switch to the compiler sufficient in this regard. This really is just a shortcut mechanism.

In our original program in section 1.1, the Main function called the method System.Windows.Forms.Application.Run. In our new listing the using directive allows us to shorten this call to Application.Run. The long form is called the *fully qualified name* since the entire namespace is specified. Imagine if you had to use the fully qualified name throughout your code. Aside from tired fingers, you would have long, cluttered lines of code. As a result, our new code is a bit easier to read:

```
public static void Main()
{
    Application.Run(new MyForm());
}
```

Since Application is not a C# keyword or a globally available class, the compiler searches the System and System.Windows.Forms namespaces specified by the using directive in order to locate the System.Windows.Forms.Application class.

You can also specify an alias with the using keyword to create a more convenient representation of a namespace or class. For example,

```
using WF-alias = System.Windows.Forms
```

With this alias defined, you can then refer to the Application class as

```
WF-alias.Application.Run(new MyForm());
```

Alternatively, an alias for a specific type can be created. For example, a shortcut for the `Application` class can be defined with:

```
using MyAppAlias = System.Windows.Forms.Application
```

This would permit the following line in your code:

```
MyAppAlias.Run(new MyForm());
```

Typically, the `using` directive simply indicates the namespaces employed by the program, and this is how we use this directive in our program. For example, rather than the fully qualified names `System.Windows.Forms.Button` and `System.Windows.Forms.PictureBox`, we simply use the `Button` and `PictureBox` names directly.

It is worth noting that there is also a `Button` class in the `System.Web.UI.WebControls` namespace. The compiler uses the correct `System.Windows.Forms.Button` class because of the `using` keyword, and because the `System.Web` namespace is not referenced by our program.

When we look at Visual Studio .NET in chapter 2, you will see that Visual Studio tends to use the fully qualified names everywhere. This is a good practice for a tool that generates code to guarantee that any potential for ambiguity is avoided.

1.2.2 Fields and properties

Let's go back to our use of the `Button` and `PictureBox` classes. The top of our class now defines two member variables, or *fields* in C#, to represent the button and the picture box on our form. Here, `Button` and `PictureBox` are classes in the Windows Forms namespace that are used to create a button and picture box *control* on a `Form`. We will tend to use the terms class and control interchangeably for user interface objects in this book.[3]

```
public class MyForm : Form
{
   private Button btnLoad;
   private PictureBox pboxPhoto;
```

Fields, like all types in C#, must be initialized before they are used. This initialization occurs in the constructor for the `MyForm` class.

```
public MyForm()
{
   // Create and configure the Button
   btnLoad = new Button();
   btnLoad.Text = "&Load";
   btnLoad.Left = 10;
   btnLoad.Top = 10;
```

---

[3] Or, more formally, we will use the term *control* to refer to an instance of any class derived from the `Control` class in the `System.Windows.Forms` namespace.

```
// Create and configure the PictureBox
pboxPhoto = new PictureBox();
pboxPhoto.BorderStyle = System.Windows.Forms.BorderStyle.Fixed3D;
pboxPhoto.Width = this.Width / 2;
pboxPhoto.Height = this.Height / 2;
pboxPhoto.Left = (this.Width - pboxPhoto.Width) / 2;
pboxPhoto.Top = (this.Height - pboxPhoto.Height) / 2;
. . .
```

Note the use of the new keyword to initialize our two fields. Each control is then assigned an appropriate appearance and location. You might think that members such as Text, Left, BorderStyle, and so on are all public fields in the Button and PictureBox classes, but this is not the case. Public member variables in C++, as well as in C#, can be a dangerous thing, as these members can be manipulated directly by programmers without restrictions. A user might accidentally (or on purpose!) set such a variable to an invalid value and cause a program error. Typically, C++ programmers create class variables as protected or private members and then provide public access methods to retrieve and assign these members. Such access methods ensure that the internal value never contains an invalid setting.

In C#, there is a class member called *properties* designed especially for this purpose. Properties permit controlled access to class fields and other internal data by providing read, or get, and write, or set, access to data encapsulated by the class. Examples later in the book will show you how to create your own properties. Here we use properties available in the Button and PictureBox classes.[4]

We have already seen how the Text property is used to set the string to appear on a form's title bar. For Button objects, this same property name sets the string that appears on the button, in this case "&Load." As in previous Windows programming environments, the ampersand character '&' is used to specify an access key for the control using the Alt key. So typing Alt+L in the application will simulate a click of the Load button.

Windows Forms controls also provide a Left, Right, Top, and Bottom property to specify the location of each respective side of the control. Here, the button is placed 10 pixels from the top and left of the form, while the picture box is centered on the form.

The Width and Height properties specify the size of the control. Our code creates a picture box approximately 1/2 the size of the form and roughly centered within it. This size is approximate because the Width and Height properties in the Form class actually represent the width and height of the outer form, from edge to edge.[5]

---

[4] As we will see in later chapters, the properties discussed here are inherited from the Control class.

[5] The ClientRectangle property represents the size of the internal display area, and could be used here to truly center the picture box on the form.

1.2.3 The Controls property

The final lines in the `MyForm` constructor add the button and picture box controls to the form using the `Controls` property. The `Controls` property returns an instance of the `Control.ControlCollection` class. The `ControlCollection` class is defined within the `Form` class, and defines an `Add` method that adds a control to a form. Note that the `Controls` property can be used to retrieve the controls on a form as well.

```
public MyForm()
{
   . . .

   // Add our new controls to the Form
   this.Controls.Add(btnLoad);
   this.Controls.Add(pboxPhoto);
}
```

When a control is added to a form, it is placed at the end of the *z-order* of the stack of controls on the form. The term z-order is used for both the set of forms in the application and the set of controls on a particular form, and indicates the order of windows stacked on the screen or controls stacked on a form, much like stacking dishes on a table.

The end of the z-order is bottom of the stack. You can think of this as the view a chandelier has of a table. If the tabletop is the form, and a cup and saucer are controls, in your code you would first add the cup control to the table, then add the saucer control so that it appears underneath the cup. This can be a bit unintuitive, so make sure you understand this point when programmatically adding controls to your forms.

The term z-order comes from the fact that the screen is two-dimensional, and is often treated as a two-axis coordinate system in the X and Y directions. The imaginary axis perpendicular to the screen is called the z-axis. This concept of z-order will be important later in the chapter when we have overlapping controls.

Now that our controls are placed on the form, we can use them to load and display an image.

1.3   Loading files

The next change to our little program will permit the user to click the Load button and display a selected file in the picture box control. The result appears in figure 1.4, and looks very much like our previous screen, with the addition of the selected image.

Figure 1.4
The image loaded into the PictureBox control here is stretched to exactly fit the control's display area.

Revise your program in accordance with listing 1.3. Once again the changes are shown in bold type, and the version number has been incremented, this time to 1.3.

Listing 1.3   The OpenFileDialog class is now used to load an image file

```
[assembly: System.Reflection.AssemblyVersion("1.3")]

namespace MyNamespace
{
  using System;
  using System.Drawing;
  using System.Windows.Forms;

  public class MyForm : System.Windows.Forms.Form
  {
    Button btnLoad;
    PictureBox pboxPhoto;

    public MyForm()
    {
      this.Text = "Hello Form 1.3";

      // Create and configure the Button
      btnLoad = new Button();
      btnLoad.Text = "&Load";
      btnLoad.Left = 10;
      btnLoad.Top = 10;
      btnLoad.Click += new System.EventHandler(this.OnLoadClick);

      // Create and configure the PictureBox
      pboxPhoto = new PictureBox();
      pboxPhoto.BorderStyle = System.Windows.Forms.BorderStyle.Fixed3D;
      pboxPhoto.Width = this.Width / 3;
      pboxPhoto.Height = this.Height / 3;
      pboxPhoto.Left = (this.Width - pboxPhoto.Width) / 2;
      pboxPhoto.Top = (this.Height - pboxPhoto.Height) / 2;
      pboxPhoto.SizeMode = PictureBoxSizeMode.StretchImage;
```

```
    // Add our new controls to the Form
    this.Controls.Add(btnLoad);
    this.Controls.Add(pboxPhoto);
  }

  private void OnLoadClick(object sender, System.EventArgs e)
  {
    OpenFileDialog dlg = new OpenFileDialog();

    dlg.Title = "Open Photo";
    dlg.Filter = "jpg files (*.jpg)|*.jpg|All files (*.*)|*.*" ;

    if (dlg.ShowDialog() == DialogResult.OK)
    {
      pboxPhoto.Image = new Bitmap(dlg.OpenFile());
    }

    dlg.Dispose();
  }
  public static void Main()
  {
  Application.Run(new MyForm());
  }
  }
}
```

Note that there is a new namespace reference:

```
    using System.Drawing;
```

This is required for the Bitmap class used to load the image file. As you'll recall, the using keyword allows us to shorten to fully qualified name System.Drawing.Bitmap to the more manageable Bitmap. To include the definition of the Bitmap class, the System.Drawing.dll assembly is required when the program is compiled. The new compiler command for our program is below. Note that we use the short form /r of the /reference switch.

```
> csc MyForm.cs /r:System.dll
  /r:System.Windows.Forms.dll /r:System.Drawing.dll
```

Run the new program. Click the Load button and you will be prompted to locate a JPEG image file. If you do not have any such files, you can download some sample images from the book's website at www.manning.com/eebrown. Select an image, and it will be loaded into the image window. Figure 1.4 shows a window with a selected image loaded. If you think this image looks a little distorted, you are correct. We'll discuss this point in more detail later in the chapter.

As before, let's take a look at our changes in some detail.

1.3.1   Events

If you think about it, Windows applications spend a large amount of time doing nothing. In our example, once the window is initialized and controls drawn, the application waits for the user to click the Load button. This could happen immediately or hours later. How an application waits for such user interactions to occur is an important aspect of the environment in which it runs. There are really only two possible solutions: either the application has to check for such actions at regular intervals, or the application does nothing and the operating system kicks the program awake whenever such an action occurs.

Waiting for a user action can be compared to answering the phone. Imagine if there were no ringer and you had to pick up your phone and listen for a caller every couple of minutes to see if someone was calling. Even ignoring the extra time a caller might have to wait before you happened to pick up the receiver, it would be difficult to perform any other activities because you would constantly have to interrupt your work to check the phone. The ringer allows you to ignore the phone until it rings. You can fall asleep on the couch while reading this book (not that you would, of course) and rely on the phone to wake you up when someone calls (unless you turn off the ringer, but that is a separate discussion).

Similarly, Windows would grind to a halt if applications were actively looking for user actions all the time. Instead, applications wait quietly on the screen, and rely on the operating system to notify them when an action requires a response. This permits other applications to perform tasks such as checking for new email and playing your music CD between the time you run a program and actually do something with it. The interval between running the program and using it may only be seconds, but to a computer every fraction of a second counts.

Internally, the Windows operating system passes messages around for this purpose. When the user clicks the Load button, a message occurs that indicates a button has been pressed. The `Application.Run` method arranges for the application to wait for such messages in an efficient manner.

The .NET Framework defines such actions as *events*. Events are pre-defined situations that may occur. Examples include the user clicking the mouse or typing on the keyboard, or an alarm going off for an internal timer. Events can also be triggered by external programs, such as a web server receiving a message, or the creation of a new file on disk. In C#, the concept of an event is built in, and classes can define events that may occur on instances of that class, and enable such instances to specify functions that receive and process these events.

While this may seem complicated, the result is simply this: when the user clicks the mouse or types on the keyboard, your program can wake up and do something. In our program, we want to do something when the user clicks the Load button. The `Button` class defines an event called `Click`. Our program defines a method called `OnLoadClick` to handle this event. We link these two together by registering our method as an *event handler* for the `Click` event.

```
btnLoad.Click += new System.EventHandler(this.OnLoadClick);
```

Since it is possible to have more than one handler for an event, the += notation is used to add a new event handler without removing any existing handlers. When multiple event handlers are registered, the handlers are typically called sequentially in the same order in which they were added. The System.EventHandler is a *delegate* in C#, and specifies the format required to process the event. In this case, EventHandler is defined internally by the .NET Framework as

```
public delegate void EventHandler(object sender, EventArgs e);
```

A *delegate* is similar to a function pointer in C or C++ except that delegates are type-safe. The term *type-safe* means that code is specified in a well-defined manner that can be recognized by a compiler. In this case, it means that an incorrect use of a delegate is a compile-time error. This is quite different than in C++, where an incorrect use of a function pointer may not cause an error until the program is running.

By convention, and to ensure interoperability with other languages, event delegates in .NET accept an object parameter and an event data parameter. The object parameter receives the source, or sender, of the event, while the event data parameter receives any additional information for the event. Typically, the sender parameter receives the control that received the event. In our case, this is the actual Button instance. The e parameter receives an EventArgs instance, which does not by default contain any additional information.

We will discuss events and delegates in more detail later in the book, most notably in chapters 3 and 9. For now, simply recognize that OnLoadClick is an event handler that is invoked whenever the user clicks the Load button.

The next section looks at the implementation of the OnLoadClick method in more detail.

1.3.2 The OpenFileDialog class

Once our OnLoadClick event handler is registered, we are ready to load a new image into the application. The signature of the OnLoadClick method must match the signature of the EventHandler delegate by being a void function that accepts an object and EventArgs parameter. Note how this is a private method so that it is not available except within the MyForm class.

```
private void OnLoadClick(object sender, System.EventArgs e)
{
  OpenFileDialog dlg = new OpenFileDialog();

  dlg.Title = "Open Photo";
  dlg.Filter = "jpg files (*.jpg)|*.jpg|All files (*.*)|*.*" ;

  if (dlg.ShowDialog() == DialogResult.OK)
  {
    pboxPhoto.Image = new Bitmap(dlg.OpenFile());
  }

  dlg.Dispose();
}
```

The `System.Windows.Forms.OpenFileDialog` class is used to prompt the user to select an image to display. This class inherits from the more generic `FileDialog` class, which provides a standard framework for reading and writing files. A summary of this class is given in .NET Table 1.2.

```
OpenFileDialog dlg = new OpenFileDialog();

dlg.Title = "Open Photo";
dlg.Filter = "jpg files (*.jpg)|*.jpg|All files (*.*)|*.*" ;
```

The `Title` property for this class sets the string displayed in the title bar of the dialog, while the `Filter` property defines the list of file types that can be seen in the dialog. The format of the `Filter` property matches the one used for file dialogs in previous Microsoft environments. The vertical bar character '|' separates each part of the string. Each pair of values in the string represents the string to display in the dialog and the regular expression to use when displaying files, respectfully. In our example, the dialog box presents two options for the type of file to select. This first is "jpg files (*.jpg)" which will match all files of the form `*.jpg`; while the second is "All files (*.*)" which will match all files of the form `*.*`.

Once the `OpenFileDialog` object is created and initialized, the `ShowDialog` method displays the dialog and waits for the user to select a file. This method returns a member of the `DialogResult` enumeration, which identifies the button selected by the user.

```
if (dlg.ShowDialog() == DialogResult.OK)
{
  pboxPhoto.Image = new Bitmap(dlg.OpenFile());
}
```

If the user clicks the OK button, the `ShowDialog` method returns the value `DialogResult.OK`. If the user clicks the Cancel button, the `ShowDialog` method returns the value `DialogResult.Cancel`. When the OK button has been clicked, the selected file is loaded as a `Bitmap` object, which is our next topic.

TRY IT! Note that no error handling is performed by our code. Try selecting a non-image file in the dialog to see how the program crashes and burns. We will talk about handling such errors in the next chapter.

Before we move on, note the final line of our `OnLoadClick` handler.

```
dlg.Dispose();
```

While the garbage collector frees us from worrying about memory cleanup, non-memory resources are still an issue. In this case, our `OpenFileDialog` object allocates operating system resources to display the dialog and file system resources to open the file via the `OpenFile` method. While the garbage collector may recover these resources eventually, such resources may be limited and should always be reclaimed manually by calling the `Dispose` method.

The `FileDialog` class is a common dialog that supports interacting with files on disk. This class is *abstract*, meaning you cannot create an instance of it, and serves as the base class for the `OpenFileDialog` and `SaveFileDialog` class. The `FileDialog` class is part of the `System.Windows.Forms` namespace and inherits from the `CommonDialog` class.

Note that a `FileDialog` object should call the `Dispose` method when finished to ensure that nonmemory resources such as file and window handles are cleaned up properly.

Public Properties	AddExtension	Gets or sets whether the dialog box automatically adds the file extension if omitted by the user.
	CheckFileExists	Gets or sets whether the dialog box displays a warning if the specified file does not exist.
	FileName	Gets or sets the string containing the selected file name.
	FileNames	Gets the array of strings containing the set of files selected (used when the `OpenFileDialog.Multiselect` property is true).
	Filter	Gets or sets the file name filter string, which determines the file type choices for a file dialog box.
	InitialDirectory	Gets or sets the initial directory displayed by the file dialog box.
	RestoreDirectory	Gets or sets whether the dialog box restores the current directory to its original value before closing.
	ShowHelp	Gets or sets whether the Help button appears on the dialog.
	Title	Gets or sets the title bar string for the dialog box.
Public Methods	Reset	Resets all properties for the dialog box to their default values.
	ShowDialog (inherited from `CommonDialog`)	Displays a common dialog box and returns the `DialogResult` enumeration value of the button selected by the user.
Public Events	FileOk	Occurs when the Open or Save button is clicked on a file dialog box.
	HelpRequested (inherited from `CommonDialog`)	Occurs when the Help button is clicked on a common dialog box.

The `Dispose` method is the standard mechanism for cleaning up such resources. We will discuss this method in more detail in chapter 6.

1.3.3   Bitmap images

So far we have discussed how our application responds to a click of the Load button and enables the user to select an image file. When the user clicks the OK button in the open file dialog box, the `OnLoadClick` method loads an image into the

PictureBox control. It does this by creating a new `Bitmap` object for the selected file and assigning it to the `Image` property of the `PictureBox` control.

```
if (dlg.ShowDialog() == DialogResult.OK)
{
    pboxPhoto.Image = new Bitmap(dlg.OpenFile());
}
```

The support for image files has been steadily improving with each new development environment from Microsoft, and the .NET Framework is no exception. While the .NET classes do not provide all the functionality you might like (as we shall see), it does provide a number of improvements over the previous support provided by the MFC (Microsoft Foundation Class) library. One of them is the `PictureBox` control to make image display a little easier. All we have to do is set the `Image` property to a bitmap image and the framework takes care of the rest.

Our friend, the new keyword, creates the `Bitmap`. Once again, we see how garbage collection makes our life easier. In C++, the memory allocated for this `Bitmap` would need to be tracked and eventually freed with a call to `delete`. In C#, we create the object and forget about it, relying on the garbage collector to clean it up when a new image is loaded by the `OnLoadClicked` method and the existing `Bitmap` replaced.

The `OpenFileDialog` class provides a couple of ways to access the selected file. The `FileName` property retrieves the path to the selected file. In our code, we opt for the `OpenFile` method to open this file with read-only permission. The open file is passed to the `Bitmap` constructor to load the image.

The constructed bitmap is assigned to the `Image` property of our `pboxPhoto` variable. This property can hold any object which is based on the `Image` class, including bitmaps, icons, and cursors.

How this image appears within the picture box control depends on the `PictureBox.SizeMode` property. In our case, we set this property so that the image is shrunk and/or expanded to fit the boundaries of the `PictureBox` control.

```
pboxPhoto.SizeMode = PictureBoxSizeMode.StretchImage;
```

TRY IT!   If you're feeling slightly adventurous, you should now be able to add a second `Button` and second `PictureBox` to the form. Label the second button "Load2" and implement an `OnLoad2Click` event handler that loads a second image into the second `PictureBox` control.

As an alternate modification, change the `Main` method to receive the array of command-line arguments passed to the program in an `args` variable. Load the first parameter in `args[0]` as a `Bitmap` object and assign it to the `PictureBox` control for the `MyForm` class. To do this, you will need to add a new constructor to the `MyForm` class that receives the name of an image file.

1.4 Resizing forms

The final topic we touch on in this chapter is resizing forms. For readers familiar with MFC programming in Visual C++, you will know that it can take some work to properly resize a complicated form. The folks at Microsoft were likely aware of this and sought to simplify this task in .NET.

Before looking at our new code listing, try resizing our existing program to see what happens. The position of each control is fixed relative to the top-left corner of the form, as shown in figure 1.5.

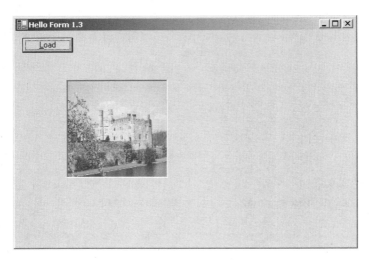

Figure 1.5
Version 1.3 of our application uses the default resize behavior, with both controls anchored to the top and left of the window.

We would prefer the `PictureBox` control to resize automatically along with the window, as is shown in figure 1.6. Fortunately, Windows Forms controls provide a couple of properties to achieve this effect, namely the `Anchor` and `Dock` properties.

Figure 1.6
Version 1.4 of our application anchors the picture box control to all sides of the window, so that it resizes automatically whenever the window is resized.

Revise your code so that it matches listing 1.4. This new code sets the Anchor property for each control, and uses the version number 1.4. As before, the changes to our code from section 1.3 are shown in bold.

Listing 1.4   The PictureBox resizes based on the Anchor property setting

```
[assembly: System.Reflection.AssemblyVersion("1.4")]

namespace MyNamespace
{
  using System;
  using System.Drawing;
  using System.Windows.Forms;

  public class MyForm : System.Windows.Forms.Form
  {
    private Button btnLoad;
    private PictureBox pboxPhoto;

    public MyForm()
    {
      // Constructor
      this.Text = "Hello Form 1.4";
      this.MinimumSize = new Size(200,200);

      // Create and configure the Button
      btnLoad = new Button();
      btnLoad.Text = "&Load";
      btnLoad.Left = 10;
      btnLoad.Top = 10;
      btnLoad.Click += new System.EventHandler(this.OnLoadClick);
      btnLoad.Anchor = AnchorStyles.Top | AnchorStyles.Left;

      // Create and configure the PictureBox
      pboxPhoto = new PictureBox();
      pboxPhoto.BorderStyle = System.Windows.Forms.BorderStyle.Fixed3D;
      pboxPhoto.Width = this.Width / 2;
      pboxPhoto.Height = this.Height / 2;
      pboxPhoto.Left = (this.Width - pboxPhoto.Width) / 2;
      pboxPhoto.Top = (this.Height - pboxPhoto.Height) / 2;
      pboxPhoto.SizeMode = PictureBoxSizeMode.StretchImage;
      pboxPhoto.Anchor = AnchorStyles.Top | AnchorStyles.Bottom
        | AnchorStyles.Left | AnchorStyles.Right;

      // Add our new controls to the Form
      this.Controls.Add(btnLoad);
      this.Controls.Add(pboxPhoto);
    }

    protected void OnLoadClick(object sender, System.EventArgs e)
    {
      OpenFileDialog dlg = new OpenFileDialog();

      dlg.Title = "Open Photo";
      dlg.Filter = "jpg files (*.jpg)|*.jpg|All files (*.*)|*.*" ;
```

```
        if (dlg.ShowDialog() == DialogResult.OK)
        {
          pboxPhoto.Image = new Bitmap(dlg.OpenFile());
        }

        dlg.Dispose();
      }

    public static void Main()
    {
      Application.Run(new MyForm());
    }
  }
}
```

◼

As an aside, figure 1.6 exposes a problem with our application that will need to be fixed. Since the image scales along with our PictureBox control, the *aspect ratio* changes as well. The aspect ratio is the ratio of the height of an image to its width. A standard 4-inch by 6-inch photograph, for example, has an aspect ratio of two-thirds (4 divided by 6). As the form is resized the image is distorted to fit the control, which affects the aspect ratio. We will fix this in chapter 7. In the meantime, keep in mind that our program exhibits what can only be called a bug.

While we have only added three lines here, they lead us to some interesting discussion points.

1.4.1 Desktop layout properties

The first change in our program sets the MinimumSize property to define the minimum possible size for the form. This ensures that the form never becomes so small that the PictureBox disappears and our image cannot be seen.

The MinimumSize property is a Size structure representing the minimum width and height of the form. As you may recall, structures are value types and store their data directly, either on the stack or as part of the containing type. As we discussed in section 1.1.3, the new keyword is used to create a new value type. When one value type is assigned to another, as we do here, the contents of the original type are copied into the target type. As a result, the fact that the newly allocated Size structure is destroyed when the MyForm constructor is finished has no effect on the value stored within the MyForm class.

```
    public MyForm()
    {
      . . .
      this.MinimumSize = new Size(200,200);
      . . .
    }
```

Note that the `System.Drawing` namespace defines a number of structures that are used in a similar manner, including the `Size`, `Point`, and `Rectangle` structures. We will encounter these types repeatedly throughout the book.

The `MinimumSize` property is one of a number of properties that control how a form behaves on the Windows Desktop. While not directly related to our discussion, this is a good place to introduce these properties as a set. Figure 1.7 illustrates how these properties relate to the desktop.

A brief explanation of each property shown in figure 1.7 is provided in the following table:

Property	Type	Description
ControlBox	bool	Whether to include a control box (upper-left icon) on the form.
DesktopBounds	Rectangle	The bounds (area) of the form on the desktop.
DesktopLocation	Point	The location of the upper left corner of the form on the desktop.
FormBorderStyle	FormBorderStyle	This defines whether the form is a dialog box, whether it is resizable, and what type of outer border is used.
Icon	Icon	The icon, or picture, used to represent the form. This appears in the control box and on the taskbar.
MaximizedBounds	Rectangle	The bounds of the form when it is maximized. This property is protected.
MaximizeBox	bool	Whether to include a maximize box on the form. Note that this is only shown if the `ControlBox` property is `true`.
MaximumSize	Size	The maximum size to which the form can be resized.
MinimizeBox	Size	Whether to include a minimize box on the form. Note that this is only shown if the `ControlBox` property is `true`.
MinimumSize	Size	The minimum size to which the form can be resized.
ShowInTaskBar	Bool	Whether to show the form on the Windows taskbar.

1.4.2   The Anchor property

The remaining two lines added to our program use the `Anchor` property to fix the control on the form in relation to the form's edges.

```
// Create and configure the Button
. . .
btnLoad.Anchor = AnchorStyles.Top | AnchorStyles.Left;

// Create and configure the PictureBox
. . .
pboxPhoto.Anchor = AnchorStyles.Top | AnchorStyles.Bottom
  | AnchorStyles.Left | AnchorStyles.Right;
```

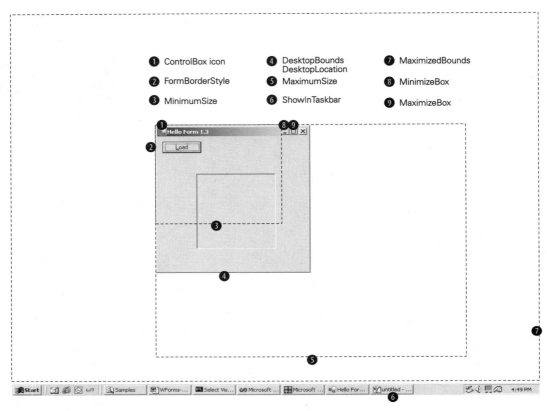

Figure 1.7 The properties for the Form class that relate to the Windows desktop define the size, appearance, and position of the form on the desktop.

All controls in the .NET Framework support the Anchor property for this purpose. The property is set using the AnchorStyles enumeration, discussed in .NET Table 1.3..

<table>
<tr><td colspan="3">.NET Table 1.3 AnchorStyles enumeration</td></tr>
<tr><td colspan="3">The AnchorStyles enumeration specifies the settings available for the Anchor property in the Control class, and by inheritance all controls in the .NET Framework. The enumeration is part of the System.Windows.Forms namespace. An Anchor property is set for a control object using a bitwise or (with the vertical bar '|' operator) of the desired values.</td></tr>
<tr><td rowspan="5">**Enumeration values**</td><td>Bottom</td><td>Control is anchored to the bottom edge of its container.</td></tr>
<tr><td>Left</td><td>Control is anchored to the left edge of its container.</td></tr>
<tr><td>None</td><td>Control is not anchored to its container. When an Anchor property is set to None, the control moves half the distance that its container is resized in all directions.</td></tr>
<tr><td>Right</td><td>Control is anchored to the right edge of its container.</td></tr>
<tr><td>Top</td><td>Control is anchored to the top edge of its container.</td></tr>
</table>

The `Anchor` property preserves the distance from the control to the anchored edge or edges of its container. Here, the container for the button and picture box controls is the `Form` itself. There are also other containers such as the `Panel` and `GroupBox` controls that we will encounter in chapters 7 and 9 that can hold anchored controls as well.

You can think of an anchor as being much like a boat tethered to a floating pier at the edge of a lake. The lake is "resized" as the water level rises and falls, but the distance of the boat from the pier remains constant based on the length of the tether.

For example, if a control is anchored 10 pixels from the left edge of its container, it will remain 10 pixels from the left edge regardless of the size of the container. If a control is anchored to opposite sides then the control expands or shrinks so that the distance from its edges to the anchored edges remain constant.

In our code, the `Button` is anchored to the top and left of the form, which is the default setting for the `Anchor` property. As a result our Load button remains in the upper left corner of the display window as the form is resized. The `PictureBox` control is anchored to all four sides so that it expands as the application window expands and shrinks as the window shrinks.

TRY IT! Change the `Anchor` settings in your program to experiment with this property. In particular, set this property for the `btnLoad` control to `AnchorStyles.None`. You will find that the control moves half the distance the form is resized in this case. Expand the form by 10 pixels horizontally, and the Load button will be 5 additional pixels from the left edge.

While you're at it, take out the `MinimumSize` property and see what happens. For the more adventurous, use the desktop properties from figure 1.7 such as `ControlBox` and `MaximumSize` to see the effect on your program.

1.4.3   The Dock property

The use of `Anchor` is fine when you have a set of controls and need to define their resize behavior. In the case where you want to use as much of the form as possible, the `Anchor` property does not quite work. While you could position the control at the edges of the form and anchor it to all sides, this is not the most elegant solution. Instead the framework provides the `Dock` property for this purpose.

The `Dock` property is related to `Anchor` in that it also affects the resizing of controls on a form. In our previous analogy of the boat tethered to a floating pier, the boat itself is "docked" to the shore, in that it remains at the edge of the lake as the water rises and falls. Similarly, the `Dock` property establishes a fixed location for a control within its container by fixing it flush against a side of the form.

Like `Anchor`, the `Dock` property takes its values from an enumeration, in this case the `DockStyle` enumeration. Note that one enumeration is plural (`AnchorStyles`) since a control can be anchored to multiple sides, while the other enumeration is singular (`DockStyle`) since a control is docked to no sides, one side, or all sides. More details on this enumeration appear in .NET Table 1.4.

The `DockStyle` enumeration specifies the settings available for the `Dock` property in the `Control` class, and by inheritance all controls in the .NET Framework. This enumeration is part of the `System.Windows.Forms` namespace. If a `Dock` property other than `None` is set for a control then the `Anchor` setting for that control is set to the top and left edges

	Bottom	Control is positioned flush against the bottom edge of its container.
	Fill	Control is positioned flush against all sides of its container.
	Left	Control is positioned flush against the left edge of its container.
Enumeration values	None	Control is not docked to its container. This is the default, and indicates that the `Anchor` property is used to maintain the control's position within its container.
	Right	Control is positioned flush against the right edge of its container.
	Top	Control is positioned flush against the top edge of its container.

We can see how the `Dock` property works by changing our program so that the `PictureBox` control fills the entire form. Also change the version number in your program code to 1.5 (not shown here).

```
pboxPhoto.Top = (this.Height - pboxPhoto.Height) / 2;
pboxPhoto.SizeMode = PictureBoxSizeMode.StretchImage;
pboxPhoto.Dock = DockStyle.Fill;

// Add our new controls to the Form
this.Controls.Add(btnLoad);
this.Controls.Add(pboxPhoto);
```

Compile and run the program again. After loading an image your form should look something like figure 1.8. Note how the Load button is still visible since it is added to the form first and is therefore higher in the z-order stack than the image.

Note that if multiple controls are set to the same `Dock` value, the z-order of the controls determines the order in which the controls are docked. The top, or first, control in the z-order stack is placed flush against the docked edge. The next control is placed flush against the first control, and so on. The exception is the `DockStyle.Fill` value. In this case the controls appear on top of one another, and the z-order determines which control is seen.

Figure 1.8   This PictureBox control in this window is docked to fill the entire client area of the form.

TRY IT! Modify the order in which the controls are added to the form (add the `PictureBox` first and the `Button` second) to change the z-order of the button and box. This will cause the button to be below (or behind) the image so that it no longer appears. However, the button is still there, and you can use the access key Alt+L to load an image.

While you are at it, try setting the `Dock` property for the `Button` to `DockStyle.Top`. How does this affect the application window, and how does the z-order for these controls affect their placement on the form?

Of course, you can experiment with other `Dock` settings as well.

We will use the `Dock` and `Anchor` properties throughout the book, so more examples with these properties are yet to come.

1.5   *Recap*

Before we move on, let's quickly review what we covered in this chapter. These chapter recaps will be quick, and will introduce the subsequent chapter as well.

In this chapter we did a whirlwind tour of .NET terms and C# features. We showed how to build and run an application containing a blank form, and added a Load button to select an image file and a picture box control to display this file. We discussed different members of C# classes such as constructors, methods, properties, and events, and saw how .NET executes a program. We also looked at how to use the `OpenFileDialog` class to open a file, and the `Anchor` and `Dock` properties for setting the position and resize behavior of a control.

We intentionally ignored Visual Studio .NET in this chapter. Instead we edited code by hand and used the command-line compiler to build and link our program. In the next chapter we will examine how to build the identical program using Visual Studio .NET, and use the opportunity to present some additional details about the world of .NET.

The concepts presented here will be discussed in more detail as we progress through the book. So if you missed it the first time, you will have a second chance to figure it out.

C H A P T E R   2

Getting started with Visual Studio .NET

2.1   Programming with Visual Studio .NET 35
2.2   Adding controls 43
2.3   Loading files 54
2.4   Resizing forms 61
2.5   Recap 65

This chapter will take a look at Microsoft's newest interactive development environment, or IDE. This, of course, is Visual Studio .NET, sometimes referred to as Visual Studio 7.0 or VS .NET.[1] Visual Studio .NET provides a number of advances over previous versions of Microsoft's development environments that make it worth a look. The environment does use a lot of resources, which may make it inappropriate for some older machines with less memory or for savvy developers that prefer a good text editor and a set of build files.

Either method of development is possible with this book. Since Visual Studio is intended as the development environment of choice for .NET, the rest of this book will use Visual Studio in its examples. If you are comfortable using command-line programs and/or makefiles, you should be able to follow these examples and associated code excerpts to write the code in your favorite editor.

---

[1]   Early versions of this environment, including the Beta2 version, were called Visual Studio.NET, with no space. This was later changed, but you will likely see both versions of the name. The official name includes the extra space.

Do not discount the use of Visual Studio, however. Even relatively modest Windows applications require a number of files and classes to create the resulting program. When working in a text editor, you the programmer must remember the required files, the classes, their member names, and other information. Visual Studio attempts to organize such information on your behalf and alleviates the need to track all of these pieces. In addition, Visual Studio provides some graphical shortcuts intended to ease the layout and programming of your applications. How much they actually help your efforts will depend on your personal preferences. Do, however, take a look and make a conscious decision. As an aside, it is interesting to note that almost all of Visual Studio .NET was written in C#.

Since this book is not specifically about Visual Studio .NET, this is the only chapter that focuses solely on this new environment. Additional information on the environment will be discussed as it arises while building our application, so pay close attention to the procedures shown here. In particular, you should know how to do the following in Visual Studio .NET by the end of this chapter.

- Start a new Windows Forms project.
- Add and place controls on a form.
- Modify properties of a control, including the variable name for the control.
- Add a `Click` event handler to a `Button` control.

In order to concentrate on the environment, most of this chapter will recreate the photo application already presented in chapter 1. We will call our new program "MyPhotos" and follow the sections from the previous chapter to create a very similar application. This application will be used throughout the rest of the book as we add and refine the features and capabilities of the MyPhotos application.

Lest you get bored, there are some new topics thrown in here as well. In particular, we will look more closely at two topics:

- Assembly attributes such as version numbers.
- Exception handling in C#.

2.1 Programming with Visual Studio .NET

Version 1.1 of the MyForm program was a blank form. A similar application is the default starting point in Visual Studio .NET. In this section we will create an initial MyPhotos application using Visual Studio .NET instead of a text editor. Of course, we are still programming in C#, just using the graphical tools provided by Visual Studio instead of the command-line tools used in chapter 1. In this section we will create a program very similar to that shown in figure 1.1 in the first chapter, on page 4.

As in chapter 1, this discussion assumes you have installed the .NET SDK and Visual Studio .NET on your PC. We also assume you have some knowledge of Windows, such as the ability to start the Visual Studio .NET program. The initial window of this program is shown in figure 2.1.

1 **Toolbox**
Used to add new controls to a form

2 **Links**
These display various information and resources available. The **Get Started** link is shown.

3 **Recent projects**
Quick access to recent projects

4 **Dockable windows**
One-click access (via the tabs) to various windows in the environment

5 **New Project button**
Click here to create a new project

6 **Solution Explorer**
Displays the files and resources in your solution. Note that this area contains other dockable windows.

7 **Dynamic Help**
Instant help on topics related to your current activities.

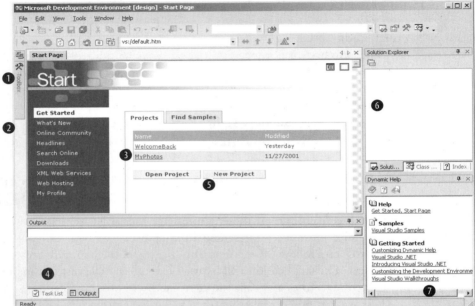

Figure 2.1   Components of the initial Visual Studio .NET window that relate to the discussion in this chapter. The exact placement of some of these windows may vary.

As a way to structure our discussion, this chapter as well as subsequent chapters will use the Action-Result table format described in the introduction to present the steps required to create the sample code discussed in each chapter. These tables provide numbered instructions for the task, including the actions to perform and the result of these actions.

In this section we will create a Visual Studio project for our application, compile and run this application from within Visual Studio, and look at the source code generated by Visual Studio in contrast to the program we wrote in section 1.1.

2.1.1   Creating a project

To begin, let's create a Visual Studio project called "MyPhotos" for our new application. This application will duplicate the functionality presented in section 1.1. The following table enumerates the steps required. We discuss the term *project* and other aspects of the application following this table.

	Action	**Result**
		CREATE THE MYPHOTOS PROJECT

	Action	Result
1	Start Visual Studio. NET. **How-to** Locate the appropriate item in the Start menu.	The Microsoft Development Environment displays with the Start Page shown. **Note:** This window is illustrated in figure 2.1. You may want to consider closing the Dynamic Help window (by clicking the X in the upper right corner of this window) while using this book. While quite useful in that it provides help related to your current activities, this window also uses quite a bit of CPU and memory resources.
2	Click the New Project button.	The New Project dialog box appears.
3	Under Project Types, select Visual C# Projects.	A list of C# Templates appears.
4	Under Templates, select Windows Application.	
5	In the Name field, enter "MyPhotos".	**Note:** The Location entry may vary depending on which version of Windows you are using. To avoid any confusion, this book will use the directory "C:\Windows Forms\Projects." In your code, use the default setting provided by the environment.

	Action	Result
6	Click the OK button.	The new MyPhotos project is created. The Solution Explorer now contains the files in this solution, and the main window displays a blank form.

Visual Studio .NET has a lot of information and a ton of features. We will cover some features in this section, and others as we develop our application. On the right side of the Visual Studio window, you will see the Solution Explorer window. This window shows the contents of the current solution, namely the projects in the solution and files in these projects.

Visual Studio uses projects and solutions to manage application development. Conceptually, a *project* is a collection of files that produce a .NET application, such as a library (.dll) or executable (.exe). A *solution* is a collection of projects that are grouped together for development or deployment purposes. When a solution has only one project, the two words are somewhat equivalent.

The MyPhotos solution is stored on disk in a file called "MyPhotos.sln." This solution holds a single project called MyPhotos, stored in the C# project file "MyPhotos.csproj." The Solution Explorer window shows the MyPhotos solution containing the MyPhotos project. This project displays four items:

- *References*—the list of assemblies referenced by the project. These are provided to the compiler using the /references switch we saw in chapter 1. You can expand this entry to see the default list of assemblies for the project, or wait until chapter 5 where we add an assembly to this list.

- *App.ico*—the icon for the application. We will discuss icons in chapter 12.

- *AssemblyInfo.cs*—a file containing the assembly information for the project. We talk about this file in section 2.2.1.
- *Form1.cs*—a file containing the default `Form` class created for our application. We look at the contents of this file below.

We will discuss the meaning and use of these items later in this chapter and throughout the book.

2.1.2 Executing a program

Our MyPhotos project is in fact a fully functional application. To see this, let's compile and run the application from within Visual Studio.

COMPILE AND RUN THE MYPHOTOS APPLICATION		
	Action	**Result**
1	Compile the project. **How-to** a. Click the Build menu. b. Select the Build Solution item. **Alternately** Use the keyboard shortcut Ctrl+Shift+B.	This compiles the project and creates an executable file. **Note:** The default keyboard shortcut is Ctrl+Shift+B. Depending on your keyboard setting, you may see a different shortcut in your application. Click on the "My Profile" option on the Start pge to see your setting.
2	Run the application. **How-to** a. Click the Debug menu. b. Select the Start Without Debugging item. **Alternately** Use the keyboard shortcut Ctrl+F5.	The MyPhotos application executes, displaying our not-so-exciting blank form. **Note:** This window is very similar to the original MyForm application written in chapter 1. Here and throughout the book, you can run applications with or without debugging. The result should be the same in either case.

Note that we have not written any code to create this application. The code has been generated for us by Visual Studio. By default, Visual Studio displays the Windows Forms Designer window for the default `Form` class created in the project, which presents a graphical display of the form. We can also display the source code for the Form1.cs file containing this default class.

2.1.3 Viewing the source code

As in section 1.1, our application here is not all that glamorous. The source code is quite similar to the code from chapter 1. The following table shows how to view this code so that we can discuss it in more detail.

View the code generated by Visual Studio .NET		
	Action	**Result**
1	Right-click the Form1.cs file in the Solution Explorer window.	A menu of options appears. 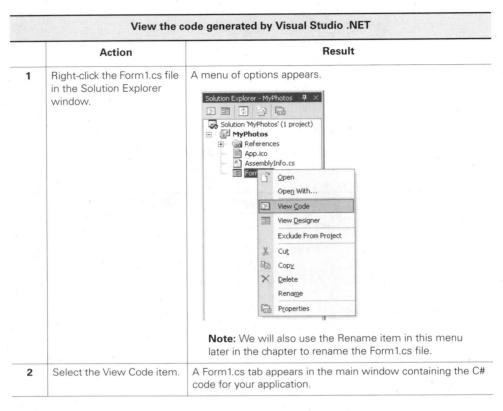 **Note:** We will also use the Rename item in this menu later in the chapter to rename the Form1.cs file.
2	Select the View Code item.	A Form1.cs tab appears in the main window containing the C# code for your application.

A listing of the Form1.cs code that appears in Visual Studio is shown below.

```
using System;
using System.Drawing;
using System.Collections;
using System.ComponentModel;
using System.Windows.Forms;
using System.Data;

namespace MyPhotos
{
  /// <summary>
  /// Summary description for Form1.               ➊  XML documentation
  /// </summary>
  public class Form1 : System.Windows.Forms.Form
  {
    /// <summary>
    /// Required designer variable.
    /// </summary>
    private System.ComponentModel.Container components = null;
                                                  Internal components variable ➋
    public Form1()
    {
```

```
        //
        // Required for Windows Form Designer support
        //
        InitializeComponent();

        //
        // TODO: Add any constructor code after InitializeComponent call
        //
    }

    /// <summary>
    /// Clean up any resources being used.
    /// </summary>
    protected override void Dispose( bool disposing )      ❸ Dispose
    {                                                          method
        if( disposing )
        {
            if (components != null)
            {
                components.Dispose();
            }
        }
        base.Dispose( disposing );
    }

    #region Windows Form Designer generated code
    /// <summary>
    /// Required method for Designer support - do not modify
    /// the contents of this method with the code editor.
    /// </summary>
    private void InitializeComponent()
    {
        this.components = new System.ComponentModel.Container();
        this.Size = new System.Drawing.Size(300,300);
        this.Text = "Form1";
    }
    #endregion

    /// <summary>                                          Region for designer
    /// The main entry point for the application.            generated code  ❹
    /// </summary>
    [STAThread]                        ❺ Declare thread as single
    static void Main()                   threaded apartment
    {
        Application.Run(new Form1());
    }
    }
}
```

This code for MyPhotos looks a lot like our original MyForm application. The namespace MyPhotos is used, and a class Form1 is created that is based on the System.Windows.Forms.Form class. Some key differences to notice are listed on page 42. Note that the numbers here correspond to the numbered annotations in the above code.

❶ Visual Studio inserts comments for documenting your program and its methods. The C# language defines a standard for XML documentation of code. Such lines must begin with three slashes and precede certain C# constructs such as classes, properties, and namespaces. There is a standard for what this documentation should look like that is summarized in appendix A. Check out the online documentation for complete details. The C# compiler csc accepts a /doc switch that gathers all such documentation lines and generates HTML reference pages. Visual Studio will do this for your code using the Build Comment Web Pages… menu item located in the top-level Tools menu.

```
/// <summary>
/// Summary description for Form1.
/// </summary>
```

❷ The Windows Forms Designer requires this field in order to ensure that components are properly managed on the form at run time, and specifically for components that are not also Windows Forms controls. We will discuss this field later in chapter 13 when we talk about specific components such as the ImageList class.

```
private System.ComponentModel.Container components;
```

❸ The use of garbage collection in .NET means that you have no idea when memory will be freed from objects no longer in use. Since some objects use critical system resources such as file handles or database connections that should be cleaned up as quickly as possible, a Dispose method is provided to do just this. All Windows Forms controls provide a Dispose method, and it is normally an error to use an object after its Dispose method has been called. We will discuss this method in greater detail in chapter 5.

```
protected override void Dispose( bool disposing )
{
```

❹ A special InitializeComponent method is created for initializing the controls for the form. This method is processed by the Windows Forms Designer window whenever this design window is displayed. While Microsoft recommends that you do not edit this method manually; if you are very careful, manual changes can be made. By default, this region is hidden in the source code window using the C# preprocessor #region directive. The #region directive defines a block of code that can be expanded and collapsed in editors such Visual Studio .NET.

```
#region Windows Form Designer generated code
/// <summary>
/// Required method for Designer support - do not modify
/// the contents of this method with the code editor.
/// </summary>
private void InitializeComponent()
{
  this.components = new System.ComponentModel.Container();
  this.Size = new System.Drawing.Size(300,300);
```

```
        this.Text = "Form1";
    }
    #endregion
```

It is worth noting here that the `InitializeComponent` method is called from the `Form1` constructor. In chapter 1, we initialized our `Form` object in the constructor as well. Visual Studio uses a separate method for this purpose in order to encapsulate the auto-generated code for the program.

❺ This line assigns the `STAThread` attribute to our `Main` function. This ensures that the main application thread runs as a single threaded apartment so that operations such as drag and drop and the clipboard will work correctly. Strictly speaking, we should have done this in chapter 1 as well (we did not in order to keep the number of discussion points down). Apartments and threading are a bit beyond our discussion here, so for now just accept that this line is needed for the form to properly interact with the clipboard and other parts of the Windows operating system.

```
        [STAThread]
```

Congratulations are once again in order for creating your first Windows Forms program, this time in Visual Studio .NET. Sit back in your chair to savor your accomplishment, and join me in section 2.2 when you are ready to add some controls to your program.

2.2   Adding controls

In this section we use Visual Studio .NET to add the `Button` and `PictureBox` controls to our form. Before we do, let's take a look at the AssemblyInfo.cs file in our project.

2.2.1   The AssemblyInfo file

When you create a C# Windows application project, an AssemblyInfo.cs file is created to define various attributes for the program assembly. This includes the version number shown in the Version tab when you display the program's properties dialog box from Windows Explorer. An *attribute* in C# is a declarative tag that affects the settings or behavior exhibited by an assembly, type (such as a class), or type member (such as a method or property). All attributes are based on the `System.Attribute` class defined in the .NET Framework as part of the `System.Reflection` namespace.

The AssemblyInfo.cs file makes use of some assembly-related attributes defined by this namespace. These settings are defined using the standard format for attributes targeted at the assembly file:

```
        [assembly: <attribute>(<setting>)]
```

The various attribute classes defined for this purpose include the `AssemblyVersionAttribute` class supporting the file version number settings. In C#, the

`Attribute` portion of the class name can be omitted, resulting in a version number setting something like the following:

```
[assembly: AssemblyVersion("1.0")]
```

A summary of the attributes used by this file are shown in the following table:

Common attributes in AssemblyInfo.cs file

Attribute	Description
AssemblyTitle	The title for this assembly
AssemblyDescription	A short description of the assembly
AssemblyCompany	The company name for the assembly
AssemblyProduct	The product name for the assembly
AssemblyCopyright	The copyright string for the assembly
AssemblyVersion	The version string for the assembly

Most of these attributes accept a string that specifies the value for the attribute. One exception is the `AssemblyVersion` attribute. The version number is used internally for comparing expected and actual version numbers of other assemblies, namely programs or libraries, used by your application. The version number format is a string specified as follows:

```
Major.Minor.Build.Revision
```

These are all expected to be integers. The first two values are for the major and minor version number used by most products these days. Changes in these numbers normally represent incompatible changes with previous versions; that is, version 2.1 is not compatible with version 2.2 of the same library.

The build number is for different compiles of the same minor version of an assembly. Occasionally this might introduce incompatibilities, but often version 2.1.17 will operate the same as version 2.1.42, although perhaps with some slight problems in the earlier build that will have been fixed in the later build. The revision number is for bug fixes or other incidental updates, and should not normally break compatibility.

In .NET, the build and revision number can be inserted automatically by the compiler. This is done by inserting an asterisk (*) in place of one or both of these numbers.

The automated build number is the number of days since January 1, 2000 in local time, and the automated revision number is the number of seconds since the previous midnight, local time, modulo 2. These automated values ensure that a new build and revision number is generated for each compile, that the build number always increases, and that the revision number increases within a generated build. It should be noted that this scheme is good for thousands of years, and that the revision number will never be larger than a 32-bit integer. Some examples and interpretations of version number strings are shown in the following table.

Assembly version number examples

Version String	Major #	Minor #	Build #	Revision #
"1"	1	0	0	0
"2.1"	2	1	0	0
"3.2.1"	3	2	1	0
"4.3.2.1"	4	3	2	1
"5.4.*"	5	4	Days since 1 Jan 2000 in local time.	Seconds since midnight, local time, divided by 2.
"6.5.4.*"	6	5	4	Seconds since midnight, local time, divided by 2.

In our application, we will set the version number equal to the current section number. The following steps set the version number for our application to 2.2. While we are here, we will also assign values to other settings in the AssemblyInfo.cs file, and use the `ProductVersion` property of the `Application` class to include this version number in the title bar automatically.

	SET THE VERSION NUMBER FOR THE MYPHOTOS PROJECT	
	Action	**Results**
1	Display the project's AssemblyInfo.cs file. **How-to** In the Solution Explorer window, double click the name of the file.	The source code for this file appears in the main window.
2	Find the `AssemblyVersion` line and change the version number to "2.2".	`[assembly: AssemblyVersion("2.2")]`

3	Set the other assembly attributes to reasonable values.	In my code, I used the following settings.
		
		`[assembly: AssemblyTitle("MyPhotos")]`
		`[assembly: AssemblyDescription("Sample application`
		`    for Windows Forms Programming with C#")]`
		`[assembly: AssemblyConfiguration("")]`
		`[assembly: AssemblyCompany("Manning`
		`    Publications Co.")]`
		`[assembly: AssemblyProduct("MyPhotos")]`
		`[assembly: AssemblyCopyright("Copyright`
		`    (C) 2001")]`
		`[assembly: AssemblyTrademark("")]`
		`[assembly: AssemblyCulture("")]`

4	Display the Form1.cs source code file.	

	Action	Results
5	Locate the `Form1` constructor.	```public Form1
{
. . .```
6	At the end of the constructor, add code to include the version number in the title bar.	```// Set the application title bar
Version ver
    = new Version(Application.ProductVersion);

this.Text = String.Format("MyPhotos {0:#}.{1:#}",
    ver.Major, ver.Minor);
}```

Note: This code uses the `Version` class to decode the version string. The constructor of this class accepts a string and provides access to the individual parts of the corresponding version number. |

In your applications, you can set the build and revision numbers explicitly, or have .NET generate them automatically. We will change the version number repeatedly throughout this book as a way to indicate which section of the book corresponds to the current application. You can change or not change the version number as you wish. On the book's web site, these version numbers are used to identify the file associated with a specific section.

In your own applications, a version number identifies a specific instance of a product that your customers or friends are using. This is useful for documentation and support reasons, and for indicating to your customers when new features and functionality are added to a product. Note that it is common practice to include the version number in a dialog box, often called an About box, that is available from a top-level Help menu in an application.

Of course, the class `Form1` is not the most descriptive name, so let's rename this class next.

2.2.2 Renaming a form

One other change before we add some controls to our form. Visual Studio created the class `Form1` in our project. Let's rename this file and associated class to `MainForm`.

RENAME THE FORM1 CLASS AND FILE TO MAINFORM

	Action	Result
1	Rename the Form1.cs file in the Solution Explorer window to MainForm.cs. **How-to** a. Right-click the Form1.cs file in the Solution Explorer window. b. Select the Rename item. c. Type the new name "Main-Form.cs" for the file. d. Press the Enter key.	The file is renamed. The designer and code windows are also renamed to reflect the new file name.
2	If not already shown, display the MainForm.cs window containing our source code. **How-to** Click the MainForm.cs tab in the main window.	
3	Replace all occurrences of the string "Form1" with "MainForm." **How-to** a. Type the Ctrl+H key to display the Replace dialog. b. Type "Form1" for the *Find what:* text and "MainForm" for the *Replace with* text, as shown in the graphic. c. Click the Replace All button. **Note:** The Ctrl+H key is a shortcut for the Replace menu item located in the Find and Replace submenu under the top-level Edit menu.	The Replace dialog box should appear as follows. 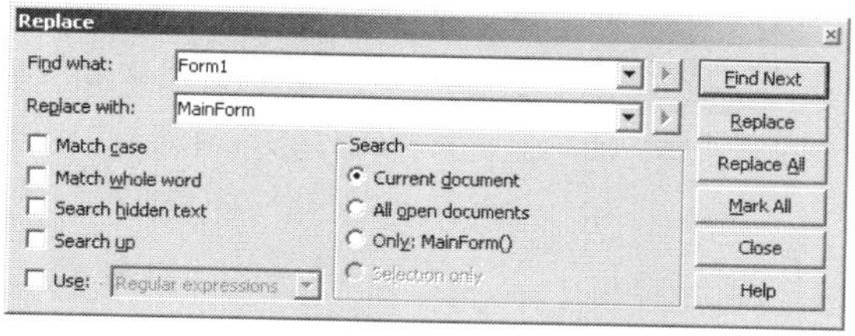 After the Replace All button is clicked, all four occurrences of the string are replaced in the code.
4	Click the Close button.	The Replace dialog disappears.

With an explanation of versions and the renaming of our main form out of the way, we can get back to the topic of placing controls on our form.

2.2.3 The Toolbox window

Finally, we are ready to insert the controls onto the form. In future chapters, we will not include the excruciating details of adding controls to forms and setting their properties with the Forms Designer, so make sure you understand the process here.

If you recall, in chapter 1 we inserted a `Button` and a `PictureBox` on our form. We will do the same here using Visual Studio.

	ADD THE CONTROLS TO OUR FORM	
	Action	**Result**
1	Click the MainForm.cs [Design] tab.	The Windows Form Designer appears, displaying our blank form.
2	Click the Toolbox tab on the upper left side of the window. **Note:** Your Toolbox may appear on the right or left, depending on your settings. If the Toolbox tab is not visible, select the Toolbox item from the View menu.	The Toolbox window appears. 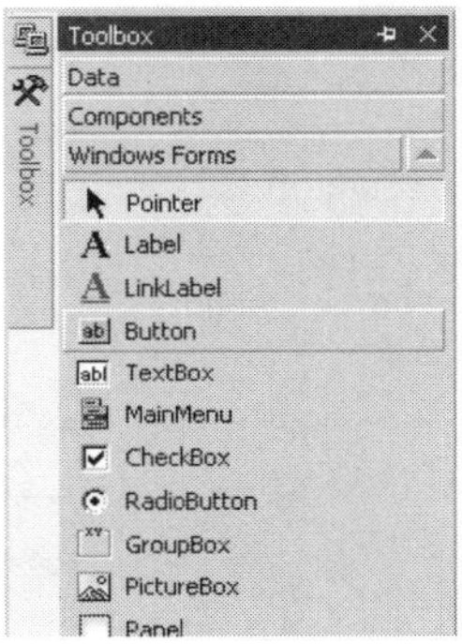 **Note:** The order of controls in your window may be different than what you see here. The contents of this window can be customized, and new controls can be added. Look up "toolbox, customizing" in the online documentation for more details on this latter point.
3	Click the Button item in the Toolbox window.	The Button item is now highlighted.
4	Click the blank form.	A new `Button` object appears on the form. 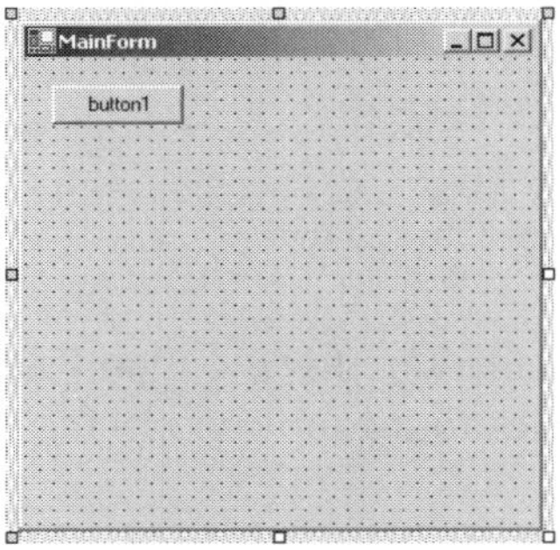

	Action	Result
5	Similarly, add a `Picture-Box` object to the form.	A new `PictureBox` appears on the form. **Note:** The order in which controls are added establishes the tab order and the z-order for these controls. All controls support the `TabIndex` property for this purpose, which we discuss later in the chapter.
6	Arrange the controls so that the `Button` is at the top left and the `PictureBox` roughly in the middle. **How-to** Move each control by clicking it and dragging it around the form. You can also click and drag a control's corners or edges to resize the control.	Your form should now look something like this.

Our controls are now on the form. Each control is named based on the type of control. The `Button` is called `button1`, while the `PictureBox` is called `pictureBox1`. Visual Studio .NET automatically creates a name for each new control based on the class name followed by a number. A second `Button` object added to the form would be called `button2`, and so forth. As for the `Form1` class earlier in this chapter, we would prefer more descriptive names for our controls, so we rename these items in the following table.

In addition, we need to set the properties for our controls similar to the settings in chapter 1. Since we have set our control's position and size graphically, there is no need to assign the positional properties such as `Left` and `Height` here. In chapter 1, we also set the `Text` property of the button to "&Load" and the `BorderStyle` property of the `PictureBox` control to `Fixed3D`.

Visual Studio provides a special Properties window where the properties and name of a control can be viewed and modified. We can use these to update our controls. We will set the `Button` properties first by continuing our previous steps.

	RENAME THE CONTROLS AND DEFINE THEIR PROPERTIES	
	Action	**Result**
7	Display the properties for the `Button` control. **How-to** a. Right-click the `Button` control to display a list of options. b. Select the Properties item. c. If the controls are not shown alphabetically, click the A-Z button of the Properties window.	The Properties window appears with the properties for the `button1` control displayed. **Note:** On your PC, the Properties window may appear below or to the right of the main window. You can move it by dragging its tab, located below the window, to a new location. I prefer this window on the right side of Visual Studio .NET to allow a longer list of properties to be displayed. We will always display properties alphabetically in the book, rather than by category. This will make it easier to discuss and find required properties. You can display the entries either way in your own application.
8	Rename the control from "button1" to "btnLoad." **How-to** a. Locate the (Name) entry at the top of the list. b. Click the "button1" text after this property.[1] c. Type the new name "btnLoad."	The variable associated with the button is renamed. 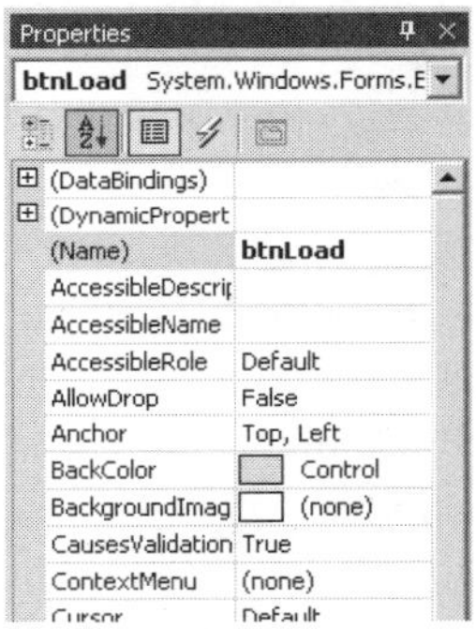 ![Properties window showing btnLoad System.Windows.Forms.E with properties: (DataBindings), (DynamicPropert), (Name) btnLoad, AccessibleDescri, AccessibleName, AccessibleRole Default, AllowDrop False, Anchor Top, Left, BackColor Control, BackgroundImag (none), CausesValidation True, ContextMenu (none), Cursor Default]
9	Modify the `Text` property for the button to be "&Load." **How-to** a. Locate the Text entry in the Properties window. b. Change its value to "&Load."	**Note:** As in chapter 1, the ampersand (&) is used to indicate the access key for the button. Also notice that the `TabIndex` property for this control is set to 1, since it was the first control added to the form.

	Action	Result
10	Display the `PictureBox` control properties. **How-to** Right-click the control and select Properties. **Alternately** You can select the `pictureBox1` entry from the dropdown list at the top of the Properties window.	The properties for the `PictureBox` control are shown.
11	Set the `(Name)` property to "pbxPhoto".	
12	Set the `BorderStyle` property to `Fixed3D`.	**Note:** The `BorderStyle` property is displayed as a drop-down list since this property is based on a fixed set of values, in this case those taken from the `BorderStyle` enumeration.
13	Display the properties for our `MainForm` object. **How-to** Click the title bar of the form, or select the `MainForm` entry from the dropdown list.	
14	Set the `Text` property to "MyPhotos"	This setting immediately appears in the title bar of the form in the designer window. **Note:** We already added code to assign a new title bar in the constructor of our class, but it's nice to have a default title bar regardless.

Before we compile and run this code, let's check out the MainForm.cs source code generated by Visual Studio .NET to see how this code has changed in response to our actions. Take a look at the region marked `Windows Form Designer generated code` in the source file. You may need to click the plus (+) sign in front of this region to display this block of code. This region defines the `InitializeComponent` method where properties and other settings are defined. Your code should look something like this:

```
#region Windows Form Designer generated code
/// <summary>
/// Required method for Designer support - do not modify
/// the contents of this method with the code editor.
/// </summary>
```

```
private void InitializeComponent()                     Create the
{                                                      controls    ❶
    this.btnLoad = new System.Windows.Forms.Button();
    this.pbxPhoto = new System.Windows.Forms.PictureBox();
    this.SuspendLayout();         ❷   Suspend layout logic
    //
    // btnLoad                    ❸   Control sections
    //
    this.btnLoad.Location = new System.Drawing.Point(16, 16);
    this.btnLoad.Name = "btnLoad";
    this.btnLoad.TabIndex = 0;              ❹   Set standard
    this.btnLoad.Text = "&Load";               control
    //                                         settings
    // pbxPhoto
    //
    this.pbxPhoto.BorderStyle = System.Windows.Forms.BorderStyle.Fixed3D;
    this.pbxPhoto.Location = new System.Drawing.Point(40, 80);
    this.pbxPhoto.Name = "pbxPhoto";
    this.pbxPhoto.Size = new System.Drawing.Size(216, 160);
    this.pbxPhoto.TabIndex = 1;
    this.pbxPhoto.TabStop = false;
    //                                 Set control ❺
    // MainForm                            location
    //                                     and size
    this.AutoScaleBaseSize = new System.Drawing.Size(5, 13);
    this.ClientSize = new System.Drawing.Size(292, 273);
    this.Controls.AddRange(new System.Windows.Forms.Control[] {
                            this.pbxPhoto,
                            this.btnLoad});
    this.Name = "MainForm";                          Add controls
    this.Text = "MyPhotos 2.2";                        to form  ❻
    this.ResumeLayout(false);      ❼   Resume
}                                      layout logic
#endregion
```

A couple of points here are worth highlighting. The numbers from the previous code
excerpt match the numbers in the following list.

❶ As we saw in chapter 1, control variables are classes and therefore represent reference
types. In order to create an actual object for each control, the new keyword is used.

```
this.btnLoad = new System.Windows.Forms.Button();
this.pbxPhoto = new System.Windows.Forms.PictureBox();
```

❷ To ensure that the .NET Framework does not attempt to lay out the form while it is
being created, the normal layout logic is suspended to prevent layout-related activities
and events from occurring. The SuspendLayout method is available to all Windows Forms controls for this purpose.

```
this.SuspendLayout();
```

❸ To make the generated code easier to read and understand for both programmers and book authors, the settings for each control are defined in their own labeled section. The comments here indicate which control variable is configured by the subsequent code.

```
//
// btnLoad
//
```

❹ The properties we set in the Windows Forms Designer are defined in each control's section. The Name property is always set to the variable name of the control, while the TabIndex property is also set for each control, starting with zero (0), to establish the tab order for the controls on the form.

```
this.btnLoad.Name = "btnLoad";
this.btnLoad.TabIndex = 0;
this.btnLoad.Text = "&Load";
```

❺ The size and location of each control is determined automatically by Visual Studio .NET and defined here. The settings are defined using structures such as Point and Size from the System.Drawing namespace. A structure, unlike a class, is a value type, so the new statement creates these objects on the stack and copies their value into the appropriate property.

```
this.pbxPhoto.Location = new System.Drawing.Point(40, 80);
. . .
this.pbxPhoto.Size = new System.Drawing.Size(216, 160);
. . .
this.AutoScaleBaseSize = new System.Drawing.Size(5, 13);
this.ClientSize = new System.Drawing.Size(292, 273);
```

❻ Once all of the controls are created and initialized, they can be added to the form. Visual Studio adds the controls in one statement using the AddRange method available to the Form.Controls property. Note how this method accepts an array of Control objects. All Windows Forms controls are based on the Control class, as we shall see in chapter 4. Note the use of square brackets to declare the array type, with the elements for the Control[] array defined in the subsequent braces.[2] The order of the controls in the array defines the initial z-order of the controls.

```
this.Controls.AddRange(new System.Windows.Forms.Control[] {
                                this.pbxPhoto,
                                this.btnLoad});
```

❼ At the end of the InitializeComponent method, normal layout processing must be resumed. The ResumeLayout method accepts a boolean value indicating whether an immediate layout should occur or not. For Visual Studio, an immediate layout is not necessary, so the method is invoked with false.

```
this.ResumeLayout(false);
```

---

[2] For more details on declaring arrays in C#, see the discussion in appendix A.

When you have finished reviewing the code, compile and run the program as before. As in chapter 1 for version 1.2 of the MyForm application, this version displays our controls but does not allow you to do anything with them. Enabling the user to load an image is our next topic.

2.3   *Loading files*

Now that the controls are on the form, we can load an image into the `PictureBox` control using the `OpenFileDialog` class. Up until this point we really haven't typed any C# code for our MyPhotos application. We simply set values via Visual Studio and let the environment do the work on our behalf. In this section we finally get our hands dirty. The result of our labors will allow a file to be selected as shown in figure 2.2.

Figure 2.2   The dialog used to select a file in our application. This dialog is created using the OpenFileDialog class.

There are a couple of topics worth discussing here. First we will discuss how to support the dialog shown in figure 2.2. Then we will discuss how to handle the case where the user selects an invalid file.

2.3.1   Event handlers in Visual Studio .NET

As discussed in chapter 1, an event is a predefined action that a program can respond to, such as a user clicking a button or resizing a window. In chapter 1 we handled the event that occurs when the user clicks on the Load button. Here we will do the same using Visual Studio rather than a text editor.

As before, the Load button handler will allow the user to select a file and then load a `Bitmap` image of the file into our `PictureBox` control. If you recall, this involves setting a `Click` event handler for the button and using the `OpenFileDialog` class to prompt the user for an image to load.

Let's duplicate our code from chapter 1 in Visual Studio. Our code for the event handler will be identical to that already shown and discussed, so if you skipped ahead and missed this discussion, go back to chapter 1

Set the version number of the application to 2.3.

	IMPLEMENT A CLICK HANDLER FOR THE BTNLOAD BUTTON	
	Action	**Result**
1	Display the MainForm.cs [Design] window (the Windows Forms Designer window).	
2	Add a `Click` event handler for the Load button. **How-to** Double-click the Load button.	The MainForm.cs source code window is displayed with a new btnLoad_Click method added. ```protected void btnLoad_Click(object sender,\n System.EventArgs e)\n{\n\n}``` **Note:** Visual Studio uses the naming convention for all event handlers consisting of the variable name, followed by an underscore, followed by the event name.
3	Add our code to handle the `Click` event. **How-to** Cut and paste your previous code, or enter the code shown here by hand.	```protected void btnLoad_Click(object sender,\n System.EventArgs e)\n{\n OpenFileDialog dlg = new OpenFileDialog();\n\n dlg.Title = "Open Photo";\n dlg.Filter = "jpg files (*.jpg)|*.jpg"\n + "|All files (*.*)|*.*";\n\n if (dlg.ShowDialog() == DialogResult.OK)\n {\n pbxPhoto.Image = new Bitmap(dlg.OpenFile());\n }\n\n dlg.Dispose();\n}``` **Note:** Some of these lines do not fit this table. The dlg.Filter line, in particular, should be a single string. Here and throughout the book, we will reformat the code to fit the table in a way that is equivalent to the code in the online examples.

	Action	**Result**
4	Set the `SizeMode` property for the `PictureBox` control to `StretchImage`. **How-to** a. Display the designer window. b. Right-click the `PictureBox` control. c. Select Properties. d. Locate the `SizeMode` property. e. Set its value to `StretchImage`.	When an image is displayed, the entire image will now be stretched and distorted to fit within the box. **Note:** In the Properties window, notice how nondefault properties for a control are displayed in **bold** type.

Before we discuss the code here, it is worth calling attention to the statement completion feature of Visual Studio .NET, both what it is and how to disable it. If you typed in the above code by hand, then you probably noticed how Visual Studio pops up with class member information as you type. Figure 2.3 shows what you might see after entering part of the first line of the `btnLoad_Click` method. After you type "new," Visual Studio pops up a list of possible classes. The list changes to reflect the characters you type, so that after typing "Ope" the list will look something like the figure. At this point, you can press the Enter key to have Visual Studio automatically finish your typing with the highlighted entry.

Notice in this figure how Visual Studio uses a different icon for namespaces, structures, classes, and enumerations. In the figure, `OleDB` is a namespace, `OpenFileDialog` is a class, and `Orientation` is an enumeration type. We will not discuss these types here, other than `OpenFileDialog`. A structure type is not shown in this figure, but you can scroll through the list in Visual Studio to find a structure such as `Point` or `Size`.

Figure 2.3   An example of statement completion for the new keyword in Visual Studio after typing the letters "Ope."

The feature applies to variables and classes as well. As another example, when you begin typing the next line to set the `Title` property of the dialog box, you may see something like figure 2.4. Here Visual Studio displays the class properties, methods, and events available to the `dlg` variable. These correspond to the members of the `OpenFileDialog` class.

Once again note how Visual Studio uses different icons for different types. In the figure, `ShowDialog` is a method and `Title` is a property. You can scroll through the dialog to locate an event such as `Disposed` or `FileOk` in order to see its icon.

You will notice other statement completion popups as you type as well. One particularly nice feature is that signatures of methods are displayed as you type, and you can step through the various overloaded versions of a method using the arrow keys. In addition, as you will see in chapter 5, Visual Studio automatically picks up the classes and structures defined in your solution and incorporates them into these popup menus. Any documentation provided by <summary> tags within these classes is included as well, providing an automated forum for conveying important comments about a particular member to other programmers.

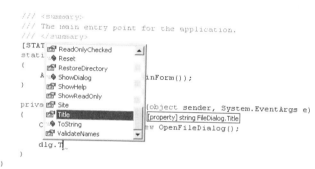

Figure 2.4
An example of statement completion for a class variable after typing the letter "T" for an OpenFileDialog class instance. Notice the small popup indicating that Title is declared as a string property in the FileDialog class.

Of course, like any feature, all these popup windows require a certain amount of CPU and system resources. If you are running Visual Studio on a slower machine, or do not want such windows popping up, you can turn statement completion off in the Options dialog box. Click the Options item under the top-level Tools menu to display this dialog. Click the Text Editor settings, select the C# item, followed by the General item. This dialog is shown in figure 2.5.

As you can see in the figure, you can disable the automatic listing of members, the display of parameter information, or both of these features. Other option settings are available here as well, of course. Feel free to look around and use the ever-ready Help button for any questions you may have.

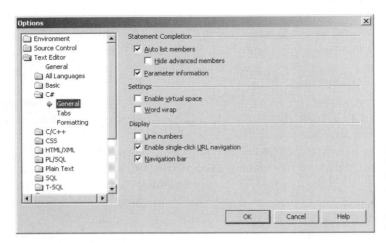

**Figure 2.5
The Visual Studio
Options dialog box
can be used to en-
able or disable the
statement comple-
tion feature.**

Back to our `btnLoad_Click` method, the code used here matches the code used for the MyForm program in chapter 1. Take another look at the `InitializeCompo-nent` method in the Windows Form Designer generated code region. You will notice that Visual Studio has added the `Click` event handler for the `btnLoad` control.

```
this.btnLoad.Click += new System.EventHandler(this.btnLoad_Click);
```

Compile and run the application to verify that the program can now load and display an image. Try loading different images into the program.

If you recall, we noted in chapter 1 that this code presumes the selected file can be turned into a `Bitmap` object. If you select a nonimage file, the program exits in a most unfriendly manner. This is a fine opportunity to fix this problem, so we'll make it the subject of our next section.

2.3.2   Exception handling

You may well be familiar with exception handling, since a number of C++ develop-ment environments, including earlier Microsoft environments, support this feature. Newer languages such as Java also support exceptions. Exception handling came into existence as a common way to deal with errors in a program. In our application, we expect the user to select a JPEG or other image file that can be opened as a `Bitmap` object. Most of the time, no error occurs. However, if a corrupted or invalid JPEG file is selected, or if the operating system is low on memory, then this creates an exceptional condition where it may not be possible to create our `Bitmap`. Since such situations will certainly occur, a way to recognize such errors is required.

Since some C++ programmers may not be familiar with exception handling, we will look at some alternative approaches before discussing exceptions in .NET. As one approach, we could use static creation methods that include an error field. For exam-ple, our code might look like the following:

```
// Wrong way #1 to support error handling
int err = 0;
Bitmap bm = Bitmap.CreateObject(dlg.OpenFile(), err);
if (err != 0) {
  // An error occurred
  if (err == bad_file_error) {
     // Indicate to the user that the file could not be loaded.
  }
  else if (err == memory_error) {

    // Indicate that memory is running low.

  }

  return;    // on error abort the event handler
}

// Assign the newly created Bitmap to our PictureBox
pbxPhoto.Image = bm;
```

This code would certainly work, but it requires extra variables and the programmer must check for errors every time a bitmap is created. This might be problematic if the programmer forgets or a new error is added which is not handled by the code. Then our design is for naught and bad things will happen. In critical production code, the mishandling of errors can lead to serious problems such as corrupted database information, unexpected stock trades, or other actions that a user or a program would not normally allow to happen. So this solution does not provide the best guarantees for program and data stability.

A second way to handle errors is to provide a global GetLastError function. This solution was used by Microsoft prior to the MFC environment, and is still used in some cases within MFC. It looks something like this:

```
// Wrong way #2 to support error handler
Bitmap bm = new Bitmap(dlg.OpenFile());
int err = GetLastError();
if (err != 0) {

  // Handle error values much like the above code

}
```

This is more elegant than the previous method, but has all the same problems. Programmers may forget to use it, and error codes change from release to release.

Exceptions provide a solution to these problems by forcing a programmer to deal with them, and provide guarantees that the program will exit if they do not. When an exception is not caught by a program, the program will exit. A forced exit is much safer than continuing to run in an error state and risk compromising critical data.

More formally, an *exception* is an unexpected error, or exceptional condition, that may occur in a program. Code that creates such a condition is said to *throw* the exception, and code that processes the condition is said to *catch* the exception. In .NET, exceptions are implemented as classes. Almost all exceptions inherit from the `Sys`-`tem.Exception` class.

One problem with exceptions in other languages is that they are expensive to support. Modern languages like Java and C# have done away with this problem by designing exceptions into the language so that compilers can handle them cheaply and gracefully.

The format used to process exceptions is the well-known `try`-`catch` blocks used in distributed computing interfaces and C++ development environments for many years. A portion of code where exceptions may be caught is enclosed in a `try` block, and the portion of code that handles an exception is enclosed in a `catch` block. We will discuss this syntax in more detail in a moment. First, let's add such a block to the code where we create the `Bitmap` object. Here is our existing code:

```
if (dlg.ShowDialog() == DialogResult.OK)
{
   imgPhoto.Image = new Bitmap(dlg.OpenFile());
}
```

The following table details how to catch exceptions in this code.

	CATCH EXCEPTIONS IN THE btnLoad_Click METHOD	
	Action	**Result**
1	Edit the MainForm.cs source file and locate the `btnLoad_Click` method.	**Note:** You can search this file by hand, or use the drop-down box in the top portion of the source code window to select this method explicitly.

2	Insert a `try` block around the `Bitmap` creation code.	The changes to the existing code are shown in bold.
		
		 ```if (dlg.ShowDialog() == DialogResult.OK)```
		```{```
		   ```try```
		   ```{```
		      ```imgPhoto.Image = new Bitmap(dlg.OpenFile());```
		   ```}```
		```}```

3	Add a `catch` block to catch any exceptions that may occur in the `try` block.	```if (dlg.ShowDialog() == DialogResult.OK)```
		```{```
		   ```try```
		   ```{```
		      ```imgPhoto.Image = new Bitmap(dlg.OpenFile());```
		   ```}```
		   ```catch (Exception ex)```
		   ```{```
		      ```// Handle exception```
		   ```}```
		```}```
		
		Note: Event handlers in Visual Studio .NET tend to use an "e" parameter for the event parameter to the call. To ensure we avoid a conflict, we will use `ex` as a standard variable name for an `Exception` object.

In C#, the `catch` clause takes an exception class name, and a variable to use in referring to this class. The block is executed if one of the statements in the `try` block throws this class as an exception. The `catch` clause can leave this class name out to catch any exception. Here, we catch all `Exception` class objects, which is generally all exceptions in .NET. For example, the `OpenFileDialog.OpenFile` method can throw a file I/O exception using the `IOException` class. Since this class derives from the `Exception` class, it will be caught by our handler. Other exceptions such as `OutOfMemoryException` may also occur, and are caught by our block as well.[3]

HANDLE EXCEPTIONS IN THE BTNLOAD_CLICK METHOD		
	Action	**Results and Comments**

4	Handle the exception by displaying a message to the user.
	
	Note: In this case, we return to the caller without loading an image.
		One way to do this is as follows:
		<pre>catch (Exception ex)
		{
		    // Handle exception
		    MessageBox.Show(
		        "Unable to load file: " + ex.Message);
		}</pre>

This code uses a class we have not seen before: the `MessageBox` class. This class is used to display a simple dialog box. We discuss this class in detail in chapter 8. For now, just copy the code and trust me.

The `Message` property for the `ex` variable is used in our dialog to insert the message string describing the exception provided by the `Exception` object. This and other members of the `Exception` class are summarized in .NET Table 2.1.

We will use exceptions throughout the book to handle errors in a similar manner. Other concepts associated with exceptions will be presented as they are required by our sample program.

Our MyPhotos application is now in line with our MyForm application from section 1.3, with the slight improvement of handling any exception that occurs while opening the file. Our last task in this chapter is to enable the form to resize gracefully using the `Anchor` property.

2.4 Resizing forms

Our final task in this chapter is to set the behavior for resizing using the `Anchor` property for our controls, and establish a minimum size for the form so that our `PictureBox` control does not disappear. This will finish our duplication of the application created in chapter 1. The remainder of this book will use Visual Studio .NET when discussing applications changes, so we will carry the MyPhotos application into chapter 3 and beyond.

---

[3] A more formal discussion of exceptions and the exception handling syntax appears in appendix A.

Figure 2.6
The application is resized here via the Picture-Box.Anchor property.

.NET Table 2.1   Exception class

The `Exception` class represents a generic exceptional condition, and serves as the base class for all exception classes in .NET. This class is part of the `System` namespace, and provides information required to raise (`throw`) and process (`catch`) exceptions. Note that it is possible for unmanaged code to throw exceptions that will not be seen as `Exception` objects. These exceptions can be caught using an empty `catch` clause.

Public Properties	HelpLink	Gets a link to help information associated with this exception.
	InnerException	Gets the inner (nested) exception associated with this object, if any.
	Message	Gets the message text assigned to the exception.
	Source	Gets or sets a string containing the source of the exception, such as the name of the application or object that generated the error.
	StackTrace	Gets the stack trace as a string. By default, the stack is captured just before the exception is thrown.
	TargetSite	Gets the `MethodBase` object for the method that threw this exception.
Public Methods	GetBaseException	Returns the original `Exception` that caused the current exception to be thrown. Useful when a chain of nested exceptions is received.
	SetHelpLink	Sets the string returned by the `HelpLink` property.
	ToString (overridden from `Object`)	Returns the fully qualified name of the exception, and possibly other information such as the message text, the name of the inner exception, and a stack trace.

2.4.1 Assign the Anchor property

In chapter 1 we set the Anchor property for our Button control to Top and Left, and for our PictureBox control to Top, Bottom, Left, and Right. In Visual Studio .NET, the default value of Top and Left is already set for our button, so we only need to modify the property for the pbxPhoto control. The result of this change when running the application is shown in figure 2.6.

Set the version number of the application to 2.4.

SET THE ANCHOR PROPERTY FOR THE PBXPHOTO CONTROL	
Action	**Result**
1 Display the properties for the PictureBox control.	
2 Use the Anchor property to anchor this control to all four sides of the form. **How-to** a. Click the down arrow for the Anchor item setting. b. Click the corresponding value to select Top, Bottom, Left, and Right. c. Click outside the drop-down dialog to set the selected values.	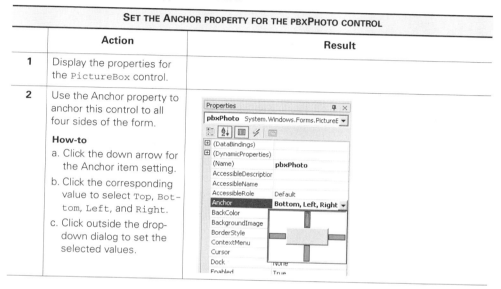

Visual Studio recognizes that the Anchor property is an enumeration containing a set of or'd values, so it breaks apart the value into its components.[4] For the PictureBox control, this displays the value as "Top, Bottom, Left, Right." If you look in the InitializeComponent method generated by Visual Studio, you will notice that this value is set much like our code in chapter 1. Note that the Button.Anchor property is not set in this method since it uses the default value.

```
this.pbxPhoto.Anchor = (((System.Windows.Forms.AnchorStyles.Top
    | System.Windows.Forms.AnchorStyles.Bottom)
    | System.Windows.Forms.AnchorStyles.Left)
    | System.Windows.Forms.AnchorStyles.Right);
```

---

[4]   This occurs because the AnchorStyles enumeration has the FlagsAttribute attribute assigned. An attribute is a C# construct that defines a behavior or configuration setting for a type, in this case the fact that the enumeration allows a bitwise combination of its member values.

2.4.2 Assign the MinimumSize property

To match our application from chapter 1, we also need to set the MinimumSize property to ensure that the window will never be so small that the PictureBox disappears. This is done with the following steps:

	SET THE MINIMUMSIZE PROPERTY FOR THE PBXPHOTO CONTROL	
	Action	**Result**
1	Display the properties for the Form object.	
2	Set the value of the MinimumSize property to "200, 200"	The code in InitializeComponent sets this new value. `this.MinimumSize = new System.Drawing.Size(200, 200);`

Compile and run the application to verify that the program resizes similar to figure 2.6. Once again note that the aspect ratio is not preserved by our application. This is a known bug that we will fix later in the book.

Now that we have duplicated the MyForm program from chapter 1, you might take a look at the source code in MainForm.cs and compare it to our final MyForm.cs listing. Other than some of the differences we pointed out at the start of this chapter, you will see that the code is much the same.

TRY IT! First, change the Anchor setting for the PictureBox control to use Dock instead. In the Properties window, you will notice a dropdown for this property similar to the one shown for the Anchor property, as in figure 2.7. Here you select the section of the box to dock against, namely the Top, Left, Right, Bottom, Fill (in the middle), or None. In figure 2.7, the DockStyle.Fill value is selected. If the picture box covers up the Load button, right-click the picture box and select the "Send to Back" option to send the control to the

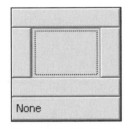

Figure 2.7   The Dock property dropdown window.

end of the z-order. Compile and run the program to see the new behavior.

Second, for the adventurous, try adding a second Button and PictureBox control to the application using Visual Studio .NET, similar to the task suggested at the end of chapter 1. Name the button btnLoad2 and set the text on the label to "Loa&d2" with a Click event handler that loads a second image and displays it in the second PictureBox named pbxPhoto2. You can use the anchor property for these, or set the Dock property for the first picture box to DockStyle.Top, and for the second picture box to DockStyle.Fill.

2.5   Recap

In this chapter, we recreated the application from chapter 1 using Visual Studio .NET. While much of the code was quite similar, we saw how Visual Studio generates the `InitializeComponent` method for initializing the controls created in the Windows Forms Designer window. We discussed the AssemblyInfo.cs file generated by Visual Studio, and how version numbers are specified within this file. We also looked at exception handling, and its integration into C# and use by the .NET Framework.

This ends part 1 of the book. The MyPhotos application will serve as the basis for much of the rest of the book. Part 2 begins a systematic discussion of Windows Forms controls, and will begin with the MyPhotos project created in this chapter.

Basic Windows Forms

If you have actually read part 1 of this book, then you have a good idea where we are going here. Chapter 2 constructed our program using Visual Studio .NET and extended the discussion of the .NET architecture and Windows Forms programming provided in chapter 1. Here we pick up where chapter 2 left off and provide a somewhat systematic discussion of basic Windows Forms development. The goal here is to cover the essential concepts and classes needed in most Windows Forms applications.

Following our practice in chapter 2, the complete steps required to create each example are provided. For the most part, the MyPhotos application is used throughout the book. In a couple places we create alternate applications to provide variety and because I felt the topics were better presented separately.

For all applications, the code used for each section in the book is available on the book's web site at www.manning.com/eebrown. Follow the instructions and links to the version number corresponding to the desired section in order to retrieve the appropriate files.

We begin this part of the book with chapter 3 on "Menus," and add various types of menus to the MyPhotos application. This chapter also presents the foundations of the Windows Forms class hierarchy and the handling of events in Visual Studio .NET. By the end of this chapter our application will be able to load a photographic image from disk and display it in various ways within the main window.

Chapter 4 covers "Status bars" containing both simple text and a set of panels. A status bar is used to provide feedback to the user during potentially long operations, and to summarize what is displayed in the main window. An introduction to the .NET drawing interface is presented by way of a custom status bar panel.

Chapter 5 on "Reusable libraries" steps out of Windows Forms momentarily to create a reusable photo album library. This chapter discusses collection classes in .NET and the concept of *interfaces*. A detailed discussion of the penultimate ancestor, the `object` class, is also provided.

Chapter 6 integrates our new library into the MyPhotos application during the course of presenting "Common file dialogs." A new menu bar is created and file dialogs are used to access, store, and load image and album data on disk. The idea of *painting* on a Form is also introduced.

Chapter 7 takes the painting idea further in "Drawing and scrolling." Painting on both form and panel controls is discussed, and automated scrolling is introduced and used to scroll an image that is larger than the display area.

Chapter 8 continues the discussion of the Form class as it relates to "Dialog boxes." The difference between *modal* and *modeless* dialogs is discussed, and the most basic of modal dialogs, the message box, is presented. A custom modal and nonmodal dialog is created, and the relationship between closing and disposing of objects is covered in detail.

Chapter 9 on "Basic controls" begins a systematic review of the standard Windows Forms controls available in the .NET Framework. The concept of *form inheritance* is discussed, and dialogs including labels, text boxes, and buttons are created. The difference between `Panel` and `GroupBox` objects is presented, and concepts such as C# delegates and control validation are also covered.

Chapter 10 presents "List controls," namely the `ListBox` and `ComboBox` controls. Various aspects of these controls such as single and multiple selection, dynamic update, and owner-drawn list items are presented while creating a new MyAlbumEditor application. The new application leverages the library built in chapter 5 to support reading and writing of photo album data.

Chapter 11 rounds out our discussion on controls with the hot topic of "More controls." Additional controls are presented and used in the MyAlbumEditor application, including the `TabControl`, `TabPage`, `DateTimePicker`, and `MonthCalendar` controls. Here we discuss how to move an existing set of controls into a container control, customized data strings, and processing click events within a month calendar control.

Chapter 12 returns to the MyPhotos application to present "A .NET assortment." Topics presented here include keyboard and mouse events, image buttons, and form and application icons.

The final topic in this part is "Tool bars and tips" in chapter 13. A `ToolBar` control is added to the application, along with various styles of `ToolBarButton` components. Tool tips for controls using the `ToolTip` class are also presented here and used with the dialog boxes created in chapter 9.

Part 3 of this book will expand on these chapters to cover more advanced Windows Forms topics.

C H A P T E R   3

Menus

3.1   The nature of menus 70
3.2   Menu bars 74
3.3   Click events 85

3.4   Popup events and shared handlers 88
3.5   Context menus 97
3.6   Recap 101

Menu bars provide a good starting point for our discussion in this part of the book. Menus provide a convenient way to group similar or related commands in one place. Most users are familiar with the menu bar concept and expect standard menus such as File, Edit, and Help to appear in their applications. Even novice computer users quickly learn that clicking a menu on the menu bar displays a dropdown list of commands.

Menus became popular on Windows applications in the late 1980s, following their success on the Apple Macintosh. Prior to menus, users had to cope with a wide array of interfaces offered by desktop applications. The function keys still found at the top of computer keyboards were developed in part as a standard way to access common functions in an application, and some programs even went so far to provide a plastic template that sat on top of these function keys to help users remember the available commands.

Perhaps because of this history, many developers take the usefulness and popularity of menus for granted and do not spend sufficient time laying out a consistent, usable interface for their application. While graphical elements such as menus, toolbars, and other constructs make applications much more friendly, this is not an excuse to ignore good user design and rely on customers to become "experienced" to make effective use of the interface.

Well, if that little lecture doesn't get your creative juices flowing, then nothing will. Back in .NET-land, Visual Studio .NET provides a rather intuitive interface for the construction of menus that does away with some of the clunkiness found in earlier Windows development environments from Microsoft. No more dealing with menus in one place, the application in another place, and the menu handlers in a third place.

This chapter will cover the following aspects of menu creation and handling:

• Defining different types of menus

• Creating and modifying menus and menu items

• Handling menu events

• Handling multiple menus from a single event handler

• Cloning (as in copying) menu items from one menu to another

The examples in this chapter assume you have the code for MyPhotos version 2.4 available, as developed with Visual Studio .NET in the previous chapter. You can use this code with or without Visual Studio as a starting point for the tasks covered here. If you did not work through chapter 2, download the project from the book's web site at http://www.manning.com/eebrown. Follow the links and instructions on the page to retrieve version 2.4 of the application.

3.1 THE NATURE OF MENUS

Before we add some menus to our application, we should talk about the different kinds of menu structures and the classes that support them in the .NET Framework. The traditional *menu bar*, sometimes called the *main menu* or an *anchored menu*, is a set of menus shown horizontally across the top of most applications. The menus in a

typical menu bar display a dropdown list of commands when they are activated with the mouse or by a keyboard accelerator. Figure 3.1 shows an example of a menu bar containing a File, View, and Help menu. The View menu is exposed, and a submenu of the Image menu item is displayed as well.

Another type of menu is a *context menu*, also called a *popup menu* or *shortcut menu*. A context menu is a menu that appears in a particular situation, or context. Typically, a context menu contains a set of commands or menus related to a specific graphical element of the application. Such menus appear throughout the Windows environment at the right-click

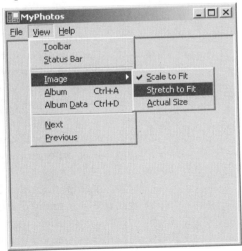

Figure 3.1 A traditional menu bar provides a set of menus across the top of an application

of the mouse. For example, right-click the Windows desktop, any program icon on your screen, or even the Windows start menu, and a context menu will pop up with a set of commands related to the desktop display, the program, or the start menu, respectively. Newer keyboards contain an accelerator key designed to simulate this behavior at the cursor's current location.

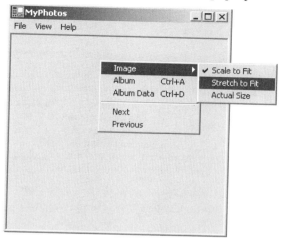

Figure 3.2 A context menu provides a set of commands or menus related to a specific portion of an application.

Context menus in .NET are typically associated with a specific control, the contents of which may change to reflect the condition of the control or type of item selected within the control. Note that context menu items can also contain submenus similar to those appearing in the menu bar. Figure 3.2 shows an example of a context menu associated with the main window of the application.

3.1.1 THE MENU CLASS

All menus in .NET derive from the Menu class. This class provides the core capabilities required by all menus, such as access to the parent menu, if any, and the collection of submenu items for the menu. The Menu class, summarized in .NET table 3.1, is *abstract,* meaning you cannot create an instance of it.

You will note in .NET table 3.1 that the Menu.MenuItems property contains a collection of MenuItem objects. This is an odd notion for object-oriented environments, since Menu is the base class of MenuItem, yet it uses this derived class as part of its definition. Such an arrangement is not disallowed, and is useful in situations like this when an object should contain instances of its own type.

3.1.2 THE MENU CLASS HIERARCHY

Before we plunge into specific types and examples of menus, it is useful to step back and consider the class hierarchy for the Menu class. A *class hierarchy* is the set of classes from which a particular class is derived, and gives some indication of the purpose and capabilities behind the specific class. The class hierarchy for the Menu class is also interesting because it is all or part of the class hierarchy for most Windows Forms controls. As you can see from figure 3.3, there are three classes beside Menu in this hierarchy.

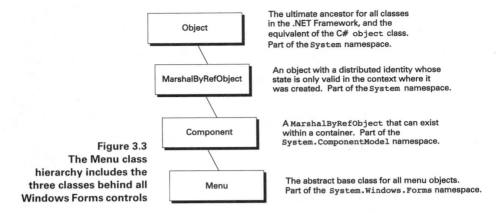

The ultimate ancestor for all classes in the .NET Framework, and the equivalent of the C# `object` class. Part of the `System` namespace.

An object with a distributed identity whose state is only valid in the context where it was created. Part of the `System` namespace.

A `MarshalByRefObject` that can exist within a container. Part of the `System.ComponentModel` namespace.

The abstract base class for all menu objects. Part of the `System.Windows.Forms` namespace.

**Figure 3.3
The Menu class hierarchy includes the three classes behind all Windows Forms controls**

The `Menu` class derives from the `Component` class, which derives from the `MarshalByRefObject` class, which derives from the `Object` class. All classes in C#,

.NET Table 3.1 Menu class		
The `Menu` class is the base class for all menus in the .NET Framework. This abstract class is part of the `System.Windows.Forms` namespace, and inherits from the `System.ComponentModel.Component` class.		
Public Properties	Handle	Gets the window handle for the menu. Used as a back door to special operations not supported by the framework.
	IsParent	Gets whether this menu contains any `MenuItem` objects.
	MdiListItem	Gets the `MenuItem`, if any, that will display the list of MDI child forms currently open in the application.
	MenuItems	Gets the `MenuItemCollection` object that holds the list of `MenuItem` objects attached to this menu, or null if no items are attached.
Public Methods	GetContextMenu	Returns the `ContextMenu` object that contains this menu, or `null`.
	GetMainMenu	Returns the `MainMenu` object that contains this menu, or `null`.
	MergeMenu	Merges a given `Menu` object into the current menu.
Public Events	Disposed (inherited from `Component`)	Occurs when the component is disposed, such as when the `Dispose` method is called for the component.

even internal types such as int and char, implicitly derive from the object class.[1] In the .NET Framework, this class is equivalent to the Object class. We will discuss this class in more detail in chapter 5.

The MarshalByRefObject class is an object that must be marshaled by reference. *Marshaling* is a method of passing an item from one context so that it can be understood in another context. A typical use for marshaling is in remote procedure calls between two different machines, where each parameter of a function call must be converted into a common format (that is, marshaled) on the sending machine so that it may be interpreted on the receiving machine. In the .NET world, Windows controls are MarshalByRefObject objects since they are only valid in the process that creates them, and can be used outside this process only by reference.[2]

The Component class is the base implementation of the IComponent interface. A *component is* an object that can exist within a container, and allows cleanup of non-memory resources via the Dispose method. This class supports the IDisposable interface as well the IComponent interface. We'll cover interfaces in chapter 5, so don't get caught up in the terminology here. Since graphical controls exist within a Form window or other container control, all Windows Forms controls ultimately derive from this class.

3.1.3 DERIVED CLASSES

The .NET Framework derives three menu classes from the abstract Menu to support menu bars, context menus, and the menu items they contain.

- The MainMenu class represents a main menu for an application. MainMenu objects contain a collection of MenuItem objects to display in the menu bar.
- The ContextMenu class represents a context menu associated with a specific control. ContextMenu objects also contain a collection of MenuItem objects to display when this menu pops up.
- The MenuItem class represents a menu item that appears within another menu. An instance of a MenuItem can contain a collection of MenuItem objects to appear as the submenu of this item. While an unrestricted number of submenus are permitted, it is a good idea to keep such menu hierarchies limited to no more than two or three levels. Too many submenu levels can be confusing for users and are best avoided when possible.

We will discuss each class separately, beginning with the MainMenu class.

---

[1] It is worth noting that object, as a class, is a reference type, whereas types such as int and char are value types. When a value type is used as an object instance, the value type is converted to a reference type via a process called boxing. This process is totally hidden from the programmer, but does have performance implications. See appendix A for a discussion of this concept in more detail.

[2] The details of marshalling is totally hidden for most Windows Forms applications, so you do not really need to know any of this. Hopefully, you find it somewhat interesting if not useful.

3.2 MENU BARS

So, let's do it. Looking at our MyPhotos application, it would be nice to replace the Load button with a menu option. This will allow more space in our window for the displayed image, and permit additional commands to be added in the future related to loading images. As an added benefit, it provides a nice example for this book, which is, of course, our ultimate goal.

Our new application using a menu bar is shown in figure 3.4. A Load and Exit menu have been added to a File menu on the main menu bar. The Load menu item will replace our Load button from the previous chapter. Notice how these menu items are separated by a small line. Such a line is called a *menu separator*. A View menu is also shown, which will be discussed later in this section.

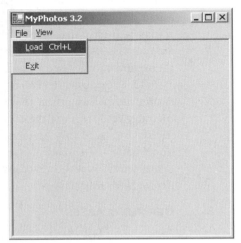

Figure 3.4 Notice in this File menu how the Load item displays Ctrl+L as its keyboard shortcut.

As you may expect, the menu bar will appear in our code as a `MainMenu` object. Menus such as the File menu are represented as `MenuItem` objects contained within the `MainMenu` object. The dropdown menus underneath the File menu are also `MenuItem` objects. This includes the menu separator as well as the Load and Exit menu items.

3.2.1 ADDING THE MAIN MENU

The steps to add the `MainMenu` object to our application are shown below. As already mentioned, this book uses Visual Studio .NET for all example programs. If you are writing the code by hand and using the C# compiler on the command-line, read through the steps and use the code inside or following the task description as a model for your own program. Note that this and most other tables at the beginning of a section change the version number in the program as a way to track our progress throughout the book and as a link to the online code at the book's web site. If you recall, the version number is modified in the AssemblyInfo.cs file of the project.

Before we add the menu, we need to remove the existing Load button from the form.

Set the version number of the application to 3.2.

	REMOVE THE LOAD BUTTON	
	Action	**Result**
1	Remove the Load button from the form. **How-to** a. Display the MainForm.cs [Design] window. b. Right-click the Load button. c. Select the Delete option. **Alternately** Simply select the button and hit the Delete key.	Visual Studio automatically removes all generated code related to the button from the InitializeComponent method of the MainForm.cs file. **Note:** When a control is deleted, the declaration of any event handlers are removed, but the actual event handling code, in this case our btnLoad_Click method, must be removed manually. We will remove this code later in the chapter.
2	Display the properties for the PictureBox control. **How-to** a. Right-click on the control. b. Select Properties. **Alternately** Click the control and use the keyboard shortcut Alt-Enter.	The property values for this control are displayed.
3	Set the value of the Dock property to Fill. **How-to** a. Locate the Dock property. b. Display the dropdown window for this property. c. Click the center button.	Clicking the center button as shown in the graphic sets the value of the Dock property to Fill, so that the PictureBox control takes up the entire display window of the form. **Note:** When the Dock property is set to a value other than None, the Anchor property is automatically set to its default value of Top and Left.

With the Load button gone, our way is now clear to move this functionality into a menu bar. We continue the above steps and add a menu bar to our form.

	CREATE THE MAIN MENU BAR	
4	Display the Toolbox window. **How-to** a. Click the View menu in Visual Studio. b. Select the Toolbox option. **Alternately** Click the wrench and hammer icon on the left side of Visual Studio.	A list of available controls is displayed.

	CREATE THE MAIN MENU BAR *(continued)*	
5	Drag a MainMenu object from the Toolbox onto your form.	A MainMenu object called mainMenu1 is added to your form. This object is displayed in a new area called the *component tray* below the form where objects appear that may not have a physical presence in the window. Such objects include timers, database connections, and main menus. **Note:** An example of the component tray showing the mainMenu1 object appears later in this chapter in figure 3.9, on page 99.

Let's take a look at the source code generated by these actions in the MainForm.cs window. If this window is not shown, right-click the mainMenu1 object and select View Code. You will note that the Windows Forms Designer has added the mainMenu1 variable to the MainForm class.

```
private System.Windows.Forms.MainMenu mainMenu1;
```

The InitializeComponent method we discussed in chapter 2 initializes this variable and attaches it to the form. An object for this variable is created using the new keyword. As we mentioned in part 1, the this keyword refers to the current class instance, just as it does in C++.

```
this.mainMenu1 = new System.Windows.Forms.MainMenu();
```

At the end of the method, the MainMenu object is attached to the form using the Form.Menu property. This property sets or retrieves a MainMenu object to appear as the main menu bar for the application, and can be used to swap in and out different menu bars to customize how the menu looks for specific situations. We will only use a single MainMenu object in this chapter. See .NET Table 3.2 for additional details on the MainMenu class.

```
this.Menu = this.mainMenu1;
```

Also notice in the code how the Anchor property setting for the PictureBox control has been replaced by the Dock property.

```
this.pbxPhoto.Dock = System.Windows.Forms.DockStyle.Fill;
```

The MainMenu class is a container class that holds a collection of MenuItem objects to appear as a menu bar on a Windows form. This class is part of the System.Windows.Forms namespace, and inherits from the Menu class. A main menu is assigned to a specific window using the Menu property in the Form class. See the .NET Table 3.1 on page 72 for a list of members inherited from Menu.

Public Properties	RightToLeft	Gets or sets whether text displayed by the menu should use a right-to-left alignment. This is useful when displaying a language such as Hebrew or Arabic which reads from right to left.
Public Methods	CloneMenu	Returns a new MainMenu as a duplicate of the current menu.
	GetForm	Returns the Form object that contains this menu, or null if this menu is not contained by a Form.

3.2.2   ADDING THE FILE MENU

With a MainMenu on our form to act as the menu bar, we can now add the menus that should appear. Each menu is created using the MenuItem class. In this section we will create the top-level File menu only. In the next section we will create the dropdown menu that appears when the user clicks on this menu.

	CREATE THE FILE MENU	
	Action	**Result**
1	Edit the menu bar in the MainMenu.cs [Design] window. **How-to** Click on the mainMenu1 variable that appears below the window.	An empty menu bar appears at the top of the form. The space for the first top-level menu contains the words "Type Here."
2	Type in a top-level File menu as "&File.	A File menu appears on the form. 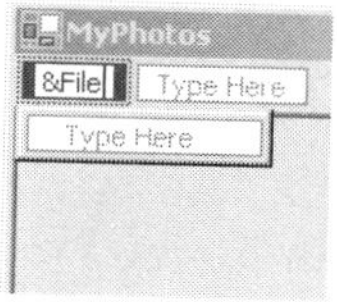 **Note:** The ampersand (&) specifies the character, in this case F, to use as the access key for this menu. Such access keys are used with the Alt key. In our application the File menu can be displayed by clicking on it or with the access key Alt-F.

3	Modify the (Name) property for this menu to be "menuFile."	The (Name) setting represents the variable name used for the object in the MainForm.cs source code. Changing this value automatically changes all generated instances of the variable for this control to the new name.
	How-to a. Display the Properties window for the new File menu item. b. Click on the (Name) entry. c. Enter the text "menuFile."	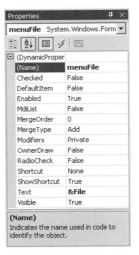

Note: The string "&File" we entered for the menu appears in the Text property.

Your application now contains a File menu on the menu bar. In the source code, the menuFile variable is created as a private MenuItem object within the class.

```
private System.Windows.Forms.MenuItem menuFile;
```

The InitializeComponent method now contains additional lines to initialize this menu and add it to our MainMenu object. The relevant lines are extracted here.

```
private void InitializeComponent()
{
   . . .
   this.menuFile = new System.Windows.Forms.MenuItem ();
   . . .
   //
   // mainMenu1
   //
   this.mainMenu1.MenuItems.AddRange(new
          System.Windows.Forms.MenuItem[] { this.menuFile } );
   //
   // menuFile
   //
   this.menuFile.Index = 0;
   this.menuFile.Text = "&File";
   . . .
}
```

Note in particular how the File menu is added to our `mainMenu1` object by creating an array of `MenuItem` objects with `menuFile` as the only entry. This code also sets an `Index` property, which we will discuss in the next section.

3.2.3 ADDING THE DROPDOWN MENU

So far, we have added the main menu and inserted a File menu in it. Next we will create the dropdown menu that appears when this menu is clicked.

	CREATE THE FILE DROP-DOWN MENU	
	Action	**Result**
1	Create a Load menu item within the File menu. Use the text "&Load." **How-to** a. Make sure the designer window is displayed. b. Click on the File menu. c. Type in "&Load" below the File menu where it says *Type Here*	The Load menu appears as the first item in the drop-down list for the File menu.
2	Display the Properties window for the Load menu item and set the following property values: **Settings** | **Property**	**Value**	 | (Name)	menuLoad	 | Shortcut	CtrlL	 | Text	&Load		The modified properties are displayed in the Properties window. **Note:** The `Shortcut` property defines a keyboard shortcut, in this case Ctrl+L, that immediately invokes the menu as if it were clicked, without actually displaying the menu. The access key Alt+L for this menu can be used to select this menu from the keyboard after the File menu has been displayed.
3	Add a menu separator after the Load menu. **How-to** Enter a dash character '–' as the next menu item.	A menu separator is added to the dropdown menu. **Note:** By definition, a menu separator in .NET is a `Menu-Item` with its `Text` property set to a single dash. We will leave the (Name) of the separator as the default value.

	Create the File drop-down menu *(continued)*	
	Action	**Result**
4	Finally, add the Exit menu item. **Settings** **Property** / **Value** (Name) / menuExit Text / E&xit	The File menu is now complete. **Note:** Of course, the Windows keyboard shortcut Alt-F4 can always be used to close the application. There is no need to add this keystroke to our menu as it is imposed by the operating system.

As you might expect, the code generated for the MainForm.cs file uses `MenuItem` objects to add this dropdown list to the File menu, with the objects initialized in the `InitializeComponent` method. The relevant code from the source file is shown here.

```
private System.Windows.Forms.MenuItem menuLoad;
private System.Windows.Forms.MenuItem menuItem1;
private System.Windows.Forms.MenuItem menuExit;
. . .
private void InitializeComponent()
{
  . . .
  this.menuLoad = new System.Windows.Forms.MenuItem();
  this.menuItem1 = new System.Windows.Forms.MenuItem();
  this.menuExit = new System.Windows.Forms.MenuItem();
  . . .
  //
  // menuFile
  //
  this.menuFile.Index = 0;
  this.menuFile.MenuItems.AddRange(new System.Windows.Forms.MenuItem[]{
                                   this.menuLoad,
                                   this.menuItem1,
                                   this.menuExit});
  this.menuFile.Text = "&File";
  //
  // menuLoad
  //
  this.menuLoad.Index = 0;
  this.menuLoad.Shortcut = System.Windows.Forms.Shortcut.CtrlL;
  this.menuLoad.Text = "&Load";
  //
  // menuItem1
  //
```

❶ **Create File drop-down menu**

❷ **Define keyboard shortcut**

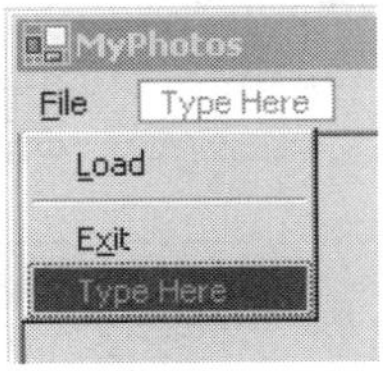

```
        this.menuItem1.Index = 1;                    Create menu
        this.menuItem1.Text = "-";               ❸ separator
        //
        // menuExit
        //
        this.menuExit.Index = 2;                 ❹ Set menu index
        this.menuExit.Text = "E&xit";
        . . .
    }
```

Some aspects of this code are worth highlighting:

❶ As we saw for our main menu, the items to appear under the File menu are added by constructing an array of the desired MenuItem objects and assigning them to the menuFile.MenuItems property. Note that this array does not establish the order in which these items will appear. The display order is established by the menu index assigned to each object.

❷ The Ctrl+L shortcut for the Load menu is defined through the use of the System.Windows.Forms.Shortcut enumeration.

❸ This line creates our separator menuItem1 by setting its Text property to a dash (-).

❹ The Index property defines the zero-based position of the menu item within its parent menu. This position establishes the order in which menu items are displayed. In our code, the dropdown list for the File menu should display the Load menu, then a separator, and then the Exit menu. This is done by setting the Index property for these objects to 0, 1, and 2, respectively.

Our code uses a few of the properties provided by the MenuItem class. Other properties will be used as we progress through this and subsequent chapters. An overview of the MenuItem class appears in .NET Table 3.3.

If you wish to see the application so far, compile and run the code to view the File menu. You will notice that the menu bar contains only a single item, which is perhaps a bit boring. We do not want a boring application, so we will double the number of menus in our next section.

The MenuItem class represents a menu within a MainMenu or ContextMenu object, or a sub-menu of another MenuItem object. MenuItem objects are displayed to the user, while Main-Menu and ContextMenu objects simply establish a container in which MenuItem objects can appear. The MenuItem class is part of the System.Windows.Forms namespace, and inherits from the Menu class. See .NET Table 3.1 on page 72 for a list of members inherited from this base class.

Public Properties	Checked	Gets or sets whether a check mark appears next to the text of the menu item.
	Enabled	Gets or sets whether the menu item is enabled. A disabled menu is displayed in a gray color, cannot be selected, and does not display any child menu items.
	Index	Gets or sets the position of the menu item within its parent menu.
	MergeOrder	Gets or sets the value of the relative position for the menu when it is merged with another.
	OwnerDraw	Gets or sets whether Windows draws the menu (false) or the application will draw the item (true). Used to create custom menus.
	Parent	Gets the Menu object that is the parent of this menu.
	RadioCheck	If Checked is true, gets or sets whether to display a radio button next to the menu instead of a checkmark.
	Shortcut	Gets or sets the shortcut key for this menu item.
	ShowShortcut	Gets or sets whether to display the Shortcut setting when displaying the menu.
	Text	Gets or sets the text to display for the menu. The character following an ampersand (&) is used as an access key.
	Visible	Gets or sets whether to display the menu item.
Public Methods	CloneMenu	Creates a copy of the MenuItem.
	MergeMenu	Merges this menu with another MenuItem.
	PerformClick	Generates a Click event for this item.
	PerformSelect	Generates a Select event for this item.
Public Events	Click	Occurs when the user clicks the menu or accesses it via an accelerator or shortcut key.
	DrawItem	Occurs when the OwnerDraw property is true and a request is made to draw the menu item.
	MeasureItem	Occurs when the size of the menu item is required before drawing it.
	Popup	Occurs before the menu item displays its list of child menus.
	Select	Occurs when the menu is highlighted using the mouse or keyboard.

3.2.4 ADDING A VIEW MENU

We have seen how to add simple menu items and menu separators, so here we will do something different. Let's add a menu with a submenu to see how the displayed image should appear in the window. This will give us an opportunity to cover checked menus as well. Figure 3.5 shows the View menu we will create as it appears in Visual Studio.

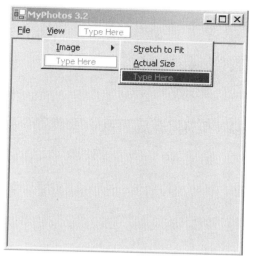

Figure 3.5
Menus in Windows Forms Designer are similar to their appearance in an application, with the addition of a "Type Here" wherever a new menu item can be added.

The View menu and its single menu item Image are created similar to the manner in which the File menu was previously created.

	CREATE THE VIEW MENU	
	Action	**Result**

1	Add a top-level View menu to the right of our existing File menu.
	
	Settings
	
	Property / **Value**
	(Name) / menuView
	Text / &View
		A new `MenuItem` object called `menuView` is created in the MainForm.cs source code
		
		`private System.Windows.Forms.MenuItem menuView;`
		
		This object is initialized in the `InitializeComponent` method as well.
		
		``private void InitializeComponent()
		{
		  this.menuView
		    = new System.Windows.Forms.MenuItem ();
		  . . .
		  menuView.Index = 1;
		  menuView.Text = "&View";
		  . . .
		}```

2	Underneath the View menu, add an Image menu item.	A new `MenuItem` called `menuImage` is created and initialized in the source code.

Settings

Property	Value
(Name)	menuImage
Text	&Image

So far this is similar to our File menu. We continue by creating the submenu to appear when the user clicks the Image menu.

CREATE THE IMAGE SUBMENU	
Action	**Result**

3	Add the "Stretch to Fit" submenu item and assign its properties.
	
	How-to
	Enter this menu to the right of the Image item (not underneath it).
		The new menu appears in Visual Studio .NET as in Figure 3.5. A new `MenuItem` is created in the MainForm.cs source file as well.
		
		`private System.Windows.Forms.MenuItem`
		`    menuStretch;`
		`. . .`

Settings

Property	Value
(Name)	menuStretch
Text	S&tretch to Fit

4	Add the "Actual Size" submenu item.	These changes are reflected in the MainForm.cs source code. In particular, note how the collection of menus in the `menuImage` submenu is initialized to contain our two new values:
		
		`this.menuImage.MenuItems.AddRange(new`
		`        System.Windows.Forms.MenuItem[] {`
		`            this.menuStretch,`
		`            this.menuActual});`

Settings

Property	Value
(Name)	menuActual
Text	&Actual Size

The code generated in MainForm.cs for the View menu is very similar to the code we looked at previously, so we will not discuss it in more detail. Realize that all of our visible menus are `MenuItem` objects regardless of what level they appear on. The View menu, the Image menu item, and the Stretch to Fit submenu item are all objects of type `MenuItem`.

TRY IT!   Compile and run the application to see the menus in action. Notice how the shortcut for the Load menu is displayed within the menu. Try setting the `ShowShortcut` property for this menu to `false` in order to prevent this shortcut from appearing on the menu. Note that the keyboard shortcut still works, the user is just not told about it in the menu bar.

Sit back for a moment and think about what we have done here. If you have used Visual C++ with MFC, you should realize that the secret macros and magic interface files required by this environment are gone. In their place are well-designed objects that can quickly and easily be used to create arbitrarily complex menu structures.

If you have been following the examples with Visual Studio .NET, also realize that you have not written any code thus far. This will change when we add event handlers for our menus in the next section.

3.3   CLICK EVENTS

Of course, a menu is not very useful if you can't make it do something. In this section we'll define some event handlers for our menus and examine how event handlers work in more detail than we covered in chapter 2. This section builds on the MyPhotos version 3.2 project constructed in section 3.2, or available on the book's web site.

Events for Windows Forms controls can be added from the Windows Forms Designer window, or in the Properties window. We will discuss each method separately.

3.3.1   ADDING HANDLERS VIA THE DESIGNER WINDOW

As you might guess, Visual Studio adds a `Click` event handler whenever you double-click a menu control in the Windows Forms Designer. We already saw this behavior for buttons in chapter 2. Let's use this feature to add a handler to the Load menu here.

Set the version number of the application to 3.3.

	ADD CLICK HANDLER FOR THE LOAD MENU	
	Action	**Result**
1	Display the MainForm.cs [Design] window.	

2	Add a `Click` handler for the Load menu
	
	How-to
	a. Click on the File menu.
	b. Double-click on the Load menu.
	
	Note: This double-click method only works for the `Click` event. We will see how to add events more generally in the next section.
		A new event handler for the Load menu is added and the cursor is placed in the MainForm.cs code window within the newly added handler.
		
		```protected void menuLoad_Click(object sender,\n System.EventArgs e)\n{\n}```
		
		The new handler is also registered as a `Click` handler for the Load menu in the `InitializeComponent` method.
		
		```menuLoad.Click += new System.EventHandler\n (this.menuLoad_Click);```

| 3 | Copy the code from the now defunct `btnLoad_Click` into our new method and delete the old method.

Note: Unless you removed it, the code for `btnLoad_Click` should still be present in your code. After copying this code, remove the method. | This code is identical to the code used with our Load button in chapter 2; it is just invoked via a menu rather than a button.

```csharp
protected void menuLoad_Click
    (object sender, System.EventArgs e)
{
  OpenFileDialog dlg = new OpenFileDialog();

  dlg.Title = "Load Photo";
  dlg.Filter = "jpg files (*.jpg)"
      + "|*.jpg|All files (*.*)|*.*";

  if (dlg.ShowDialog() == DialogResult.OK)
  {
    try
    {
      pbxPhoto.Image = new
          Bitmap(dlg.OpenFile());
    }
    catch (Exception ex)
    {
      MessageBox.Show(
          "Unable to load file: "
              + ex.Message);
    }
  }

  dlg.Dispose();
}
``` |

Since this code matches the handler we discussed in chapter 2 for the Load button, we will not discuss it again.

Compile the application to verify that the Load menu now works as expected. You should be able to load a new image using the menu bar via the mouse, using the access keys Alt+F and then Alt+L, or using the keyboard shortcut Ctrl+L.

3.3.2 ADDING HANDLERS VIA THE PROPERTIES WINDOW

Double-clicking our controls in Visual Studio is fine when we wish to add a `Click` event handler for a menu item. What about other types of events? The .NET classes provide a rich set of events for everything from keyboard presses and mouse clicks to redrawing a control. To support these and other events, Visual Studio provides a more generic way to add an event handler than the double-click we have used thus far.

This is done using the Properties window. We have seen how this window provides the list of properties associated with a specific control. It also provides the list of events for each control and allows new event handlers to be added. Figure 3.6 shows the relevant elements of the Properties window. Note the small toolbar buttons between the object dropdown and the list of object members. The Properties button is the default and displays a list of properties for the current object. If you click the Events button, this window displays a list of events. The events for the `menuExit` object are shown in the figure.

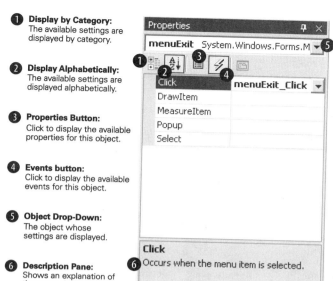

1. **Display by Category:** The available settings are displayed by category.

2. **Display Alphabetically:** The available settings are displayed alphabetically.

3. **Properties Button:** Click to display the available properties for this object.

4. **Events button:** Click to display the available events for this object.

5. **Object Drop-Down:** The object whose settings are displayed.

6. **Description Pane:** Shows an explanation of the currently selected item.

Figure 3.6
The Properties window displays both the properties and events for the controls on the form.

As you can see in the figure, our `menuExit` object supports five different events. These correspond to the events for the `MenuItem` class shown in .NET Table 3.3 on page 82. To the right of these events, the registered event handlers are displayed, with a `menuExit_Click` method shown as the handler for the `Click` event. To add a specific type of event, you simply need to double-click the entry in this window. We will illustrate this by defining a `Click` event handler for the Exit menu.

	Action	Result
ADD CLICK HANDLER FOR THE EXIT MENU		
1	Display the Properties window for the Exit menu.	The available properties for the `menuExit` object are shown.
2	Click the Events button in the Properties toolbar.	The events for the `menuExit` object are displayed.
3	Double-click on the Click item listed in the window.	A `menuExit_Click` handler is added to the `menuExit` object. The new method is registered and defined in the `InitializeComponent` method, and the cursor is located within this new method. ```protected void menuExit_Click (object sender, System.EventArgs e) {```
4	Call the `Form.Close` method within this handler.	``` this.Close(); }``` **Note:** Note how the code for this event handler is split across steps 3 and 4 of this table. We will do this throughout the book as a convenient way to discuss different sections of code for a single member of a class.

The `Form.Close` method is used to exit the application. This method closes the associated form, or the entire application if the form was the startup form for the application.

As you may have noticed in chapter 1, the `Application` class provides an `Exit` method that we could use instead here. This call forces all message loops started by `Application.Run` methods to exit, and closes any forms associated with them as well.

In our existing code, either method would close the application. As we will see in chapter 9, however, the `Close` method ensures that all nonmemory resources associated with a form are disposed, and invokes the `Form.Closing` event to permit additional processing as required. As a result, use of the `Close` method is normally preferred in an Exit menu rather than the `Application.Exit` method.

TRY IT! Once again, compile and run the code to verify that the Load and Exit menus now work. If you feel like experimenting, modify the `Enabled` and `Visible` properties for the Exit menu to see how they change the behavior of this menu.

Our handling of the File menu is now complete. Next we will handle the items in the View menu.

3.4 *POPUP EVENTS AND SHARED HANDLERS*

The File menu is fairly straightforward as menus go. There is a Load item, a separator, and an Exit item. Each menu item raises a `Click` event when pressed, and the associated event handler performs the appropriate operations. Our View menu will handle things a little differently. This menu contains a single Image menu, which in turn points to a submenu with two entries. When a `MenuItem` object contains a nonempty collection in its `MenuItems` property, the `Click` event for that menu is not raised. This makes sense, as the submenu automatically pops up when the parent menu is clicked, making a `Click` event a bit extraneous.

This is the case for the File and View menus on the menu bar. These menus never raise a `Click` event. The same applies to the Image menu, since it is the parent of the `MenuItem` objects `menuStretch` and `menuActual`. Rather than `Click` events, menus such as the Image menu raise a `Popup` event just before their submenu is displayed. This permits an event handler to modify the contents or appearance of the submenu as dictated by the application. An example of this type of handler can be found in the Windows operating system. Display the My Computer window and look at the File menu. The contents of the File menu changes depending on what type of file is currently selected.

In .NET, `Popup` events can be associated with any `MenuItem` or `ContextMenu` object that contains a collection of `MenuItem` objects in their `MenuItems` property.

In this section we will use a `Popup` event associated with the Image menu to control how our two submenu items appear when displayed. Before we do this, we will need a `Click` event handler for our submenu items.

3.4.1 DEFINING A SHARED HANDLER

The submenu for the Image menu item pops up whenever the Image menu is clicked. Our submenu items are selected by the user to control how the image should appear in the window. To implement this behavior, we will alter the `SizeMode` property of our `PictureBox` control depending on which menu was selected. The `SizeMode` values for these menus are as follows

The SizeMode settings for the Image submenu items

MenuItem	SizeMode Setting	Description
Stretch to Fit	StretchImage	As we have already seen, this value causes the image to be stretched or shrunk to exactly fit the display area.
Actual Size	Normal	This displays the actual image data in the display area with the upper left corner of the image in the upper left corner of the display area.

One way to implement this behavior would be to handle the `Click` event for each `MenuItem` in the preceding table, and modify the `SizeMode` setting appropriately in each handler. A fine idea, but not our approach. Instead, this is a great opportunity to see the power of event handlers in .NET, not to mention lay the groundwork for some features we will explore later in this chapter and in other chapters.

For our implementation, we will use a single event handler for both `MenuItem` objects. This handler will also be employed when we discuss context menus later in the chapter, and will ensure consistency between our menu bar and context menu as we add more features in future chapters. To facilitate this amazing behavior, we will define a new structure to hold the `SizeMode` value depending on the `Index` setting of the menu.

Set the version number of the application to 3.4.

	DEFINE ARRAY FOR SIZEMODE SETTINGS	
	Action	**Result**
1	Locate the `MainForm` constructor in the MainForm.cs window.	

| 2 | Add a private array of `PictureBoxSizeMode` values called modeMenu-Array just before the constructor. | `/// <summary>`
`/// Mode settings for the View->Image submenu.`
`/// The order here must correspond to the order`
`/// of menus in the submenu.`
`/// </summary>`
`private PictureBoxSizeMode[] modeMenuArray =`
`{`
`   PictureBoxSizeMode.StretchImage,`
`   PictureBoxSizeMode.Normal`
`};`

Note: To enter the comment preceding the array definition, type in three slashes (/ / /) in Visual Studio and it will automatically expand to a <summary> comment block. |
| 3 | Add a private integer _selectedImageMode after the array. | `private int _selectedImageMode = 0;`

Note: This variable will hold the currently selected display mode for the image. |

With these variables available, a `Click` handler for both the `menuStretch` and `menuActual` menu items can now be implemented. One possible implementation for this handler is shown below:

```
// An example (not our approach) of a shared event handler
protected void menuImage_ChildClick (object sender, System.EventArgs e)
{
  if (sender == (object)menuStretch)
  {
    // Code for Stretch to Window click
  }
  else
  {
    // Code for Actual Size click
  }
}
```

This implementation uses the `sender` parameter provided to the handler to identify which menu was selected. This is an excellent idea and would work just fine. Because all classes ultimately derive from `object`, you can compare the `sender` parameter to your window control variables in order to identify which control raised the event. This is a common tactic used to handle a set of menus with a shared implementation.

In order to provide even more flexibility, we will favor an implementation that is not based on a comparison such as that shown here. This will allow us to modify our menus without the need to modify the code for this handler.

If you recall, the order of the menus within the parent menu `menuImage` is set using the `Index` property. The value of this property can be used as an index into the `modeMenuArray` variable to locate the proper `SizeMode` value.

Since our handler is not specific to any one item, we will call the handler menuImage_ChildClick. Let's create the code required before we discuss this further. This code continues the previous steps that created the variables used by this handler.

	ADD SHARED CLICK HANDLER FOR IMAGE SUBMENU	
	Action	**Result**

4	In the MainForm.cs [Design] window, add a Click event handler for the Stretch to Fit menu called menuImage_ChildClick.
	
	How-to
	a. Display the Properties window for the Stretch to Fit menu.
	b. Click the Events button to show the list of events.
	c. Click the space to the right of the Click item.
	d. Enter the handler "menuImage_ChildClick" by hand.
	e. Press the Enter key.
		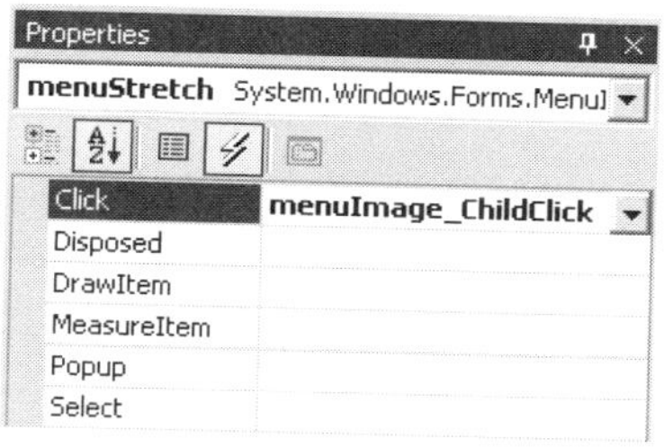 The new method is registered with the menuStretch object in the InitializeComponent method of the MainForm.cs source file:
		`menuStretch.Click +=`
		`    new System.EventHandler (`
		`        this.menuImage_ChildClick);`
		The MainForm.cs code window is shown with the cursor at the beginning of this new method.
		`protected void menuImage_ChildClick`
		`    (object sender, System.EventArgs e)`
		`    {`
		`    }`

5	Add this method as the Click handler for the Actual Size menu as well.
	
	How-to
	a. Display the events for the Actual Size menu.
	b. Click to the right of the Click item.
	c. Click the down arrow.
	d. Select the menuImage_ChildClick event handler from the list.
	
	Note: This down arrow is shown in the graphic for the prior step. Clicking this arrow displays a list of possible event handlers from your code.
		The selected handler is registered with the Actual Size menu in the InidializeComponent method of the MainForm.cs source file.
		`menuActual.Click +=`
		`    new System.EventHandler (`
		`        this.menuImage_ChildClick);`

We now have one event handler that receives the Click event for two different menus. Note how the handler is registered for each menu in the same way as our previous Click handlers.

Continuing with our previous steps, we can now implement this handler.

	Action	Result
IMPLEMENT THE MENUIMAGE_CHILDCLICK EVENT HANDLER.		
6	First, make sure sender is a MenuItem object.	```protected void menuImage_ChildClick (object sender, System.EventArgs e) { if (sender is MenuItem) {``` **Note:** Readers familiar with C# will recognize that this implementation requires two casts, one to perform the is statement, another to cast the sender parameter to a MenuItem object. This can be avoided using the as keyword, which we will discuss later in the book.
7	Create a local MenuItem instance from sender.	```MenuItem mi = (MenuItem)sender;```
8	Set the SizeMode property to the appropriate array value based on the selected menu.	```_selectedImageMode = mi.Index; pbxPhoto.SizeMode = modeMenuArray[mi.Index];```
9	Invalidate the PictureBox control to redisplay the image.	``` pbxPhoto.Invalidate(); } }```

The code for the menuImage_ChildClick handler introduces a few new concepts. We duplicate it here so we can discuss it in more detail.

```
protected void menuImage_ChildClick (object sender, System.EventArgs e)
{
  if (sender is MenuItem)                    ❶ Verify sender is MenuItem object
  {
    MenuItem mi = (MenuItem)sender;          ❷ Downcast sender to MenuItem instance

    _selectedImageMode = mi.Index;           ❸ Assign new
    pbxPhoto.SizeMode = modeMenuArray[mi.Index];    display settings

    pbxPhoto.Invalidate();                   ❹ Invalidate
  }                                             PictureBox
}                                               control
```

Let's look at the new concepts introduced here:

❶ In C++, there is no built-in mechanism for knowing if a variable is a certain type, making it difficult to safely downcast a variable from a base class (such as object) to a derived class (such as MenuItem). In C#, the is keyword provides a way to check that an object (such as the sender parameter) is in fact a specific type (in this case, a MenuItem instance).

❷ The key to this code is the ability to treat `sender` as a `MenuItem` object. The `Index` property is not available in the `object` class, so we need to convert our variable of type `object` into a variable of type `MenuItem`. Since the conversion is "down" the class hierarchy, such a conversion is called a downcast. In C++ such operations are dangerous since `object` might be something other than the target class type. In C#, downcasting is much safer. In fact, an illegal cast of an object throws an exception of type `InvalidCastException`. We verify that sender is a `MenuItem` object to ensure that an exception will not be thrown here.

❸ The `Index` parameter is used to set the currently selected mode as well as an index into the `modeMenuArray` variable for determining the new value for the `SizeMode` property.

❹ Windows Forms controls support the `Invalidate` method. This method invalidates the contents of the control so that the system will redraw, or paint, any changes onto the screen. In this case, we want the control to redraw the image with our new `SizeMode` setting.

Look carefully at what we have done here. This code is based solely on the index of the menu within its parent. We can add new menu items to our View menu or even use an alternate menu with a similar list of items. As long as we keep our `modeMenuArray` up to date, this method will reset the `SizeMode` property appropriately.

TRY IT! Compile your code and verify that the `PictureBox.SizeMode` property is altered when you select a different submenu item. The `PictureBox.SizeMode` property contains more than just the two settings we use here. Add a menu item to the Image menu called `menuCenter` with text Center Image to handle the `CenterImage` value for this property. You will need to add a new `MenuItem` to the menuImage menu and modify the `modeMenuArray` definition to include this new value.

We now have a `Click` handler that will modify the way an image is displayed based on the user's selection. Unfortunately, our interface does not indicate the current display mode in the Image submenu. We will address this problem in the next section by adding a check mark to the current value.

3.4.2 HANDLING POPUP EVENTS

Users appreciate feedback on the current settings for an application. Our current interface does not yet do this. The user has to understand the possible displays modes in order to know what is currently selected and to choose a different setting. A nicer interface would somehow highlight the current selection in the `menuImage` submenu. This would immediately indicate what mode is currently displayed, and help our user make a more informed selection.

If you look at the `MenuItem` class, there is a `Checked` property that, when `true`, will display a check mark next to the menu. This property could be set whenever the selection is modified, and our user would see the appropriate feedback. Of course, as our program changes, there might be other commands or user interactions that alter the display mode of the image. A better approach would ensure that the display modes are checked or unchecked as they are displayed to the user. This approach is more robust in the face of future changes, creating an application that users, documenters, and testers will appreciate for years to come.

The Popup event is designed for just this purpose. This event occurs just before a submenu is displayed, so that its appearance or contents can be modified and then immediately displayed to the user. In Visual Studio, a Popup event handler is added from the Properties window much like we added a Click event in the previous section.

		IMPLEMENT A POPUP HANDLER FOR IMAGE MENU	
	Action	**Result**

1	Add a Popup event handler for the Image menu.
	
	How-to
	a. Display the events for the Image menu in the Properties window.
	b. Double-click the Popup entry
		A Popup event handler is added for the menuImage object. The beginning of this code is shown here:
		
		``csharp
		protected void menuImage_Popup
		   (object sender, System.EventArgs e)
		{
		``

2	Verify that the sender is a MenuItem object.	```csharp
		if (sender is MenuItem) {
		{
		``

3	Determine if an image has been loaded into the application.	```csharp
		bool bImageLoaded
		   = (imgPhoto.Image != null);
		``

4	Set the Enabled and Checked properties for each submenu item.	```csharp
		foreach (MenuItem mi in
		         ((MenuItem)sender).MenuItems)
		{
		   mi.Enabled = bImageLoaded;
		   mi.Checked
		      = (this._selectedImageMode == mi.Index);
		}
		}
		}
		``

Our new handler downcasts the sender object to a MenuItem instance similar to the menuImage_ChildClick handler we already discussed. The handler is repeated below so we can note a few points in the code.

```csharp
protected void menuImage_Popup (object sender, System.EventArgs e)
{
  if (sender is Menu)
  {
    bool bImageLoaded = (pbxPhoto.Image != null);      ❶ Determine if an image is loaded

    Menu parentMenu = (Menu)sender;
    foreach (MenuItem mi in parentMenu.MenuItems)      ❷ Iterate over each submenu item
    {
```

```
        mi.Enabled = bImageLoaded;
        mi.Checked = (this._selectedImageMode == mi.Index);
      }
    }
  }
```

Note that the parentMenu variable here could be defined as a MenuItem object. The Menu type is a base class and allows our handler to accommodate other Menu types in the future. In addition, a couple of C# keywords we have not seen before are worth a special mention.

❶ Unlike C and C++, C# has a built-in boolean type called bool. As a result, boolean expressions such as the one here evaluate to true or false, rather than 0 or 1 as in C. In this case, the bImageLoaded variable will be set to true only after an image has been assigned to the Image property of the pbxPhoto object.

❷ In addition to the for loop used in C and other languages, C# also defines a foreach loop. A foreach loop iterates over the objects in an array or other container object, with the advantage that you don't have to worry about the starting or ending index, or whether the container is empty. The language ensures that each entry in the given container is passed to the loop code. In this case, the loop executes for each MenuItem contained in the given menuImage menu. Within the loop, each MenuItem is enabled only if an image has been loaded, and a check mark is set using the Checked property based on whether the index of the menu item matches the selected image mode.

You may also notice that there is nothing in this handler to indicate that these menu items are part of a specific menu structure. This will be useful in our upcoming discussion on context menus.

Compile and run the application to verify that the menus work correctly, and the display mode of the image changes depending on the menu selection. Figure 3.7 shows the application with an image displayed in Actual Size mode.

Unfortunately, this figure reveals another problem with our PictureBox control. In the figure, the image is larger than the display area, but there is no way to see the rest of the image without resizing the window. While this is possible when the image is small enough, a high-resolution image may contain more pixels than our screen. Ideally, the application should display scroll bars here. Since the PictureBox control does not support scroll bars, this is not possible.

You may be wondering about a book that teaches you how to build an application that doesn't quite work, and you should. Be patient until chapter 7, where we will get rid of our not-quite-right PictureBox control in order to fix this problem.

Figure 3.7
Our Actual Size display mode only shows a portion of the image. The window must be resized to view more.

TRY IT! Okay, I admit this has nothing to do with our application. Still, if you want to have fun with a `Popup` event, add a new menu `menuCounter` at the bottom of the View menu called "Counter" and insert a single menu called "Popup" in its submenu. Define a `Popup` event for the `menuCounter` menu (which Visual Studio will call `menuCounter_Popup`). In this handler, dynamically create a new `MenuItem` object and add it to the end of the `menuCounter` submenu. Set the `Text` property to your new menu to "Count #," where # is the number of pop-ups that have occurred on your new menu. To do this, add a static integer `popupCount` to the `MainForm` class to track the number of pop-ups. The lines to create the new menu in your `Popup` handler will look something like the following.

```
MenuItem mi = new MenuItem();
mi.Text = "Count " + popupCount.ToString();
menuCounter.MenuItems.Add(mi);
```

This example illustrates how easy it is to create controls on the fly with the .NET Framework, and how a parent menu can change the contents of its submenu using the `Popup` event handler. This might be used, for example, to display a list of files most recently opened by an application.

If all this makes no sense to you, download the code for this TRY IT! from the book's web site. Have a look at the `menuCounter_Popup` handler to see the code required.

This concludes our discussion of the main menu in our application. Some of you may be disappointed that we did not look at owner-drawn menus, such as menus that display an icon or other image in addition to or instead of a text string. If this applies to you, skip ahead and go read chapter 4. There we discuss owner-drawn status bar panels, which use a similar mechanism to that required for owner-drawn menus. In the meantime, the rest of us will move on to context menus.

3.5   CONTEXT MENUS

While the creation of context menus requires a little extra effort by a programmer, they also improve the usability of an application greatly and should be seriously considered for any application. The ability of a user to right-click a control and instantly see a list of commands is a powerful mechanism that experienced users especially appreciate. Context menus are typically associated with a specific graphical control, but can also be brought up programmatically. As a result, context menus provide quick access to commands immediately relevant to what the user is currently trying to accomplish or understand.

Most controls in the `System.Windows.Forms` namespace have a `Context-Menu` property that specifies a `ContextMenu` object to associate with the control. Like the `Menu` property on `Form` objects, this setting can be changed dynamically to allow different context menus to display depending on the state of the control.

In this section we will add a context menu to our `PictureBox` control that will match the contents of the View menu. The contents and behavior of our context menu will be inherited from the View menu items. As you will see, our careful handling of these menus earlier in the chapter will make processing events for our context menu a snap. Figure 3.8 shows this context menu both before and after an image has been loaded by the user.

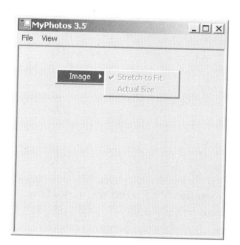 

Figure 3.8   In both the main View menu and the context menu, the display options are disabled before an image is loaded.

3.5.1 CREATING A CONTEXT MENU

We will begin by simply adding a new context menu to our application and associating it with the pbxPhoto control. The next section will discuss how to populate this menu with our existing menu items.

Set the version number of the application to 3.5.

ADD A CONTEXT MENU		
	Action	**Result**
1	Add a ContextMenu object to the form in the MainForm.cs [Design] window. **How-to** a. Open the Toolbox window. b. Drag a ContextMenu object onto the form.	The new object appears below the form next to the existing MainMenu object. **Note:** The Visual Studio window for this step is a bit too big for this space, but is shown in figure 3.9.

2	Rename the new context menu to ctxtMenuView.
	
	How-to
	Use the Properties window to modify the (Name) setting for the object.
		The new name is displayed both below the form and in the Properties window.
		
		All instances of the ContextMenu object in the source code MainForm.cs are renamed as well.
		
		`private System.Windows.Forms.ContextMenu`
		   `ctxtMenuView;`

3	Associate this new context menu with our PictureBox control.
	
	How-to
	a. Display the properties for the pbxPhoto object.
	b. Locate the Context-Menu property.
	c. Click to the right of this entry.
	d. Click the down arrow.
	e. Select the ctxtMenu-View item from the list.
		The down arrow for the ContextMenu property displays the list of available ContextMenu objects available in the form. In our case, only the ctxtMenuView is shown.
		
		In the InitializeComponent method of our MainForm class, the selected context menu is assigned to the property.
		
		`private void InitializeComponent()`
		`{`
		  `. . .`
		   `pbxPhoto.ContextMenu = this.ctxtMenuView;`

When you are finished, your Visual Studio .NET window should look something like figure 3.9. Visual Studio generates all the necessary source code for these changes, excerpts of which appear in the steps shown in the previous table.

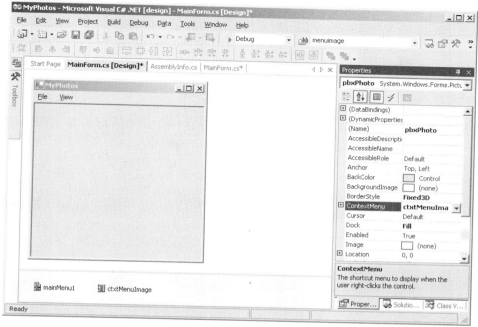

Figure 3.9 The component tray below the designer window is used for objects that do not have a representation on the form itself.

The .NET ContextMenu class is essentially a container for the MenuItem objects that appear within the menu. An overview of this class is shown in .NET Table 3.4.

.NET Table 3.4   ContextMenu class

The ContextMenu class is a popup menu that appears at the current cursor location when a user right-clicks an associated object. This class is part of the System.Windows.Forms namespace, and inherits from the Menu class. Context menus are typically associated with a graphical control, and are displayed automatically at a right-click of the mouse within the control. The Control class contains a ContextMenu property inherited by most controls that establishes a context menu to automatically display for the control. See the Menu class description in .NET Table 3.1 on page 72 for a list of inherited members.

Public Properties	RightToLeft	Indicates whether text in the control should be displayed right to left.
	SourceControl	Gets the last Control object that displayed this context menu.
Public Methods	Show	Displays the menu at a specified position within a given control.
Public Events	Popup	Occurs before a context menu displays its list of child menus.

3.5.2 ADDING MENU ITEMS

We are now ready to add menu items to our context menu. Within Visual Studio, you can click the `ctxtMenuView` object in the designer window to display a "Type Here" message on your form much like it did for the `MainMenu` object. You can enter the items to include on this menu and create submenus and handlers as we discussed earlier in the chapter.

We could use this feature to manually enter the contents of the main View menu into our context menu. The behavior and events would have to be set manually for each menu, and the menu would require updating every time the View menu changes. While this could be done, it would be ideal if we could simply copy the contents of the existing View menu into our new context menu, and inherit the behavior and event handlers already established.

Fortunately, the `MenuItem` class provides a `CloneMenu` method to create a duplicate copy of a menu item. This permits us to very quickly create our context menu with the identical behavior as the existing View menu in the menu bar.

	CLONE THE VIEW MENU ITEMS INTO THE CONTEXT MENU	
	Action	**Result**
1	Create a private `DefineContextMenu` method at the end of the MainForm.cs source file.	```private void DefineContextMenu()
{```
2	For each `MenuItem` in the View menu, clone the menu and add it to our context menu.	```// Copy the View menu into ctxtMenuView
foreach (MenuItem mi in menuView.MenuItems)
{
ctxtMenuView.MenuItems.Add
(mi.Index, mi.CloneMenu());
}
}```
3	Call the new `DefineContextMenu` method from the end of the `MainForm` constructor.	```public MainForm()
{
. . .
DefineContextMenu();
}``` **Note:** Unlike C++, C# does not require forward declarations of functions. The method may be used at the beginning of the file even though it is not defined until the end of the file.

In the implementation of `DefineContextMenu`, note how a `foreach` loop is used to iterate over the items in the View menu. Each item is added to the `ctxtMenuView` context menu using the `MenuItems` property of the class. The identical menu index is used for the new menu so that the order of menus in the context menu will match the order used in the View menu. This feature is important, since the `foreach` loop does not provide any guarantees on the order in which `MenuItem` objects are presented to the loop.

Compile and run this application to see our new context menu in action. The `CloneMenu` method provides a *deep copy*, in that it duplicates not only the Image menu item, but its child menu items and all event handlers associated with each menu. Because of our careful construction of the `Popup` and `Click` event handlers earlier in the chapter, these handlers work without any changes.

It is important to realize that the `MenuItem` objects within our context menu are not the same as those under the View menu. In particular, if you manually modify an item (such as the `menuStretch` menu), it will have no effect on the context menu. This may seem a bit strange to programmers used to managing memory in their application, since there are no pointers or other mechanisms required to track these new `MenuItem` objects. The references to these objects from the context menu are tracked internally as part of the garbage collection system, leaving us to concentrate on our next subject instead of worrying about memory management.

3.6   RECAP

That's it for menus in .NET. In this chapter we showed how both menu bars and context menus can be created, modified, and handled within the .NET Framework by adding these controls to our MyPhotos application. We looked at submenus, and showed how a single event handler can be used by multiple menu objects.

The shared event handlers we created supported both our menu bar as well as our context menu. The contents of our context menu were cloned, or copied, based on the contents of the top-level View menu so that the behavior and processing of both constructs were identical.

We also examined some C# keywords such as the `is`, `in`, and `foreach` keywords, as well as the `bool` type. We looked at the Properties window in Visual Studio .NET in more detail, and used this window to add various events to our program.

Future chapters will rely on our knowledge of menus and the C# and Visual Studio items we have learned here. The next chapter will take us to the bottom of the application window, where the status bar normally resides.

More .NET   One resource for menus specifically and .NET in general is the GotDotNet web site at www.gotdotnet.com. This site is currently managed by Microsoft, and bills itself as the ".NET Framework Community Website."

General information about the .NET Framework can also be found on the Microsoft Developer Network at msdn.microsoft.com. These and other Internet sites with information on .NET are listed in appendix D.

C H A P T E R   4

Status bars

4.1   The Control class 103
4.2   The StatusBar class 105
4.3   Status bar panels 110
4.4   Owner-drawn panels 118
4.5   Recap 125

Most applications stuff a lot of information and features into a single window. Most users do not use all of these features, but there is often a core subset that all users would appreciate having at their fingertips. A status bar is a good place for this type data, as it can provide quick feedback related to the current task or cursor position. My word processor, for example, indicates the current page number, total number of pages, column and line position of the cursor, whether the Insert key has been pressed (which I seem to hit constantly while aiming for the Page Down key), and other information I may want to know at a glance. This helps me keep track of how this book is shaping up, when the Insert key has been pressed, and where these words you are reading will appear on the page.

Status bars can also contain graphical information such as the status of the printer, whether the application is connected to the Internet, and pretty much anything else you can draw or animate.

In this chapter, we will look at status bars in Windows Forms by adding the status bar shown in figure 4.1. As you can see, this status bar contains three areas, called *panels.* You can place any number of panels on a status bar, or you can use a status bar with no panels and simply display text.

Figure 4.1
Our status bar will include the optional sizing grip graphic at the lower right of the control. A user can click this graphic to resize the form.

4.1 THE CONTROL CLASS

Before we venture into the `StatusBar` class, it is worth looking at the classes behind this and all other Windows Forms controls. In chapter 3 we saw how the `Menu` class derived from the `Object`, `MarshalByRefObject`, and `Component` classes. The hierarchy for the `StatusBar` class is shown in figure 4.2.

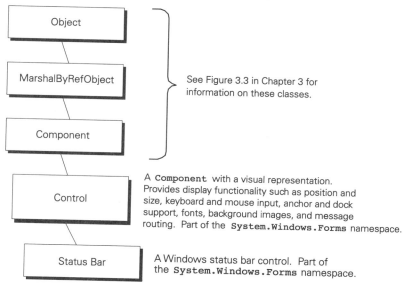

Figure 4.2   The StatusBar class hierarchy includes the base class for all Windows Forms controls: the Control class.

The `Control` class for Windows Forms is a component with a visual representation on the desktop. This class is part of the `System.Windows.Forms` namespace, and inherits from the `System.ComponentModel.Component` class. This class encapsulates the standard functionality used by all Windows Forms controls.

Public Properties	AllowDrop	Gets or sets whether to allow drag and drop operations in this control. Drag and drop operations are discussed in chapter 18.
	Anchor	Gets or sets the anchor setting for the control. The `Dock` property gets or sets the dock setting for the control.
	BackColor	Gets or sets the background color of the control.
	ContextMenu	Gets or sets the context menu for the control.
	Controls	Gets or sets the collection of controls contained by this control.
	ClientRectangle	Gets the client area of the control. The `DisplayRectangle` property gets the display area.
	Cursor	Gets or sets the `Cursor` to display when the mouse is over the control.
	Enabled	Gets or sets whether the control is enabled.
	Location	Gets or sets the location of the control. The edges are available via the `Top`, `Bottom`, `Left`, and `Right` properties.
	Parent	Gets or sets the parent of this control.
	TabIndex	Gets or sets the tab index of the control.
	TabStop	Gets or sets whether the user can use the Tab key to give the focus to the control.
	Text	Gets or sets the text associated with this control.
	Visible	Gets or sets whether control is visible. This also affects any controls contained by this control.
Public Methods	BringToFront	Brings the control to the front of the z-order. A similar `SendToBack` method also exists.
	GetNextControl	Returns the next or previous control in the tab order.
	Invalidate	Invalidates all or part of the control and forces a paint message to be sent to it.
	PointToClient	Converts a screen location to client coordinates.
Public Events	Click	Occurs when the control is clicked.
	KeyPress	Occurs when a key is pressed while the control has focus.
	MouseUp	Occurs when a mouse button is released within the control.
	Paint	Occurs when all or part of the control should be repainted.

The `Control` class extends the `Component` class we saw in chapter 3. All controls are components, and therefore support the `IComponent` and `IDisposable` interfaces. Controls can act as containers for other controls, although not all controls actually do so. The premier example of such a container is the `Form` class, which we have been using for our application window all along. The class hierarchy for the `Form` class is discussed in chapter 7.

All controls are also disposable. When you are finished with a control, you should call the `Dispose` method inherited from the `Component` class to clean up any non-memory resources used by the control.

The `Control` class forms the basis for all windows controls in .NET, and provides many of the properties, methods, and events we have already seen such as the `Left`, `Top`, `Width`, and `Height` properties, the `Invalidate` method, and the `Click` event. An overview of the `Control` class is provided in .NET Table 4.1. Note that only a portion of the many members of this class are shown in the table. Consult the online documentation for the complete list of members.

The `StatusBar` class is just one of many controls derived from the `Control` class. We will look at the `StatusBar` class in more detail in a moment, and other control classes throughout the rest of the book.

4.2   THE STATUSBAR CLASS

Now that we have seen the class hierarchy, let's turn our attention to the `StatusBar` class itself. Typically, an application has only one status bar, although its contents may change as the application is used in different ways. Two types of information are normally displayed on a status bar.

- *Simple text*—the status bar can display a text string as feedback on the meaning of menu commands and toolbars. This is often referred to as flyby text since it displays as the cursor moves over, or flies by, the associated control. A simple string can also display status information on what the application is currently doing. For example, we will use the status bar to display a message while the application is loading a selected image. On a slower machine or for a large image, this will tell our user that the application is busy and currently unavailable.

- *State or attribute information*—another type of data often provided is relevant information about the application or an object displayed by the application. This information is usually divided into separate areas called status bar panels (or status bar indicators or panes). Such information can include both text and graphical data. In this chapter, we will use a status bar panel to display the image size in pixels of the displayed image.

This section will implement the first type of information to display the status bar shown in figure 4.3. As before, this chapter builds on the application constructed in the previous chapter.

Figure 4.3
The status bar shown here uses the Text property of the StatusBar class to display a string to the user.

4.2.1 ADDING A STATUS BAR

As you might expect, a status bar can be added to our application in Visual Studio by dragging one from the Toolbox window onto the form.

Set the version number of the application to 4.2.

ADD A STATUS BAR		
	Action	**Result**
1	Place a status bar at the base of the MyPhotos application. **How-to** a. Display the MainForm.cs [Design] window. b. Drag a `StatusBar` object from the Toolbox window onto the form.	The new status bar appears in the designer window. For lack of a better choice, we'll use the default name `statusBar1`.
2	Set the `Text` property for the `StatusBar` control to "Ready."	

Before we interact with our new status bar, let's take a look at the code so far. An excerpt of the code in our MainForm.cs source file is shown below.

```
. . .
private System.Windows.Forms.StatusBar statusBar1;
. . .
private void InitializeComponent()
{
  . . .
  this.statusBar1 = new System.Windows.Forms.StatusBar();
  . . .
  //
  // statusBar1
  //
  this.statusBar1.Location = new System.Drawing.Point(0, 233);
  this.statusBar1.Name = "statusBar1";
  this.statusBar1.Size = new System.Drawing.Size(292, 20);
  this.statusBar1.TabIndex = 2;              ❶ Set the tab order
  this.statusBar1.Text = "Ready";                for status bar
  . . .
  pbxPhoto.Dock = System.Windows.Forms.DockStyle.Fill;
  . . .
  this.Controls.AddRange(new System.Windows.Forms.Control[] {
                            this.statusBar1,
                            this.pbxPhoto});
}
```

Add the status bar before the picture box ❷

This looks very similar to code we have seen before. As usual, though, there are some points worth highlighting.

❶ This line is a little strange. You do not normally tab into a status bar, so why set a tab index? Visual Studio does this to ensure that each control has a unique index, but it does not mean that you can tab to the status bar control. By default, the StatusBar sets the TabStop property (inherited from the Control class) to false. So the status bar is not a tab stop (by default), even though Visual Studio sets a TabIndex for it.

❷ If you recall, the order in which controls are added establishes the z-order stack (which controls are in front or behind the others). This is important here since the pbxPhoto control takes up the entire window (with Dock set to Fill). By adding the status bar first, this insures this control is on top, docked first, and therefore visible. In the Forms Designer window, you can right-click a control to select the Bring to Front or Send to Back item and modify the z-order.[1] You might try this to verify that the status bar is hidden if you run the application with pbxPhoto at the top of the z-order.

---

[1] You can also change the order in which controls are added by rearranging their order in the Initial-izeComponent method. While Microsoft recommends against this, it does work.

❸ Set the Dock property   I know, there is no number 3 in the code. I'm just trying to see if you're paying attention. The default setting for the `Dock` property in the `Control` class is `DockStyles.None`. The `StatusBar` class overrides this setting to use `DockStyles.Bottom` by default. This ensures the status bar appears docked at the bottom of the form. Since this is the default, Visual Studio does not set this value in the code, so there is no number 3.

A summary of the `StatusBar` class is shown in .NET Table 4.2. One feature noticeably missing from the `StatusBar` class is flyby text. In the MFC classes, menu and toolbar objects can set help messages that appear in the status bar as the cursor passes over the corresponding control. This feature may well be included in a future release of the .NET Framework.

.NET Table 4.2 StatusBar class		
The `StatusBar` class is a control used to show a status bar on a form. This class can display either a textual string or a collection of panels in the form of `StatusBarPanel` objects. Whether the text or panels appear is determined by the value of the `ShowPanels` property. The `StatusBar` class is part of the `System.Windows.Forms` namespace, and inherits from the `Control` class. See .NET Table 4.1 on page 104 for a list of members inherited from the `Control` class, and .NET Table 4.3 on page 116 for more information on the `StatusBarPanel` class.		
Public Properties	Dock (inherited from `Control`)	Gets or sets the dock setting for the control. The default value for status bars is `DockStyles.Bottom`.
	Panels	Gets the `StatusBarPanelCollection` class containing the set of `StatusBarPanel` objects managed by this status bar.
	ShowPanels	Gets or sets whether the panels (if `true`) or text (if `false`) should be displayed on the status bar. Defaults to `false`.
	SizingGrip	Gets or sets whether a sizing grip should be displayed in the corner of the status bar. This grip can be used to resize the form. Defaults to `true`.
	TabStop (inherited from `Control`)	Gets or sets whether the control is a tab stop on the form. The default value for status bars is `false`.
	Text (inherited from `Control`)	Gets or sets the text for the status bar. This is displayed on the status bar only if `ShowPanels` is set to `false`.
Public Events	DrawItem	Occurs when an owner-drawn status bar panel must be redrawn.
	PanelClick	Occurs when a panel on the status bar is clicked.

4.2.2 ASSIGNING STATUS BAR TEXT

In our application, we will add some helpful text when an image is loaded and displayed. This will let the user know when a file is loading, and when it is complete.

		SET THE STATUS BAR TEXT	
	Action	**Result**	

1	Locate the `menuLoad_Click` method in the MainForm.cs code window.	`protected void menuLoad_Click`
		  `(object sender, System.EventArgs e)`
		`{`
		    `OpenFileDialog dlg = new OpenFileDialog();`
		    `. . .`	

2	Define a status bar message before and after an image is loaded.	The changes to the `try-catch` block in this method are shown in bold.	

```
try
{
   statusBar1.Text
       = "Loading " + dlg.FileName;
   pbxPhoto.Image
       = new Bitmap(dlg.OpenFile());
   statusBar1.Text
       = "Loaded " + dlg.FileName;
}
catch (Exception ex)
{
   statusBar1.Text
       = "Unable to load " + dlg.FileName;
   MessageBox.Show(
       "Unable to load file: "
           + ex.Message);
}
```

Whether or not the user sees the `"Loading..."` message depends on the speed of his or her machine and the size of the image. After an image is successfully loaded, the `"Loaded..."` message displays as per figure 4.5 at the beginning of this section.

Since the assignment of the status bar text occurs within a `try` block, it is important to consider the implications of an exception occurring. If an exception is thrown while preparing the file for display in the `PictureBox` control, then the "Loading…" line will still be present on the status bar. To make sure this doesn't happen, we assign the status bar text to a more appropriate value in our exception handler.

Of course, other text messages could be added to our application as well. We will see additional examples as we progress through the book.

TRY IT!   You can implement flyby, or temporary, help text for menu items using the `Select` event in the `MenuItem` class. This event occurs when the cursor is placed over the menu. Handle this event for the Load menu to display the text "Loads a photo to display in the window" on the status bar whenever the cursor hovers over this menu item.

    The `Form` class provides the `MenuStart` and `MenuComplete` events to capture when the menu associated with a form has and then loses focus.

You can use these events to enable and disable the display of help text in the status bar. The easiest way to do this here is to set the `Text` property of the status bar to empty whenever the menu loses focus. Either handle the event in the `MainForm` class or override the protected `OnMenuComplete` method in your `Form` class.

In a form with status bar panels, the `MenuStart` and `MenuComplete` events can be used to toggle between displaying the panels and displaying flyby text on the corresponding status bar. The panels are hidden in the handler for the `MenuStart` event, and redisplayed in the handler for the `MenuComplete` event.

4.3   STATUS BAR PANELS

Now that we have seen how to add a status bar and display simple text, we can talk about status bar panels. Panels provide a nice way to encapsulate a specific nugget of information in a single location. As we will see, panels can present both text and graphical information to your users.

When designing an application, do not crowd so many panels into your status bar that it becomes cluttered and unusable. Make sure the information you provide is desired and useful to your users. An example of an extraneous panel might be the book and pencil graphic that animates whenever you type into Microsoft Word. A pretty little graphic, but who needs to be told when they are typing? Keep your panel information to a minimum, and your users will thank you.

For our application, let's add three panels to provide some information on the displayed image. These panels are shown

Figure 4.4   Status bar panels can be displayed with no border, a sunken border, or a raised border (not shown).

in figure 4.4. The first panel will display the filename of the image; the second the image's dimensions in pixels; and the third will be an owner-drawn panel displaying the percentage of the image currently shown. The following table summarizes these panels. We will use the `sbpnl` prefix to identify these variables as `Status-BarPanel` objects.

StatusBarPanel objects for our application

Panel Name	Contents	Notes
sbpnlFileName	The file name of the image currently displayed.	Later in the book, we will change this panel to display a user-supplied caption. For now, the file name of the image will suffice.
sbpnlImageSize	The dimensions of the image in pixels.	We will write the text for this panel as "*width* x *height*," as shown in figure 4.4.
sbpnlImagePercent	The percentage of the image currently shown.	The percent of image that is shown only changes in the Actual Size display mode. We will show a graphical bar taking up the equivalent percent of the panel.

In this section we will add the new panels to our status bar, and define some text for the first two panels. The final panel is an owner-drawn panel, and is the subject of section 4.4.

4.3.1 Adding panels to a status bar

Let's begin by adding our three panels to the status bar. In Visual Studio, panels are not added via the Toolbox, but rather through the Panels item in the Property window. If you are not using Visual Studio, you can create `StatusBarPanel` objects like you would any other object for your form.

Set the version number of the application to 4.3.

		ADD STATUS BAR PANELS	
	Action		**Result**
1	In the designer window, display the Properties window for the `statusBar1` control.	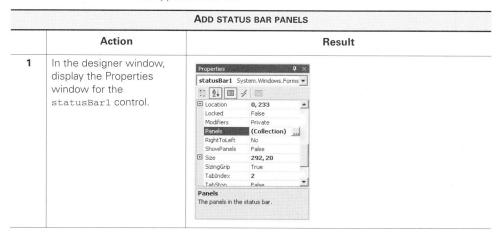	

ADD STATUS BAR PANELS *(continued)*

<table>
<tr><th></th><th>Action</th><th>Result</th></tr>
<tr><td>2</td><td>Display the StatusBarPanel Collection Editor dialog for the status bar.

How-to
a. Click the Panels entry in the Properties window.
b. Click the small ... button that appears.

Note: The <code>Panels</code> property holds the collection of panels for the status bar.</td><td>The StatusBarPanel Collection Editor dialog appears, where panels for the status bar can be added and removed.

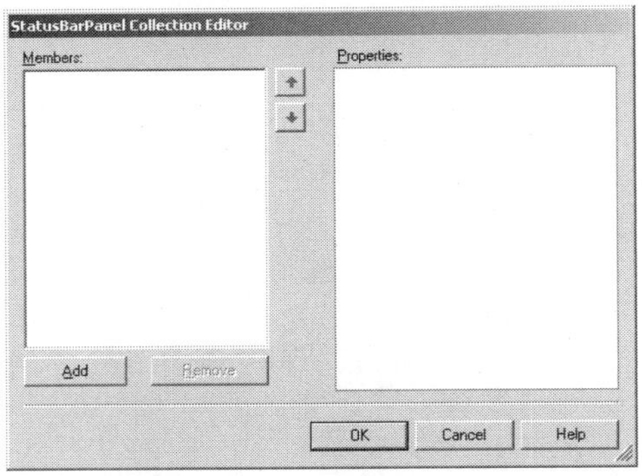
</td></tr>
<tr><td>3</td><td>Add a new panel for the control.

How-to
a. In the Editor window, click the Add button.
b. Set the panel's properties as shown below.

Settings
<table><tr><th>Property</th><th>Value</th></tr><tr><td>(Name)</td><td>sbpnlFileName</td></tr><tr><td>AutoSize</td><td>Spring</td></tr><tr><td>BorderStyle</td><td>None</td></tr><tr><td>ToolTipText</td><td>Image File Name</td></tr></table></td><td>The first panel (number 0) is added to the dialog. Panels are shown in the Members column on the left, and properties are shown on the right.

The dialog after all three panels have been added is shown below in Step 5.</td></tr>
<tr><td>4</td><td>Add the second panel.

Settings
<table><tr><th>Property</th><th>Value</th></tr><tr><td>(Name)</td><td>sbpnlImageSize</td></tr><tr><td>AutoSize</td><td>Contents</td></tr><tr><td>ToolTipText</td><td>Image Size</td></tr></table></td><td>The second panel is added as panel number 1 in the dialog.

Note: The arrow buttons in the center of the Editor dialog are used to alter the order in which panels will appear. We will use this feature in chapter 6 when we add an additional panel to our status bar.</td></tr>
</table>

	Action	Result
5	Add the third panel (panel 2).	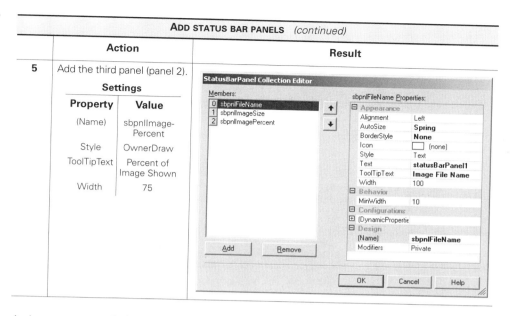

Settings

Property	Value
(Name)	sbpnlImage-Percent
Style	OwnerDraw
ToolTipText	Percent of Image Shown
Width	75

As is our custom, let's look at an excerpt of the code generated by these actions.

```
private System.Windows.Forms.StatusBarPanel sbpnlImagePercent;
private System.Windows.Forms.StatusBarPanel sbpnlImageSize;
private System.Windows.Forms.StatusBarPanel sbpnlFileName;
. . .

private void InitializeComponent()
{
   . . .
    this.sbpnlFileName = new System.Windows.Forms.StatusBarPanel();
    this.sbpnlImageSize = new System.Windows.Forms.StatusBarPanel();
    this.sbpnlImagePercent = new System.Windows.Forms.StatusBarPanel();
    ((System.ComponentModel.ISupportInitialize)
              (this.sbpnlFileName)).BeginInit();
    ((System.ComponentModel.ISupportInitialize) =
              (this.sbpnlImageSize)).BeginInit();
    ((System.ComponentModel.ISupportInitialize)
              (this.sbpnlImagePercent)).BeginInit();
    . . .
    //
    // sbpnlFileName
    //
    this.sbpnlFileName.AutoSize =
          System.Windows.Forms.StatusBarPanelAutoSize.Spring;
    this.sbpnlFileName.BorderStyle =
          System.Windows.Forms.StatusBarPanelBorderStyle.None;
    this.sbpnlFileName.Text = "statusBarPanel1";
    this.sbpnlFileName.ToolTipText = "Image File Name";
```

❶ **Begin panel initialization**

❷ **Set panel properties**

❸ **Set tool tip text**

```
//
// sbpnlImageSize
//
this.sbpnlImageSize.AutoSize =
        System.Windows.Forms.StatusBarPanelAutoSize.Contents;
this.sbpnlImageSize.Text = "statusBarPanel2";
this.sbpnlImageSize.ToolTipText = "Image Size";
this.sbpnlImageSize.Width = 97;
//
// sbpnlImagePercent
//
this.sbpnlImagePercent.Style =
        System.Windows.Forms.StatusBarPanelStyle.OwnerDraw
this.sbpnlImagePercent.Text = "statusBarPanel3";
this.sbpnlImagePercent.ToolTipText = "Percent of Image Shown";
this.sbpnlImagePercent.Width = 75;
. . .
this.statusBar1.Panels.AddRange(new
        System.Windows.Forms.StatusBarPanel[] {
                                        this.sbpnlFileName,
                                        this.sbpnlImageSize,
                                        this.sbpnlImagePercent});

. . .
((System.ComponentModel.ISupportInitialize)
        (this.sbpnlFileName)).EndInit();
((System.ComponentModel.ISupportInitialize)
        (this.sbpnlImageSize)).EndInit();
((System.ComponentModel.ISupportInitialize)
        (this.sbpnlImagePercent)).EndInit();
    . . .
}
```

Set panel properties ❷

Set panel properties ❷

Update StatusBar object ❹

Some of the properties here are a little different than we have seen before. The Status-BarPanel is not a control, but rather a Component object similar to our menu object.

❶ The StatusBarPanel object must be fully initialized before it can be used within the StatusBar control. The ISupportInitialize interface specifies that this object uses a simple transacted notification for batch initialization. When creating such an object, use of the BeginInit and EndInit methods supported by this interface should be used to ensure proper initialization.

❷ Since panels exist within a status bar control, properties exist to indicate how to draw the panel within the containing control. See .NET Table 4.3 for a summary of all properties in the StatusBarPanel class. Some properties used here are briefly explained in the following list.

  • AutoSize indicates whether the panel is automatically sized within the status bar, and if so how. This property uses the StatusBarPanelAutoSize enumeration, with the following values:

StatusBarPanelAutoSize Value	Description
Contents	The width of the panel expands or contracts to fit the actual contents of the panel.
None	The width of the panel is fixed based on the Width property setting. This is the default.
Spring	The width of the panel expands or contracts to share the available space with other panels that have the Spring size setting.

- BorderStyle indicates the type of border to use for the panel, taken from the StatusBarPanelBorderStyle enumeration:

StatusBarPanelBorderStyle Value	Description
None	The panel is displayed with no border.
Raised	The panel is displayed with a raised border.
Sunken	The panel is displayed with a sunken border. This is the default.

- Style indicates how the panel should be drawn, taken from the StatusBarPanelStyle enumeration:

StatusBarPanelStyle Value	Description
OwnerDraw	The panel is drawn by the owner, using the DrawItem event in the StatusBar class.
Text	The panel is drawn by the system using the Text property of the panel.

As you can see from the code, two of our panels display text in the status bar, and one of them is an owner-drawn panel. Each of the AutoSize values are used.

❸ Panels provide a built-in tool tip mechanism in the ToolTipText property. These appear when the cursor hovers over the corresponding panel. We will look at the ToolTips class in chapter 13 as a way to support tool tips for classes derived from the Control object.

❹ Finally, note the changes to our statusBar1 variable. The set of panels is added to the Panels property using the AddRange method.

```
this.statusBar1.Panels.AddRange(new
        System.Windows.Forms.StatusBarPanel[] {
                                        this.sbpnlFileName,
                                        this.sbpnlImageSize,
                                        this.sbpnlImagePercent});
```

The StatusBarPanel class is a component that appears as a panel within a StatusBar control. This class is part of the System.Windows.Forms namespace, and inherits from the System.ComponentModel.Component class. A panel must be associated with a StatusBar instance with its ShowPanels property set to true in order to appear on a form.

Public Properties	Alignment	Gets or sets the HorizontalAlignment for the panel's text.
	AutoSize	Gets or sets how the panel is sized within the status bar.
	BorderStyle	Gets or sets the type of border to display for the panel, if any.
	MinWidth	Gets or sets the minimum width for the panel.
	Parent	Gets the StatusBar object that contains this panel.
	Style	Gets or sets the style used to draw the panel.
	Text	Gets or sets the text for the panel.
	ToolTipText	Gets or sets the tool tip for the panel.
	Width	Gets the current width or sets the default width for the panel.
Public Methods	BeginInit	Begins initialization of the panel when used within a form or other component.
	EndInit	Ends initialization of the panel when used within a form or other component.

4.3.2   ASSIGNING PANEL TEXT

With our panels defined, we simply set the Text property value for each panel to have the text displayed by the application. This only works for panels with their Style property set to Text, of course. We will look at our owner-drawn panel in section 4.4. Since our panels only have meaning after an image is loaded, we assign their values as part of the Click event handler for the Load button, as indicated by the following steps.

	SET THE TEXT TO APPEAR IN THE PANELS	
	Action	**Result**
1	In the menuLoad_Click method, set the ShowPanels property to false while the image is loading.	```private void menuLoad_Click``` ``` (object sender, System.EventArgs e)``` ```{``` ``` . . .``` ``` try``` ``` {``` ``` statusBar1.ShowPanels = false;```

	Action	Result

2	Initialize the `sbpnlFileName` and `sbpnlImageSize` panels after the image is successfully loaded.	`statusBar1.Text = "Loading " + dlg.FileName;`
		
		`pbxPhoto.Image = new Bitmap(dlg.OpenFile());`
		
		`statusBar1.Text = "Loaded " + dlg.FileName;`
		`this.sbpnlFileName.Text = dlg.FileName;`
		`this.sbpnlImageSize.Text`
		`  = String.Format("{0:#} x {1:#}",`
		`      pbxPhoto.Image.Width,`
		`      pbxPhoto.Image.Height);`

3	Set the `ShowPanels` property to `true` so the panel text will appear.	`statusBar1.ShowPanels = true;`
		`  }`
		`    . . .`
		`  }`

Look again at the new `try` block.

```
try
{
    statusBar1.ShowPanels = false;        ❶ Disable the
    statusBar1.Text = "Loading " + dlg.FileName;   panels

    pbxPhoto.Image = new Bitmap(dlg.OpenFile());

    statusBar1.Text = "Loaded " + dlg.FileName;
    this.sbpnlFileName.Text = dlg.FileName;
    this.sbpnlImageSize.Text
      = String.Format("{0:#} x {1:#}",
          pbxPhoto.Image.Width, pbxPhoto.Image.Height);   ❷ Create image
    statusBar1.ShowPanels = true;                            size string
}
```

Two items are worth noting in this code:

❶ The `ShowPanels` property is set to `false` while an image is loading so that the `StatusBar.Text` property setting will appear, and set to `true` after the image is loaded and the panels are set.

❷ The `Format` method used here is a static method provided by the `String` class for constructing a string. We could spend a chapter covering this and other features available in C# strings generally and the .NET `System.String` class specifically, but instead will assume you can look this one up in the documentation. In the code shown here, the `"{0:#} x {1:#}"` string indicates that two parameters are required, both of them integers.

Build and run the application to see these panels in action. Resize the window to see how the panels react. You will notice that the first panel resizes automatically along with the window, while the second two panels maintain their initial size. This is consistent with the `AutoSize` settings we used for these objects.

4.4 OWNER-DRAWN PANELS

So what about this owner-drawn panel? Text panels do not need to worry about drawing their text onto the panel, as the .NET Framework handles this internally. There are some cases where text just will not do, and these situations requiring manual drawing of the panel.

Drawing of panels and other objects in .NET are handled through use of the `System.Drawing` namespace, sometimes referred to as GDI+ since it is based on an update to the graphical drawing interface provided by Microsoft. Components such as menus, status bars, and tabs that contain drawable components support a `DrawItem` event that occurs when an item in the component should be drawn. Controls derived from the `Control` class provide a `Paint` event for this purpose. Both types of drawing make use of the `Graphics` class discussed in this section in order to draw the item.

This section will examine how owner-drawn status bar panels are supported, and draw the `sbpnlImagePercent` panel for our application. A similar discussion would apply to owner-drawn menu items or other objects supporting the `DrawItem` event. The result of our changes is shown in figure 4.5.

Figure 4.5
The third status bar panel here indicates that 30 percent of the image is visible in the window.

As you can see in the figure, when the image is displayed in Actual Size mode, the third panel will show a numeric and visual representation of how much of the image is displayed. Before we draw this panel, let's take a closer look at the `DrawItem` event.

4.4.1 THE DRAWITEM EVENT

The `DrawItem` event is used by a number of classes to draw an item contained within some sort of larger collection. For instance, the `MenuItem`, `ListBox`, and `ComboBox` classes all include a `DrawItem` event for custom drawing of their contents. These classes use the `DrawItemEventArgs` class to provide the data associated with the event. The `StatusBar` class uses a derived version of this class, but the bulk of the drawing information is in the base class. An overview of this base class is provided in .NET Table 4.4.

The `DrawItemEventArgs` class is an event object used when handling `DrawItem` events in a number of classes. This class is part of the `System.Windows.Forms` namespace, and inherits from the `System.EventArgs` class. Practically, this class is used to manually draw list box items, menu items, status bar panels and other objects.

The `StatusBarDrawItemEventArgs` class extends this class for use with `StatusBar` objects. This class includes a public `Panel` property to indicate which panel requires drawing.

Public Properties	Bounds	Gets the `Rectangle` of the area to be drawn with respect to the entire graphical area for the object.
	Font	Gets a suggested `Font` to use for any text. Typically, this is the parent's `Font` property.
	ForeColor	Gets a suggested `Color` to use for foreground elements, such as text. Typically, this is `SystemColors.WindowText`, or `SystemColors.HighlightText` if the object is selected.
	Graphics	Gets the `Graphics` object to use for painting the item.
	Index	Gets the index of the item to be painted. The exact meaning of this property depends on the object.
	State	Gets additional state information on the object, using the `DrawItemState` enumeration. Examples include whether the item is selected, enabled, has the focus, or is checked (for menus).
Public Methods	DrawBackground	Draws the `Bounds` rectangle with the default background color.
	DrawFocusRectangle	Draws a focus rectangle in the `Bounds` area.

For the `StatusBar` class, the `StatusBarDrawItemEventArgs` class derives from the `DrawItemEventArgs` class and is received by `StatusBar.DrawItem` event handlers. The `Panel` property provided by this class is useful both for identifying the panel and when the text assigned to the panel is needed.

When a `DrawItem` event handler is invoked, the default property values are what you might expect. The `Bounds` property is set to the display rectangle of the panel to draw. This rectangle is with respect to the rectangle for the containing status bar, so the upper left corner of a panel's bounds is not (0,0). The `Font` and `ForeColor` properties are set to the font information for the `StatusBar` object; the `Graphics` property to an appropriate drawing object, the `Index` to the zero-based index number of the panel, and `State` is typically set to `DrawItemState.None`. The `DrawItem` event is called once for each panel drawn.

The `System.Drawing` namespace provides access to basic graphics functionality provided by the graphical device interface (GDI+). The classes in this namespace are used when drawing to any display device such as a screen or printer, and to represent drawing primitives such as rectangles and points.

Classes	Brush	An abstract class representing an object used to fill the interior of a graphical shape. For example, the `Graphics.FillRectangle` method uses a brush to fill a rectangular area on a drawing surface. Classes derived from this class include the `SolidBrush` and `TextureBrush` classes.
	Brushes	A sealed class that provides `Brush` objects for all standard colors. For example, the `Brushes.Red` property can be used to fill shapes with a solid red color.
	Font	Represents a font that defines how text is drawn. This includes the font style and size as well as the font face.
	Graphics	Represents a GDI+ drawing surface. Members are provided to draw shapes, lines, images, and other objects onto the drawing surface.
	Image	An abstract class for image objects such as `Bitmap`.
	Pen	Represents an object used to draw lines and curves. A pen can draw a line in any color and specify various styles such as line widths, dash styles, and ending shapes (such as arrows). For example, the `Graphics.DrawRectangle` method uses a pen to draw the outline of a rectangular area on a drawing surface.
	Region	Represents the interior of a graphics shape composed of rectangles and paths.
	SystemColors	A sealed class that provides `Color` objects for the colors configured in the local Windows operating system. For example, the `SystemColors.Control` property returns the color configured for filling the surface of controls. Similar classes also exist for `Brush`, `Pen`, and `Icon` objects based on the local system configuration.
	Color	Stores a color value. A number of static colors are defined, such as `Color.Red`, or a custom color can be created from an alpha component value and a set of RGB values.
Structures	Point	A two-dimensional point as an integral x and y coordinate.
	PointF	A two-dimensional point as a floating point x and y coordinate.
	Rectangle	Stores the location and size of a rectangular region within a two-dimensional area. All coordinates are integral values.
	Size	Represents the size of a rectangular region as an integral width and height.
	SizeF	Represents the size of a rectangular region as a floating point width and height.

A number of classes are available in the `System.Drawing` namespace for drawing status bar panels, menu items, and other objects. An overview of this namespace is provided in .NET Table 4.5. Rather than provide detailed coverage of this namespace in any one chapter of the book, we will visit members of this namespace as required by our application. In particular, we will use this namespace again in chapter 7 when drawing on `Form` and `Panel` controls, and also in chapter 10 when discussing owner-drawn list boxes.

4.4.2   DRAWING A PANEL

So let's draw the panel in our application. If you recall, we want this panel to show what percentage of the image is shown in the `PictureBox` control. To do this, we need to handle the `DrawItem` event. We will build this code step by step. The complete code for the handler is shown following the table.

Set the version number of the application to 4.4.

<table>
<tr><th colspan="3">ADD DRAWITEM HANDLER</th></tr>
<tr><th></th><th>Action</th><th>Result</th></tr>
<tr>
<td>1</td>
<td>Handle the `DrawItem` event for the `StatusBar` control in the MainForm.cs [Design] window.

How-to

In the Properties window for the status bar, double-click the DrawItem entry.</td>
<td>An event handler for the `DrawItem` event is added to the control.

```
protected void statusBar1_DrawItem
    (object sender,
        StatusBarDrawItemEventArgs sbdevent)
{
```
</td>
</tr>
<tr>
<td>2</td>
<td>In this handler, check that the panel to draw is the sbpnlImagePercent panel.

Note: This `if` statement is not strictly necessary. Still, since the event relates to the entire status bar and not just this panel, this provides some robustness against future changes.</td>
<td>

```
if (sbdevent.Panel == sbpnlImagePercent)
{
    // Calculate the percent of the image shown
    // Calculate the rectangle to fill
    // Draw the rectangle in the panel
    // Draw the text on top of the rectangle
}
}
```

Note: The four comments here are the four steps that must be performed to draw the panel. Each step is performed in the subsequent four steps of this table.</td>
</tr>
</table>

	Action	Result
3	Calculate what percentage of the image appears in the window. **How-to** a. If the `SizeMode` setting for the image is `StretchImage`, use 100% of the panel. b. Otherwise, divide the smaller of the display area and the image size by the total image area. c. For simplicity, use integer percent values.	```// Calculate the percent of the image shown` `int percent = 100;` `if (pbxPhoto.SizeMode` ` != PictureBoxSizeMode.StretchImage)` `{` ` Rectangle dr = pbxPhoto.ClientRectangle;` ` int imgWidth = pbxPhoto.Image.Width;` ` int imgHeight = pbxPhoto.Image.Height;` ` percent = 100 * Math.Min(dr.Width, imgWidth)` ` * Math.Min(dr.Height, imgHeight)` ` / (imgWidth * imgHeight);` `}```
4	Calculate the rectangular region to fill. **How-to** Use the event's `Bounds` property and adjust its `Width` based on the calculated percent.	```// Calculate the rectangle to fill` `Rectangle fillRect = sbdevent.Bounds;` `fillRect.Width = sbdevent.Bounds.Width` ` * percent / 100;```
5	Draw this rectangle in the panel. **How-to** a. Use the `Graphics` object for the event. b. Paint the rectangle with the `FillRectangle` method, using a `SlateGray` brush.	```// Draw the rectangle in the panel` `sbdevent.Graphics.FillRectangle(` ` Brushes.SlateGray, fillRect);``` **Note:** We could also have used the `ForeColor` property of the event as the color here. This code illustrates using the `Brushes` class, which provides access to a `Brush` object for all standard colors available in the framework.
6	Draw the percentage value in the panel. **How-to** Use the `DrawString` method for the `Graphics` object.	```// Draw the text on top of the rectangle` `sbdevent.Graphics.DrawString(` ` percent.ToString() + "%",` ` sbdevent.Font,` ` Brushes.White,` ` sbdevent.Bounds);``` **Note:** White is a good color choice if used with the default desktop colors. It may not be a good choice if custom desktop colors are used.

The complete code for this handler is shown as follows:

```
protected void statusBar1_DrawItem (object sender,
     StatusBarDrawItemEventArgs sbdevent)
{
  if (sbdevent.Panel == sbpnlImagePercent)
```

```
{
  // Calculate the percent of the image shown
  int percent = 100;
  if (pbxPhoto.SizeMode != PictureBoxSizeMode.StretchImage)
  {
    Rectangle dr = pbxPhoto.ClientRectangle;
    int imgWidth = pbxPhoto.Image.Width;
    int imgHeight = pbxPhoto.Image.Height;
    percent = 100 * Math.Min(dr.Width, imgWidth)
      * Math.Min(dr.Height, imgHeight) / (imgWidth * imgHeight);
  }

  // Calculate the rectangle to fill
  Rectangle percentRect = sbdevent.Bounds;
  percentRect.Width = sbdevent.Bounds.Width * percent / 100;

  // Draw the rectangle in the panel
  sbdevent.Graphics.FillRectangle(Brushes.SlateGray, percentRect);

  // Draw the text on top of the rectangle
  sbdevent.Graphics.DrawString(percent.ToString() + "%",
    sbdevent.Font, Brushes.White, sbdevent.Bounds);
}
}
```

The Graphics class used in this handler provides a rich set of drawing capabilities, from circles, ellipses, and rectangles to polygons, pie shapes, and bezier curves. Here we use the FillRectangle method, which requires a Brush object to use when "painting" the rectangle. In chapter 7, we will make additional use of this class. See .NET Table 4.6 for an overview of some of the more interesting members of this class.

It should be noted that the statusBar1_DrawItem handler is invoked each time a panel must be redrawn. As a result, care should be taken in handlers such as this to avoid expensive calculations or other operations that might adversely affect the performance of the application. For example, if we had generated a custom Brush object while filling the rectangle here, such an operation would be performed each time the handler is invoked, potentially using an excessive amount of memory over the life of the application. Of course, our choice of the SlateGray color might not be the best choice either, as it might interfere with colors the user has selected for their desktop. A better option here might be to determine a color programmatically based on the user's desktop settings, and generate a single Brush object the first time the event handler is invoked that is reused for the life of the application.

You can compile and run this code so far if you like, but we do need to make one more change. When the PictureBox.SizeMode property is StretchImage, the complete image (100%) is always shown. When SizeMode is set to Normal, the amount of image shown varies as the size of the client area changes. As a result, when the user changes this setting, we need to make sure that our panel is redrawn by invalidating the contents of the status bar.

The Graphics class is a drawing object that encapsulates a drawing surface , or more specifically a graphical device interface (GDI+) drawing surface. This class is part of the System.Drawing namespace, and inherits from the System.MarshalByRefObject class. Drawing the outline of a shape typically requires a Pen object, while drawing a filled-in shape typically requires a Brush object.

This class contains a large number of members, but the list here should provide some idea of the supported functionality.

Public Static Properties	FromHdc	Returns a Graphics instance from a given handle to a device context.
	FromHwnd	Returns a Graphics instance from a given window handle.
Public Properties	Clip	Gets or sets as a Region object the portion of the graphics area available for visible drawing.
	DpiX	Gets the horizontal resolution supported by the object.
	DpiY	Gets the vertical resolution supported by the object.
	PageUnit	Gets or sets the GraphicsUnit value specifying the unit of measure for page coordinates.
	SmoothingMode	Gets or sets the SmoothingMode value indicating how shapes are rendered with this object.
	TextRenderingHint	Gets or sets the TextRenderingHint value indicating how text is rendered with this object.
Public Methods	Clear	Fills the entire drawing surface with a specified color.
	DrawCurve	Draws a curve specified as an array of points using a given Pen.
	DrawEllipse	Draws the outline of an ellipse (which might be a circle) bounded by a given rectangle using a given Pen.
	DrawLine	Draws a line using a given Pen.
	DrawRectangle	Draws the outline of a rectangle using a given Pen.
	FillClosedCurve	Fills the interior of a closed curve specified as an array of points using a given Brush.
	FillEllipse	Fills the interior of an ellipse (which might be a circle) bounded by a given rectangle using a given Brush.
	FillRectangle	Fills the interior of a rectangle using a given Brush.
	MeasureString	Returns the size a given string would occupy using a given Font.

If you recall, our menus invoke the `menuImage_ChildClick` method to alter the display mode by assigning a new `SizeMode` value.

INVALIDATE STATUS BAR	
Action	**Result**
7	Modify the `menuImage_Child-Click` method to force a redraw of the status bar.	`protected void menuImage_ChildClick(object sender, System.EventArgs e)` ...

```
protected void menuImage_ChildClick(object sender,
        System.EventArgs e)
{
    if (sender is MenuItem)
    {
        MenuItem mi = (MenuItem)sender;

        nSelectedImageMode = mi.Index;
        pbxPhoto.SizeMode
            = this.modeMenuArray[mi.Index];
        pbxPhoto.Invalidate();
        statusBar1.Invalidate();
    }
}
```

Now the status bar will be redrawn whenever the `SizeMode` property is altered. Note that this change highlights another advantage of our decision in chapter 3 to handle the `Click` of an Image submenu item with a shared handler. If we decided to add additional display modes in the future, this code will ensure that the status bar is redrawn correctly each time it changes.

Compile and run your application to verify that the code works as expected. Display an image in both Stretch to Fit and Actual Size mode to see how the owner-drawn status bar panel behaves when the application is resized.

4.5 RECAP

This chapter introduced the `StatusBar` class and showed how both text and panel information are displayed in this control. We looked at how to switch between the display of text and panels in a status bar, and discussed how various properties can be used to alter the appearance and behavior of status bar panels.

We also presented the base class of all Windows Forms controls by looking at the `Control` class in some detail. A discussion of owner-drawn panels and the use of the `DrawItem` and `Paint` events led to a discussion of the `System.Drawing` namespace in general, and the `Graphics` class in particular.

The next chapter takes us out of the Windows Forms namespace briefly in order to discuss reusable libraries.

C H A P T E R   5

Reusable libraries

5.1 C# classes and interfaces 127
5.2 Class libraries 133
5.3 Interfaces revisited 145
5.4 Robustness issues 151
5.5 Recap 160

This chapter is our chance to lean back in our respective chairs, take stock of where we've been, and plan for the future. Before we jump back into the Windows Forms classes in chapter 6, we will build some infrastructure and introduce some important programming concepts. Some of you may be familiar or comfortable with these concepts; others may not. The discussion will attempt to provide enough material to review what is needed without getting too bogged down in the minute details.

Looking at our MyPhotos application, it would be great if this application turned out to be somewhat useful. As such, it is worth laying the proper groundwork for the road ahead. So far, we have built an application with the following features:

- A title bar where the name and version number of the program are displayed.

- A menu bar where the user can access commands such as loading an image.

- A main window that displays a single photo at a time (stretched and distorted, but displayed nonetheless).

- A status bar where information about the displayed photo appears.

So now what? In this book, there are a number of features that still need to be covered. Tool bars, dialog boxes, splitters, and printing, to name a few. In order to do this we will need more than a single photograph in our application. If we can display one, why not more than one. Let's display multiple photos. We will call this, of course, a photo album.

To keep this chapter somewhat manageable, we will not muck with our main application window here. We will focus instead on creating a photo album abstraction, and wait until chapter 6 to integrate it into our application. Specifically, we will perform the following tasks in this chapter:

- Create a `PhotoAlbum` class to represent a collection of photograph files.
- Create a `Photograph` class to represent a single photograph.
- Compile the `PhotoAlbum` and `Photograph` classes into an external library.

Before we write any code for these classes, a short design discussion is in order.

5.1 C# CLASSES AND INTERFACES

Within our application, we need to represent the album in a way that facilitates the required actions, such as "add an image," "move to the next photo," and so forth. You may immediately think of some sort of array, and this will be our approach. This section will present a short design discussion as a way to introduce some terminology we require and lay the groundwork for writing our code.

Each photo is an image file located somewhere on disk. While a simple list of files could be stored in an array of strings, we should not be too hasty here. Requirements change, as do applications. We may want to add additional features to our photo album later, so it makes sense to encapsulate our album in a class to make this possible. Classes in C# are very similar to classes in the C++ and Java languages. We will create a `PhotoAlbum` class to represent a single photo album, and provide a set of methods that external users of the class, such as our MyPhotos application, can use to retrieve and modify the contents of the album.

What will our album contain? We already mentioned the idea of array file names. Since we would like to provide quick access to the images, we could also consider an array of `Bitmap` objects. Not a bad idea, except that a bitmap can be pretty large. A full color image such as a photograph uses 24 bits, or three bytes per pixel: one each for a red, blue, and green color. Do the math and you'll find that a 640×480 pixel image takes up around 900K in memory, or almost 1 MB. A system with 32 MB of RAM will run out of memory fairly quickly, and even 128 or 256 MB systems will feel the pinch. Of course, virtual memory will allow us to use more than the available physical memory, but the performance will not make our users happy. Instead of bitmaps, we will stick with the file names of our images, and create `Bitmap` objects as required. To accommodate both types of information, and to extend this definition in the future, we will create a `Photograph` class to encapsulate the concept of a single photograph. Our album will contain zero or more photographs.

One more feature here: once we build our `PhotoAlbum` and `Photograph` classes, they could be useful in other programs that wish to use our concept of a photo album. For example, a genealogy program for creating family trees might want to link to a photo album of a specific person or family. So we will place our new classes in a library that other programs can reuse. In Windows parlance, such a library is called a Dynamic Link Library, or DLL.

5.1.1 INTERFACES

As you might expect, the .NET Framework provides a number of classes that can help us here. These classes implement common data structures such as arrays, stacks, queues, and hash tables. Before the ever-appropriate table summarizing such classes, this is a good place to introduce the idea of an interface.

An *interface* is an abstraction of an abstraction, and should be familiar to programmers of COM or its UNIX ancestor, the distributed computing environment (DCE). While a class encapsulates a data structure and its operations, an interface encapsulates a type of data structure and its operations. This is very similar to an abstract class, except that an interface does not provide any implementations for its members, it just defines the properties, methods, and events that a class should implement in order to support the interface. In practice, an interface is a good way to encapsulate a common idea for use by a number of possibly unrelated classes, while an abstract class is a good way to encapsulate a common idea for use by a number of related classes.

For example, the .NET `ICloneable` interface defines a type of class that can be cloned, or copied, from an existing class instance to a new one.[1] This concept applies to the `Array`, `Brush`, `Font`, `String`, and a number of other classes throughout the .NET Framework. Languages such as C++ provide multiple inheritance for this type of support. In C++, `ICloneable` could be an abstract class and inherited where needed. In C# and Java, only single inheritance is supported, so this is not possible. Instead, both languages provide interfaces as a way to encapsulate common functionality that can be used by a wide range of classes.

For example, the `Brush` class supports the `ICloneable` interface. We used this abstract class in chapter 4 to create an owner-drawn status bar panel. `Brush` objects can be cloned to create a new copy of an existing `Brush`. You can create an instance of a `Brush`, since it is a class, but you cannot create an instance of an `ICloneable` except as a by-product of an existing class that happens to support this interface.

The .NET Framework provides interfaces for everything from enumerating members of a set to transferring data between applications. Some interfaces related to our current discussion on albums are listed in the following table.

---

[1] Generally speaking, cloning in .NET always produces a *deep copy* of an object, as we saw for the menu classes in chapter 3.

Interfaces related to data collections

Interface	Description	Sample Members
IEnumerable	Interface that supports the creation of an enumerator class for iterating over the elements in a collection. **Usage** Supporting this interface allows the C# foreach statement to be used with instances of a class or structure.	GetEnumerator method, which returns a class that supports the IEnumerator interface.
IEnumerator	Interface for stepping through the elements in a collection.	Current property, to retrieve the current element from the collection. MoveNext method, which advances to the next element in the collection. Reset method, which sets the enumerator just before the first element.
ICollection	An IEnumerable interface that provides sizing and synchronization capabilities. This interface is the basis for all collections in the .NET Framework.	Count property, to retrieve the number of elements in the collection. SyncRoot property, to retrieve an object for synchronizing multi-threaded access to the collection. CopyTo method, which copies the elements in the collection into an Array object.
IList	An ICollection interface that provides indexing of its elements. **Usage** Supporting this interface allows a class or structure to be treated as an array. This permits objects to be used as targets of data bound controls, as discussed in chapter 17.	Item property, to support array-style indexing of elements using [brackets], much like a [ ] override in C++. Add method, which adds a new element to the collection. Contains method, which determines if the collection contains a specific object. Remove method, to remove the element from the collection at a given index value.

5.1.2 DATA COLLECTION CLASSES

Looking over the interfaces in the table, the IList interface seems particularly appropriate for the task at hand. This allows elements to be added and removed from the collection, and supports array-style indexing. Some of the data collection classes in the .NET Framework are shown in the following table. Note, in particular, those classes in the table that support the IList interface.

Some .NET classes related to data collections

Class	Description	Interfaces supported
Array	The base class for all array objects. This class is abstract.	ICloneable, IList, ICollection, IEnumerable
ArrayList	A dynamically-sized array.	ICloneable, IList, ICollection, IEnumerable
CollectionBase	An abstract class for creating a strongly typed collection.	IList, ICollection, IEnumerable
DataView	A customized view of a database table.	IList, ICollection, IEnumerable, and others
Hashtable	A collection of values stored based on a hash code of the value, called a key.	ICloneable, ICollection, IEnumerable, IDictionary, and others
Queue	A FIFO queue; a first in, first out collection of objects.	ICloneable, ICollection, IEnumerable
SortedList	A sorted collection of keys and values accessible by both key and index.	ICloneable, ICollection, IEnumerable, IDictionary
StringCollection	A collection of string objects.	IList, ICollection, IEnumerable
Stack	A LIFO queue; a last in, first out collection of objects.	ICloneable, ICollection, IEnumerable

Since we do not have a database here, the DataView class is not appropriate. If all we wanted was a collection of file names, the StringCollection class would work, but then our PhotoAlbum would not be very extensible. This leaves us with a simple array or the ArrayList or CollectionBase classes. A simple fixed-size array is not appropriate since we would like our album to grow dynamically. So we are left to choose between the ArrayList and CollectionBase classes.

Either class would work here, and both classes can be quite useful. An overview of the ArrayList class is shown in .NET Table 5.1. Deriving our PhotoAlbum class from ArrayList would look like this:

```
// Deriving PhotoAlbum from ArrayList (not our approach)
public class PhotoAlbum : System.Collections.ArrayList
{
    // Inherits all properties and methods from ArrayList
}
```

An advantage of this approach is that we would not need to implement many of the methods, since they would be directly inherited from ArrayList. A disadvantage is that all methods would accept any object, and not just our Photograph objects. If you look at the documentation, you will see that the methods in ArrayList operate on object instances. For example, the PhotoAlbum.Add method would have the following signature:

```
// PhotoAlbum.Add when derived from ArrayList
public int Add( object value );
```

So while this would be a very easy implementation, the methods in our PhotoAlbum class would not be type-safe, and therefore not so robust.

The ArrayList class is a collection of indexed objects where the number of objects can change dynamically. This class is part of the System.Collections namespace, and is very similar to the Array class for fixed-length collections of objects. The ArrayList class supports the ICloneable, IEnumerable, ICollection, and IList interfaces.

Public Properties	Capacity	Gets or sets the maximum number of objects the list can contain.
	Count	Gets or sets the actual number of objects in the array.
Public Methods	Add	Adds an object to the end of the array.
	AddRange	Adds the elements from an ICollection interface to the end of the array.
	Clear	Removes all objects from the array.
	Contains	Determines if an object is in the array. Comparison is done using the Object.Equals method.
	CopyTo	Copies the ArrayList, or a portion of it, into a one-dimensional Array object.
	IndexOf	Returns the zero-based index of the first occurrence of the given object in the array, or −1 if the object is not found. Comparison is done using the Object.Equals method.
	Remove	Removes an object from the array.
	RemoveAt	Removes the object at a given index from the array.
	Sort	Sorts the array, using an IComparable interface to compare objects.
	TrimToSize	Sets the capacity of the array to the actual number of objects in it.

Let's instead take a look at the CollectionBase class. An overview of this class is shown in .NET Table 5.2. This class is an abstract class, and requires derived classes to implement the additional methods required to support the appropriate interfaces. This requires a little more work on our part, but creates a nicer interface that works with Photograph objects directly.

Before we create our implementation, note that an alternative implementation would incorporate a private ArrayList object in a class derived directly from System.Object. This alternative would look something like the following:

```
// PhotoAlbum implementation with private ArrayList (not our approach)
class PhotoAlbum
{
  // internal (not inherited) ArrayList
```

```
private ArrayList _photoArray;

// Constructor and other wrappers

// Custom Add wrapper
public int Add(Photograph photo)
{
    return _photoArray.Add(photo);
}
}
```

This would work just fine and be similar to our actual implementation derived from `CollectionBase`. Our implementation is more appropriate than this alternative, since the `CollectionBase` class is designed for just this purpose, and does in fact provide access to an `ArrayList` member through a protected property.

.NET Table 5.2   CollectionBase class

The `CollectionBase` class is an abstract class for creating strongly typed collections. A class is *strongly typed* if it only allows a specific type or types in its methods, rather than a generic type such as an `object`. Strongly typed classes allow the compiler to ensure that the proper objects are passed to methods in the class, and can prevent errors that would otherwise occur only at runtime.

The `CollectionBase` class is part of the `System.Collections` namespace. It supports the `IEnumerable`, `ICollection`, and `IList` interfaces. A complete list of the public members defined by this class is as follows. Derived classes must implement the additional methods to support the required interfaces.

Public Properties	Count	Gets or sets the actual number of objects in the array.
Public Methods	Clear	Removes all objects from the array.
	GetEnumerator	Returns an enumerator that can iterate through the elements in the collection using the `IEnumerator` interface.
	RemoveAt	Removes the object at a given index from the array.
Protected Properties	InnerList	Gets an `ArrayList` instance representing the collection instance. This can be used when implementing derived classes to modify the collection.
	List	Gets an `IList` instance representing the collection instance. This can be used when implementing derived classes to modify the collection.
Protected Methods	OnClear	Performs additional custom processing before clearing the contents of the collection. This can be used by derived classes to perform any required actions before the collection is cleared.
	OnInsert	Performs additional custom processing before inserting an element into a collection. A number of other protected methods are provided, with a similar purpose.

5.2   CLASS LIBRARIES

Finally, we are ready to specify our album class. We have decided to base this on `Col-lectionBase`, and use our own `Photograph` object for the elements. As we discussed in the previous section, the `CollectionBase` class provides a limited set of methods, so it will be up to us to implement the appropriate class members to support the required interfaces.

As a result, our `PhotoAlbum` class will look something like the following. Since this is a photo album and we expect to display photos from it, we will also add some methods to manage the current position within the album.

```
public class PhotoAlbum : CollectionBase        ❶ Inherit from
{                                                  CollectionBase class

  // Default constructor

  // The IEnumerable interface is provided by CollectionBase
  // This allows the use of foreach with an album

  // ICollection members

  // IList members

  // Position operations
  //      - Get/Set current position (as index).
  //      - Get photograph at current position.
  //      - Move to the next photograph.
  //      - Move to the previous photograph.
}           ❷ End of PhotoAlbum class
```

Some syntactic points here:

❶ As already mentioned, classes in C# support inheritance from a single class only, in this case from the `CollectionBase` class, although multiple interfaces can be specified. This is the same as Java, and a break from C++. Also unlike the C++ language, C# classes do not support private or protected inheritance.

❷ If you haven't realized it by now, also note that there are no header files in C#. Like Java, the entire class is specified in a single file. For C++ programmers, also note that a semicolon (;) is not required after the class definition.

The `Photograph` class will hold the original file name for the image, and the `Bit-map` object when necessary. Its definition will look something like this:

```
public class Photograph          ❸ Inherit from System.Object
{

  // Create a new instance from a file name.

  // Properties:
  //    - get the file name for the Photograph
  //    - get the Bitmap for the Photograph

  // Methods:
  //    - see if two Photographs are equal
}
```

One additional point here:

❸ It is worth noting that all classes in C# implicitly inherit from the `object` class even when it is not specified. This ensures that all classes have a common ancestor. So even though it is not shown, our `Photograph` class inherits from the base `System.Object` class implicitly, which is equivalent to the C# `object` class.

Now that we understand the framework for our classes, let's perform the actual implementation. This section will create the class library in Visual Studio, discuss creating such a library using the command line tools, and provide the initial implementation of our `PhotoAlbum` and `Photograph` classes.

5.2.1 CREATING THE CLASS LIBRARY

Enough preparation: time to create our library. If you are not using Visual Studio .NET here, create your library as a separate directory and place the files discussed here in it. We'll give you some hints for building this from the command line later in the chapter.

In this section we will create a new project as part of our MyPhotos solution. This project will build the new MyPhotoAlbum library. We will create a top-level namespace called `Manning` for this project, and reference the new library from our MyPhotos project.

Set the version number of the application to 5.2.

CREATE A REUSABLE LIBRARY IN VISUAL STUDIO .NET		
	Action	**Result**
1	Add a new project to the MyPhotos solution. **How-to** a. Click the File menu in Visual Studio .NET. b. Click on the Add Project menu. c. Select the New Project… item.	

	Action	Result
2	Configure the new project as a class library named "MyPhotoAlbum." **How-to** a. Select Visual C# Projects as the Project Type. b. Select Class Library as the Template. c. Enter "MyPhotoAlbum" for the name of the project.	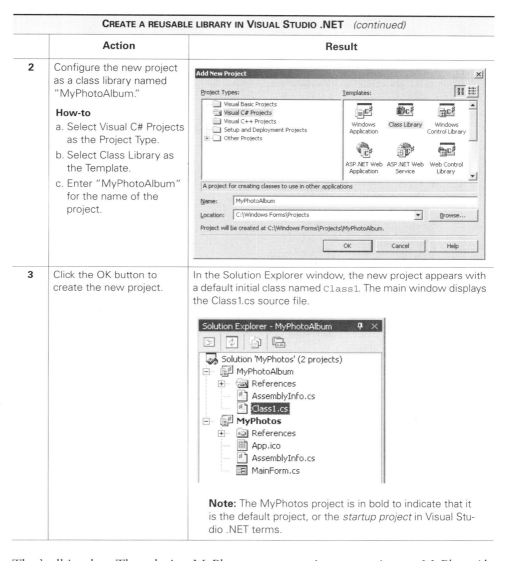
3	Click the OK button to create the new project.	In the Solution Explorer window, the new project appears with a default initial class named `Class1`. The main window displays the Class1.cs source file. **Note:** The MyPhotos project is in bold to indicate that it is the default project, or the *startup project* in Visual Studio .NET terms.

That's all it takes. The solution MyPhotos now contains two projects: a MyPhotoAlbum project to create a DLL library, and a MyPhotos project to create a Windows Forms application. You will note that the new project has its own AssemblyInfo.cs file to support an independent version number for the library.

We do not want a class called Class1, so let's rename it to PhotoAlbum. We will also adjust the version number of our new project to reflect the current section number.

RENAME THE CLASS1.CS CLASS FILE	
Action	**Result**
4 Set the MyPhotoAlbum version number to 5.2. **How-to** a. Double-click the AssemblyVersion.cs file. b. Modify the `Assembly-Version` line to contain the desired version number.	When you compile the MyPhotoAlbum library, the new version number is included, and will be visible when displaying the properties for the generated library assembly. **Note:** Your main window now displays two AssemblyInfo.cs tabs for the corresponding files in each project. Make sure you keep track of which is which. The displayed file is always selected in the Solution Explorer window, which identifies the project that contains the file. To display the Solution Explorer window while editing a file, use the keyboard shortcut Ctrl+Alt+L.
5 Rename the Class1.cs file name to PhotoAlbum.cs. **How-to** a. Right-click on the Class1.cs file. b. Select Rename. c. Enter "PhotoAlbum.cs" for the file name.	The Class1.cs tab in the main window is renamed as well.

6   Rename the `Class1` class name to `PhotoAlbum`.
 	
How-to
a. Double-click the PhotoAlbum.cs file.
b. Change the three instances of "Class1" to "PhotoAlbum" in the code.
	The PhotoAlbum.cs file should look like this:
	
	`using System;`
	
	`namespace MyPhotoAlbum`
	`{`
	`    /// <summary>`
	`    /// Summary description for PhotoAlbum.`
	`    /// </summary>`
	`    public class PhotoAlbum`
	`    {`
	`        public PhotoAlbum()`
	`        {`
	`            //`
	`            // TODO: Add Constructor Logic here`
	`            //`
	`        }`
	`    }`
	`}`

Visual Studio automatically uses the project name as the namespace for all files in the project. Here, the PhotoAlbum class is in the MyPhotoAlbum namespace, so that our class called PhotoAlbum will not interfere with anyone else who may have a class called PhotoAlbum. By convention, namespaces should specify the company name, followed by the project name. Since our library might be used outside of this book (hey, you never know!), we should follow this convention as well. We will use the publisher's name Manning as our top-level namespace.

	Action	Result

7	Modify the entire MyPhotoAlbum namespace to exist within the `Manning` namespace
	
	How-to
	Enter the bolded text into the PhotoAlbum.cs file. When you type the final brace, Visual Studio will automatically reformat the lines as shown.
	
	Note: We have not made a similar change in the MyPhotos application since in this project the namespace is not likely to be used outside of the application itself.
		The PhotoAlbum.cs file should now look as follows:
		
		<pre>using System;
		
		namespace Manning
		{
		  namespace MyPhotoAlbum
		  {
		    /// <summary>
		    /// Summary description for PhotoAlbum.
		    /// </summary>
		    public class PhotoAlbum
		    {
		      public PhotoAlbum()
		      {
		        //
		        // TODO: Add Constructor Logic here
		        //
		      }
		    }
		  }
		}</pre>

Our library is now ready; all we need to do is add code. One last task before we do this is to make certain we can use our library from within the MyPhotos application project. For this to work, the MyPhotos project must include a reference to the MyPhotoAlbum class. This corresponds to the `/reference` switch on the C# compiler (csc.exe) that we saw in chapter 1, and is a bit like linking a library into your program in C++. Since there are no header files in C#, a reference is all we need to start using classes from the library in our project.

	REFERENCE MYPHOTOALBUM FROM THE MYPHOTOS PROJECT	
	Action	Result
8	Display the Add Reference dialog box for the MyPhotos project. **How-to** a. Click the MyPhotos project in the Solution Explorer window. b. Click on the Project menu. c. Select the Add Reference item. **Alternately** Right-click on the References entry under the MyPhotos project in the Solution Explorer window, and select Add Reference.	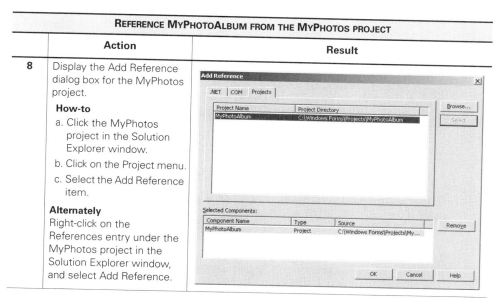

	Action	Result
9	Reference the MyPhotoAlbum project. **How-to** a. Click the Projects tab. b. Click the MyPhotoAlbum project. c. Click the Select button. d. Click OK to add the selected project.	The MyPhotoAlbum assembly appears in Solution Explorer under the References entry for the MyPhotos project.

It is important to realize that our new reference refers to the assembly produced by the MyPhotoAlbum project, and not the project itself. Visual Studio automatically uses the correct path when compiling the MyPhotos project to pick up the most recent MyPhotoAlbum library from the corresponding project.

If you are not using Visual Studio .NET to build your program, you will need to establish the correct library location manually. The command-line tools discussed in chapter 1 are used for this purpose. The next section provides a short discussion on this topic.

5.2.2 USING THE COMMAND-LINE TOOLS

As we saw in chapter 1, you can build Windows Forms applications without using Visual Studio .NET. The interactive environment makes a number of tasks easier, but also uses memory and other system resources. On a computer with limited resources, this can present some problems. If you have a favorite editor and are comfortable working with makefiles, you can create the examples in this book without using Visual Studio .NET.

To create a class library such as MyPhotoAlbum.dll, create a MyPhotoAlbum directory for the library and place the required source files in it. In this case you would create a PhotoAlbum.cs file to hold the `PhotoAlbum` class source code, and create other files as required. You can create an AssemblyInfo.cs file as well, or simply include the version number and other assembly information at the top of your file as we did in chapter 1. The C# compiler (csc.exe) discussed in chapter 1 is used to produce both executables and libraries. The `/target` switch specifies the type of output file to produce.

C# compiler output options (/target switch)

Switch	Output	Comments
/target:exe	Creates a console application (.exe).	This is the default.
/target:library	Creates a library file (.dll).	The library generated is an assembly that can be referenced by other .NET applications.
/target:module	Creates a library module (.dll).	This option does not produce an assembly manifest for the file. Such a file cannot be loaded by the .NET runtime until it is incorporated in an assembly manifest using the /addmodule switch. This permits collections of files to become a single assembly.
/target:winexe	Creates a Windows application (.exe).	When a Windows application is run in a console window, the console does not wait for the application to exit. This is different than a console application, where the console does in fact wait.

The /out switch can be used to specify the output file name. Both /out and /target must appear before any source file names.

For example, the following line will create a library assembly called MyPhotoAlbum.dll using a single source file PhotoAlbum.cs.

```
> csc /target:library /out:MyPhotoAlbum.dll PhotoAlbum.cs
  /r:System.dll
```

To use this library with your MyPhotos application, you will need to include a /r reference when compiling the application. For example, if your library was in a directory called C:\MyProjects\MyPhotoAlbum, then you would use the following switch when compiling the MyPhotos application:

```
/r:C:\MyProjects\MyPhotoAlbum
```

5.2.3   CREATING THE PHOTOALBUM CLASS

No matter how you compile your library, we are now ready to implement the PhotoAlbum class. These next two sections take us through the initial implementation of this and the Photograph class. If you find typing all this code a bit tedious (or are a really bad typist!), don't be afraid to download the final code from the book's web site and simply read the accompanying text. For the rest of us, let's forge ahead.

	IMPLEMENT PHOTOALBUM CLASS	
	Action	**Result**
1	Display the PhotoAlbum.cs file in the main window.	

2	Add some class documentation.	`/// <summary>`
		`/// The PhotoAlbum class represents a`
		`///   collection of Photographs.`
		`/// </summary>`

	Action	**Result**
IMPLEMENT PHOTOALBUM CLASS *(continued)*		
| **3** | Define `CollectionBase` as the base class. | ```csharp
public class PhotoAlbum : CollectionBase
{
``` |
| **4** | Create an empty default constructor. | ```csharp
public PhotoAlbum()
{
   // Nothing to do
}
```<br><br>**Note:** It's a good idea to add a short comment in situations like this to inform the poor guy or gal who eventually supports your code that you created an empty constructor on purpose. |

You may notice here that the MyPhotoAlbum project does not compile. Try to do so and the compiler returns an error something like the following:

Error   The type or namespace name 'CollectionBase' could not be found (are you missing a using directive or an assembly reference?)

This is because `CollectionBase` is part of the `System.Collections` namespace. It turns out this namespace is part of the system library, so there is no need for another reference in our project. We could fix the error by declaring the class as follows:

```csharp
public PhotoAlbum : System.Collections.CollectionBase
{
   . . .
```

Since we may use other objects or names from the `System.Collections` namespace, we will instead simply indicate that our class will use this namespace at the top of the file.

	Action	**Result**
USE SYSTEM.COLLECTIONS NAMESPACE		
| **5** | Add a `using` directive to the PhotoAlbum.cs file for the `System.Collections` namespace. | You should now have two `using` directives present:<br><br>```csharp
using System;
using System.Collections;
``` |

Now the project should compile with no errors. Before we implement any members for this class, let's also take a look at the `Photograph` class.
```

CREATING THE PHOTOGRAPH CLASS

The `Photograph` class represents a photograph stored in a file. Earlier, we laid out this class as follows.

```
public class Photograph
{
  // Create a new instance from a file name.

  // Properties:
  //   - get the file name for the Photograph
  //   - get the Bitmap for the Photograph

  // Methods:
  //   - see if two Photographs are equal
}
```

While we could implement this class within the PhotoAlbum.cs file, it makes more sense to separate these two classes into two separate files. In this section we create this new class file and add some initial properties for the class. The following steps create our Photograph.cs source file.

	ADD A PHOTOGRAPH CLASS FILE	
	Action	**Result**
1	Open the dialog to add a new class for the MyPhotoAlbum project. **How-to** a. In Solution Explorer, click the MyPhotoAlbum project. b. Open the Project menu. c. Select Add Class.... **Alternately** Right-click on the MyPhotoAlbum project and select Add Class... from the Add submenu.	The Add New Item dialog opens with the Class template selected. 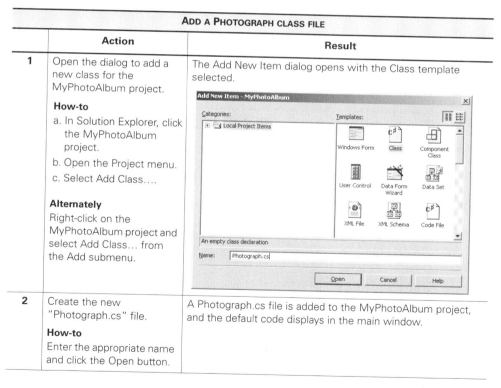
2	Create the new "Photograph.cs" file. **How-to** Enter the appropriate name and click the Open button.	A Photograph.cs file is added to the MyPhotoAlbum project, and the default code displays in the main window.

	ADD A PHOTOGRAPH CLASS FILE *(continued)*	
	Action	**Result**
3	Add some class documentation.	``` . . . /// <summary> /// The Photograph class represents a single /// photo and its properties. /// </summary> public class Photograph . . . ```

Once again, let's modify the namespace to be `Manning.MyPhotoAlbum`.

	MODIFY THE NAMESPACE	
	Action	**Result**

4	Modify the namespace to be `Manning.MyPhotoAlbum`.	```
		. . .
		namespace Manning
		{
		   namespace MyPhotoAlbum
		   {
		      . . .
		   }
		}
		``

We now have a fully functional class as part of our library. Of course, it doesn't do anything yet. Let's start by tracking the file name and bitmap for the photograph.

	DEFINE THE FILE AND BITMAP PROPERTIES	
	Action	**Result**

5	Create private member variables to track the file name and any `Bitmap` object.	```
		public class Photograph
		{
		   private string _fileName;
		   private Bitmap _bitmap;
		``
		Note: Here and elsewhere in the book, we indicate that a variable is `private` and not available outside of the containing class by prefixing it with an underscore.

6	Create a constructor to initialize these members from a given file name.	```
		public Photograph(string fileName)
		{
		   _fileName = fileName;
		   _bitmap = null;
		}
		``
		Note: We allow a `Photograph` to be created with an invalid file name.

7	Create a `FileName` property to return the current file name.	```
		public string FileName
		{
		   get { return _fileName; }
		}
		``

	Action	Result
| 8 | Create an `Image` property to return the corresponding `Bitmap` object.<br><br>**Note:** We intentionally ignore any error here. We will fix this later in the chapter. | ```csharp
public Bitmap Image
{
  get
  {
    if (_bitmap == null)
    {
      _bitmap = new Bitmap(_fileName);
    }
    return _bitmap;
  }
}
``` |

This is the first time we've created our own properties, so it is worth a short discussion. A property in C# is created much like a method. You define an access level, a type, and a name for the property. By convention, property and method names begin with a capital letter. The lack of parentheses after the name informs the compiler that this is a property and not a method.

Inside the braces, the *access methods* for the property are defined. The access methods provide read access, via the `get` keyword, or write access, via the `set` keyword. The `get` access method must return the defined type, while the `set` access method uses the reserved word `value` to access the value provided on the right side of the equals sign '='. For example, if we wanted users of our `Photograph` class to set the `FileName` property, we could code this as follows:

```csharp
public string FileName
{
  get { return _fileName; }
  set { _fileName = value; }  // example only, not in our code
}
```

Of course, in an actual implementation it might be good to verify that the `value` provided to the `set` call is a real file and does indeed represent a photograph. For our purposes, the `Photograph` class is tied to a specific file name, so we do not provide a `set` implementation here. In this case the `FileName` property is said to be *read-only,* since the value can be read but not written.

Practically, properties permit safe access to a class without the need to expose internal variables or other features. To duplicate the `get` and `set` functionality for a file name member in C++, programmers typically provide methods such as `SetFile-Name` and `GetFileName` for this purpose. Properties formalize this concept for C# so that all programs use a standard mechanism for this style access.

Since properties are invoked similar to methods, additional calculations can be performed as part of their definition. In the code for the `Image` property, for example, the `Bitmap` is created as required before returning it to the user.

```csharp
public Bitmap Image
{
  get
```
```

```
    {
      if (_bitmap == null)
      {
        _bitmap = new Bitmap(_fileName);
      }
      return _bitmap;
    }
  }
```

Astute readers will note here that the given file may or may not exist and may or may not be an actual image file. We will handle any exception that occurs as a result of such an error in a moment.

We now have enough to link our classes into the main application. One problem remains: the MyPhotoAlbum project will once again not compile. Now the error is something like this:

Error   The type or namespace name 'Bitmap' could not be found (are you missing a using directive or an assembly reference?)

This is because `Bitmap` is part of the `System.Drawing` namespace, which is referenced by our MyPhotos project, but not the MyPhotoAlbum project. Unlike `System.Collections`, this namespace is provided in a separate library, namely the System.Drawing.dll library. We need to reference this DLL and then use it in our class.

	ADD SYSTEM.DRAWING REFERENCE	
	Action	**Result**
9	Display the Add Reference dialog for the MyPhotoAlbum project.	
10	Add System.Drawing.dll as a reference. **How-to** a. Click the .NET tab. b. Locate and click the System.Drawing.dll item from the list. c. Click the Select button. d. Click the OK button.	The `System.Drawing` assembly appears in the References list for the MyPhotoAlbum project.

11	Add a `using` directive for the `System.Drawing` namespace at the top of the file.	The Photograph.cs file now contains two `using` directives:
		`using System;`
		`using System.Drawing;`

Now the project should compile with no errors in Visual Studio .NET. If you are not using Visual Studio, multiple files can be included in the library by simply providing the list of files to the compiler. An example of how this might look is shown here.

```
>   csc /target:library /out:MyPhotoAlbum.dll PhotoAlbum.cs
    Photograph.cs /r:System.dll /r:System.Drawing.dll
```

Before we deal with the possible exception that can occur in the `Photo-graph.Image` property, let's return to our `PhotoAlbum` class to make some initial use of the `Photograph` class.

5.3   INTERFACES REVISITED

Back in our `PhotoAlbum` class, we are ready to implement the interfaces required. As you'll recall, an interface defines the set of required members, but does not provide any implementation. Supporting an interface requires that we define the class as support-ing the interface, and include the required members for that interface within the class.

For the `PhotoAlbum` class, the `CollectionBase` class defines itself as supporting the `IEnumerable`, `ICollection`, and `IList` interfaces. An implementation for the single method `GetEnumerator` required by the `IEnumerable` interface is provided by `CollectionBase`. As a result, we are left to implement the `ICollection` and `IList` interfaces. A list of `ICollection` members is provided in the following table:

PhotoAlbum members required for the ICollection interface

	Name	Implementation Notes
Properties	Count	This property is provided by `CollectionBase`.
	IsSyncronized	For simplicity, we will not provide a synchronized interface for the `PhotoAlbum` class. As a result, this property will always return `false`.
	SyncRoot	
Methods	CopyTo	

The `IList` interface has a slightly longer list of members. Some of them are already provided by the `CollectionBase` class, but the bulk of them will be implemented using the protected `CollectionBase.List` property.

PhotoAlbum members required for the IList interface

	Name	Implementation Notes
Properties	IsFixedSize	This method will always return `false`.
	IsReadOnly	This method will always return `false`.
	Item	This property enables array-style indexing for our class.

PhotoAlbum members required for the IList interface *(continued)*

	Name	Implementation Notes
	Add	
	Clear	This method is provided by `CollectionBase`.
	Contains	
Methods	IndexOf	
	Insert	
	Remove	
	RemoveAt	This method is provided by `CollectionBase`.

We will examine the implementation of these interfaces separately.

5.3.1 ### SUPPORTING THE ICOLLECTION INTERFACE

The implementation of the `ICollection` members will use the protected `List` property from our base class, so let's get to it. We will make these and our `IList` members virtual to allow any subclass to override them as needed.

Set the version number for the application to 5.3.

		SUPPORT THE ICOLLECTION INTERFACE	
	Action	**Result**	
1	Display the PhotoAlbum.cs file.		

2	Implement the `IsSynchronized` property.	`public virtual bool IsSynchronized`
		`{`
		`    get { return false; }`
		`}`	

3	Implement the `SyncRoot` property.	`public virtual object SyncRoot`
		`{`
		`    get { return List.SyncRoot; }`
		`}`	

4	Implement the `CopyTo` method.	`public virtual void CopyTo`
		`    (Photograph[] array, int index)`
		`{`
		`    List.CopyTo(array, index);`
		`}`
		
		Note: We require the array parameter to be an array of `Photograph` objects. The `ICollection` interface defines the `CopyTo` method as `CopyTo(Array array, int index)`. Since a `Photograph[]` is also an `Array`, our declaration is an acceptable implementation even though it is more restrictive than the method defined by the interface.	

5.3.2 SUPPORTING THE ILIST INTERFACE

Our implementation for `IList` will be very similar in spirit to our implementation for `ICollection`. A key difference between the signatures of the `IList` members and our implementation is that we will use the `Photograph` class explicitly rather than the more generic `object`. Since a `Photograph` is still an `object` instance, a construct that requires an `IList` instance will still be able to use our `PhotoAlbum` object.

This may seem a bit boring and tedious, but it needs to be done for a complete implementation. Note that C# does not support C++ style templates at this time, which would have been handy for implementing this and other interfaces.

	SUPPORT THE ILIST INTERFACE	
	Action	**Result**
1	Display the PhotoAlbum.cs file.	

2	Implement the `IsFixedSize` property.	`public virtual bool IsFixedSize`
		`{`
		`    get { return false; }`
		`}`

3	Implement the `IsReadOnly` property.	`public virtual bool IsReadOnly`
		`{`
		`    get { return false; }`
		`}`

4	Implement the `Item` property.
	
	Note: The `Item` property is the C# indexer, so we simply implement indexing to support this property.
		`public virtual Photograph this[int index]`
		`{`
		`    get { return (Photograph)(List[index]); }`
		`    set { List[index] = value; }`
		`}`

5	Implement the `Add` method.	`public virtual int Add(Photograph photo)`
		`{`
		`    return List.Add(photo);`
		`}`

6	Implement the `Contains` method.	`public virtual bool Contains(Photograph photo)`
		`{`
		`    return List.Contains(photo);`
		`}`

7	Implement the `IndexOf` method.	`public virtual int IndexOf(Photograph photo)`
		`{`
		`    return List.IndexOf(photo);`
		`}`

8	Implement the `Insert` method.	`public virtual void Insert`
		`        (int index, Photograph photo)`
		`{`
		`    List.Insert(index, photo);`
		`}`

9	Implement the `Remove` method.	`public virtual void Remove(Photograph photo)`
		`{`
		`    List.Remove(photo);`
		`}`

These methods simply use the equivalent version in the protected `List` property, except that our implementation will only accept `Photograph` objects. The `Item` property is worth noting since it defines zero-based array-style indexing for our class, such as `myAlbum[1]` to specify the second `Photograph` in an album. The syntax defines an *indexer* for the class. Indexers define array-style access to a class, using a syntax employing access methods similar to the declaration of properties. An indexer is defined using the `this` keyword to refer to the class itself, with the `index` variable defining the index value within the definition. In this manner the indexer defines retrieval and assignment access to the array of `Photograph` objects in the collection. Any collection class can be treated as an indexed array through the use of a similar indexer definition.

```
public virtual Photograph this[int index]
{
  get { return (Photograph)(List[index]); }
  set ( List[index] = value; }
}
```

5.3.3 IMPLEMENTING ALBUM POSITION OPERATIONS

This is a good place to insert the position operations for tracking the current location within an album. This position will be used by our application to display the current photo from the album as well as other tasks.

From a design perspective, we will use the word "Current" as a prefix for these operations. This is the name of a property used by the `IEnumerator` interface, and is consistent with the meaning we intend here. We will add the following members to our class:[2]

PhotoAlbum position members

Member	Description
CurrentPosition property	Gets or sets the index of the current position within the album. By definition, the first position is always zero (0), and the last position is one less than the number of `Photographs` in the album.
CurrentPhoto property	Gets the `Photograph` object at the current position. This will use the `CurrentPosition` property as an index into the collection to ensure that we will always retrieve a valid photo.
CurrentNext method	Moves the current position to the next photograph. Returns a boolean indicating if there was a next photo (`true`) or if the end of the album has been reached (`false`).
CurrentPrevious method	Moves the current position to the previous photograph. Returns a boolean indicating if there was a previous photo (`true`) or if the beginning of the album has been reached (`false`).

---

[2] Some might argue for using the `GetEnumerator` method to track the position, or for creating a mechanism similar to database cursors to allow an application to track multiple locations within the album at the same time. The former is problematic if the application inserts or removes photos while the enumerator is active. The latter is a good idea, but a bit beyond what we intend to cover in this chapter.

Let's add these members to our implementation. Internally, this will also require a private integer to track the current position. This private member is not part of our exported implementation, so it was not shown in the previous table.

	Action	Result
	IMPLEMENT ALBUM POSITION OPERATIONS	
1	In the PhotoAlbum.cs file, add a private integer `_currentPos`.	```/// <summary>
/// Tracks the current index position
/// when displaying the album.
/// </summary>
private int _currentPos = 0;```
2	Add the `CurrentPosition` property to get or set this position. **How-to** For the `get` access method, simply return the current value. For the `set` access method, make sure the given `value` is in range.	```public int CurrentPosition
{
    get { return _currentPos; }

    set
    {
        if (value <= 0)
        {
            _currentPos = 0;
        }
        else if (value >= this.Count)
        {
            _currentPos = this.Count - 1;
        }
        else
        {
            _currentPos = value;
        }
    }
}``` |
| 3 | Ensure that this value is reset when the album is cleared.

How-to
Override the `OnClear` method.

Note: This protected method is provided by the `CollectionBase` class to permit collection-specific code to be executed before the `Clear` method is invoked. | ```protected override void OnClear()
{
    _currentPos = 0;
    base.OnClear();
}```

Note: The base keyword used here is provided by C# as a convenient way to reference the base class of the current object. |
| 4 | Implement the `CurrentPhoto` property. | ```public Photograph CurrentPhoto
{
    get
    {
        if (this.Count == 0)
            return null;

        return this[CurrentPosition];
    }
}``` |

	Action	Result

5	Implement the `CurrentNext` method.
	
	How-to
	Use the `CurrentPosition` property to set and get the current index.
		``csharp
		public bool CurrentNext()
		{
		    if (CurrentPosition+1 < this.Count)
		    {
		        CurrentPosition ++;
		        return true;
		    }
		
		    return false;
		}
		``

6	Implement the `CurrentPrev` method.	```csharp
		public bool CurrentPrev()
		{
		    if (CurrentPosition > 0)
		    {
		        CurrentPosition --;
		        return true;
		    }
		
		    return false;
		}
		``

We can now add photographs to and remove photographs from our album, and track the current position for display purposes. Since we expect the `CurrentPosition` property to return a valid index, we should also update this setting whenever a `Photograph` is removed from the album.

ENSURE ALBUM POSITION REMAINS VALID		
	Action	Result

7	In the PhotoAlbum.cs file, override the `OnRemoveComplete` method.
	
	Note: This protected method is called after an object is removed from the contained collection.
		``csharp
		protected override void OnRemoveComplete
		    (int index, object val)
		{
		    CurrentPosition = _currentPos;
		    base.OnRemoveComplete(index, val);
		}
		``

As you can see, this code ensures that the current position is updated whenever an object is removed from the collection. This includes both the `Remove` and `RemoveAt` methods. By resetting the property, we ensure that the `_currentPos` variable is reset as appropriate for the new bounds of the album.

With the interfaces for our `PhotoAlbum` class fully implemented, let's head back to the `Photograph` class to deal with various issues related to the robustness of our new library.

5.4 ROBUSTNESS ISSUES

While our classes are basically ready, there are some additional issues that will affect the robustness of our application in future chapters. This section will address a number of these issues in order to make our library a bit more sturdy. These topics apply more generally to any class library, so are probably worth considering while developing your own libraries as well.

This section will look at the following areas:

- Handling the potential exception when a bitmap is created.
- Ensuring that photographs are compared as expected.
- Cleaning up system resources used by our classes.
- Associating a file name with an album.

We will examine each issue separately.

5.4.1 HANDLING AN INVALID BITMAP

We discussed the concept of exceptions in chapter 2. Here, there is a potential exception when we create our `Bitmap` object for the `Image` property. Look back at our definition of this property.

```
public Bitmap Image
{
  get
  {
    if (_bitmap == null)
    {
      _bitmap = new Bitmap(_fileName);
    }
    return _bitmap;
  }
}
```

If the file is an invalid bitmap, or cannot be loaded for some reason, this presents a real problem. On the one hand, this is an error, so perhaps we should return `null` or allow the exception to be thrown. On the other hand, the caller is expecting to display a `Bitmap`, and checking for `null` or an exception every time seems a bit cumbersome, not to mention the issue of what the caller should then display in lieu of a `Bitmap` object.

As an alternative approach, we will instead create a special bitmap to return whenever the file cannot be loaded. This provides a `Bitmap` that the caller can display in any situation, but still indicates that something is wrong. We will create a private static member of our `Photograph` class to hold this special image, and provide a new property to indicate if a valid image for the current `Photograph` exists.

Let's see how this looks.

Set the version number of the MyPhotoAlbum library to 5.4.

		HANDLE THE BITMAP EXCEPTION
	Action	**Result**
1	In the Photograph.cs file, create a private static member to hold a `Bitmap` object.	```private static Bitmap _invalidImageBitmap = null;```
2	Add a public property to retrieve this bitmap. **How-to** Create a 100×100 pixel image that contains a red X to indicate it is invalid.	```public static Bitmap InvalidPhotoImage\n{\n get\n {\n if (_invalidImageBitmap == null)\n {\n // Create the "bad photo" bitmap\n Bitmap bm = new Bitmap(100, 100);\n Graphics g = Graphics.FromImage(bm);\n g.Clear(Color.WhiteSmoke);\n\n // Draw a red X\n Pen p = new Pen(Color.Red, 5);\n g.DrawLine(p, 0, 0, 100, 100);\n g.DrawLine(p, 100, 0, 0, 100);\n\n _invalidImageBitmap = bm;\n }\n\n return _invalidImageBitmap;\n }\n}```
3	Use this new property as the bitmap to return if the image file cannot be loaded.	```public Bitmap Image\n{\n get\n {\n if (_bitmap == null)\n {\n try\n {\n _bitmap = new Bitmap(_fileName);\n }\n catch\n {\n _bitmap = InvalidPhotoImage;\n }\n }\n return _bitmap;\n }\n}```
4	Also add a new property `IsImageValid` to identify if a valid image file is present.	```public bool IsImageValid\n{\n get\n {\n return (_bitmap != InvalidPhotoImage);\n }\n}```

There is quite a bit of new code here (at least, by our standards in this chapter), so let's take a look at some of the more important pieces. First, look at the `Invalid-PhotoImage` property.

```
public static Bitmap InvalidImageBitmap
{
  get
  {
    if (_invalidImageBitmap == null)
    {
      // Create the "bad photo" bitmap
      Bitmap bm = new Bitmap(100, 100);        ❶ Create the new bitmap

      Graphics g = Graphics.FromImage(bm);     ❷ Construct Graphics object
      g.Clear(Color.WhiteSmoke);

      Pen p = new Pen(Color.Red, 5);           ❸ Draw a red X
      g.DrawLine(p, 0, 0, 100, 100);
      g.DrawLine(p, 100, 0, 0, 100);

      _invalidImageBitmap = bm;
    }

    return _invalidImageBitmap;
  }
}
```

The get implementation shown here creates and initializes the _invalidImage-Bitmap object the first time the property is invoked.

❶ First, a new Bitmap of size 100×100 pixels is constructed.

❷ Next, a Graphics object is generated to treat the Bitmap as a drawing surface using the static Graphics.FromImage method.

❸ Finally, a new red Pen is constructed with a width of five pixels and two lines are drawn corner to corner on the bitmap image to create a big red X. The Pen class is part of the System.Drawing namespace discussed in chapter 4. We could have used the Pen object returned by the Red property of the Pens class. This pen has a width of one pixel, so we opted to create our own pen instead.

Since the _invalidImageBitmap member variable is static, this code is executed the first time the property is called, and the image is then re-used as needed for all PhotoAlbum objects in the application. In the Photograph.Image property, an exception raised while creating the bitmap is caught and the _bitmap field is set to our invalid image.

```
try
{
  _bitmap = new Bitmap(_fileName);
}
catch
{
  _bitmap = InvalidImageBitmap;
}
```

Notice how an exception class is not specified in the catch clause. This ensures that all exceptions will be caught regardless of their origin.

Finally, a new `IsImageValid` property compares the photo's bitmap to the static invalid image variable to see if they are equal. If they are, then the original photo is not a valid photograph.

```
public bool IsImageValid
{
  get
  {
    return (_bitmap != InvalidPhotoImage);
  }
}
```

Interestingly enough, if neither the `_bitmap` nor the `_invalidImageBitmap` variables has been initialized, then this comparison will generate both `Bitmap` objects in order to compare them.

This handles any possible exception our code might encounter when creating a bitmap from a given file name. One other subtle but very important change we need to make is how `Photograph` objects are compared. We will take this up next.

5.4.2 OVERRIDING METHODS IN THE OBJECT CLASS

As we have repeatedly indicated, all classes in C# implicitly inherit from the `object` class, which is the same as `System.Object` class. In this section we look at the `Object` class in some detail, and override some of the methods inherited from this class in our `Photograph` class.

You may wonder why there is both an `object` and an `Object`, and the answer is both simple and confusing. The `object` class is part of the C# language definition, and all types, be they built-in or specific to your program, ultimately inherit from `object`.

Separate from the language definition is the .NET Framework, containing classes and namespaces used to generate programs and services of every kind. Within the .NET Framework is the `System.Object` class. In Microsoft's C# compiler, the `System.Object` class is equivalent to the C# `object` class. So `object` and `Object` are different but functionally equivalent. In this book, we have used and will continue to use both classes interchangeably, with a preference toward the language-specific `object`. An overview of the `Object` class is shown in .NET Table 5.3.

Note that a similar discussion applies to the classes `string` and `System.String` as well.

Look closely at the `Equals` method in the table. In our `Photograph` class, we would like two `Photographs` to be equal if they represent the same file. So far, however, this will not be the case. Since `Photograph` is a reference type, two objects will be equal only if they refer to the same physical storage on the heap. It doesn't matter if both objects internally represent the same image file. If they are different references, they are not equal. This behavior should come as no surprise to the seasoned Java coders among us, but might seem a little strange to programmers accustomed to C++ or Visual Basic behavior.

The `Object` class is the base class for all objects in C#, including the built-in types such as `int` and `bool`, and is part of the `System` namespace. The `System.Object` class is equivalent to the C# language `object` class in the .NET Framework.

Public Static Methods	Equals	Determines if two objects are equal.
	ReferenceEquals	Determines if two objects both refer to the same object instance.
Public Methods	Equals	Determines whether a given object is the same as this object. Performs bitwise equality for value types, and object equality for reference types.
	GetHashCode	Returns an integer suitable for use as a hash code for the object. Objects which are equal (based on the `Equals` method) return the same value, so you should override this method if you override `Equals`.
	GetType	Returns the `Type` object representing the C# language metadata associated with the object.
	ToString	Returns a `string` that represents the current object. By default, the name of the object's type is returned, so classes should normally override this method to return a more useful value.

In order to ensure that `Photographs` compare as expected, we must override the `Equals` method. Our override will return `true` if the two photos refer to the same file.

	OVERRIDE EQUALS METHOD	
	Action	**Result**
| **1** | In the Photograph.cs file, provide an override of the `Equals` method that compares file names. | ```cs
public override bool Equals(object obj)
{
  if (obj is Photograph)
  {
    Photograph p = (Photograph)obj;

    return (_fileName.ToLower().
        Equals(p.FileName.ToLower()));
  }

  return false;
}
``` |

Some features of this code are worth noting in more detail:

1 In C#, the `override` keyword is required to override a virtual method. Using the `virtual` keyword here would cause a compile error, since the method name is already declared in the base class. The `override` keyword indicates that the `Equals` method here serves the same purpose as the inherited member and replaces this base member. To define a new meaning for an inherited member and hide the original definition, the `new` modifier is used instead of the `override` keyword.
```

```
public override bool Equals(object obj)
{
```

2 Since we must handle any object here, we only perform our comparison if the given object is a `Photograph`. We use the `is` keyword for this purpose, even though this results in the performance of two cast operations—one for the `is` keyword, and one for the actual cast.

```
    if (obj is Photograph)
    {
        Photograph p = (Photograph)obj;
```

3 The `String.Equals` method performs a case-sensitive comparison of strings. That is, "book" and "book" are equal, but "book" and "Book" are not. To ignore capitalization in our file name strings, we use the `ToLower` method to make sure the compared strings are all lower case.

```
        return (_fileName.ToLower().Equals(p.FileName.ToLower()));
    }
```

4 Note how `false` will always be returned if the given object is not a `Photograph`.

```
    return false;
}
```

It is also worth noting here that the `String` class overrides the `Equals` method to perform a value-based case-sensitive comparison of its contents, even though it is a reference type. This ensures that two `String` objects are identical as long as they contain the same set of characters in the same order.

We should also override the `GetHashCode` and `ToString` methods in our `Photograph` class. The default `GetHashCode` implementation for the `Object` class returns different hash values for different references, while the default `ToString` implementation returns the name of the type, in this case the string `"Photograph"`. Neither of these implementations really works for our purposes.

This is especially true for the `GetHashCode` method. This method should return an identical value for identical, or equal, objects. The default implementation for reference types works fine when two physically different objects are never equal. In our case, since two different photographs can now be equal, this means that two `Photograph` objects that refer to the same file name might return different hash values.[3] This would make it rather difficult to look up `Photograph` objects in a hash table. As a

---

[3] This discussion assumes you understand hashing and hash tables. Briefly, a standard hash table uses a key, or hash code, as an index into a table. Unlike an array, this key does not have to be unique for each object, since each entry in the table refers to a linked list of objects that hash to the same key. A hash table enjoys the benefits of a linked list in that items can be quickly inserted and removed, and the benefits of an array since items can be quickly located. Of course, it all depends on a table appropriate for the number of expected items, and a good hash code algorithm that produces an equal distribution of values for the stored data across the entire table.

rule, you should always (yes, always!) override `GetHashCode` if you are overriding the `Equals` method. In our case, the comparison in `Equals` is based on the file name string, so we can use the `String.GetHashCode` method in a similar fashion.

	OVERRIDE THE GETHASHCODE METHOD	
	Action	**Result**

2	Override the `GetHashCode` method.
	
	How-to
	Use the `String.GetHashCode` method on the contained file name.
		``csharp
		public override int GetHashCode()
		{
		    return this.FileName.GetHashCode();
		}
		``

Finally, we may as well override the `ToString` method here as well. The default implementation will return the string `"Photograph"` every time, which is not very illuminating. A better implementation for our purposes would return the file name associated with the photograph, which is what we will do here.

	OVERRIDE THE TOSTRING METHOD	
	Action	**Result**

3	Override the `ToString` method to return the contained file name.	```csharp
		public override string ToString()
		{
		    return this.FileName;
		}
		``

Compile the code to verify that you and I have not made any errors. These overrides of the base `Object` methods will come in useful in future chapters. Since they are found in every object, Windows Forms controls make use of these methods whenever an object must be compared with another object or a corresponding string displayed in a window. In particular, we will see in chapter 10 how list controls utilize the `ToString` method by default when displaying an object in a list. As a result, providing a reasonable `ToString` implementation for your classes is always a good idea.

The changes in this section ensure that the base object methods are properly implemented for our `Photograph` class. Another change we should make is to ensure that any system resources used by our classes are cleaned up as required.

5.4.3   DISPOSING OF RESOURCES

Our `PhotoAlbum` and `Photograph` classes are now fairly well-defined. We can create photographs from image files, add and remove photos to albums, and iterate through the contents of an album. A topic we haven't touched on is the issue of cleaning up a photo or album when we are finished.

You might be wondering why we even care. Isn't this the purpose of garbage collection? When we are finished with an album, the garbage collector will clean it up eventually, so we do not need to worry about it.

This is true to a point. The problem is that we have no idea when the garbage collector will run. It could be immediately, it could be hours later, or it could even be in conjunction with the program exiting. This is fine for the memory used by our objects, but might present a problem for the system resources in use. For example, the creation of a `Bitmap` object requires that a file be opened and loaded into memory. This requires file and other system resources. Since such resources can be limited, it is a good idea to release them when you are finished.

The preferred method for doing this is through a `Dispose` method as part of the `IDisposable` interface. This interface is summarized in .NET Table 5.4. Since the `Component` class supports the `IDisposable` interface and is the basis for most classes in the `System.Windows.Forms` namespace, most objects in the Windows Forms namespace provide a `Dispose` method for just this purpose.

.NET Table 5.4   IDisposable interface
The `IDisposable` interface indicates that an object can be disposed of. Typically, instances of objects that support this interface should always call the `Dispose` method to free any non-memory resources before the last reference to the object is discarded. This interface is part of the `System` namespace.

Public Methods	Dispose	Releases any resources used by the object.

Let's support this interface in our classes. In many cases, it is an error to reference a disposed object. In our case, we would like to be able to clear and reuse a `PhotoAlbum` instance, so we will leave the album object in a usable state after the `Dispose` method has been called.

	SUPPORT THE IDISPOSABLE INTERFACE	
	Action	**Result**

1	In the Photograph.cs source file, indicate that this class will support the `IDisposable` interface.	`public class Photograph : IDisposable`
		`{`
		`    . . .`

2	Implement the `Dispose` method.
	
	How-to
	Dispose of the contained bitmap only if it exists and is not our static `InvalidPhotoImage` bitmap.
		`public void Dispose()`
		`{`
		`    if (_bitmap != null`
		`        && _bitmap != InvalidPhotoImage)`
		`    {`
		`        _bitmap.Dispose();`
		`    }`
		
		`    _bitmap = null;`
		`}`
		`    . . .`
		`}`

3	Similarly, support the `IDisposable` interface in the PhotoAlbum.cs file.	`public class PhotoAlbum :`
		`        CollectionBase, IDisposable`
		`{`
		`    . . .`

	Action	Result
| 4 | Implement the `Dispose` method for the `PhotoAlbum` class.<br><br>**Note:** We dispose of each Photograph in the album as well here." | ```csharp
private bool _disposing = false;
public void Dispose()
{
  if (!_disposing)
  {
    _disposing = true;
    foreach (Photograph photo in this)
    {
      photo.Dispose();
    }
    Clear();
  }
}
``` |
| 5 | Ensure that the album is properly disposed of when its contents are cleared.<br><br>**How-to**<br>Update the `OnClear` method to dispose of the contents. | ```csharp
protected override void OnClear()
{
  _currentPos = 0;
  this.Dispose();
  base.OnClear();
}
``` |

Our objects can now dispose of their contents properly. Be aware that it may not always be a good idea to dispose of contained objects as we do for the `PhotoAlbum` class here. There are times when an object in a list may be in use elsewhere in the program, and it is best to let the caller or the garbage collector decide when and how to dispose of any contents. For example, if a single `Photograph` object could be stored in two `PhotoAlbum` objects at the same time, then our `PhotoAlbum.Dispose` method would not be appropriate. We will enforce the rule that a single `Photograph` can only be a member of a single album, so the implementation presented here will work just fine.

We have one more change to make before going on to chapter 6.

5.4.4   ASSOCIATING A FILE NAME WITH AN ALBUM

One final addition that hasn't fit anywhere else in this chapter is the ability to assign a file name to an album. This will come in handy when we save and open albums in chapter 6. We will do this by providing a `FileName` property in the class, as detailed by the following table.

ADD A FILE NAME PROPERTY FOR AN ALBUM		
	Action	**Result**
1	In the PhotoAlbum.cs file, create a private field to store the file name.	`private string _fileName = null;`

ADD A FILE NAME PROPERTY FOR AN ALBUM		
	Action	**Result**
| 2 | Create a public property to retrieve or define this value. | ```
public string FileName
{
   get { return _fileName; }
   set { _fileName = value; }
}
``` |
| 3 | Reset this value when the album is cleared. | ```
protected override void OnClear()
{
   _currentPos= 0;
   _fileName = null;
   this.Dispose();
   base.OnClear();
}
``` |

Note that we permit a nonexistent file name to be assigned in this property. This allows an album name to be assigned before any data is actually saved into the file.

This completes the implementation of the `PhotoAlbum` and `Photograph` classes, at least for now. As usual, we finish this chapter with a quick summary of our accomplishments.

5.5   RECAP

In this chapter we created an external library that applications everywhere can use when a photo album is required. We implemented a `Photograph` class to encapsulate a photographic image, and a `PhotoAlbum` class to encapsulate a collection of `Photograph` objects. Along the way we examined interfaces, .NET collection classes, custom bitmap creation, internals of the `Object` class, and the `IDisposable` interface.

The MyPhotoAlbum.dll library is ready for use in our MyPhotos application. Integrating this library into our application is the topic of our next chapter. This will allow us to support multiple images in our application, and set the stage for future changes to come.

More .NET   For questions on C#, Windows Forms, and other aspects of .NET, Microsoft provides a number of Internet newsgroups on a variety of topics. These are available at Microsoft's News Server at news.microsoft.com. Among the newsgroups provided are microsoft.public.dotnet.framework.windowsforms for questions about Windows Forms application development, and microsoft.public.dotnet.languages.csharp for questions about the C# programming language.

CHAPTER 6

Common file dialogs

6.1 Design issues 162
6.2 Multiple file selection 166
6.3 Paint events 169
6.4 Context menus revisited 173

6.5 Files and paths 175
6.6 Save file dialogs 181
6.7 Open file dialogs 189
6.8 Recap 193

In the previous chapter we created the `Photograph` and `PhotoAlbum` classes as a way to encapsulate a photographic image and a collection of photographs. In this chapter we make use of these classes in our application to display a photo album to the user. We will stick with our model of one photo at a time, but allow a user to move forward and backward within the album. This will permit us to focus on integrating the library without too many changes to the user interface.

In future chapters, we will expand our class library with additional functionality such as storing the date a photograph was taken, or the name of a photographer. Adding such features to a photo album will take some work by the user, which we would not want to throw away when the program exits. As a result, before any of these additional features really make sense, we need to store our photo album on the disk so it can be used again (and again and again).

How will we store our album on disk? In a file, of course, to match the chapter title. Specifically, this chapter will show how to perform the following tasks:

- Use the `PhotoAlbum` and `Photograph` classes to display, navigate, and manage a set of photographs in the MyPhotos application.
- Allow multiple images to be loaded at once using the `OpenFileDialog` class.

- Save the current album using the `SaveFileDialog` class.
- Open a previously saved album using the `OpenFileDialog` class.

Figure 6.1 shows how our application will look by the end of this chapter, with the new File menu displayed. Note that we have also added an Edit menu and a new status bar panel showing the current position within the album. In the figure, the third of a total of four photographs in the album is shown.

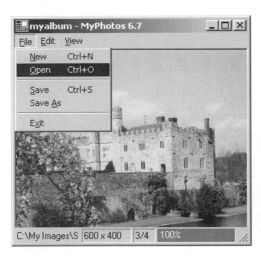

**Figure 6.1
In this chapter we implement a more traditional File menu structure for our application.**

6.1   DESIGN ISSUES

The changes planned for this chapter require that we rewrite our menu bar. Before we plunge ahead, let's do some brief design work to lay out this new main menu. It is always a good idea to sketch your graphical elements up front. You can even do this on paper. The point is to have in mind the graphical interface you wish to implement before you start writing code. While it is always possible to move menus and other objects around, it can also waste a lot of time. This is especially true if the application has to be approved by a manager, the customer, or anyone else. Doing a quick sketch on paper creates a basis for discussion and allows initial thoughts and ideas to be aired before a more formal design document or any code is written.

6.1.1   CHANGING THE MENU BAR

While we are not doing a formal design here, let's at least write down the new menu structure we will implement. As shown in the following table, in addition to the File menu changes, we will also add an Edit menu to our application.

The new menu structure for the MyPhotos application

Menu Bar	Menu Item	Shortcut	Description
File	File	Ctrl+N	Create a new photo album (the existing album is saved if necessary).
	Open	Ctrl+O	Open an existing photo album file.
	Save	Ctrl+S	Save the current album.
	Save As		Save the current album in a new file.
	Exit		Exit the application. It should offer to save the current album if any changes have been made.
Edit	Add	Ctrl+A	Add one or more photos to the album.
	Remove	Ctrl+R	Remove the displayed photo from the album.
View	Image		We will leave this menu as already implemented. This contains a submenu indicating how the image should be displayed.
	Next	Ctrl+Shift+N	Display the next image in the album, if any.
	Previous	Ctrl+Shift+P	Display the previous image in the album, if any.

It is tempting to use our own terminology and establish our own conventions here. For example, why not use an "Album" main menu instead of the File menu, or have Ctrl+N as the shortcut for View-Next rather than File-New. The short answer: don't do it. Computer users appreciate familiarity and resist change (so do most consumers and small children, but I digress). The File menu is standard in most Windows applications, and Ctrl+N is used for creating a new object (be it a document in Microsoft Word, or an image in Adobe PhotoDeluxe). Unless you are intending your application to be somewhat contrary, use existing standards where possible.

So even though Ctrl+N and Ctrl+P would make nice shortcuts for Next and Previous, we will stick with Ctrl+N for New and save Ctrl+P for when we add printing in part 3 of the book. We have already looked at menus in chapter 3, so this section will remove the existing Load menu and add our new menu structure.

Set the version number of the MyPhotos application to 6.1.

	REMOVE THE LOAD MENU	
	Action	**Results**
1	In the MainForm.cs [Designer] window, remove the Load menu from the File menu. **How-to** a. Right-click the menu item. b. Select Delete. **Alternately** Click the menu item and press the Delete key.	The menu and its properties are removed from the program. **Note:** The `menuLoad_Click` method remains in the source file. We will make use of this code when we handle the Add menu later in this chapter.

The creation of our menu requires the procedures we saw in chapter 3. The following table creates and positions the new menu items required in our application. The subsequent sections will look at the required event handlers for these menu items.

CREATE OUR NEW MENU		
Action		**Result**
2 Create the new File menu structure, as shown in the following table.		The new settings appear in the window and are reflected in the MainForm.cs file.

Settings		
MenuItem	**Property**	**Value**
New	(Name)	menuNew
	Shortcut	CtrlN
	Text	&New
Open	(Name)	menuOpen
	Shortcut	CtrlO
	Text	&Open...
separator		
Save	(Name)	menuSave
	Shortcut	CtrlS
	Text	&Save
Save As	(Name)	menuSaveAs
	Text	Save &As...
separator		
Exit	as before	

Note: Recall that a menu separator is added by creating a `MenuItem` with the `Text` property set to a single dash '-'.

3 Define a new Edit menu between the existing File and View menus.	**Note:** This space intentionally left blank.

How to
a. Click the "Type Here" entry on the menu bar, to the right of the existing View menu.
b. Enter the name "&Edit" in this space and press Enter.
c. Using the mouse, click on the new Edit menu and drag it left to appear between the File and View menus.

Settings	
Property	**Value**
(Name)	menuEdit
Text	&Edit

Note: If you are not using Visual Studio, create the new menu manually, and set the `Index` property for each of the File, Edit, and View menus to 0, 1, and 2 respectively.

	Action	Result
4	Add the dropdown menu for the Edit menu.	

Settings

MenuItem	Property	Value
Add	(Name)	menuAdd
	Shortcut	CtrlA
	Text	&Add
Remove	(Name)	menuRemove
	Shortcut	CtrlR
	Text	&Remove

	Action	Result
5	Create the View menu structure:	

Settings

MenuItem	Property	Value
Image	*as before*	
separator		
Next	(Name)	menuNext
	Shortcut	CtrlShiftN
	Text	&Next
Previous	(Name)	menuPrevious
	Shortcut	CtrlShiftP
	Text	&Previous

The source code generated here does not use anything we have not already seen and discussed in chapter 3, so we will move right along and start processing our new menus.

6.1.2 ADDING CLASS VARIABLES

Before we can implement any event handlers for our menus, and in particular before we can open and save album files, we must have a `PhotoAlbum` at our disposal in the `MainForm` class. In chapter 5 we added a reference to the MyPhotoAlbum library in the MyPhotos project, so this library is already available to our application.

Here we will add some protected variables to hold the displayed album and whether the user has made any changes to this album.

		CREATE SOME CLASS VARIABLES	
	Action		**Result**
1	At the top of the MainForm.cs file, indicate that we are using the MyPhotoAlbum namespace.		`using Manning.MyPhotoAlbum;` **Note:** Since we already reference the library (remember, no header files required), we could write the fully qualified name every time we reference an object from the library. Typing `Manning.MyPhotoAlbum.PhotoAlbum` repeatedly is not my idea of fun, so adding a `using` directive here makes sense.

	Action	Result
2	Within the `MainForm` class, add a protected album variable `_album`.	`protected PhotoAlbum _album;`
3	Add a protected boolean called `_bAlbumChanged` to track when an album is modified.	`protected bool _bAlbumChanged = false;` **Note:** This will be useful when deciding whether to save an existing album before loading a new one or closing the application. If no changes have occurred, then we will know to not save the album.

4	Create an empty album at the end of the `MainForm` constructor.	`public MainForm()`
		`{`
		`    . . .`
		`    _album = new PhotoAlbum();`
		`}`

These variables are required to implement all of our new menu items in this chapter. With these in place, it is time to do just that.

6.2 MULTIPLE FILE SELECTION

Now that we have an album in our `MainForm` class, albeit an empty one, we can add photos to it. In previous chapters, we allowed the user to read in a single photo, first using a button and later with a menu item. In our new structure, this has been replaced by the ability to add multiple photos to the album or remove the current photo from the album. Since this code builds on our original Load handler, it is a good place to begin.

As you would expect, we will provide `Click` handlers for both the Add and Remove items. The Add menu should allow one or more photos to be selected and added to the album, while the Remove menu should delete the currently displayed photo from the album. The Add menu will use the `Multiselect` property of the `OpenFileDialog` class, and is where our catchy section title comes from.

6.2.1 ADDING IMAGES TO AN ALBUM

In chapter 3, the `Click` handler for the Load menu permitted a single file to be selected using the `OpenFileDialog` class. This made sense when only a single image was managed by the application. In this chapter, the idea of an album permits multiple images to be present at the same time. As a result, our user should also be able to load multiple images at once. This is again done using the `OpenFileDialog` class, so the code for this handler will be similar to the `Click` event handler for the Load menu from chapter 3. The `Multiselect` property is provided by the `Open-FileDialog` class to indicate whether multiple files can be selected in the dialog. This and other members specific to this class are summarized in .NET Table 6.1.

The OpenFileDialog class represents a common file dialog box for loading one or more files from disk, and is part of the System.Windows.Forms namespace. This class inherits from the FileDialog class, and is the standard class for opening existing files. See .NET Table 1.2 on page 24 for a list of members inherited from the FileDialog class.

Public Properties	Multiselect	Gets or sets whether the user can select multiple files in the dialog. The FileNames property inherited from the FileDialog class should be used to retrieve the selected files.
	ShowReadOnly	Gets or sets whether the dialog should contain a read-only check box. Defaults to false.
	ReadOnlyChecked	Gets or sets whether the read only checkbox is checked. Defaults to false.
Public Methods	OpenFile	Returns a Stream with read-only access for the file specified by the FileName property.

The steps to implement a Click event handler for the Add menu are shown in the following table.

Set the version number of the MyPhotos application to 6.2.

IMPLEMENT ADD HANDLER		
	Action	**Result**
1	Open the Windows Forms Designer window for the MainForm.cs file.	As we have seen before, a graphic of the current layout for this form is displayed.

2	Add a Click event handler for the Add item under the Edit menu.
	How-to
	Double-click on the menu item.
		A new menuAdd_Click method is added to and displayed in the MainForm.cs source file.
		The line to add the handler is created by Visual Studio in the InitializeComponent method automatically:
		`menuAdd.Click += new`
		`    EventHandler (this.menuAdd_Click);`

3	Remove the menuLoad_Click handler and copy its code into the menuAdd_Click handler.	**Note:** This code opens a single file and arranges to display it in the window. Here, we just want to add the file to the album, so some changes are required. The code in the subsequent steps is based on the Load handler, although there are some differences. In particular, we do not handle any exceptions that might occur. This is done intentionally so that we can discuss the handling of such exceptions in chapter 7.

	Action	Result
| 4 | Initialize an `OpenFileDialog` instance to allow multiple selections of various image file types.<br><br>**How-to**<br>Use the `Multiselect` property to allow multiple files to be selected.<br><br>**Note:** The `Filter` setting here includes most of the common formats users are likely to see. All of these formats are supported by the `Bitmap` class. | ```csharp
protected void menuAdd_Click
    (object sender, System.EventArgs e)
{
    OpenFileDialog dlg = new OpenFileDialog();

    dlg.Title = "Add Photos";
    dlg.Multiselect = true;
    dlg.Filter
        = "Image Files (JPEG, GIF, BMP, etc.)|"
        + "*.jpg;*.jpeg;*.gif;*.bmp;"
        + "*.tif;*.tiff;*.png|"
        + "JPEG files (*.jpg;*.jpeg)|*.jpg;*.jpeg|"
        + "GIF files (*.gif)|*.gif|"
        + "BMP files (*.bmp)|*.bmp|"
        + "TIFF files (*.tif;*.tiff)|*.tif;*.tiff|"
        + "PNG files (*.png)|*.png|"
        + "All files (*.*)|*.*";
    dlg.InitialDirectory
        = Environment.CurrentDirectory;
``` |
| 5 | Invoke the dialog and process an OK response. | ```csharp
if (dlg.ShowDialog() == DialogResult.OK)
{
``` |
| 6 | Extract the array of files selected by the user. | ```csharp
string[] files = dlg.FileNames;
``` |
| 7 | Turn off the status bar panels while the images are loading. | ```csharp
statusBar1.ShowPanels = false;
statusBar1.Text
    = String.Format("Loading {0} Files",
        files.Length);
``` |
| 8 | Iterate through the array of selected files. | ```csharp
int index = 0;
foreach (string s in files)
{
``` |
| 9 | Add each image to the album if it is not already present.<br><br>**How-to**<br>Use the `IndexOf` method to see if the photo is already in the album. | ```csharp
Photograph photo = new Photograph(s);

// Add the file (if not already present)
index = _album.IndexOf(photo);
if (index < 0)
{
    index = _album.Add(photo);
    _bAlbumChanged = true;
}
}
```<br><br>**Note:** The IndexOf method relies on the Equals override we implemented in chapter 5. |
| 10 | Dispose of the nonmemory resources used by the dialog. | ```csharp
dlg.Dispose();
``` |
| 11 | Invalidate the main window to display the new settings. | ```csharp
    this.Invalidate();
    }
}
``` |

In the code, note how the `Multiselect` property is used to permit multiple file selections. This property is one of the few `OpenFileDialog` members not inherited from the `FileDialog` class.

The code also sets the `InitialDirectory` property to the current directory using the `Environment` class. This ensures that the initial directory in the dialog is always the current directory for our application. While this may not seem so relevant right now, it will become important when we implement `Click` handlers for our Save and Save As menus. We will look at the `Environment` class in more detail later in the chapter.

The `menuAdd_Click` method is similar to our original Load menu handler, but also very different. In particular, this method leaves unresolved the issue of what to display in the form, and the exception handling has been removed. We will handle these issues subsequently. For now, let's move on to the Remove menu handler.

6.2.2 REMOVING IMAGES FROM AN ALBUM

The event handler for the Remove menu uses the `CurrentPosition` property to locate the current photo and delete it from the album.

	IMPLEMENT REMOVE HANDLER	
	Action	**Result**
1	Add a `Click` handler for the Remove menu.	```protected void menuRemove_Click (object sender, System.EventArgs e) {```
2	Implement this handler to remove the current photo from the album.	```if (_album.Count > 0) { _album.RemoveAt(_album.CurrentPosition); _bAlbumChanged = true; } this.Invalidate(); }```

The `menuRemove_Click` handler uses the `RemoveAt` method from our `PhotoAlbum` class to remove the current photo. The issue of adjusting the current position in case we remove the last photo from the album is left to the `PhotoAlbum` class to handle. If you recall, the `RemoveAt` method we implemented in chapter 5 ensures that the current index remains valid after it is called through an override of the `OnRemoveComplete` method, so the current position is properly updated here.

Once again we have ignored the display issues. This is because our menu handlers will no longer interact with the `Form` window directly. Instead we will override the protected `OnPaint` method for this purpose, which is our next topic.

6.3 PAINT EVENTS

Now that we can load multiple images into our album, we need a way to make them appear in the window. In previous chapters, we have simply assigned the selected photo to the `Image` property of our `PictureBox` control and relied on the .NET Framework to deal with the rest. The framework will still do most of the work, but now we need to identify which image from our album should be drawn.

As in previous Microsoft development environments, such drawing is called *painting* in .NET. You may have noticed in chapter 3 that the `Control` class provides a `Paint` event for custom painting of a control. The event name is one piece of the support provided for each event in the .NET Framework. While we have seen these pieces in our previous use of events, this is a good place to list them more formally. The following support is required in order to define and support an event.

- *A class that defines the event data.* This is either the `System.EventArgs` class or a class derived from `System.EventArgs`. The event data for the `Paint` event is defined by the `PaintEventArgs` class. We will discuss the contents of the `PaintEventArgs` class in chapter 7.

- *A delegate for the event.* This delegate is used by Visual Studio .NET to add the event handler in the `InitializeComponent` method. By convention, the name of this delegate is the event name followed by the string "EventHandler." The `Paint` event is supported by the `PaintEventHandler` delegate. The creation of delegates is discussed in chapter 9.

- *A class that raises the event.* This class must define the event and provide a method to raise the event. By convention the method to raise the event is the string "On" followed by the event name. The protected `OnPaint` method raises the `Paint` event.

For painting of controls, the `Control` class defines the `Paint` event. Within the definition of this class, the event is defined using the `event` keyword in C#.

```
public event PaintEventHandler Paint;
```

6.3.1 DRAWING THE CURRENT PHOTOGRAPH

Returning to our code, we need a way to draw the appropriate photograph in our album. We could handle the `Paint` event directly in our `Form` or `PictureBox` control for this purpose. Instead, since the `MainForm` class derives from the `Form` class, we can override the method that raises the event directly. This technique is preferred where possible to avoid the extra overhead of creating and invoking an event handler. In this case, we will override the protected `OnPaint` method to handle the `Paint` event.

Set the version number of the MyPhotos application to 6.4.

OVERRIDE THE OnPaint METHOD		
	Action	**Result**
1	In the MainForm.cs file override the OnPaint method.	```protected override void OnPaint(PaintEventArgs e) {```

2	Only paint an image if the album is not empty.
	
	Note: The three comments here are implemented in the subsequent steps. In all cases, the status bar is invalidated.
		``if (_album.Count > 0)
		{
		    // Paint the current image
		    // Update the status bar
		}
		else
		{
		    // Indicate the album is empty
		}```
		
		`statusBar1.Invalidate();`

3	Call OnPaint in the base class.	``` base.OnPaint(e); }``` **Note:** This call is required to ensure that any Paint event handlers registered with the Form are called. As mentioned in chapter 5, the base keyword refers to the base class of the current object.
4	Paint the current image by setting the Image property of the pbxPhoto control.	```// Paint the current image Photograph photo = _album.CurrentPhoto; pbxPhoto.Image = photo.Image;```

5	Update the status bar to hold the appropriate information about the image.
	
	Note: The code here is similar to what we used in our menuLoad_Click event handler in chapter 4.
		``// Update the status bar.
		sbpnlFileName.Text = photo.FileName;
		sbpnlImageSize.Text = String.Format
		    ("{0:#} x {1:#}",
		      photo.Image.Width,
		      photo.Image.Height
		    );
		statusBar1.ShowPanels = true;```

6	When no images are present, clear the screen and display an appropriate status bar message.	```// Indicate the album is empty
		pbxPhoto.Image = null;```
		
		``statusBar1.Text = "No Photos in Album";
		statusBar1.ShowPanels = false;```

6.3.2 DISPLAYING THE CURRENT POSITION

Before we see our changes in action, it would be nice to have some indication of our current position within the album and the total album size in the window. We can do this by adding a new StatusBarPanel to hold this information, as detailed by the following steps.

ADD A NEW STATUS BAR PANEL		
	Action	**Result**
1	In the MainForm.cs Design window, display the StatusBarPanel Collection Editor for the statusBar1 control. **How-to** a. Display the properties for this control. b. Click on the Panels property item. c. Click the ... button.	The StatusBarPanel Collection Editor dialog appears as was shown in chapter 4.
2	Add a new StatusBarPanel in this dialog just before the existing sbpnlImagePercent panel. **How-to** a. Click the Add button. b. Click the up arrow in the center of the dialog to move the panel just beforethe image percent panel. c. Assign the proper settings as shown. d. Click OK to add the panel. **Settings** | Property	Value | |---|---| | (Name) | sbpnlFileIndex | | AutoSize | Contents | | ToolTipText | Image Index |	The new panel is added to the Panels collection. The source code in the InitializeComponent method is updated to define the new panel and add it to the status bar.

3	In the OnPaint method, set the text for this panel to contain the image index and album size.	sbpnlFileIndex.Text = String.Format
		("{0:#}/{1:#}",
		   _album.CurrentPosition+1,
		   _album.Count);

The preceding tables have made a number of changes to the OnPaint method. The following code pulls together all of the pieces presented in the preceding tables. We will not discuss these changes in additional detail.

```
protected override void OnPaint(PaintEventArgs e)
{
  if (_album.Count > 0)
  {
    // Paint the current image
    Photograph photo = _album.CurrentPhoto;
    pbxPhoto.Image = photo.Image;

    // Update the status bar.
    sbpnlFileName.Text = photo.FileName;
    sbpnlFileIndex.Text = String.Format("{0}/{1}",
      _album.CurrentPosition+1, _album.Count);
    sbpnlImageSize.Text = String.Format("{0} x {1}",
      photo.Image.Width, photo.Image.Height);
```

```
        statusBar1.ShowPanels = true;
    }
    else
    {
      // Indicate the album is empty
      pbxPhoto.Image = null;

      statusBar1.Text = "No Photos in Album";
      statusBar1.ShowPanels = false;
    }

    statusBar1.Invalidate();
    base.OnPaint(e);
}
```

Our code is coming along. We can add new photos to the album, and remove the photo currently displayed.

TRY IT!   Compile the code and verify that you can add and remove images to the album. Make sure you can add multiple images at once by selecting a range of images with the Shift key. This can be done by clicking the first file, holding down the Shift key, and then clicking the last file. You can also select multiple single images with the Ctrl key by clicking the first, holding down the Ctrl key, clicking the second, and so on.

Also see what happens when a nonimage file is specified. You should see our invalid image with the red X that we created in chapter 5. This indicates to the user that something is wrong, but maintains the image paradigm used by our application.

The current code does not allow us to move to the next and previous images in the album, so only the first photo in the album is ever displayed. Navigating within the album using the Next and Previous menus is our next topic.

6.4   CONTEXT MENUS REVISITED

In this section we implement the Next and Previous menu items for our application. These menus are part of the View menu on the main menu bar. If you recall, this menu was cloned and assigned to the context menu for use with the `PictureBox` control. Our careful implementation in chapter 3 ensured that the contents of the context menu always match the contents of the View menu. In fact, your application should include these menus now, as can be seen in figure 6.2.

Figure 6.2
A context menu displays keyboard shortcuts just like the main menu. As a special treat, an image not yet seen in this book is shown here.

The handlers for Next and Previous use concepts we have previously discussed, so let's get to it.

6.4.1 DISPLAYING THE NEXT PHOTOGRAPH

The Next handler uses the `CurrentNext` method from our `PhotoAlbum` class, and is implemented using the following steps.

Set the version number of the MyPhotos application to 6.4.

	IMPLEMENT HANDLER FOR THE NEXT MENU	
	Action	**Result**
1	Add a `Click` handler for the Next menu item.	```protected void menuNext_Click
(object sender, System.EventArgs e)
{```
2	Implement this handler using the `CurrentNext` method.	``` if (_album.CurrentNext())
{
this.Invalidate();
}
}```

You will note that we invalidate any image currently displayed only if a next photograph is available. It might be a good idea to beep or display a message when no next photo is available to inform the user they are at the end of the album. We will discuss how to do this in the next chapter.

6.4.2 DISPLAYING THE PREVIOUS PHOTOGRAPH

The `Click` event for the Previous menu is implemented in a similar manner.

IMPLEMENT PREVIOUS HANDLER		
	Action	**Result**
| 1 | Add a `Click` handler for the Previous menu item. | ```
protected void menuPrevious_Click
     (object sender, System.EventArgs e)
{
``` |
| 2 | Implement this handler using the `CurrentPrev` method. | ```
if (_album.CurrentPrev())
{
    this.Invalidate();
}
}
``` |

Compile and run the application to verify that your code produces the screen shown in figure 6.2 earlier in this section.

TRY IT! It would be useful to have First and Last menu items here. These would display the first or last photo in the album, respectively. Add these two menus to the View menu and provide a `Click` event handler for each menu.

6.5 FILES AND PATHS

Before we implement our save methods, a brief talk on the name of an album is in order. While we may store the album in a file such as "C:\Program Files\MyPhotos\sample.abm," such a name is a bit cumbersome for use in dialogs and on the title bar. The base file name, in this case "sample," is more appropriate for this purpose. Another issue is where exactly should album files be stored?

This section resolves these issues by defining a default directory where albums are stored and establishing a title bar based on the current album name. These features will then be used to implement a `Click` event handler for our New menu.

6.5.1 CREATING A DEFAULT ALBUM DIRECTORY

While an album file can be placed in any directory, it is nice to provide a common place for such files. This location will be used by default for both opening and saving albums. Common directories for this and other standard information are available from the `Environment` class, as summarized in .NET Table 6.2.

For our default directory, the `GetFolderPath` method provides convenient access to the special folders in the system, such as the user's My Documents directory. There are a number of special folders available, with a few of them listed in .NET Table 6.3. We are interested in the location of the My Documents directory, which corresponds to the `Personal` enumeration value.

The `Environment` class represents the current user's environment, providing the means to retrieve and specify environmental information. This class is sealed and the members defined by this class are static. The `Environment` class is part of the `System` namespace.

Public Static Properties	CurrentDirectory	Gets or sets the fully qualified path of the current directory for this process.
	ExitCode	Gets or sets the exit code for the process.
	MachineName	Gets the NetBIOS name of this local computer.
	OSVersion	Gets an `OperatingSystem` instance under which this process is currently running.
	TickCount	Gets the number of milliseconds elapsed since the system started.
	UserName	Gets the user name that started the current thread for this process.
	WorkingSet	Gets the amount of physical memory mapped to this process context.
Public Static Methods	Exit	Terminates this process and returns the specified exit code to the underlying operating system.
	GetCommandLineArgs	Returns an array of `string` objects containing the command line arguments for the current process.
	GetEnvironmentVariable	Returns the value of a specified environment variable as a `string`.
	GetEnvironmentVariables	Returns the set of all environment variables as an `IDictionary` instance.
	GetFolderPath	Returns the path of a special folder as identified by the `Environment.SpecialFolder` enumeration.
	GetLogicalDrives	Returns an array of `string` objects containing the names of the logical drives on the computer under which this process is running.

We will use this value to define a static `DefaultDir` property in our `PhotoAlbum` class. We will allow a programmer to modify this value, but this provides a starting point for album storage. To distinguish photo albums from other documents, we will create an `Albums` directory within the My Documents folder.

The `SpecialFolder` enumeration specifies various types of predefined folders in the .NET Framework. This enumeration is used by the `GetFolderPath` method in the `Environment` class. This enumeration is defined within the `Environment` class as part of the `System` namespace.

Enumeration Values	ApplicationData	The common directory where application data for the current roaming, or network, user is typically stored.
	Cookies	The directory where Internet cookies are typically stored.
	Favorites	The directory where the user's favorite items are typically stored.
	Personal	The directory where the user's documents are typically stored.
	SendTo	The directory that contains the Send To menu items.
	StartMenu	The directory that contains the Start menu items.

Let's see how this looks by creating the required code.

Set the version number of the MyPhotoAlbum library to 6.5.

	CREATE A DEFAULT ALBUM DIRECTORY	
	Action	**Result**
1	In the PhotoAlbum.cs file, indicate we are using the `system.IO` namespace.	`using System.IO;`
2	Define static members for the default directory and whether this directory has been initialized.	`static private string _defaultDir = null;` `static private bool _initializeDir = true;`

3	Define a static `InitDefaultDir` method to initialize the default directory setting.
	
	Note: The ampersand '@' in C# specifies an "as-is" string, where escape sequences normally denoted by the backslash character are ignored.
		`static private void InitDefaultDir()`
		`{`
		`  if (_defaultDir == null)`
		`  {`
		`    _defaultDir = Environment.GetFolderPath(`
		`      Environment.SpecialFolder.Personal);`
		`    _defaultDir += @"\Albums";`
		`  }`
		
		`  Directory.CreateDirectory(_defaultDir);`
		`}`

	Action	Result
4	Implement a `DefaultDir` property to retrieve or assign the default directory setting. **How-to** Use the `_initializeDir` field to ensure that the directory setting is only initialized once.	``` static public string DefaultDir { get { if (_initializeDir) { InitDefaultDir(); _initializeDir = false; } return _defaultDir; } set { _defaultDir = value; _initializeDir = true; } } ```

The `InitDefaultDir` method does much of the work for this property. If an explicit value for the default directory has not been set, then this method assigns a value based on the user's personal directory for documents, with an Albums subdirectory added.

```
static private void InitDefaultDir()
{
  if (_defaultDir == null)
  {
    _defaultDir == Environment.GetFolderPath(
        Environment.SpecialFolder.Personal);
    _defaultDir += @"\Albums";
  }
```

Since this directory, or any directory provided by the user, may or may not exist at the start of the program, we create the directories as part of our initialization.

```
    Directory.CreateDirectory(_defaultDir);
  }
```

For programmers familiar with earlier development environments from Microsoft, the lack of directory-related classes and dialogs has been a noticeably missing feature. Microsoft has provided a `Directory` class .NET containing a number of static methods for dealing with directories. This class resides in the `System.IO` namespace and should simplify the handling of directories in applications. We will not look at this class in detail here. The `CreateDirectories` method used in our code ensures that each of a string of directories in a given path exist. Note that if the `_defaultDir` setting is not a well-formed directory string, then the `CreateDirectories` method will throw an exception.

6.5.2 SETTING THE TITLE BAR

So far we have only set the title bar in our `MainForm` constructor. Realistically, we will likely want to set this from a number of places in our application, especially if we want to include information about the current album as part of the title bar.

Let's create a `SetTitleBar` method to assign the title bar based on the current album name, if any. This method requires a means of extracting the base name from the current album file. This functionality is provided by the `Path` class, as described in .NET Table 6.4. The rather cumbersome `GetFileNameWithoutExtension` method obtains the base file name without the extension.

The code for the `SetTitleBar` method is described in the following table:

Set the version number of the MyPhotos application to 6.5.

SET THE APPLICATION TITLE BAR		
	Action	**Result**
1	In the MainForm.cs code window, indicate that we are using the System.IO namespace.	`using System.IO;`

2	Add a new SetTitleBar method to the MainForm class.	`private void SetTitleBar()`
		`{`
		  `Version ver = new Version(`
		    `Application.ProductVersion);`

3	Define a default title bar when no album file is set.	`if (_album.FileName == null)`
		`{`
		  `this.Text = String.Format("MyPhotos {0:#}.{1:#}",`
		    `ver.Major, ver.Minor);`
		`}`

4	When an album file is set, include the base file name in the title bar.	`else`
		`{`
		  `string baseFile = Path.`
		    `GetFileNameWithoutExtension(`
		      `_album.FileName);`
		  `this.Text = String.Format(`
		    `"{0} - MyPhotos {1:#}.{2:#}",`
		    `baseFile, ver.Major, ver.Minor);`
		`}`
		`}`

We will make use of this new method in our implementation of a `Click` handler for the New menu.

The Path class represents an object stored on disk, whether a file or directory object. This class is sealed, and is part of the System.IO namespace. The Path class contains static methods for creating and managing disk objects.

Public Static Readonly Fields	DirectorySeparatorChar	A platform-specific directory separator character. This is the backslash character '\' on Windows systems.
	InvalidPathChars	A platform-specific array of characters. Each character is not permitted in a file system path.
	PathSeparator	A platform-specific path separator character. The semicolon ';' character on Windows systems.
Public Static Methods	ChangeExtension	Changes or removes the file extension for a file.
	GetDirectoryName	Returns the directory path of a file.
	GetExtension	Returns the extension of a file.
	GetFileName	Returns the file and extension parts of a file.
	GetFileNameWithoutExtension	Returns the file name without its extension.
	GetFullPath	Returns the fully qualified path for a given path.
	GetPathRoot	Returns the root of a given path.
	GetTempFileName	Returns a unique temporary file name and creates an empty file with that name on disk.
	HasExtension	Determines whether a path includes a file extension.

6.5.3   HANDLING THE NEW MENU

With the ability to manage an album file and directory in place, this is as good a place as any to implement a Click handler for our New menu. We will use our new SetTitleBar method to initialize the title bar for the application. This method is used here as well as later in this chapter to initialize the title bar when the current album changes.

	CREATE A CLICK EVENT HANDLER FOR THE NEW MENU	
	Action	**Result**
1	In the MainForm.cs [Design] window, add a `Click` event handler for the New menu.	```private void menuNew_Click (object sender, System.EventArgs e) {```
2	In this handler, dispose of the existing album and create a new one. **Note:** This really is poor design, since we throw away any changes to the existing album. We will fix this in chapter 8 when we discuss the `MessageBox` class.	```if (_album != null) _album.Dispose(); _album = new PhotoAlbum();```
3	Initialize the application title bar.	```// Set the application title bar SetTitleBar();```
4	Invalidate the current window.	```this.Invalidate(); }```
5	Add a call to this method in the `MainForm` constructor.	```menuNew_Click(this, EventArgs.Empty);``` **Note:** The static `EventArgs.Empty` property provides an empty `EventArgs` instance for use when calling event handlers from your code.
6	Remove the code to set the title bar from the `MainForm` constructor.	The initial title bar is now set as part of the `menuNew_Click` method.

We have made a few changes to our `MainForm` constructor here. To make sure we are all on the same page (so to speak), your constructor in Visual Studio should now look something like the following:

```
public MainForm()
{
  //
  // Required for Windows Form Designer support
  //
  InitializeComponent();

  // Additional Form initialization
  DefineContextMenu();
  menuNew_Click(this, EventArgs.Empty);
}
```

With this infrastructure in place, we can turn our attention to the methods required in the `PhotoAlbum` class.

6.6   SAVE FILE DIALOGS

So far we have used the MyPhotoAlbum library to support the creation and manipulation of an album in memory. At this point, we would like to preserve this album by storing it on disk. In this section we will handle the Save menu item to do just this. In the next section we will implement an Open menu handler to allow such an album to be reloaded and used at a later time.

We have already seen how the OpenFileDialog class is used to locate image files. As you might expect, .NET provides a SaveFileDialog class to store information to a file. A summary of this class is shown in .NET Table 6.5.

.NET Table 6.5 SaveFileDialog class		
The SaveFileDialog class represents a common file dialog box for saving a file to disk, and is part of the System.Windows.Forms namespace. This class inherits from the FileDialog class. See the FileDialog class description in .NET Table 1.2 on page 24 for a list of inherited members.		
Public Properties	CreatePrompt	Gets or sets whether the dialog should prompt the user for permission to create a specified file that does not exist. The default is false (do not prompt).
	OverwritePrompt	Gets or sets whether the dialog should prompt the user for permission to overwrite a specified file that already exists. The default is true (always prompt).
Public Methods	OpenFile	Returns a Stream object with read/write permission of the file selected by the user.

To save an album to disk, we need to implement two types of methods. The first is a Click event handler for both the Save and Save As menus. These handlers will use the SaveFileDialog class to allow a file to be selected. Second is a PhotoAlbum.Save method to write the album information into the selected file. Separating the user interface portion, in this case the file selection, from the data manipulation portion, here the actual file writes, is a common design technique that allows us to change either aspect of the task without overly affecting the other. As we shall see in future chapters, changes to how the data is stored by the PhotoAlbum.Save method will not affect the menu handlers implemented here.

6.6.1 WRITING ALBUM DATA

The Click handlers for our Save and Save As menus will rely on a Save method in the PhotoAlbum class to actually save the data, so let's implement this first. This method will accept the name of a file in which to store the data. We rely on the user interface in MainForm to provide a file name approved by the user, so if the file already exists we will simply overwrite it.

Set the version number of the MyPhotoAlbum library to 6.6.

		ADD PHOTOALBUM.SAVE METHOD
	Action	**Result**
1	Display the PhotoAlbum.cs file.	
2	At the end of the file, add the new Save method.	```
public void Save(string fileName)
{
}
```
**Note:** This method is void since an error is not expected. If something goes wrong, an Exception will be thrown. |

The format to use when creating such a file is always a question. One possibility would be to write an XML file to hold this album information. This is a good idea, but beyond the scope of this chapter, so we will stick with a simple text format. Since the file format will likely change, especially in this book, we will allow for possible future changes.

With these issues in mind, we will store each photograph in the album on a separate line, with a version number at the beginning of the file. This section will use 66 as the version number, since we are in section 6.6 of the book. The resulting file looks like this:

```
66
<path to photograph 0>
<path to photograph 1>
<path to photograph 2>
. . .
```

Our version number is likely to change in future chapters, so we will provide a constant to hold the current version.

		ADD A CURRENT VERSION CONSTANT
	Action	**Result**
| **3** | Add a static constant integer called _CurrentVersion to hold the version number. | ```
private const int _CurrentVersion = 66;
``` |

The Save method will store the version number followed by the file name of each Photograph written as a simple string.

	Action	Result
| 4 | Implement the Save method to store the album in the given file using the agreed-upon format. | ```csharp
public void Save(string fileName)
{
   FileStream fs = new FileStream(fileName,
      FileMode.Create,
      FileAccess.ReadWrite);

   StreamWriter sw = new StreamWriter(fs);

   try
   {
      sw.WriteLine(_CurrentVersion.ToString());

      // Store each file on a separate line.
      foreach (Photograph photo in this)
      {
         sw.WriteLine(photo.FileName);
      }
   }
   finally
   {
      sw.Close();
      fs.Close();
   }
}
``` |
| 5 | Implement an alternate Save method that uses the default file name. | ```csharp
public void Save()
{
   // Assumes FileName is not null
   Save(this.FileName);
}
``` |

This code uses some classes we have not seen before, so let's break our main Save method down piece by piece. Our first line opens or creates the given file name as a FileStream object. This class provides file I/O using simple byte arrays, and supports the well-known standard in, standard out, and standard error streams familiar to C and C++ programmers. Files can be open in various modes (via the FileMode enumeration), with various access levels (via the FileAccess enumeration). Different sharing options can be specified as well (not shown here) via the FileShare enumeration.

```csharp
public void Save(string fileName)
{
   FileStream fs = new FileStream(fileName,
      FileMode.Create,
      FileAccess.ReadWrite);
```

Next, we create a StreamWriter instance using the new FileStream object. Since we are using strings and not byte arrays, we need a class that provides simple string operations. The StreamWriter class does just this, and includes a constructor that accepts a FileStream instance.

```csharp
StreamWriter sw = new StreamWriter(fs);
```

The new `StreamWriter` instance is used to write our data into the file. We encapsulate the code to write the actual data in a `try` block to catch any exception that might occur.

```
try
{
```

First we write the version number as a string on the first line of the file. This line is a bit more magical than it looks. We are using a constant integer as an `object` here. While permitted, it requires the conversion of the value type `_CurrentVersion` into a reference type that can be treated as an `object` instance on the heap. This conversion is called *boxing*, since the value is "boxed" into a reference type on the heap. More information on boxing is provided in appendix A.

```
sw.WriteLine(_CurrentVersion.ToString());
```

The `Photograph` objects in the album are written using a `foreach` loop to iterate through the array. This code relies on the fact that our album contains `Photograph` objects and implements the `IEnumerable` interface. The `WriteLine` method from the `StreamWriter` class (actually, this method is inherited from the base `Text-Writer` class) writes a given string onto a single line of the file and adds the appropriate line termination characters.

```
// Store each file on a separate line.
foreach (Photograph photo in this)
{
   sw.WriteLine(photo.FileName);
}
```

You may think the magic of garbage collection obviates the need to explicitly clean up system resources such as files. As we have seen, this just isn't so. Normally the `Dispose` method is used to clean up nonmemory resources. For file objects such as `FileStream` and `StreamWriter`, the more traditional `Close` method is used. By definition, `Close` is equivalent to `Dispose` in the .NET Framework. Classes that provide a `Close` method are automatically disposed of when the `Close` method is called. We will discuss this notion in more detail in chapter 8.

Since the files must be closed even when an exception occurs, we encapsulate these lines in a `finally` block. As you may know, while a `finally` block does not catch any exceptions, any code in the block is executed regardless of whether an exception occurs or not.

```
finally
{
   sw.Close();
   fs.Close();
}
}
```

Note that closing the objects in the reverse order of which they were opened is critical. Once the `FileWriter` is closed, the `StreamWriter` is not able to write any remaining data into the file. Calling the `Close` methods in the proper order ensures all data is properly written to the file and avoids this potential error.

More .NET   In this book we take a rather straightforward approach to reading and writing files, and will stick with a simple text file to represent our album throughout the book. There are some summaries of using the `System.IO` namespace in the .NET documentation if you are interested in more details. Search for the "Working with I/O" section in the *.NET Framework Developer's Guide.*

We could also have stored our file in XML using classes from the `System.XML` namespace. The use of XML, for eXtensible Markup Language, is a great way to organize data, and is particularly useful when interacting with database systems or interfacing with remote computer systems. We opted for a simple text file in our application since many readers may not be familiar with XML. You can read up on XML in general at www.xml.org, or look up the `XmlReader` class and other members of the `System.XML` namespace in the .NET documentation.

Our new `Save` method can now be used in our MyPhotos application to save an album via our Save and Save As menus.

6.6.2   SAVING AN ALBUM AS A NEW FILE

Let's implement a handler for the Save As menu first. This handler should prompt the user to select a file where the album should be stored (using the `SaveFileDialog` class) and then use this file name to save the actual data. There are some questions to answer here about how photo albums should be saved. These questions apply more generally to any file, so are presented generically to apply to any file and not just our albums.

SaveFileDialog: questions to answer

- *Where are photo albums stored?*

  Even though you may allow the user to select any location on disk, it is a good idea to encourage a standard location for the files in your application. In our case, this location is specified by the static `DefaultDir` property in the `PhotoAlbum` class.

- *What is the file extension?*

  The selection of extension is a bit subjective. On Windows platforms, the following conventions normally apply:

  - *Use three-letter extensions.*   The one exception is .html files for HTML files, but even here the .htm extension is preferred.

  - *Keep the first letter.*   Typically, the first letter of the type of file should be the first letter of your extension. In our case, the extension for album file should begin with the letter 'a'.

- *Avoid numbers.* At a minimum, start the extension with a letter. Use a number only if it is a critical aspect the type file you are creating.
- *Avoid well-known extensions.* You will avoid confusion by using a somewhat unique combination of letters. You would not want to use extensions such as .txt (already used for Text files) or .jpg (for JPEG files). To see the list of file types currently registered on your computer, open Windows Explorer and select the Folder Options… item under the Tools menu. Click on the File Types tab to see the extensions currently in use.
- *Use an acronym.* It helps if your extension has some meaning to your users. If it makes sense, use an acronym of the full name. For example, the .gif extension is used for Graphics Interchange Format files.
- *Leave out the vowels.* Another common tactic is to leave out any vowels in the name. Examples of this include the .txt (Text) and .jpg (JPEG) extensions.

Based on these conventions, we could use alb or abm here, which both derive from Album without the vowel "u'). We will use the extension .abm.

- *What is the right title bar text?*

    Don't forget to set a custom title bar that makes sense for your dialog. The default title bar is "Save," which is not very descriptive. We will use "Save Album" for our title.

- *How should existing or nonexistent files be handled?*

    By default, the user will be prompted if they select a file that already exists (the `OverwritePrompt` property) and will not be told if the file is new (the `CreatePrompt` property). Often the default behavior is fine, but it is worth making a conscious decision for your application. We will (consciously!) use the defaults in our code.

Now that we understand the right behavior to provide, we can implement the Save As menu handler.

Set the version number of the MyPhotos application to 6.6.

IMPLEMENT HANDLER FOR SAVE AS MENU		
	Action	**Result**

1	Add a `Click` handler to the Save As menu.	`protected void menuSaveAs_Click`
		`    (object sender, System.EventArgs e)`
		`{`

2	Create a `SaveFileDialog` instance and initialize the properties as discussed.
	
	Note: In the `Filter` property setting, we permit all files to be shown, even though only the abm extension is a recognized album file. This is not necessary, but a nice convenience to allow the user to see all files in a directory.
		`SaveFileDialog dlg = new SaveFileDialog();`
		
		`dlg.Title = "Save Album";`
		`dlg.DefaultExt = "abm";`
		`dlg.Filter = "Album files (*.abm)|*.abm|"`
		`    + "All files|*.*";`
		`dlg.InitialDirectory = PhotoAlbum.DefaultDir;`
		`dlg.RestoreDirectory = true;`

3	Once a user selects a file, record the album name and save the current album using this name.	`if (dlg.ShowDialog() == DialogResult.OK)`
		`{`
		`    // Record the new album name`
		`    _album.FileName = dlg.FileName;`
		
		`    // Use Save handler to store the album`
		`    menuSave_Click(sender, e);`
		
		`    // Update title bar to include new name`
		`    SetTitleBar();`
		`}`

4	Dispose of nonmemory resources used by the dialog.	`dlg.Dispose();` `}`

You will note that our code for the menuSaveAs_Click handler is reminiscent of our previous use of the OpenFileDialog class. The album is saved only if the user clicks the OK button. The yet-to-be-implemented Save menu handler actually saves the file.

Also note the use of the RestoreDirectory property. We set this to true so that the current directory setting for the application is restored after the dialog exits. By default, this property is set to false, and the current directory for the application is modified to match the final directory in the dialog. You may recall that we set the InitialDirectory setting for our menuAdd_Click handler to the current directory via the CurrentDirectory property of the Environment class. Since we have different menus interacting with the file system in different ways, we ensure that the initial directory seen for each menu makes some amount of sense.

6.6.3 SAVING AN EXISTING ALBUM

We come at last to the Save menu handler. Here we need to select an album file name if one does not already exist, and save the actual data associated with the album.

	IMPLEMENT A CLICK HANDLER FOR THE SAVE MENU	
	Action	**Result**
1	Add a `Click` handler for the Save menu.	```protected void menuSave_Click
(object sender, System.EventArgs e)
{```
2	If an album name does not exist, use the Save As menu handler to prompt the user for an album name.	``` if (_album.FileName == null)
{
// Need to select an album file
menuSaveAs_Click(sender, e);
}```
3	If an album name exists, then simply save the file.	``` else
{
// Save the album in the current file
_album.Save();```
4	Mark that the now-saved album has no changes.	``` _bAlbumChanged = false;
}
}```

Note the neat trick we play between the Save and Save As `Click` handlers. When you save an album with no name, the Save handler calls the Save As handler to select a name, which then calls the Save handler to perform the actual save. The second time in the `menuSave_Click` method, a name will exist and the data will be saved.

Of course, whenever you interact with the file system, you should be concerned about possible exceptions. I intentionally ignored this issue here to whet your appetite for the next chapter. There, we will formally introduce the `MessageBox` class as a way to display simple dialogs to the user, most notably when an exception occurs.

Compile your code to verify that you can create an album and save it to disk. Open a saved album file in Notepad or some other text editor to see what it looks like. You should see something similar to the following:

```
66
C:\My Images\Samples\castle.jpg
C:\My Images\Samples\goose.jpg
C:\My Images\Samples\castle3.jpg
C:\My Images\Samples\gardens.jpg
```

Of course, saving the file is not very useful if you cannot also open a previously saved file. We will talk about this next.

6.7   OPEN FILE DIALOGS

So far, we have provided our application with the ability to load multiple photographs to create a photo album, step between these photographs using the Next and Previous menus, and save the album onto disk. Our final task is to open a previously saved album and display the first photo in our window. As you probably realize, we need to implement the user interface portion by handling the Open menu in our `MainForm` class, and the data portion by implementing an `Open` method for our `PhotoAlbum` class.

As before, we will begin with our `PhotoAlbum` class.

6.7.1 READING ALBUM DATA

The `Open` method will accept a file name and read the photo album stored in this file. It relies on the user interface layer in the caller to provide an actual file, and will throw an exception if an error occurs.

Set the version number of the MyPhotoAlbum library to 6.8.

	IMPLEMENT AN OPEN METHOD IN THE PHOTOALBUM CLASS	
	Action	**Result**
1	In the PhotoAlbum.cs file, add an `Open` method to the class.	```csharp\npublic void Open(string fileName)\n{\n```
2	Open the given file with read access.	```csharp\nFileStream fs = new FileStream(fileName,\n FileMode.Open,\n FileAccess.Read);\n\nStreamReader sr = new StreamReader(fs);\n```
3	Read the version string from the file and convert it to an integer. **How-to** Use the `Int32.Parse` method. This will throw an exception if the `string` is not actually an integer.	```csharp\nint version;\n\ntry\n{\n version = Int32.Parse(sr.ReadLine());\n}\ncatch\n{\n version = 0;\n}\n```
4	Clear the existing album and assign the new file name to the corresponding property.	```csharp\ntry\n{\n this.Clear();\n this.FileName = fileName;\n```
5	Read in the list of photos. **Note:** The C# `switch` statement used here allows for additional version numbers in the future.	```csharp\nswitch (version)\n{\n case 66:\n {\n // Read in the list of image files\n string name;\n do\n {\n name = sr.ReadLine();\n\n if (name != null)\n {\n // Add the name as a photograph\n Photograph p = new Photo-\ngraph(name);\n\n this.Add(p);\n }\n } while (name != null);\n break;\n }\n```

	Action	Result

6	If the version number is not recognized, throw an exception.
	
	How-to
	Use the C# `throw` keyword and create an `IOException` object.
		``default:
		    // Unknown version or bad file.
		    throw (new IOException
		        ("Unrecognized album file format"));
		}```

7	Close the file objects regardless of whether an exception occurs.
	
	Note: This disposes of any non-memory resources for our files. Make sure you close the files in the proper order.
		`` }
		    finally
		    {
		        sr.Close();
		        fs.Close();
		    }
		}```

Note how our code reads the version number as a string and converts it to an integer using the `Int32` class. The `Parse` method here throws an exception if a noninteger is provided. Since we really do not want the caller to see such an exception, we turn any exception thrown into a version number of zero to cause an unrecognized album exception to be thrown.

This code is our first use of the C# `switch` keyword. A `switch` block uses a `case` label just like C++ to identify a value to process, although C# `switch` blocks do not allow a fall through to the next `case` block unless the previous `case` has no code associated with it. Here, all our album files should be the current version 66 so only a single `case` label is required. We do not use the constant `_CurrentVersion` here since this value may change in the future.

If an invalid album file is provided, then the `default` block is executed. We throw an exception to indicate that an unexpected error occurred. Rather than creating a custom exception object here, we opt for the `IOException` class instead with an appropriate message string.

In case our `default` clause executes, or if any other unexpected problems occur, we enclose the entire code to read from the file in a `try` block.

6.7.2   OPENING AN ALBUM FILE

The `PhotoAlbum.Open` method can now be used in a `Click` handler for the Open menu of our application. We have been using the `OpenFileDialog` class to open image files. Here we will use it to open album files. As we did for our Save menus, we will preserve the current directory setting to ensure that the Add menu handler opens its file dialog at the most recent location.

Set the version number of the MyPhotos application to 6.7.

IMPLEMENT A CLICK HANDLER FOR THE OPEN MENU		
	Action	**Result**
1	Add a click handler for the Open menu item in the `MainForm` class.	```protected void menuOpen_Click (object sender, System.EventArgs e) {```
2	Save any existing album before loading the new one. **Note:** This code is not the best design. Not only does it discard a newly created album, it forces a save of the current one. We will fix this behavior in chapter 8.	```// Save the existing album, if necessary if (_bAlbumChanged && _album.FileName != null) { menuSave_Click(sender, e); }```
3	Create an `OpenFileDialog` class to select an album file.	```// Allow user to select a new album OpenFileDialog dlg = new OpenFileDialog(); dlg.Title = "Open Album"; dlg.Filter = "Album files (*.abm)|*.abm|" + "All files (*.*)|*.*"; dlg.InitialDirectory = PhotoAlbum.DefaultDir; dlg.RestoreDirectory = true;```
4	Use the `PhotoAlbum.Open` method to read the album.	```if (dlg.ShowDialog() == DialogResult.OK) { // Open the new album _album.Open(dlg.FileName);```
5	Set the new album name and invalidate the window to draw the initial photo.	```_album.FileName = dlg.FileName; _bAlbumChanged = false; this.Invalidate(); }```
6	Dispose of nonmemory resources used by the dialog.	```dlg.Dispose(); }```

Note that our implementation has an unfortunate feature of discarding a new album that has never been saved, and of saving an existing one even when the user does not wish to do so. This might not be the desired behavior, but is okay for this chapter. You may notice that we also do not handle any exceptions that might be raised by the `PhotoAlbum.Open` method, such as when the selected file does not actually represent a `PhotoAlbum` object. These problems are both addressed in chapter 8.

TRY IT!   If you would like to experiment here, create a version of the album file (use version number 67) that stores the current position in the album. This value should be saved in the album file in the line after the version number before any image files are listed.

This is a little trickier that it sounds, as you will need to handle both the old and new formats correctly. When you are finished, your application should not only write the new file version but also be able to open both the old and new file types.

6.8 RECAP

This is a good place to close out our discussion on file dialogs. In this chapter, we rewrote the menu bar and began using the MyPhotoAlbum project developed in chapter 5. We saw how to open multiple files simultaneously, and supported the ability to save and open album files from our application.

We seem to have a knack for introducing little bugs into our application. So far our image is distorted and stretched out of proportion, we are unable to scroll when the actual image is displayed, and in this chapter we threw out a newly created album while loading a new one. The next two chapters will clear up these problems while introducing the idea of drawing and scrolling on a form in chapter 7, followed by a discussion of interactive dialog boxes in chapter 8.

More .NET   The FileDialog class, as well as the OpenFileDialog and SaveFile-Dialog classes, are referred to as *common dialogs*. Common dialogs are dialog boxes provided by the .NET Framework that implement a standard interface for common functionality required by applications. The File-Dialog class inherits from the CommonDialog class directly.

Two other common dialogs provided by .NET are the ColorDialog and FontDialog classes. The ColorDialog class permits a user to select a color and corresponding Color structure, while the FontDialog class permits a user to select a font name, family, size, and corresponding Font class instance. The use of these dialogs is similar to what is shown for the FileDialog objects in this chapter, although the actual windows are quite different.

Also of note are the PageSetupDialog and PaintDialog classes. These common dialogs are used when printing from Windows Forms applications, and are discussed in chapter 18.

Finally, we should also note that common dialogs, including the Open-FileDialog and SaveFileDialog classes used in this chapter can be configured directly in the Windows Forms Designer window. They are available in the Toolbox window, and can be dragged onto the form and configured in the Properties window much like any other component. We elected not to do this here since the dialogs would then exist for the life of the form, which is not really necessary for our purposes.

C H A P T E R   7

Drawing and scrolling

7.1 Form class hierarchy 195
7.2 Image drawing 198
7.3 Automated scrolling 212
7.4 Panels 215
7.5 Recap 222

As you may have noticed, the main window for our application is built using the Form class. We have poked and prodded the edges of this class without really looking inside this complex but very important .NET object. In this and the next chapter we will investigate the Form class in more detail.

Earlier development environments from Microsoft distinguished among the different types of windows an application may display. In MFC, for example, there is one hierarchy (CFrameWnd) for framed windows such as MDI windows and control bars, another (CDialog) for dialog boxes, and yet another (CView) for the various document view classes.

The .NET Framework has taken a very different approach. In .NET, the Control class is the basis for all controls, including the various types of window objects. The Form class, as we shall see, encompasses all types of windows be they MDI frames, MDI child windows, floating tool bars, or dialog boxes.

The next two chapters will take a closer look at the Form class to understand how to interact with this object in our applications. In this chapter we will:

- Explore the Form class hierarchy.

- Draw the current photograph directly on our form.

- Automate scrolling when the image is larger than the form.
- Examine the `Panel` class, and draw our image in a `Panel` object instead of directly onto the form.

As we have done in previous chapters, we begin by looking at the class hierarchy for the `Form` object in more detail.

7.1 FORM CLASS HIERARCHY

If you have actually read this book from the beginning, you will recall that we looked at the `Menu` class hierarchy in chapter 3 and the `StatusBar` hierarchy in chapter 4. Chapter 3 introduced some of the low-level classes used by Windows Forms, and chapter 4 extended this hierarchy to include the `Control` class.

The `Form` class is based on additional extensions to enable scrolling and containment. The complete hierarchy is shown in figure 7.1.

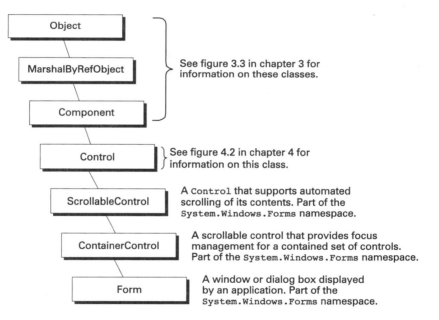

Figure 7.1 The Form class hierarchy extends the Control class discussed in chapter 4 with the functionality required for various kinds of application windows.

As you can see in the figure, the `ScrollableControl` and `ContainerControl` classes extend the `Control` class discussed in chapter 4 to support functionality required by the `Form` class. The `ScrollableControl` class adds auto-scrolling capabilities, while the `ContainerControl` adds focus management on the contained set of controls, even when the container itself does not have the focus.

7.1.1 THE SCROLLABLECONTROL CLASS

You might think that all classes with scrolling support inherit from the `Scrolla-bleControl` object. In fact, this class is only for objects which support automated scrolling for a contained set of `Control` objects. Controls such as `ListBox`, `Text-Box`, and other controls that provide scrolling of their drawing area do so independently of this object using the `ScrollBar` class, which is unrelated to the `ScrollableControl` class.

The `TextBox` and `ListBox` classes are discussed in chapters 9 and 10, respectively. The point here is that the `ScrollableControl` class is specifically designed for the scrolling support required by container objects such as forms and panels. A summary of this class is provided in the .NET Table 7.1.

We will see the members of this class in action later in the chapter when we enable scrolling within our application.

.NET Table 7.1   ScrollableControl class

The `ScrollableControl` class represents a control that supports automated scrolling. This class is part of the `System.Windows.Forms` namespace and inherits from the `System.Windows.Forms.Control` class. This class is not typically used directly. Instead, derived classes such as `Form` and `Panel` are used. See .NET Table 4.1 on page 104 for a list of members inherited from the `Control` class.

Public Properties	AutoScroll	Gets or sets whether the user can scroll the container to any contents placed outside of its visible boundaries.
	AutoScrollMargin	Gets or sets the extra margin to add to the container's contents for scrolling purposes. This ensures that the scrollable area goes slightly beyond the edge of any contained controls.
	AutoScrollMinSize	Gets or sets the `Size` object representing the minimum height and width of the scrollbars in pixels.
	AutoScrollPosition	Gets or sets the `Point` within the virtual display area to appear in the upper left corner of the visible portion of the control.
	DockPadding	Gets or sets the extra padding for the inside border of this control when it is docked.
Public Methods	SetAutoScrollMargin	Sets the `AutoScrollMargin` property.
Protected Properties	HScroll	Gets or sets whether the horizontal scroll bar is visible.
	VScroll	Gets or sets whether the vertical scroll bar is visible.

7.1.2 THE FORM CLASS

We will skip over the `ContainerControl` class from figure 7.1 and jump straight to the `Form` class. The `ContainerControl` class simply adds functionality for focus management on the contained controls. For example, an `ActiveControl` property sets or gets the `Control` object that has the focus; while the `ActivateControl` method sets the focus to a specific control. The functionality is useful, but not as glamorous as scroll bars or forms, so we skip it.

.NET Table 7.2 Form class		
The `Form` class represents any window that can be displayed by an application, including standard windows as well as modal or modeless dialog boxes and multiple document interface (MDI) windows. This class is part of the `System.Windows.Forms` namespace and inherits from the `ContainerControl` class. The contents of a form can be drawn directly by a program, consist of a collection of controls, or some combination of the two. These contents can also be larger than the visible area, with scrolling supported by the `ScrollableControl` class (see .NET Table 7.1).		
Public Static Properties	ActiveForm	Gets the `Form` currently active in the application, or `null` if no `Form` is active.
Public Properties	AcceptButton	Gets or sets the button to invoke when the Enter key is pressed.
	ControlBox	Gets or sets whether a control box appears at the left of the title bar.
	DialogResult	Gets or sets the dialog result to return when the form is a modal dialog box.
	Icon	Gets or sets the icon for the form.
	IsMdiChild	Gets whether this form is an MDI child form. MDI forms are discussed in chapter 16.
	MaximizeBox	Gets or sets whether a Maximize button appears in the title bar of the form.
	MaximumSize	Gets or sets the maximum size for a form.
	Menu	Gets or sets the MainMenu object for this form.
	Modal	Gets whether this form is displayed modally.
	ShowInTaskBar	Gets or sets whether the form is displayed in the Windows task bar.
	StartPosition	Gets or sets the initial position of the form when it is displayed.
	WindowState	Gets or sets how the form is displayed on the desktop (normal, maximized, or minimized).
Public Methods	Activate	Activates the form and gives it focus.
	Close	Closes the form.
	ShowDialog	Displays this form as a modal dialog box.
Public Events	Closing	Occurs when the form is about to close.
	Deactivate	Occurs when the form has lost the focus.
	Load	Occurs before a form is initially displayed.

On to our friend the Form class. This class can be used for just about any application window, including borderless, floating, and dialog box windows. The Control class we discussed in chapter 4 provides a number of useful members for dealing with forms. For example, the Width and Height properties determine the size of the form, the DisplayRectangle property holds the drawable area of the form, and the Cursor property gets or sets the current cursor to display. A number of common events such as Click, KeyDown, MouseUp, and Paint are also inherited from this class. Scrolling, of course, is provided by the ScrollableControl class. An overview of the members specific to the Form class is shown in .NET Table 7.2.

Once you have perused the Form overview and memorized its contents, go on to the next section where we will make some practical use of some of these members.

7.2   IMAGE DRAWING

Well, we are ready to utilize the Form class members, but where to begin? We will avoid dialog boxes and other new windows for the time being, and stick with the single form in our application. A good first topic we can cover here is drawing on a form.

As we have seen, drawing in .NET is performed using the System.Drawing namespace. We used classes from this namespace in chapter 4 when we created an owner-drawn status bar panel. Here, we continue to use the Graphics class for drawing, but will make use of some alternate members. Before we can do this, we need a place to draw. To generate such a place, we will remove the PictureBox object from our application.

7.2.1   DELETING THE PICTUREBOX CONTROL

Beside the need for a place to draw, the PictureBox control just isn't working out here. Like the Load button before it, it is just the wrong control for the task at hand. In chapter 2 we saw how this control stretched and distorted our image, and in chapter 3 we saw that scrolling was not supported when the displayed image exceeded the size of the control. So, it was nice while it lasted, but off it goes.[1]

Let's get this task out of the way so we can draw with a somewhat freer hand.

---

[1] It is, in fact, possible to extend the PictureBox control to provide this support. You can override the Paint event to draw an image with the proper aspect ratio much like we do in this chapter, and scroll bars can be added using the ScrollBar class. We do not take this approach here since we want to discuss forms and panels, so the PictureBox control is no longer needed. Chapter 15 displays a properly proportioned image within a PictureBox control, and chapter 18 provides a short discussion on how to create a custom control incorporating this functionality.

Set the version number of the MyPhotos application to 7.2.

	DELETE THE PICTUREBOX CONTROL	
	Action	**Result**
1	Display the MainForm.cs [Design] window.	
2	Delete the `PictureBox` control. **How-to** Select the Delete item from the control's context menu, or simply click on the control and press the Delete key.	The control no longer appears on the form. In the MainForm.cs file, the definition for the control (the `pbxPhoto` variable) and all references to it in the `InitializeComponent` method are removed. **Note:** nonautomated references to this variable must be removed by hand. This will be done during the course of this section.

With this task completed, our way is clear to implement the functionality previously provided by the `PictureBox` control in our `MainForm` control directly.

7.2.2 HANDLING THE IMAGE MENU

One of the unfortunate but necessary side effects of nuking the `PictureBox` control is that our processing of the Image menu no longer makes sense. We built this with the `PictureBoxSizeMode` enumeration values in mind. Since we are no longer using this control, we need to change how our menu works.

As an alternative solution, we will create our own enumerator for this purpose to use in place of the `PictureBoxSizeMode` enumeration. We could provide a long discussion of the individual changes required here, but this is chapter 7 so we'll just plunge ahead.

In this section we'll create the new enumeration and begin the process of modifying our menu handlers. The subsequent sections will address issues specific to the child menu items of the Image menu, and complete our implementation of the menu handlers.

	REPLACE THE MODEMENUARRAY MEMBER	
	Action	**Result**
1	In the MainForm.cs file, delete the `modeMenuArray` and `_selectedImageMode` fields.	

	Action	Result
| 2 | Create a private `DisplayMode` enumerator in the `MainForm` class. | ```csharp
/// <summary>
/// Mode settings for the View->Image
/// submenu.  The order and values here
/// must correspond to the index of
/// menus in the Image submenu.
/// </summary>
private enum DisplayMode
{
   StretchToFit = 0,
   ActualSize = 1
}
``` |
| 3 | Create a private instance of this enumerator called `_selectedMode`. | ```csharp
private DisplayMode _selectedMode
      = DisplayMode.StretchToFit;
``` |
| 4 | Replace the use of the old `_selectedImageMode` with the appropriate use of `_selectedMode` in the `statusBar1_DrawItem` method. | ```csharp
private void statusBar1_DrawItem
      (object sender, System.Windows.Forms.
         StatusBarDrawItemEventArgs sbdevent)
{
   if (sbdevent.Panel == sbpnlImagePercent)
   {
      // Calculate percent of image shown
      int percent = 100;
      if (_selectedMode == DisplayMode.ActualSize)
      {
         Photograph photo
            = _album.CurrentPhoto;

         Rectangle dr = this.ClientRectangle;
         int imgWidth = photo.Image.Width;
         int imgHeight = photo.Image.Height;
         percent = 100
            * Math.Min(dr.Width, imgWidth)
            * Math.Min(dr.Height, imgHeight)
            / (imgWidth * imgHeight);
      }
      . . .
   }
}
``` |
| 5 | Replace all other instances of the old `_selectedImageMode` with the new `_selectedMode`. | The instances of this variable in `menuImage_Popup`, `menuImage_ChildClick`, and `OnPaint` are replaced.

Note: Some tweaking of this code is required to make it work properly. The changes are shown in the subsequent text and will evolve throughout this section. |

Let's look at the menu handlers here to see how our new `DisplayMode` enumeration is used. The `Popup` event handler is called whenever the Image submenu is about to display, while the `Click` handler is called whenever an Image submenu is selected.

```csharp
protected void menuImage_Popup (object sender, System.EventArgs e)
{
   if (sender is MenuItem)
   {
      bool bImageLoaded = ( _album.Count > 0 );
      MenuItem miParent = (MenuItem)sender;
```
```

```
      foreach (MenuItem mi in miParent.MenuItems)
      {
        mi.Enabled = bImageLoaded;
        mi.Checked = (this._selectedMode == (DisplayMode)mi.Index);
      }
    }
  }

  protected void menuImage_ChildClick (object sender, System.EventArgs e)
  {
    if (sender is MenuItem)
    {
      MenuItem mi = (MenuItem)sender;

      _selectedMode = (DisplayMode) mi.Index;

      switch (_selectedMode)
      {
        default:
        case DisplayMode.StretchToFit:
          // Stretch image to fit the display area.
          this.Invalidate();
          break;

        case DisplayMode.ActualSize:
          // Display image at actual size.
          this.Invalidate();
          break;
      }

      statusBar1.Invalidate();
    }
  }
```

Cast integer to enumerated type ❶

Cast integer to enumerated type ❶

Handle enumeration values ❷

Invalidate current window ❸

This code raises some interesting points about the use of enumerated types.

❶ This line simply casts an integer value to an enumerated type. With the extensive error and type checking built into C#, you might think it would be an error to cast an integer to an enumeration value that does not exist. In fact, a standard C# enumeration by definition can hold any integer value, so any integer value can be cast to any enumeration type.

❷ This line uses a `switch` statement to perform the appropriate action based on the current display mode setting. Notice how the `StretchToFit` case is used as the `default` setting.

❸ Since our image will now be drawn directly on the form, we need to call the `Form.Invalidate` method to force the application to redraw the window using the new setting.

Of course, the `menuImage_ChildClick` method is not finished yet. We will fill this method in as we enable the corresponding display modes.

Before we do, one other feature is missing. Our wonderful context menu disappeared along with the PictureBox control. The menu is still around, of course, and is still initialized by the DefineContextMenu method to contain a copy of the View menu. The menu is just not hooked up to any controls at the moment, so it never appears.

We can fix this by attaching this menu to our Form class. Continuing our previous steps:

ASSOCIATE THE CONTEXT MENU WITH THE FORM		
	Action	**Result**
7	Display the properties for the MainForm object in the MainForm.cs [Design] window.	
8	Set the ContextMenu property to the ctxtMenuView menu. **How-to** Click the down arrow next to the ContextMenu property to display the available menus.	The property is set in the InitializeComponent method of the MainForm.cs source file. `this.ContextMenu = ctxtMenuView;`

Our context menu is now associated with the top-level form, and will appear whenever the user right-clicks anywhere in the window.

Your program may or may not compile here, depending on what you did to the OnPaint method when the _selectedImageMode field was removed. We'll cover this as part of the next section.

7.2.3 IMPLEMENTING THE STRETCH TO FIT OPTION

The modification of our Image menu handlers fully eradicates the PictureBox control from our application. While the PictureBox control created some problems, it also drew the current photograph for us. Now we will need to do this by hand, the result of which is shown in figure 7.2. You will note in this figure that the application is lacking the border previously shown around the image by the PictureBox control. This will be addressed later in the chapter.

The `System.Drawing` namespace expands the drawing capabilities found in previous Microsoft environments. Chapter 4 presented some information on this namespace and provided an overview of the `Graphics` class, one of the cornerstones of the .NET drawing interfaces.

In order to draw the current image from our album, we need to modify the `OnPaint` method to handle the manual drawing of the image. We will implement the Stretch to Fit menu option first as it is the most straightforward. As you'll recall, this option stretches and perhaps distorts the image to fit the entire display area of the application. This can be done with the following steps. A discussion of the resulting `OnPaint` method follows this table.

Figure 7.2   When an image is drawn directly on the form, the border and other properties provided by the PictureBox control are no longer available.

		IMPLEMENT THE STRETCH TO FIT MENU OPTION
	Action	**Result**
| **1** | Find the `OnPaint` method in the MainForm.cs file. | ```
protected override void
    OnPaint(PaintEventArgs e)
{
  if (_album.Count > 0)
  {
``` |
| **2** | When painting the current image, obtain the Graphics object from the PaintEventArgs parameter. | ```
    // Paint the current image
    Photograph photo = _album.CurrentPhoto;
    Graphics g = e.Graphics;
``` |
| **3** | To draw the current photo, use a `switch` statement to determine the current drawing mode.<br><br>**How-to**<br>For the `StretchToFit` option, use the `Graphics.DrawImage` method to fill the entire window with the image. | ```
    switch (_selectedMode)
    {
      default:
      case DisplayMode.StretchToFit:
        // Fill entire window with the image
        g.DrawImage(photo.Image,
          this.DisplayRectangle);
        break;

      case DisplayMode.ActualSize:
        break;
    }
    . . .
  }
``` |
| **4** | When the current album is empty, draw the default color in the window. | ```
  else
  {
    // Indicate the album is empty
    e.Graphics.Clear(SystemColors.Control);
    . . .
  }
``` |

These changes modify OnPaint to draw the image in the window for the StretchToFit display option, or to clear the window when an empty album is displayed. The resulting OnPaint method is shown here, with the changes just made shown in bold.

```
protected override void OnPaint(PaintEventArgs e)       ❶ Override the
{                                                          OnPaint method
  if (_album.Count > 0)
  {
    // Paint the current image
    Photograph photo = _album.CurrentPhoto;
    Graphics g = e.Graphics;

    switch (_selectedMode)
    {                                            Draw image in
      case DisplayMode.StretchToFit:            client window ❷
        // Fill the entire window with the image
        g.DrawImage(photo.Image, this.DisplayRectangle);
        break;

      case DisplayMode.ActualSize:
        break;
    }

    // Update the status bar.
    sbpnlFileName.Text = photo.FileName;
    sbpnlFileIndex.Text = String.Format("{0:#}/{1:#}",
      _album.CurrentIndex+1, _album.Count);
    sbpnlImageSize.Text = String.Format("{0:#} x {1:#}",
      photo.Image.Width, photo.Image.Height);
    statusBar1.ShowPanels = true;
  }
  else
  {
    // Indicate the album is empty
    e.Graphics.Clear(SystemColors.Control);      ❸ Clear the window
    statusBar1.Text = "No Photos in Album";
    statusBar1.ShowPanels = false;
  }

  statusBar1.Invalidate();
  base.OnPaint(e);
}
```

Your application should now compile and run. Load an image, and it should look similar to figure 7.2 shown at the start of this section. The following points are worth noting in our implementation of the OnPaint method.

❶ The OnPaint method takes a single PaintEventArgs parameter. We did not discuss this parameter in chapter 6, but a brief mention is warranted here, and an overview is provided in .NET Table 7.3. This class is similar in purpose to the DrawItemEventArgs class presented in chapter 4. The two classes are similar, except that the Paint event and PaintEventArgs class are used for controls, while the DrawItem event and DrawItemEventArgs class are used for drawing components or other objects within a control.

❷ The Graphics.DrawImage method is used to draw the current photograph in the window. The image is drawn into the area represented by the Form.DisplayRectangle property rather than the ClipRectangle area provided by the PaintEventArgs parameter. This is because ClipRectangle only represents the area that requires updating, which may not be the entire window. In our case, we need to redraw the entire image to account for changes in the display mode or the size of the drawable area.

❸ When an empty album is present, we draw over any image data that may still be present in the window. The Graphics.Clear method performs this task by painting a single color onto the form. The SystemColors class provides access to the user-definable desktop colors, with the Control property representing the default background color for 3-D controls.

Our application has now taken a step backward. The Stretch to Fit option by definition distorts the image displayed, so the behavior we have here is the same as we saw before. In addition, we have lost our nice border around the image, and resizing the form no longer works.

The border is simply cosmetic and will be addressed in due course toward the end of this chapter. This distortion problem we will address immediately. The resize issue can wait until after the next section.

.NET Table 7.3 PaintEventArgs class		
The PaintEventArgs class defines the event data required by the Paint event. This class inherits from the System.EventArgs class, and is part of the System.Windows.Forms namespace.		
Public Properties	ClipRectangle	Gets the Rectangle representing the area of the object that needs to be painted. This property is read-only.
	Graphics	Gets the Graphics to use when painting the object.

7.2.4   IMPLEMENTING A SCALE TO FIT OPTION

The Stretch to Fit option we have used so far is really a poor choice for displaying an image. Users really do not want their images distorted when displayed on the screen. This option makes a nice example to use in our book, but otherwise is not all that useful. Even so, we will keep the option available as a contrast to the more appropriate solution we are about to implement.

Ideally, an image is scaled so that it fits inside the available window space. We will call this option *Scale to Fit*, and make it the default for our application. An important aspect of this option is the calculation to determine the proper rectangle in which to draw the image. This rectangle should be centered in the available area with the same aspect ratio of the original image. Figure 7.3 illustrates the scaling of an image from its original size to fit within the display area of the application. Note that the image is not distorted since the aspect ratio of the image is preserved from its original size.

If you look closely here, you will realize that the image is centered between the base of the menu and the bottom of the window, as opposed to the top of the status bar. This is because the client area includes the status bar, even though our image does not cover it up. This is a minor problem that many users will not notice. Of course, since we have noticed, it will have to be fixed. First we need to create the code necessary to match the figure, and later we will worry about making it better.

Figure 7.3   Scaling an image from its original size to fit the display area is similar to zooming in or out of a graphic. The image looks the same; it just gets smaller or larger.

The operation of scaling a photograph to fit an available area could be a common operation in a photo album application. Because of this, let's create a method for this algorithm in our MyPhotoAlbum library so that it can be used by other applications, and perhaps later in the book. We will add this method to the Photograph class with the following signature:

```
public Rectangle ScaleToFit(Rectangle targetArea)
```

The following steps detail the implementation of this method. Once the method is available, we will look at adding our new option to the menu, and updating our handlers using this new method.

Set the version number of the MyPhotoAlbum library to 7.2.

	IMPLEMENT A SCALETOFIT METHOD IN THE PHOTOGRAPH CLASS	
	Action	**Result**
| 1 | In the Photograph.cs file, add the `ScaleToFit` method. | ```
public Rectangle ScaleToFit
    (Rectangle targetArea)
{
``` |
| 2 | Define a `Rectangle` to hold the calculated result. | ```
Rectangle result
    = new Rectangle(targetArea.Location,
                    targetArea.Size);
``` |
| 3 | Determine whether the photograph will fit best horizontally or vertically. | ```
// Determine best fit: width or height
if (result.Height * Image.Width
        > result.Width * Image.Height)
    {
``` |
| 4 | If horizontally, determine the resulting height and center the rectangle in the available space. | ```
    // Final width should match target,
    // determine and center height
    result.Height = result.Width
        * Image.Height / Image.Width;
    result.Y += (targetArea.Height
        - result.Height) / 2;
    }
``` |
| 5 | If vertically, determine the resulting width and center the rectangle in the available space. | ```
else
    {
    // Final height should match target,
    // determine and center width
    result.Width = result.Height
        * Image.Width / Image.Height;
    result.X += (targetArea.Width
        - result.Width) / 2;
    }
``` |
| 6 | Return the calculated result. | ```
    return result;
    }
``` |

Since this algorithm is a bit off-topic from Windows Forms development, we will not discuss it in much detail. This gives us a mechanism for scaling our image to the proper display size, and accounts for both horizontal and vertical images. The method returns a `Rectangle` object containing both a location and a size for the new image. That is, this method does not just provide the final size for our displayed image; it also provides the location where it should appear within the target rectangle.

With this in hand, let's turn back to our MyPhotos application. To implement our Scale to Fit menu, we need to add the menu item itself, the menu-handling logic, and the appropriate drawing code. We will begin with the menu option.

ADD SCALETOFIT MENU ITEM		
	Action	**Result**
7	In the MainForm.cs [Design] window, add a Scale To Fit menu to the top of the View menu..	

<table>
<tr><th colspan="2">Settings</th></tr>
<tr><th>Property</th><th>Value</th></tr>
<tr><td>(Name)</td><td>menuScale</td></tr>
<tr><td>Text</td><td>&Scale to Fit</td></tr>
</table>

	Action	**Result**
8	Add the `menuImage_ChildClick` method as the `Click` event handler for the `menuScale` menu item.	The handler is registered with the `Click` event associated with the menu.

The code generated by these steps is similar to the menu code generated in chapter 3 and elsewhere. In particular, note that the `Index` property settings for these menus are adjusted in the `InitializeComponent` method to reflect the insertion of the new item at the first location.

```
menuScale.Index = 0;
menuStretch.Index = 1;
menuActual.Index = 2;
```

Since the `DisplayMode` enumeration must match our menu, we need to update the values appropriately.

UPDATE DISPLAYMODE ENUMERATION		
	Action	**Result**
9	Locate the `DisplayMode` definition in the MainForm.cs source file.	`private enum DisplayMode` `{`

10	Add a `ScaleToFit` value and adjust the settings to match the Image submenu.	`    ScaleToFit = 0,`
		`    StretchToFit = 1,`
		`    ActualSize = 2`
		`}`

11	Set the default value for the `_selectedMode` field to the new setting.	`private DisplayMode _selectedMode` `    = DisplayMode.ScaleToFit;`

We also need to check each place in the code where this enumerator is used. If you do a search, you will discover the `_selectedMode` field in `menuImage_Popup`, `menuImage_ChildClick`, and `OnPaint`. The popup event is not affected by this change, but the click handler requires a change to its `switch` block.

UPDATE menuImage_ChildClick EVENT HANDLER

	Action	Result

12	Locate the menuImage_ChildClick method in the MainForm.cs source file.	```
		protected void menuImage_ChildClick
		  (object sender, System.EventArgs e)
		{
		  . . .
		``

13	Add the new display mode to the switch statement, and make it the default.	```
		switch (_selectedMode)
		{
		  default:
		  case DisplayMode.ScaleToFit:
		    // Scale image to fit display area
		    this.Invalidate();
		    break;
		
		  case DisplayMode.StretchToFit:
		    . . .
		}
		  . . .
		}
		``

The final change required to properly scale our image is in the OnPaint method. Here we simply draw the image into the Rectangle determined by our Photograph.ScaleToFit method.

UPDATE OnPaint METHOD

	Action	Result

14	Locate the OnPaint method in the MainForm.cs source file.	```
		protected override void OnPaint(PaintEventArgs e)
		{
		  . . .
		``

15	Add the new display mode to the switch statement, and make it the default.	```
		switch (_selectedMode)
		{
		  default:
		  case DisplayMode.ScaleToFit:
		    // Preserve aspect ratio of image
		    g.DrawImage(photo.Image,
		        photo.ScaleToFit(DisplayRectangle));
		    break;
		
		  case DisplayMode.StretchToFit:
		    . . .
		}
		  . . .
		}
		``

There you have it. The Scale to Fit display mode is very similar to the Stretch to Fit display mode. Both fit the image into the display area, and both draw the image into a rectangle. The difference is the rectangle into which they draw. Compile your application to verify that the image scales properly. It may be a bit hard to determine if this is working properly since a window resize does not cause the image to be redrawn. Let's address this problem next.

7.2.5 REPAINTING WHEN THE FORM IS RESIZED

Now that we are drawing directly on the form, we need to redraw our image whenever the form is resized. The `PictureBox` control used in prior chapters handled this issue automatically for us.

There is in fact a `Resize` event associated with controls. This event occurs when a control, including a `Form` object, is resized. Handling this event would allow us to invalidate the window whenever the display mode is `ScaleToFit` or `StretchToFit`. Since our `MainForm` class is derived from `Form`, we could even go directly to the protected `OnResize` method that raises this event. This would force our `OnPaint` method to be called and the window would update appropriately. A fine idea, but there is another way.

.NET Table 7.4 ControlStyles enumeration

The `ControlStyles` enumeration specifies a set of values related to the interaction of a control with the Windows desktop. These styles define how low-level Windows messages are processed by the control when a user interacts with it in various ways. This enumeration is part of the `System.Windows.Forms` namespace.

The values in this enumeration can be combined using the bitwise "or" operator. The protected `GetStyle` and `SetStyle` methods in the `Control` class can be used to modify these settings for a control.

Enumeration Values	DoubleBuffer	Whether to perform drawing in a buffer and output the result to the screen after it completes. This prevents flicker caused by redrawing the control.
	FixedHeight	Whether the control has a fixed height.
	FixedWidth	Whether the control has a fixed width.
	ResizeRedraw	Whether the control is completely redrawn when it is resized.
	Selectable	Whether the control can get the focus.
	StandardClick	Whether `OnClick` is called when the control is single-clicked. Note that the control may still call `OnClick` directly.
	StandardDoubleClick	Whether `OnDoubleClick` is called when the control is double clicked. Note that the control may still call `OnDoubleClick` directly.
	UserMouse	Whether the control does its own mouse processing. If so, then mouse messages are not passed to the control.[a]
	UserPaint	Whether the control paints itself. If so, then paint messages are not passed to the control.

a. Actually, the messages here are not passed to the underlying `NativeWindow` object, but you can think of it as the control itself. For `UserMouse`, this affects the `WM_MOUSEDOWN`, `WM_MOUSEMOVE`, and `WM_MOUSEUP` messages. For `UserPaint`, this affects the `WM_PAINT` and `WM_ERASEBKGND` messages.

The .NET Framework defines a `ControlStyles` enumeration, summarized in .NET Table 7.4, for customizing the behavior of a control. The values defined by this enumeration indicate how the control appears or responds in various situations related to desktop interaction with a user, and are useful for customizing the behavior of a `Form` or other custom control class.

The `Control` class provides a `SetStyle` method to set these styles, and a `Get-Style` method to retrieve the current setting for these styles. These methods are protected, so you must inherit from an existing control in order to modify these styles.

For our purposes, you may have noticed the `ResizeRedraw` style, which we can use to force our application to redraw itself every time the user resizes the window.

	FORCE THE FORM TO REDRAW WHEN RESIZED	
	Action	**Result**
1	Locate the `menuImage_ChildClick` method in the MainForm.cs source file.	```protected void menuImage_ChildClick` ` (object sender, System.EventArgs e)` `{` ` . . .```
2	Modify the logic when the display mode is `ScaleToFit` or `StretchToFit` to force a redraw whenever the form resizes.	```switch (_selectedMode)` `{` ` default:` ` case DisplayMode.ScaleToFit:` ` case DisplayMode.StretchToFit:` ` SetStyle(ControlStyles.ResizeRedraw,` ` true);` ` Invalidate();` ` break;` ` . . .` ` }` ` . . .` `}``` **Note:** Since the logic is the same for these two modes, we have merged these two case labels into a single block. C# allows a `case` label to fall through to the next label only if it has no code associated with it.

We will make one other change here before testing our program. When the program begins, the `ResizeRedraw` style is not set to `true`. Only after the user makes a selection will this style be set appropriately. A simple solution would be to set the `ResizeRedraw` style in the constructor for our form. This works, but does not account for any future changes to the `menuImage_ChildClick` method. Since such changes will occur in the next section, a more robust solution is to simulate an Image menu selection directly from the constructor.

Simulating a call to an event handler during control initialization is a good way to ensure that future changes to the handler are dealt with during initialization. It also allows you to make such changes in only one place. We did this in the previous chapter for the New menu. Let's do this here by continuing the previous steps.

	Action	Result
| 3 | Locate the `MainForm` constructor in the MainForm.cs source window. | ```
public MainForm()
{
    . . .
``` |
| 4 | Add a call to `menuImage_ChildClick` in this constructor.<br><br>**How-to**<br>a. Use the `menuScale` menu as the sender parameter.<br>b. Use `EventArgs.Empty` for the event parameter. | ```
    menuImage_ChildClick(menuScale,
        EventArgs.Empty);
}
```<br><br>**Note:** This call must occur after the `InitializeComponent` method has been called to ensure that the menu objects have been initialized. |

Now you can compile and run the application to see the amazing `ResizeRedraw` style in action. This code uses the static `EventArgs.Empty` property we saw in chapter 6 to provide a valid, albeit empty, event argument to the handler.

TRY IT! If you are tired of reading, modify your code to use the `Resize` event instead of the `ResizeRedraw` control style. This change reduces the processing required when an Image submenu item is selected, at the expense of additional processing whenever the window is resized. Do this by overriding the `OnResize` method for the form, and use the `_selectedMode` field to invalidate the window as required.

Another change you can make is to modify the form to do double buffering. This removes the flicker that currently occurs when resizing the image. To do this, use the following code in the `menuImage_ChildClick` method:

```
SetStyle(ControlStyles.UserPaint, true);
SetStyle(ControlStyles.DoubleBuffer, true);
SetStyle(ControlStyles.AllPaintingInWmPaint, true);
```

This completes the drawing of an image within the window. While we have lost our border, we are now able to draw the image in our window using either the Stretch to Fit or Scale to Fit display options. Our next task is to handle the Actual Size menu to draw the full-sized image in the window. This requires the use of scroll bars and will lead us into a discussion of the `Panel` class.

7.3   AUTOMATED SCROLLING

The implementation of the Actual Size menu option allows us to look at the `ScrollableControl` class in more detail. As we have seen, the actual image is often larger than the form's client area. In chapter 3, the `PictureBox` control did not support scrolling and we could only view the rest of the image by resizing the form. Here, we will use scroll bars via the `ScrollableContainer` class members to provide a more appropriate solution.

The result of our labors is shown in figure 7.4. As you can see, part of the image is shown, and scroll bars at the right and bottom of the image can be used to scroll to the remainder of the image. These scroll bars will appear and disappear automatically as needed. You may wonder where our status bar has gone. This is an unfortunate side effect drawing directly on our form, and is the reason a section 7.4 exists in this chapter. More on this later.

Figure 7.4
The scroll bars for the form appear automatically when the display area is larger than the client area.

7.3.1   PROPERTIES FOR SCROLLING

We already have the Actual Size menu available, but we need to add the appropriate processing when this menu is clicked and in the `OnPaint` method. Before we write any code, let's consider which properties we need from the `ScrollableControl` class.

ScrollableControl properties for scrolling our image

Property	Purpose
AutoScroll	Whether scrolling is enabled. We will set this to `true` for the Actual Size mode, and `false` for other display modes.
AutoScrollMinSize	The minimum size for the scrollable window. This is the display size, and not the actual client size seen by the user. We will set this to the size of the current image to ensure that the scroll bars are sized appropriately for this image.
AutoScrollPosition	The window position, in pixels, at the upper left corner of the window. This property is adjusted automatically as the window scrolls.

7.3.2   IMPLEMENTING AUTOMATED SCROLLING

Now that we have reviewed some of the properties used for automated scrolling, we can tackle the code required for the `ActualSize` display mode. We will start with the menu click, and handle the painting of the image in a moment.

When the user clicks the `ActualSize` display mode, we need to adjust not just the Actual Size display mode, but also our Scale to Fit and Stretch to Fit menus to ensure that scrolling is disabled when these modes are set. The following steps detail the changes required.

Set the version number of the MyPhotos application to 7.3.

	MODIFY MENUIMAGE_CHILDCLICK FOR ACTUALSIZE DISPLAY MODE	
	Action	**Result**
1	Locate the `menuImage_ChildClick` method in the MainForm.cs source window.	```protected void menuImage_ChildClick (object sender, System.EventArgs e) { . . . ```
2	Turn scrolling off for the `ScaleToFit` and `StretchToFit` display modes.	```switch (_selectedMode) { default: case DisplayMode.ScaleToFit: case DisplayMode.StretchToFit: // Display entire image in window AutoScroll = false; SetStyle(ControlStyles.ResizeRedraw, true); . . . ```
3	Turn scrolling on for the `ActualSize` display mode. **How-to** a. Set `AutoScroll` to true. b. Turn off the `ResizeRedraw` style for the form.	```case DisplayMode.ActualSize: // Display image at actual size AutoScroll = true; SetStyle(ControlStyles.ResizeRedraw, false); Invalidate(); break; } . . . } ```

Note here that we did not set `AutoScrollMinSize` to the size of the current image. Since different images may have different sizes, we will need to adjust this setting whenever the current image changes. One way to do this would be to modify this setting in all the places where the current image changes. This would include the Next, Previous, and Remove menu handlers, and possibly other locations in the future as well. That's a lot to keep track off. Instead, we will set this property when the image is painted so that it is updated by default whenever the image changes.

For the `Paint` operation itself, another version of the `Graphics.DrawImage` method is used to account for drawing the image into a space larger than the client area. The `DrawImage` method has a number of overloads to handle various types of drawing. See the documentation for the complete list.

MODIFY ONPAINT METHOD FOR ACTUALSIZE DISPLAY MODE	
Action	**Result**
| 4   Locate the `OnPaint` method in the MainForm.cs source window. | ```
protected override void OnPaint(PaintEventArgs e)
{
    . . .
``` |
| 5   When the display mode is `ActualSize`, draw the image into the display area. | ```
case DisplayMode.ActualSize:
    // Draw appropriate portion of image
    g.DrawImage(photo.Image,
        AutoScrollPosition.X,
        AutoScrollPosition.Y,
        photo.Image.Width,
        photo.Image.Height);
``` |
| 6   Also set the `AutoScrollMinSize` property as appropriate. | ```
    AutoScrollMinSize = photo.Image.Size;
    break;
    . . .
}
``` |

That's it! Your application will now handle all three display modes. Note how the `AutoScrollPosition` property is used for the location to appear in the upper left corner of the client area. As the window scrolls, this value is updated automatically so we can use it future `Paint` operations.

Crank it up and display your favorite set of images stretched to fit, scaled to fit, and at the actual size. Make sure you try some images of alternate sizes to ensure that the scroll bars adjust appropriately as you move through the album. Also note how the scroll bars disappear when the window is expanded to be larger than the image.

Too bad about our status bar. It really should not be part of the scrolled area here. The problem is that we are drawing and scrolling the form itself, and both the image and the status bar are part of the form. As a result, as goes the image, so goes the status bar. To fix this, we need to isolate the image portion of the form and have our image appear only in this area. The `PictureBox` control isolated the image without the ability to scroll. The `Panel` class will provide both isolation and scrolling.

7.4   PANELS

If you have prior experience with MFC, then you must know how frustrating the MFC group box control can be. A fine control, I would submit, except when you have to adjust its position, or worse, add controls inside of it. The problem, for those not familiar with this construct, is that it is just a box, with no relationship to the inside of the box. If you move the box, you have to adjust the contents separately, and vice versa. Very frustrating.

In the .NET Framework, controls can act as containers for other controls. When you move the container, the controls inside move with it. Two such containers in the `System.Windows.Forms` namespace are the `GroupBox` and `Panel` classes. When you move a .NET container, the contents move with it. The position of the inner controls are defined in relationship to the container, and the `Anchor` and `Dock` properties are used to set their resize behavior within the container just like within a form.
```

Our focus in this section will be the `Panel` class. This class can contain and position controls just like the `Form` class, and supports automated scrolling since it inherits from the `ScrollableControl` class.[2] We will not position controls within a panel in this chapter, but we will use this class to fix some of the problems we have seen when drawing directly on the form. We will draw our photo directly in a `Panel`, and solve the following problems we noticed when drawing directly on the form:

- Our image was off-center vertically for the Scale to Fit display option. The `DisplayRectangle` property included the vertical space occupied by the scroll bar, which threw our calculations off. Here, we will use the panel's `DisplayRectangle` property, so that the image will be centered exactly inside the panel.

- The 3-D border we used for the `PictureBox` control was gone. We could have attempted to draw a border inside the form using the `ControlPaint.DrawBorder3D` method, but a `Panel` provides a much easier solution. The `Panel` class provides a `BorderStyle` property much like the corresponding `PictureBox` property, so the .NET framework will draw the border for us.

- The status bar was part of the scrollable area. Since the `Form` object managed the scrolling, the `StatusBar` control on the form was caught up in the scrolling logic. In this section, the scrolling will be managed by the `Panel` class independent of the form and status bar. As a result, our status bar will return to and remain at its natural position at the base of the form.

Before we get into the required changes, figure 7.5 shows how our three display modes will appear by the end of this section. As you can see, the application looks much more polished here than when we drew directly on the form. Note especially the excellent centering, the fine border, and the well-behaved scroll bars.

Figure 7.5   This shows an image drawn inside a panel with the Scale to Fit, Stretch to Fit, and Actual Size display modes.

---

[2]   For the curious, the `GroupBox` control inherits from the `Control` class and does not support scrolling.

As you will see, the code to draw the image inside a panel is very similar to drawing the image directly on the form. We will need to add a new panel, update some of our menu handlers and the drawing of the status bar, and finally draw the image into the panel.

7.4.1 ADDING A PANEL

Adding a `Panel` object in Visual Studio is much like adding any other control. You open the Toolbox and drag a `Panel` onto the form. In the source code, the panel is added using the `Control` property of the parent form. We will look at both of these, beginning with the use of Visual Studio.

Set the version number of the MyPhotos application to 7.4.

	ADD A PANEL TO THE FORM	
	Action	**Result**
1	In the MainForm.cs [Design] window, drag a Panel control from the Toolbox onto the form.	A `Panel` control is added to the window.
2	Set the panel's properties as shown.	

Settings

Property	Value
(Name)	pnlPhoto
BorderStyle	Fixed3D
Dock	Fill

Take a look at the MainForm.cs source file to see how the panel is created. As you can see, this code looks very similar to the code for other controls from prior chapters. A private instance is created in the `MainForm` class, initialized in the `Initialize-Component` method, and added to the form using the `Form.Controls` property.

```
private System.Windows.Forms.Panel pnlPhoto;
. . .
private void InitializeComponent()
{
  . . .
  this.pnlPhoto = new System.Windows.Forms.Panel ();
  . . .
  //
  // pnlPhoto
  //
  this.pnlPhoto.BorderStyle = System.Windows.Forms.BorderStyle.Fixed3D;
  this.pnlPhoto.Dock = System.Windows.Forms.DockStyle.Fill;
  this.pnlPhoto.Name = "pnlPhoto";
  this.pnlPhoto.Size = new System.Drawing.Size(292, 233);
  this.pnlPhoto.TabIndex = 3;
  . . .
  this.Controls.AddRange(new System.Windows.Forms.Control[] {
                            this.pnlPhoto,
                            this.statusBar1});
```

The `Panel` class depends largely on its base classes for exported functionality, with the `BorderStyle` property just about the only new member added by the class. An overview of the `Panel` class appears in .NET Table 7.5.

.NET Table 7.5 Panel class		
The `Panel` class represents a scrollable control that acts as a container for other controls. This class is often used to define a region of controls within a `Form`. This class is part of the `System.Windows.Forms` namespace and inherits from the `ScrollableControl` class. See .NET Table 7.1 on page 196 for a list of members inherited from the `ScrollableControl` class.		
Public Properties	BorderStyle	Gets or sets the type of border to display around the control.
	DisplayRectangle (inherited from Control)	Gets the display area for the control. When scrolling is enabled, this property represents the entire scrollable area for the panel. The `ClientRectangle` property represents the visible portion of the control.
	Enabled (inherited from Control)	Gets or sets whether the panel is enabled. Controls within the panel are disabled whenever the panel itself is disabled.
	Visible (inherited from Control)	Gets or sets whether the panel is visible. Controls within the panel are invisible if the panel itself is invisible.

7.4.2 UPDATING THE MENU HANDLERS

With our panel on the form, we need to update the code for drawing our image to use the new panel rather than interacting with the form itself. We will begin with the menu handlers for the Image submenu.

The `menuImage_Popup` method simply sets the `Enabled` and `Checked` menu properties as required for the current display mode. This behavior does not change, so no modifications are required. The `menuImage_ChildClick` method sets scrolling properties for the form. Since our scrolling will be managed from the `Panel` object now, we need to use the corresponding `Panel` members rather than those in the `Form` itself.

	UPDATE THE MENUIMAGE_CHILDCLICK METHOD TO USE THE NEW PANEL	
	Action	**Result**
| 1 | Locate the `menuImage_ChildClick` method in the MainForm.cs source window. | ```
protected void menuImage_ChildClick
    (object sender, System.EventArgs e)
{
    . . .
``` |
| 2 | Modify the code for the `ScaleToFit` and `StretchToFit` display mode to set drawing-related properties on the `Panel` rather than the parent `Form`. | ```
case DisplayMode.ScaleToFit:
case DisplayMode.StretchToFit:
    SetStyle(ControlStyles.ResizeRedraw,
        true);
    pnlPhoto.AutoScroll = false;
    pnlPhoto.Invalidate();
    break;
``` |

	Action	Result

3	Modify the code for the `ActualSize` display mode in a similar manner.	```case DisplayMode.ActualSize:```
		 ``` SetStyle(ControlStyles.ResizeRedraw,```
		 ``` false);```
		 ``` pnlPhoto.AutoScroll = true;```
		 ``` pnlPhoto.Invalidate();```
		 ``` break;```
		 ``` . . .```
		 ```}```

That's it for our menu handlers. The `SetStyle` method is a protected member and cannot be modified for our `Panel` class, so we just force the redraw to happen at the `Form` level as we did before. This will redraw the entire form and not just our panel, but it gets the job done. In this case, the drawing required outside of our panel is not overly complex, so this extra drawing should not be a problem.

On a more complex form, it would make sense to handle the `Resize` event for the `pnlPhoto` object instead of setting a form-level style as we do here. Handling the `Resize` event would allow us to only redraw the panel itself, and not the other parts of the `Form`.

The `AutoScroll` property is a public member of the `ScrollableControl` class, so we can set its value for the `pnlPhoto` object directly.

As you can see, because the `Panel` and `Form` classes are based on a similar class hierarchy, design changes like this are very easy to make in .NET. Let's move on to our owner-drawn status bar.

7.4.3   DRAWING THE STATUS BAR PANEL

Our status bar is drawn in the `statusBar1_DrawItem` method. This method must calculate the percentage of the image shown in the window. Since the image will now be displayed inside the `Panel` object, we must modify this routine to use the `Panel` client area rather than the `MainForm` one.

	Action	Result

1	Locate the `statusBar1_DrawItem` method in the MainForm.cs file.	```protected void statusBar1_DrawItem```
		 ``` (object sender,```
		 ``` StatusBarDrawItemEventArgs sbdevent)```
		 ```{```
		 ``` . . .```

	Action	Result
2	Modify the calculation of the `percent` variable to use the panel rather than the form.	```// Calculate percent of image shown int percent = 100; if (_selectedMode == DisplayMode.ActualSize) { Photograph photo = _album.CurrentPhoto; Rectangle dr = pnlPhoto.ClientRectangle; int imgWidth = photo.Image.Width; int imgHeight = photo.Image.Height; percent = 100 * Math.Min(dr.Width, imgWidth) * Math.Min(dr.Height, imgHeight) / (imgWidth * imgHeight); } . . . }```

Once again this change simply uses our private `Panel` field rather than the `this` keyword. Our last change is to draw the image inside the panel rather than on the form itself.

7.4.4 DRAWING THE IMAGE

When drawing the image on the form, we were able to override the protected `OnPaint` method that raises the `Paint` event. For the `Panel` object, we do not have access to protected members, so we must use the public `Paint` event to update the panel. Internally in the Windows Forms library, of course, the `Panel` control will use its own version of the `OnPaint` method to invoke our event handler.

	Action	Result
ADD A PAINT HANDLER FOR THE PNLPHOTO OBJECT		
1	Add a `Paint` event handler for the panel. **How-to** Double-click the `Panel` control. **Note:** The `Paint` event is the default event for the panel control in Visual Studio. Other events can be added via the Properties window.	Visual Studio generates the appropriate code in the source file. ```protected void pnlPhoto_Paint (object sender, System.Windows.Forms.PaintEventArgs e) { }```

Note that the `Paint` event handler receives a `PaintEventArgs` instance containing the event data. As we saw earlier in the chapter, this class contains the `Graphics` object for drawing inside the panel. Our code uses this object in the same way as when the image was drawn in the form. Continuing our previous steps:

Transfer the drawing code into the new Paint handler

<table>
<tr><th></th><th>Action</th><th>Result</th></tr>
<tr><td>2</td><td>In the pnlPhoto_Paint method, use the given Graphics to draw the image when the album is not empty.</td><td><pre>
protected void pnlPhoto_Paint
  (object sender,
   System.Windows.Forms.PaintEventArgs e)
{
  if (_album.Count > 0)
  {
    // Paint the current photo
    Photograph photo = _album.CurrentPhoto;
    Graphics g = e.Graphics;
</pre></td></tr>
<tr><td>3</td><td>Copy the switch statement for drawing the image from the existing OnPaint method.</td><td><pre>
    switch (_selectedMode)
    {
      . . .
    }
  }
  else
  {
    // No image to paint
  }
}
</pre></td></tr>
<tr><td>4</td><td>Update this switch block to use the pnlPhoto object as appropriate.</td><td><pre>
    switch (_selectedMode)
    {
      default:
      case DisplayMode.ScaleToFit:
        // Preserve aspect ratio of image
        g.DrawImage(photo.Image,
          photo.ScaleToFit(
              pnlPhoto.DisplayRectangle));
        break;

      case DisplayMode.StretchToFit:
        // Fill entire panel with image
        g.DrawImage(photo.Image,
            pnlPhoto.DisplayRectangle);
        break;

      case DisplayMode.ActualSize:
        // Draw portion of image
        g.DrawImage(photo.Image,
            pnlPhoto.AutoScrollPosition.X,
            pnlPhoto.AutoScrollPosition.Y,
            photo.Image.Width,
            photo.Image.Height);
        pnlPhoto.AutoScrollMinSize
            = photo.Image.Size;
        break;
    }
</pre></td></tr>
<tr><td>5</td><td>If the album is empty, draw the standard system control color onto the panel.</td><td><pre>
  else
  {
    // No image to paint
    e.Graphics.Clear(SystemColors.Control);
  }
}
</pre></td></tr>
</table>

	Action	Result
| 6 | Remove the corresponding drawing code from the existing `OnPaint` method. | The `OnPaint` method now looks as follows:<br><br>```csharp
protected override void OnPaint
    (PaintEventArgs e)
{
    if (_album.Count > 0)
    {
        // Paint the current image
        Photograph photo = _album.CurrentPhoto;

        // Update the status bar.
        pnlFileName.Text = photo.Caption;
        pnlFileIndex.Text
            = String.Format("{0:#}/{1:#}",
                    _album.CurrentIndex+1,
                    _album.Count);
        pnlImageSize.Text
            = String.Format("{0:#} x {1:#}",
                    photo.Image.Width,
                    photo.Image.Height);
        statusBar1.ShowPanels = true;
    }
    else
    {
        // Indicate the album is empty
        statusBar1.Text = "No Photos in Album";
        statusBar1.ShowPanels = false;
    }
``` |
| 7 | At the end of this method, invalidate the panel to ensure it is redrawn. | ```csharp
    // Ensure contained controls are redrawn
    pnlPhoto.Invalidate();
    statusBar1.Invalidate();
    base.OnPaint(e);
}
``` |

It may look like a lot of code, but the number of changes is actually quite small, as indicated by the few number of bolded lines. The program is all set now. Verify that your code compiles and runs properly. Change display modes, use different-sized images, and resize the form to observe the effect.

TRY IT! If you are feeling brave, try adding a Fit to Width menu item to the Image submenu. This should preserve the aspect ratio of the image by scaling the image to match the width of the panel window. You will need to add a `FitToWidth` enumeration value to the `DisplayMode` enumeration. Calculate the height using code similar to the `Photograph.ScaleToFit` method where the width is preserved. The tricky part is setting the `pnlPhoto.AutoScrollMinSize` property appropriately and drawing the image into this same rectangle.

7.5 RECAP

This chapter has looked at some drawing and scrolling aspects of the `Form` class. In particular, we removed the `PictureBox` control from our application and learned how to draw our image directly onto the form. We used the protected `OnPaint` method and made use of the automated scroll bars inherited by the `Form` class to scroll our image. This did not work exactly as we wanted, so we modified our code to use the `Panel` class instead as a way to draw the image independent of the rest of the form.

The next chapter will continue our investigation of the `Form` class by looking at dialog boxes.

C H A P T E R   8

Dialog boxes

8.1   Message boxes 225
8.2   The Form.Close method 233
8.3   Modal dialog boxes 237
8.4   Modeless dialogs 252
8.5   Recap 262

So far we have only used a single window in our MyPhotos application. We have changed its appearance in each chapter, adding controls such as a menu bar, status bar, and panel, but all controls, events, painting, and other activities have occurred within our one `Form` window. In this chapter we branch out.

The previous chapter introduced the `Form` class and demonstrated drawing and scrolling in both it and the `Panel` class. Both of these classes can be used to support intricate drawing interfaces from those seen in basic drawing applications such as Microsoft Paint to a full-fledged Internet browser window.

Another common use for `Form` classes is the creation of dialog boxes. The `Form` class, as well as the `Panel` class, allows other controls to be positioned and managed inside its boundaries. In this chapter we look at how dialog boxes are created for both simple message boxes and more complex custom dialogs. This will consist of the following topics.

- Create simple message dialogs with the `MessageBox` class.

- Discuss the use of `Close` and `Dispose` for `Form` objects.

- Use the `OnClosing` method to intercept when a form or dialog box closes.

- Explain the difference between modal and modeless dialogs.
- Create dialog boxes using the `Form` class.

Before we get into generating custom dialog boxes, we will first look at how simple messages are displayed using the `MessageBox` class.

8.1 MESSAGE BOXES

Developers, especially object-oriented developers, are always looking for shortcuts. Classes such as `OpenFileDialog` and `SaveFileDialog` not only provide a standard way to prompt a user for files, they also save programmers a lot of time and effort by encapsulating the required window display and interaction code. Another common task programmers face is the need to display a simple message to the user. Our photo album application, for example, should really display an error message when an album cannot be saved successfully, or it could pose a question by asking the user if they would like to save the album to an alternate file location.

The .NET Framework provides a `MessageBox` class for this purpose. This class is very similar to the MFC function of the same name. This section will show how this class is used to handle simple interactions with a user. While this class is not actually a `Form` object, it is the most basic type of modal dialog box.

All dialog boxes are either modal or modeless. A *modal* dialog box requires the user to respond before the associated program will continue. *Modeless* or *nonmodal* dialog boxes allow the application to continue while the dialog box is displayed.

All `MessageBox` windows are modal, while `Form` windows are modal if invoked via the `Form.ShowDialog` method and modeless if invoked via the `Form.Show` method.

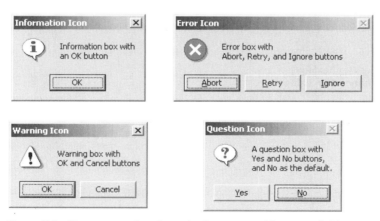

Figure 8.1   These examples show the four types of icons available to MessageBox dialogs.

Figure 8.1 shows some sample message boxes with various settings. Note the different button configurations, and how the Question Icon dialog has defined No as the default button. An overview of the `MessageBox` class is provided in .NET Table 8.1.

.NET Table 8.1 MessageBox class		
The `MessageBox` class represents a modal dialog box that displays a message or question to the user and waits for their response. This class is part of the `System.Windows.Forms` namespace. A `MessageBox` cannot be instantiated as an object with the `new` keyword; instead the static `Show` method is used to display the dialog. By default, a message box displays with no icon and a single OK button. The `Show` method is overloaded to allow these and other settings to be customized. There are four enumerations used for this purpose: `MessageBoxButtons`, `MessageBoxIcon`, `MessageBoxDefault-Button`, and `MessageBoxOptions`. In the following table, the enumeration values for some of these four types are included, since these types are only used with the `MessageBox.Show` method.		
Public Static Methods	Show	Displays a message box and returns the `DialogResult` enumeration value corresponding to the button selected by the user.
MessageBoxButtons Enumeration Values	OK	The message box should contain an OK button only.
	OKCancel	The message box should contain an OK and Cancel button.
	YesNo	The message box should contain a Yes and No button.
	YesNoCancel	The message box should contain a Yes, No, and Cancel button.
MessageBoxIcon Enumeration Values	Error	The message box should contain an error symbol, a white X in a red circle. Use this for unexpected problems that prevent an operation from continuing.
	Information	The message box should contain an information symbol, a lower case letter 'i' in a circle. Use this for general messages about the application such as a status or notification.
	Question	The message box should contain a question mark symbol. Use this for Yes/No questions where a choice by the user is required.
	Warning	The message box should contain a warning symbol, an exclamation point in a yellow triangle. Use this for problems that may interfere with the ability of an operation to continue.
MessageBoxDefault-Button Enumeration Values	Button1	The first button in the message box is the default.
	Button2	The second button is the default.
	Button3	The third button is the default.

8.1.1 THE MESSAGEBOX.SHOW METHOD

A `MessageBox` instance cannot be instantiated. Instead, the `Show` method is used to create the message dialog and return the result. There are a number of overloads available for this method, from a version that takes a single message string to one that accepts a parameter for everything from the title bar text to which button should be the default. Various forms of this method are shown in the following signatures. The comment preceding each signature refers to the characters in bold.

```
// The return value indicates which button was clicked by the user
public static DialogResult Show( string text );

// Displays the dialog in front of the specified window object
public static DialogResult Show( IWin32Window owner, string text );

// Accepts a message string and title bar caption
public static DialogResult Show( string text, string caption );

// Displays the dialog with the specified buttons
public static DialogResult Show( IWin32Window owner,
                                 string text,
                                 string caption,
                                 MessageBoxButtons buttons );

// The penultimate Show method: an icon, default button, and options
public static DialogResult Show( IWin32Window owner,
                                 string text,
                                 string caption,
                                 MessageBoxButtons buttons,
                                 MessageBoxIcon icon,
                                 MessageBoxDefaultButton defaultButton,
                                 MessageBoxOptions options );
```

Turning back to our MyPhotos application, the addition of a message box would be beneficial in some of the situations we have already encountered. These include:

- When an error occurs while trying to open an existing album.
- When an error occurs while trying to save the current album.
- When the current album has changed and is about to be discarded.

We will add a `MessageBox` to our program for each of these instances.

8.1.2 CREATING AN OK DIALOG

When we are unable to open a selected album, there is not much to do other than inform the user that something is wrong. We will use an error dialog since a failure here is not normally expected. The resulting dialog is shown in figure 8.2.

Figure 8.2
This message box is displayed when the album contains an unrecognized version number.

Let's add the code to create this dialog whenever an unexpected problem occurs while opening the file

Set the version number of the MyPhotos application to 8.1.

	HANDLE EXCEPTION IN MENUOPEN_CLICK METHOD	
	Action	**Result**
| 1 | Locate the `menuOpen_Click` method in the MainForm.cs source file. | ```csharp
private void menuOpen_Click
    (object sender, System.EventArgs e)
{
    . . .
``` |
| 2 | Enclose the code to open the album in a `try` block. | ```csharp
if (dlg.ShowDialog() == DialogResult.OK)
{
    try
    {
        // Open the new album.
        _album.Open(dlg.FileName);

        _album.FileName = dlg.FileName;
        _bAlbumChanged = false;
        this.Invalidate();
    }
``` |
| 3 | Catch any `Exception` that occurs. | ```csharp
catch (Exception ex)
``` |
| 4 | Display the dialog in the catch block. | ```csharp
    {
        MessageBox.Show(this,
            "Unable to open file " + dlg.FileName
            + "\n (" + ex.Message + ")",
            "Open Album Error",
            MessageBoxButtons.OK,
            MessageBoxIcon.Error);
    }
}
    . . .
}
```

Note: The text string is constructed using the + (plus sign) notation for strings. Also note that a new line is inserted in the dialog with the \n character. |

In this code, we cheated a little by catching any and all `Exception` objects in the `catch` block. It is normally safer to catch specific exceptions that may occur so you can provide feedback or take actions based on the specific error. In this code, an `IOException` will occur if an unexpected error occurs during a file I/O operation. If you recall, the `PhotoAlbum.Open` method throws an `IOException` explicitly if the version number in the file is not recognized.

It is also worth noting that we ignore the result returned by the `Show` method, since there is only a single OK button in the dialog.

8.1.3 CREATING A YESNO DIALOG

As an alternate example, what happens when an error occurs while saving an album? We could simply display an OK dialog as we did while opening an album. This would just duplicate the previous code, so we will do something different. Instead, we will allow the user to save the album under an alternate file name. This permits the user to save the album to an alternate location that is less likely to fail, or retry the save to the same location. The new message box is shown in figure 8.3.

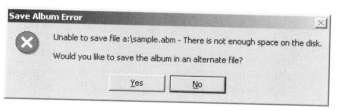

Figure 8.3
This message box is displayed when an exception occurs in the `menuSave_Click` method.

The steps required to generate this message dialog are shown in the following table:

	HANDLE EXCEPTION IN MENUSAVE_CLICK METHOD	
	Action	**Result**
1	Locate the `menuSave_Click` method in the MainForm.cs file.	```private void menuSave_Click``` ```(object sender, System.EventArgs e)``` ```{``` ```. . .```
2	Enclose the code to save the album in a `try` block.	```else``` ```{``` ``` try``` ``` {``` ``` // Save album in current file``` ``` _album.Save();``` ``` _bAlbumChanged = false;``` ``` }```
3	Catch any exception that occurs.	```catch (Exception ex)``` ```{```
4	Within the `catch` block, display the dialog and record the selected button.	```string msg = "Unable to save file {0}"``` ``` + " - {1}\nWould you like to save"``` ``` + " the album in an alternate file?";``` ```DialogResult result``` ``` = MessageBox.Show(this,``` ``` String.Format(msg,``` ``` _album.FileName, ex.Message),``` ``` "Save Album Error",``` ``` MessageBoxButtons.YesNo,``` ``` MessageBoxIcon.Error,``` ``` MessageBoxDefaultButton.Button2);```
5	If the user wishes to save under an alternate name, prompt the user for the new file name. **How-to** Use the Save As menu handler.	```if (result == DialogResult.Yes)``` ```{``` ``` menuSaveAs_Click(sender, e);``` ```}``` ``` }``` ```. . .``` ```}```

Unlike our message for the Open handler, this code makes use of the result returned by the `Show` method. This result is a `DialogResult` enumeration that indicates the button pressed. The values in this enumeration are shown in .NET Table 8.2, and correspond to the kinds of buttons typically found in Windows dialogs.

.NET Table 8.2	DialogResult enumeration	
	The `DialogResult` enumeration represents a value returned by a dialog box. This class is part of the `System.Windows.Forms` namespace, and is used with all dialog boxes in Windows Forms. In particular, a `DialogResult` is returned by the `MessageBox.Show` method as well as the `ShowDialog` method in both the `Form` class and common dialogs derived from the `CommonDialog` class. This enumeration is also used by the `Button` class to indicate the result to automatically return from a modal dialog when the button is clicked.	
Enumeration Values	Abort	The dialog return value is Abort. Typically, this means the user clicked an Abort button.
	Cancel	The dialog returns Cancel, typically from a Cancel button.
	Ignore	The dialog returns Ignore, typically from an Ignore button.
	No	The dialog returns No, typically from a No button.
	None	The dialog returns nothing, indicating that the dialog box is still running.
	OK	The dialog returns OK, typically from an OK button.
	Retry	The dialog returns Retry, typically from a Retry button.
	Yes	The dialog returns Yes, typically from a Yes button.

You can compile and run this code if you would like to see the message boxes we created. You can generate an open error easily enough by selecting a file that is not, in fact, an album file. A save error can be generated by attempting to save to a read-only CD, or by filling up a floppy disk and then saving a file to it.

Our last example will generate a message box for closing an existing album.

8.1.4   Creating A YesNoCancel dialog

Our final example is the case where an album has changed but is about to be discarded. This can occur when the application is about to exit, when loading a new album with the Open menu item, and when creating a new album with the New menu item.

To handle these situations in a consistent way, we will create a protected method to gracefully close the current album for all three cases using the dialog in figure 8.4. We will call this method `CloseCurrentAlbum` and have it return a boolean value indicating whether the album was closed or the user clicked the Cancel button.

Figure 8.4   This dialog is displayed when an album is about to be discarded.

The three buttons in our dialog will correspond to the following behavior in our `CloseCurrentAlbum` method:

- Yes will save the album, then close the album and return `true`.
- No will not save the album, then close the album and return `true`.
- Cancel will not save or close the album and return `false` to indicate that the calling operation should be canceled.

To close the album, `CloseCurrentAlbum` will clear the album and related settings. The following steps create this method:

	ADD A CLOSECURRENTALBUM METHOD	
	Action	**Result**
1	Add the `CloseCurrentAlbum` method to the MainForm.cs source code window.	```protected bool CloseCurrentAlbum()
{```
2	Offer to save the album if it has been modified.	```if (_bAlbumChanged)
{
// Offer to save the current album```
3	Define an appropriate message to display. **Note:** We vary the message text depending on whether the current album has a name or not.	```string msg;
if (_album.FileName == null)
msg = "Do you want to save the "
+ "current album?";
else
msg = String.Format("Do you want to "
+ "save your changes to \n{0}?",
_album.FileName);```
4	Display the message box and record the result.	```DialogResult result
= MessageBox.Show(this, msg,
"Save Current Album?",
MessageBoxButtons.YesNoCancel,
MessageBoxIcon.Question);```
5	Perform the action requested by the user.	```if (result == DialogResult.Yes)
menuSave_Click(this,EventArgs.Empty);
else if (result == DialogResult.Cancel)
{
// Do not close the album
return false;
}
}```
6	Close the album and return true. **Note:** This action is only performed if the Yes or No button was selected.	```// Close the album and return true
if (_album != null)
_album.Dispose();
_album = new PhotoAlbum();
SetTitleBar();
_bAlbumChanged = false;
return true;
}```

We will use this new method in three different places to ensure that the user has the option of saving any changes he or she might make to the album.

- In `menuNew_Click` to save the existing album before a new album is created.
- In `menuOpen_Click` to save the album before a new album is selected.
- In `menuExit_Click` to save the album before the application exits.

We will modify the handlers for the New and Open menus here. The Exit menu presents some additional issues, which we will take up in the next section. The following table continues our previous steps.

UPDATE THE HANDLERS FOR THE NEW AND OPEN MENUS		
	Action	**Result**
| 7 | Modify the `menuNew_Click` method to use the `CloseCurrentAlbum` method. | ```
protected void menuNew_Click
    (object sender, System.EventArgs e)
{
    if (this.CloseCurrentAlbum() == true)
    {
        // Make sure the window is redrawn
        this.Invalidate();
    }
}
``` |
| 8 | Modify the `menuOpen_Click` method to use the `CloseCurrentAlbum` method.<br><br>**Note:** The new code here replaces the previous code in this method to save the current album. The remainder of this method stays the same. | ```
protected void menuOpen_Click
    (object sender, System.EventArgs e)
{
    // Save the existing album, if necessary
    if (this.CloseCurrentAlbum() == false)
    {
        // Cancel this operation
        return;
    }

    OpenFileDialog dlg = new OpenFileDialog();
    . . .
}
``` |

These changes make our application much more user-friendly by interacting with the user when they are about to discard a modified album.

TRY IT!   Before moving on, create a `MessageBox` dialog in the `menuRemove_Click` method, where the current photograph is removed without any confirmation by the user. Add a question box here to verify that the user does indeed want to remove the current photo.

Another place where a message box could be used is at the beginning and end of the album. Modify the Next and Previous menus to display an information dialog whenever the user tries to move before the beginning of the album or past the end.[1]

For the Exit menu, life is not so easy. We will pick up this topic in the next section.

---

[1]   The interface designers among us will argue that the Previous and Next commands should be disabled at the beginning and end of the album, respectively. Why allow the user to invoke a menu item that does not work? I would not disagree, and if you prefer this approach, please go right ahead.

8.2 THE FORM.CLOSE METHOD

In this section we pick up the thread of our previous discussion on the CloseCurrentAlbum method by discussing the Close and Dispose methods. You may think this is a little off-topic from dialog boxes, but in fact it is quite relevant. One of the key issues for C# programming in .NET is when to call the Dispose method to clean up window handlers and other nonmemory resources. This section will discuss this topic as it relates to dialog boxes, and introduce the Closing event as a way to intercept a user's request to close a form.

8.2.1 The relationship between Close and Dispose

Before we return to the topic of calling CloseCurrentAlbum when our application exits, let's look at the relationship between Close and Dispose in .NET. It's actually quite simple: they are the same. For all classes in the .NET Framework, a call to Close is equivalent to calling the Dispose method, and a call to Dispose is equivalent to calling the Close method. The term "close" traditionally applies to objects like files and windows, and .NET has preserved this terminology. When you are finished with a form or a file, it seems silly to require a call to both Close and Dispose, so it makes sense to merge these two concepts together. The .NET design team could have chosen to use a common name for all classes, but programmers naturally expect to close objects such as forms and files, and closing objects like arrays or drawing objects seems a bit odd. Instead, the designers chose to use both methods and define them to be equivalent.

For Form objects, the behavior of the form itself varies depending on whether the object is displayed as a modal or modeless window. For a modeless window, displayed with the Form.Show method, the nonmemory resources are automatically cleaned up when the form is closed. This makes life much easier for us programmers, since we do not have to remember anything in this case. You cannot use a modeless Form after it is closed since all of its resources are gone. The Hide method should be used if you simply want to remove a Form from the desktop and display it later via the Show method. We will see this in chapter 13 when we use a tool bar button to hide the modeless dialog created in section 8.4 of this chapter.

For modal windows, displayed with the Form.ShowDialog method, there is a problem in that the dialog is typically accessed after the window disappears. As a result, a modal dialog must call Dispose explicitly to release its nonmemory resources. Typically, a modal dialog is created and destroyed in the same block of code. For example:

```
{
    MyModalDialog dlg = new MyModalDialog();

    // Initialize any dlg settings

    if (dlg.ShowDialog() == DialogResult.OK)
    {
        // Use dlg settings to do something
```

```
    }
      dlg.Dispose()
}
```

In this code, if the resources for the `dlg` variable disappeared after the `ShowDialog` method returned, you could not access any of its settings. For this reason, .NET only calls the `Hide` method after a user responds to a modal dialog, so that the dialog settings may still be accessed. This can be a little confusing since we still say the user closes the dialog, even though the dialog's `Close` method is not actually called.

Fortunately, modal dialog boxes tend to have *deterministic scope*, meaning that you can predict when the dialog will be created and destroyed. The application waits until the user responds to a modal dialog, so it's clear where the `Dispose` method must be called. We have already seen this method used with `OpenFileDialog` and `SaveFileDialog` objects in chapter 6, both of which are modal dialogs.

The C# language provides a `using` statement to call `Dispose` on our behalf in deterministic situations such as this. We have seen how the `using` directive defines an alias or shortcut for an object or members of a namespace. The `using` statement defines the scope in which a given object should exist. The syntax is as follows:

```
using (object)
{
    // Do something with object
}
```

At the end of the block of code associated with the statement, the identified object is automatically disposed. For example, the previous code for the `My ModalDialog` object can be written as follows to cause `Dispose` to be called automatically at the end of the block:

```
{
    using (MyModalDialog dlg = new MyModalDialog)
    {
        // Initialize any dlg settings

        if (dlg.ShowDialog() == DialogResult.OK)
        {
            // Use dlg settings to do something
        }
    }
}
```

As another example, here is how our `menuSaveAs_Click` handler looks with this statement. The changes from our current implementation are shown in bold.

```
private void menuSaveAs_Click(object sender, System.EventArgs e)
{
    using (SaveFileDialog dlg = new SaveFileDialog())
    {
```

```
dlg.Title = "Save Album";
dlg.DefaultExt = "abm";
dlg.Filter = "abm files (*.abm)|*.abm";
dlg.InitialDirectory = PhotoAlbum.DefaultDir;
dlg.RestoreDirectory = true;

if (dlg.ShowDialog() == DialogResult.OK)
{
  // Record the new album name
  _album.FileName = dlg.FileName;

  // Use Save handler to store the album
  menuSave_Click(sender, e);

  //Update title bar to include new name
  SetTitleBar();
}
}
}
```

In general, any object that supports the IDisposable interface can be used with the using statement in this manner. In particular, you will recall that we supported this interface in our PhotoAlbum and Photograph classes in chapter 5, so we could use this statement with our album and photo objects.

For the remainder of the book, we will generally employ the using statement in our examples to dispose of nonmemory resources rather than calling the Dispose method explicitly.

8.2.2   INTERCEPTING THE FORM.CLOSE METHOD

Let's get back to our application and the CloseCurrentAlbum method. Since our application is a modeless dialog, Close will be called when the application exits. In fact, we call the Close method explicitly in the Click handler for our Exit menu.

We could certainly use the CloseCurrentAlbum method in our Click event handler. While this would work for the Exit menu, it does not work for the case where the application exits via the Alt+F4 keyboard shortcut or the Close option on the system menu.[2]

To handle both situations, the Form class provides a Closing event that occurs whenever the form is about to close. The protected OnClosing method is invoked whenever the Close method is called, and it in turn raises the Closing event by invoking any registered event handlers. The signature for this method is as follows:

```
protected virtual void OnClosing(CancelEventArgs ce);
```

---

[2] The *system menu*, as you may know, is the menu of operating system commands that appears when you click the control box icon in the upper left corner of a window. You can also right-click an application's title bar or its entry in the task bar to display this menu.

As you can see, this method receives a `CancelEventArgs` object. This class defines a `Cancel` property to help determine whether the application will actually exit. If this property is set to `true` by an override of the `OnClosing` method or a `Closing` event handler, then the close operation is cancelled and the application will continue to run. The `Cancel` property has a default value of `false`, so that the close operation is not cancelled and the application will exit.

We will override the `OnClosing` method in our `MainForm` class to make sure the `CloseCurrentAlbum` method is called regardless of how the application exits.

Set the version number of the MyPhotos application to 8.2.

	OVERRIDE THE ONCLOSING METHOD	
	Action	**Result**

1	Override the `OnClosing` method in the MainForm.cs source window.	`protected override void OnClosing`
		    `(CancelEventArgs ce)`
		`{`

2	Within this method, call the `CloseCurrentAlbum` method to see if the current album should be saved.	`if (this.CloseCurrentAlbum() == false)`
3	If the user clicked the Cancel button, then cancel the close operation.	`    ce.Cancel = true;` **Note:** This cancels the Close operation so that the application does not exit.

4	Otherwise, allow the application to close.	`else`
		    `ce.Cancel = false;`
		
		Note: Since `false` is the default value, these lines are not strictly required. They are here simply to illustrate the setting when the application is permitted to exit.

5	Remember to call `OnClosing` in the base class.	`    base.OnClosing(ce);`
		`}`
		
		Note: This call ensures that logic internal to the `Form` class is performed, and ensures that any `Closing` event handlers for the form are called before the application exits. Of course, any registered handler can prevent the application from exiting by setting `ce.Cancel` to true.

Compile and run the application to see this method in action. Add a few photos and try to exit the application using the Exit menu, the Alt+F4 key, and the Close option from the system menu. In all cases, you should be queried by the `CloseCurrent-Album` method with the question dialog for saving the current album. If you select the Cancel button the application will not, in fact, exit.

Before we go on, we should point out that our `OnClosing` override can be written more succinctly by taking advantage of the boolean value returned by our close album method.

```
protected override void OnClosing(CancelEventArgs ce)
{
  ce.Cancel = (!this.CloseCurrentAlbum());

  base.OnClosing(ce);
}
```

Now that we know all about closing a dialog box, let's see how to create one of our own.

8.3   MODAL DIALOG BOXES

In earlier chapters, we added controls such as a `Button`, `PictureBox`, and `StatusBar` to our main form, and displayed and managed these objects within the `Form` class on behalf of our application. In this section we will see how a dialog box can be created and displayed to further our understanding of the `Form` object.

As a way to introduce this concept, we will add the ability to assign a caption to an image. This caption will be a text string supplied by the user. The dialog box shown in figure 8.5 will allow the user to modify this value. The base file name of the image will be used as the default caption.

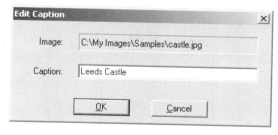

Figure 8.5
Our dialog box will contain three text labels, a text box, and two buttons.

In order to support this dialog, we will need to modify three aspects of our application:

1 *Data layer.*   Our `Photograph` class must support a caption on an image, and our `PhotoAlbum` class must store and retrieve these captions when saving and opening files.

2 *Presentation layer.*   We need a class to display our form as a dialog box. We will call this class `CaptionDlg`. This class must provide the interface and a means for returning a new caption value set by the user.

3 *Application layer.*   Our `MainForm` class must provide access to the new interface, and the link between the interface layer in our `CaptionDlg` class and the data layer in our MyPhotoAlbum library.

We will address each of these layers separately in order to create our new dialog.

8.3.1 ADDING CAPTIONS TO PHOTOS

Let's begin with the data layer. In this section we will support captions on photographs, and in the next section store and retrieve captions in our photo album files. In the Photograph class, we need to track the caption value, and allow external classes to set and get this value. These changes are detailed by the following steps.

Set the version number of the MyPhotoAlbum library to 8.3.

	ADD A CAPTION TO THE PHOTOGRAPH CLASS	
	Action	**Result**
1	In the Photograph.cs file, add a private _caption field to hold the caption for the object.	``` private string _fileName; private Bitmap _bitmap; private string _caption; ```

2	Initialize the caption to the base name of the file in the constructor.
	How-to
	a. Add a using System.IO statement at the top of the file.
	b. Use the Path class to retrieve the base file name.
		``
		using System.IO;
		. . .
		public Photograph(string fileName)
		{
		  _fileName = fileName;
		  _bitmap = null;
		  _caption = Path.
		    GetFileNameWithoutExtension(_fileName);
		}
		``

3	Add a Caption property.	```
		public string Caption
		{
		``

4	Implement the get accessor to return the current caption.	``` get { return _caption; } ```

5	Implement the set accessor to revert to the default on null, and otherwise use the given value.	```
		set
		{
		  if (value == null || value.Length == 0)
		  {
		    _caption = Path.
		      GetFileNameWithoutExtension(_fileName);
		  }
		  else
		  {
		    _caption = value;
		  }
		}
		}
		``
		Note: The value keyword is used as a string object here since the containing property is of type string.

We now have the ability to set captions for individual photographs. This will not do us much good unless our album class preserves these captions in the album file. For this we need to modify the Open and Save methods.

Before we do, note that we can make immediate practical use of our caption in the `MainForm` class. The `sbpnlFileName` status bar panel has previously displayed the entire path to the file, which may not fit when the window is small. The photo's caption seems like a much better choice here.

Set the version number of the MyPhotos application to 8.3.

		DISPLAY THE CAPTION VALUE IN THE STATUS BAR	
	Action	**Result**	

6	Locate the `OnPaint` method in the MainForm.cs source code.	`protected override void OnPaint`
		`    (PaintEventArgs e)`
		`{`
		`    . . .`	

7	Modify the `sbpnlFileName` status bar panel to display the caption.	`if (_album.Count > 0)`
		`{`
		`    . . .`
		`    // Update the status bar.`
		`    sbpnlFileName.Text = `**`photo.Caption;`**
		`    . . .`
		`}`
		`. . .`
		`}`	

8.3.2 Preserving caption values

Our new caption values must be saved whenever an album is saved to disk, and loaded when an album is opened. To do this, we need to create a new version of our album file, while still preserving the ability to read in our existing files. Fortunately, we established a version number for these files in chapter 6, so the changes required are not too extensive. First, let's look at the changes to our `Save` method.

		UPDATE THE SAVE METHOD TO STORE CAPTIONS	
	Action	**Result**	
1	In the PhotoAlbum.cs file, modify the version constant to be 83.	`private const int _CurrentVersion = `**`83;`**	

2	Modify our `foreach` loop in the `Save` method to store both the file name and caption, each on a separate line.	`public void Save(string fileName)`
		`{`
		`    . . .`
		`    // Store the data for each photograph`
		`    foreach (Photograph photo in this)`
		`    {`
		`        sw.WriteLine(photo.FileName);`
		`        `**`sw.WriteLine(photo.Caption);`**
		`    }`
		`}`	

Note that the rest of our `Save` method works as before. In particular, the current version number is written as the first line of the file. Since we updated the constant for this number, the value written to our new album files is updated as well.

Next we need to modify our `Open` method to read the new file format. We will also preserve backward compatibility with our older version. This can be done by handling our previous version number 66 in addition to our new one. We continue the previous table with the following steps.

UPDATE THE OPEN METHOD TO READ CAPTIONS		
	Action	**Result**
| 3 | Modify the `switch` block in the `Open` method to recognize both the old and current version. | ```
public void Open(string fileName)
{
    . . .
    switch (version)
    {
      case 66:
      case 83:
      {
        string name;
``` |
| 4 | Modify the `do..while` loop to read the caption when a newer version of the file is opened. | ```
        do
        {
          name = sr.ReadLine();

          if (name != null)
          {
            Photograph p = new Photograph(name);

            if (version == 83)
            {
              // Also read the caption string
              p.Caption = sr.ReadLine();
            }

            this.Add(p);
          }
        } while (name!= null);
        break;
    . . .
}
``` |

Our data layer is complete. We can add individual captions to photographs, and these captions are preserved as the album is saved and opened. Next we turn our attention to the new `Form` required.

8.3.3   CREATING THE CAPTIONDLG FORM

With our data layer ready, we can turn to the presentation layer. This requires the dialog previously shown in figure 8.5. In this section we create a new `Form` class to hold the dialog, and look at what settings should be set to turn the default form into a standard dialog box. In the next section we will add some properties to this class so that our `MainForm` class can interact with the dialog.

In previous Windows development environments, an explicit class such as `CDialog` created a dialog box directly. It would certainly be possible to create a `FormDialog` class in .NET derived from the `Form` class for this purpose, and perhaps Microsoft will do so in the future. Until this happens, you will have to create your own dialog class or modify each dialog form separately to have dialog box behavior. The following table summarizes the properties required to turn the default `Form` into a somewhat standard dialog box.

Turning the default Form into a dialog box

Property	Default	Value for Dialog Box	Comments
AcceptButton	(none)	OK button instance	For a modal dialog, set to the OK or other `Button` the user will click when finished.
CancelButton	(none)	Cancel button instance	For a modal dialog, set to the Cancel or other `Button` the user will click to abort dialog.
FormBorderStyle	Sizable	FixedDialog	This creates a fixed-sized window with a thick dialog-style border, and no control box on the title bar. Assuming the `ControlBox` setting is `true`, the system menu is still available by right-clicking on the title bar. This value is based on the `FormBorderStyle` enumeration.
HelpButton	False	True or False	Set to `true` if you would like the question mark box to appear on the title bar. The `HelpRequested` event fires when this box is clicked. Note that the question box only appears if the `MaximizeBox` and `MinimumBox` properties are both `false`.
MaximizeBox	True	False	Removes the Maximize button from the title bar.
MinimizeBox	True	False	Removes the Minimize button from the title bar.
ShowInTaskBar	True	False	Does not display the dialog on the Windows task bar.
StartPosition	WindowsDefault-Location	CenterParent	Establishes the initial position for the form. Typically, a dialog box is centered over the parent window.
Size	300, 300	(varies)	For a fixed size dialog, set the window to an appropriate size.

Of course, you may need to modify other properties as well, but these settings establish the appropriate features for a standard dialog box. We can use this table to create a dialog in our application.

CREATE THE CAPTIONDLG CLASS		
	Action	**Result**
1	Add a new form called "CaptionDlg" to the MyPhotos project. **How-to** a. Right-click the MyPhotos project in Solution Explorer. b. Expand the Add menu. c. Select Add Windows Form… under the Add menu to display the Add New Item dialog. d. Enter "CaptionDlg" as the name of the form. e. Click the Open button.	The new file is added to the MyPhotos project and a CaptionDlg.cs [Design] window displays your new form.
2	Modify the form's properties to make this create a somewhat standard dialog. **Settings** | **Property**	**Value** | |---|---| | FormBorderStyle | FixedDialog | | MaximizeBox | False | | MinimizeBox | False | | ShowInTaskBar | False | | Size | 350, 160 | | StartPosition | CenterParent | | Text | Edit Caption |	The form in the designer window should now look something like this.

If you compare these settings to the previous table, you will see that we have not set the `AcceptButton` and `CancelButton` properties yet. This is because the required buttons are not yet on our form. We will look at some of the code generated in the CaptionDlg.cs file in a moment. Before we do, let's continue our changes to add the required controls to our form.

ADD CONTROLS TO THE CAPTIONDLG FORM

<table>
<tr><th></th><th>Action</th><th>Result</th></tr>
<tr><td>3</td><td>Before adding any controls, lock the toolbox open.

How-to
Open the Toolbox window and click the push-pin graphic at the top right of this window.</td><td>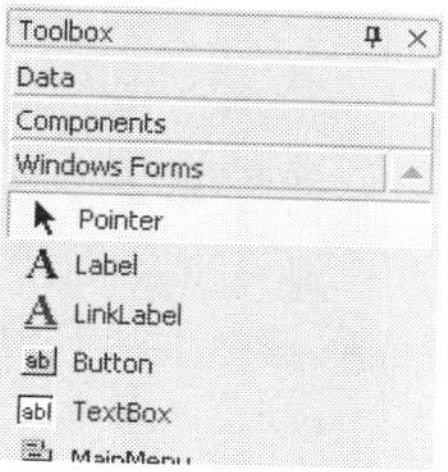

Note: The order of controls in your toolbox may differ from those shown here. You can sort this list alphabetically by right-clicking on the Windows Forms title and selecting the Sort Items Alphabetically option.</td></tr>
<tr><td>4</td><td>Add an OK button to the base of the form.

How-to
Drag a <code>Button</code> control from the toolbox onto the form, and assign its properties as indicated.

Settings
<table><tr><th>Property</th><th>Value</th></tr><tr><td>(Name)</td><td>btnOK</td></tr><tr><td>DialogResult</td><td>OK</td></tr><tr><td>Text</td><td>&OK</td></tr></table>
Note: We discuss the meaning of the <code>DialogResult</code> property later in the chapter.</td><td>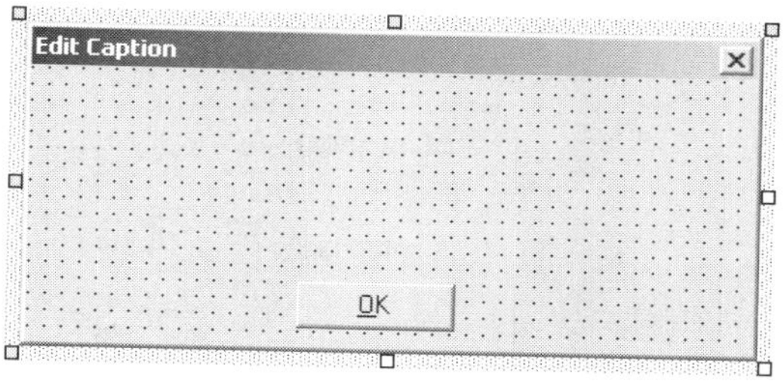
</td></tr>
<tr><td>5</td><td>Add a Cancel button to the form, and position the two buttons as shown in the graphic.

Settings
<table><tr><th>Property</th><th>Value</th></tr><tr><td>(Name)</td><td>btnCancel</td></tr><tr><td>DialogResult</td><td>Cancel</td></tr><tr><td>Text</td><td>&Cancel</td></tr></table></td><td>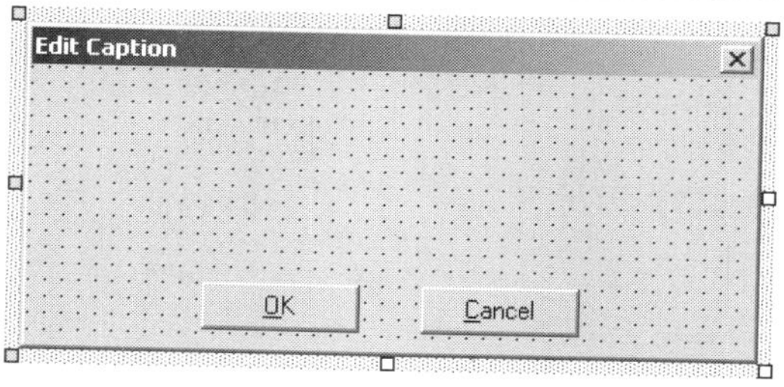

Note: There is a bit of black magic involved in positioning controls. The Format menu in Visual Studio .NET provides commands for positioning and aligning controls. These appear on the Layout toolbar, and you can experiment with these while creating this form.</td></tr>
</table>

	Action	Result

6 — Create the Image and Caption labels on the form.

How-to
Drag two `Label` controls onto the form, and resize and position them as in the graphic.

Settings

Label	Property	Value
Image	Text	Image:
	TextAlign	MiddleRight
Caption	Text	Caption:
	TextAlign	MiddleRight

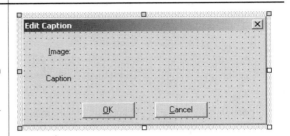

Note: For the Visual C++ programmers among us, the `Label` class is similar to the `CStatic` class found in the MFC library.

7 — Create a `lblImage` label on the form.

Note: We could also use a read-only `TextBox` control here. Labels and text boxes are discussed in detail in chapter 9.

Settings

Property	Value
(Name)	lblImage
BorderStyle	Fixed3D
Text	image file name
TextAlign	MiddleLeft

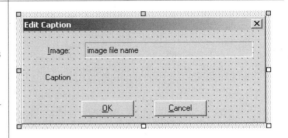

8 — Create a text box to hold the image caption.

How-to
Drag a `TextBox` control onto the form.

Settings

Property	Value
(Name)	txtCaption
Text	image caption

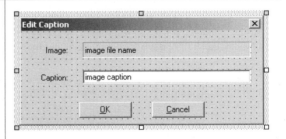

Note: Again for Visual C++ programmers, the `TextBox` class is similar to the `CEdit` class found in the MFC library.

	Action	**Result**
9	Set the tab order for the controls on the form. **How-to** a. Click the top-level View menu. b. Select the Tab Order item. c. Click the controls in the desired order, starting with number 0, as shown in the graphic. d. Press the Esc key to save the new tab order.	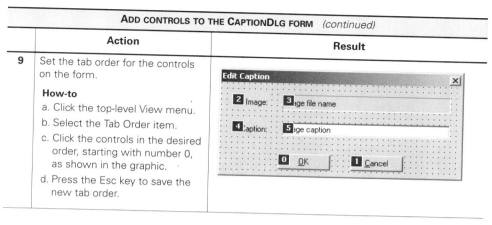

Well, that took a while. Placing controls on a form is not a difficult task, but it can take some time. This is another reason sketching out your interface up front is a good idea before you spend too much time in the designer window.

As you might expect, the code generated in the CaptionDlg.cs source file is quite similar to what we have seen for our `MainForm` class in previous chapters. As a quick recap, here is a summary of the code you will find in this file.

- The `CaptionDlg` class is derived from the `Form` class.

```
public class CaptionDlg : System.Windows.Forms.Form
{
```

- Each control is created as a private member of the class. The organization used by Visual Studio can be a bit confusing, so I have used the power of cut and paste to rearrange these code excerpts to be a bit more logical. If you recall, the `components` member is required by Visual Studio to manage certain controls on the form.

```
private System.Windows.Forms.Button btnOK;
private System.Windows.Forms.Button btnCancel;
private System.Windows.Forms.Label label1;
private System.Windows.Forms.Label label2;
private System.Windows.Forms.Label lblImage;
private System.Windows.Forms.TextBox txtCaption;
/// <summary>
/// Required designer variable.
/// </summary>
private System.ComponentModel.Container components = null;
```

- The controls are initialized in the `InitializeComponent` method, which is called from the `CaptionDlg` constructor.

```
#region Windows Form Designer generated code
/// <summary>
```

```
/// Required method for Designer support - do not modify
/// the contents of this method with the code editor.
/// </summary>
private void InitializeComponent()
{
```

- Inside the `InitializeComponent` method, the controls are first created using the new keyword.

```
this.btnOK = new System.Windows.Forms.Button ();
this.btnCancel = new System.Windows.Forms.Button ();
this.label1 = new System.Windows.Forms.Label ();
this.label2 = new System.Windows.Forms.Label ();
this.lblImage = new System.Windows.Forms.Label ();
this.txtCaption = new System.Windows.Forms.TextBox ();
```

- Next the nondefault properties are set for each control. This section is quite long, so the following code is only an excerpt of this portion of the file:

```
this.SuspendLayout();
//
// btnOK
//
this.btnOK.DialogResult = System.Windows.Forms.DialogResult.OK;
this.btnOK.Location = new System.Drawing.Point(82, 88);
this.btnOK.Name = "btnOK";
this.btnOK.TabIndex = 0;
this.btnOK.Text = "&OK";
//
// btnCancel
//
this.btnCancel.DialogResult
    = System.Windows.Forms.DialogResult.Cancel;
this.btnCancel.Location = new System.Drawing.Point(187, 88);
this.btnCancel.Name = "btnCancel";
this.btnCancel.TabIndex = 1;
this.btnCancel.Text = "&Cancel";
//
// label1
//
this.label1.Location = new System.Drawing.Point(32, 8);
this.label1.Name = "label1";
this.label1.Size = new System.Drawing.Size(48, 23);
this.label1.TabIndex = 2;
    . . .
```

- Finally, the `Form` itself is initialized, and the controls are added to the form using the `Form.Controls` property.

```
//
// CaptionDlg
//
```

```
        this.AutoScaleBaseSize = new System.Drawing.Size(5, 13);
        this.ClientSize = new System.Drawing.Size(344, 125);
        this.ControlBox = false;
        this.Controls.AddRange(new System.Windows.Forms.Control[] {
                                       this.txtCaption,
                                       this.lblImage,
                                       this.label2,
                                       this.label1,
                                       this.btnCancel,
                                       this.btnOK});
        this.FormBorderStyle
           = System.Windows.Forms.FormBorderStyle.FixedDialog;
        this.MaximizeBox = false;
        this.MinimizeBox = false;
        this.Name = "CaptionDlg";
        this.ShowInTaskbar = false;
        this.StartPosition
           = System.Windows.Forms.FormStartPosition.CenterParent;
        this.Text = "CaptionDlg";
        this.ResumeLayout(false);
    }
    #endregion
```

Our dialog box is now ready from a display perspective. There is still the matter of making sure our main form can make use of it to edit a caption for an image. For this, we will need to add some properties to our `CaptionDlg` class.

8.3.4 ADDING PROPERTIES TO THE CAPTIONDLG FORM

So far we have modified our data layer to understand photograph captions, and created a dialog to use for editing this caption. To integrate this dialog with the rest of our application, we need to ensure that the `MainForm` class can set the text to appear in the `Label` and `TextBox` controls of a `CaptionDlg` instance before the dialog is displayed, and retrieve the modified `TextBox` value after the dialog is finished. We must also ensure that the result of the dialog, whether the user pressed OK or Cancel, can be detected by the caller.

If we were programming in C++, we might create `SetImage`, `SetCaption`, and `GetCaption` methods to allow the `lblImage` and `txtCaption` values to be modified. In C#, the property construct provides a slightly more elegant solution.

	ADD IMAGELABEL AND CAPTION PROPERTIES TO OUR DIALOG	
	Action	**Result**
1	Add an `ImageLabel` property to the CaptionDlg.cs source window.	`public string ImageLabel` `{`

	Action	**Result**

2	Implement `set` for this property to modify the text for the `lblImage` label.	```set { lblImage.Text = value; }```
		`}`
		
		Note: This code relies on the .NET Framework to display this value in the control and deal with an empty or `null` string.

3	Add a `Caption` property.	`public string Caption` `{`
4	Implement `set` for this property to modify the text for the `txtCaption` text box.	`set { txtCaption.Text = value; }`
5	Implement `get` to return this text value.	`get { return txtCaption.Text; }` `}`

These properties will allow the values in the dialog to be set and retrieved as appropriate. Our last task is to return the appropriate value based on which button the user selects.

We have already seen how the `DialogResult` enumeration encapsulates the possible values returned by the `MessageBox.Show` method. For `Form` objects, the `ShowDialog` method returns this enumeration for a similar purpose. Here, we would like this method to return `DialogResult.OK` if the user clicks the OK button or presses the Enter key, and `DialogResult.Cancel` if the user clicks the Cancel button or presses the Esc key.

The `Form` class handles the keyboard values, namely the Enter and Esc keys, directly via the `AcceptButton` and `CancelButton` properties. We will look at returning the proper value from the `ShowDialog` method in a moment.

	ALLOW THE DIALOG TO BE CLOSED VIA THE KEYBOARD	
	Action	**Result**
6	From the CaptionDlg.cs [Design] window, assign the OK button as the accept button for the form, to be activated when the user presses the Enter key. **How-to** a. Display the properties for the form. b. Click the down arrow to the right of the `Accept-Button` entry in the list. c. Select `btnOK`.	

	Action	Result

7	Similarly, set the `CancelButton` property to the `btnCancel` button.	These settings assign each property to the selected button object in the `InitializeComponent` method of the CaptionDlg.cs source file.
		
		`this.AcceptButton = this.btnOK;`
		`this.CancelButton = this.btnCancel;`

The `Form` now invokes the OK or Cancel button when the user presses the Enter or Esc key, respectively.

We also need to ensure that the `ShowDialog` method returns the proper result when one of these buttons is clicked or invoked via the keyboard. The `Button` class provides a `DialogResult` property for this purpose. When this property is set, clicking the corresponding button will automatically hide the parent form and return the selected result.[3] We already set these properties to the appropriate values while creating the buttons, so the `InitializeComponent` method already defines these settings.

```
btnOK.DialogResult = System.Windows.Forms.DialogResult.OK;
btnCancel.DialogResult = System.Windows.Forms.DialogResult.Cancel;
```

We will see how the settings interact with the `ShowDialog` method when we display the dialog from our `MainForm` class. This is our next topic.

8.3.5 DISPLAYING THE DIALOG IN THE MAINFORM CLASS

We can now turn to our `MainForm` class in order to invoke the dialog and edit a photo's caption. We do this via our menu bar, of course. Since we are editing an aspect of the photo, we will place a Caption menu item under the Edit menu. This section defines our new menu and creates a `Click` handler for this menu to display the `CaptionDlg` form to the user.

We will begin by adding a new menu item to our main form.

	Action	Result
	ADD A CAPTION ITEM TO THE EDIT MENU	
1	Click the Edit menu in the MainForm.cs [Design] window.	
2	Add a menu separator after the Remove menu item.	

---

[3] The term "hide" here is intentional. Pursuant to our earlier discussion on the equivalence of `Close` and `Dispose`, modal dialog boxes must be disposed of manually to allow their members to be accessed after `ShowDialog` returns. As a result, the framework only hides our dialog by calling the `Hide` method when the OK or Cancel button is clicked.

	Action	Result
3	Add a "&Caption..." menu under the separator.	

Settings

Property	Value
(Name)	menuCaption
Enabled	False
Text	&Caption...

We set the `Enabled` property for the menu to `false` since an image will not be shown when the application starts.

To enable this menu, we could use the existing `OnPaint` method of our form. A simpler approach is to add a `Popup` event handler for the parent Edit menu, and enable or disable the Caption menu as required just before it displays.

	Action	Result
	ENABLE THE CAPTION MENU IN A POPUP HANDLER	
	Action	Result

4	Add a `Popup` event handler for the Edit menu.
	
	How-to
	Double-click the Popup item in the list of events for the Edit menu.
		`public void menuEdit_Popup`
		`    (object sender, EventArgs e)`
		`{`

5	Set the `Enabled` property for the Caption menu based on whether an image is currently displayed.	`    menuCaption.Enabled = (_album.Count > 0);` `}`

Our Caption menu is enabled whenever photographs are available and therefore displayed, and disabled when the album is empty.

The final task in this section is to implement a `Click` handler for our menu. This handler will display our `CaptionDlg` form and modify the caption as required. This task continues the previous steps and pulls together all the changes we have made in this section.

	Action	Result
6	Add a `Click` event handler for the Caption menu.	```protected void menuCaption_Click
(object sender, System.EventArgs e)
{```
7	Get the current photograph.	```Photograph photo = _album.CurrentPhoto;
if (photo == null)
return;   // no current photo``` **Note:** Since the user can only click the Caption menu if an image is displayed, the value of `photo` should never be `null`. It never hurts to be safe, though.
8	Use the `CaptionDlg` object to modify the caption.	```using (CaptionDlg dlg = new CaptionDlg())
{``` **Note:** Congratulations, you have just created a `Form`. The using statement will clean up the dialog's resources when we are finished.
9	Initialize the dialog with the settings from the current `Photograph`.	```dlg.ImageLabel = photo.FileName;
dlg.Caption = photo.Caption;```
10	Display the dialog.	```if (dlg.ShowDialog() == DialogResult.OK)
{```
11	If the user clicks OK, modify the `Photograph` object to use the new settings.	```photo.Caption = dlg.Caption;
this._bAlbumChanged = true;```
12	Also update the caption text in the status bar as well.	``` sbpnlFileName.Text = photo.Caption;
statusBar1.Invalidate();
}
}
}```

If you are familiar with the MFC library, this code will be reminiscent of how you might use the `CDialog` class to perform a similar task. One major difference is how the object is created and destroyed. In MFC you would create the dialog on the stack and rely on C++ to destroy the object by calling its destructor when the stack is cleaned up. In C#, of course, the memory for our dialog is cleaned up by the garbage collector. To ensure that its nonmemory resources are cleaned up immediately, we create the dialog within a `using` statement.

The dialog does not appear to the user until the ShowDialog method is called, at which point the entire application waits until the user clicks the OK or the Cancel button.

```
if (dlg.ShowDialog() == DialogResult.OK)
{
  photo.Caption = dlg.Caption;
  this._bAlbumChanged = true;
  sbpnlFileName.Text = photo.Caption;
  statusBar1.Invalidate();
}
```

If the user clicks the OK button, `DialogResult.OK` is returned and any new caption he or she entered is stored in the photograph and propagated to the status bar. Note how we set `_bAlbumChanged` to `true` to indicate the album has changed. If the user clicks the Cancel button, `DialogResult.Cancel` is returned and the photograph's caption will not be altered.

Our dialog is now complete. It is displayed via the Caption menu and initialized with the current image file and caption settings. The user can modify the caption and click OK to save it. The new caption appears on the status bar and is stored in the album file when the album is saved.

We will see more modal dialogs as we continue our trip through Windows Forms. Before we end the chapter, let's also discuss modeless dialogs.

8.4 MODELESS DIALOGS

In the previous section we created a dialog box to allow the user to edit the caption for a photograph. Modal dialog boxes tend to be in and out. You open it, you do something, you close it. Modeless dialog boxes tend to show some information relevant to the program. In a stock analysis program, for example, you might have a stock ticker window that runs independently of the program. This would be a modeless, or nonmodal, dialog and would update continuously with stock information, perhaps related to a displayed portfolio or to what the user is viewing in the main application window.

In this section we will create a modeless dialog to display the location of the mouse pointer within the image window, and the color of the image at this location. This information will update continuously as the location of the mouse pointer changes, using the dialog in figure 8.6. As you can see in the figure, the pixel position of the mouse pointer within the image is shown as an X and Y coordinate, along with the color in RGB or red, blue, and green, coordinates. This par-

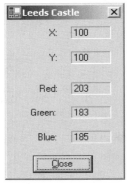

Figure 8.6
Our modeless dialog will show the position in image coordinates and RGB color of the pixel indicated by the current location of the cursor.

ticular figure indicates that the mouse pointer is over the image at pixel (100, 100) of the image, and the current color at that pixel has an RGB value of (203, 183, 185).

As for our caption dialog, we will need to make sure our three layers can support this dialog.

- *Data layer.* The position and color of the current pixel is based on the location of the mouse pointer within the displayed bitmap. Since this information is already available, no changes are necessary here.

- *Presentation layer.* As before, we will need a `Form`-based class to display the dialog. Since we are showing information about the current pixel, we will call this class `PixelDlg` and store it in the file PixelDlg.cs.

- *Application layer.* Our application will again tie the data and presentation together. To do this, we will create a new menu item under the View menu called "Pixel Data."

Since no changes are required to the data layer in this case, we will begin with the presentation layer

8.4.1 CREATING THE PIXELDLG FORM

The creation of a dialog is much the same whether it is a modal or modeless dialog. First you create a new Form class for the dialog, update the property settings, lay out the controls on the form, and finally add code to set or process the controls as required.

So let's begin by creating the dialog.

Set the version number of the MyPhotos application to 8.4.

CREATE THE PIXELDLG CLASS		
	Action	**Result**
1	Add a new form to the MyPhotos project with the name "PixelDlg."	The new class is added to the MyPhotos project, and a design window for the class is displayed.
2	Set the properties for the form as indicated. **Settings** | **Property**	**Value** | |---|---| | FormBorderStyle | FixedSingle | | MaximizeBox | false | | MinimizeBox | false | | Size | 150, 230 | | Text | Pixel Values | **Note:** The border style FixedSingle used here is similar to FixedDialog, except that the control box appears on the form. Since this will be a modeless dialog, it also seems appropriate to use the default setting of true for the ShowInTaskbar property.	

	Action	Result
3	Create and arrange the five Label objects on the left side of the dialog. **How-to** a. Drag Label objects from the Toolbox onto the form. Note that you can repeatedly double-click the Label entry in the Toolbox to add successive Label controls to the form. b. Set the TextAlign properties for these labels to TopRight. c. Set the Text property for these labels to X, Y, Red, Green, and Blue, respectively. **Note:** You can set the TextAlign property for all controls at once using the following technique: a. Using the mouse, click the form and drag a box around all five controls. The Properties window now displays the common properties for the five selected controls. b. Set the TextAlign property to the desired value.	
4	Create and arrange the five Label objects on the right side of the dialog. **How-to** a. Place the new Label objects on the form. b. Set the BorderStyle property for each label to Fixed3D. c. Set the (Name) property to lblXVal, lblYVal, lblRedVal, lblGreenVal, and lblBlueVal, respectively.	

	Action	Result
5	Add a `Button` object to the base of the form and set its properties. **Settings** 	

Property	Value
(Name)	btnClose
Text	&Close

The code generated here is very similar to the code we saw earlier in this chapter for the `CaptionDlg` class, so we will not look at this code in detail. Instead, we will move on to the internal class members required by this new form.

8.4.2 ADDING CLASS MEMBERS TO PIXELDLG

There really isn't a lot of work to do here. We need to allow our main application to modify the display values, and make sure the dialog exits when the Close button is clicked. We will use properties for the display values, and handle the `Click` event to close the form.

You may recall that we did not handle any events for our `CaptionDlg` form. Since this was a modal dialog, we took advantage of the `DialogResult` property in the `Button` class. When the corresponding button is clicked and a modal dialog is displayed via the `ShowDialog` method, this property closes the form and returns the assigned result to the caller. Here, such a scheme is not possible since we are creating a modeless dialog. Thus our need for a `Click` event handler.

The steps here are similar to what we have done before, so let's get to it.

	Action	Result
ADD THE REQUIRED PIXELDLG CLASS MEMBERS		
	Action	**Result**

1	In the PixelDlg.cs [Design] window, add a `Click` handler for the Close button.	`protected void btnClose_Click`
		 `    (object sender, System.EventArgs e)`
		 `{`

2	Implement this method to close the form.	`    Close();` `}`

3	Add an `XVal` property to set the value for the X label.	`public int XVal`
		 `{`
		 `    set { lblXVal.Text = value.ToString(); }`
		 `}`

	ADD THE REQUIRED PIXELDLG CLASS MEMBERS	(continued)
	Action	**Result**
| 4 | Add a YVal property to set the value for the Y label. | ```csharp
public int YVal
{
    set { lblYVal.Text = value.ToString(); }
}
``` |
| 5 | Add RedVal, GreenVal, and BlueVal properties for their respective labels. | ```csharp
public int RedVal
{
    set { lblRedVal.Text = value.ToString(); }
}

public int GreenVal
{
    set { lblGreenVal.Text = value.ToString(); }
}

public int BlueVal
{
    set { lblBlueVal.Text = value.ToString(); }
}
``` |

This ensures our dialog can be closed, and provides the properties necessary to update the labels from our main form. Note how the `Form.Close` method is used to close the form, just like in the Exit menu handler for our main application window. The .NET framework keeps track of which form is the top-level application window, so the `Close` method here closes just the `PixelDlg` window and not the entire application. As you'll recall, this method disposes of any nonmemory resources allocated by the form as well.

One other change we should make is to allow the standard keyboard shortcuts to close the dialog. Since there is a single button on our form, we will support both the Enter and Esc keys for this purpose. Continuing the previous steps:

	SUPPORT KEYBOARD SHORTCUTS TO CLOSE PIXELDLG FORM	
	Action	**Result**
6	In the PixelDlg.cs [Design] window, display the properties for the `PixelDlg` form.	
7	Set both the `AcceptButton` property and the `CancelButton` property to `btnClose`.	The properties are set in the `InitializeComponent` method of the PixelDlg.cs source file.

Our `PixelDlg` form is ready to go. Next we need to invoke this form from the main window.

8.4.3 DISPLAYING THE MODELESS PIXELDLG FORM

For our `CaptionDlg` form, we displayed it as a modal dialog box using the `Form.ShowDialog` method. This method displays the form and waits until it exits, preventing the parent form from accepting any external input until this occurs. For a modeless dialog a different method is required that will allow the parent form to continue execution.

The `Form.Show` method is used for this purpose. The `Show` method is inherited from the `Control` class and sets a control's `Visible` property to `true`. For a `Form`, this means it displays in a modeless fashion. The `Show` method is a `void` method since no immediate result is returned.

As for our modal dialog, we will display the form from an item on the menu bar.

	ADD PIXEL DATA MENU TO INVOKE THE PIXELDLG FORM	
	Action	**Result**
1	Display the View menu in the MainForm.cs [Design] window.	
2	Add a separator at the end of the menu.	
3	Add a Pixel Data menu item. **Settings** **Property** **Value** (Name) menuPixelData Text Pi&xel Data...	

Before we use this to display the dialog, let's ponder what support we need for our new dialog. Since this is a modeless dialog, it will display while the main form is displayed. So the user may change which photo is displayed, or modify the display mode used. Such changes will require that we modify what is displayed in the dialog.

To facilitate this, we will track whether the dialog is currently displayed, and which photo is currently represented by the dialog. Let's continue the previous steps and add these class members.

	ADD CLASS MEMBERS TO TRACK PIXELDLG SETTINGS	
	Action	**Result**
4	In the MainForm.cs window, add a private member to hold the `PixelDlg` form object.	`private PixelDlg _dlgPixel = null;`
5	Also add an integer to hold the current photo represented in this form.	`private int _nPixelDlgIndex;`

These members will be used to update the dialog as the main window changes. In particular, we can use these members to create the dialog in the menu handler.

	Action	Result
	IMPLEMENT MENUPIXELDATA_CLICK EVENT HANDLER	

6	Add a click handler for the Pixel Data menu.	<pre>protected void menuPixelData_Click
		        (object sender, System.EventArgs e)
		{</pre>

7	If the dialog has not been created or the existing dialog has been disposed, create a new dialog.	<pre>if (_dlgPixel == null || _dlgPixel.IsDisposed)
		{
		    _dlgPixel = new PixelDlg();
		    _dlgPixel.Owner = this;
		}</pre>
		Note: The Owner property used here ensures that the PixelDlg form is minimized and maximized along with the parent form.

8	Assign the initial data to display in the dialog.	<pre>_nPixelDlgIndex = _album.CurrentPosition;
		Point p = pnlPhoto.PointToClient(
		                    Form.MousePosition);
		UpdatePixelData(p.X, p.Y);</pre>

9	Finally, display the dialog.	<pre>_dlgPixel.Show();
		}</pre>

The code to create and display the dialog should seem familiar, but what about that code in step 8 of our task. Let's talk about it.

The first line in step 8 simply assigns the current photo index to the _nPixelDlgIndex variable. No problem there.

```
_nPixelDlgIndex = _album.CurrentIndex;
```

The next line converts the current screen coordinates of the mouse pointer to its coordinates within in the main Panel object. This uses the static Form.MousePosition property to retrieve the screen coordinates of the mouse pointer as a Point instance. This point contains the current X and Y position of the pointer on the screen in pixels.

The location on the screen is not what we need. We need to know the location of the mouse pointer within the main Panel object. That is, in the pnlPhoto control. This can then be used to calculate what part of the image is at that location.

The PointToClient method does this conversion. It accepts a point in screen coordinates and returns the same point in client coordinates. If the given point happens to be outside the control, the returned Point will contain values outside the display area of the control.

```
Point p = pnlPhoto.PointToClient(Form.MousePosition);
```

The final line calls an as-yet-undefined UpdatePixelData method. We will write this method in the next section to accept the current position of the mouse pointer in Panel coordinates and fill in the appropriate values of the PixelDlg form.

```
UpdatePixelData(p.X, p.Y);
```

8.4.4 UPDATING THE PixelDlg FORM

So far we have created and displayed our form as a modeless dialog. In this section we will implement the code to update this dialog based on the current location of the mouse pointer in the pnlPhoto control. We will account for the fact that a photo might not be displayed, and that the mouse pointer may be located outside of the panel.

This code for UpdatePixelData is a bit long, so let's get to it.

	IMPLEMENT UpdatePixelData METHOD	
	Action	**Result**
1	In the MainForm.cs window, add an UpdatePixelData method to the end of the file.	```protected void UpdatePixelData``` ```(int xPos, int yPos)``` ```{```
2	Return immediately if the PixelDlg does not exist or is not visible.	```if (_dlgPixel == null || !_dlgPixel.Visible)``` ``` return;```
3	Get the currently display photo.	```Photograph photo = _album.CurrentPhoto;```
4	Display all zeros if a Photograph is not displayed or the given coordinates are outside the display area. **Note:** The question mark '?' syntax here works the same as in C++.	```Rectangle r = pnlPhoto.ClientRectangle;``` ```if (photo == null``` ``` || !(r.Contains(xPos,yPos)))``` ```{``` ``` _dlgPixel.Text = ((photo == null)``` ``` ? " " : photo.Caption);``` ``` _dlgPixel.XVal = 0;``` ``` _dlgPixel.YVal = 0;``` ``` _dlgPixel.RedVal = 0;``` ``` _dlgPixel.GreenVal = 0;``` ``` _dlgPixel.BlueVal = 0;``` ``` _dlgPixel.Update();``` ``` return;``` ```}```
5	Display the caption for the current image in the title bar of our dialog.	```_dlgPixel.Text = photo.Caption;```
6	Use a switch statement to determine the current display mode. **Note:** The calculation here depends on how the image is displayed, so a switch statement is required.	```// Calc x and y position in the photo``` ```int x = 0, y = 0;``` ```Bitmap bmp = photo.Image;``` ```switch (this._selectedMode)``` ```{```
7	Implement the Actual Size display mode logic. **Note:** In this mode, the display area and image area are equivalent.	```case DisplayMode.ActualSize:``` ``` // Panel coords equal image coords``` ``` x = xPos;``` ``` y = yPos;``` ``` break;```

	Action	Result
8	Implement the Stretch to Fit display mode logic. **Note:** In this mode, the image fills the entire display area, so we convert from display position to image location.	```case DisplayMode.StretchToFit: // Translate panel coords to image x = xPos * bmp.Width / r.Width; y = yPos * bmp.Height / r.Height; break;```
9	Implement the Scale to Fit display mode logic. **How-to** a. Calculate the rectangle containing the image using the `ScaleToFit` method in the `Photograph` class. b. If the mouse pointer is outside this rectangle, it is not in the image. c. Otherwise, convert this rectangle into image coordinates.	```case DisplayMode.ScaleToFit: // Determine image rectangle. Rectangle r2 = photo.ScaleToFit(r); if (!r2.Contains(xPos, yPos)) return; // Mouse outside image // Translate r2 coords to image x = (xPos - r2.Left) * bmp.Width / r2.Width; y = (yPos - r2.Top) * bmp.Height / r2.Height; break; }```
10	Retrieve the color of the pixel at the calculated image location. **How-to** Use the `Bitmap.GetPixel` method.	```// Extract color at calculated location Color c = bmp.GetPixel(x, y);```
11	Finally, update the pixel dialog with the appropriate values. **How-to** For the RGB color values, use the `R`, `G`, and `B` properties in the `Color` structure.	```// Update PixelDlg with new values _dlgPixel.XVal = x; _dlgPixel.YVal = y; _dlgPixel.RedVal = c.R; _dlgPixel.GreenVal = c.G; _dlgPixel.BlueVal = c.B; _dlgPixel.Update(); }```

And there you have it. This method updates the `PixelDlg` form each time it is called. Since the explanation of each step is embedded in the table, we will not discuss this code further.

Our final task is to make sure this method is called each time the mouse pointer moves or the displayed photograph changes.

8.4.5 UPDATING PIXELDLG AS THE MOUSE MOVES

In the previous section we waded through the logic necessary to convert the current mouse pointer location in panel coordinates to the corresponding image coordinates to update the `PixelDlg` form correctly. Next, we need to ensure that `UpdatePixelData` is called whenever appropriate.

The most obvious time is whenever the location of the mouse pointer changes. There is a MouseMove event inherited from the Control class for this purpose. The protected OnMouseMove method raises this event, so we could override OnMouse-Move in our Form class. In this case, we would have to convert from Form coordinates to Panel coordinates, so handling the event for the Panel class is probably a better choice. More importantly, by handling mouse pointer movements in the Panel object directly, our code is only called when the movement occurs inside the panel.

	CALL THE UPDATEPIXELDATA METHOD WHEN THE MOUSE MOVES	
	ACTION	RESULT
1	In the MainForm.cs [Design] window, add a MouseMove event handler for the pnlPhoto object.	```protected void pnlPhoto_MouseMove (object sender, System.Windows.Forms.MouseEventArgs e) {```
2	Call the UpdatePixelData method with the current mouse pointer coordinates.	```UpdatePixelData(e.X, e.Y); }```

The MouseMove event handler receives a MouseEventArgs parameter containing, among other event data, an X and Y property defining the current coordinates of the mouse pointer in the control's coordinates. We will discuss this and other mouse events in chapter 12, so we will not go into more detail on this handler here.

The one other instance when the pixel values must be updated is when the displayed image changes. The easiest place to track this is when the Panel is painted in the pnlPhoto_Paint method. Continuing the previous steps:

	CALL UPDATEPIXELDATA WHEN CURRENT PHOTO CHANGES	
	Action	Result
3	Locate the pnlPhoto_Paint method in the MainForm.cs source file.	```protected void pnlPhoto_Paint(. . .) {```
4	Call UpdatePixelData if a new photo is displayed.	```// Update PixelDlg if photo has changed if ((_dlgPixel != null) && (_nPixelDlgIndex != _album.CurrentPosition)) { _nPixelDlgIndex = _album.CurrentPosition; Point p = pnlPhoto.PointToClient(Form.MousePosition); UpdatePixelData(p.X, p.Y); } // Paint the current photo, if any if (_album.Count > 0) { . . . } }```

This code uses the same `Form.MousePosition` method and nonstatic `Panel.Point-ToClient` we saw earlier in this section.

Our modeless dialog is finished. Compile your code, show your friends, and otherwise verify that the dialog works properly. Note how both the form and the dialog can be manipulated at the same time, and how the dialog behaves when you display the next or previous image in an album, with the mouse cursor both inside and outside the panel control.

TRY IT! One nice change you could make here is to modify the cursor used for the Panel control to use a small cross-hair rather than the normal arrow. Do this by changing the `Cursor` property for the `Panel` class to use the `Cross` cursor.

Another interesting change is to allow the user to hide the `PixelDlg` window using the main application's menu bars. One way to do this is to modify the `Text` displayed for the `menuPixelData` menu to be "Hide Pi&xel Data" whenever the dialog is displayed and back to "Pi&xel Data" whenever the dialog is hidden or closed. Set the appropriate menu text in the `menuView_Popup` handler, and use the `Hide` method or the `Visible` property to hide the dialog.

Before we move on to the next topic, let's give a quick summary of what we covered in this chapter.

8.5 RECAP

In this chapter we looked at dialog boxes. We began with simple dialogs using the `MessageBox` class, and then created a custom modal dialog based on the `Form` class, followed by a custom modeless dialog. Along the way we discussed the difference between modal and modeless dialog boxes, caught potential exceptions when opening and saving our album files, examined the relationship between the `Close` and `Dispose` methods, saw how to intercept a closing window using the `OnClosing` method, and learned how to track the mouse pointer within a panel control.

We are not done with dialog boxes. Since our main form is getting rather full, future topics will require dialogs in order to continue this book and expand the capabilities of our program. In particular, the next chapter will create a dialog for both our current album and the individual photos in the album as a way to introduce specific Windows Forms controls in more detail.

C H A P T E R   9

Basic controls

9.1   Form inheritance 264
9.2   Labels and text boxes 271
9.3   Button classes 290
9.4   Recap 313

The .NET Framework provides a number of controls for use in Windows Forms applications. This chapter will introduce the most basic of these, namely the `Label`, `TextBox`, `Button`, `RadioButton`, and `CheckBox` controls. These controls date back to the original version of Windows,[1] and before that to other graphical environments in other operating systems, so they must be somewhat useful. In practice, labels, text boxes, and the various button types are critical in almost any Windows application, so it is worth spending a little time to see how they are added to and utilized by applications.

As usual, we will discuss the classes for these controls in the context of our MyPhotos application. This will require that we do some work on our `PhotoAlbum` and `Photograph` classes. Our controls are not very useful unless they can be integrated into an application, so these changes should illustrate how similar constructs can be used in your own applications. In addition, such changes present opportunities to discuss additional concepts such as the .NET `DateTime` structure and the C# `delegate` keyword.

---

[1]   List boxes and combo boxes were part of this version as well, but we will leave these controls to the next chapter.

Specific Windows Forms concepts we will cover in this chapter include:

- Form inheritance: what is it and how do you do it?
- Basic Windows Forms controls: the `Label`, `TextBox`, `Button`, `RadioButton`, and `CheckBox` classes.
- Container controls such as `Panel` and `GroupBox` objects.

In addition, we will also look at the following related concepts:

- The C# `delegate` keyword.
- The `System.DateTime` structure.
- Keyboard and focus events for controls.
- Using the `Control.Tag` property.

To enable our discussion of all this and more, we will create two modal dialog boxes for our form, shown in the first section as figure 9.1. These will represent various settings the user can modify on an individual photograph or entire album. While we will discuss each control generally, these two dialogs will serve to demonstrate the creation and usage of each control as we move through the chapter.

We begin our discussion with form inheritance.

9.1 FORM INHERITANCE

The concept of object inheritance is often explained with the canonical `Employee` class derived from a `Person` class. The derived class, in this case `Employee`, inherits the properties and functionality found in the parent class, e.g., `Person`. For example, the `Person` class might provide properties and methods for tracking the address of a person. The `Employee` class inherits these members and supports this functionality without the addition of any new code.[2]

The .NET Framework allows a similar behavior for Forms. You can create a form, and then reuse that form in the creation of additional forms. The parent form defines various members and controls that child forms will inherit. Controls on the form define their access level, such as `private`, `protected`, or `public`, just like members of any other class. A child form can modify these controls to the extent of their assigned access level.

For our application, we would like to add the two dialogs shown in figure 9.1. The first is for editing the properties of a specific photograph, and the second for editing the properties of an album. While the contents of these two windows are entirely different, they are both modal dialog boxes and share a common set of buttons at the base of the form and a panel at the top.

---

[2] The overview of C# in appendix B provides additional information on inheritance.

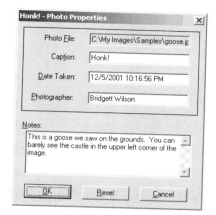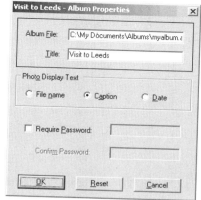

Figure 9.1 These dialogs are created using only the controls discussed in this chapter.

We could just be very careful here, and ensure that the two dialogs appear and behave in a similar manner. But who wants to be careful? Instead, this is a great chance to use a common `Form` for both windows to see how form inheritance works.

In this section we will create the base window and a derived window for use in subsequent sections. Since our new windows will be specific to the `PhotoAlbum` and `Photograph` classes, we will create these objects in the `MyPhotoAlbum` library.

9.1.1 CREATING A BASE FORM

A base form is created just like any other form object. Since our base form does not use any settings we haven't seen in earlier chapters, let's whip through the creation of this new window. Before we do, you may recall that we modified the namespace for the `Photograph` and `PhotoAlbum` classes in chapter 5 to include the `Manning` prefix. Rather than continue to do this by hand, we can modify the project properties so that this namespace is used by default.

Set the version number of the MyPhotoAlbum to 9.1.

	MODIFY THE NAMESPACE FOR FILES IN THE MYPHOTOALBUM PROJECT	
	Action	**Result**
1	Set the default namespace for the MyPhotoAlbum project to `Manning.MyPhotoAlbum`. **How-to** a. Right-click the MyPhotoAlbum project in the Solution Explorer window. b. Select Properties. c. In the MyPhotoAlbum Property Pages window, make sure the General settings are shown. d. Modify the Default Namespace setting to be "Manning.MyPhotoAlbum."	This ensures that all future classes created for this project will use the `Manning.MyPhotoAlbum` namespace.

This ensures that any new objects added to the project will be created with this namespace. With this change in place, we can create our base form.

Here we will just create the form and its controls. Later in this section we will create some infrastructure that will be useful in our derived forms later in the chapter.

	CREATE THE BASEEDITDLG FORM	
	Action	**Result**
2	Add a new `Form` to the MyPhotoAlbum project called "BaseEditDlg."	The new class appears in the Solution Explorer window and the BaseEditDlg.cs [Design] window is displayed.
3	Add the three buttons to the form. Assign their settings and position as shown.	

Settings

Button	Property	Value
OK	(Name)	btnOk
	DialogResult	OK
	Text	&OK
Reset	(Name)	btnReset
	Text	&Reset
Cancel	(Name)	btnCancel
	DialogResult	Cancel
	Text	&Cancel

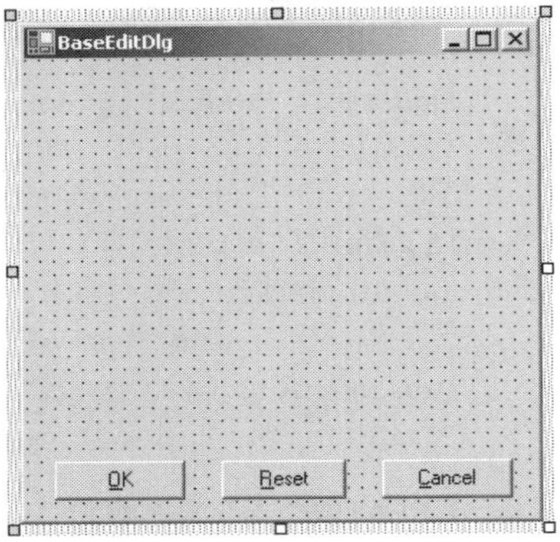

4	Add a `Panel` to the top of the form.	

Settings

Property	Value
BorderStyle	FixedSingle
Modifiers	Protected

Note: The `Modifiers` property used here establishes the accessibility level of the control. The three buttons use the default setting of Private. The Protected setting creates a `protected` control so that it can be modified in subclasses.

	Action	Result
5	Set the properties for the `BaseEditDlg` form to make it a dialog box.	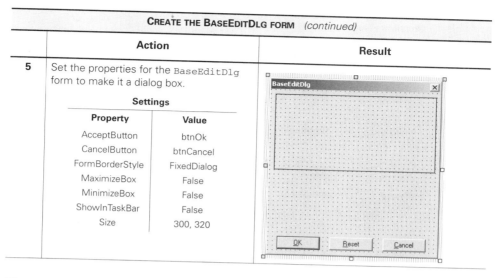

Settings

Property	Value
AcceptButton	btnOk
CancelButton	btnCancel
FormBorderStyle	FixedDialog
MaximizeBox	False
MinimizeBox	False
ShowInTaskBar	False
Size	300, 320

The code generated here is similar to code we have seen for other forms in our application. The one exception is the `panel1` control. The three buttons are defined as `private` controls as have all the controls we created in earlier chapters. The `panel1` object is a `protected` control. As we shall see, this will allow our child forms to modify the settings of this panel, and in particular change its size to accommodate the desired collection of controls.

```
namespace Manning.MyPhotoAlbum
{
  /// <summary>
  /// Base form window.
  /// </summary>
  public class BaseEditDlg : System.Windows.Forms.Form
  {
    private System.Windows.Forms.Button btnOk;
    private System.Windows.Forms.Button btnReset;
    private System.Windows.Forms.Button btnCancel;
    protected System.Windows.Forms.Panel panel1;
```

The cause of this change is the `Modifiers` property setting. This is not an actual property in the C# sense, and does not appear in the documentation for the `Button` class. This setting appears in the Properties window within Visual Studio to allow the access level for a control to be set. There are five possible values of this setting, as shown in the following table:

Possible values for the Modifiers property

Value	C# equivalent	Comments for Form inheritance
Public	public	Any class, regardless of where and how it is defined, can modify the control. This is not typically used, since you do not normally want any object to modify the location, size, or other internal control settings of your form.
Protected	protected	Any subclass of the form, regardless of where it is defined, can modify the control.
Protected Internal	protected internal	Any subclass of the form that is defined in the same assembly can modify the control.
Internal	internal	Any class in the same assembly, regardless of how it is defined, can modify the control. This is safer than public access, since you typically have control over the classes common to an assembly.
Private	private	No subclass can modify the control. This is the default setting.

Based on the table, we could have used either the `Protected` or `Protected Internal` setting here. Since there is no reason to prevent derived forms in external assemblies from modifying the `Panel` control, the `Protected` value will work just fine.

Before we move on, notice that our subclasses will not be able to add `Click` handlers for our private buttons. The OK and Cancel buttons have assigned actions due to their `DialogResult` setting. When either button is clicked, the dialog is deactivated and the appropriate value returned. We will require a way to save our modified settings when the OK button is clicked, and we need a way to perform an action when the Reset button is clicked.

As a solution, let's add two protected methods that child classes can implement to handle these situations. We will create a `SaveSettings` method to store the modified values, and a `ResetSettings` method to handle a click of the Reset button. This continues our previous steps.

	CREATE OVERRIDABLE METHODS FOR OK AND RESET BUTTONS	
	Action	**Result**
6	Create a protected virtual method for resetting the form.	```protected virtual void ResetSettings()
{
// Subclasses override to reset form
}```
7	Add a `Click` handler for the Reset button to invoke this new method.	```private void btnReset_Click
(object sender, System.EventArgs e)
{
ResetSettings();
}```
8	Create a protected virtual method for saving the dialog settings when a form is deactivated. This should return whether the save was successful.	```protected virtual bool SaveSettings()
{
// Subclasses override to save form
return true;
}```

	Action	Result
9	Override the `OnClosing` method for the form to invoke this new method when the user clicks the OK button. **Note:** This method is discussed in detail in chapter 8. Note how the settings are saved only if a subclass has not cancelled the operation.	```csharp\nprotected override void OnClosing\n (CancelEventArgs e)\n{\n if (!e.Cancel && (this.DialogResult\n == DialogResult.OK))\n {\n e.Cancel = ! SaveSettings();\n }\n\n base.OnClosing(e);\n}\n```

The `ResetSettings` and `SaveSettings` methods are now available to our derived forms. Compile your code to make the base form available for inheritance.

Next, let's create a derived form for editing a photograph's settings. The `BaseEditDlg` form will act as the parent of this new form.

9.1.2 Creating a derived form

A new form is derived from an existing form the same way that any new class is derived from an existing class. The base form is defined as the parent class of the new form.

```csharp
public class PhotoEditDlg : Manning.MyPhotoAlbum.BaseEditDlg
{
  // class definition goes here
}
```

In our case, we will create a derived form and leave the addition of new members for the subsequent sections. Visual Studio supports the creation of inherited forms graphically via an Add Inherited Form… menu in the Project menu, or the context menu of the project itself. This is detailed in the following steps.

	DERIVE THE PHOTOEDITDLG FORM FROM THE BASEEDITDLG FORM	
	Action	**Result**
1	Open the Add New Item dialog to add a new `PhotoEditDlg` form inherited from the existing `BaseEditDlg` form. **How-to** a. In the Solution Explorer window, right-click on the MyPhotoAlbum project. b. Select Add Inherited Form… from the Add menu. c. Enter the name "PhotoEditDlg."	The Add New Item dialog displays with the Inherited Form template selected by default.

	Action	Result
2	Click the Open button to display the Inheritance Picker dialog.	This window is shown in the next step.
3	Define `BasedEditDlg` as the base class for the new form. **Note:** If you get an error here, it likely means that your `BaseEdit-Dlg` form was never compiled. Visual Studio looks for inheritable forms in the existing assembly, so you must compile before you can inherit.	
4	Click the OK button in the Inheritance Picker dialog to create the class file and add it to the MyPhotoAlbum project. **Settings** Set the `Text` property to "PhotoEditDlg" to distinguish this window from our base form.	A new file PhotoEditDlg.cs is added to the project and the PhotoEditDlg.cs [Design] window is displayed. **Note:** Notice the small graphic on the existing controls here. This graphic indicates that these controls are inherited by the form.

View the code generated in the PhotoEditDlg.cs file, an excerpt of which follows. You will note that the new class is based on the BaseEditDlg class, and does not yet contain any controls of its own.

```
namespace Manning.MyPhotoAlbum
{
  public class PhotoEditDlg : Manning.MyPhotoAlbum.BaseEditDlg
  {
    private System.ComponentModel.IContainer components = null;

    . . .

    #region Designer generated code
```

```
/// <summary>
/// Required method for Designer support - do not modify
/// the contents of this method with the code editor.
/// </summary>
private void InitializeComponent()
{
  components = new System.ComponentModel.Container();
  . . .
}
#endregion
. . .
    }
  }
```

Take a look at the properties for the `PhotoEditDlg` object. The form has inherited all of the settings from our `BaseEditDlg` form to make it into a dialog box. The buttons and panel from the base class appear on the form as well, and you can examine the properties for the individual buttons. Note in particular that the OK, Reset, and Cancel buttons are private and cannot be modified, while the protected `Panel` can.

We will leave the topic of inherited forms for now and move on to specific controls for our `PhotoEditDlg` form. Before we do, it is worth realizing how powerful this feature really is. For example, a standard form for a database table could be created. Applications that use this table can customize the form for their specific needs, or libraries that extend the existing database can build a new form based on the original. In many cases, changes to the original database can be encoded in the base class in such a way that no changes are required in the inherited forms.

When you need a set of forms in your application based on a common concept or theme, consider creating a base form from which other forms can be derived.

9.2 LABELS AND TEXT BOXES

In our MyPhotos application, we have already used the `Label` and `TextBox` classes while creating dialog boxes in chapter 8. Here we will look at these classes in a bit more detail as we place them on our `PhotoEditDlg` form.

To do this, we need to come up with some reasonable properties in our `Photograph` class that will facilitate the creation of these and other controls. The following features will serve our purposes rather well:

- *Caption*—a caption for the photo. We created this property in chapter 8.
- *Date*—the date the photograph was taken. We will present this as a string on our form here, and convert our dialog to use the `DateTimePicker` control in chapter 11.
- *Photographer*—the person who took the photo. For now, we will treat this setting as a string. Later in the book this setting will be taken from a list of possible photographers.
- *Notes*—random notes or other comments about the photograph.

A dialog to support these new settings is shown in figure 9.2. This dialog will be constructed and discussed over the next few sections. In this section we will create the infrastructure required in the `Photograph` class to support these new settings, add the required controls to the dialog, and invoke the dialog from the main form of our `MyPhotos` class. We also look at some of the settings and events provided by the `TextBox` class for modifying the behavior or appearance of the control.

We will start with the changes required in our `Photograph` class.

Figure 9.2
Our Photo Properties dialog adds Label and Textbox controls to our inherited form.

9.2.1 EXPANDING THE PHOTOGRAPH CLASS

In order to support the date, photograph, and notes settings in our photos, we need to make a few changes. This section adds these features to our `Photograph` object, as well as the ability to read and write photographs, and update the `Save` and `Open` methods in our `PhotoAlbum` class.

We begin with some variables to hold these values and properties to provide external access.

Set the version number of the MyPhotoAlbum library to 9.2.

ADD NEW MEMBERS TO THE PHOTOGRAPH CLASS	
Action	**Result**
1 In the Photograph.cs file, add some variables to hold the new settings. **Note:** The `DateTime` structure used here represents a specific day and time.	``` . . . private string _caption; private DateTime _dateTaken; private string _photographer; private string _notes; ```

	Action	Result
| 2 | Initialize these new settings in the constructor. | ```csharp
public Photograph(string fileName)
{
    _fileName = fileName;
    _bitmap = null;
    _caption = Path.
        GetFileNameWithoutExtension(fileName);
    _dateTaken = DateTime.Now;
    _photographer = "unknown";
    _notes = "no notes provided";
}
``` |
| 3 | Add properties to set and retrieve these values.<br><br>**Note:** A Caption property was added in chapter 8, and is not shown here. | ```csharp
public DateTime DateTaken
{
    get { return _dateTaken; }
    set { _dateTaken = value; }
}

public string Photographer
{
    get { return _photographer; }
    set { _photographer = value; }
}

public string Notes
{
    get { return _notes; }
    set { _notes = value; }
}
``` |

This code is similar to member fields and properties we have seen before, except for the DateTime structure. This structure represents an instant in time measured in 100 nanosecond units since 12:00:00 AM on January 1, 0001, with a maximum value of 11:59:59 PM on December 31, 9999. Each nanosecond unit of time is called a *tick*. Members of this structure allow you to add, subtract, format, and otherwise manipulate date and time values. A related TimeSpan structure represents an interval of time. You can look up these structures in the .NET Framework documentation for more information on these types.

With our fields and properties defined, we next need to store and retrieve these values in the Save and Open methods of our PhotoAlbum class. Since the Photograph class is becoming a bit more complex, we will create Read and Write methods in this class to encapsulate the logic required. The Write method will store a photo into an open StreamWriter object, while various Read methods will accept an open StreamReader and return a Photograph object.

In our PhotoAlbum class, we will use these new methods to save and load a new version of our album file. It will be version 92, to match the current section of the book.

Let's continue our previous steps and create Read and Write methods in our Photograph class.

	Action	Result

4	Create a public `Write` method in the Photograph.cs file to store a `Photograph` into a given file.
	
	How-to
	a. Store the file name, caption, and photographer as a string.
	b. Convert the `DateTime` to a number of ticks and store this value.
	c. Since the notes may span multiple lines, store the length of this string and write its value as an array of characters.
		<pre>public void Write(StreamWriter sw)
		{
		    // First write the file and caption.
		    sw.WriteLine(this.FileName);
		    sw.WriteLine(this.Caption);
		
		    // Write the date and photographer
		    sw.WriteLine(this.DateTaken.Ticks);
		    sw.WriteLine(this.Photographer);
		
		    // Finally, write any notes
		    sw.WriteLine(this.Notes.Length);
		    sw.Write(this.Notes.ToCharArray());
		    sw.WriteLine();
		}</pre>

5	Create a `ReadVersion66` and `ReadVersion83` method to read in the data in the existing formats.
	
	Note: These methods are static since they create a new `Photograph` instance from the data provided by the given stream.
		<pre>static public Photograph
		      ReadVersion66(StreamReader sr)
		{
		  String name = sr.ReadLine();
		  if (name != null)
		    return new Photograph(name);
		  else
		    return null;
		}
		
		static public Photograph
		      ReadVersion83(StreamReader sr)
		{
		  String name = sr.ReadLine();
		  if (name == null)
		    return null;
		
		  Photograph p = new Photograph(name);
		  p.Caption = sr.ReadLine();
		  return p;
		}</pre>

	Action	Result

6	Create a static `ReadVersion92` method to read in a `Photograph` for our new version 92 of an album file.
	
	How-to
	
	a. Load the file name and caption using the `ReadVersion83` method.
	
	b. Read the date as a string and convert it to a `long` integer to instantiate a `DateTime` object.
	
	c. Read the photographer as a string.
	
	d. For the notes, read in the number of characters and use this value to read an equivalent-sized array of characters. This array can then be used to create a string.
	
	e. After the `Notes` property is set, a final `ReadLine` call is required to clear the final line in preparation for reading the next `Photograph` object.
		<pre>static public Photograph
		    ReadVersion92(StreamReader sr)
		{
		  // Use ReadVer83 for file and caption
		  Photograph p = ReadVersion83(sr);
		  if (p == null)
		    return null;
		
		  // Read date (may throw FormatException)
		  string data = sr.ReadLine();
		  long ticks = Convert.ToInt64(data);
		  p.DateTaken = new DateTime(ticks);
		
		  // Read the photographer
		  p.Photographer = sr.ReadLine();
		
		  // Read the notes size
		  data = sr.ReadLine();
		  int len = Convert.ToInt32(data);
		
		  // Read the actual notes characters
		  char[] notesArray = new char[len];
		  sr.Read(notesArray, 0, len);
		  p.Notes = new string(notesArray);
		  sr.ReadLine();
		
		  return p;
		}</pre>

7	Create a public `delegate` to use when selecting the appropriate reader.	<pre>public delegate Photograph
		    ReadDelegate(StreamReader sr);</pre>

Before we update the `Save` and `Open` methods in the `PhotoAlbum` class, a short discussion of our sudden use of the `delegate` keyword is in order.

We briefly mentioned in chapter 1 that a delegate acts much like a function pointer in C++. It identifies the signature for a method without actually defining a method. The advantage of C# delegates is that they are type safe. It is impossible to assign a nonconforming method to a delegate.

In our code, we create a delegate called `ReadDelegate`. This delegate encapsulates methods that accept a single `StreamReader` parameter and return a `Photograph` object. It just so happens that this matches the signature of the three read methods we created in the prior steps. This delegate can be used to great advantage when opening an album. Let's see how this looks.

	UPDATE THE SAVE AND OPEN METHODS IN PHOTOALBUM CLASS	
	Action	**Result**
8	In the `PhotoAlbum.cs` source code window, set the current version constant to 92.	`private const int CurrentVersion = 92;`

9	Modify the `Save` method to use the new `Photograph.Write` method. **Note:** The initial part of this method creates the `FileStream` and `StreamWriter` objects. This code does not change, and is not shown here. Similarly, the code for the `finally` clause is also not shown.	```
		public void Save(string fileName)
		{
		    . . .
		    try
		    {
		        sw.WriteLine(
		            _CurrentVersion.ToString());
		
		        // Store each photo separately
		        foreach (Photograph photo in this)
		        {
		            photo.Write(sw);
		        }
		
		        this._fileName = fileName;
		    }
		    finally
		    . . .
		}
		``

10	Modify the `Open` method to use the new `ReadDelegate` delegate.	```
		public void Open(string fileName)
		{
		    . . .
		    try
		    {
		        Clear();
		        this._fileName = fileName;
		        Photograph.ReadDelegate ReadPhoto;
		``

11	In the `switch` statement, select the correct version of the `Photograph` reader. **How-to** Use a `new` statement to instantiate a new version of the `delegate` for each version.	```
		switch (version)
		{
		    case 66:
		        ReadPhoto = new
		            Photograph.ReadDelegate(
		                Photograph.ReadVersion66);
		        break;
		
		    case 83:
		        ReadPhoto = new
		            Photograph.ReadDelegate(
		                Photograph.ReadVersion83);
		        break;
		
		    case 92:
		        ReadPhoto = new
		            Photograph.ReadDelegate(
		                Photograph.ReadVersion92);
		        break;
		
		    default:
		        // Unknown version or bad file.
		        throw (new IOException(. . .));
		}
		``

	Action	Result
12	Use the reader delegate to load the individual photographs. **Note:** The code for the `finally` clause remains the same and is not shown here.	```// Read each photograph in the album\nPhotograph p = ReadPhoto(sr);\nwhile (p != null)\n{\n this.Add(p);\n p = ReadPhoto(sr);\n}\n}\nfinally\n. . .\n}```

This neat little use of delegates makes our code much more readable. A delegate instance is declared just like any other variable, except that in this case the type is our delegate.

```
Photograph.ReadDelegate ReadPhoto;
```

This variable is assigned by creating a new instance of the delegate object, providing a method with a matching signature. Note that in our case the method happens to be `static`. A delegate tracks both an object and a method, allowing both internal and static members of a class to be used. In our code, when the version number is 92, the `PhotoReader` variable is initialized as follows. If the method provided does not match the signature assigned to the delegate, a compiler error is generated. Such compiler-time checking is a big advantage of delegates in C# over function pointers in C++.

```
case 92:
    ReadPhoto = new Photograph.ReadDelegate(Photograph.ReadVersion92);
    break;
```

The delegate is then used like any other function call to invoke the assigned method.

```
// Read each photograph in the album
Photograph p = ReadPhoto(sr);
while (p != null)
{
    this.Add(p);
    p = ReadPhoto(sr);
}
```

Our `PhotoAlbum` class is now ready. Let's get back to our `PhotoEditDlg` form and begin creating our new form.

9.2.2 CREATING THE PHOTOEDITDLG PANEL AREA

Looking back at the `PhotoEditDlg` dialog we wish to create, let's focus on the `Panel` control at the top of the form. In chapter 7 we made use of the `Panel` class for its drawing and scrolling capabilities. Here, we will use this class as a container for other controls to improve the overall appearance of our form. While we will not enable scrolling in our panel, realize that controls can be placed outside of the visible portion of a panel and made accessible via the automated scroll bars discussed in chapter 7.

We have used the `Label` and `TextBox` controls previously in our program, so let's update our panel before we talk about these classes in more detail. As you recall, the `Panel` object is inherited from the base form, but is modifiable by our class since it has a protected access level.

	CREATE THE PANEL AREA OF THE PHOTOEDITDLG FORM	
	Action	**Result**
1	In the PhotoEditDlg.cs [Design] window, modify the `Text` property for the new dialog to be "Photo Properties."	
2	Add the four `Label` controls to the left side of the panel, as shown in the graphic. Resize the panel control if necessary. Set the properties for each label as shown. **Note:** In this step you are placing the controls inside the `Panel`, rather than inside the `Form`. This is an important distinction.	

Settings

Label	Property	Value
label1	Text	Photo &File:
	TextAlign	MiddleRight
label2	Text	Cap&tion:
	TextAlign	MiddleRight
label3	Text	&Date Taken:
	TextAlign	MiddleRight
label4	Text	&Photographer:
	TextAlign	MiddleRight

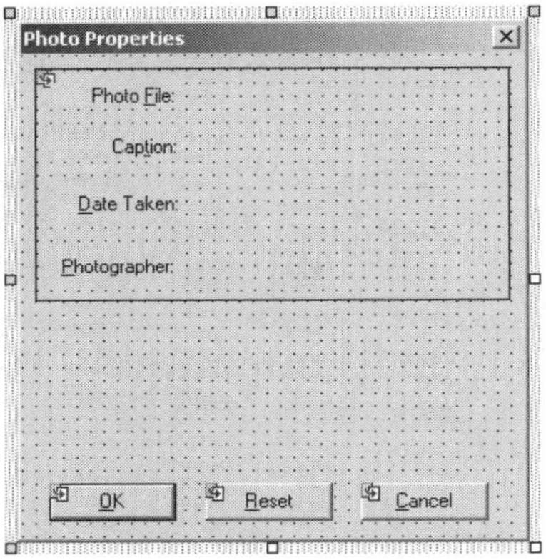

	Action	Result

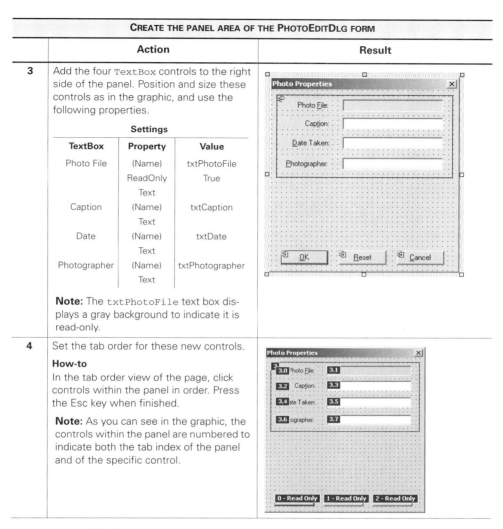

3 — Add the four `TextBox` controls to the right side of the panel. Position and size these controls as in the graphic, and use the following properties.

Settings

TextBox	Property	Value
Photo File	(Name)	txtPhotoFile
	ReadOnly	True
	Text	
Caption	(Name)	txtCaption
	Text	
Date	(Name)	txtDate
	Text	
Photographer	(Name)	txtPhotographer
	Text	

Note: The `txtPhotoFile` text box displays a gray background to indicate it is read-only.

4 — Set the tab order for these new controls.

How-to
In the tab order view of the page, click controls within the panel in order. Press the Esc key when finished.

Note: As you can see in the graphic, the controls within the panel are numbered to indicate both the tab index of the panel and of the specific control.

Note that the labels and text boxes here are defined within the `Panel` control, rather than within the form. In the `InitializeComponent` method, the controls are added to the `Panel` object much like we have seen other controls added to the `Form` class in previous chapters.

```
this.panel1.Controls.AddRange(new System.Windows.Forms.Control[] {
                            this.txtPhotographer,
                            this.txtDate,
                            this.txtCaption,
                            this.txtPhotoFile,
                            this.label4,
                            this.label3,
                            this.label2,
                            this.label1 });
```

The setting of the tab order in the final step, which internally assigns the `TabIndex` property for each control, is very important here. We could have set these values explicitly in steps 2 and 3, but the method in step 4 allowed us to set all controls at once. Since the `Label` and `TextBox` controls are located within the `Panel` object, the tab order defined applies only within the panel, so the `TabIndex` values for our labels and text boxes start at zero.

While label controls do not participate in the tab order, their `TabIndex` setting is still utilized. When you tab to or activate a label, the next control in the tab order will receive focus. This is the same behavior provided by the MFC `CStatic` class in Visual C++.

.NET Table 9.1 Label class

The `Label` class is a control that displays a text string or image within a form. This class is part of the of the `System.Windows.Forms` namespace, and inherits from the `Control` class. A `Label` object can be assigned a tab index, but when activated the next control in the tab order will always receive focus. See .NET Table 4.1 on page 104 for a list of members inherited from the `Control` class.

Public Properties	AutoSize	Gets or sets whether the label should automatically resize to display its contents.
	BorderStyle	Gets or sets the border for the label, taken from the `BorderStyle` enumeration. The default is `None`.
	FlatStyle	Gets or sets the flat style for the label, using the `FlatStyle` enumeration. The default is `Standard`.
	Image	Gets or sets the image to appear on the label.
	ImageList	Gets or sets an `ImageList` object to associate with the label. The `ImageIndex` property determines which image is displayed on the label.
	PreferredHeight	Gets the height of the control, in pixels, assuming a single line of text is displayed.
	PreferredWidth	Gets the width of the control, in pixels, assuming a single line of text is displayed.
	TextAlign	Gets or sets the text alignment to use for text in the control.
	UseMnemonic	Gets or sets whether an ampersand (&) in the `Text` property is interpreted as an access key prefix character.
Public Events	AutoSizeChanged	Occurs when the value of the `AutoSize` property changes.
	TextAlignChanged	Occurs when the value of the `TextAlign` property changes.

This tab order behavior is especially relevant for the assigned access key, also called a mnemonic. For example, the ampersand character "&" in the Photo File label defines the 'F' character as the access key. Typing the keystroke Alt+F sets the focus to this label. When you do this, the `txtPhotoFile` control actually receives the focus. Similarly, typing Alt+P for the Caption label will set the focus to the `txtCaption` control. Such mnemonics are very useful for users, myself included, who prefer to avoid the mouse and keep their fingers on the keyboard.

Labels include other features as well, of course. As we saw in chapter 8, they can display a border and define an alignment for displayed text. These and other features of the `Label` class are summarized in .NET Table 9.1. The `Label` class is also the parent of the `LinkLabel` class, which adds the ability to perform an action when the text on the label is clicked, similar to an HTML link in a web browser. We will use the `LinkLabel` class in chapter 18 while discussing how to include ActiveX controls on a form.

We will use `Label` objects again in future sections. For now, let's move on to discuss some of the features of our `TextBox` controls, and the `TextBox` class in general.

9.2.3 CREATING THE MULTILINE TEXT BOX

The `TextBox` controls on our form are used to display various properties of the `Photograph` object. We have already created the text box controls within the panel area. In this section we create the text box for displaying the `Photograph.Notes` property in our dialog, and implement the protected members we defined in our base class earlier in the chapter.

As we saw in the previous section, text boxes can be editable or read-only. In some ways a read-only text box is similar to a `Label` object with a 3D border. The major difference is that a text box supports cut and paste operations, while a label does not. The existing `CaptionDlg` form in our application used a 3D label to illustrate this point, so you can verify this for yourself if you prefer.

As a result, a read-only `TextBox` should be used when displaying text that a user may wish to copy. This, in fact, is why our `PhotoEditDlg` form uses a read-only `TextBox` to display the photograph's file name.

The `TextBox` class is based on the `TextBoxBase` class, which provides much of the core functionality for text controls. An overview of this base class appears in .NET Table 9.2.

The TextBoxBase class is a control that displays editable text and can interact with the Clipboard class to permit cut and paste operations. This class is part of the of the System.Windows.Forms namespace, and inherits from the Control class. Both the TextBox and RichTextBox classes are derived from this abstract class. See .NET Table 4.1 on page 104 for a list of members inherited from the Control class, and .NET Table 9.3 on page 288 for an overview of the TextBox class.

Public Properties	AcceptsTab	Gets or sets whether a multiline text box displays a Tab character or moves focus to the next control when the Tab key is pressed.
	CanUndo	Gets or sets whether the user can undo the previous edit performed in the text box.
	Lines	Gets or sets the array of strings representing the lines of text in the control.
	MaxLength	Gets or sets the maximum number of characters the control will accept.
	Multiline	Gets or sets whether this is a multiline text box.
	ReadOnly	Gets or sets whether the text is read-only.
	SelectedText	Gets or sets the currently selected text in the control. The SelectedStart property indicates the location of the first selected character.
	WordWrap	Gets or sets whether a multiline control automatically wraps to the next line as required.
Public Methods	AppendText	Appends a string to the existing text in the control.
	Copy	Copies the current text into the Clipboard.
	Paste	Replaces the current selection with the contents of the Clipboard.
	ScrollToCaret	Ensures the current caret position is visible in a multiline text box.
	SelectAll	Selects all text in the control. The Select method can be used to select a substring.
	Undo	Undoes the last edit operation in the text box.
Public Events	AcceptsTab-Changed	Occurs when the AcceptsTab property changes.
	Multiline-Changed	Occurs when the Multiline property changes.

As shown in the table, the TextBoxBase class provides a Multiline property that indicates whether a derived control can accept multiple lines of text. The bottom part of our PhotoEditDlg form is designed to show off such a text box. This control displays descriptive text about the photo, and automatically scrolls if the text becomes too long. The following steps add this control to our dialog:

ADD A MULTILINE TextBox TO THE PhotoEditDlg FORM	
Action	**Result**

#	Action	Result
1	Add the Notes label to the PhotoEditDlg form in the PhotoEditDlg.cs [Design] window.. **Settings** 	Property	Value	 	AutoSize	True	 	TabIndex	4	 	Text	Notes:		The AutoSize property causes the label to resize to exactly fit its Text value.
2	Add the multiline TextBox control to the form. **Settings** | Property	Value	 | (Name)	txtNotes	 | AcceptsReturn	True	 | Multiline	True	 | ScrollBars	Vertical	 | TabIndex	5	 | Text			 **Note:** The Multiline property must be set to true before the control can be resized to contain multiple lines of text. The AcceptsReturn property causes the control to treat an Enter key as a new line rather than allowing the parent form to invoke the OK button.

Our form is now ready, except for the internal logic to process the user's changes.

Since our dialog is intended to edit a Photograph object within a PhotoAlbum collection, we need a reference to the associated PhotoAlbum object within the dialog. We should also implement the methods necessary to handle the OK and Reset buttons, namely the ResetSettings and SaveSettings methods provided by the BaseEditDlg class.

The following steps detail these changes:

INTERACTING WITH THE PHOTOALBUM OBJECT	
Action	**Result**
| **3** In the PhotoEditDlg.cs file add a private `PhotoAlbum` variable to hold the album containing the photo to display. | ```csharp
private PhotoAlbum _album;
``` |
| **4** Modify the constructor to accept a `PhotoAlbum` parameter. | ```csharp
public PhotoEditDlg(PhotoAlbum album)
{
``` |
| **5** Within the constructor, set the album variable and call `ResetSettings` to initialize the dialog's controls. | ```csharp
   // This call is required . . . .
   InitializeComponent();

   // Initialize the dialog settings
   _album = album;
   ResetSettings();
}
``` |
| **6** Implement the `ResetSettings` method to set the controls to their corresponding settings in the current photograph. | ```csharp
protected override void ResetSettings()
{
   Photograph photo = _album.CurrentPhoto;

   if (photo != null)
   {
     txtPhotoFile.Text = photo.FileName;
     txtCaption.Text = photo.Caption;
     txtDate.Text
         = photo.DateTaken.ToString();
     txtPhotographer.Text = photo.Photographer;
     this.txtNotes.Text = photo.Notes;
   }
}
``` |
| **7** Implement `SaveSettings` to save the contents of the form to the current photograph. **Note:** Here, the settings are always stored successfully, so this method always returns true. | ```csharp
protected override bool SaveSettings()
{
   Photograph photo = _album.CurrentPhoto;

   if (photo != null)
   {
     photo.Caption = txtCaption.Text;
     // Ignore txtDate setting for now
     photo.Photographer = txtPhotographer.Text;
     photo.Notes = txtNotes.Text;
   }

   return true;
}
``` |

Our dialog is complete, at least for now. Applications can use it to display and modify information about a photograph. The one exception is the date a photograph was taken. While it is certainly possible to convert a string provided by the user into a `DateTime` structure, this is not really the best way to specify a date on a form. Instead, the `DateTimePicker` control is provided especially for this purpose. We will look at this control in chapter 11, and simply ignore the value of `txtDate` for now.

The next step is to use this new dialog in our main application. This is the topic of the next section.
```

9.2.4 Adding PhotoEditDlg to our main form

Now that our new dialog is ready, we need to display it in our MyPhotos application. This section integrates the dialog into our application, much like we integrated the CaptionDlg form in chapter 8.

The CaptionDlg form does present a slight problem, in that it already allows the caption to be edited, just like our new PhotoEditDlg form. We could keep this dialog around and provide two ways to edit a photograph's caption. This might be a little confusing to users, so we will instead remove CaptionDlg from our application.

The step to remove this dialog follows. We will integrate the PhotoEditDlg dialog into our application in a moment.

Set the version number of the MyPhotos application to 9.2.

	REMOVE THE CAPTIONDLG FORM	
	Action	**Result**
1	In the Solution Explorer window, delete the CaptionDlg form. **How-to** a. Right-click on the CaptionDlg.cs file. b. Select Delete from the popup menu. c. Click OK in the confirmation box. **Alternately** Click on the file and press the Delete key.	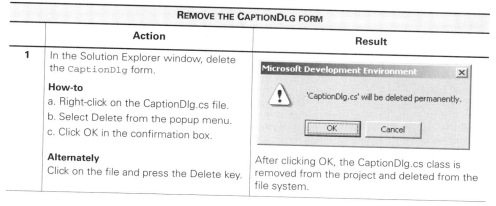 After clicking OK, the CaptionDlg.cs class is removed from the project and deleted from the file system.

With the caption dialog gone, our way is clear to display the PhotoEditDlg form from our main window. We will reuse the menuCaption menu for this purpose, renamed and revamped by the following steps:

DISPLAY THE PHOTOEDITDLG FORM FROM THE MAIN WINDOW	
Action	**Result**
2 Double-click the MainForm.cs file in the Solution Explorer window.	The Windows Forms Designer window appears for this form.
3 Modify the properties for the Caption menu item under the Edit menu. **Settings** | **Property**	**Value** | |---|---| | (Name) | menuPhotoProp | | Text | &Photo Properties... | **Note:** We could elect to use this menu under its previous name. This could prove confusing in the future, so we instead rename the control in line with its new purpose.	
4 Rename the `Click` event for this menu to menuPhotoProp_Click.	
5 Replace the old handler with an implementation to display the PhotoEditDlg form. **Note:** The old handler was called menuCaption_Click.	```csharp\nprivate void menuPhotoProp_Click\n (object sender, System.EventArgs e)\n{\n if (_album.CurrentPhoto == null)\n return;\n\n using (PhotoEditDlg dlg\n = new PhotoEditDlg(_album))\n {\n if (dlg.ShowDialog()\n == DialogResult.OK)\n {\n _bAlbumChanged = true;\n\n sbpnlFileName.Text\n = _album.CurrentPhoto.Caption;\n statusBar1.Invalidate();\n }\n }\n}\n```
6 Update the `Popup` event handler for the Edit menu to use the new menu.	```csharp\nprivate void menuEdit_Popup\n (object sender, System.EventArgs e)\n{\n menuPhotoProp.Enabled\n = (_album.Count > 0);\n}\n```

Since the dialog itself handles the initialization and storage of any changes made by the user, and the using statement disposes of the dialog when we are finished, there is not much work required by our handler. When the user clicks OK, we mark that the album has changed and update the status bar with any new caption entered by the user.

So let's see if your code actually works. Compile and run the application and open a previously saved album file. Display the Photo Properties dialog. Note in particular the following features:

- The differences between the read-only and editable text boxes.
- Label text cannot be highlighted, while text within text boxes can, even when read-only.
- Use the access key for a label and notice how the following text box receives focus.
- Press the Enter key while editing a single-line text box. The dialog behaves as if you had clicked the OK button.
- Press the Enter key while editing within the Notes text box. Since we set the `AcceptsReturn` property to `true`, this adds a new line within the Notes box and does not deactivate the window.
- Right-click on any text box. The default context menu will appear. This context menu contains various commands for editing text, and is shown in figure 9.3. The items in this menu correspond to methods in the `TextBoxBase` class, as shown in .NET Table 9.2.

While our form is working just fine, there are some features missing that might make our dialog a little more friendly. These are the subject of the next section.

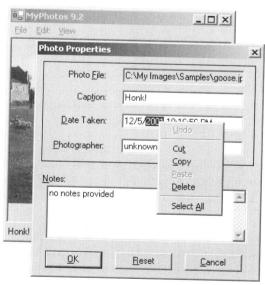

Figure 9.3
The standard context menu for Text-Box controls, shown here for the Date Taken text box, disables commands that are not currently available.

9.2.5 USING TextBox CONTROLS

So let's add some interesting features to our text boxes. Most of the events for `TextBox` controls are inherited from the `Control` and `TextBoxBase` classes. Members specific to the TextBox class appear in .NET Table 9.3. Here we will look more closely at the KeyPress event and the TextChanged event.

The keyboard events inherited from the Control class are especially interesting, and consist of the KeyDown, KeyPress, and KeyUp events. These events are inherited from the Control class, and occur when a key on the keyboard is pushed down and released while the control has focus. The KeyDown event occurs when the key is first pressed. The KeyPress event activates while the key is held down and repeats while the key remains held down. The KeyUp event occurs when the key is released. These events can be used to fine-tune your interfaces as the user types on the keyboard.

.NET Table 9.3 TextBox class		
The TextBox class represents a TextBoxBase control that displays a single font. This control is part of the System.Windows.Forms namespace, and inherits from the TextBoxBase control. Through its parent class, text boxes can support single or multiple lines, and interact with the clipboard to cut, copy, or paste text.		
Public Properties	AcceptsReturn	Gets or sets whether the Enter key in a multiline text box adds a new line of text or activates the default button for the form.
	CharacterCasing	Gets or sets how the control modifies the case of entered characters. This can be used to display all uppercase or lowercase letters in the text box.
	PasswordChar	Gets or sets the character used to mask the text display in the control. When this property is set, cutting or copying to the clipboard is disabled.
	ScrollBars	Gets or sets which scrollbars should appear in a multiline text box.
	TextAlign	Gets or sets how displayed text is aligned within the control.
Public Events	TextAlignChanged	Occurs when the TextAlign property has changed.

We will look at the keyboard events in more detail in chapter 12, but let's do a quick example here. Suppose we wanted the Caption property to only contain letters or numbers. No punctuation characters and no symbols. The KeyPress event receives keyboard characters as they are typed, and allows the event handler to handle or ignore them. The KeyPressEventArgs class is used with this event, and provides a KeyChar property to get the character pressed, and a Handled property to get or set whether the character has been handled. If Handled is set to true, then the control will not receive the character.

The obvious, albeit incorrect, way to implement such a handler would be as follows:

```
private void txtCaption_KeyPress(object sender, KeyPressEventArgs e)
{
```

```
char c = e.KeyChar;

// Ignore all non-alphanumerics - not our approach
e.Handled = !(Char.IsLetter(c) || Char.IsDigit(c));
}
```

This implementation uses members of the System.Char class to see if the category of the character is a letter or number. It may look good, but it also causes all other characters to be ignored by the control, such as spaces and backspaces. Clearly, this is not what we want.

Instead, we will allow all control and white space characters past our event handler. This will permit the keyboard shortcuts to work, and also allows spaces in our captions.

	ADD KEYPRESS EVENT HANDLER FOR TXTCAPTION CONTROL	
	Action	**Result**
1	In the PhotoEditDlg.cs Design window, add a KeyPress event for the txtCaption text box control.	`private void txtCaption_KeyPress` `(object sender, KeyPressEventArgs e)` `{`
2	Implement this handler to only permit letters and numbers to appear in captions.	`char c = e.KeyChar;` `e.Handled = !(Char.IsLetterOrDigit(c)` `    || Char.IsWhiteSpace(c)` `    || Char.IsControl(c));` `}`

The caption text box will only receive letters, digits, white space, and all control characters. This may or may not be a good idea, by the way, since a caption such as "one-way street" is now not permitted, since the dash '-' is a punctuation character. Feel free to remove this handler if you do not want this behavior in your program.

Another feature we could add to our dialog is to display the caption for the photograph in the title bar. Of course, this caption can be edited, and we would not want the text box and the title bar to display different values.

The TextChanged event occurs as text is entered, and can be used here to update the title bar while the user is typing. We could also implement this feature using the KeyPress event we just saw, but would have to deal with the delete and backspace keys as well as some text-editing controls. The TextChanged approach is a bit more straightforward.

Let's continue our previous steps and make this change.

UPDATE TITLE BAR DURING TXTCAPTION MODIFICATION	
Action	**Result**
3 Add a `TextChanged` event for the `txtCaption` text box control. **How-to** This is the default event for text boxes, so you can just double-click the control.	```private void txtCaption_TextChanged` ` (object sender, System.EventArgs e)` `{```
4 Modify the title bar to include the modified text from the control.	``` this.Text = String.Format(` ` "{0} - Photo Properties",` ` txtCaption.Text);` `}```

Compile and run your application to view these new changes. Verify that the caption can contain only letters and numbers, and that the title updates automatically as the caption is modified.

TRY IT! As an exercise in using some of the methods available to `TextBox` controls, see if you can create the standard context menu for text boxes manually and assign it to the `Notes` control. You will need to add a `ContextMenu` object to the form and assign it to the `txtNotes.ContextMenu` property. Assigning this property automatically disables the default context menu. Add the eight menu items to the menu, namely Undo, a separator, Copy, Cut, Paste, Delete, another separator, and Select All. To make your menu different than the standard one, also add a Clear menu item at the end of the context menu to clear the text in the box.

To process this menu, you will need a `Popup` event handler for the menu itself to enable or disable the menu items as appropriate. You will need to use the `CanUndo`, `SelectedText`, `SelectionLength`, and `SelectionStart` properties, and the `Copy`, `Cut`, `Paste`, `SelectAll`, and `Undo` methods as part of your implementation.

If you run into difficulties, visit the book's web site and download the code required for this change.

This ends our discussion of `Label` and `TextBox` objects for now. We will see these objects again in the next section and elsewhere in the book. Our next topic will create the Album Properties dialog box as a way to introduce the button classes in the .NET Framework.

9.3 BUTTON CLASSES

So just what is a button, exactly? For graphical interfaces, a button is a control that establishes a specific state, typically some form of on or off. Buttons are used to perform immediate actions in an interface, define the behavior for a specific feature, or turn a setting on or off. Figure 9.4 shows various styles of buttons in Windows Forms. More generally, the various types of buttons are as follows.

- A *push button*—is a button that performs some immediate action, such as displaying or deactivating a dialog, or modifying the values in the window. In Windows Forms, the `Button` class represents a push button.

- A *check box button*—allows a user to turn a specific option on or off, such as whether a file should be saved as read-only or not. In .NET, the `CheckBox` class can represent either a check box button or a *toggle button*. A toggle button appears as a normal button, but preserves an up or down state to represent a checked or unchecked mode, respectively.

- A *radio button*—sometimes called an *option button*, is used to select from a set of mutually exclusive options. When one of a group of radio buttons is selected, the other radio buttons in the group are automatically deselected. Radio buttons can be displayed normally or as toggle buttons. Windows Forms provides the `RadioButton` class for the creation of these objects. All radio buttons in the same container are automatically part of the same group. Use container classes such as `GroupBox` and `Panel` to support multiple groups of radio buttons on your forms.

Figure 9.4
The three types of buttons in various styles. Note how both check boxes and radio buttons can appear as toggle buttons.

In figure 9.4, note how each button supports a normal three-dimensional style as well as a flat style. In addition, note that toggle buttons appear identical to regular push buttons. Unlike push buttons, a toggle button preserves an in or out state when they are pressed.

All buttons in .NET inherit from the `ButtonBase` class. This class provides common functionality for all buttons, including the flat style setting and whether to display an image on the button. An overview of this class appears in .NET Table 9.4.

The `ButtonBase` class represents a control that can be displayed as a button. It is an abstract class in the `System.Windows.Forms` namespace, and inherits from the `Control` class. The `Button`, `CheckBox`, and `RadioButton` classes all inherit from this class. See .NET Table 4.1 on page 104 for a list of members inherited from the `Control` class.

Public Properties	FlatStyle	Gets or sets the flat style appearance of the button.
	Image	Gets or sets an image to display on the button.
	ImageAlign	Gets or sets the alignment of an image on the button.
	ImageIndex	Gets or sets an image to display on the button as an index into the `ImageList` property.
	ImageList	Gets or sets an `ImageList` object to associate with the button control.
	TextAlign	Gets or sets the alignment of text on the button.

In the MyPhotos application, we have already used a number of push buttons in our application, and we've seen how the `DialogResult` property can be used to automatically exit a modal dialog when a button is clicked. An overview of the `Button` class appears in .NET Table 9.5. In this section we build a dialog window for editing album properties to permit modification of internal album settings by the user. Our hidden agenda, of course, is to demonstrate the various types of buttons.

The `Button` class represents a standard push button. A button may display text, an image, or both text and an image. This class is part of the `System.Windows.Forms` namespace, and inherits from the `ButtonBase` class. See .NET Table 9.4 for details on this base class.

Public Properties	DialogResult	Gets or sets a value that is returned to the parent form when the button is clicked.
Public Methods	PerformClick	Generates a `Click` event for the button.

We will illustrate various styles of buttons in a dialog box for editing the properties of a photo album. To do this, we need to start with some reasonable properties for our `PhotoAlbum` class that will lend themselves to button objects. The following features will serve our purposes rather well.

- *Title*—a title or name for the album. As you may guess, this will be a `TextBox` control.
- *Photo display name*—which `Photograph` setting should be used as the short display name for the photo. This will be either the base file name, the caption, or the date assigned to the photo. This property has three possible values, making it perfect as a `RadioButton` example.

- *Password*—if present, a password is required to open the album. We will use a `CheckBox` to indicate whether a password is desired, and `TextBox` controls to accept and confirm the password.

A dialog to support these new settings is shown in figure 9.5. Of course, we will need some additional infrastructure in our `PhotoAlbum` class to support these new settings.

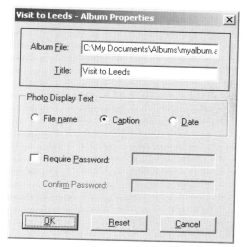

Figure 9.5
Note how the AlbumEditDlg modifies the Panel control inherited from BaseEditDlg as compared with the PhotoEditDlg just completed. This is possible since the panel is a protected member of the base form.

9.3.1 EXPANDING THE PHOTOALBUM CLASS

In order to support title, display name, and password settings in our albums, we need to make a few changes. For starters, let's add some variables to hold these values and properties to provide external access.

Set the version number of the MyPhotoAlbum library to 9.3.

ADD NEW SETTINGS TO THE PHOTOALBUM CLASS	
Action	**Result**

1 In the PhotoAlbum.cs file, add some variables to hold the new title, password, and display option settings.	`private string _title;`
	`private string _password;`
	
	`public enum DisplayValEnum {`
	`    FileName, Caption, Date`
	`};`
	`private DisplayValEnum _displayOption`
	`    = DisplayValEnum.Caption;`

ADD NEW SETTINGS TO THE PHOTOALBUM CLASS	
Action	**Result**
| 2    Add properties to set and retrieve these values. | ```
public string Title
{
  get { return _title; }
  set { _title = value; }
}

public string Password
{
  get { return _password; }
  set { _password = value; }
}

public DisplayValEnum DisplayOption
{
  get { return _displayOption; }
  set { _displayOption = value; }
}
``` |
| 3    Modify the `OnClear` method to reset these settings when the album is cleared. | ```
protected override void OnClear()
{
  _currentPos = 0;
  _fileName = null;
  _title = null;
  _password = null;
  _displayOption = DisplayValEnum.Caption;
  . . .
}
``` |

Next, we need to store and retrieve these values in the Save and Open methods. This will also require us to create a new version of our file. The new version will be 93, to match the current section of the book. Continuing the previous steps:

UPDATE SAVE METHOD IN PHOTOALBUM CLASS	
Action	**Result**
4 Change the current version setting to 93.	```private const int CurrentVersion = 93;```
| 5    Update the Save method to store the new album settings. | ```
public void Save(string fileName)
{
  . . .
  try
  {
    sw.WriteLine
        (CurrentVersion.ToString());

    // Save album properties
    sw.WriteLine(_title);
    sw.WriteLine(_password);
    sw.WriteLine(Convert.ToString(
        (int)_displayOption));

    // Store each photo separately
    . . .
}
``` |
```

Similar changes are required for the `Open` method. To make this code a little more readable, we will extract the code to read the album data into a separate method.

	UPDATE OPEN METHOD IN PHOTOALBUM CLASS	
	Action	**Result**

6	Modify the `Open` method to use a new `ReadAlbumData` method.	<pre>public void Open(string fileName)
		{
		  . . .
		  try
		  {
		    // Initialize as a new album
		    Clear();
		    this._fileName = fileName;
		    ReadAlbumData(sr, version);
		
		    // Check for password
		    // (we'll deal with this shortly)
		
		    Photograph.ReadDelegate PhotoReader;
		    switch (version)
		    {
		      . . .
		      case 92:
		      case 93:
		        PhotoReader =
		          new Photograph.ReadDelegate(
		            Photograph.ReadVersion92);
		        break;
		      . . .
		    }
		    . . .
		  }</pre>

7	Implement the new `ReadAlbumData` to read in the album-related information from an open stream.	<pre>protected void ReadAlbumData
		    (StreamReader sr, int version)
		{
		  // Initialize settings to defaults
		  _title = null;
		  _password = null;
		  _displayOption
		      = DisplayValEnum.Caption;
		
		  if (version >= 93)
		  {
		    // Read album-specific data
		    _title = sr.ReadLine();
		    _password = sr.ReadLine();
		    _displayOption = (DisplayValEnum)
		        Convert.ToInt32(sr.ReadLine());
		  }
		
		  // Initialize title if none provided
		  if (_title == null || _title.Length == 0)
		  {
		    _title = Path.
		      GetFileNameWithoutExtension(_fileName);
		  }
		}</pre>

Our `PhotoAlbum` class can now store and retrieve these settings in the album file. We can make immediate use of these new settings within the `PhotoAlbum` class.

9.3.2 USING THE NEW ALBUM SETTINGS

Before we create the Album Properties form, let's make use of our new settings within the `PhotoAlbum` class. The title is not used internally, but the password and display settings are for internal use. The display option indicates which `Photograph` property should be displayed to represent the photo for the album. This will be used by our main form to decide which string to display on the status bar panel.

The password setting is required when opening the album. When this field is set, the `Open` method should prompt for the password before it reads in the file. This requires a small dialog box to request this string from the user.

We will provide support for the display option first.

	Action	Result
	SUPPORT DISPLAY TEXT OPTION	
1	In the PhotoAlbum.cs file, add a new `GetDisplayText` method to return the display string for a given `Photograph` object.	```public string GetDisplayText(Photograph photo)``` ``` {```

2	Implement this method by using the `DisplayOption` property to determine the appropriate value to return.	``` switch (this._displayOption)```
		``` {```
		``` case DisplayValEnum.Caption:```
		``` default:```
		``` return photo.Caption;```
		
		``` case DisplayValEnum.Date:```
		``` return photo.DateTaken.ToString("g");```
		
		``` case DisplayValEnum.FileName:```
		``` return Path.GetFileName(photo.FileName);```
		``` }```
		``` }```

3	Also add a `CurrentDisplay-Text` property to return this value for the current photo.	```public string CurrentDisplayText```
		``` {```
		``` get { return GetDisplayText(CurrentPhoto); }```
		``` }```

This code is fairly straightforward. One new feature is the ability to provide a formatting code to the `DateTime.ToString` method.

```
return photo.DateTaken.ToString("g");
```

The `"g"` string used here causes the short form of the associated `DateTime` structure to be returned. We will discuss additional formatting conventions for `DateTime` structures when we discuss the `DateTimePicker` control in chapter 11.

For the password setting, we require a new dialog to permit this string to be entered by the user when an album is opened. The following steps create the dialog for this purpose:

		CREATE A PASSWORD DIALOG	
		Action	**Result**
4		Create a new Windows Form called PasswordDlg in the MyPhotoAlbum project.	The PasswordDlg.cs file is created and added to the project, and its design window is displayed.

5 — Create the form as shown, using the following settings.

Settings

Control	Property	Value
Label	Text	*as shown*
TextBox	(Name)	txtPassword
	Password-Char	*
Button	(Name)	btnOk
	DialogResult	OK
	Text	&OK
Form	AcceptButton	btnOk
	ControlBox	False
	FormBorderStyle	FixedDialog
	ShowInTaskbar	False
	Size	262, 142
	Text	Enter Password

Note: The PasswordChar property setting for the TextBox control masks the user's entry with the given character. When this property is set, the Clipboard cut and copy operations are disabled (the paste operation is still permitted).

6	Create a Password property to retrieve the value of the txtPassword control.	`public string Password`
		`{`
		`    get { return txtPassword.Text; }`
		`}`

We will use this dialog to request a password when an album is opened. The point here is to illustrate the PasswordChar property, and not to create a secure mechanism for handling passwords.

		ENFORCE (INSECURE) PASSWORD MECHANISM	
		Action	**Result**
7		In the PhotoAlbum.cs code window, indicate that this class uses the Windows Forms namespace.	`using System.Windows.Forms;`

	Action	Result
| **8** | Use the new `PasswordDlg` form in the `PhotoAlbum.Open` method to receive a password from the user. | ```csharp
public void Open(string fileName)
{
  . . .
  try
  {
    . . .
    // Check for password
    if (_password != null && _password.Length > 0)
    {
      using (PasswordDlg dlg = new PasswordDlg())
      {
        dlg.Text = String.Format(
          "Opening album {0}",
          Path.GetFileName(_fileName));
        if ((dlg.ShowDialog() == DialogResult.OK)
          && (dlg.Password != _password))
        {
          throw new ApplicationException(
            "Invalid password provided");
        }
      }
    }
  }
  . . .
}
``` |

Our `PhotoAlbum` class is now ready. Each `PhotoAlbum` instance supports the new title, password, and display option settings. These settings are saved in the album file, and in the `Open` method an album cannot be loaded unless the proper password is provided.[3]

Let's get back to the matter at hand and create our Album Properties dialog.

9.3.3 CREATING THE AlbumEditDlg PANEL AREA

With our new infrastructure in place, we are ready to create the `AlbumEditDlg` form. This section will inherit the new dialog from our base form, and add controls to the panel at the top of the form.

---

[3]   Of course, the password mechanism here is quite insecure. A user can examine the album file by hand in order to discern the password. We could make this scheme more secure by using the password as a scrambling mechanism on the file. For example, rather than storing the password string in the file, call `GetHashCode` on the password string and XOR each character in the file with this hash code and the byte-sum of the password characters. The scrambled result is then stored in the file. The validity of the password is checked by using it to unscramble the version number of the file to see if it makes sense. If so, then the password is presumed to be valid. Again, this is not a totally secure mechanism, but it is slightly better then that shown in the text. For more information on security in .NET in general and the `System.Security` namespace in particular, see the book *.NET Security* by Tom Cabanski from Manning Publications.
```

The `Panel` control inherited from the `BaseEditDlg` form will display the album file and the title in our new `AlbumEditDlg` form. The following steps create the new form class and the controls contained by the panel.

	Action	Result
	CREATE THE ALBUMEDITDLG FORM AND ITS PANEL CONTROLS	

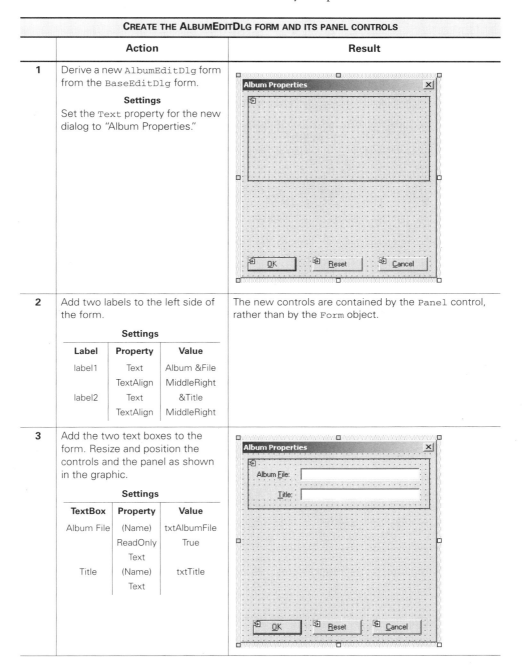

1 — Derive a new `AlbumEditDlg` form from the `BaseEditDlg` form.

Settings
Set the `Text` property for the new dialog to "Album Properties."

2 — Add two labels to the left side of the form.

Settings

Label	Property	Value
label1	Text	Album &File
	TextAlign	MiddleRight
label2	Text	&Title
	TextAlign	MiddleRight

The new controls are contained by the `Panel` control, rather than by the `Form` object.

3 — Add the two text boxes to the form. Resize and position the controls and the panel as shown in the graphic.

Settings

TextBox	Property	Value
Album File	(Name)	txtAlbumFile
	ReadOnly	True
	Text	
Title	(Name)	txtTitle
	Text	

With these steps completed, we are ready to add our button controls.

9.3.4 USING RADIO BUTTONS

The bottom part of our dialog will contain some radio and check box buttons. We will begin with the radio buttons in the middle of the form.

Radio buttons display a set of mutually exclusive options. In our case, they indicate which Photograph setting should be used to represent the photograph in a main window. Radio buttons in .NET work much the same as radio buttons in other graphical environments. An overview of this class appears in .NET Table 9.6.

In our code, three radio buttons will collectively set the _displayOption setting for the album. Since these are the only radio buttons on the form, it is not necessary to group them within a container control. We will anyway, since it improves the overall appearance of the form.

.NET Table 9.6	RadioButton class	
The RadioButton class represents a button that displays one of a possible set of options. Radio buttons are usually grouped together, and only one button may be checked at any one time. By default, when a radio button is clicked, it is automatically selected and all radio buttons in the same group are deselected. This behavior can be disabled using the AutoCheck property. The parent container for this control defines its group. So if four radio buttons are contained within a form, then only one of the four buttons may be checked at any one time. Use container classes such as GroupBox and Panel to provide multiple independent groups of radio buttons on a single form. This control is part of the System.Windows.Forms namespace, and inherits from the ButtonBase class. See .NET Table 9.4 on page 292 for members inherited from this class.		
Public Properties	Appearance	Gets or sets whether the control appears as a normal radio button or as a toggle button.
	AutoCheck	Gets or sets the behavior of related radio buttons when this button is clicked. If true, then the framework automatically deselects all radio buttons in the same group; if false, other radio buttons in the same group must be deselected manually.
	CheckAlign	Gets or sets the alignment of the click box portion of the control.
	Checked	Gets or sets whether the control is checked.
Public Methods	PerformClick	Sends a Click event to the control.
Public Events	AppearanceChanged	Occurs when the Appearance property changes.
	CheckedChanged	Occurs when the Checked property changes.

A Panel control could be used here, of course, but this is a good opportunity to create a GroupBox control. The GroupBox class inherits directly from the Control class to provide a collection of control objects with no scrolling capabilities. A group box includes a simple border, and the `Text` property for this control displays an optional label as part of the border. In general, use a group box control to provide simple containment of controls, especially when you wish to provide a label for the group.

The `Panel` and `GroupBox` controls are similar in that they are both used to contain controls. The `Panel` class provides some advanced features such as automated scrolling and configurable borders, while the `GroupBox` control provides a simple border with an optional label.

The steps to create the radio buttons on our form are provided in the following table. Note in particular how the `Tag` property inherited from the `Control` class is used to hold the enumeration value associated with the button.

	CREATE THE GROUP BOX SECTION OF THE ALBUMEDITDLG FORM	
	Action	**Result**
1	In the AlbumEditDlg.cs [Design] window, drag a `GroupBox` control from the Toolbox onto the form.	A `GroupBox` object is added to the form.
2	Set the `Text` property of the `GroupBox` control to "Phot&o Display Text."	This text is shown in the graphic for step 3.
3	Add three `RadioButton` buttons within this `GroupBox`, and position as in the graphic. **Settings** <table><tr><th>Button</th><th>Property</th><th>Value</th></tr><tr><td>File name</td><td>(Name)</td><td>rbtnFileName</td></tr><tr><td></td><td>Text</td><td>File &name</td></tr><tr><td>Caption</td><td>(Name)</td><td>rbtnCaption</td></tr><tr><td></td><td>Text</td><td>Ca&ption</td></tr><tr><td>Date</td><td>(Name)</td><td>rbtnDate</td></tr><tr><td></td><td>Text</td><td>&Date</td></tr></table>	

4	In the `AlbumEditDlg` constructor, initialize the `Tag` property for each control to contain the corresponding enumeration value.	`public AlbumEditDlg()`
		`{`
		`    . . .`
		`    // Initialize radio button tags`
		`    this.rbtnCaption.Tag = (int)`
		`        PhotoAlbum.DisplayValEnum.Caption;`
		`    this.rbtnDate.Tag = (int)`
		`        PhotoAlbum.DisplayValEnum.Date;`
		`    this.rbtnFileName.Tag = (int)`
		`        PhotoAlbum.DisplayValEnum.FileName;`
		`}`

	Action	**Result**
5	Add a private field to the `AlbumEditDlg` class to hold the currently selected radio button.	`private PhotoAlbum.DisplayValEnum` `  _selectedDisplayOption;`

6	Create a `DisplayOption_Click` method to serve as the `Click` event handler for all three buttons.	`private void DisplayOption_Click`
		`    (object sender, System.EventArgs e)`
		`{`
		`  RadioButton rb = sender as RadioButton;`
		
		`  if (rb != null)`
		`    this._selectedDisplayOption =`
		`      (PhotoAlbum.DisplayValEnum)rb.Tag;`
		`}`

7	Add this new method as the `Click` handler for each of the three radio buttons.	

Before we discuss the new code here, the tab behavior of `RadioButton` and `GroupBox` controls is worth a mention.

For radio button controls, all radio buttons in a group are treated as a single tab index. When you tab to a group of radio buttons, the selected button receives the focus, and then the left and right arrow keys alter the selected button.

The tab behavior for the `GroupBox` control is much like the `Label` class, in that it never receives the focus directly. Instead, the first control in the box receives the focus. In our form, when you tab to the group box, or use the access key Alt+O, the currently selected radio button receives the focus on behalf of the group. We will set the tab order for our controls shortly, after which we can see this behavior for ourselves.

As for the code changes here, let's look at them in a bit more detail. Here is an excerpt of the AlbumEditDlg.cs source file after the previously mentioned code modifications have been made.

```
namespace Manning.MyPhotoAlbum
{
  public class AlbumEditDlg : Manning.MyPhotoAlbum.BaseEditDlg
  {
    . . .
    private PhotoAlbum.DisplayValEnum _selectedDisplayOption;

    public AlbumEditDlg(PhotoAlbum album)
    {
      // This call is required by the Windows Form Designer
      InitializeComponent();

      // Initialize radio button tags
      this.rbtnCaption.Tag = (int)PhotoAlbum.DisplayValEnum.Caption;
      this.rbtnDate.Tag = (int)PhotoAlbum.DisplayValEnum.Date;
      this.rbtnFileName.Tag = (int)PhotoAlbum.DisplayValEnum.FileName;
    }

    #region Designer generated code
```

Assign tag values ❶

```
    . . .
    private void InitializeComponent()
    {
      . . .
      this.panel1.SuspendLayout();              ❷ Suspend
      this.groupBox1.SuspendLayout();              layout logic
      this.SuspendLayout();
      //
      // groupBox1
      //                                                        Add radio
      this.groupBox1.Controls.AddRange(                        buttons to
                         new System.Windows.Forms.Control[] {  group box ❸
                                  this.rbtnCaption,
                                  this.rbtnFileName,
                                  this.rbtnDate});
      this.groupBox1.Location = new System.Drawing.Point(8, 104);
      this.groupBox1.Name = "groupBox1";
      this.groupBox1.Size = new System.Drawing.Size(280, 56);
      this.groupBox1.TabIndex = 4;
      this.groupBox1.TabStop = false;
      this.groupBox1.Text = "Phot&o Display Text";
      //
      // rbtnFileName
      //
      this.rbtnFileName.Location = new System.Drawing.Point(8, 24);
      this.rbtnFileName.Name = "rbtnFileName";
      this.rbtnFileName.Size = new System.Drawing.Size(80, 24);
      this.rbtnFileName.TabIndex = 0;
      this.rbtnFileName.Text = "File &name";          Set click
      this.rbtnFileName.Click += new                  handler ❹
            System.EventHandler(this.DisplayOption_Click);
      . . .
      this.Controls.AddRange(new System.Windows.Forms.Control[] {
                                  this.groupBox1,
                                  this.panel1});
      . . .
      this.panel1.ResumeLayout(false);
      this.groupBox1.ResumeLayout(false);          Add controls to form ❺
      this.ResumeLayout(false);
    }                                               Record selected
    #endregion                                     radio button ❻

    . . .
    private void DisplayOption_Click(object sender, System.EventArgs e)
    {
      RadioButton rb = sender as RadioButton;

      if (rb != null)
        this._selectedDisplayOption = (PhotoAlbum.DisplayValEnum)rb.Tag;
    }
  }
}
```

Let's look at the numbered sections of this code in a little more detail.

❶ The `Tag` property contains an object to associate with the control. This provides a general mechanism for associating any data with any control. In our case, we use this property to hold the `DisplayValEnum` enumeration value corresponding to the individual buttons.

❷ Visual Studio suspends the layout logic for all container controls during initialization, including our group box. This ensures that the controls do not perform any layout of their contained objects during initialization.

❸ As we saw for our `Panel` control previously, the contained controls, in this case the three radio buttons, are added directly to the `GroupBox` control. This means that layout-related values, such as the `Anchor` and `Dock` properties, apply within the `GroupBox` container, and not within the `Form`.

❹ The `Click` handler for our three radio buttons is set using the standard += notation for events.

❺ It is interesting to note that the form itself only contains two controls so far. These are the `Panel` control and the `GroupBox` control.

❻ The shared click handler, `DisplayOption_Click`, receives a radio button object and records its `Tag` value as the currently selected radio button. We will use this selected value to save the settings for our dialog box when the user clicks OK.

Also note the use of the C# as keyword in our shared click handler. An `as` statement works much like a cast, except that the value `null` is assigned if the provided variable is not of the given type, as opposed to the `InvalidCastException` that is thrown when a cast operation fails. This handler could also be written as follows, although the following code is slightly less efficient since the `sender` parameter is checked twice—once for the `is` statement and once for the cast.

```
private void DisplayOption_Click(object sender, System.EventArgs e)
{
    // Our click handler using the is statement - not our approach
    if (sender is RadioButton)
    {
        RadioButton rb = (RadioButton) sender;
        this._selectedDisplayOption = (PhotoAlbum.DisplayValEnum)rb.Tag;
    }
}
```

Before we hook up this new form to our application, let's create the check box control on our form as well.

9.3.5   USING CHECK BOX BUTTONS

The `CheckBox` control is similar to a radio button. While a radio button is used for a set of mutually exclusive options, a check box is used for a single option that can be turned on or off. A check box normally appears as a small square followed by a textual description of the option. The settings for this control are rather similar to those provided for RadioButton objects, and are summarized in .NET Table 9.7.

.NET Table 9.7   CheckBox class

The CheckBox class represents a button that displays an option to the user. Typically, a check box represents one of two states, either *checked* or *unchecked*. A three-state check box can also be established, with an additional *intermediate* state. This third state is useful when used with a set of objects, where some objects have the option checked and some unchecked.

This control is part of the System.Windows.Forms namespace, and inherits from the ButtonBase class. See .NET Table 9.4 on page 292 for members inherited from the Button-Base class.

Public Properties	Appearance	Gets or sets whether the control appears as a normal check box button or as a toggle button.
	AutoCheck	Gets or sets whether the control is checked automatically or manually. The default is true.
	Checked	Gets or sets whether the control is checked.
	CheckState	Gets or sets the state of a three-state check box as a CheckState enumeration value. This is either Checked, Unchecked (the default), or Intermediate.
	ThreeState	Gets or sets whether the check box displays three states. The default is false.
Public Events	CheckedChanged	Occurs when the Checked property changes.
	CheckStateChanged	Occurs when the CheckState property changes.

Check boxes are normally used in one of two ways. The first is as a simple on or off state. For example, we could have elected to add a check box indicating whether the album can be modified. If yes, then photographs could be added to and removed from the album. If no, then any attempt to modify the album could throw an InvalidOperationException object. In a Windows dialog box, this option could be represented as a check box, which the user would click to turn modifications on or off.

Another common usage for a check box is to enable or disable a set of controls related to a specific option. This is the type of check box we will create here. In our case, the check box relates to whether the photo album has a password associated with it or not. If it does, then controls to set this password will be enabled on our form. If it does not, then these controls will be disabled.

Let's begin by adding the CheckBox and related controls to our AlbumEditDlg form. These steps also add some logic for processing the check box and associated controls. We discuss the events used here following the table.

CREATE THE PASSWORD SECTION OF THE ALBUMEDITDLG FORM	
Action	**Result**

1 In the AlbumEditDlg.cs [Design] window, drag a CheckBox control from the Toolbox window onto the form.

Settings

Property	Value
(Name)	cbtnPassword
Text	Require &Password

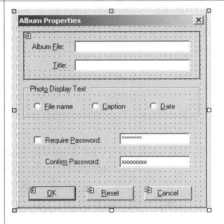

2 Add a text box to receive the password, and an additional label and text box to confirm the password. Set the size and position of these controls as shown in the graphic.

Settings

Control	Property	Value
First TextBox	(Name)	txtAlbumPwd
	Enabled	False
	PasswordChar	*
Label	(Name)	lblConfirmPwd
	Enabled	False
	Text	Confir&m Password
	TextAlign	MiddleLeft
Second TextBox	(Name)	txtConfirmPwd
	Enabled	False
	PasswordChar	x

Note: Since the default value for the CheckBox is unchecked, these controls are set to disabled by default. We will enable them when the user clicks the check box.

Also, notice the two different settings for PasswordChar used here. This is done only for illustrative purposes. Generally, you should use the same password character for all controls in a window.

	Action	Result
3	Use the tab order view to assign the `TabIndex` properties for the controls in the dialog, using the order shown in the graphic.	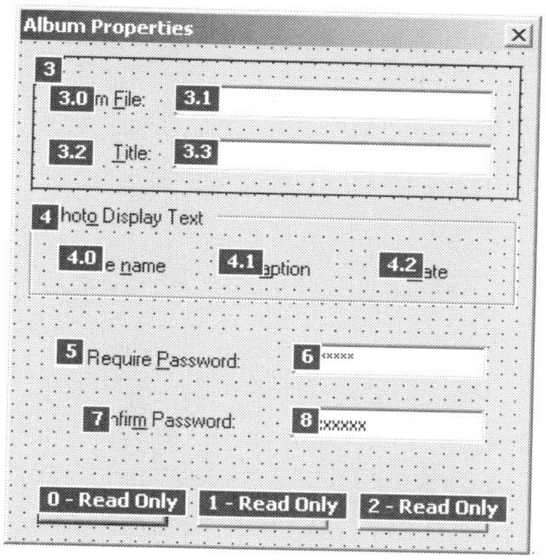
| 4 | Add a `CheckedChanged` handler for the `CheckBox` object to enable the controls when the box is checked.<br><br>**How-to**<br>This is the default event for the `CheckBox` control, so simply double-click on the control. | ```csharp
private void cbtnPassword_CheckedChanged
    (object sender, System.EventArgs e)
{
  // Enable pwd controls as required.
  bool enable = cbtnPassword.Checked;
  txtAlbumPwd.Enabled = enable;
  lblConfirmPwd.Enabled = enable;
  txtConfirmPwd.Enabled = enable;

  if (enable)
  {
    // Assign focus to pwd text box
    txtAlbumPwd.Focus();
  }
}
``` |
| 5 | Add a `Validating` event handler to the `txtAlbumPwd` control.<br><br>**Note:** The `Validating` and `Validated` events allow custom validation to be performed on a control. | ```csharp
private void txtAlbumPwd_Validating
  (object sender, System.
    ComponentModel.CancelEventArgs e)
{
  if (txtAlbumPwd.TextLength == 0)
  {
    MessageBox.Show(this,
    "The password for the album "
    + "cannot be blank",
    "Invalid Password",
      MessageBoxButtons.OK,
      MessageBoxIcon.Error);
    e.Cancel = true;
  }
}
``` |

BUTTON CLASSES

	Action	Result

6	Add a `ValidPasswords` method to return whether the two passwords match.	```csharp
		private bool ValidPasswords()
		{
		    if ((cbtnPassword.Checked)
		        && (txtConfirmPwd.Text
		            != txtAlbumPwd.Text))
		    {
		        MessageBox.Show(this,
		          "The password and confirm "
		          + "values do not match",
		          "Password Error",
		          MessageBoxButtons.OK,
		          MessageBoxIcon.Error);
		        return false;
		    }
		
		    return true;
		}```

This code demonstrates a couple of new concepts, such as setting the focus and validating the contents of a control. Let's look at these changes in a bit more detail.

```csharp
private void cbtnPassword_CheckedChanged        ❶ Handle the
    (object sender, System.EventArgs e)            CheckedChanged
{                                                  event
    // Enable the password controls as required
    bool enable = cbtnPassword.Checked;
    txtAlbumPwd.Enabled = enable;
    lblConfirmPwd.Enabled = enable;
    txtConfirmPwd.Enabled = enable;

    if (enable)
    {
        // Assign focus to password control    ❷ Set focus to
        txtAlbumPwd.Focus();                      txtAlbumPwd
    }                                             control
}

private void txtAlbumPwd_Validating
    (object sender, System.ComponentModel.CancelEventArgs e)
{                                                  Handle the   ❸
    if (txtAlbumPwd.TextLength == 0)               Validating
    {                                              event
        MessageBox.Show(this,
          "The password for the album cannot be blank",
          "Invalid Password",
          MessageBoxButtons.OK,
          MessageBoxIcon.Error);

        e.Cancel = true;
    }
}

private bool ValidPasswords()
{
```

```
if ((cbtnPassword.Checked)
    && (txtConfirmPwd.Text != txtAlbumPwd.Text))
{
  MessageBox.Show(this,
    "The password and confirm values do not match",
    "Password Error",
    MessageBoxButtons.OK,
    MessageBoxIcon.Error);

  return false;
}

return true;
}
```

The numbered sections in this code warrant the following commentary.

❶ The `AutoCheck` property handles the `Click` event automatically on behalf of our `CheckBox` control. To process the change in button state that occurs when this happens, we handle the `CheckedChanged` event. The value of the `Checked` property is used to enable or display the associated controls, as required.

❷ When our radio button is checked, the focus, by default, would remain with the `cbtnPassword` control. Typically, when a user checks this button, he or she would immediately want to edit the password field. Calling the `Focus` method does this automatically and saves the user an extra step.

❸ The `Validating` event is one of a series of events related to entering and leaving a control. Collectively, these events are sometimes referred to as the *focus events*. The focus events, in the order in which they occur, are as follows: `Enter`, `GotFocus`, `Leave`, `Validating`, `Validated`, and `LostFocus`. These events can be used to fine-tune the behavior of a control as the user moves from one control to the next.

The validation events, namely `Validating` and `Validated`, occur during and after validation whenever the `CausesValidation` property is set to `true`. This property defaults to `true`, so the validation events normally occur. The `Validating` event receives a `CancelEventArgs` parameter much like the `OnClosing` event we discussed for the `Form` class in chapter 6. The `CancelEventArgs.Cancel` property is used to cancel the operation when the validation fails.

In our case, we want to verify that the password provided is not blank. When this occurs, we display a message box to inform the user of the problem, and cancel the operation to indicate that validation has failed. The .NET Framework returns focus to the control, forcing the user to correct the problem.

Our check box example does have one drawback. If the user clicks the check box, then he or she is forced to enter a password before leaving the txtAlbumPwd control. This could be a little frustrating if the user then wishes to uncheck the check box. We alleviate this a little by providing a default text string in the txtAlbumPwd control. From a book perspective, this was a good place to demonstrate the Focus method and validation events, so we will allow this little design anomaly to remain. In practice, an alternative might be to ensure that the password is nonempty as part of the ValidPasswords method.

This completes our discussion of check boxes. The last step here is to add the logic to reset and save our dialog box values, and display the form from our MyPhotos application.

9.3.6 Adding AlbumEditDlg to our main form

The final task required so that we can see our AlbumEditDlg dialog in action is to handle the reset and save logic required and link the dialog into our application. Let's make this happen.

	FINISH THE ALBUMEDITDLG FORM	
	Action	**Result**
1	In the AlbumEditDlg.cs source window, add a private PhotoAlbum variable to hold the album to edit.	`private PhotoAlbum _album;`
2	Modify the constructor to accept a PhotoAlbum parameter.	`public AlbumEditDlg(`**`PhotoAlbum album`**`)` `{`

3	Within the constructor, set the album variable and call ResetSettings to initialize the dialog's controls.	`    . . .`
		`    // Initialize the dialog settings`
		`    _album = album;`
		`    ResetSettings();`
		`}`

	Action	Result

4	Implement `ResetSettings` to set the controls to their corresponding settings in the current photograph.
	
	How-to
	a. Assign the album file name and title text boxes.
	b. Place the album title in the title bar as well.
	c. Set the radio buttons based on the `DisplayOption` setting for the album.
	d. Check the check box button if the album contains a non-empty password.
	e. Assign both password text boxes to the current password.
		``csharp
		protected override void ResetSettings()
		{
		    // Set file name
		    txtAlbumFile.Text = _album.FileName;
		
		    // Set title, and use in title bar
		    this.txtTitle.Text = _album.Title;
		    this.Text = String.Format(
		        "{0} - Album Properties",
		        txtTitle.Text);
		
		    // Set display option values
		    _selectedDisplayOption
		        = _album.DisplayOption;
		    switch (_selectedDisplayOption)
		    {
		      case PhotoAlbum.DisplayValEnum.Date:
		        this.rbtnDate.Checked = true;
		        break;
		
		      case PhotoAlbum.DisplayValEnum.FileName:
		        this.rbtnFileName.Checked = true;
		        break;
		
		      case PhotoAlbum.DisplayValEnum.Caption:
		      default:
		        this.rbtnCaption.Checked = true;
		        break;
		    }
		
		    string pwd = _album.Password;
		    cbtnPassword.Checked
		        = (pwd != null && pwd.Length > 0);
		    txtAlbumPwd.Text = pwd;
		    txtConfirmPwd.Text = pwd;
		}
		``

5	Implement the `SaveSettings` method to store the results after the user has clicked OK.
	
	How-to
	a. Use the `ValidPasswords` method to verify the passwords settings.
	b. Store the new settings only if the passwords were valid.
	c. Return whether the settings were successfully stored.
		``csharp
		protected override bool SaveSettings()
		{
		    bool valid = ValidPasswords();
		
		    if (valid)
		    {
		        _album.Title = txtTitle.Text;
		        _album.DisplayOption
		            = this._selectedDisplayOption;
		
		        if (cbtnPassword.Checked)
		          _album.Password = txtAlbumPwd.Text;
		        else
		          _album.Password = null;
		    }
		
		    return valid;
		}
		``

6	Add a `TextChanged` event handler to the `txtTitle` control to update the title bar as the title text is modified.	```csharp
		private void txtTitle_TextChanged
		    (object sender, System.EventArgs e)
		{
		    this.Text = String.Format(
		        "{0} - Album Properties",
		        txtTitle.Text);
		}
		``

BUTTON CLASSES

This completes the dialog. Now let's invoke this dialog from our main application window.

Set the version number of the MyPhotos application to 9.3.

	DISPLAY THE ALBUMEDITDLG FORM	
	Action	**Result**
7	In the MainForm.cs [Design] window, add a new Album Properties menu item to the Edit menu.	

Settings

Property	Value
(Name)	menuAlbumProp
Text	A&lbum Properties

| 8 | Add a `Click` handler for this menu to display the `AlbumEditDlg` form. | (see code below) |

```
private void menuAlbumProp_Click
    (object sender, System.EventArgs e)
{
  using (AlbumEditDlg dlg
        = new AlbumEditDlg(_album))
  {
    if (dlg.ShowDialog()
        == DialogResult.OK)
    {
      // Update window with changes
      this._bAlbumChanged = true;
      SetTitleBar();
      this.Invalidate();
    }
  }
}
```

| 9 | Also, make use of the new `CurrentDisplayText` property in the `OnPaint` method. | (see code below) |

```
protected override void OnPaint(. . .)
{
  if (_album.Count > 0)
  {
    . . .
    // Update the status bar.
    sbpnlFileName.Text
        = _album.CurrentDisplayText;
    . . .
  }
}
```

And we are finished. Compile and run the application to display properties for an album. Note the following aspects of the Album Properties dialog:

- This dialog can be displayed for an empty album, as opposed to the Photo Properties dialog, which requires at least one photograph in the album in order to appear.

- The title bar updates as the title changes.

- The radio buttons receive focus as a group. If you use the Tab key to move through the form, this is readily apparent. Note how the arrow keys can be used to modify the selected radio button from the keyboard.

- The radio buttons receive focus when you type the access key Alt+O to activate the `GroupBox` control.
- Modifying the display option for the album alters the `Photograph` setting displayed in the status bar of the main form.
- The password entry controls are enabled and disabled automatically as the `CheckBox` control is clicked. Note how the `txtPassword` control receives focus automatically when the controls are enabled.
- Try to enter a blank password or an invalid confirmation password to see how the validation behaves for these controls.

Feel free to experiment with some of the settings here. Also make sure the album and photograph settings are saved and restored properly whenever you close and later open an album.

TRY IT!   Use the `Appearance` property to modify the radio buttons in the `AlbumEditDlg` form to be toggle buttons rather than normal radio buttons. Compile and run the program to see the toggle button behavior in action. Users typically expect normal radio buttons for situations like this, so make sure you have a good reason for using an alternate appearance when you choose to do so.

9.4   RECAP

In this chapter we reviewed the basic controls in Windows Forms, namely the `Label`, `TextBox`, `Button`, `RadioButton`, and `CheckBox` controls. The majority of applications include one or more of these controls, and many dialogs are based exclusively on these classes. We examined the members, focus behavior, and some special features of each control, and used each control in our dialogs.

We also examined how one `Form` can be based on another `Form` using form inheritance. We constructed a base form and used it while building our two dialogs in Visual Studio .NET. During this process we also took a look at the container controls `Panel` and `GroupBox` as a way to logically arrange controls on a form, and in particular to define a distinct group for a set of radio buttons.

Along the way we looked at access modifiers for controls on a form, the `DateTime` structure, the C# `delegate` keyword, keyboard events, the `Tag` property, and focus events. You can review these topics by looking back through the chapter or by locating the appropriate page number using the book's index.

There are a number of other controls in .NET, of course. The next chapter continues our discussion on controls in Windows Forms with a detailed discussion of the `ListBox` and `ComboBox` controls.

List controls

10.1 List boxes 315

10.2 Multiselection list boxes 325

10.3 Combo boxes 333

10.4 Combo box edits 339

10.5 Owner-drawn lists 343

10.6 Recap 352

This chapter continues our discussion of the Windows Forms controls available in the .NET Framework. The controls we saw in chapter 9 each presented a single item, such as a string of text or a button with associated text. In this chapter we will look at some controls useful for presenting collections of items in Windows-based applications.

While it is certainly possible to use a multiline `Textbox` control to present a scrollable list of items, this control does not allow the user to select and manipulate individual items. This is where the `ListBox` and other list controls come in. These controls present a scrollable list of objects that can be individually selected, highlighted, moved, and otherwise manipulated by your program. In this chapter we will look at the `ListBox` and `ComboBox` controls in some detail. We will discuss the following topics:

- Presenting a collection of objects using the `ListBox` class.
- Supporting single and multiple selections in a list box.
- Drawing custom list items in a list box.
- Displaying a selection using the `ComboBox` class.
- Dynamically interacting with the items in a combo box.

Note that the `ListView` and `TreeView` classes can also be used with collections of objects. These classes are covered in chapters 14 and 15.

We will take a slightly different approach to presenting the list controls here. Rather than using the MyPhotos application we have come to know and love, this chapter will build a new application for displaying the contents of an album, using the existing MyPhotoAlbum.dll library. This will demonstrate how a library can be reused to quickly build a different view of the same data. Our new application will be called MyAlbumEditor, and is shown in figure 10.1.

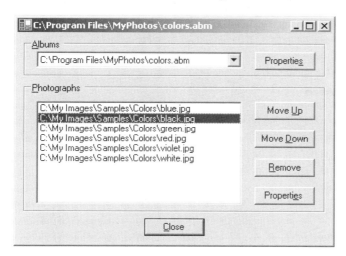

**Figure 10.1
The MyAlbumEditor application does not include a menu or status bar.**

10.1   LIST BOXES

A list box presents a collection of objects as a scrollable list. In this section we look at the `ListControl` and `ListBox` classes. We will create a list box as part of a new MyAlbumEditor application that displays the collection of photographs in a `Photo-Album` object. We will also support the ability to display our `PhotoEditDlg` dialog box for a selected photograph.

Subsequent sections in this chapter will extend the capabilities of this application with multiple selections of photographs and the use of combo boxes.

10.1.1   CREATING A LIST BOX

The `ListBox` and `ComboBox` controls both present a collection of objects. A list box displays the collection as a list, whereas a combo box, as we shall see, displays a single item, with the list accessible through an arrow button. In the window in figure 10.1, the photo album is displayed within a `ComboBox`, while the collection of photographs is displayed in a `ListBox`. Both of these controls are derived from the `ListControl` class, which defines the basic collection and display functionality required in both controls. A summary of this class appears in .NET Table 10.1.

The ListControl class is an abstract class for presenting a collection of objects to the user. You do not normally inherit from this class; instead the derived classes ListBox and ComboBox are normally used.

This class is part of the System.Windows.Forms namespace, and inherits from the Control class. See .NET Table 4.1 on page 104 for a list of members inherited by this class.

Public Properties	DataSource	Gets or sets the data source for this control. When set, the individual items cannot be modified.
	DisplayMember	Gets or sets the property to use when displaying objects in the list control. If none is set or the setting is not a valid property, then the ToString property is used.
	SelectedIndex	Gets or sets the zero-based index of the object selected in the control.
	SelectedValue	Gets or sets the value of the object selected in the control.
	ValueMember	Gets or sets the property to use when retrieving the value of an item in the list control. By default, the object itself is retrieved.
Public Methods	GetItemText	Returns the text associated with a given item, based on the current DisplayMember property setting.
Public Events	DataSourceChanged	Occurs when the DisplaySource property changes
	DisplayMemberChanged	Occurs when the DisplayMember property changes.

Let's see how to use some of these members to display the list of photographs contained in an album. The following steps create a new MyAlbumEditor application. We will use this application throughout this chapter to demonstrate how various controls are used. Here, we will open an album and display its contents in a ListBox using some of the members inherited from ListControl.

	Action	Result
	CREATE THE MYALBUMEDITOR PROJECT	

1	Create a new project called "MyAlbumEditor."
	
	 How-to
	 Use the File menu, or the keyboard shortcut Ctrl+Shift+N. Make sure you close your existing solution, if any.
		The new project appears in the Solution Explorer window, with the default `Form1` form shown in the designer window.
		
		 Solution Explorer - MyAlbumEditor
		 Solution 'MyAlbumEditor' (1 project)
		   MyAlbumEditor
		     References
		     App.ico
		     AssemblyInfo.cs
		     Form1.cs

2	Rename the Form1.cs file to MainForm.cs.	
3	In the MainForm.cs source file, rename the C# class to `MainForm`.	```\npublic class MainForm:System.Windows.Forms.Form\n{\n . . .\n```

4	Add the MyPhotoAlbum project to the solution.
	
	 How-to
	 a. Right-click on the MyAlbumEditor solution.
	 b. Select Existing Project… from the Add menu.
	 c. In the Add Existing Project window, locate the MyPhotoAlbum directory.
	 d. Select the MyPhotoAlbum.csproj file from within this directory.
		Solution Explorer - MyAlbumEditor
		 Solution 'MyAlbumEditor' (2 projects)
		   MyAlbumEditor
		     References
		       MyPhotoAlbum
		       System
		       System.Data
		       System.Drawing
		       System.Windows.Forms
		       System.XML
		     App.ico
		     AssemblyInfo.cs
		     MainForm.cs
		   MyPhotoAlbum
		     References
		     AlbumEditDlg.cs
		     AssemblyInfo.cs
		     BaseEditDlg.cs
		     PasswordDlg.cs
		     PhotoAlbum.cs
		     PhotoEditDlg.cs
		     Photograph.cs

5	Reference the MyPhotoAlbum project within the MyAlbumEditor project. **How-to** Right-click the References item in the MyAlbumEditor project and display the Add Reference dialog.	

These steps should be familiar to you if you have been following along from the beginning of the book. Since we encapsulated the `PhotoAlbum` and `Photograph` classes in a separate library in chapter 5, these objects, including the dialogs created in chapter 9, are now available for use in our application. This is quite an important point, so I will say it again. The proper encapsulation of our objects in the MyPhoto-

Album library in chapters 5 and 9 makes the development of our new application that much easier, and permits us to focus our attention on the list controls.

With this in mind, let's toss up a couple of buttons and a list so we can see how the ListBox control works.

Set the version number of the MyAlbumEditor application to 10.1.

CREATE THE CONTROLS FOR OUR NEW APPLICATION		
	Action	**Result**
6	Drop two GroupBox controls onto the form. **How-to** As usual, drag them from the Toolbox window.	

Settings

GroupBox	Property	Value
First	Anchor	Top, Left, Right
	Text	&Albums
Second	Anchor	Top, Bottom, Left, Right
	Text	&Photo-graphs

7	Drop a Button control into the Albums group box, a Listbox control into the Photographs group box, and a Button control at the base of the form.

Settings

Control	Property	Value
Open Button	(Name)	btnOpen
	Anchor	Top, Right
	Text	&Open
ListBox	(Name)	lstPhotos
	Anchor	Top, Bottom, Left, Right
Close Button	(Name)	btnClose
	Anchor	Bottom
	Text	&Close

Note: A couple points to note here. First, the Anchor settings define the resize behavior of the controls within their container. Note that the Button and ListBox here are anchored within their respective group boxes, and not to the Form itself.

Second, since our application will not have a menu bar, we use the standard Close button as the mechanism for exiting the application.

	Action	Result
8	Set the properties for the `MainForm` form. **Settings** | **Property**	**Value**
---	---
AcceptButton	btnClose
Size	400, 300
Text	MyAlbumEditor | **Note:** When you enter the new Size setting, note how the controls automatically resize within the form based on the assigned Anchor settings.	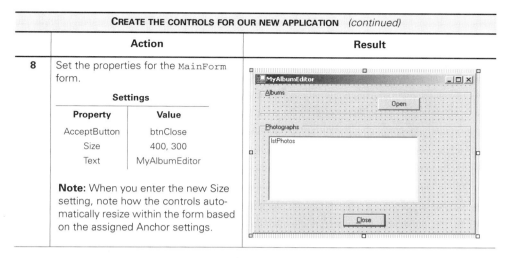

Our form is now ready. You can compile and run if you like. Before we talk about this in any detail, we will add some code to make our new `ListBox` display the photographs in an album.

Some of the new code added by the following steps mimics code we provided for our MyPhotos application. This is to be expected, since both interfaces operate on photo album collections.

	Action	Result
	DISPLAY THE CONTENTS OF AN ALBUM IN THE LISTBOX CONTROL	
9	In the MainForm.cs file, indicate we are using the `Manning.MyPhotoAlbum` namespace.	```. . .
using Manning.MyPhotoAlbum;```
10	Add some member variables to track the current album and whether it has changed.	```private PhotoAlbum _album;
private bool _bAlbumChanged = false;```
11	Override the `OnLoad` method to initialize the album. **Note:** The OnLoad method is called a single time after the form has been created and before the form is initially displayed. This method is a good place to perform one-time initialization for a form.	```protected override void OnLoad
    (EventArgs e)
{
  // Initialize the album
  _album = new PhotoAlbum();

  base.OnLoad(e);
}``` |
| 12 | Add a `Click` handler for the Close button to exit the application. | ```private void btnClose_Click
    (object sender, System.EventArgs e)
{
  Close();
}``` |

	Action	Result
| 13 | Add a `CloseAlbum` method to close a previously opened album.<br><br>**How-to**<br>Display a dialog to ask if the user wants to save any changes they have made. | ```csharp
private void CloseAlbum()
{
    if (_bAlbumChanged)
    {
        _bAlbumChanged = false;

        DialogResult result
            = MessageBox.Show("Do you want "
            + "to save your changes to "
            + _album.FileName + '?',
            "Save Changes?",
            MessageBoxButtons.YesNo,
            MessageBoxIcon.Question);

        if (result == DialogResult.Yes)
        {
            _album.Save();
        }
    }

    _album.Clear();
}
``` |
| 14 | Override the `OnClosing` method to ensure the album is closed on exit. | ```csharp
protected override void OnClosing
    (CancelEventArgs e)
{
    CloseAlbum();
}
``` |
| 15 | Add a Click handler for the Open button to open an album and assign it to the `ListBox`.<br><br>**How-to**<br>a. Close any previously open album.<br>b. Use the `OpenFileDialog` class to allow the user to select an album.<br>c. Use the `PhotoAlbum.Open` method to open the file.<br>d. Assign the album's file name to the title bar of the form.<br>e. Use a separate method for updating the contents of the list box. | ```csharp
private void btnOpen_Click
    (object sender, System.EventArgs e)
{
    CloseAlbum();

    using (OpenFileDialog dlg
            = new OpenFileDialog())
    {
        dlg.Title = "Open Album";
        dlg.Filter = "abm files (*.abm)"
            + "|*.abm|All Files (*.*)|*.*";
        dlg.InitialDirectory
            = PhotoAlbum.DefaultDir;

        try
        {
            if (dlg.ShowDialog()
                    == DialogResult.OK)
            {
                _album.Open(dlg.FileName);
                this.Text = _album.FileName;
                UpdateList();
            }
        }
        catch (Exception)
        {
            MessageBox.Show("Unable to open "
                + "album\n" + dlg.FileName,
                "Open Album Error",
                MessageBoxButtons.OK,
                MessageBoxIcon.Error);
        }
    }
}
``` |
```

	Action	Result
16	Implement a protected `UpdateList` method to initialize the `ListBox` control.	```protected void UpdateList()\n{\n lstPhotos.DataSource = _album;\n}```

That's it! No need to add individual photographs one by one or perform other complicated steps to fill in the list box. Much of the code is similar to code we saw in previous chapters. The one exception, the `UpdateList` method, simply assigns the `DataSource` property of the `ListBox` control to the current photo album.

```
protected void UpdateList()
{
   lstPhotos.DataSource = _album;
}
```

The `DataSource` property is part of the *data binding* support in Windows Forms. Data binding refers to the idea of assigning one or more values from some source of data to the settings for one or more controls. A data source is basically any array of objects, and in particular any class that supports the `IList` interface.[1] Since the `PhotoAlbum` class is based on `IList`, each item in the list, in this case each `Photograph`, is displayed by the control. By default, the `ToString` property for each contained item is used as the display string. If you recall, we implemented this method for the `Photograph` class in chapter 5 to return the file name associated with the photo.

Compile and run your code to display your own album. An example of the output is shown in figure 10.2. In the figure, an album called colors.abm is displayed, with each photograph in the album named after a well-known color. Note how the `GroupBox` controls display their keyboard access keys, namely Alt+A and Alt+P. When activated, the focus is set to the first control in the group box, based on the assigned tab order.

---

[1] We will discuss data binding more generally in chapter 17.

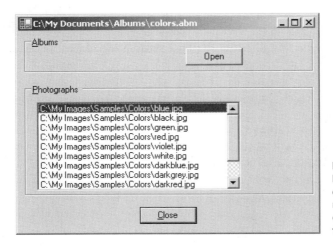

Figure 10.2
By default, the ListBox control displays a scroll bar when the number of items to display exceeds the size of the box.

You will also note that there is a lot of blank space in our application. Not to worry. These spaces will fill up as we progress through the chapter.

TRY IT! The `DisplayMember` property for the `ListBox` class indicates the name of the property to use for display purposes. In our program, since this property is not set, the default `ToString` property inherited from the `Object` class is used. Modify this property in the `UpdateList` method to a property specific to the `Photograph` class, such as "FileName" or "Caption." Run the program again to see how this affects the displayed photographs.

The related property `ValueMember` specifies the value returned by members such as the `SelectedValue` property. By default, this property will return the `object` instance itself.

10.1.2 HANDLING SELECTED ITEMS

As you might expect, the `ListBox` class supports much more than the ability to display a collection of objects. Particulars of this class are summarized in .NET Table 10.2. In the MyAlbumEditor application, the list box is a single-selection, single-column list corresponding to the contents of the current album. There are a number of different features we will demonstrate in our application. For starters, let's display the dialogs we created in chapter 9.

The album dialog can be displayed using a normal button. For the `PhotoEdit-Dlg` dialog, we would like to display the properties of the photograph that are currently selected in the list box. As you may recall, this dialog displays the photograph at the current position within the album, which seemed quite reasonable for our MyPhotos application. To make this work here, we will need to modify the current position to correspond to the selected item.

The ListBox class represents a list control that displays a collection as a scrollable window. A list box can support single or multiple selection of its items, and each item can display as a simple text string or a custom graphic. This class is part of the System.Windows.Forms namespace, and inherits from the ListControl class. See .NET Table 10.1 on page 316 for a list of members inherited by this class.

Public Static Fields	DefaultItemHeight	The default item height for an owner-drawn ListBox object.
	NoMatches	The value returned by ListBox methods when no matches are found during a search.
Public Properties	DrawMode	Gets or sets how this list box should be drawn.
	ItemHeight	Gets or sets the height of an item in the list box.
	Items	Gets the collection of items to display.
	MultiColumn	Gets or sets whether this list box should support multiple columns. Default is false.
	SelectedIndices	Gets a collection of zero-based indices for the items selected in the list box.
	SelectedItem	Gets or sets the currently selected object.
	SelectedItems	Gets a collection of all items selected in the list.
	SelectionMode	Gets or sets how items are selected in the list box.
	Sorted	Gets or sets whether the displayed list should be automatically sorted.
	TopIndex	Gets the index of the first visible item in the list.
Public Methods	BeginUpdate	Prevents the control from painting its contents while items are added to the list box.
	ClearSelected	Deselects all selected items in the control.
	FindString	Returns the index of the first item with a display value beginning with a given string.
	GetSelected	Indicates whether a specified item is selected.
	IndexFromPoint	Returns the index of the item located at the specified coordinates.
	SetSelected	Selects or deselects a given item.
Public Events	DrawItem	Occurs when an item in an owner-drawn list box requires painting.
	MeasureItem	Occurs when the size of an item in an owner-drawn list box is required.
	SelectedIndex-Changed	Occurs whenever a new item is selected in the list box, for both single and multiple selection boxes.

The following steps detail the changes required to display our two dialogs.

	DISPLAY THE PROPERTY DIALOGS	
	Action	**Result**
1	In the MainForm.cs [Design] window, add two buttons to the form as shown in the graphic. **Settings** | Button	Property	Value | |---|---|---| | album | (Name) | btnAlbumProp | | | Anchor | Top, Right | | | Text | Propertie&s | | photo | (Name) | btnPhotoProp | | | Anchor | Top, Right | | | Text | Properti&es |	
| 2 | Add a Click event handler for album's Properties button.<br><br>**How-to**<br>a. Within this handler, display an Album Properties dialog box for the current album.<br>b. If the user modifies the properties, mark the album as changed and update the list. | ```csharp
private void btnAlbumProp_Click
    (object sender, System.EventArgs e)
{
  using (AlbumEditDlg dlg
        = new AlbumEditDlg(_album))
  {
    if (dlg.ShowDialog()
        == DialogResult.OK)
    {
      _bAlbumChanged = true;
      UpdateList();
    }
  }
}
``` |
| 3 | Add a Click event handler for the photograph's Properties button to display the PhotoEditDlg form.<br><br>**How-to**<br>a  Within the handler, if the album is empty then simply return.<br>b. Set the current position in the album to the selected photograph.<br>c. Display a Photo Properties dialog box for the photograph at the current position.<br>d. If the user modifies the properties, mark the album as changed and update the list. | ```csharp
private void btnPhotoProp_Click
    (object sender, System.EventArgs e)
{
  if (_album.Count == 0)
    return;

  if (lstPhotos.SelectedIndex >= 0)
  {
    _album.CurrentPosition
      = lstPhotos.SelectedIndex;
  }

  using (PhotoEditDlg dlg
        = new PhotoEditDlg(_album))
  {
    if (dlg.ShowDialog()
        == DialogResult.OK)
    {
      _bAlbumChanged = true;
      UpdateList();
    }
  }
}
``` |

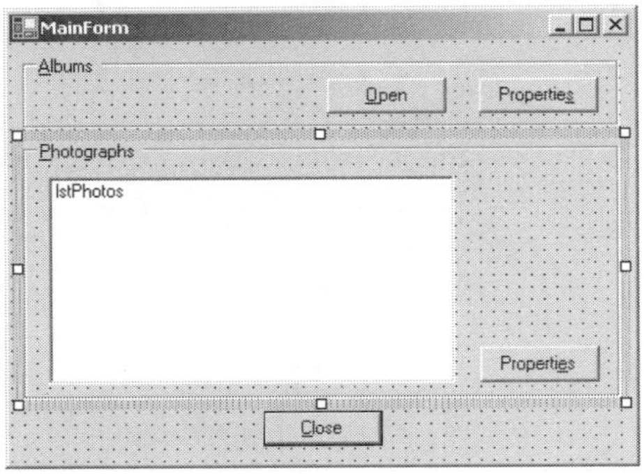

	Action	Result

4	Also display the photograph's properties when the user double-clicks on the list.
	
	How-to
	Handle the `DoubleClick` event for the `ListBox` control.
		``csharp
		private void lstPhotos_DoubleClick
		    (object sender, System.EventArgs e)
		{
		  btnPhotoProp.PerformClick();
		}
		``

In the code to display the Photograph Properties dialog, note how the `SelectedIndex` property is used. If no items are selected, then `SelectedIndex` will contain the value −1, and the current position in the album is not modified. When a photograph is actually selected, the current position is updated to the selected index. This assignment relies on the fact that the order of photographs in the `ListBox` control matches the order of photographs in the album itself.

```csharp
if (lstPhotos.SelectedIndex >= 0)
    _album.CurrentPosition = lstPhotos.SelectedIndex;
```

For both dialogs, a C# `using` block ensures that any resources used by the dialog are cleaned up when we are finished. We also call `UpdateList` to update our application with any relevant changes made. In fact, neither property dialog permits any changes that we would display at this time. Even so, updating the list is a good idea in case we add such a change in the future.

Compile and run your application to ensure that the dialog boxes display correctly. Note how easily we reused these dialogs in our new application. Make some changes and then reopen an album to verify that everything works as you expect.

One minor issue with our application occurs when the album is empty. When a user clicks the photo's Properties button, nothing happens. This is not the best user interface design, and we will address this fact in the next section.

So far our application only allows a single item to be selected at a time. List boxes can also permit multiple items to be selected simultaneously—a topic we will examine next.

10.2 MULTISELECTION LIST BOXES

So far we have permitted only a single item at a time to be selected from our list. In this section we enable multiple item selection, and add some buttons to perform various actions based on the selected items. Specifically, we will add Move Up and Move Down buttons to alter the position of the selected photographs, and a Remove button to delete the selected photographs from the album.

10.2.1 Enabling multiple selection

Enabling the `ListBox` to allow multiple selections simply requires setting the right property value, namely the `SelectionMode` property, to the value `MultiSimple` or `MultiExtended`. We discuss this property in detail later in the section.

Whenever you enable new features in a control, in this case enabling multiple selection in our list box, it is a good idea to review the existing functionality of the form to accommodate the new feature. In our case, what does the Properties button in the Photographs group box do when more than a single item is selected? While we could display the properties of the first selected item, this seems rather arbitrary. A more logical solution might be to disable the button when multiple items are selected. This is, in fact, what we will do here.

Since the Properties button will be disabled, we should probably have some other buttons that make sense when multiple items are selected. We will add three buttons. The first two will move the selected items up or down in the list as well as within the corresponding `PhotoAlbum` object. The third will remove the selected items from the list and the album.

The steps required are shown in the following table:

Set the version number of the MyAlbumEditor application to 10.2.

	ENABLE MULTIPLE SELECTIONS IN THE LIST BOX	
	Action	**Result**
1	In the MainForm.cs [Design] window, modify the `SelectionMode` property for the list box to be `MultiExtended`.	This permits multiple items to be selected similarly to how files can be selected in Windows Explorer.
2	Add three new buttons within the Photographs group box as shown in the graphic.	

Settings

Button	Property	Value
Move Up	(Name)	btnMoveUp
	Anchor	Top, Right
	Text	Move &Up
Move Down	(Name)	btnMoveDown
	Anchor	Top, Right
	Text	Move &Down
Remove	(Name)	btnRemove
	Anchor	Top, Right
	Text	&Remove

	Action	Result

3	Set the `Enabled` property for the four buttons in the Photographs group box to `false`.
	
	How-to
	a. Click the first button.
	b. Hold down the Ctrl key and click the other buttons so that all four buttons are highlighted.
	c. Display the Properties window.
	d. Set the Enabled item to False.
	
	Note: This technique can be used to set a common property for any set of controls on a form to the same value.
		The code in the `InitializeComponent` method for all four buttons is modified so that their Enabled properties are set to false.
		
		`btnMoveUp.Enabled = false;`
		`. . .`
		`btnMoveDown.Enabled = false;`
		`. . .`

4	Rewrite the `UpdateList` method to add each item to the list manually.
	
	Note: The `BeginUpdate` method prevents the list box from drawing the control while new items are added. This improves performance and prevents the screen from flickering.
		This allows us to manipulate and modify the individual items in the list, which is prohibited when filling the list with the `DisplaySource` property.
		
		<pre>private void UpdateList()
		{
		    lstPhotos.BeginUpdate();
		    lstPhotos.Items.Clear();
		    foreach (Photograph photo in _album)
		    {
		        lstPhotos.Items.Add(photo);
		    }
		    lstPhotos.EndUpdate();
		}</pre>

5	Handle the `SelectedIndexChanged` event for the `ListBox` control.
	
	How-to
	This is the default event for all list controls, so simply double-click on the control.
		<pre>private void
		    lstPhotos_SelectedIndexChanged
		        (object sender, System.EventArgs e)
		{
		    int numSelected
		        = lstPhotos.SelectedIndices.Count;</pre>

6	Implement this handler to enable or disable the buttons in the Photographs group box based on the number of items selected in the list box.
	
	Note: The Move Up button should be disabled if the first item is selected. The Move Down button should be disabled if the last item is selected. The `GetSelected` method is used to determine if a given index is currently selected.
		<pre> bool someSelected = (numSelected > 0);
		
		    btnMoveUp.Enabled = (someSelected
		        && !lstPhotos.GetSelected(0));
		    btnMoveDown.Enabled = (someSelected
		        && (!lstPhotos.GetSelected(
		            lstPhotos.Items.Count - 1)));
		    btnRemove.Enabled = someSelected;
		
		    btnPhotoProp.Enabled
		        = (numSelected == 1);
		}</pre>

MULTISELECTION LIST BOXES

You can compile and run this code if you like. Our new buttons do not do anything, but you can watch them become enabled and disabled as you select items in a newly opened album.

We assigned the `MultiExtended` selection mode setting to the `List-Box.SelectionMode` property, which permits selecting a range of items using the mouse or keyboard. This is one of four possible values for the `SelectionMode` enumeration, as described in .NET Table 10.3.

TRY IT! Change the list box selection mode to `MultiSimple` and run your program to see how the selection behavior differs between this and the `Multi-Extended` mode.

Our next task will be to provide an implementation for these buttons. We will pick up this topic in the next section.

10.2.2 HANDLING THE MOVE UP AND MOVE DOWN BUTTONS

Now that our list box allows multiple selections, we need to implement our three buttons that handle these selections from the list. This will permit us to discuss some collection and list box methods that are often used when processing multiple selections in a list.

We will look at the Move Up and Move Down buttons first. There are two problems we need to solve. The first is that our `PhotoAlbum` class does not currently provide an easy way to perform these actions. We will fix this by adding two methods to our album class for this purpose.

.NET Table 10.3 SelectionMode enumeration		
The `SelectionMode` enumeration specifies the selection behavior of a list box control, such as the `ListBox` and `CheckedListBox` classes. This enumeration is part of the `System.Windows.Forms` namespace.		
	None	Items cannot be selected.
	One	A single item can be selected using a mouse click or the space bar key.
Enumeration Values	MultiSimple	Multiple items can be selected. Items are selected or deselected using a mouse click or the space bar.
	MultiExtended	Multiple items can be selected. This extends simple selection to permit a range of items to be selected using a drag of the mouse or the Shift, Ctrl, and arrow keys.

The second problem is that if we move an item, then the index value of that item changes. For example, if we want to move items 3 and 4 down, then item 3 should move to position 4, and item 4 to position 5. As illustrated in figure 10.3, if we first move item 3 down, it becomes item 4. If you then move item 4 down, you would effectively move the original item 3 into position 5.

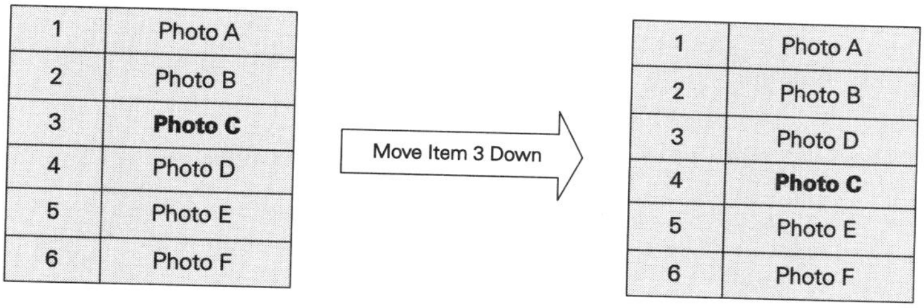

Figure 10.3 When the third item in the list is moved down, the original fourth item moves into position 3.

The trick here, as you may realize, is to move item 4 first, and then move item 3. In general terms, to move multiple items down, we must move the items starting from the bottom. Conversely, to move multiple items up, we must start at the top.

We will begin with the new methods required in the PhotoAlbum class.

Set the version number of the MyPhotoAlbum library to 10.2.

	IMPLEMENT MOVE METHODS IN PHOTOALBUM CLASS	
	Action	**Result**
1	In the PhotoAlbum.cs window, add a MoveBefore method to move a photograph at a specified index to the previous position. **How-to** a. Ensure the given index is valid. b. Remove the Photograph at this index from the list. c. Insert the removed photograph at the new position.	```csharp\npublic void MoveBefore(int i)\n{\n if (i > 0 && i < this.Count)\n {\n Photograph photo = this[i];\n this.RemoveAt(i);\n this.Insert(i-1, photo);\n }\n}\n```
2	Add a MoveAfter method to move a photograph at a specified index to the subsequent position.	```csharp\npublic void MoveAfter(int i)\n{\n if (i >= 0 && i < this.Count-1)\n {\n Photograph photo = this[i];\n this.RemoveAt(i);\n this.Insert(i+1, photo);\n }\n}\n```

With these methods in place, we are ready to implement Click event handlers for our Move Up and Move Down buttons. These handlers are shown in the following steps:

	Action	Result

HANDLE THE MOVE BUTTONS

	Action	Result
| **3** | Implement a `Click` event handler for the Move Up button.<br><br>**Note:** We could have used a `foreach` loop over the indices array here. This was written as a `for` loop to be consistent with the implementation of the Move Down handler. | ```csharp
private void btnMoveUp_Click
    (object sender, System.EventArgs e)
{
    ListBox.SelectedIndexCollection indices
        = lstPhotos.SelectedIndices;
    int[] newSelects = new int[indices.Count];

    // Move the selected items up
    for (int i = 0; i < indices.Count; i++)
    {
        int index = indices[i];
        _album.MoveBefore(index);
        newSelects[i] = index - 1;
    }

    _bAlbumChanged = true;
    UpdateList();

    // Reset the selections.
    lstPhotos.ClearSelected();
    foreach (int x in newSelects)
    {
        lstPhotos.SetSelected(x, true);
    }
}
``` |
| **4** | Implement the `Click` handler for the Move Down button. | ```csharp
private void btnMoveDown_Click
    (object sender, System.EventArgs e)
{
    ListBox.SelectedIndexCollection indices
        = lstPhotos.SelectedIndices;
    int[] newSelects = new int[indices.Count];

    // Move the selected items down
    for (int i = indices.Count - 1;
        i >= 0;
        i--)
    {
        int index = indices[i];
        _album.MoveAfter(index);
        newSelects[i] = index + 1;
    }

    _bAlbumChanged = true;
    UpdateList();

    // Reset the selections.
    lstPhotos.ClearSelected();
    foreach (int x in newSelects)
    {
        lstPhotos.SetSelected(x, true);
    }
}
``` |

Both of these methods employ a number of members of the `ListBox` class. Let's examine the Move Down button handler in detail as a way to discuss these changes.

```
private void btnMoveDown_Click(object sender, System.EventArgs e)
{
  ListBox.SelectedIndexCollection indices = lstPhotos.SelectedIndices;
  int[] newSelects = new int[indices.Count];

  // Move the selected items down
  for (int i = indices.Count - 1; i >= 0; i--)
  {
    int index = indices[i];
    _album.MoveAfter(index);
    newSelects[i] = index + 1;
  }

  _bAlbumChanged = true;
  UpdateList();

  // Reset the selections.
  lstPhotos.ClearSelected();
  foreach (int x in newSelects)
  {
    lstPhotos.SetSelected(x, true);
  }
}
```

❶ **Retrieve the selected items**

❷ **Move selected items down**

❸ **Update the list box**

❹ **Reselect the items**

The following points are highlighted in the code:

❶ A local `indices` variable is created to hold the index values of the selected items. The `SelectedIndices` property returns a `ListBox.SelectedIndexCollection` instance containing an array of the selected index values. The related `Selected-Items` property returns the actual objects selected. Note that an array of integers is also created to hold the new index positions of the objects after they have been moved.

❷ Starting from the bottom of the list, each selected item is moved down in the album. Note that the MoveDown button is disabled if the last item is selected, so we know for certain that `index + 1` will not produce an index which is out of range.

❸ Once all the changes have been made to our album, we update the list box with the new entries. Note that the `UpdateList` method has a side effect of clearing the current selections from the list.

❹ Once the list has been updated, the items need to be reselected. The `newSelects` array was created for this purpose. The `ClearSelected` method is used to remove any default selections added by the `UpdateList` method, and the `SetSelected` method is used to select each entry in the array.

You can run the application here if you like to see how these buttons work. The next section discusses the Remove button implementation.

10.2.3   HANDLING THE REMOVE BUTTON

The Remove button is a bit like the Move Down button. We have to be careful that the removal of one item does not cause us to remove incorrect entries on subsequent items. We will again loop through the list of selected items starting from the end to avoid this problem.

Also note that by removing the selected photographs, we are making an irreversible change to the photo album. As a result, this is a good place to employ the `MessageBox` class to ensure that the user really wants to remove the photos.

	HANDLE THE REMOVE BUTTON	
	Action	**Result**
1	Add a `Click` handler to the Remove button.	```csharp private void btnRemove_Click (object sender, System.EventArgs e) { ```
2	Implement this handler to confirm with the user that they really want to remove the selected photos. **How-to** Use the `MessageBox` class with the `Question` icon.	```csharp string msg; int n = lstPhotos.SelectedItems.Count; if (n == 1) msg = "Do your really want to " + "remove the selected photo?"; else msg = String.Format("Do you really want to " + "remove the {0} selected photos?", n); DialogResult result = MessageBox.Show(msg, "Remove Photos?", MessageBoxButtons.YesNo, MessageBoxIcon.Question); ```
3	If the user says `Yes`, then remove the selected items. **How-to** Use the `SelectedIndices` property.	```csharp if (result == DialogResult.Yes) { ListBox.SelectedIndexCollection indices = lstPhotos.SelectedIndices; for (int i = indices.Count - 1; i >= 0; i--) { _album.RemoveAt(indices[i]); } _bAlbumChanged = true; UpdateList(); } } ```

This code uses the `SelectedItems` property to retrieve the collection of selected objects. This property is used to determine how many items are selected so that our message to the user can include this information.

```csharp
    int n = lstPhotos.SelectedItems.Count;
```

To perform the deletion, we use the `SelectedIndices` property to retrieve the index numbers of each selected object. Since our list is based on the `PhotoAlbum` class, we know that the index in the list box corresponds to the index in the album. Removing a selection is a simple matter of removing the object at the given index from the album.

```csharp
    ListBox.SelectedIndexCollection indices = lstPhotos.SelectedIndices;
    for (int i = indices.Count - 1; i >= 0; i--)
    {
      _album.RemoveAt(indices[i]);
    }
```

Compile and run the application to see the Remove button and the rest of the interface in action. Note that you can remove photographs and move them around and still decide not to save these changes when the album is closed.

If you look at our application so far, there is still some space available in the Albums group box. This space is intended for a ComboBox control holding the list of available albums. Now that we have seen different ways to use the ListBox control, it's time to take a look at the other .NET list control: the ComboBox class.

10.3   COMBO BOXES

A list box is quite useful for presenting a list of strings, such as the photographs in an album. There are times when only one item will ever be selected, or when the extra space necessary to display a list box is problematic or unnecessary. The ComboBox class is a type of ListControl object that displays a single item in a text box and permits selection from an associated list box. Since a user can enter new values into the text box control directly, a ComboBox allows additional items to be added much more simply than a ListBox control.

Features specific to the ComboBox class are shown in .NET Table 10.4. As you can see, a number of members are reminiscent of members from both the ListBox class and the TextBox class. The TextBox area of the control is sometimes called the editable portion of the control, even though it is not always editable, and the ListBox portion may be called the dropdown portion, since the list drops down below the text box portion for some display styles.

10.3.1   CREATING A COMBO BOX

In our MyAlbumEditor application, we will add a ComboBox control to permit quick and easy access to the list of albums stored in the default album directory. The entries for this control will be taken from the album file names discovered in this directory, and the user will not be able to add new entries by hand. Figure 10.4 shows how our application will look after this change, with the ComboBox dropdown list displayed.

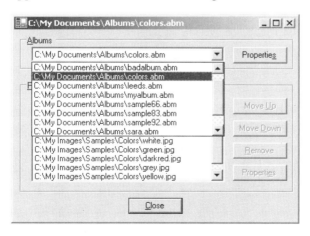

Figure 10.4
The dropdown list for a Combo-Box is hidden until the user clicks on the small down arrow to reduce the amount of space required for the control on the

The ComboBox class is a ListControl object that combines a TextBox control with a List-Box object. A user can select an item from the list or enter an item manually. A ComboBox can be displayed with or without the list box portion shown and with or without the text box portion editable, depending on the setting of the DropDownStyle property. When the list box portion is hidden, a down arrow is provided to display the list of available items. This class is part of the System.Windows.Forms namespace, and inherits from the ListControl class. See .NET Table 10.1 on page 316 for a list of members inherited by this class.

Public Properties	DrawMode	Gets or sets how elements in the list are drawn in a window.
	DropDownStyle	Gets or sets the style used to display the edit and list box controls in the combo box.
	DropDownWidth	Gets or sets the width of the list box portion of the control.
	DroppedDown	Gets or sets whether the combo box is currently displaying its list box portion.
	Items	Gets or sets the collection of items contained by this combo box.
	MaxDropDownItems	Gets or sets the maximum number of items permitted in the list box portion of the control.
	MaxLength	Gets or sets the maximum number of characters permitted in the text box portion of the control.
	SelectedItem	Gets or sets the currently selected item in the control.
	SelectedText	Gets or sets any text that is selected in the text box portion of the control.
	Sorted	Gets or sets whether the items in the control are sorted alphabetically.
Public Methods	BeginUpdate	Prevents the control from painting its contents while items are added to the list box.
	SelectAll	Selects all text in the text box portion of the control.
Public Events	DrawItem	Occurs when an owner-drawn combo box requires repainting.
	DropDown	Occurs just before the dropdown portion of a combo box is displayed.
	SelectionChange-Committed	Occurs when the selected item in the control has changed and that change is confirmed.

The steps required to create the combo box for our application are as follows:

Set the version number of the MyAlbumEditor application to 10.3.

	REPLACE OPEN BUTTON WITH A COMBOBOX CONTROL	
	Action	**Result**
1	Delete the Open button in the MainForm.cs [Design] window.	The button and all related code added by Visual Studio are removed from the MainForm.cs source file. Any nonempty event handlers, in this case `btnOpen_Click`, remain in the file and must be removed manually.
2	Drag a `ComboBox` control into the left side of the Albums group box as shown in the graphic. **Settings** 	**Property**	**Value** (Name) | cmbxAlbums Anchor | Top, Left, Right DropDownStyle | DropDownList Sorted | True	
| 3 | Replace the `btnOpen_Click` method in the MainForm.cs source file with an `OpenAlbum` method to open a given album file. <br><br> **Note:** Most of the existing code for the `btnOpen_Click` method is removed. Any exception that occurs here will be the responsibility of the caller. | ```csharp
private void OpenAlbum(string fileName)
{
    CloseAlbum();

    // Open the given album file
    _album.Open(fileName);
    this.Text = _album.FileName;

    UpdateList();
}
``` |
| 4 | Set the `Enabled` property for the Properties button in the Albums group box to `false`. | **Note:** We will enable this button when a valid album is selected in the combo box control. |
| 5 | Initialize the contents of the combo box in the `OnLoad` method. <br><br> **How-to** <br> Use the static `GetFiles` method from the `Directory` class to retrieve the set of album files in the default album directory. | ```csharp
protected override void
    OnLoad(EventArgs e)
{
    // Initialize the album
    _album = new PhotoAlbum();

    // Initialize the combo box
    cmbxAlbums.DataSource
        = Directory.GetFiles(
            PhotoAlbum.DefaultDir, "*.abm");

    base.OnLoad(e);
}
``` |
| 6 | At the top of the file, indicate that we are using objects in the `System.IO` namespace. | ```csharp
. . .
using System.IO;
``` |
```

As we saw for our `ListBox` control, the `DataSource` property provides a quick and easy way to assign a collection of objects to the `cmbxAlbums` control. In this case, the `Directory.GetFiles` method returns an array of strings containing the set of file names in the given directory that match the given search string.

Our `ComboBox` is created with the `DropDownStyle` property set to `DropDownList`. This setting is taken from the `ComboBoxStyle` enumeration, and indicates that the list box associated with the combo box should not be displayed by default, and that the user cannot manually enter new values into the control. A complete list of values provided by the `ComboBoxStyle` enumeration is shown in .NET Table 10.5.

.NET Table 10.5 ComboBoxStyle enumeration		
The `ComboBoxStyle` enumeration specifies the display behavior of a combo box control. This enumeration is part of the `System.Windows.Forms` namespace.		
Enumeration Values	DropDown	The text portion of the control is editable. The list portion is only displayed when the user clicks an arrow button on the control. This is the default.
	DropDownList	The text portion of the control is not editable. The list portion is only displayed when the user clicks an arrow button on the control.
	Simple	The text portion of the control is editable, and the list portion of the control is always visible.

Feel free to compile and run your program if you like. The combo box will display the available albums, without the ability to actually open an album. Opening an album requires that we handle the `SelectedItemChanged` event for our combo box, which is the topic of the next section.

10.3.2 HANDLING THE SELECTED ITEM

Our `ComboBox` currently displays a selected album, but it doesn't actually open it. The previous section replaced the `Click` handler for the now-deleted Open button with an `OpenAlbum` method, so all we need to do here is recognize when a new album is selected and open the corresponding album.

The one issue we must deal with is the case where an invalid album exists. While we initialized our control to contain only album files ending with ".abm," it is still possible that one of these album files contains an invalid version number or other problem that prevents the album from loading. The following steps handle this case by disabling the Properties button and `ListBox` control when such a problem occurs. An appropriate error message is also displayed in the title bar.

	Action	Result
1	Add a `SelectedItemChanged` handler to the combo box control.	```private void cmbxAlbums_SelectedIndexChanged(object sender, System.EventArgs e) {```
2	In the implementation of this handler, make sure the selected item is a new album. **Note:** If the selected album has not actually changed, there is no need to reload it.	```string albumPath = cmbxAlbums.SelectedItem.ToString(); if (albumPath == _album.FileName) return;```
3	Try to open the album.	```try { CloseAlbum(); OpenAlbum(albumPath);```
4	If the album is opened successfully, enable the album Properties button, and set the background color of the list box to normal window color.	```btnAlbumProp.Enabled = true; lstPhotos.BackColor = SystemColors.Window; }```
5	When an error occurs, display a message in the title bar to reflect this fact.	```catch (Exception) { // Unable to open album this.Text = "Unable to open selected album";```
6	Also clear the list box, set its background color to match the surrounding controls, and disable the album Properties button on the form.	```lstPhotos.Items.Clear(); lstPhotos.BackColor = SystemColors.Control; btnAlbumProp.Enabled = false; } }```

This code provides both text and visual cues on whether the selected album was successfully opened. Note how the `SelectedItem` property is used to retrieve the current selection. Even though we know this is a `string`, the framework provides us an `object` instance, so `ToString` must be called to extract the actual text.

```
string albumPath = cmbxAlbums.SelectedItem.ToString();
```

When the selected album opens successfully, the `ListBox` background is painted the normal window color as defined by the system and the Properties button in the Albums group box is enabled. Figure 10.1 at the beginning of this chapter shows the interface with a successfully opened album. When the album fails to open, the exception is caught and the title bar on the form is set to indicate this fact. In addition, the `ListBox` background is painted the default background color for controls and the `Button` control is disabled.

```
catch (Exception)
{
  // Unable to open album
  this.Text = "Unable to open selected album";
  lstPhotos.Items.Clear();
  lstPhotos.BackColor = SystemColors.Control;
  btnAlbumProp.Enabled = false;
}
```

An example of this situation appears in figure 10.5. The specified album, badalbum.abm, could not be opened, and between the title bar and the window this fact should be fairly clear.

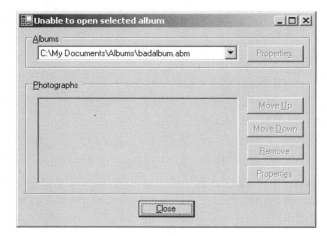

Figure 10.5
When the selected album cannot be loaded, only the Close button remains active.

TRY IT! The ComboBox in our application does not allow the user to manually enter a new album. This could be a problem if the user has created some albums in other directories. To fix this, add a ContextMenu object to the form and associate it with the Albums group box. Add a single menu item called "Add Album..." to this menu and create a Click event handler to allow the user to select additional album files to add to the combo box via the OpenFileDialog class.

Note that you have to modify the ComboBox to add the albums from the default directory manually within the OnLoad method. At present, since the DataSource property is assigned, the Items collection cannot be modified directly. Use BeginUpdate and EndUpdate to add a set of albums via the Add method in the Items collection, both in the OnLoad method and in the new Click event handler.

The next section provides an example of how to handle manual edits within a combo box.

10.4 COMBO BOX EDITS

The `ComboBox` created in the previous section used a fixed set of list entries taken from a directory on the disk. This permitted us to use the `DataSource` property for the list of items, and the `DropDownList` style to prevent the user from editing the text entry.

In this section we will create another `ComboBox` that permits manual updates to its contents by the user. Such a control is very useful when there are likely to be only a few possible entries, and you want the user to create additional entries as necessary. It so happens that we have just this situation for the `Photographer` property of our `Photograph` class.

Within a given album, there are likely to be only a handful of photographers for the images in that album. A combo box control is a good choice to permit the user to select the appropriate entry from the drop-down list. When a new photographer is required, the user can enter the new name in the text box.

Figure 10.6 shows how this combo box will look. You may notice that this list only displays four photographers, whereas our previous album combo box displayed eight album files at a time. A `ComboBox` control displays eight items by default. We will shorten the size here so that the list does not take up too much of the dialog window.

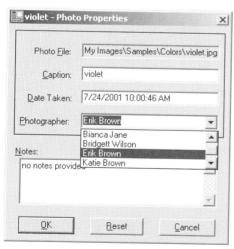

Figure 10.6
Note how the dropdown for the ComboBox extends outside of the Panel control. This is permitted even though the control is contained by the panel.

We will add this control to the MyAlbumEditor application in two parts. First we will create and initialize the contents of the control, and then we will support the addition of new photographers by hand.

10.4.1 REPLACING THE PHOTOGRAPHER CONTROL

The creation of our combo box within the `PhotoEditDlg` form is much like the one we created for the MyAlbumEditor application, with the exception of a few settings. The steps required to create this control are shown in the following table:

Set the version number of the MyPhotoAlbum library to 10.4.

	ADD THE PHOTOGRAPHER COMBO BOX	
	Action	**Result**
1	In the PhotoEditDlg.cs [Design] window, delete the `TextBox` control associated with the Photographer label.	The control is removed from the form, and the code generated by Visual Studio is removed as well. The subsequent steps modify the manually entered code associated with this control.
2	Place a `ComboBox` control on the form where the text box used to be. **Settings** **Property** / **Value** (Name) / cmbxPhotographer MaxDropDown / 4 Sorted / True Text / photographer	The `MaxDropDown` property here specifies that the list portion of the combo box displays at most four items at a time, with any remaining items accessible via the scroll bar.
3	Modify the ResetSettings method to initialize the items in the new combo box if necessary	```protected override void ResetSettings()\n{\n // Initialize the ComboBox settings\n if (cmbxPhotographer.Items.Count == 0)\n {```
4	First add the "unknown" photographer to ensure that the list is never empty.	```// Create the list of photographers\ncmbxPhotographer.BeginUpdate();\ncmbxPhotographer.Items.Clear();\ncmbxPhotographer.Items.\n Add("unknown");```
5	Then add to the `ComboBox` control any other photographers found in the album. **How-to** Use the `Items.Contains` method to check that a photographer is not already in the list. **Note:** This code is not terribly efficient, since it rescans the entire list each time the method is called. A better solution might be to modify the `PhotoAlbum` class to maintain the list of photographers assigned to `Photograph` objects in the album.	```foreach (Photograph ph in _album)\n{\n if (ph.Photographer != null\n && !cmbxPhotographer.Items.\n Contains(ph.Photographer))\n {\n cmbxPhotographer.Items.\n Add(ph.Photographer);\n }\n}\ncmbxPhotographer.EndUpdate();\n}```

	Action	Result
6	Select the photographer of the current photo in the combo box.	```Photograph p = _album.CurrentPhoto;

if (p != null)
{
    txtPhotoFile.Text = p.FileName;
    txtCaption.Text = p.Caption;
    txtDate.Text
        = p.DateTaken.ToString();
    cmbxPhotographer.SelectedItem
        = p.Photographer;
    txtNotes.Text = p.Notes;
}
}
``` |
| 7 | Update the SaveSettings method to save the photographer entered into the combo box.

Note: We will stop ignoring the txt-Date setting in the next chapter. | ```protected override bool SaveSettings()
{
    Photograph p = _album.CurrentPhoto;

    if (p != null)
    {
        p.Caption = txtCaption.Text;
        // Ignore txtDate setting for now
        p.Photographer
            = cmbxPhotographer.Text;
        p.Notes = txtNotes.Text;
    }

    return true;
}
``` |

Note how this code uses both the SelectedItem and Text properties for the ComboBox control. The SelectedItem property retrieves the object corresponding to the item selected in the list box, while the Text property retrieves the string entered into the text box. Typically these two values correspond to each other, but this is not always true, especially when the user manipulates the text value directly, as we shall see next.

10.4.2 UPDATING THE COMBO BOX DYNAMICALLY

With our control on the form, we now need to handle manual entries in the text box. This is normally handled via events associated with the ComboBox control. The Validated event, discussed in chapter 9, can be used to verify that a user-provided entry is part of the list and also add it to the list if necessary. The TextChanged event can be used to process the text while the user is typing.

We will handle both of these events in our code. First, let's add a Validated event handler, and then add code to auto-complete the entry as the user types.

VALIDATE THE PHOTOGRAPHER ENTRY		
	Action	**Result**
1	Add a Validated event handler for the cmbxPhotographer control.	```csharp\nprivate void cmbxPhotographer_Validated\n (object sender, System.EventArgs e)\n{\n```
2	To implement this handler, get the text currently entered in the control.	```csharp\nstring pg = cmbxPhotographer.Text;\n```
3	If the cmbxPhotographer control does not contain this text, then add the new string to the combo box.	```csharp\nif (!cmbxPhotographer.Items.Contains(pg))\n{\n _album.CurrentPhoto.Photographer = pg;\n cmbxPhotographer.Items.Add(pg);\n}\n```
4	Set the selected item to the new text.	```csharp\ncmbxPhotographer.SelectedItem = pg;\n}\n```

Our `ComboBox` is now updated whenever the user enters a new photographer, and the new entry will be available to other photographs in the same album.

Another change that might be nice is if the dialog automatically completed a partially entered photographer that is already on the list. For example, if the photographer "Erik Brown" is already present, and the user types in "Er," it would be nice to complete the entry on the user's behalf.

Of course, if the user is typing "Erin Smith," then we would not want to prevent the user from doing so. This can be done by causing the control to select the auto-filled portion of the name as the user types. You will be able to experiment with this behavior yourself after following the steps in the subsequent table.

AUTO-COMPLETE THE TEXT ENTRY AS THE USER TYPES		
	Action	**Result**
5	Add a TextChanged event handler for the cmbxPhotographer control.	```csharp\nprivate void cmbxPhotographer_TextChanged\n (object sender, System.EventArgs e)\n{\n```
6	Search for the current text in the list portion of the combo box.	```csharp\nstring text = cmbxPhotographer.Text;\nint index\n = cmbxPhotographer.FindString(text);\n```
7	If found, then adjust the text in the control to include the remaining portion of the matching entry.	```csharp\nif (index >= 0)\n{\n // Found a match\n string newText = cmbxPhotographer.\n Items[index].ToString();\n cmbxPhotographer.Text = newText;\n\n cmbxPhotographer.SelectionStart\n = text.Length;\n cmbxPhotographer.SelectionLength\n = newText.Length - text.Length;\n}\n}\n```

This code uses the `FindString` method to locate a match for the entered text. This method returns the index of the first object in the list with a display string beginning with the specified text. If no match is found, then a −1 is returned.

```
int index = cmbxPhotographer.FindString(text);
```

When a match is found, the text associated with this match is extracted from the list and assigned to the text box portion of the control.

```
if (index >= 0)
{
  // Found a match
  string newText = cmbxPhotographer.Items[index].ToString();
  cmbxPhotographer.Text = newText;
```

The additional text inserted into the text box is selected using the `SelectionStart` and `SelectionLength` properties. The `SelectionStart` property sets the cursor location, and the `SelectionLength` property sets the amount of text to select.

```
  cmbxPhotographer.SelectionStart = text.Length;
  cmbxPhotographer.SelectionLength = newText.Length - text.Length;
}
```

TRY IT!   The list portion of the control can be forced to appear as the user types with the `DroppedDown` property. Set this property to `true` in the `Text-Changed` handler to display the list box when a match is found.

You may have realized that this handler introduces a slight problem with the use of the backspace key. When text is selected and the user presses the backspace key, the selected text is deleted rather than the previously typed character as a user would normally expect. Fix this behavior by handling the `KeyPress` event, discussed in chapters 9 and 12, to force the control to delete the last character typed rather than the selected text.

Before leaving our discussion of `ListControl` objects, it is worth noting that the controls we have discussed so far all contain textual strings. The .NET Framework automatically handles the drawing of these text strings within the list window. It is possible to perform custom drawing of the list elements, in a manner not too different than the one we used for our owner-drawn status bar panel in chapter 4.

As a final example in this chapter, let's take a look at how this is done.

10.5   OWNER-DRAWN LISTS

Typically, your `ListBox` and `ComboBox` controls will each display a list of strings. You assign objects to the list, and the `ToString` method is used to retrieve the string to display in the list. The `string` value of a specific property can be displayed in place of the `ToString` method by setting the `DisplayMember` property for the list. The .NET Framework retrieves and draws these strings on the form, and life is good.

There are times when you do not want to display a string, or when you would like to control exactly how the string looks. For these situations you must draw the list manually. This is referred to as an *owner-drawn list*, and the framework provides specific events and other mechanisms for drawing the list items in this manner.

In this section we modify our main `ListBox` control for the application to optionally include a small representation of the image associated with each photograph. Such an image is sometimes called a *thumbnail*, since it is a "thumbnail-sized" image. An example of our list box displaying these thumbnails is shown in figure 10.7. As you can see, the list includes a thumbnail image as well as the caption string from the photograph.

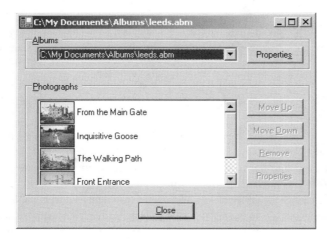

Figure 10.7
The ListBox here shows both the image and the caption for each photograph. Note how none of the items are selected in this list.

We will permit the user to switch between the thumbnail and pure text display using a context menu associated with the list box. This menu will be somewhat hidden, since users will not know it exists until they right-click on the list control. A hidden menu is not necessarily a good design idea, but it will suffice for our purposes. We will begin our example by adding this new menu.

10.5.1   ADDING A CONTEXT MENU

Since we would like to dynamically switch between an owner-drawn and a framework-drawn control, we need a way for the user to select the desired drawing method. We will use a menu for this purpose, and include a check mark next to the menu when the thumbnail images are shown. Context menus were discussed in chapter 3, so the following steps should be somewhat familiar.

Set the version number of the MyAlbumEditor application to 10.5.

	ADD A CONTEXT MENU	
	Action	**Result**
1	Add a ContextMenu control named ctxtPhotoList to the form in the MainForm.cs [Design] window.	
2	Add a single menu item to this context menu. **Settings** **Property** / **Value** (Name) / menuThumbs Text / &Thumbnail	
3	Set the ContextMenu property for the ListBox control to this new menu.	
4	Add a Click handler for the new menu item to reverse the Checked state of this menu.	```private void menuThumbs_Click\n (object sender, System.EventArgs e)\n{\n menuThumbs.Checked = ! menuThumbs.Checked;```
5	When checking the menu, set the DrawMode for the Photographs list to be owner-drawn.	``` if (menuThumbs.Checked)\n {\n lstPhotos.DrawMode\n = DrawMode.OwnerDrawVariable;\n }```
6	When unchecking the menu, set the DrawMode to its default setting. Also reset the default item height.	``` else\n {\n lstPhotos.DrawMode = DrawMode.Normal;\n lstPhotos.ItemHeight\n = lstPhotos.Font.Height + 2;\n }\n}```

The Click handler for our new menu simply toggles its Checked flag and sets the drawing mode based on the new value. The DrawMode property is used for both the ListBox and ComboBox controls to indicate how each item in the list will be drawn. The possible values for this property are shown in .NET Table 10.6. Since the size of our photographs in an album may vary, we allow the size of each element in the list to vary as well. As a result, we use the DrawMode.OwnerDrawVariable setting in our code.

The ItemHeight property contains the default height for each item in the list. When the DrawMode property is set to Normal, we set this property to the height of the current font plus 2 pixels. For our owner-drawn list, the item height depends on the size of the photograph we wish to draw. This requires that we assign the item height dynamically, and this is our next topic.

The `DrawMode` enumeration specifies the drawing behavior for the elements of a control. This enumeration is part of the `System.Windows.Forms` namespace. Controls that use this enumeration include the `ListBox`, `CheckedListBox`, and `ComboBox` classes, although the `CheckedListBox` class only supports the `Normal` setting.

Enumeration Values	Normal	All elements in the control are drawn by the .NET Framework and are the same size.
	OwnerDrawFixed	Elements in the control are drawn manually and are the same size.
	OwnerDrawVariable	Elements in the control are drawn manually and may vary in size.

10.5.2   SETTING THE ITEM HEIGHT

Since a `ListBox` normally holds text in a specific font, the default height of each list box item is just large enough to accommodate this font. In our case, we want to draw an image in each item, so the height of the default font is likely a bit on the small side. We can assign a more appropriate item height by handling the `MeasureItem` event. This event occurs whenever the framework requires the size of an owner-drawn item.

Note that this event does not occur with the setting `DrawMode.OwnerDrawFixed`, since the items are by definition all the same size. For this setting, the `ItemHeight` property should be assigned to the common height of the items. Since we are using the `DrawMode.OwnerDrawVariable` setting, this event will occur each time a list item must be custom drawn.

The `MeasureItemEventArgs` class provides the event data necessary to determine the size of an owner-drawn item. This class is part of the `System.Windows.Forms` namespace, and inherits from the `System.EventArgs` class.

Public Properties	Graphics	Gets the graphics object to use when calculating measurements.
	Index	Gets the index of the item to measure.
	ItemHeight	Gets or sets the height of the specified item.
	ItemWidth	Gets or sets the width of the specified item.

A `MeasureItem` event handler receives a `MeasureItemEventArgs` class instance to permit an application to set the width and height of a given item. Specifics of this class are shown in .NET Table 10.7. In our case, we are drawing an image followed by a string. We will fit the image into a 45×45 pixel box, and use the `Caption` property as the string portion.

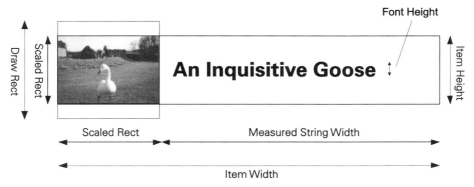

Figure 10.8   This figure shows the various measurements used to calculate a list item's width and height.

The following steps implement the code required for the `MeasureItem` event. Figure 10.8 illustrates the various measurements used to determine the width and height of the item.

	CALCULATE THE LIST ITEM SIZE DYNAMICALLY	
	Action	**Result**
1	In the MainForm.cs window, add a static `Rectangle` to the `MainForm` class to hold the drawing rectangle for the image.	`private static Rectangle _drawRect` `    = new Rectangle(0,0,45,45);`

2	Add a `MeasureItem` event handler for the `lstPhotos` list box.	`private void lstPhotos_MeasureItem`
		`    (object sender,`
		`        Windows.Forms.MeasureItemEventArgs e)`
		`{`

3	Calculate the size of the image when scaled into the drawing rectangle.	`Photograph p = _album[e.Index];`
		`Rectangle scaledRect`
		`    = p.ScaleToFit(_drawRect);`

4	Calculate the item's height.	`e.ItemHeight = Math.Max(scaledRect.Height,` `    lstPhotos.Font.Height) + 2;`

5	Calculate the item's width.	`e.ItemWidth = scaledRect.Width + 2`
		`    + (int) e.Graphics.MeasureString(`
		`        p.Caption, lstPhotos.Font).Width;`
		`}`

For the item's height, this code uses the larger of the scaled item's height and the `ListBox` control's font height, plus 2 pixels as padding between subsequent items in the list.

```
e.ItemHeight = Math.Max(scaledRect.Height, lstPhotos.Font.Height) + 2;
```

For the item's width, the width of the scaled image plus the width of the drawn string is used, plus 2 pixels as padding between the image and the text. To do this, the

`Graphics.MeasureString` method is used to calculate the size of the string when drawn with the `Font` object used by the `ListBox` control.

```
e.ItemWidth = scaledRect.Width + 2
    + e.Graphics.MeasureString(p.Caption, lstPhotos.Font);
```

Our final task is to draw the actual items using the `DrawItem` event.

10.5.3   DRAWING THE LIST ITEMS

As you may recall, the `DrawItem` event and related `DrawItemEventArgs` class were discussed in chapter 4. See .NET Table 4.4 on page 119 for an overview of the `DrawItemEventArgs` class.

Before we look at how to draw the list items in our application, let's make a small change to the Photograph class to improve the performance of our drawing. Since we may have to draw an item multiple times, it would be nice to avoid drawing the thumbnail from the entire image each time. To avoid this, let's create a `Thumbnail` property in our `Photograph` class to obtain a more appropriately sized image.

Set the version number of the MyPhotoAlbum library to 10.5.

	STORE A THUMBNAIL IMAGE IN THE PHOTOGRAPH OBJECT	
	Action	**Result**
1	In the Photograph.cs file, create an internal _thumbnail field to store the new thumbnail image.	`. . .` `private Bitmap _thumbnail = null;`

2	Update the `Dispose` method to properly dispose of the new object.	`public void Dispose()`
		`{`
		`    if (_bitmap != null`
		`        && _bitmap != InvalidPhotoImage)`
		`        _bitmap.Dispose();`
		
		`    if (_thumbnail != null)`
		`        _thumbnail.Dispose();`
		
		`    _bitmap = null;`
		`    _thumbnail = null;`
		`}`

3	Add a static constant to store the default width and height for a thumbnail.	`private const int ThumbSize = 90;`

	Action	Result

4	Add a property to retrieve the thumbnail.
	
	Note: While we draw our list items into a 45-pixel box, we draw our thumbnail into a 90-pixel box. Aside from the fact that we might want to use the Thumbnail property in other code, it is beneficial, when downsizing an image, to have an original image with a higher resolution than the final size.
		<pre>public Bitmap Thumbnail
		{
		  get
		  {
		    if (_thumbnail == null)
		    {
		      // Create the "thumbnail" bitmap
		      Rectangle sr = this.ScaleToFit(
		          new Rectangle(0,0,
		                  ThumbSize,ThumbSize));
		      Bitmap bm = new Bitmap(sr.Width,
		                  sr.Height);
		      Graphics g = Graphics.FromImage(bm);
		      GraphicsUnit u = g.PageUnit;
		      g.DrawImage(this.Image,
		              bm.GetBounds(ref u));
		
		      _thumbnail = bm;
		    }
		
		    return _thumbnail;
		  }
		}</pre>

This ensures that we will not have to load up and scale the full-size image every time we draw an item. With this property in place, we have everything we need to draw our list items.

	Action	Result
HANDLE THE DrawItem EVENT TO DRAW A LIST ITEM		

5	Add a static Brush field to the MainForm.cs file.	<pre>private static SolidBrush _textBrush
		    = new SolidBrush(SystemColors.WindowText);</pre>
		Note: This will improve the performance of our handler by eliminating the need to recreate a brush each time an item is drawn.

6	Add a DrawItem event handler for the ListBox control.	<pre>private void lstPhotos_DrawItem
		  (object sender,
		   System.Windows.Forms.DrawItemEventArgs e)
		{</pre>

7	To implement this method, get the Graphics and Photograph objects required for this handler.	<pre>Graphics g = e.Graphics;
		Photograph p = _album[e.Index];</pre>

	Action	Result

8	Calculate the `Rectangle` that will contain the thumbnail image.
	
	How-to
	a. Use `e.Bounds` to obtain the bounding rectangle for item.
	b. Adjust this rectangle based on the size of the scaled image.
		<pre>Rectangle scaledRect
		    = p.ScaleToFit(_drawRect);
		Rectangle imageRect = e.Bounds;
		imageRect.Y += 1;
		imageRect.Height = scaledRect.Height;
		imageRect.X += 2;
		imageRect.Width = scaledRect.Width;</pre>

9	Draw the thumbnail image into this rectangle.
	
	How-to
	a. Use `DrawImage` to paint the thumbnail into the rectangle.
	b. Use `DrawRectangle` to paint a black border around the image.
		<pre>g.DrawImage(p.Thumbnail, imageRect);
		g.DrawRectangle(Pens.Black, imageRect);</pre>

10	Calculate the `Rectangle` that will contain the caption for the image.
	
	How-to
	Use the bounding rectangle without the image area and centered vertically for the current font.
		<pre>Rectangle textRect = new Rectangle(
		    imageRect.Right + 2,
		    imageRect.Y + ((imageRect.Height
		                - e.Font.Height) / 2),
		    e.Bounds.Width - imageRect.Width - 4,
		    e.Font.Height);</pre>

11	If the current item is selected, make sure the text will appear selected as well.
	
	How-to
	a. Use the `State` property to determine if this item is selected.
	b. Use the system `Highlight` color for the background.
	c. Use the `HighlightText` color for the actual text.
		<pre>if ((e.State & DrawItemState.Selected)
		        == DrawItemState.Selected)
		{
		  _textBrush.Color
		      = SystemColors.Highlight;
		  g.FillRectangle(_textBrush, textRect);
		  _textBrush.Color
		      = SystemColors.HighlightText;
		}</pre>
		Note: The `State` property used here defines the state settings for the current item. This contains an or'd set of values taken from the `DrawItemState` enumeration. The code here is preferred over the use of a method such as `ListBox.GetSelected` since these and other methods may not reflect recent user changes until after the `DrawItem` event is processed.

	Action	Result
12	If the current item is not selected, make sure the text will appear normally. **How-to** a. Use the system `Window` color for the background. b. Use the `WindowText` color for the actual text.	```\nelse\n{\n _textBrush.Color = SystemColors.Window;\n g.FillRectangle(_textBrush, textRect);\n _textBrush.Color\n = SystemColors.WindowText;\n}\n```
13	Draw the caption string in the text rectangle using the default font.	```\ng.DrawString(p.Caption, e.Font,\n _textBrush, textRect);\n}\n```

Well done! You've just created your first owner-drawn list box. This code provides a number of features that should be useful in your own applications. It includes how to draw the image as well as the string for the item, and how to handle selected and deselected text. Compile and run the application. Click the Thumbnail context menu and watch the list display thumbnails. Click it again and the list reverts to normal strings.

TRY IT!　Our list box currently displays the file name for each photograph when DrawMode is Normal, and the caption string when DrawMode is OwnerDrawVariable. It would be nice if the user could select which string to display in either mode.

Try implementing this change by adding additional entries to the ListBox control's context menu. Add a parent menu called "Display As," and a submenu to allow the user to select between "File Name," "Caption," and "Photographer." Based on their selection, set the DisplayMember property for the list to the appropriate property string.

In normal draw mode, the framework picks up the DisplayMember property automatically. For the DrawItem event, you will need to retrieve the appropriate string based on the DisplayMember value. You can use string comparisons to do this, or use the System.Reflection namespace classes and types. This namespace is not discussed in detail in this book, but the following code excerpt can be used at the end of your DrawItem event handler to dynamically determine the value associated with the property corresponding to a given string.

```
PropertyInfo pi = typeof(Photograph).
  GetProperty(lstPhotos.DisplayMember);
object propValue = pi.GetValue(p, null);
g.DrawString(propValue.ToString(), e.Font,
  _textBrush, textRect);
```

This completes our discussion of list controls. The next section provides a quick recap of the chapter just in case you have already forgotten.

10.6 RECAP

This chapter discussed the basic list classes in the .NET Framework, namely the ListBox and ComboBox controls. We created a new application for this purpose, the MyAlbumEditor application, and built this application from the ground up using our existing MyPhotoAlbum library.

We began with a discussion of the common base class for list controls, namely the ListControl class, followed by a discussion of both single and multiple selection in the ListBox class. We saw how to enable and disable controls on the form based on the number of items selected, and how to handle double clicks for quick access to a common operation.

For the ComboBox class, we created a noneditable ComboBox to hold the list of available album files. Modifying the selected value automatically closed the previous album and opened the newly selected one. We then looked at an editable ComboBox for our photographer setting in the PhotoEditDlg dialog box. We discussed how to dynamically add new items to the list, and how to automatically select an existing item as the user is typing.

We ended with a discussion of owner-drawn list items by providing the option of displaying image thumbnails in our list box. We saw how to draw both images and text, including selected text.

There are additional controls than those discussed in chapters 9 and 10, of course. We will see some of these in the next chapter, and others as we continue our progression through the book. In chapter 11 we continue with our new MyAlbumEditor application, and look at Tab pages as a way to organize large amounts of information on a single form.

C H A P T E R   1 1

More controls

11.1 Tab controls 354
11.2 Tab pages 359
11.3 Dates and Times 366
11.4 Calendars 372
11.5 Recap 381

Chapters 9 and 10 examined basic controls such as buttons and labels, and list controls such as the `ListBox` class. In this chapter we discuss the tab controls and controls for displaying dates and times. Tab controls are especially useful when used to separate a large number of controls into logical groups within a single region of a form. The date controls, of course, are used to present and specify `DateTime` structures in a form.

The specific controls discussed in this chapter are the following:

- TabControl
- TabPage
- DateTimePicker
- MonthCalendar

Since the MyAlbumEditor project served us so well in chapter 10, we will continue to use this project here as well. Of course, any changes we make to our MyPhotoAlbum library will be available when we return to the MyPhotos project in chapter 12.

We begin our discussion with tab controls.

11.1 TAB CONTROLS

Tab controls are used to compact a large amount of data into a single form by segmenting the data into different screens, or *tab pages*. One of the more well-known examples of this construct is the Properties window associated with files and directories in the Windows file system. Right-click on a directory and select the Properties item, and you will see a window similar to figure 11.1. This figure shows the properties for the MyAlbumEditor directory containing the project we began in chapter 10. There are three tab pages available to display different types of directory properties: General, Web Sharing, and Sharing. The exact tabs displayed on your system may differ depending on which version of Windows you are running and the specific features installed and enabled.

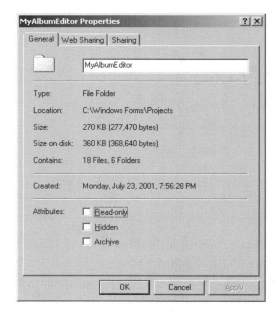

Figure 11.1
Users switch to a different tab page by clicking on the desired tab, or using the keyboard shortcut Ctrl+Tab.

You can create windows similar to figure 11.1 using the Windows Forms classes `Tab-Control` and `TabPage`. The `TabControl` class is a container for one or more `TabPage` objects, with each `TabPage` instance holding the tab information and set of controls to display for a specific page. Since I haven't shown you a class diagram for a few chapters, take a look at figure 11.2 showing the class hierarchy for the tab and tab page controls. It is also worth noting that the complete class hierarchy of all Windows Forms controls is shown in appendix C.

As shown in figure 11.2, the `TabControl` class inherits directly from the `Control` class we discussed in chapter 3. We will look at the members of this class in a moment. The `TabPage` class, on the other hand, inherits from the `Panel` class. This makes sense, since each page in a tab control contains a collection of controls, exactly like a `Panel` object. This also permits tab pages to automatically scroll if the display area exceeds the size of the window by using members of the `ScrollableControl` class. We saw how to enable this type of scrolling for `Form` and `Panel` objects in chapter 7.

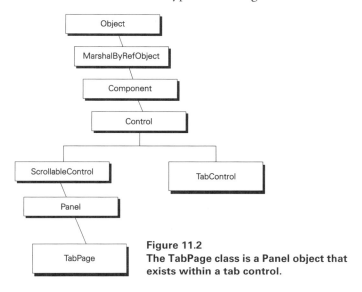

Figure 11.2
The TabPage class is a Panel object that exists within a tab control.

In this chapter we will look at the details of both the `TabControl` and the `TabPage` class. We examine the `TabControl` class first.

11.1.1   THE TABCONTROL CLASS

The `TabControl` class provides a container in which to manage a collection of `TabPage` objects. This container class provides members to control the location, appearance, and behavior of the pages in the control. Details on this class are provided in .NET Table 11.1.

Tab controls are often forgotten or perhaps forsaken by programmers. It is not uncommon to see a user interface packed full of buttons, labels, text boxes, and other controls. Often these are collected into group boxes to separate the information into logical groups. While such interfaces are very functional, they may not be so effective since users must process so much information at once. Visual Studio .NET allows multiple tab pages to be created for an interface quite easily, so perhaps programmers will think to use these constructs more often in the future. As a rule of thumb, make sure the controls in each tab page are all related, and try to limit yourself to no more than seven controls per page. The number seven here is not completely arbitrary, as user interface research has shown that this is a reasonable maximum number of items to present to a user at once.[1]

---

[1]   See the references listed in the bibliography for more information on this and other aspects of good user interface design.

The `TabControl` class is a control that presents a collection of tab pages to the user. Each tab page is represented by a `TabPage` class instance. This class is part of the `System.Windows.Forms` namespace, and inherits from the `Control` class. See .NET Table 4.1 on page 104 for a list of members inherited from the `Control` class, and .NET Table 11.2 on page 360 for details on the `TabPage` class.

Public Properties	Alignment	Gets or sets the area of the control where tabs are displayed, called the *tab strip*. Defaults to the top of the control.
	Appearance	Gets or sets how the tabs are displayed, such as a normal tab or 3D button.
	DrawMode	Gets or sets how the tabs are drawn in the control.
	HotTrack	Gets or sets whether the tabs change their appearance when the mouse passes over them.
	ImageList	Gets or sets the list of images to use on the control's tabs.
	ItemSize	Gets or sets the default size of each tab.
	Multiline	Gets or sets whether more than one line of tabs can be displayed.
	RowCount	Gets the number of rows currently displayed on the control's tab strip.
	SelectedIndex	Gets or sets the index of the currently selected tab page.
	SelectedTab	Gets or sets the currently selected `TabPage` object.
	ShowToolTips	Gets or sets whether the tool tips for each tab page should be displayed.
	SizeMode	Gets or sets how the tabs for the control are sized.
	TabCount	Gets the number of tab pages in the control.
	TagPages	Gets the collection of `TabPage` objects contained by this control.
Public Methods	GetTabRect	Returns the bounding `Rectangle` for a specified tab.
Public Events	DrawItem	Occurs when a tab must be drawn.
	SelectedIndexChanged	Occurs when a new tab page is selected.

11.1.2 CREATING A TAB CONTROL

Let's create a new tab control for our MyAlbumEditor project. We will do this by creating a new form to display the collection of images in an album. While this is not necessarily an efficient use of memory, it does provide a nice example of tab controls and tab pages. Figure 11.3 shows the new dialog with our favorite album displayed.

Note how the photograph's base file name is used as the text for each tab page, and how the full file path appears as a tool tip associated with each tab.

Figure 11.3
Each tab page in the tab control for this window displays an image stretched to fit a PictureBox control.

You may think that we need to add a new `Form` class to our project using Visual Studio .NET. This would certainly work, but you do not need a new file in Visual Studio every time a new form is required. Instead, we will create this form by hand. We will add a new `MenuItem` object to the context menu built in section 10.5 to provide access to this new form.

This section creates the new menu item and associated `Click` handler. The next section discusses tab pages, and will continue the implementation of this new form.

Set the version number of the MyAlbumEditor application to 11.1.

	ADD A NEW CONTEXT MENU ITEM	
	Action	**Result**
1	In the MainForm.cs [Design] window, add a menu separator to the `ContextMenu` object on the form.	
2	Add a new Images menu.	

		Settings	
	Property	**Value**	
	(Name)	menuImages	
	Text	&Images...	

| 3 | Add a `Click` handler for this menu. | `private void menuImages_Click`
`    (object sender, System.EventArgs e)`
`{`
`}` |

As you may recall, this context menu is associated with the lstPhotos control. Whenever the user right-clicks on list and selects our new item, the menuImages_Click handler will execute. In this handler we will create our new form.

The steps to create a tab control on a form programmatically are shown in the following table. The next section will add the individual tab pages to this form.

	IMPLEMENT THE CLICK EVENT HANDLER TO CREATE A NEW FORM	
	Action	**Result**

4	Create a new Form in the Click handler.	`private void menuImages_Click`
		`    (object sender, System.EventArgs e)`
		`{`
		`    Form imagesDlg = new Form();`

5	Create a TabControl object for the form.	`TabControl tcImages = new TabControl();`

6	Suspend the layout of both objects while the individual tab pages are created.	`imagesDlg.SuspendLayout();`
		`tcImages.SuspendLayout();`
		`// Create a tab page for each photo`
		`// (see next section)`

7	Initialize the tab control.
	
	Settings
	
	Property / **Value**
	Dock / Fill
	HotTrack / True
	ShowToolTips / True
		`tcImages.Dock = DockStyle.Fill;`
		`tcImages.HotTrack = true;`
		`tcImages.ShowToolTips = true;`

8	Initialize the form to contain the tab control.
	
	Settings
	
	Property / **Value**
	ShowInTaskbar / False
	Size / 400, 300
	Text / *as shown*
		`imagesDlg.Controls.Add(tcImages);`
		`imagesDlg.ShowInTaskbar = false;`
		`imagesDlg.Size = new Size(400, 300);`
		`imagesDlg.Text = "Images in "`
		`    + Path.GetFileName(_album.FileName);`

9	Resume layout of the container controls.	`tcImages.ResumeLayout();` `imagesDlg.ResumeLayout();`
10	Display the form as a modal dialog.	`imagesDlg.ShowDialog();` **Note:** We ignore the value returned by the ShowDialog method.
11	Dispose of the form.	`    imagesDlg.Dispose();` `}`

As you can see, this code creates a Form with a single TabControl object docked to fill the entire window area. The *hot tracking* feature causes a tab's text to change color as the mouse passes over the tab. Both this feature and tool tips are enabled for all tab pages in the control.

```
tcImages.Dock = DockStyle.Fill;
tcImages.HotTrack = true;
tcImages.ShowToolTips = true;
```

For the `Form` itself, a standard resizable window is used. The `tcImages` tab control is displayed on the form, and the base name of the album is assigned to the title bar. You can change this form into a more standard modal dialog box if you prefer, using the settings discussed in chapter 8. In our current code, only the `ShowInTaskBar` and `Size` properties are assigned.

```
imagesDlg.Controls.Add(tcImages);
imagesDlg.ShowInTaskbar = false;
imagesDlg.Size = new Size(400, 300);
imagesDlg.Text = "Images in " + Path.GetFileName(_album.FileName);
```

We display the form as a modal dialog to force the user to close this window before continuing with the application. Note that a Close button is not provided, so the user must close the form using the title bar, the system menu, or the keyboard shortcut Alt+F4.[2] After the `ShowDialog` method returns, we clean up the system resources assigned to the form by calling the `Dispose` method.

```
imagesDlg.ShowDialog();
imagesDlg.Dispose();
```

The application will run just fine with these changes. Of course, all you will see is a very empty `TabControl` object. We fill this in with `TabPage` controls in the next section.

11.2   TAB PAGES

Tab pages are the heart and soul of a tab control. They define the tabs displayed to the user and the layout of controls that appear when each page is displayed. An overview of the `TabPage` class is provided in .NET Table 11.2. As you can see, most of the behavior for tab pages is inherited from the `Panel` class. Normally, the .NET Framework displays each tab as a simple text string, as specified by the `Text` property for each page inherited from the `Control` class. Tabs are owner-drawn tabs if the `DrawMode` property for the containing tab control is set to `OwnerDrawFixed`. In this case, the `DrawItem` event for the `TabControl` must be handled to draw each tab by hand.

---

[2]   Of course, the `Form` object does not actually close in the technical sense of invoking the `Close` method. Since this is a modal dialog box, the framework only calls the `Hide` method here to permit additional access to the `Form` and its members. The word "close" is used here for lack of a better word.

The `TabPage` class represents a `Panel` object with an associated tab that exists within a `TabControl` object. It contains the set of controls and the tab for a single *sheet*, or *page*, of the tab control. The appearance and location of the tab is controlled by the TabControl class, as discussed in .NET Table 11.1.

This class is part of the `System.Windows.Forms` namespace, and inherits from the `Panel` class. An overview of the `Panel` class is provided in .NET Table 7.5 on page 218.

Public Properties	ImageIndex	Gets or sets an index into the `ImageList` associated with the `TabControl` object for this page. The corresponding image is displayed on this page's tab.
	ToolTipText	Gets or sets a string to display as the tool tip for this tab.

In our application, we will use normal textual tabs that are drawn by the framework. This section creates tab pages by hand and using Visual Studio .NET. First, we will finish the code started in the previous section to display the images associated with an album.

11.2.1   CREATING TAB PAGES DYNAMICALLY

Time for us to finish the `menuImages_Click` handler begun in section 11.1.2. This handler responds to the `Click` event for the Images menu associated with our List-Box control in the MyAlbumEditor application. We will create a `TabPage` control for each image in the album.

Set the version number of the MyAlbumEditor application to 11.2.

	CREATE THE TAB PAGES FOR THE IMAGESDLG FORM	
	Action	**Result**

1	Display the MainForm.cs file and locate the `menuImages_Click` event handler.	`private void menuImages_Click`
		`    (object sender, System.EventArgs e)`
		`{`

2	Insert a `foreach` loop to iterate over the photographs in the album.	`Form imagesDlg = new Form();`
		`TabControl tcImages = new TabControl();`
		`   . . .`
		
		`// Create a tab page for each photo`
		`foreach (Photograph photo in _album)`
		`{`

3	In the loop, create a `TabPage` object for the photo.	`string shortFileName`
		`    = Path.GetFileName(photo.FileName);`
		`TabPage newPage`
		`    = new TabPage(shortFileName);`
		
		`newPage.SuspendLayout();`

	Action	Result
4	Create a `PictureBox` control containing the image for this photo. **Settings** | Property	Value
---	---
BorderStyle	Fixed3D
Dock	Fill

SizeMode	StretchImage		```PictureBox pbox = new PictureBox();```
			```pbox.BorderStyle = System.Windows.```
			`    Forms.BorderStyle.Fixed3D;`
			```pbox.Dock = DockStyle.Fill;```
			```pbox.Image = photo.Image;```
			```pbox.SizeMode```
			`    = PictureBoxSizeMode.StretchImage;`

5	Add the picture box to the page.	```newPage.Controls.Add(pbox);```
6	Set the `ToolTipText` property for the page to the full file name of the photo.	```newPage.ToolTipText = photo.FileName;```

7	Add the new tab page to the tab control.	```tcImages.TabPages.Add(newPage);```
		```newPage.ResumeLayout();```
		`}`
		
		`. . .`
		```imagesDlg.ShowDialog();```
		```imagesDlg.Dispose();```
		`}`

This code will now create the required tab pages for each image, resulting in the dialog shown previously in figure 11.2. The complete implementation of the `menuImages_Click` handler is shown in the subsequent code. Since the individual lines were discussed in the previous tables, additional commentary is not provided. The annotated set of lines in this code is referenced in the TRY IT! text following the code.

```
private void menuImages_Click(object sender, System.EventArgs e)
{
  Form imagesDlg = new Form();
  TabControl tcImages = new TabControl();

  imagesDlg.SuspendLayout();
  tcImages.SuspendLayout();

  // Create a tab page for each photo
  foreach (Photograph photo in _album)
  {
    string shortFileName = Path.GetFileName(photo.FileName);
    TabPage newPage = new TabPage(shortFileName);

    newPage.SuspendLayout();

    // Create the PictureBox for this photo
    PictureBox pbox = new PictureBox();
    pbox.BorderStyle = System.Windows.Forms.BorderStyle.Fixed3D;
    pbox.Dock = DockStyle.Fill;
```

Display the image on the page ❶

```
pbox.Image = photo.Image;
pbox.SizeMode = PictureBoxSizeMode.StretchImage;

newPage.Controls.Add(pbox);
newPage.ToolTipText = photo.FileName;

tcImages.TabPages.Add(newPage);
newPage.ResumeLayout();
}

// Initialize the tab control
tcImages.Dock = DockStyle.Fill;
tcImages.HotTrack = true;
tcImages.ShowToolTips = true;

// Initialize the form
imagesDlg.Controls.Add(tcImages);
imagesDlg.ShowInTaskbar = false;
imagesDlg.Size = new Size(400, 300);
imagesDlg.Text = "Images in " + Path.GetFileName(_album.FileName);

tcImages.ResumeLayout();
imagesDlg.ResumeLayout();

// Display the dialog as modal and ignore any result
imagesDlg.ShowDialog();
imagesDlg.Dispose();
}
```

Compile and run your program to see this new dialog. This dialog is resizable, and the controls automatically resize with the window since we set the `Dock` property to `Fill` for our controls.

TRY IT! The `TabControl` here is created with the default behavior. You can change the location and style for the tabs by altering the `Alignment` and `Appearance` properties. Try setting these properties to alternate values to see how the control then appears. Also set the `Multiline` property to `true` and resize the form to see how multiple rows of tabs are displayed.

For a more complicated change, you will note that each image is displayed in a `PictureBox` control much like an image was displayed way back in chapter 2. This, of course, has the problem that the image is stretched and distorted as the window is resized. Fix this by replacing the use of the `PictureBox` control in the prior code block with a `Paint` event handler for the `TabPage` object. This code is annotated as ❶ in the prior code block with "Display the image on the page." As part of this change, assign the photo to the `Tag` property of the `newPage` object so you can retrieve this photo in the `Paint` handler. The replaced code should look something like the following:

```
// Assign a Paint event handler to draw this photo
newPage.Tag = photo;
newPage.Paint += new System.EventHandler(this.newPage_Paint);
```

Implement the `newPage_Paint` event handler to retrieve the `Photograph` stored in the sender's `Tag` parameter and paint the image with the proper aspect ratio. This should be similar to how we painted the image within the `Panel` for the `ScaleToFit` display option in chapter 7.

This example is a good reminder that Visual Studio .NET is not needed to create Windows Forms applications. Visual Studio provides a number of nice features that are useful for handling layout and complexity issues, as we have seen. Still, it is good to remember that Visual Studio is just a tool and not a required part of the C# language or the .NET Framework.

That said, managing a number of controls on multiple tab pages would get rather confusing without Visual Studio available. We will see how to use Visual Studio to create tab controls and pages next.

11.2.2 CREATING TAB PAGES IN VISUAL STUDIO

In this section we will replace the existing Photographs group box in the MyAlbum-Editor application with a tab control. This control will contain the controls currently in the Photographs group box. Here we will only create a single tab page. A second tab page will be added later in the chapter. Figure 11.4 shows how this new window will look.

Figure 11.4
The Photos tab will contain the controls we created in chapter 10. The tab, shown here on the left, can be placed on any side of the tab control.

As you can see, the `ListBox` and four `Button` controls have been moved inside a Photos tab page. To make this change, we need to delete the `GroupBox` control. If we delete the group box directly, we will also delete the contained controls. While we could delete the `GroupBox`, add the `TabControl` and a `TabPage`, and then recreate the controls inside, it would be much nicer if we could somehow move the controls into a tab page directly. This is, in fact, what we will do.

The solution is to use cut and paste just like you might when moving text around in a document. We will cut the controls from the group box and then paste them inside of a tab page. The steps required are described in the following table:

	Action	Result
	REPLACE THE GROUPBOX WITH A TABPAGE	
1	In the MainForm.cs [Design] window, highlight the set of controls inside the Photographs group box. **How-to** a. Click the ListBox control. b. Hold down the Ctrl key and click the four Button controls. **Alternately** Click inside the GroupBox control and drag a focus rectangle to include all five controls.	
2	Cut the selected controls to the Clipboard. **How-to** Select Cut from the Edit menu. **Alternately** Use the keyboard shortcut Ctrl+X.	
3	Delete the Photographs group box control from the form.	
4	Drag a TabControl object onto the form, and resize it to be about the same size as the deleted Photographs group box.	

	Action	Result
5	Add a `TabPage` object within the tab control. **How-to** a. Right-click the `TabControl` object. b. Select Add Tab from the menu. **Alternately** You can use the `TabPages` property of the tab control to display the TabPage Collection Editor dialog.	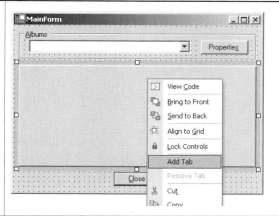
6	Insert the controls inside the `TabPage` control. Resize and position the controls if necessary. **How-to** a. Click inside the `TabPage` object to make it the active control. b. Select Paste from the Edit menu. **Alternately** Click inside the control and use the keyboard shortcut Ctrl+V.	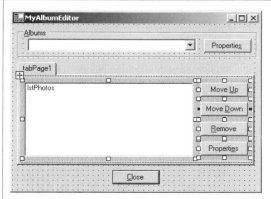
7	Set the properties for the tab control and page. **Settings**<table><tr><td>Control</td><td>Property</td><td>Value</td></tr><tr><td>TabControl</td><td>(Name)</td><td>tcPhotos</td></tr><tr><td></td><td>Alignment</td><td>Left</td></tr><tr><td></td><td>Anchor</td><td>Top, Bottom, Left, Right</td></tr><tr><td>TabPage</td><td>(Name)</td><td>tabPhotos</td></tr><tr><td></td><td>Text</td><td>Photos</td></tr></table>	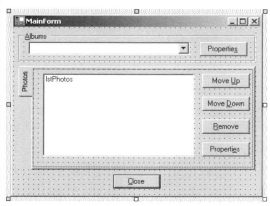

	Action	Result
8	Manually reestablish the event handlers for the controls. This includes the `DoubleClick`, `DrawItem`, `MeasureItem`, and `SelectedIndexChanged` event handlers for the list box, and the `Click` handlers for each of the four button controls. **How-to** Use the Events listing in the Properties window, and select the existing methods from the appropriate dropdown lists.	The event handlers for the controls are assigned to the appropriate events. **Note:** This step is required whenever a control is cut from one location and pasted into another. The event handlers are not preserved, although the properties of the controls are.

The Photographs group box is now replaced with a Photos tab page. This tab is aligned on the left side of the tab control. The `Alignment` property uses the `TabAlignment` enumeration, with possible values `Top`, `Bottom`, `Left`, and `Right`.

As you may have noticed, when the `Alignment` property for a tab control is `Left` or `Right`, the `Multiline` property is automatically set to `true`. Compile and run the application to make sure the controls still behave as expected, including multiple selection and the owner-drawn list feature via the Thumbnails menu.

We will add a second `TabPage` later in the chapter to display the set of dates associated with the album in a calendar format. This will enable a discussion of the `MonthCalendar` class. Before we can do this, we will first provide the appropriate support for the `DateTaken` property of the `Photograph` class.

11.3   DATES AND TIMES

We will return to tab pages and our MyAlbumEditor application in a moment. In this section we finally preserve the Date Taken value entered by the user in our `PhotoEditDlg` form. As you may recall, in chapter 9 we intentionally ignored this value to avoid converting the user-entered string value into a date. At the time we said there was a better way to deal with date constructs. In this section we finally see exactly what this looks like.

Dealing with dates and times is one of those issues that prevent some programmers from getting a good night's sleep. With 3600 seconds in an hour, and 24 hours in a day, and different days per month, and leap years almost but not quite every four years, it's no wonder. Fortunately, most languages and environments these days provide direct support for date-time values to simplify handling of these constructs. In the .NET Framework, this support extends to Windows Forms controls as well.

In chapter 5 we saw how the `DateTime` structure is used to represent a date-time value within a program. In this section we will look at representing a date-time value on a form using the `DateTimePicker` class, as summarized in .NET Table 11.3. This class displays a date and/or time to the user, and allows the user to change the values from the keyboard or from a dropdown calendar control. The dropdown calendar is based on the `MonthCalendar` class, which we will examine in the next section.

.NET Table 11.3 DateTimePicker class		
The `DateTimePicker` class represents a date and/or time value on a form. It allows the user to select a specific date and/or time, and presents this selection in a specified format. The `DateTime` value is presented in a text box control, with a down arrow providing access to a calendar from which an alternate date can be selected. The various parts of the `DateTime` value can alternately be modified using an up-down button or the arrow keys on the keyboard. This class is part of the `System.Windows.Forms` namespace, and inherits from the `Control` class. See .NET Table 4.1 on page 104 for a list of members inherited from this class.		
Public Properties	CalendarFont	Gets or sets the Font to apply to the calendar portion of the control.
	CalendarForeColor	Gets or sets the foreground color for the calendar.
	Checked	When the `ShowCheckBox` property is `true`, gets or sets whether the check box is checked.
	CustomFormat	Gets or sets the custom date-time format.
	Format	Gets or sets how the date-time value is formatted in the control.
	MaxDate	Gets or sets the maximum date-time value for the control.
	MinDate	Gets or sets the minimum date-time value for the control.
	ShowCheckBox	Gets or sets whether a check box displays to the left of the selected date.
	ShowUpDown	Gets or sets whether an up-down control is used to adjust the date-time value.
	Value	Gets or sets the `DateTime` value assigned to the control. Default is the current date and time.
Public Events	CloseUp	Occurs when the dropdown calendar is dismissed and disappears.
	DropDown	Occurs when the dropdown calendar is shown.
	FormatChanged	Occurs when the `Format` property changes.
	ValueChanged	Occurs when the `Value` property changes.

11.3.1   DATES AND TIMES

Our Photo Properties dialog with a `DateTimePicker` control in place is shown in figure 11.5. As you can see, the dropdown calendar control is displayed for the object.

Figure 11.5
The DateTimePicker shown here displays the Long date format, which is the default.

We can add this control to our dialog using the following steps. We will begin with the default display settings for this control, and look at how to modify these settings later in the section.

Set the version number of the MyPhotoAlbum application to 11.3.

	REPLACE THE DATE TEXT BOX WITH A DATETIMEPICKER CONTROL	
	Action	**Result**
1	In the PhotoEditDlg.cs [Design] window, delete the `TextBox` control next to the Date Taken label.	
2	Place a `DateTimePicker` control where the text box used to be. **Settings** <table><tr><td>**Property**</td><td>**Value**</td></tr><tr><td>(Name)</td><td>dtpDateTaken</td></tr><tr><td>TabIndex</td><td>5</td></tr></table>	**Note:** The location of this control is shown in figure 11.5.

3	Locate the `ResetSettings` method in the MainForm.cs source file.	`protected override void ResetSettings()`
		`{`
		`    // Initialize the ComboBox settings`
		`    . . .`

4	Set the `Value` property for the date and time control.
	
	How-to
	Use the `DateTaken` property.
		`Photograph photo = _album.CurrentPhoto;`
		
		`if (photo != null)`
		`{`
		`    txtPhotoFile.Text = photo.FileName;`
		`    txtCaption.Text = photo.Caption;`
		`    `**`dtpDateTaken.Value = photo.DateTaken;`**
		`    cmbxPhotographer.SelectedItem`
		`        = photo.Photographer;`
		`    txtNotes.Text = photo.Notes;`
		`}`
		`}`

	Action	**Result**
5	Locate the `SaveSettings` method.	`protected override void SaveSettings()` `{`

6	Set the `DateTaken` property to the date-time value specified by the user.	`Photograph photo = _album.CurrentPhoto;`
		
		`if (photo != null)`
		`{`
		`    photo.Caption = txtCaption.Text;`
		`    `**`photo.DateTaken = dtpDateTaken.Value;`**
		`    photo.Photographer`
		`        = cmbxPhotographer.Text;`
		`    photo.Notes = txtNotes.Text;`
		`}`
		`}`

REPLACE THE DATE TEXT BOX WITH A DATETIMEPICKER CONTROL *(continued)*

And there you have it. One `DateTimePicker` control ready to work. Compile and run the application, and set the dates for your photographs as appropriate. Make sure your albums preserve the selected date after exiting and restarting the program.

.NET Table 11.4   DateTimePickerFormat enumeration

The `DateTimePickerFormat` enumeration specifies how to display a date-time value in a `DateTimePicker` control. This enumeration is part of the `System.Windows.Forms` namespace. For each value, the default setting for the U.S. English culture is provided. The format codes used here correspond to the codes supported by the `DateTimeFormatInfo` class.

Enumeration Values	Custom	A custom format is used, as specified by the `CustomFormat` property.
	Long	The long date format is used. In Windows, this is typically "dddd, MMMM dd, yyyy" for U.S. English environments. This is the default value.
	Short	The short date format is used. In Windows, this is typically "MM/dd/yyyy" for U.S. English environments.
	Time	The time format is used. In Windows, this is typically "HH:mm:ss tt" for U.S. English environments.

You may have noticed that our control does not display the time. By default, the date and time control displays what .NET calls the *long date*. This includes the day of the week and month written out in the local language as well as the two-digit day and four-digit year. The format used by the control is specified by the `Format` property, using the `DateTimePickerFormat` enumeration described in .NET Table 11.4. As you can see from the table, various values allow either the date or time to be displayed in a format specified by the operating system.

11.3.2   CUSTOMIZING A DATETIMEPICKER CONTROL

As can be seen in .NET Table 11.4, a custom display setting for the `DateTime-Picker` control is used when the `Format` property is set to `DateTimePicker-`

Format.Custom. The CustomFormat property contains the string value to use in this case. A number of format codes are available within this string. These codes are managed by the sealed DateTimeFormatInfo class. The following table shows a number of these codes, along with some corresponding properties in the DateTimeFormatInfo class, which can be especially useful when operating in a multi-language environment. Consult the .NET documentation for the complete list of codes and additional information on the specified properties.

Date-time codes for the DateTimeFormatInfo class

Pattern	Description	Default U.S. English Values	DateTimeFormatInfo Property
d	Day of the month.	1 to 31	
dd	Two-digit day of the month.	01 to 31	
ddd	Abbreviated day of the week.	Sun to Sat	AbbreviatedDayNames
dddd	Full day of the week.	Sunday to Saturday	DayNames
M	Numeric month.	1 to 12	
MM	Two-digit numeric month.	01 to 12	
MMM	Abbreviated month name.	Jan to Dec	AbbreviatedMonthNames
MMMM	Full month name.	January to December	MonthNames
y	Year without century.	1 to 99	
yy	Two-digit year without century.	01 to 99	
yyyy	Four-digit century.	0001 to 9999	
gg	Period or era, if any.	B.C. or A.D.	
h	Hour on a 12-hour clock.	1 to 12	
hh	Two-digit hour on a 12-hour clock.	01 to 12	
H	Hour on a 24-hour clock.	1 to 24	
HH	Two-digit hour on a 24-hour clock.	01 to 24	
m	Minute.	0 to 59	
mm	Two-digit minute.	00 to 59	
s	Second.	0 to 59	
ss	Two-digit second.	00 to 59	
tt	AM/PM designator.	AM or PM	AMDesignator and PMDesignator
:	Default time separator.	: (a colon)	TimeSeparator
/	Default date separator.	/ (a slash)	DateSeparator
'c'	Displays the specified character. For example, 's' will display the character s rather than the number of seconds.		

Let's modify our date and time control to display a customized value. We will include both the date and time in the display.

DISPLAY A CUSTOM DATE-TIME VALUE IN THE DATETIMEPICKER CONTROL	
Action	**Result**
1 Display the properties for the `DateTimePicker` control in the PhotoEditDlg.cs [Design] window.	
2 Modify this control to display a custom format string.	The control displays the new format within Visual Studio.

Settings

Property	Value
CustomFormat	MM/dd/yy 'at' hh:mm tt
Format	Custom

If you compile and run these changes, you will find that the dropdown calendar still appears. The time values can be modified by hand or with the arrow keys. You might try using some alternate format strings, or setting the ShowUpDown property to true as a way to experiment with these customized settings.

The DateTimePicker class is great for displaying a single date-time value. When multiple dates or a range of dates are required, the MonthCalendar class can be used. We will discuss this control next.

More .NET As an alternative to a DateTimePicker control, another option here is to create separate controls for the month, day, and year, and if necessary the time of day. While the TextBox or ComboBox controls could be used for this purpose, you could also use the DomainUpDown and NumericUpDown controls. These controls are derived from the UpDownBase control, which in turn is based on the ContainerControl class presented in chapter 7.

The up-down controls present a text-box-like window that displays a range of values. The DomainUpDown control presents a string value taken from a collection of objects, while the NumericUpDown control presents a numeric value, optionally over a defined range.

For separate month, day, and year controls, the properties for the DateTime-FormatInfo class shown earlier in this section may be used to obtain the default set of month strings for display within a DomainUpDown control. The day and year values can be displayed in a NumericUpDown control, with the range set based on the current month and the requirements of the application.

11.4   CALENDARS

Sometimes a single date will not do. A scheduling program, for example, might need to show a calendar with meeting days highlighted, or display a meeting that covers a range of dates. The MonthCalendar class allows one or more months to be displayed on a Form, with individual days highlighted or a range of days selected.

Since our PhotoAlbum class permits each photograph to specify its own date, it seems appropriate to demonstrate the calendar control by highlighting the days in a calendar on which a photograph was taken. We will do this by adding a second TabPage object to our MyAlbumEditor main window. The result of our changes is shown in figure 11.6. Note how some dates are in bold to indicate one or more photographs were taken that day. If the user clicks on a date, a context menu pops up containing the corresponding photographs. When a photograph is selected from this context menu, the properties for that photograph are displayed.

The interface in figure 11.6 provides a very different view of our album. While the order of photographs in the album is not apparent, the specific days that a collection of pictures was taken is immediately available.

This section will discuss the month calendar control in general and add the control to a new tab page in our application. We will discuss how to bold the dates when photographs were taken, and how to process and respond to mouse clicks made within the control.

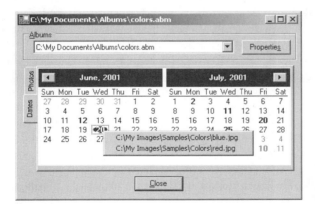

Figure 11.6
The MonthCalendar control will automatically display multiple months as it is resized.

11.4.1   ADDING A MONTHCALENDAR CONTROL

An overview of the MonthCalendar class is provided in .NET Table 11.5. This class handles the entire range of dates possible in DateTime objects, which is basically any date with a four-digit century. This class is a good way to display a series of dates related to an object or collection of objects.

.NET Table 11.5   MonthCalendar class

The `MonthCalendar` class represents a control that displays one or more months to the user. Days in each month can be displayed in bold, and the user can select single or multiple dates. This class is part of the `System.Windows.Forms` namespace, and inherits from the `Control` class. See .NET Table 4.1 on page 104 for a list of members inherited from this class.

Public Properties	AnnuallyBoldedDates	Gets or sets an array of `DateTime` objects that indicate which days to show in bold on an annual basis.
	BoldedDates	Gets or sets an array of `DateTime` objects of specific dates to show in bold.
	MaxDate	Gets or sets the maximum date. The user will not be able to display months occurring after this date.
	MaxSelectionCount	Gets or sets the maximum number of dates that can be selected in the control. Defaults to seven (7).
	ScrollChange	Gets or sets the number of months to scroll per click of a scroll button. Defaults to one (1).
	SelectionRange	Gets or sets the range of dates selected in the control.
	SelectionStart	Gets or sets the initial date of the range selected in the control.
	ShowToday	Gets or sets whether to display the `TodayDate` value at the bottom of the control.
	ShowTodayCircle	Gets or sets whether the `TodayDate` value is circled.
	TodayDate	Gets or sets the `DateTime` value used as today's date.
Public Methods	AddAnnuallyBoldedDate	Adds a day to display in bold on an annual basis.
	GetDisplayRange	Retrieves the range of dates displayed by the control.
	HitTest	Determines which aspect of the month calendar control is located at a specific point.
	RemoveBoldedDate	Removes a specific date from the list of nonrecurring bolded dates.
	SetDate	Selects the given date in the control.
Public Events	DateChanged	Occurs when the current date in the control is modified, such as when a new month is displayed.
	DateSelected	Occurs when the dates selected in the control are modified.

In our case, we will display the dates associated with a collection of photographs. Let's begin by adding a new `TabPage` containing a `MonthCalendar` control to our form.

Set the version number of the MyAlbumEditor application to 11.4.

CREATE THE DATES TAB PAGE		
	Action	**Result**

1	In the MainForm.cs [Design] window, add a second tab page to the `TabControl` object.

Settings

Property	Value
(Name)	tabDates
Text	Dates

2	Add a `MonthCalendar` control to this page.

Settings

Property	Value
(Name)	monthCalDates
Dock	Fill
MaxSelection-Count	1
ShowToday	False

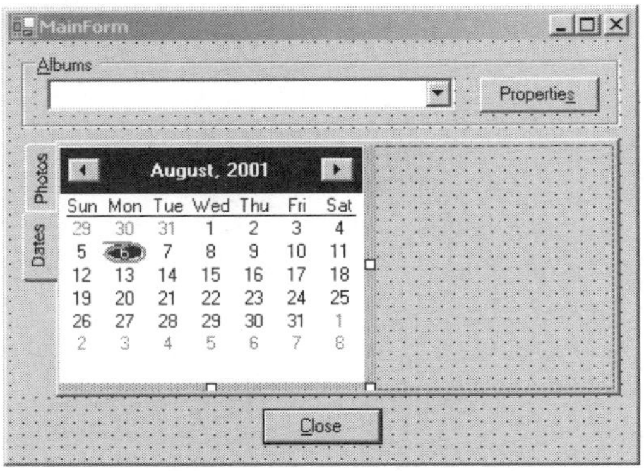

Note: Your `MonthCalendar` control will circle the current date, which is likely not the date shown in the graphic.

You will note that the `Dock` property for our month calendar object is set to `Fill`. This ensures that the number of months displayed will expand to fill the entire tab page as the form is enlarged. As we will see in the next section, months before the `MinDate` property value and after the `MaxDate` value will not be accessible from this control.

11.4.2 INITIALIZING A CALENDAR

Now that our `MonthCalendar` control is on the form, we can hook it up to our `PhotoAlbum` class. We do not want to initialize the calendar needlessly, so we will only do so when the Dates tab is displayed. By the same token, we do not want to initialize the `lstPhotos` list box needlessly, so we need to ensure that this only occurs when the Photos tab is displayed. Since we used the method `UpdateList` for our list box, we will create an `UpdateCalendar` method to initialize and update our `MonthCalendar` control.

The following steps are required for this change:

	INITIALIZE THE MONTH CALENDAR CONTROL	
	Action	**Result**
| 1 | In the MainForm.cs source file, add an `UpdateCalendar` method to update the `MonthCalendar` control in the Dates tab. | ```csharp
private void UpdateCalendar()
{
    // Initialize MonthCalendar control
``` |
| 2 | In this method, calculate the range of dates used by photographs in this album. | ```csharp
DateTime minDate = DateTime.MaxValue;
DateTime maxDate = DateTime.MinValue;

DateTime[] dates
    = new DateTime[_album.Count];
``` |
| 3 | For each `Photograph` in the album, record its date and adjust the minimum and maximum date as required. **Note:** We could use a `foreach` loop here, of course. A `for` loop works a little better since an index for the `dates` array is required. | ```csharp
for (int i = 0; i < _album.Count; i++)
{
    DateTime newDate
        = _album[i].DateTaken;
    dates[i] = newDate;

    if (newDate < minDate)
        minDate = newDate;

    if (newDate > maxDate)
        maxDate = newDate;
}
``` |
| 4 | Assign the `MonthCalendar` properties based on the calculated date values. **Note:** The `SelectionStart` property ensures that the initial date for the album is displayed by the calendar. | ```csharp
if (_album.Count > 0)
{
    monthCalDates.BoldedDates = dates;
    monthCalDates.MinDate = minDate;
    monthCalDates.MaxDate = maxDate;
    monthCalDates.SelectionStart = minDate;
}
}
``` |
| 5 | Add a new `UpdatePhotographs` method to update the appropriate tab page. **How-to** Use the `SelectedTab` property of the `tcPhotos` control. | ```csharp
private void UpdatePhotographs()
{
    if (tcPhotos.SelectedTab == tabPhotos)
        UpdateList();
    else if (tcPhotos.SelectedTab == tabDates)
        UpdateCalendar();
}
``` |
| 6 | Modify the `OpenAlbum` method to update the appropriate tab page. | ```csharp
private void OpenAlbum(string fileName)
{
    CloseAlbum();

    _album.Open(fileName);
    this.Text = _album.FileName;

    UpdatePhotographs();
}
``` |
| 7 | In the MainForm.cs [Design] window, handle the `SelectedIndexChanged` event for our tab control. **Note:** This is the default event for tab controls, and occurs whenever a new tab is selected by the user. | ```csharp
private void tcPhotos_SelectedIndexChanged
    (object sender, System.EventArgs e)
{
    UpdatePhotographs();
}
``` |
```

	Action	Result

8	Update the `SelectedIndexChanged` event handler for our combo box control to enable or disable the controls as required.
	
	Note: We take a slightly different approach here than we used earlier in the chapter. The final effect is the same.
		``csharp
		private void cmbxAlbums_SelectedIndexChanged
		    (object sender, System.EventArgs e)
		{
		  . . .
		  try
		  {
		    CloseAlbum();
		    OpenAlbum(albumPath);
		    tcPhotos.Enabled = true;
		    btnAlbumProp.Enabled = true;
		  }
		  catch (Exception)
		  {
		    // Unable to open album
		    this.Text = "Unable to . . . album";
		    tcPhotos.Enabled = false;
		    lstPhotos.Items.Clear();
		    monthCalDates.RemoveAllBoldedDates();
		    btnAlbumProp.Enabled = false;
		  }
		}
		``

Our calendar, as well as our list box, is updated whenever an album is opened and whenever the user displays an alternate tab page. Compile and run the application if you would like to see this in action. The next section processes the user's mouse clicks in the control to provide access to the `PhotoEditDlg` form associated with a selected date.

11.4.3 HANDLING MOUSE CLICKS IN A CALENDAR CONTROL

Our `MonthCalendar` control is on the form and displays the dates assigned to an album's photographs in bold. The next step is to handle clicks by the user and link them up with associated photographs.

We will handle the `MouseDown` event for this purpose, and create a `Context-Menu` object on the fly to display any photos associated with the selection point. The `MonthCalendar` class also provides the `DateChanged` event that occurs whenever a valid date is clicked. We could use this event instead, although the current mouse position would still be required to display the context menu. Since the `MouseDown` event provides the mouse location directly, this event seems a more logical choice.

We will discuss mouse events in more detail in the next chapter. Like the `Mouse-Move` event used in chapter 8, a `MouseDown` event handler receives a `MouseEvent-Args` that includes the current position of the mouse. We will use this position both to determine which aspect of the calendar the user clicked on and to display the context menu at the appropriate location.

Before we see how to add this handler, one other item is needed. When we create `MenuItem` objects for the context menu, we will need a way to retrieve the associated `Photograph` object if the user later selects the menu. While the `Control` class provides a `Tag` property that associates an `object` instance with a control, the `MenuItem` class has no such property. As a result, we have to deal with this unfortunate omission ourselves. In chapter 3, we created an array indexed by the menu location that linked a display mode to the menu. Now that we are more experienced, we will simply create a new class derived from `MenuItem` for a similar purpose.

	CREATE A CUSTOM MENUITEM CLASS TO HOLD THE ALBUM INDEX	
	Action	**Result**
1	Within the `MainForm` class definition, define a new `PhotoMenuItem` class based on the `MenuItem` class within the `MainForm` class.	`private class PhotoMenuItem : MenuItem` `{`
2	Add a public field in this class to hold the integer album index associated with the menu.	`    public int tag;` `}`

As you will see, this very simple class will make our click handling much more efficient. Let's take a look at this code.

	HANDLE A MOUSE CLICK IN THE CALENDAR CONTROL	
	Action	**Result**

3	Add an event handler for the `MouseDown` event in the `MonthCalendar` control.	`private void monthCalDates_MouseDown`
		`    (object sender,`
		`        System.Windows.Forms.MouseEventArgs e)`
		`{`

4	Determine if the user clicked on a date.
	How-to
	Use the `HitTest` method.
		`MonthCalendar.HitTestInfo info`
		`    = monthCalDates.HitTest(e.X, e.Y);`
		`if (info.HitArea`
		`        == MonthCalendar.HitArea.Date)`
		`{`

5	If so, create a new context menu to hold any photographs associated with this date.	`ContextMenu ctxtPhotoCal` `    = new ContextMenu();`
6	Iterate through the photos in the album.	`for (int i = 0; i < _album.Count; i++)` `{`

7	Look for any photographs taken on the same date as the date clicked by the user.
	How to
	Use the `Date` property to obtain only the date portion of the `DateTime` objects.
		`if (_album[i].DateTaken.Date`
		`        == info.Time.Date)`
		`{`

	Action	Result
8	If a matching photo is found, create a new `PhotoMenuItem` object for this photo. **How-to** a. Initialize the `tag` field to the photograph's index. b. Initialize the `MenuItem.Text` property to the image file name. c. Set a `Click` handler for this menu item.	```csharp\nPhotoMenuItem newItem\n = new PhotoMenuItem();\n\nnewItem.tag = i;\nnewItem.Text = _album[i].FileName;\nnewItem.Click += new\n EventHandler(\n ctxtPhotoCal_MenuClick);\n```
9	Add this new item to the context menu.	```csharp\nctxtPhotoCal.MenuItems.Add(newItem);\n }\n }\n```
10	If one or more matching photographs were found, display the context menu. **How-to** Use the `Show` method at the current mouse location.	```csharp\nif (ctxtPhotoCal.MenuItems.Count >= 1)\n{\n ctxtPhotoCal.Show(monthCalDates,\n new Point(e.X, e.Y));\n}\n }\n}\n```
11	Create a private `DisplayPhoto-EditDlg` method to accept an album index and display the associated dialog. **Note:** This method returns a boolean value indicating whether the user modified any settings.	```csharp\nprivate bool DisplayPhotoEditDlg(int index)\n{\n _album.CurrentPosition = index;\n\n using (PhotoEditDlg dlg\n = new PhotoEditDlg(_album))\n {\n if (dlg.ShowDialog() == DialogResult.OK)\n {\n _bAlbumChanged = true;\n return true;\n }\n }\n\n return false;\n}\n```
12	Implement a `ctxtPhoto-Cal_MenuClick` method to handle any context menu selection and display the associated Photo Properties dialog.	```csharp\nprivate void ctxtPhotoCal_MenuClick\n (object sender, System.EventArgs e)\n{\n PhotoMenuItem mi = sender as PhotoMenuItem;\n\n if ((mi != null)\n && (DisplayPhotoEditDlg(mi.tag)))\n {\n UpdateCalendar();\n }\n}\n```

	Action	Result
13	Update the `Click` handler for the photo's Properties button on the Photos tab page to use the new `DisplayPhotoEditDlg` method.	```private void btnPhotoProp_Click (object sender, System.EventArgs e) { if (_album.Count == 0) return; if (lstPhotos.SelectedIndex >= 0) { if (DisplayPhotoEditDlg(lstPhotos.SelectedIndex)) { UpdateList(); } } }```

When the user clicks on the `MonthCalendar` control, this code will find and display any photographs associated with a selected date. Note how the `HitTest` method is used to retrieve information about the selected point. This method returns a `Hit-TestInfo` object. The `HitTestInfo` class is defined within the `MonthCalendar` class, and provides a `HitArea` property containing the type of area clicked by the user, and a `Time` property containing the `DateTime` value corresponding to the selected item. The possible values for the `HitArea` property are defined by the `MonthCalendar.HitArea` enumeration, as described in .NET Table 11.6.

```
private void monthCalDates_MouseDown
    (object sender, System.Windows.Forms.MouseEventArgs e)
{
  MonthCalendar.HitTestInfo info = monthCalDates.HitTest(e.X, e.Y);
  if (info.HitArea == MonthCalendar.HitArea.Date)
  {
```

Another important part of this code is the definition and use of the `PhotoMenuItem` class. Without this class, we would be forced to search for a selected photograph based on the file name stored in the `Text` property of the menu. This rather simple extension to `MenuItem` provides an efficient method of communicating a photograph's index from the context menu to a menu item's `Click` handler.

```
private class PhotoMenuItem : MenuItem
{
  // An integer field to store a photograph's index
  public int tag;
}
```

Because this class is still a `MenuItem` instance, we can use it just like any other menu item object. We can set the `Text` property, establish a `Click` event handler, and add the menu to our context menu.

```
PhotoMenuItem newItem = new PhotoMenuItem();

newItem.tag = i;
```

```
newItem.Text = _album[i].FileName;
newItem.Click += new EventHandler(ctxtPhotoCal_MenuClick);

// Add this item to the context menu
ctxtPhotoCal.MenuItems.Add(newItem);
```

After the context menu has been displayed, the `Click` handler receives the menu item object selected by the user. We downcast the given `object` into a `PhotoMenuItem` instance in order to retrieve the index in the photo album and display the appropriate Photo Properties dialog.

```
private void ctxtPhotoCal_MenuClick(object sender, System.EventArgs e)
{
  PhotoMenuItem mi = sender as PhotoMenuItem;

  if ((mi != null) && (DisplayPhotoEditDlg(mi.tag)))
  {
    UpdateCalendar();
  }
}
```

Compile and run the application to see how all this code works. Click on a date where one or more photographs were taken and be amazed as a context menu pops up with the corresponding photos. Also try clicking on other aspects of the control to see what happens. In particular, see what happens when you click on the month and year in the title of the control. Note that your ability to alter the month and year displayed is restricted by the range of dates represented in the photo album.

More .NET The `PhotoMenuItem` class developed in this section extends the `MenuItem` object provided by the Windows Forms namespace. This technique is useful when you need a class that is similar to an existing control, and the ability to downcast objects in C# ensures that you can access the additional members of your derived class in a type-safe manner.

You can also build custom controls by extending the `Control` class directly. Windows Forms also provides a `UserControl` class that is specifically intended for building customized container controls. The Project menu in Visual Studio .NET includes an Add User Control item for creating such a control. There is a walkthrough in the .NET documentation entitled "Authoring a User Control with Visual C#" that introduces this concept.

Custom controls can also be tightly integrated into the Toolbox and other parts of Visual Studio .NET. The `System.Windows.Forms.Design` namespace contains the classes and other types to support such integration. If you are interested in this topic, search for more information at any of the .NET web sites listed in appendix D. In particular, as of this writing there is an article by Shawn Burke entitled "Writing Custom Designers for .NET Components" at the Microsoft Developer Network at msdn.microsoft.com.

The HitArea enumeration specifies the possible display areas in a MonthCalendar control. Typically, this is used when analyzing a specific point in a calendar control using the HitTest method. This enumeration is defined within the MonthCalendar class, and is part of the System.Windows.Forms namespace.

Enumeration Values	CalendarBackground	The specified point is part of the calendar's background.
	Date	The specified point is part of a specific date of the current month in the calendar. The Time property of the MonthCalendarInfo.HitTestInfo class is set to the corresponding DateTime value.
	DayOfWeek	The point is part of a day abbreviation, such as "Mon." The Time property should contain the date on the top row of the calendar.
	NextMonthButton	The point is part of the next month button at the top right of the control.
	NextMonthDate	The point is part of a date from the next month in the control.
	Nowhere	The point is not in the MonthCalendar control, nor is it in an active portion of the control. This is the default.
	PrevMonthButton	The point is part of the previous month button at the top left of the control.
	PrevMonthDate	The point is part of a date from the previous month in the control.
	TitleBackground	The point is over the background of a month's title.
	TitleMonth	The point is over a month name in the title of the control.
	TitleYear	The point is over a year value in the title of the control.
	TodayLink	The point is over the "today" link at the bottom of the control.
	WeekNumbers	The point is over a week number when these values are displayed. The Time property should contain the first date of that week.

11.5   RECAP

In this chapter we created tab controls and tab pages dynamically and using Visual Studio .NET. We modified our MyAlbumEditor application to use a tab control in place of the Photographs group box used in chapter 10. We then added a second tab to contain a calendar control displaying the dates when photographs in the album were taken, and permitted the user to click on a date to view the properties associated with the corresponding photographs.

We also examined the `DateTimePicker` class, and used this control in our `PhotoEditDlg` form to present the `DateTaken` property of a `Photograph` object. This led to a discussion of the formats used to display custom date-time strings.

In chapter 12 we will take up an assortment of different topics related to Windows Forms application development.

A .NET assortment

12.1 Keyboard events 384
12.2 Mouse events 387
12.3 Image buttons 393
12.4 Icons 405
12.5 Recap 409

In the last three chapters we looked at various controls available in the Windows Forms namespace, and demonstrated the use of these controls in applications. In this chapter we take a break from this aspect of Windows Forms development, and turn our attention to interacting with the keyboard and mouse, and the placement of images within certain controls.

For this discussion we return to the MyPhotos application we left in chapter 9. As usual, the Visual Studio.NET solution is available on the book's web site in case you have misplaced your copy. We will examine the following topics:

- Keyboard events

- Mouse events

- Placing images on button controls

- Icons in a form and an application

Our discussion will present each concept in a separate section, beginning with the keyboard events.

12.1 KEYBOARD EVENTS

We looked briefly at keyboard events in chapter 9 while discussing the `TextBox` class. There we used the `KeyPress` event to limit what characters could appear in a text box control. In this section we look more generically at keyboard events, and use them in our application to provide some quick shortcuts for the user.

There are three distinct events that occur whenever a key is pressed and released. Note that we did not say whenever a character is pressed and released. A character may involve multiple key presses. For example, the letter 'A' requires the use of the Shift key and the A key, typically abbreviated as Shift+A (of course, this is not true if the Caps Lock key is pressed, but you understand).

The three keyboard events are summarized in the following table. These events occur for a control in the order shown in the table whenever the control has the focus.

Keyboard events

Event	Description	Event Argument
KeyDown	Occurs when a key on the keyboard is pressed down.	`KeyEventArgs` class
KeyPress	Occurs when a character is pressed on the keyboard, and again each time the character is repeated while it continues to be pressed.	`KeyPressEventArgs` class
KeyUp	Occurs when a key on the keyboard is released.	`KeyEventArgs` class

12.1.1 HANDLING THE KEYPRESS EVENT

The `KeyPress` event is used for generic handling of keyboard characters. Event handlers of this type receive an instance of the `KeyPressEventArgs` class as its event parameter. See .NET Table 12.1 for an overview of this class.

.NET Table 12.1 KeyPressEventArgs class		
The `KeyPressEventArgs` class is the event argument class associated with the `KeyPress` event. This class represents the keyboard character pressed by the user. It is part of the `System.Windows.Forms` namespace, and inherits from the `System.EventArgs` class.		
Public Properties	Handled	Gets or sets whether the keyboard character was handled. If `true`, then the control will not receive the character.
	KeyChar	Gets the `char` value corresponding to the keyboard character pressed.

It is important to realize that this event, as well as the `KeyDown` and `KeyUp` events, is received by the control that currently has the focus. In particular, they are not normally received by parent controls such as `Panel` and `Form` objects that contain the control. Normally this is a good thing. The per-character behavior is defined by each control, with no need for parental involvement. For example, if you are handling the

`KeyPress` event to force a text box to contain only integer values, you do not want to spend precious operating system cycles percolating this event up through the set of containing objects for the text box. A parent control such as a `Panel` or `GroupBox` will only receive a keyboard event if it specifically has the focus.

This presents a slight problem for subclasses of the `ContainerControl` object, and in particular the `Form` object. As you may recall, a `ContainerControl` object manages the focus for the contained controls, and does not receive the focus directly. There are plenty of situations where you would like to initiate an action from the keyboard regardless of the current control.

The good folks at Microsoft created the `KeyPreview` property in the `Form` class for just this purpose. When this property is set to `true`, the `Form` object will receive all keyboard events before they are passed to the current control. If the event handler sets the `Handled` property to `true`, then the current control will not receive the keyboard key or corresponding character.

Let's create an example of this in our MyPhotos program by handling the plus '+' and minus '−' characters. The plus character will display the next photograph in the album, while the minus will display the previous photograph. We would like these to occur at the `Form` level, and not just in our `Panel` object where the image is displayed. The following table presents the steps required for this change.

Set the version number of the MyPhotos application to 12.1.

	MAP THE PLUS AND MINUS KEYS TO THE NEXT AND PREVIOUS MENUS	
	Action	**Result**
1	In the MainForm.cs [Design] window, modify the `KeyPreview` property for the `MainForm` object to be `true`.	
2	Override the protected `OnKeyPress` method in the MainForm.cs source file.	```protected override void OnKeyPress
(KeyPressEventArgs e)
{```
3	When a plus sign '+' is pressed, invoke the Next menu handler.	```switch (e.KeyChar)
{
case '+':
e.Handled = true;
menuNext.PerformClick();
break;```
4	When a minus sign '-' is pressed, invoke the Previous menu handler.	```case '-':
e.Handled = true;
menuPrevious.PerformClick();
break;```
5	For all other characters, do nothing. This permits the character to be sent to child controls.	```default: // do nothing
break;
}```
6	Don't forget to call the base class at the end of the method.	```base.OnKeyPress(e);
}```

We could have used an `if` statement in this code, especially with only two items to check. Since we may add behavior for additional characters in the future, a `switch` statement seems like a good idea. Note how we used the `MenuItem.PerformClick` method to simulate a user click of the appropriate menu. We could have called the `Click` event handler directly, of course, but this solution is a bit more elegant.

It should be noted here that not all characters are received by the `KeyPress` and other keyboard events. Depending on the control, some characters may be preprocessed and unavailable by default in this event. The protected `IsInputKey` and `IsInputChar` methods can be used to determine whether a specific character is preprocessed in a derived control.

Let's move on to the `KeyDown` and `KeyUp` events.

12.1.2 HANDLING OTHER KEYBOARD EVENTS

The `KeyDown` and `KeyUp` events are useful to fine-tune an application's behavior as keyboard keys are pressed and released, and for handling noncharacter keys such as the function or arrow keys. Handlers for these events receive an instance of the `KeyEventArgs` class as their event parameter. This class is summarized in .NET Table 12.2.

.NET Table 12.2 KeyEventArgs class		
The `KeyEventArgs` class is the event argument class associated with the `KeyDown` and `KeyUp` events. This class represents the keyboard key pressed down or released by the user. It is part of the `System.Windows.Forms` namespace, and inherits from the `System.EventArgs` class.		
Public Properties	Alt	Gets whether the Alt key was pressed.
	Control	Gets whether the Ctrl key was pressed.
	Handled	Gets or sets whether the event was handled.
	KeyCode	Gets the specific keyboard key pressed as a value in the `Keys` enumeration.
	KeyData	Gets the combination of keyboard keys pressed at the same time using the `Keys` enumeration values.
	KeyValue	Gets the `int` character value corresponding to the keyboard combination.
	Modifiers	Gets the combination of modifier keys pressed or released using the `Keys` enumeration values. This is a combination of the `Ctrl`, `Shift`, and `Alt` values, or `None` if no keys were pressed.
	Shift	Gets whether the Shift key was pressed.

We will demonstrate the use of the `KeyEventArgs` class by setting the Page Up and Page Down keys to invoke the Previous and Next menus, respectively. We will use the `KeyDown` event for this purpose. We have already set the `KeyPreview` property to receive keyboard events in our `Form`, so all we have to do is override the `OnKeyDown` method here.

	Action	Result
| 1 | In the MainForm.cs source window, override the OnKeyDown method. | ```
protected override void OnKeyDown
    (KeyEventArgs e)
{
``` |
| 2 | Invoke the Previous menu when the Page Up key is pressed down. | ```
switch (e.KeyCode)
{
    case Keys.PageUp:
        e.Handled = true;
        menuPrevious.PerformClick();
        break;
``` |
| 3 | Invoke the Next menu when the Page Down key is pressed down. | ```
    case Keys.PageDown:
        e.Handled = true;
        menuNext.PerformClick ();
        break;
``` |
| 4 | Do nothing by default. | ```
    default: // do nothing
        break;
}

base.OnKeyDown(e);
}
``` |

Run the program to see how this code works. Open an album and make sure all four keys we handled work as expected.

TRY IT! Modify the OnKeyDown method to recognize the Home and End keys as well. Have the Home key display the first photograph in the album, and the End key display the last.

As an alternate approach, modify this method so that Shift+PageDown will display the last photograph, and Shift+PageUp the first photograph in the album. To implement this change, you will need to modify the method to check the Shift property within the PageUp and PageDown case blocks.

That's probably enough for our quick look at keyboard events. Let's also take a look at mouse events.

12.2 MOUSE EVENTS

The mouse device has gone through its own little evolution since it was invented by Xerox Corporation almost 30 years ago. The number of buttons have varied from one to three, and the shape has evolved from a rather uncomfortable rectangle to the hand-fitting contours found in most modern versions. The mouse wheel is a rather recent addition, permitting automated scrolling from the comfort of your mouse. An even newer addition is a five-button mouse, with the extra buttons intended for backward/forward navigation in applications such as web browsers.

Regardless of the type mouse you own, the possible events in .NET are the same. In chapter 8 we used the MouseMove event to update the PixelDlg form as the mouse pointer changed position. In the previous chapter we used the MouseDown event in our MonthCalendar control to pop up a context menu when the user clicked on a date. Here, we look at mouse events in general.

Mouse events are somewhat similar to keyboard events. Mouse buttons go down and up just like keyboard keys, and the events MouseDown and MouseUp occur accordingly. Since the mouse also controls the mouse pointer, there are events related to pointer movement as well. The complete list of mouse events is shown in the following table. These events occur with respect to a specific control.

Mouse events

Event	Description	Event Argument
MouseDown	Occurs when a mouse button is pressed down while the pointer is over the control.	MouseEventArgs class
MouseEnter	Occurs when the mouse pointer enters the control.	MouseEventArgs class
MouseHover	Occurs when the mouse pointer remains, or hovers, over a control for a configurable amount of time.	MouseEventArgs class
MouseLeave	Occurs when the mouse pointer leaves the control.	MouseEventArgs class
MouseMove	Occurs when the mouse pointer moves over the control.	MouseEventArgs class
MouseUp	Occurs when a mouse button is released while the pointer is over the control.	MouseEventArgs class
MouseWheel	Occurs when the mouse wheel moves while the control has focus. The read-only MouseWheelPresent property in the SystemInformation class indicates whether the operating system believes a mouse wheel is present.	MouseEventArgs class

12.2.1 THE MOUSEEVENTARGS CLASS

As you can see from the table, all mouse event handlers received an instance of the MouseEventArgs class as their event parameters. A summary of this class appears in .NET Table 12.3. We will illustrate mouse events a few different ways in this chapter. Our first example will combine the keyboard support we examined in the previous chapter with mouse events.

12.2.2 HANDLING MOUSE EVENTS

Since we have seen a couple of mouse events before, let's make a change that involves both keyboard and mouse events. Keeping with our theme of the Previous and Next menus, let's modify the mouse button behavior in our Panel control so that the left and right buttons invoke the Previous and Next menus, respectively, when the Ctrl key is pressed.

The `MouseEventArgs` class is the event argument class associated with the mouse events. This class represents information about the mouse device and the mouse pointer position when the event occurs. It is part of the `System.Windows.Forms` namespace, and inherits from the `System.EventArgs` class.

Properties	Button	Gets the `MouseButtons` enumeration value corresponding to the mouse button pressed by the user.
	Clicks	Gets the number of times the mouse button was pressed and released. Note that the `DoubleClick` event should normally be used to process double-clicks of the mouse.
	Delta	Gets a signed integer representing the number of detents the mouse wheel has rotated. A *detent* is a rotation of the mouse wheel by one notch.
	X	Gets the x-coordinate of the current mouse pointer position.
	Y	Gets the y-coordinate of the current mouse pointer position.

This requires handling both the `KeyDown` and `KeyUp` events to track when the Ctrl key is held down, and the `MouseDown` event to map a mouse click to the appropriate menu. Once we have done this, we will discover some additional changes that will improve our interface. First, let's take a look at how to track the Ctrl key.

Set the version number of the MyPhotos application to 12.2.

	TRACK WHEN THE CTRL KEY IS HELD DOWN	
	Action	**Result**
1	In the MainForm.cs window, create a boolean field to identify when the Ctrl key is held down.	`private bool ctrlKeyHeld = false;`

2	Modify the `OnKeyDown` method to set this field to `true`.	`protected override void OnKeyDown`
		`    (KeyEventArgs e)`
		`{`
		`    switch (e.KeyCode)`
		`    {`
		`        . . .`
		`        case Keys.ControlKey:`
		`            ctrlKeyHeld = true;`
		`            break;`
		`        . . .`
		`    }`
		`    . . .`
		`}`

	Action	Result
3	Override the OnKeyUp method to set this field to false.	```protected override void OnKeyUp
    (KeyEventArgs e)
{
  switch (e.KeyCode)
  {
    case Keys.ControlKey:
      ctrlKeyHeld = false;
      break;

    default: // do nothing
      break;
  }

  base.OnKeyUp(e);
}``` |

Note that we use the `ControlKey` value from the `Keys` enumeration in our `switch` statement. There is also a `Control` value for the `Keys` enumeration that is used for the `Modifiers` property of the `KeyEventArgs` class which will not work here.

With this in place, we can now use the `MouseDown` event to invoke the Next and Previous menus when the Ctrl key is held. Continuing the previous steps:

	MODIFY THE MOUSE BEHAVIOR WHEN THE CTRL KEY IS HELD	
	Action	**Result**
4	In the MainForm.cs [Design] window, add a MouseDown event handler for the Panel control.	```private void pnlPhoto_MouseDown
(object sender, System.Windows.
Forms.MouseEventArgs e)
{```
5	If the Ctrl key is currently held down, see which button was pressed.	```if (ctrlKeyHeld)
{
switch (e.Button)
{```
6	For the left mouse button, invoke the Previous menu.	```case MouseButtons.Left:
menuPrevious.PerformClick();
break;```
7	For the right mouse button, invoke the Next menu.	```case MouseButtons.Right:
menuNext.PerformClick();
break;```
8	Do nothing if any other button is pressed.	```default: // do nothing
break;
}
}
}```

This looks good, right? Well, not exactly. If you run the program, you'll find that this code mostly works as long as you do nothing else while the Ctrl key is pressed. When you press the right mouse button, the next photo is displayed but the context menu also pops up. In addition, if you use a keyboard accelerator such as Ctrl+O, or you happen to open a menu while holding the Ctrl key, you may see some unexpected behavior. There are really four issues that should be addressed here:

1 There is no feedback. The user cannot tell that an alternate behavior will occur when the Ctrl key is pressed. Aside from reading the nonexistent documentation, the user must somehow figure out that this feature is available.

2 The context menu is displayed while the Ctrl key is pressed.

3 If the Ctrl key is released outside of the form, the ctrlKeyHeld field is not reset.

4 If the Ctrl key is released while displaying the menu, again the ctrlKeyHeld field is not reset.

For the first problem, we can fix this by using an alternate cursor when the Ctrl key is held. The second problem can be addressed by turning off the context menu when Ctrl is pressed. The other problems require that we handle the event that occurs in these situations. The following steps make these changes to finish our example.

	MARK CTRL KEY RELEASED WHEN APPROPRIATE	
	Action	**Result**
9	Modify the OnKeyDown method so that when the Ctrl key is pressed: a. An alternate cursor is used. b. The context menu is disabled.	```protected override void OnKeyDown
(KeyEventArgs e)
{
. . .
case Keys.ControlKey:
ctrlKeyHeld = true;
pnlPhoto.Cursor = Cursors.SizeWE;
this.ContextMenu = null;
break;
. . .```
10	Create a ReleaseCtrlKey method to encapsulate the logic now required when the Ctrl key is released.	```private void ReleaseControlKey()
{
ctrlKeyHeld = false;
pnlPhoto.Cursor = Cursors.Default;
this.ContextMenu = ctxtMenuView;
}```
11	Use this new method in override of the OnKeyUp method.	```protected override void OnKeyUp
(KeyEventArgs e)
{
switch (e.KeyCode)
{
case Keys.ControlKey:
ReleaseControlKey();
break;
. . .
}
}```
12	Override the OnDeactivate method to release the Ctrl key when the Form is deactivated.	```protected override void OnDeactivate
    (EventArgs e)
{
    if (ctrlKeyHeld)
      ReleaseControlKey();

    base.OnDeactivate(e);
}``` |

	Action	Result
13	Override the `OnMenuStart` method to release the Ctrl key when a menu is selected.	```protected override void OnMenuStart` ` (EventArgs e)` `{` ` if (ctrlKeyHeld)` ` ReleaseControlKey();` ` `   base.OnMenuStart(e);` `}```

Note how the form's `ContextMenu` property is set to `null` and then back to `ctxt-MenuView` to disable and then enable the context menu. The cursor to display for the `Panel` is modified using the `Cursor` property inherited from the `Control` class.

The `Cursors` class provides access to various mouse pointer cursors available in the operating system. The actual cursor for many of the properties in this class can be reconfigured by the user, so the actual images associated with a specific setting may change. While we could list the available properties in the `Cursors` class, it would not be very helpful without the graphics to go with it. Instead, figure 12.1 shows a sampling of the default graphics in Windows 2000 as seen in the Properties window of Visual Studio .NET. Check out this window in your version of Visual Studio to see the cursors in use on your system.

Run the program to make sure it works as expected. There are now way too many ways to invoke the Next and Previous menus. We have the menus themselves, the access keys with the Alt+V and Alt+N/P, the keyboard shortcuts Ctrl+Shift+N and Ctrl+Shift+P, the keyboard characters plus '+' and minus '–', the Page Down and Page Up keys, and finally the mouse buttons while holding down the Ctrl key. While this may be a bit overboard for many applications, it provides a good sampling of the various types of interfaces you might consider using in your applications. Consider your choices wisely, and document them well, and you may even put a smile on your customer's face.

This brings us to the end of our keyboard and mouse events discussion. Our next topic will be image buttons.

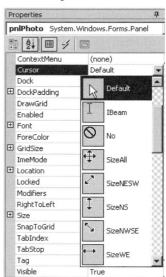

Figure 12.1 The cursor graphic can be modified through the Mouse Properties window available from the Control Panel.

12.3 IMAGE BUTTONS

So far the buttons in this book have contained text strings only. In fact, both button and label controls support the display of an image instead of or in addition to text. In this section we will look at images on buttons. Supporting images on labels is quite similar.

For button controls, imaging support is defined by the `ButtonBase` class, so this discussion applies equally well to the `Button`, `RadioButton`, and `CheckBox` objects. A summary of this class was provided in .NET Table 9.4 on page 292. For our purposes, we will focus on the `Image` property for assigning an image to a button, and the `ImageAlign` property to specify how the image is aligned within the button. An index into a list of images can also be specified using the `ImageIndex` and `ImageList` properties. We will cover image lists when we discuss toolbars in chapter 13.

As our example, we will add the ability to move to the next or previous photograph in our `PhotoEditDlg` form. Currently, when a user wants to edit the properties of two different images, he or she must display and edit the dialogs separately from the main form, so this change provides a nice shortcut for this type task. Figure 12.2 shows the dialog with our new changes. As you can see, two small image buttons have been added to the top of the form.

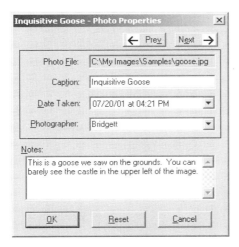

**Figure 12.2
Buttons can display text only, an image only, or both an image and text. The Prev and Next buttons in this figure display both types of data.**

This change will require more modifications than you might imagine. Our current dialog code does not make any allowances for more than a single photo. To take a somewhat incremental approach to this change, we will first add these buttons with only text displayed, and later replace the text with an image.

12.3.1 IMPLEMENTING NEXT AND PREV BUTTONS

We have been placing buttons on forms since chapter 1, so this section will run through the steps required to add and manage our new buttons. A number of steps are required here to convert our dialog from using the positional methods in the PhotoAlbum class to an index-based scheme that can support our new buttons.

To begin, let's add the new buttons to our window. In order to fit additional controls in our `PhotoEditDlg` form, we need to do some redecorating. As you'll recall, this form inherits its size from the `BaseEditDlg` form, so we are not able to resize the form itself. Our first task, then, is to squeeze the existing controls together a bit and insert our new buttons at the top of the form.

Set the version number of the MyPhotoAlbum library to 12.3.

ADD THE NEXT AND PREV BUTTONS		
	Action	**Result**
1	In the PhotoEditDlg.cs [Design] window, adjust the existing controls so there is room for the new buttons at the top of the form. **How-to** a. Resize the Notes text box to be one grid size smaller in height. b. Move the Notes label down as well. c. Resize the base of the Panel to be closer to the bottom control. d. Move the Panel down two grid sizes.	**Note:** The instructions here simply reflect how I made this change, using the default grid size of 8. Your form may vary a little, so do whatever appears to work best.
2	Add a Next button to the top of the form. **Settings** **Property** — **Value** (Name) — btnNext Size — 60, 20 Text — N&ext	
3	Add a Prev button to the left of the Next button. **Settings** **Property** — **Value** (Name) — btnPrev Size — 60,20 Text — Pre&v	
4	Adjust the tab order for the form's controls to have a reasonable sequence.	**Note:** The order does not affect our discussion, so use whatever sequence makes the most sense to you.

Each of these buttons will require a `Click` handler, and this is where it gets a bit tricky. You might be tempted to implement these handlers as follows:

```
private void btnNext_Click(object sender, System.EventArgs e)
{
  // Increment the current position (not our approach)
  _album.CurrentNext();
}
```

```
private void btnPrev_Click(object sender, System.EventArgs e)
{
  // Decrement the current position (not our approach)
  _album.CurrentPrev();
}
```

Unfortunately, life is not so simple. There are two major problems with this approach. The first is that the parent form, in this case the main form of our MyPhotos application, may rely on the existing value of the current album position. This code might adversely affect some activity in the application, or even cause a fatal error.

The second problem is that any changes made to the existing photograph are discarded whenever the user views a new photograph. Clicking the Next button should not throw out the changes already made.

As a result, we need to take a different approach. To resolve the first problem, that of adversely affecting the parent form, we will use a direct index into the album rather than modifying the current album position. We will address the second problem, that of not discarding user changes, in a moment.

	ACCESS THE ALBUM USING AN INDEX VALUE	
	Action	**Result**
5	Create an _index member in the PhotoEditDlg class.	`private int _index;`
6	Initialize this field in the constructor. **Note:** This field must be initialized before the call to the ResetSettings method.	```public PhotoEditDlg(PhotoAlbum album)` `{` ` . . .` ` // Initialize the dialog settings` ` _album = album;` ` _index = album.CurrentPosition;` ` ResetSettings();` `}```
7	Update the remainder of the file to access the current photograph using this new field rather than the CurrentPhoto method. **Note:** This requires updating the Reset-Settings, SaveSettings, and cmbxPhotographer_Validated methods.	For example, in the ResetSettings method: ```protected override void ResetSettings()` `{` ` . . .` ` Photograph photo = _album[_index];` ` . . .```
8	Also in the ResetSettings method, enable or disable the Next and Prev buttons based on the current index.	```btnPrev.Enabled = !(_index == 0);` `btnNext.Enabled` ` = !(_index == _album.Count - 1);` `}```

These changes will allow us to modify the index value in our event handlers, and the current album position will not be affected. The second problem, that of saving any changes made, requires that we save the existing photograph before moving on to the next or previous one. Of course, we do not want to do this unless the user has actually made some changes. As a result, we will track the original values for the photograph, and later compare these against the new values when moving to a new photograph.

The following steps continue our changes and build the infrastructure needed to do this. Following this table, we will make use of this infrastructure to save any changes made by the user.

	TRACK WHEN PHOTOGRAPH SETTINGS ARE MODIFIED	
	Action	**Result**

9	Create variables to hold the original caption, date taken, and photographer values.
	
	Note: The file name cannot be changed, and the Notes value will require a different approach.
		``csharp
		private string _origCaption;
		private DateTime _origDateTaken;
		private string _origPhotographer;
		``

10	Create a SetOriginals method to initialize these variables.	```csharp
		protected void SetOriginals()
		{
		    Photograph photo = _album[_index];
		
		    if (photo != null)
		    {
		      _origCaption = photo.Caption;
		      _origDateTaken = photo.DateTaken;
		      _origPhotographer = photo.Photographer;
		    }
		}
		``

11	Ensure these values are initialized in the constructor.	```csharp
		public PhotoEditDlg(PhotoAlbum album)
		{
		    . . .
		    // Initialize the dialog settings
		    _album = album;
		    _index = album.CurrentPosition;
		    ResetSettings();
		    SetOriginals();
		}
		``

You may have noticed that the Notes text box value is suspiciously missing here. While comparing a string object to the Text property works fine for a single-line TextBox control, it is not the preferred method for multiline text boxes. Instead, the Lines property should be compared line by line with the original settings. This is a little more work than we want to do, so we will simply mark this text box modified whenever the user modifies the text.

Recording whether the Notes text has changed will allow us to conditionally save a photograph's new settings, which we will do as part of the following steps:

	Action	Result
| 12 | Create a variable to hold whether the notes value has changed. | ```csharp
private bool _modifiedTxtNotes;
``` |
| 13 | Modify the SetOriginals method to reset this variable. | ```csharp
protected void SetOriginals()
{
    . . .
    if (photo != null)
    {
        . . .
        _modifiedTxtNotes = false;
    }
}
``` |
| 14 | Add a TextChanged event handler for the Notes text box to update this variable whenever the user changes the text. | ```csharp
private void txtNotes_TextChanged
    (object sender, System.EventArgs e)
{
    if (txtNotes.Focused)
        _modifiedTxtNotes = true;
}
``` |
| 15 | Create a NewControlValues method to determine if any of photograph's controls have been modified. | ```csharp
protected bool NewControlValues()
{
    bool result =
        ((_origCaption != txtCaption.Text)
        || (_origDateTaken != dtpDateTaken.Value)
        || (_origPhotographer !=
                cmbxPhotographer.Text)
        || (_modifiedTxtNotes));

    return result;
}
``` |
| 16 | Add a variable to track whether any changes have been saved. | ```csharp
private bool _hasChanged = false;
``` |
| 17 | Modify the SaveSettings method to save the changes made to the photograph.<br><br>**Note:** The _hasChanged field is required to track whether any photograph has been modified, as opposed to the current photo displayed. | ```csharp
protected override bool SaveSettings()
{
    if (NewControlValues())
    {
        // Save the photograph's settings
        Photograph photo = _album[_index];

        if (photo != null)
        {
            photo.Caption = txtCaption.Text;
            photo.DateTaken = dtpDateTaken.Value;
            photo.Photographer
                = cmbxPhotographer.Text;
            photo.Notes = txtNotes.Text;
            _hasChanged = true;
        }
    }
    return true;
}
``` |
| 18 | Add a HasChanged property so a caller can determine if any photographs were saved. | ```csharp
public bool HasChanged
{
    get { return _hasChanged; }
}
``` |
```

With these changes in place, we can finally add the click handlers for our buttons.

	HANDLE THE CLICK EVENT FOR THE NEXT AND PREV BUTTONS	
	Action	**Result**
19	Add a `Click` handler for the Next button.	```private void btnNext_Click
    (object sender, System.EventArgs e)
{
   SaveSettings();

   if (_index < _album.Count - 1)
   {
      _index ++;
      ResetSettings();
      SetOriginals();
   }
}``` |
| **20** | Add a `Click` handler for the Prev button. | ```private void btnPrev_Click
    (object sender, System.EventArgs e)
{
   SaveSettings();

   if (_index > 0)
   {
      _index --;
      ResetSettings();
      SetOriginals();
   }
}``` |

As we said at the start of all this, these buttons required more changes than you might initially expect. As a final change, we need to modify the `Click` handler for our Photo Properties menu to account for the new changes.

Set the version number of the MyPhotos application to 12.3.

	UPDATE THE CLICK HANDLER TO DISPLAY THE DIALOG	
	Action	**Result**
21	Update the `Click` handler for the `menuPhotoProp` control to use the `HasChanged` property.	```private void menuPhotoProp_Click
    (object sender, System.EventArgs e)
{
   if (_album.CurrentPhoto == null)
      return;

   using (PhotoEditDlg dlg
          = new PhotoEditDlg(_album))
   {
      if (dlg.ShowDialog() == DialogResult.OK)
      {
         _bAlbumChanged = dlg.HasChanged;
         if (_bAlbumChanged)
         {
            // Redraw to pick up any changes
            this.Invalidate();
         }
      }
   }
}``` |

Our buttons are now ready to go. Compile and run your code to make sure the buttons work as expected. Our next topic is the creation of bitmap objects for these buttons.

12.3.2 DRAWING BITMAPS FOR OUR BUTTONS

The creation of graphics for a new product is typically left to the graphic designers and marketing folks. Still, you never know when you may feel the urge to draw a bitmap or icon yourself, so let's look at how to create them from scratch. Fortunately, Microsoft provides a fairly extensive collection of bitmaps, cursors, and icons that can be used within our application. We'll talk about where to find these in a moment.

A bitmap is created much like any other item in a project. We will begin by creating a bitmap object for our Next button. Later in this section we'll create another bitmap for our Prev button.

<table>
<tr><th colspan="3">CREATE THE NEXT BUTTON BITMAP</th></tr>
<tr><th></th><th>Action</th><th>Result</th></tr>
<tr>
<td>1</td>
<td>In the Solution Explorer window, add a bitmap file "NextButton.bmp" to the MyPhotoAlbum project.

How-to
a. Right-click the MyPhoto-Album project name.
b. Open the Add submenu.
c. Select Add New Item to display the Add New Item dialog box.
d. Click Resources from the list of Categories
e. Click Bitmap File from the available Templates.
f. Enter "NextButton.bmp" as the name.

Alternately
The Add New Item dialog can be displayed using the keyboard shortcut Ctrl+Shift+A.</td>
<td>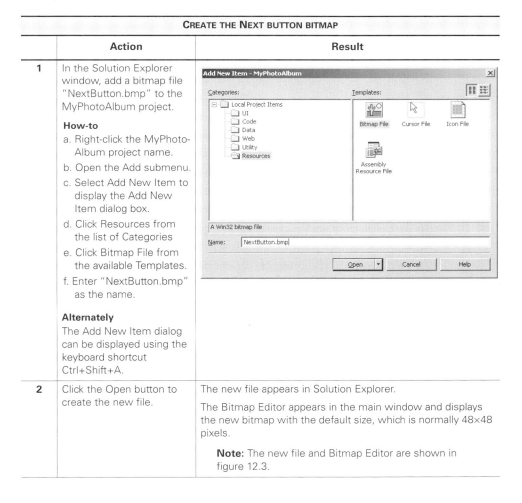</td>
</tr>
<tr>
<td>2</td>
<td>Click the Open button to create the new file.</td>
<td>The new file appears in Solution Explorer.

The Bitmap Editor appears in the main window and displays the new bitmap with the default size, which is normally 48×48 pixels.

Note: The new file and Bitmap Editor are shown in figure 12.3.</td>
</tr>
</table>

	Action	Result
3	Modify the bitmap to have size 18 ×18 pixels. **How-to** a. Right-click within the Bitmap Editor window. b. Select the Properties item c. Set the Height and Width items to 18.	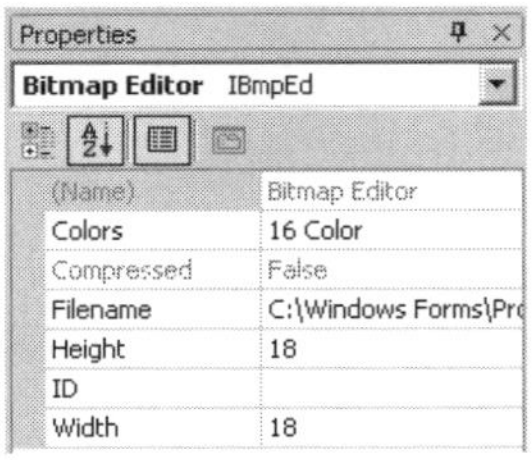 **Note:** The `Colors` property here is used to select between Monochrome, 16 Color, 256 Color, and True Color images. For our purposes, the default of 16 Color is fine.
4	Edit the pixels for the bitmap to create a right-direction arrow. **How-to** Copy the graphic shown here, or create your own version of this arrow.	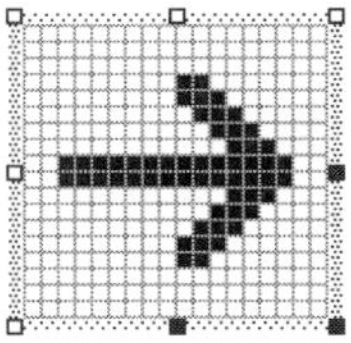

This completes our Next button. Figure 12.3 shows Visual Studio .NET with this button displayed. If you are feeling creative, the editor supports a wide range of drawing controls, in many ways similar to the Microsoft Paint application installed with the Windows operating systems. In the figure, the drawing controls are available in the bottom row of toolbar buttons, and the Colors window is shown on the left side of the window. If not shown, the Colors window is displayed by right-clicking within the Bitmap Editor window and selecting the Show Colors Window item.

A bitmap for the Prev button can be created in a similar manner as described in the previous table. An alternate method of creating this file is used in the following steps:

	Action	Result
	CREATE THE PREV BUTTON BITMAP	
5	Make a copy of the NextButton.bmp file. **How-to** a. Right-click on the file and select Copy. b. Right-click on the MyPhotoAlbum project name and select Paste.	A new bitmap file called "Copy of NextButton.bmp" is added to the project.
6	Rename this file to "PrevButton.bmp."	

	Action	Result

7	Flip the existing bitmap horizontally to create a left-pointing arrow.
	
	How-to
	a. Double-click on the PrevButton.bmp file name to display the Bitmap Editor window.
	b. Right-click within the window to display its popup menu.
	c. Select the Flip Horizontal item.
		
		  ✂ Cut
		  📋 Copy
		  📋 Paste
		  ✕ Delete
		  Add Class...
		  Invert Colors
		  Flip Horizontal
		  Flip Vertical
		  Rotate 90 Degrees
		  Show Colors Window
		  Use Selection as Brush
		  Adjust Colors...

Our two bitmaps are now ready for use. The next step is to assign these bitmaps to the buttons on our form.

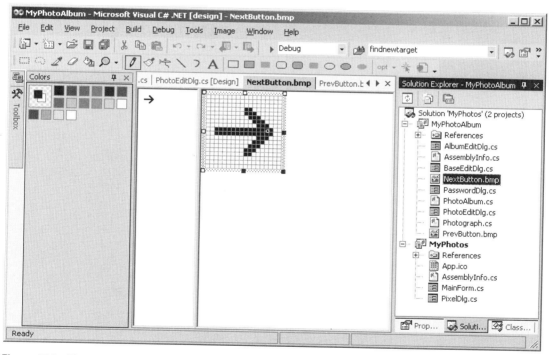

Figure 12.3   The Bitmap Editor window displays both an actual size and a per-pixel view of the bitmap.

12.3.3 PLACING IMAGES ON OUR BUTTONS

We have created the buttons in our `PhotoEditDlg` form, and created bitmaps for these buttons within our project. The next step is to reconfigure our buttons to display these images. A button can contain both an image and text string, or only an image, or only text. For our example, we will include both the image and text on our buttons.

The steps required are as follows:

	ADD THE BITMAP IMAGES TO THE BUTTONS	
	Action	**Result**
1	In the PhotoEditDlg.cs [Design] window, modify the Next button to display its text on the left side and image on the right side of the button. **Settings** | **Property**	**Value** | | ImageAlign | MiddleRight | | TextAlign | MiddleLeft |	See the graphic in step 2.
2	Assign the NextButton.bmp bitmap to the `Image` property of the `btnNext` control. **How-to** a. If necessary, save any changes to the NextButton.bmp file. b. Click on the Image item in the Properties window. c. Click the **...** button. d. Locate and open the NextButton.bmp file.	
3	Modify the Prev button to display its text on the right side and image on the left side of the button. **Settings** | **Property**	**Value** | | ImageAlign | MiddleLeft | | TextAlign | MiddleRight |	
4	Assign the PrevButton.bmp bitmap to the `Image` property of the `btnPrev` control.	

As you can see, the `ImageAlign` and `TextAlign` properties are used to set the location of the image and text within the button area. These take their values from the `ContentAlignment` enumeration, with all nine possible combinations of Top, Middle, and Bottom with Left, Center, and Right represented. Both properties use the `MiddleCenter` value by default.

Assigning the `Image` property is a simple matter of locating the desired file in the file system. The source code generated in the `InitializeComponent` method by this action is rather interesting. Here is an excerpt of the PhotoEditDlg.cs file.

```
private void InitializeComponent()                    Load the PhotoEditDlg  ❶
{                                                              resources
  System.Resources.ResourceManager resources
      = new System.Resources.ResourceManager(typeof(PhotoEditDlg));
  . . .
  this.btnNext = new System.Windows.Forms.Button();
  this.btnPrev = new System.Windows.Forms.Button();
  . . .
  //                                                    Load a specific
  // btnNext                                           bitmap resource  ❷
  //
  this.btnNext.Image = ((System.Drawing.Bitmap)
                        (resources.GetObject("btnNext.Image")));
  this.btnNext.ImageAlign
     = System.Drawing.ContentAlignment.MiddleRight;
  . . .
  this.btnNext.Text = "Nex&t";
  this.btnNext.TextAlign = System.Drawing.ContentAlignment.MiddleLeft;
  this.btnNext.Click += new System.EventHandler(this.btnNext_Click);
  //
  // btnPrev
  //
  this.btnPrev.Image = ((System.Drawing.Bitmap)
                        (resources.GetObject("btnPrev.Image")));   ❷
  this.btnPrev.ImageAlign = System.Drawing.ContentAlignment.MiddleLeft;
  . . .
}
```

You will note that the names of our original files, NextButton.bmp and PrevButton.bmp, do not appear in this listing. Instead, these files are encapsulated in a culture-specific resource for our library. A *culture-specific resource* is a text string, image, and other language or culture-specific object used in an application, library, dialog, or other construct. The term *resource* is often used as an abbreviation for such objects. A few comments on the previous code are in order:

❶ Visual Studio creates a resource file specifically for the MyPhotoAlbum project. This file is called PhotoEditDlg.resx and appears in the MyPhotoAlbum project directory. When your program is compiled in Visual Studio, this file is compiled into a .resources file based on the fully qualified name of the dialog. The resgen.exe compiler is used to generate resource files from the command line. In our application, the

.resources file, called Manning.MyPhotoAlbum.PhotoEditDlg.resources, appears in the obj directory under the MyPhotoAlbum project directory, and is included in the final MyPhotoAlbum.dll assembly produced by the compiler. The ResourcesManager class is part of the System.Resources namespace, and loads the .resources file for the given object type, in this case the Manning.MyPhotoAlbum.PhotoEditDlg type, so that the specific resources in this file may be accessed.

❷ A specific resource, in these cases our bitmap files, is loaded from the .resources file using the GetObject method. This returns the object corresponding to the given name, which can safely be typecast to the more appropriate Bitmap class.

The important points to take away from this discussion are that .resx files are used to encapsulate language-specific objects, and get compiled into .resources files for access by a program. These concepts are the basis for localization support in .NET, permitting the resources required to run a program in the United States to be encapsulated and later converted to run the same program in France, New Zealand, or Botswana with language and cultural requirements taken into account.

As long as we're here, take a quick look at the PhotoEditDlg.resx file. Such files use an XML format to encapsulate resource objects, permitting graphical programs such as Visual Studio as well as text editors like Notepad to view and edit their contents. An excerpt of this file, including the btnNext control's image definition, is shown as it appears on my computer. We won't go into the details of XML or the .resx file format here, but it is useful to see how the bitmap for the Next button, named btnNext.Image, is specified. Be careful not to change these entries, as you may adversely affect your program.

```xml
<?xml version="1.0" encoding="utf-8"?>
<root>
  . . .
  <xsd:schema id="root" . . . >
  . . .
  </xsd:schema>
  . . .
  <data name="btnNext.Image" type="System.Drawing.Bitmap, System.Drawing, Version=1.0.3300.0,
      Culture=neutral, PublicKeyToken=b03f5f7f11d50a3a"
      mimetype="application/x-microsoft.net.object.bytearray.base64">
    <value>
```
      Qk1OAQAAAAAAAHYAAAAoAAAAEgAAABIAAAABAAQAAAAAAAAAADEDgAAxA4AABAAAAAQAAAAAAA/wAA
      gP8AgAD/AICA/4AAP+AAID/gIAA/8DAwP+AgID/AAD//wD/AP8A/////wAA//8A/////wD////////
      /////wASAP//////////wASAP//////////wASAP/////wD////wASAP/////wAP///wASAP//
      ////AA///wASAP//////8AD//wASAP///////wAP/wASAP8AAAAAAAA/wASAP8AAAAAAAA/wASAP//
      /////wAP/wASAP//////8AD//wASAP//////AA///wASAP/////wAP///wASAP/////wD////wASAP//
      /////wASAP//////////wASAP//////////wASAA==
    </value>
  </data>
  . . .
</root>
```
```

This completes our rather long discussion of bitmap images. Personally, I am the kind of programmer who keeps good graphic artists employed, so we will not do any more hand-drawing of images or other graphics in this book. Fortunately for us, Microsoft provides a fairly large collection of images that can be imported into your programs. These are installed by default along with Visual Studio .NET, and they normally appear in the directory "C:\Program Files\Microsoft Visual Studio .NET\Common7\ Graphics." There are subdirectories for bitmaps, cursors, icons, metafiles, and even some videos.[1]

For the purposes of our discussions, we will use the term *common image directory* to refer to this directory rather than using the full directory name every time. In particular, we will use this directory for our next topic, which is icons.

12.4 ICONS

As long as we are talking about images, let's take a quick look at icons as well. An icon is an image used to represent an object in the operating system, typically an application or other program. Icons are much like bitmaps, except they provide *transparency*, meaning that a certain color in the icon will blend in with the background when it is displayed. If the icon is displayed on a red background, the transparent areas appear red as well. If the icon is displayed on a purple background, the transparent areas appear purple. This behavior permits Windows icons to appear on the desktop and in file system windows as if they do not have a border. In fact, all icons are rectangular in shape.

The `System.Drawing` namespace provides an `Icon` class to create and manipulate icons in your programs. It's a fine class, but we are not going to discuss it. Instead, we are going to focus on how to assign icons to your project and to specific forms. We will look at the `Icon` property of the `Form` class, and discuss how icons can be created and assigned to this property.

Before we do, it is worth mentioning that icons can be included in a project just like any other object. You can create new icons from the Add New Item dialog and edit them in Visual Studio as we did for our bitmap files earlier in the chapter. Unlike bitmaps, icons store multiple image types, or image sizes, in a single file. The most typical types are 16×16 and 32×32 pixels, so you should generally stick with these formats. New icons in Visual Studio are created with these two types by default, using 16 available colors, and the Icon Editor permits types to be deleted and custom types of various sizes and colors to be assigned.

---

[1] Of course, if you customized your installation settings when installing Visual Studio .NET, or modified the installation directory, then these files may not exist on your machine or might be in an alternate directory. You can reinstall Visual Studio .NET to add these graphics in order to follow the text, or use alternate graphics in place of the ones we use in the remainder of the book.

12.4.1 REPLACING THE ICON ON A FORM

 So let's talk icons. In the MyPhotos project, we will assign a new icon to our main form. By default, Visual Studio uses the graphic at the left as the icon on all forms.

This icon has been fine so far, but it would be nice to have a custom icon that represents a photo album in some manner. One such image is shown as the icon in figure 12.4. Microsoft provides this icon in the common image directory discussed at the end of the previous section.

Figure 12.4
By default, an application displays the small image associated with an icon in its title bar.

The following steps assign this icon to our form.

Set the version number of the MyPhotos application to 12.4.

	ASSIGN A NEW ICON TO THE MAIN FORM	
	Action	**Result**
1	In the Properties window for the `MainForm` form, locate the Icon entry in the list of properties.	

	Action	Result
2	Assign the icon file "icons/Writing/BOOKS02.ICO" from the common image directory as the icon for the form. **How-to** a. Click the **...** button in the Icon entry for the form's properties. b. In the resulting file dialog, locate the common image directory, namely the Common7\Graphics directory under the Visual Studio .NET installation directory. c. Open the indicated file.	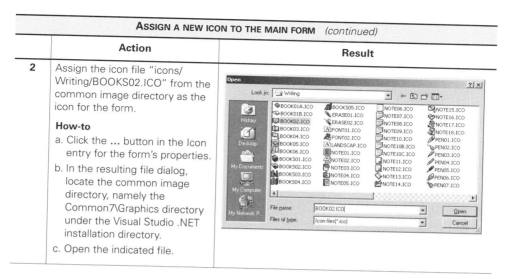

The selected icon is shown in the designer window, and will now be used whenever the application executes. The code generated here is very similar to the code we saw for our bitmap images.

```
private void InitializeComponent()
{
    System.Resources.ResourceManager resources = new
        System.Resources.ResourceManager(typeof(MainForm));
    . . .
    this.Icon = ((System.Drawing.Icon)
            (resources.GetObject("$this.Icon")));
    . . .
}
```

If you look in the MyPhotos project directory in the file system, you will see a Main-Form.resx file in which the icon data is specified. As we discussed in section 12.3, this is compiled into the MyPhotos.MainForm.resources file when the program is compiled, and the data from this file is included in the MainForm.exe executable assembly for the program.

In a similar manner, we can assign an icon for the `PixelDlg` form in the project.

	Action	Result
	ASSIGN A NEW ICON TO THE PIXEL DIALOG FORM	
	Action	**Result**
3	In the Properties window for the `PixelDlg` form, set the `Icon` property for this dialog to contain the icons/Writing/PENCIL02.ICO icon from the common image directory.	

Compile and run the application to verify that these icons now appear on their respective forms. This method can be used to assign an existing icon to any form. Of course, a custom icon can be created and assigned to a form as well. We discuss this in the next section.

At times you may prefer that an icon not appear in a form. The `ControlBox` property for the `Form` class removes the icon as well as the system menu and its shortcuts from the title bar. As an alternate method, we saw in chapter 8 how setting the form's `FormBorderStyle` property to `FixedDialog` removes the icon without affecting the presence of the system menu. Either technique may be used in your applications, depending on the desired behavior.

12.4.2 REPLACING THE APPLICATION ICON

You might think that the icon for the application is based on the icon assigned to the main form, namely the form containing the `Main` entry point for the assembly. A fine notion, but not true. In fact, the application icon is totally separate from the icons assigned to any forms within the application. One reason for this is that applications will not always contain a main form, and console applications and libraries may not contain any forms at all.

By default, Visual Studio creates an application icon as part of all Windows Forms projects. This is the App.ico file we first saw back in chapter 2. Double-clicking on this file in the Solution Explorer window will display the Icon Editor window, and permit the icon to be edited much like we edited bitmaps earlier in the chapter. Since icons contain multiple image types, you need to edit each image type when you alter the default or any other icon file. You can select the image type to display in the Icon Window by selecting the Current Icon Image Types submenu from the Icon Editor window's popup menu.

For our purposes, we will simply select an icon from the set of images provided by Microsoft in the common image directory. The current application icon, visible by double-clicking the App.ico file or looking at the MyPhotos.exe file in the MyPhotos project's bin directory, looks a bit like this:

We would prefer to use the same icon we assigned to the `MainForm` window as the application icon, so let's see exactly how to do this.

	ASSIGN A NEW APPLICATION ICON TO THE MYPHOTOS PROJECT	
	Action	**Result**
1	In the Solution Explorer window, delete the Apps.ico icon file from the MyPhotos project.	The file is deleted permanently.

	Action	Result
2	Display the Property Pages dialog for the project. **How-to** a. Right-click the MyPhotos project. b. Select the Properties item.	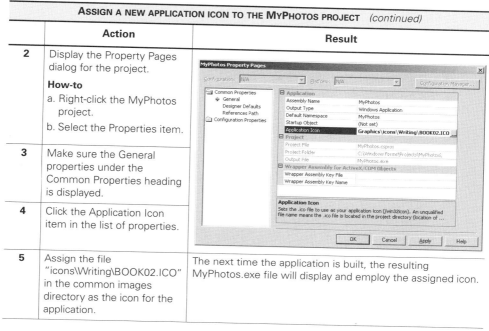
3	Make sure the General properties under the Common Properties heading is displayed.	
4	Click the Application Icon item in the list of properties.	
5	Assign the file "icons\Writing\BOOK02.ICO" in the common images directory as the icon for the application.	The next time the application is built, the resulting MyPhotos.exe file will display and employ the assigned icon.

There is no visual indication of the change. Rebuild the application and check out the bin directory. The MyPhotos.exe program file is now displayed with the assigned icon.

12.5 *RECAP*

This chapter jumped around the Windows Forms namespace to cover various topics related to application development. We began by talking about keyboard and mouse events, and made use of these events in our MyPhotos application. Keyboard event handlers receive a `KeyPressEventArgs` parameter for `KeyPress` events, and a `KeyEventArgs` parameter for `KeyDown` and `KeyUp` events. All mouse event handlers receive a `MouseEventArgs` parameter.

We also discussed the creation of image buttons. We saw how to create custom bitmaps using our precision drawing skills in Visual Studio, and placed these bitmaps on a button in the `PhotoEditDlg` form in the MyPhotoAlbum project.

Our final topic was the use of icons for the control box of a `Form` window, and the windows icon associated with an application. We discussed how to customize the icon for a form as well as an application.

Along the way we discussed cursors, including the `Cursors` class supported by Windows Forms. We briefly touched on resource files, and looked at some examples of .resx files and how Visual Studio accesses items within these files using members of the `System.Resources` namespace.

The final chapter in part 2 of the book will look at the `ToolBar` control and the use of tool tips.

C H A P T E R   1 3

Toolbars and tips

13.1 Toolbars 411
13.2 Image lists 416
13.3 Toolbar buttons 420
13.4 Tool tips 430
13.5 Recap 434

In this final chapter of part 2 of the book, we round out our discussion of basic Windows Forms programming with the `ToolBar` and `ToolTip` classes. You may wonder why these concepts were not presented earlier in our discussion, and they certainly could have been. The reason is either poor planning or clever organization—you decide which. These two concepts are not necessarily related, but they do make for a catchy chapter title.

Toolbars in Windows Forms applications are created using the `ToolBar` and `ToolBarButton` classes. We will look at these classes along with the `ImageList` class in the first three sections of the chapter. Image lists are used by toolbars and other controls to hold a set of images available for display within the control. The final section in the chapter will examine tool tips and the `ToolTip` class.

Specific topics we will look at in this chapter include:

- Adding a toolbar to a window.

- Creating toolbar buttons: push buttons, separators, dropdown menus, and toggle buttons.

- Associating menu commands with a toolbar button.

- Interacting with toolbar buttons.
- Creating and managing image lists.
- Providing tool tips for controls in a form.

We begin our discussion with toolbars.

13.1 TOOLBARS

Toolbars were added to windowing environments as an alternate shortcut method for common tasks, especially menu bar items. While keyboard shortcuts are fine for more experienced users, they do not have a graphical presence in the window. Toolbars provide a graphic for each shortcut button, so users should be able to quickly perform common tasks without the need to hunt through the menus or documentation all the time.

At least that was the theory. Personally, I prefer keyboard shortcuts, and find the plethora of toolbars a distraction in many interfaces. While common tasks such as opening and closing a file or selection of a bold or italic font style have developed somewhat standard graphical buttons, I have trouble deciphering many of the tiny graphics shown on many toolbars and prefer to search for keyboard shortcuts instead. When creating toolbars in your programs, make sure their meaning is clear, and do not use a toolbar as an excuse to avoid keyboard shortcuts and access keys. Some users prefer the keyboard over the mouse, so it is a good idea to provide keyboard as well as mouse access to program functions.

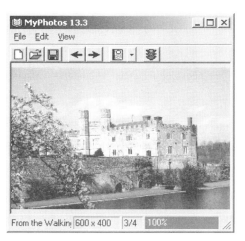

Figure 13.1   Our toolbar will use a raised-button appearance for displaying its buttons. A flat appearance is also possible.

But I digress. Let's get back to toolbars in .NET. Whether you employ them yourself or not, your users will likely expect them. In this section we will look at the ToolBar class in detail, create a blank toolbar in our MyPhotos project, and also introduce the ToolBarButton class. Later sections will look at image lists and the creation of the various kinds of toolbar buttons. By the end of section 13.3, our efforts will produce the interface shown in figure 13.1.

13.1.1   THE TOOLBAR CLASS

As you might expect, there is a ToolBar class in the Windows Forms namespace, and a corresponding .NET Table with some details about this class, namely .NET Table 13.1. A ToolBar control is a bit like the StatusBar or TabControl objects, in that they all serve primarily as containers for other graphical objects.

The `ToolBar` class represents a control that displays `ToolBarButton` objects on a form. Such objects typically provide shortcuts to menu commands and other commonly used tasks. This class is part of the `System.Windows.Forms` namespace, and inherits from the `Control` class. See .NET Table 4.1 on page 104 for a list of members inherited from `Control`.

Public Properties	Appearance	Gets or sets the display style of the toolbar.
	AutoSize	Gets or sets whether the toolbar adjusts its size automatically based on the contained buttons and the docking style.
	Buttons	Gets or sets the collection of `ToolBarButton` objects contained by the control.
	ButtonSize	Gets or sets the size of the toolbar's buttons. If not set, the button size will default to 24 pixels wide by 22 pixels high, or a size appropriate for the largest button in the collection.
	Divider	Gets or sets whether to display a divider in the toolbar. The default is `true`.
	DropDownArrows	Gets or sets whether dropdown menus in the control display a down arrow next to the button. The default is `false`.
	ImageList	Gets or sets the collection of `Image` objects available to buttons in the control.
	ImageSize	Gets the size of the images in the `ImageList` assigned to the control.
	ShowToolTips	Gets or sets whether tool tips for the buttons in the control are displayed. The default is `false`.
	TextAlign	Gets or sets the alignment of toolbar button text in relation to any image assigned to the button.
	Wrappable	Gets or sets whether multiple rows of buttons should be displayed when necessary.
Public Events	ButtonClick	Occurs when a button on the toolbar is clicked.
	ButtonDropDown	Occurs when a dropdown button on the toolbar is clicked.

13.1.2   ADDING A TOOLBAR

A toolbar is typically docked to the top of a window, although it can also be docked to the left, right, or bottom of a form. The following steps add a toolbar to the top of our `MainForm` window.

Set the version number of the MyPhotos application to 13.1.

	Action	**Result**
		ADD A TOOLBAR TO THE MAINFORM WINDOW

	Action	Result
1	In the MainForm.cs [Design] window, drag a `ToolBar` object onto the form. **How-to** a. Click the `ToolBar` item in the Toolbox window. b. Click the title bar of the form to add the control.	A toolbar is displayed on the form. **Note:** You need to be careful here. If you drop the toolbar on the `Panel` object, the `ToolBar` will happily place itself inside the panel. By dropping it onto the title bar of the form, you ensure that it is part of the `Form` itself.
2	Bring the `Panel` control to the front of the z-order. **How-to** Select Bring to Front from the panel's popup menu.	The toolbar and a portion of our panel appear in the graphic for step 3.
3	Set the properties for the toolbar as follows. **Settings** | Property	Value | |---|---| | (Name) | toolBarMain | | TextAlign | Right |	 **Note:** The `TextAlign` property takes its values from the `ToolBarTextAlign` enumeration, with possible values `Underneath` and `Right`. The default is `Underneath`.

As you can see, the `Dock` property of a `ToolBar` is set to `Top` by default. Visual Studio also sets the `DropDownArrows` and `ShowToolTips` properties to `true`, even though the default for both settings is `false`.

The code generated here is nothing unusual, so we will move on to the `ToolBarButton` class.

13.1.3   THE TOOLBARBUTTON CLASS

By themselves, toolbars do not present much information to the user. These objects take on meaning and purpose once they have one or more toolbar buttons placed on them. In this section we look at the `ToolBarButton` class in some detail. We will hold off discussing exactly how to place our buttons on the toolbar until section 13.3, after we have introduced the idea of an image list in section 13.2.

An overview of the `ToolBarButton` class appears in .NET Table 13.2. This object is a component, so it does not inherit any properties from the `Control` class. As a result, a number of control-like properties such as `Enabled`, `Tag`, and `Visible` are defined explicitly by this class.

The `ToolBarButton` class represents a button that appears within a toolbar control. These buttons typically provide shortcuts to menu commands and other commonly used tasks for the associated form. This class is part of the `System.Windows.Forms` namespace, and inherits from the `System.ComponentModel.Component` class.

Public Properties	DropDownMenu	Gets or sets the `Menu` object to display as the menu for a button with a dropdown style. While this property is of type `Menu`, a `ContextMenu` instance should normally be provided.
	Enabled	Gets or sets whether this button is active.
	ImageIndex	Gets or sets the index into the parent toolbar's `ImageList` property to display on this button.
	Parent	Gets the `ToolBar` object containing this toolbar button.
	PartialPush	Gets or sets whether a button with a toggle style is displayed as partially pushed.
	Pushed	Gets or sets whether a button with a toggle style is displayed as pushed.
	Rectangle	Gets the bounding rectangle for the toolbar button.
	Style	Gets or sets the display style for this button.
	Tag	Gets or sets an `object` instance to associate with this toolbar button.
	Text	Gets or sets the text string to display on the button.
	ToolTipText	Gets or sets the tool tip string to associate with the button.
	Visible	Gets or sets whether the button is shown on the toolbar.

Toolbar buttons can display a text string, an image, or both an image and text. They appear in one of four styles, based on the `Style` property setting. The possible styles are defined by the `ToolBarButtonStyle` enumeration. The values in this enumeration appear in .NET Table 13.3. In our application, we will create at least one button in each style in order to see how these appear in our toolbar.

The `ToolBarButtonStyle` enumeration specifies the various styles available to toolbar buttons placed within a toolbar. The style for a specific `ToolBarButton` is defined by the `Style` property for that button.

Enumeration Values	DropDownButton	A dropdown menu that displays a `Menu` object when clicked. This menu may be owner-drawn, permitting arbitrary windows to be displayed.
	PushButton	A standard push button. This is the default value for the `Style` property in the `ToolBarButton` class.
	Separator	A space or line separating sets of buttons, depending on the value of the `Appearance` property for the associated toolbar.
	ToggleButton	A standard toggle button.

As for images on our buttons, we will use the common images provided by Microsoft with Visual Studio .NET. These are installed by default into the directory "C:\Program Files\Microsoft Visual Studio .NET\Common7\Graphics," and we will continue to use the term *common image directory* introduced in chapter 12 to refer to this directory. If you are not using Visual Studio, have not installed these files, or are feeling especially creative, you can construct or find your own image files here instead of the common ones employed in the examples.

We will create ten toolbar buttons altogether in order to demonstrate various styles and behaviors. The following table summarizes the name, style, and purpose of each button. It also shows the menu item associated with each button. In most cases, clicking a toolbar button will be identical to selecting the associated menu item.

Toolbar buttons for our application

Name	Button Style	Purpose	Menu Item
tbbNew	PushButton	Open a new album.	menuNew
tbbOpen	PushButton	Open an existing album.	menuOpen
tbbSave	PushButton	Save the current album.	menuSave
default	Separator		
tbbNext	PushButton	Display the next photo.	menuNext
tbbPrevious	PushButton	Display the previous photo.	menuPrev
default	Separator		
tbbImage	DropDownButton	Select the image display mode.	menuImages
default	Separator		
tbbPixelData	ToggleButton	Show/Hide the Pixel Data dialog.	menuPixelData

Each of these buttons, except the separators, of course, will require a different image. The images placed on toolbar buttons are stored in an `ImageList` object associated with the parent toolbar. Image lists are used by a number of Windows Forms controls to manage the images displayed or available within the control. As a result, we will hold off on creating our toolbar buttons until section 13.3 in order to take a look at this rather important construct.

13.2 IMAGE LISTS

There are a number of controls that require one or more images in order to display their contents. Often, the requirement is for a set of images, rather than a single image. For example, the set of toolbar buttons in a `ToolBar` object, or the images required for a set of `Button` controls on a form. The Windows Forms namespace provides the `ImageList` class for managing such collections of images. As we shall see in chapters 14 and 15, this class is also utilized by the `ListView` and `TreeView` controls.

This section examines the `ImageList` class in some detail, and creates a set of images for use in the toolbar we created in the previous section.

.NET Table 13.4 ImageList class		
The `ImageList` class represents a collection of `Image` objects. Typically, this class is used to support one or more Windows Forms controls in the management and display of images within the control. Classes that use image lists include the `Button`, `ToolBar`, `ListView`, and `TreeView` classes. This class is part of the `System.Windows.Forms` namespace, and inherits from the `System.ComponentModel.Component` class.		
Public Properties	ColorDepth	Gets or sets the color depth for images in the list.
	Handle	Gets the Win32 handle for the image list.
	HandleCreated	Gets whether the underlying Win32 handle has been created.
	Images	Gets the collection of images for this image list. Use this collection to add, remove, and otherwise manage the list's images programmatically.
	ImageSize	Gets or sets the size for images in the list.
	ImageStream	Gets or sets the `ImageListStreamer` object to associate with this list. This object manages the data associated with the list.
	TransparentColor	Gets or sets the color to treat as transparent in the list's images.
Public Methods	Draw	Draws an indicated image in a specified `Graphics` object.
Public Events	RecreateHandle	Occurs when the underlying Win32 handle is recreated for the list.

13.2.1 THE IMAGELIST CLASS

The ImageList class, summarized in .NET Table 13.4, provides a convenient way to store and access images required by various objects. An `ImageList` component works much like an array of `Image` objects, and can be thought of as such. Classes that use this construct specify an index into the list, designating which image they wish to display. Typically, a class that uses such a list provides an `ImageList` property to specify a list to use, and classes that display an image out of such lists provide an `ImageIndex` property to indicate which image to display.

In Visual Studio .NET, an `ImageList` can be associated with a `Form` graphically and assigned to one or more controls within that form using the Windows Forms Designer and the Properties windows. Visual Studio creates the list within the set of `components` for the `Form`, so that it is disposed when the application disposes of the `Form` via the `Close` or `Dispose` methods. We will look at the code generated for this purpose in a moment.

13.2.2 CREATING AN IMAGE LIST

For the `ToolBar` object we created in our `MainForm` class, we need an `ImageList` containing the set of images required for our `ToolBarButton` objects. We will use some of the bitmaps and icons in the common image directory provided with Visual Studio. If you skipped chapter 12, or were simply not paying attention, this directory is typically "C:\Program Files\Microsoft Visual Studio .NET\Common7\Graphics."

The following steps create an `ImageList` and associate the required image files with it.

Set the version number of the MyPhotos application to 13.2.

	CREATE AN IMAGE LIST FOR OUR TOOLBAR	
	Action	**Result**
1	Associate an `ImageList` component with the `MainForm` form in the MainForm.cs [Design] window. **Note:** Windows Forms components such as the `ImageList` class are available from the Toolbox window, just like Windows Forms controls.	The new image list is shown in the component tray area below the form.
2	Set the `(Name)` property for the image list to `imageListToolBar`.	
3	Display the Image Collection Editor window. **How-to** Click the **...** button next to the Images item in the Properties window.	A blank Image Collection Editor dialog box appears. This dialog with all eight images added is shown in step 5.

	Action	Result
4	Add an image for creating a new album to the collection. **How-to** a. Click the Add button. b. In the file dialog, locate the NEW.BMP file under the common image directory in the "bitmaps/OffCtlBr/Small/Color" directory. c. Click the Open button to add the image.	The image appears as member 0 within the Image Collection Editor dialog.
5	Similarly, add the following images files to the collection. • bitmaps/OffCtlBr/Small/Color/OPEN.BMP • bitmaps/OffCtlBr/Small/Color/SAVE.BMP • icons/arrows/ARW08LT.ICO • icons/arrows/ARW08RT.ICO • icons/Writing/BOOK02.ICO • icons/Traffic/TRFFC10C.ICO • icons/Traffic/TRFFC10A.ICO	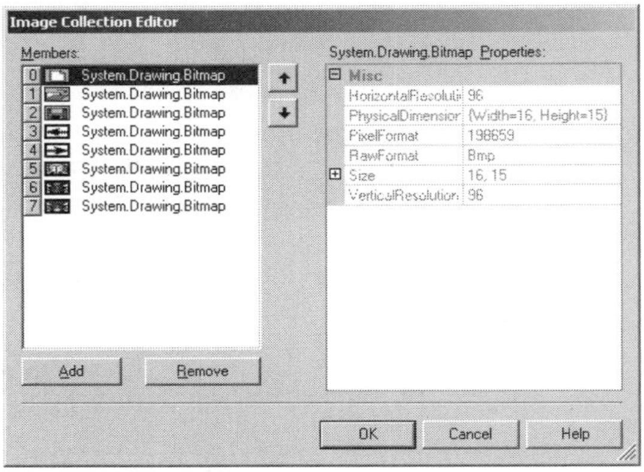
6	Click the OK button to save the changes.	The assigned images are stored in the image list.

This creates a collection of all the images we will need for our toolbar. An excerpt of the code generated by these changes is as follows.

```
. . .
namespace MyPhotos
{
  . . .
  public class MainForm : System.Windows.Forms.Form
  {
    . . .
    private System.ComponentModel.IContainer components = null;
    . . .
    private System.Windows.Forms.ImageList imageListToolBar;
    . . .
    protected override void Dispose( bool disposing )
    {
      if( disposing )
      {
```

```
          if (components != null)
          {
            components.Dispose();        ❶ Dispose of the
          }                                 components object
        }
      base.Dispose( disposing );
    }
    . . .
    private void InitializeComponent()
    {                                                  Create the image  ❷
      . . .                                           list within the
      this.imageListToolBar                           components container
          = new System.Windows.Forms.ImageList(this.components);
      . . .
      //
      // imageListToolBar                                   Load the  ❸
      //                                                image stream
      this.imageListToolBar.ColorDepth                  for the list
          = System.Windows.Forms.ColorDepth.Depth8Bit;
      this.imageListToolBar.ImageSize = new System.Drawing.Size(16, 16);
      this.imageListToolBar.ImageStream
          = ((System.Windows.Forms.ImageListStreamer)
            (resources.GetObject("imageListToolBar.ImageStream")));
      this.imageListToolBar.TransparentColor
          = System.Drawing.Color.Transparent;
      . . .
    }
```

The annotated lines merit some additional discussion.

❶ This line disposes of the components container, which in turn disposes of any components contained within this object. The controls on the form are contained within the Form object itself. As a result, the resources allocated to the controls in the form are disposed by the Form.Dispose method itself. This works for components such as the MainMenu and StatusBarPanel objects as well, since the menu is assigned to the form, and status bar panels are contained within status bar controls.

❷ This line initializes an ImageList object and assigns it to the components container. This is required to ensure that the list is properly disposed of by the Form object's Dispose method. If you create your own ImageList objects manually, be sure to dispose of the object when you are finished in order to free any Windows or file system resources assigned to the list.

❸ Like the bitmap files we created in the previous chapter, a ResourcesManager object is used to retrieve the stream of image data from a .resources file. This data is retrieved as an ImageListStream object. This object is assigned to the ImageStream property and used internally by the ImageList class to manage and access the images in the collection.

On this last point for our code, note that the MyPhotos project directory in the file system contains a MainForm.resx file that defines the binary form of the image stream for our list. This is very similar to how our bitmap images were defined for our Button objects in the previous chapter. An excerpt of this file follows. In addition to the definition of the image stream, note how the positioning of objects displayed in the component tray area of Visual Studio, such as the location of our imageList-ToolBar object, are also stored in this file

```
<?xml version="1.0" encoding="utf-8"?>
<root>
  . . .
  <data name="imageListToolBar.Location" type="System.Drawing.Point,
  System.Drawing,
    Version=1.0.3300.0, Culture=neutral,
PublicKeyToken=b03f5f7f11d50a3a">
<value>255, 17</value>
</data>
<data name="imageListToolBar.ImageStream"
  mimetype="application/x-microsoft.net.object.binary.base64">
 <value>
```

AAEAAAD/////AQAAAAAAAAMAgAAAFpTeXN0ZW0uV2luZG93cy5Gb3JtcywgVmVyc2lvbj0xLjAuMzMw

MC4wLCBDDdWx0dXJlPW5ldXRyYWwsIFB1YmxpY0tleVva2VuPWI3N2E1YzU2MTkzNGUwODkFAQAACZT

eXN0ZW0uV2luZG93cy5Gb3Jtcy5JbWFnZUxpc3RTdHJlYW1lcgEAAAERGF0YQcCAgAAAAkDAAAADwMA

```
  . . .
 </value>
  . . .
</root>
```

This completes our discussion on image lists for now. Let's get back to the ToolBar for our application and create the ToolBarButton components using the images we just assigned to our list.

13.3   TOOLBAR BUTTONS

Now that we have some understanding of image lists, we can return to the topic of toolbar buttons. This section adds the ten buttons, both images and separators, we decided to place on our toolbar. The discussion is divided into two parts. First we will look at the most basic of styles, the push button. Then we'll tackle the dropdown and toggle styles of ToolBarButton objects.

13.3.1   ADDING A PUSH BUTTON

We have a toolbar and we have an image list, so let's get to it. We will start with the push buttons related to the File menu, and later hook up these buttons to their corresponding menu item, after which we will create the buttons associated with the Next and Previous menu items.

Set the version number of the MyPhotos application to 13.3.

	ADD THE TOOLBAR BUTTONS FOR THE FILE MENU	
	Action	**Result**
1	In the MainForm.cs [Design] window, modify the properties for the `toolBarMain` control. **Settings** | Property	Value
---	---
ButtonSize	16, 16
ImageList	imageListToolBar		The images in our image list are now available to any buttons placed on the toolbar.
2	Display the ToolBarButton Collection Editor window. **How-to** In the toolbar's Properties window, click the **...** button associated with the Buttons item.	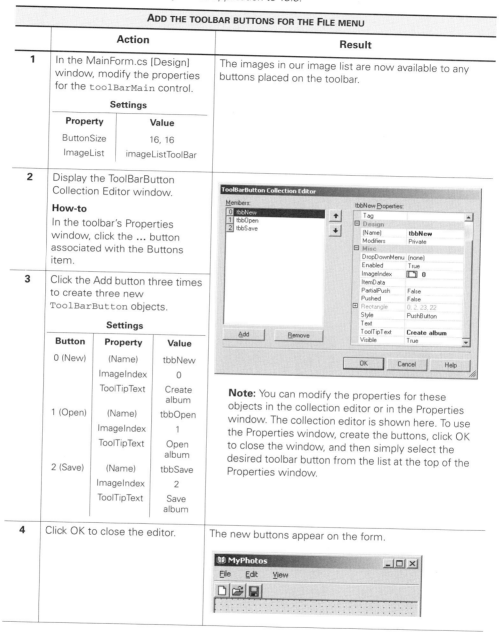
3	Click the Add button three times to create three new `ToolBarButton` objects. **Settings** 	Button	Property	Value
0 (New)	(Name)	tbbNew
	ImageIndex	0
	ToolTipText	Create album
1 (Open)	(Name)	tbbOpen
	ImageIndex	1
	ToolTipText	Open album
2 (Save)	(Name)	tbbSave
	ImageIndex	2
	ToolTipText	Save album		**Note:** You can modify the properties for these objects in the collection editor or in the Properties window. The collection editor is shown here. To use the Properties window, create the buttons, click OK to close the window, and then simply select the desired toolbar button from the list at the top of the Properties window.
4	Click OK to close the editor.	The new buttons appear on the form.

Our `ToolBar` now contains three toolbar buttons. Visual Studio displays the images associated with each button in the designer window. If text is assigned to a button,

Visual Studio will display this as well, assuming the button provides room for the text to appear.

The next step is to link these to operations within our form. The `ButtonClick` event in the `ToolBar` class is used for this purpose. Event handlers for this event receive a `ToolBarButtonClickEventArgs` parameter that contains a `Button` property. This property retrieves the `ToolBarButton` instance clicked by the user.

One means for handling our button clicks uses a series of `if` statements. The code would look something like the following:

```
private void toolBarMain_ButtonClick(object sender,
    System.Windows.Forms.ToolBarButtonClickEventArgs e)
{
  // Determine which button was clicked - not our approach
  if (e.Button == tbbNew)
  {
    menuNew.PerformClick();
  }
  else if (e.Button == tbbOpen)
  {
    menuOpen.PerformClick();
  }
  else if (e.Button == tbbSave)
  {
    menuSave.PerformClick();
  }
}
```

This can get a bit unwieldy as the number of buttons increase. A more elegant approach takes advantage of the `Tag` property for `ToolBarButton` instances. This property holds an `object` instance, and in particular can hold a `MenuItem` object to associate with the button. Since we would like our buttons to perform the same action as the corresponding menu item, we will associate the proper menu item with each of our buttons. Continuing our prior steps:

	SET THE TAG PROPERTY FOR THE TOOLBAR BUTTONS	
	Action	**Result**
5	Create a new `InitToolBarButtons` method in the MainForm.cs code window.	`private void InitToolBarButtons()` `{`

6	Set the `Tag` property for each toolbar button to the corresponding `MenuItem` object.	`  tbbNew.Tag = menuNew;`
		`  tbbOpen.Tag = menuOpen;`
		`  tbbSave.Tag = menuSave;`
		`}`

7	Add a call to this new method from the `MainForm` instance constructor.	`public MainForm()`
		`{`
		`    . . .`
		`    InitToolBarButtons();`
		`}`

Our implementation of the `ButtonClick` handler for our toolbar can now take advantage of these settings to simply invoke the `Click` event handler associated with the corresponding menu item.

	HANDLE THE BUTTONCLICK EVENT FOR THE TOOLBAR	
	Action	**Result**
8	Add a `ButtonClick` event handler for the `ToolBar` control. **How-to** This is the default event for toolbars, so simply double-click the toolbar control in the MainForm.cs [Design] window.	```private void toolBarMain_ButtonClick (object sender, System.Windows.Forms. ToolBarButtonClickEventArgs e) {```
9	Implement this handler using the `Tag` property of the `ToolBarButton` component.	```// Handle menu buttons MenuItem mi = e.Button.Tag as MenuItem; if (mi != null) mi.PerformClick(); }```

Note how the `as` keyword is used to ensure that the `Tag` property does, in fact, refer to a `MenuItem` object. If a new button is added without an associated menu, then this code is safely ignored.

We can also use this method for the Next and Previous toolbar buttons. The following steps also define a separator button to differentiate between these two sets of buttons.

	ADD THE NEXT AND PREVIOUS TOOLBAR BUTTONS	
	Action	**Result**
10	In the ToolBarButton Collection Editor, add three new toolbar buttons. **Settings** 	Button	Property	Value
3	Style	Separator
4 (Prev)	(Name)	tbbPrevious
	ImageIndex	3
	ToolTipText	Previous image
5 (Next)	(Name)	tbbNext
	ImageIndex	4
	ToolTipText	Next image		
11	Update the `InitToolBarButtons` method for these new buttons.	```private void InitToolBarButtons() { tbbNew.Tag = menuNew; tbbOpen.Tag = menuOpen; tbbSave.Tag = menuSave; tbbPrevious.Tag = menuPrevious; tbbNext.Tag = menuNext; }```

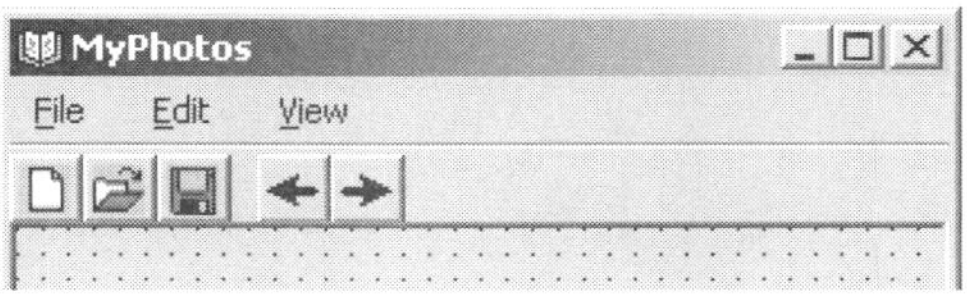

Our `ButtonClick` event handler automatically handles these buttons based on their associated menu items, so no further changes are needed. Compile and run the program to make use of these buttons. Note how the tool tips pop up when the mouse hovers over these buttons.

TRY IT! Two things to try here. First, modify the `Appearance` property for the toolbar to be `Flat`. The buttons will no longer have a three-dimensional appearance, and the separator will be a line between the two sets of buttons.

Second, modify the `Dock` property for the toolbar to be `Left`. This places the control on the left side of the form. Run the program to verify that everything still works as expected.

There are two other types of toolbar buttons, namely the `DropDownButton` and `ToggleButton` styles. The next two sections take a look at these alternate button styles.

13.3.2 ADDING A DROPDOWN BUTTON

To create a dropdown menu on our form, we will make use of our existing Images submenu displayed via the `menuImages` menu item created way back in chapter 3, and updated in chapter 6. The changes are detailed by the following steps, and discussed in the subsequent text.

	ADD A DROPDOWN BUTTON	
	Action	**Result**
1	In the MainForm.cs [Design] window, add a new `ContextMenu` object to the `MainForm` window.	A second context menu appears in the component tray.
2	Set the (Name) for the menu to `ctxtMenuImage`.	
3	Assign the `menuImage_Popup` event handler as the `Popup` event handler for the `ctxtMenuImage` menu.	**Note:** If you look at our implementation of this event handler back in chapter 3, you will find that we cast the `sender` parameter to a `Menu` object, rather than a `MenuItem` object, so that it would work with any type of menu.

4	Modify the `DefineContextMenu` method to copy the contents of the `menuImage` menu into the new context menu.
	
	 Note: This clones the submenus of the `menuImage` object and assigns them to the `ctxtMenuImage` object. We created and discussed this method in chapter 3.
		``
		private void DefineContextMenu()
		{
		  //Copy View menu into ctxtMenuView
		  . . .
		  // Copy Image menu into ctxtMenuImage
		  foreach (MenuItem mi in
		      menuImage.MenuItems)
		  {
		    ctxtMenuImage.MenuItems.
		    Add(mi.Index, mi.CloneMenu());
		  }
		}
		``

	Action	Result
5	In the ToolBarButton Collection Editor, add two new toolbar buttons.	

Settings

Button	Property	Value
6	Style	Separator
	(Name)	tbbImage
	DropDownMenu	ctxtMenuImage
7 (Image)	ImageIndex	5
	Style	DropDownButton
	ToolTipText	Set display mode

Note: The down arrow to the right of the image appears because the toolbar's `DropDownArrow` property is `true`. Set this property to `false` to display the button without the arrow.

Our new toolbar button requires a new context menu, which we use as the dropdown menu for our new button. Even though the `DropDownMenu` property for the `Tool-BarButton` class is defined as a type of `Menu` object, a `ContextMenu` instance is required to properly display a dropdown menu beneath the button. We could have used the `ctxtMenuView` context menu, although we would then display the entire View menu beneath the toolbar button.

Compile, run, open, click, and otherwise make sure the new button works. The .NET Framework does all the hard work here. When the button is clicked, the menu item collection associated with the `ctxtMenuImage` menu is displayed. This causes the `Popup` event associated with this menu to fire, invoking the `menuImage_Popup` event handler. Figure 13.2 shows the application with the popup menu displayed for our new button.

Figure 13.2
When the down arrow for a toolbar button is shown, as it is here, the user must click on this arrow to display the associated menu.

Of course, you don't always have an existing menu in your menu bar to clone and use in your dropdown toolbar buttons. A custom `ContextMenu` object can be created and assigned to the button. If desired, you can also draw your own menu items similar to how we drew a custom status bar panel in chapter 4 and list box items in chapter 10.

Alternately, you may wish to forgo a menu entirely and create a custom window to associate with your button. This can be done as well. The `ButtonDropDown` event occurs for the parent `ToolBar` control whenever a dropdown menu on the control is clicked. Event handlers for this event receive a `ToolBarButtonClickEvent-Args` class instance as the event parameter. This class contains a `Button` property to retrieve the dropdown `ToolBarButton` instance that was clicked. The `Rectangle` property for the button identifies the location of the button and can be used to properly place a small window or other graphical object at the proper location.

Our last style of button is a toggle button.

13.3.3   ADDING A TOGGLE BUTTON

Our final toolbar button will illustrate the `ToggleButton` style to show and hide the pixel data dialog created in chapter 8. Toggle buttons, as you may recall from chapter 9, provide two different states: one when the button is pressed in, and one when it is not.

We will do something a little different here that seems appropriate for our example. If you are keeping track of the images available in our image list, you may realize there are two images left, while only one more button. We will use one image when the button is pushed in, and the other when it is not. Figure 13.3 shows our application with the button pressed in and the `PixelDlg` form displayed.

Figure 13.3
The toggle button on our toolbar displays a green light when the pixel dialog is shown, and a red light otherwise.

This will require some coordination with the rest of the application to make sure the button is never pressed when the pixel dialog is hidden. We'll begin by creating the button and implementing the `ButtonClick` event support.

	ADD THE TOGGLE TOOLBAR BUTTONS	
	ACTION	**RESULT**
1	In the ToolBarButton Collection Editor, add two new toolbar buttons. **Settings**<table><tr><th>Button</th><th>Property</th><th>Value</th></tr><tr><td>8</td><td>Style</td><td>Separator</td></tr><tr><td></td><td>(Name)</td><td>tbbPixelData</td></tr><tr><td>9 (Pixel)</td><td>ImageIndex</td><td>6</td></tr><tr><td></td><td>Style</td><td>ToggleButton</td></tr><tr><td></td><td>ToolTipText</td><td>Show pixel data</td></tr></table>	
2	Implement an `AssignPixelData` method in the MainForm.cs code window to adjust the button settings based a specified value. **How-to** Display the green light icon when the button is pushed, and the red light otherwise. **Note:** This will be used by various methods to update the toggle button as the state of the pixel data dialog changes.	<pre>protected void
AssignPixelToggle(bool push)
{
tbbPixelData.Pushed = push;
if (push)
{
tbbPixelData.ImageIndex = 7;
tbbPixelData.ToolTipText
= "Hide pixel data";
}
else
{
tbbPixelData.ImageIndex = 6;
tbbPixelData.ToolTipText
= "Show pixel data";
}
}</pre>
3	Update the `ButtonClick` event handler to adjust the state of both the dialog and the button when the toggle is clicked. **How-to** a. When the button is pushed, invoke the Pixel Data menu to ensure the dialog is displayed. b. Otherwise, hide the dialog if it is currently displayed. c. Also call the `AssignPixelToggle` method to update the button settings.	<pre>private void toolBarMain_ButtonClick
    (object sender,
        ToolBarButtonClickEventArgs e)
{
  // Handle menu buttons
  . . .
  // Handle Pixel Data button
  if (e.Button == tbbPixelData)
  {
    if (e.Button.Pushed)
    {
      // Display pixel dialog
      menuPixelData.PerformClick();
    }
    else if (this._dlgPixel != null
          && _dlgPixel.Visible)
    {
      // Hide pixel dialog
      _dlgPixel.Hide();
    }

    // Update the button settings
    AssignPixelToggle(e.Button.Pushed);
  }
}</pre> |

These changes implement the correct functionality for the button. When the button is pushed, a `Click` event for the `menuPixelData` menu is performed, which displays the dialog. When the button is unpushed,[1] the dialog is hidden using the `Hide` method. In this later case we ensure that the dialog exists and is shown before trying to hide it. The `AssignPixelToggle` method adjusts the image and the tool tip to reflect the new state of the button.

You can run the program to see the button in action. If you do, you may notice that there are two problems we still need to address:

- The button is not pushed when the pixel data dialog is displayed using the View menu item.
- The button is not unpushed when the dialog is closed manually.

For the first problem, we simply need to adjust the button in the `Click` event handler for this menu. Let's do this before we discuss the second problem.

	UPDATE THE TOGGLE BUTTON WHEN THE PIXEL DATA MENU IS SELECTED	
	Action	**Result**
4	Locate the `menuPixelData_Click` event handler in the MainForm.cs code window.	```private void menuPixelData_Click (object sender, System.EventArgs e) {```
5	Update this method to adjust the toggle button settings.	```if (_dlgPixel == null || _dlgPixel.IsDisposed) { _dlgPixel = new PixelDlg(); _dlgPixel.Owner = this; } _nPixelDlgIndex = _album.CurrentPosition; Point p = pnlPhoto.PointToClient(Form.MousePosition); UpdatePixelData(p.X, p.Y); AssignPixelToggle(true); _dlgPixel.Show(); }```

Our second problem, that of the user closing the pixel data dialog by hand, is more problematic. Since this dialog is a nonmodal window, this dialog can be closed at any time. So we need a mechanism for notifying our main window whenever the dialog is closed.

If you recall, and as shown in step 5 in the previous table, the `MainForm` form is defined as the owner of the `PixelDlg` form. This ensures that both windows are

---

[1] I know, I know. There is no such word as "unpushed." You know what I mean. I thought about the word "released," but unpushed seems much more packed with meaning.

shown when either window is displayed or minimized. We can take advantage of this relationship to ensure that our main window is notified when the pixel dialog is closed.

The trick is to force the `MainForm` window to activate whenever the `PixelDlg` dialog is closed. Our main form will then receive an `Activated` event, at which time we can update our button. Since the `MainForm` class derives directly from `Form`, we can handle this event by overriding the protected `OnActivated` method.

The following steps implement this mechanism.

	UPDATE THE TOGGLE BUTTON WHEN THE PIXELDLG FORM IS CLOSED	
	Action	**Result**
6	In the PixelDlg.cs code window, override the `OnClosing` method to activate the owner of the dialog, if any. **Note:** Since the dialog may not be fully closed here if the `Main-Form.OnActivated` method runs immediately, we set the `Visible` property to `false` to ensure the correct behavior occurs. Also note that overriding the `OnClosed` method instead does not work because the `Owner` property is no longer valid once the dialog has been closed.	```csharp\nprotected override void OnClosing\n (CancelEventArgs e)\n{\n Visible = false;\n if (this.Owner != null)\n Owner.Activate();\n\n base.OnClosing(e);\n}\n```
7	Back in the MainForm.cs code window, override the `OnActivated` method.	```csharp\nprotected override void\n OnActivated(EventArgs e)\n{\n```
8	If the pixel dialog does not exist, then make sure our button is not pushed down.	```csharp\n// Update toggle button if required\nif (_dlgPixel == null\n || _dlgPixel.IsDisposed)\n{\n AssignPixelToggle(false);\n}\n```
9	Otherwise, set the button state based on the `Visible` property of the pixel dialog.	```csharp\nelse\n AssignPixelToggle(_dlgPixel.Visible);\n\nbase.OnActivated(e);\n}\n```

This code ensures that whenever the user closes the `PixelDlg` form, the main form is activated and the toggle toolbar button immediately updated. Compile and run the application to ensure that it works as expected.

TRY IT! Add two new menus to the top of the View menu called `menuToolBar` and `menuStatusBar`. Implement these menus to show and hide the corresponding controls in the application. Use the `Visible` property inherited from the `Control` class to identify the control's current state and set it to the opposite one. If you are careful, you can implement a single `Click` handler for both menus by using the `sender` parameter and observing that both objects are `Control` instances. When you run the program with these changes, note how the control shows or hides their contained buttons or panels as well.

This completes our discussion of toolbars. We now move on to the mostly unrelated but similarly named `ToolTip` class.

13.4 TOOL TIPS

You never know when a good tip might come in handy. In Windows applications, tool tips provide short and quick explanations of the purpose of a control or other object. A number of classes provide their own tool tip mechanism through a `ToolTipText` property, in particular the `StatusBarPanel`, `TabPage`, and `ToolBarButton` classes. For classes derived from the `Control` object, the `ToolTip` class handles this logic in a general fashion.

.NET Table 13.5 ToolTip class		
The `ToolTip` class is a component that provides a small popup window for a control. This window normally contains a short phrase describing the purpose of the control, and appears whenever the mouse hovers over the control for a configurable amount of time. This class is part of the `System.Windows.Forms` namespace, and supports the `IExtenderProvider` interface. The `ToolTip` class derives from the `System.ComponentModel.Component` class.		
Public Properties	Active	Gets or sets whether the `ToolTip` is currently active. When `false`, no tool tips will appear. The default is `true`.
	AutomaticDelay	Gets or sets the default delay time in milliseconds. Whenever this property is set, the `AutoPopDelay`, `InitialDelay`, and `ReshowDelay` properties are initialized. The default is 500.
	AutoPopDelay	Gets or sets the time in milliseconds before a displayed tool tip will disappear. The default is ten times the `AutomaticDelay` setting.
	InitialDelay	Gets or sets the time in milliseconds before a tool tip will appear when the mouse is stationary. The default is the `AutomaticDelay` setting.
	ReshowDelay	Gets or sets the time in milliseconds after the first tool tip is displayed before subsequent tool tips are displayed as the mouse moves from one assigned control to another. The default is one-fifth (1/5) the `AutomaticDelay` setting.
	ShowAlways	Gets or sets whether to display the tool tip for an inactive control. The default is `false`.
Public Methods	GetToolTip	Retrieves the tool tip string associated with a given control.
	RemoveAll	Removes all tool tip strings defined in this component.
	SetToolTip	Associates a tool tip string with a given control.

13.4.1 THE TOOLTIP CLASS

An overview of the `ToolTip` class is provided in .NET Table 13.5. Note that a `ToolTip` object is not strictly speaking a control, although it is sometimes referred to as such. Normally, a single `ToolTip` object is used to create the tips for all controls in a single `Form`.

13.4.2 Creating tool tips

While it is certainly possible to assign tool tips for our `MainForm` controls in the `MyPhotos` project, this would not be a very exciting example. Since menu objects are not controls, we cannot assign tool tip text to our menu items. As we saw earlier in this chapter and in chapter 4, the `ToolBar` and `StatusBar` controls provide their own tool tip mechanism. That leaves the `Panel` object, which is only a single control.

Instead, we will look to our now-famous MyPhotoAlbum library for a rich source of tool tip hungry controls. Figure 13.4 shows the `PhotoEditDlg` form with a tool tip displayed for the Date Taken text box.

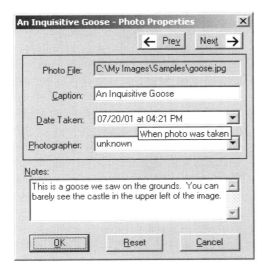

Figure 13.4
The framework displays tool tip text just below the mouse cursor, which in most cases will not obscure the control's contents from view.

Let's crank up an Action-Result table and create a `ToolTip` object for this dialog. Once the tool tip exists, we can discuss how to associate specific messages with individual controls.

Set the version number of the MyPhotoAlbum library to 13.4.

	Action	Result
	ADD A TOOL TIP OBJECT TO THE PHOTOEDITDLG FORM	
1	In the PhotoEditDlg.cs [Design] window, add a `ToolTip` object to the form.	The new object appears in the component tray below the form designer.
2	Set the (Name) for the tool tip to "toolTipPhotos."	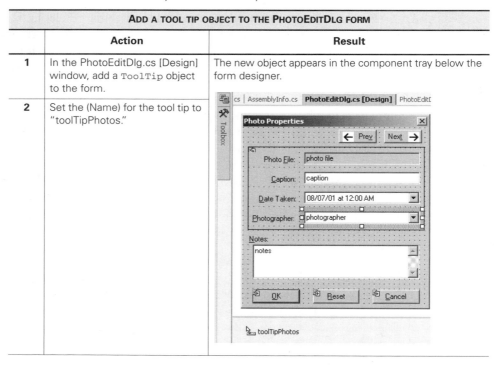

As usual, the new object is defined within the `PhotoEditDlg` class and initialized in the `InitializeComponent` method.

```
private System.Windows.Forms.ToolTip toolTipPhotos;
. . .
private void InitializeComponent()
{
    . . .
    this.toolTipPhotos = new System.Windows.Forms.ToolTip(this.components);
    . . .
}
```

As we saw for the `ImageList` in our MyPhotos application, the `ToolTip` is created within the `Form` object's `components` container to ensure that the object is disposed of when the `Form` itself is disposed.

We can add a series of tool tip strings for our controls using Visual Studio directly. This table continues our previous steps.

	Action	Result
3	Add the tool tip "Previous photo" for the Prev button control on the form. **How-to** a. Display the properties for the button in the Properties window. b. Locate the new entry "ToolTip on toolTip-Photos" that is now present c. Enter the string "Previous photo."	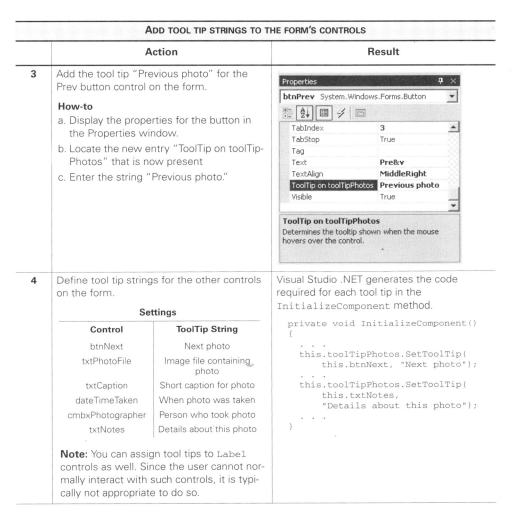

4	Define tool tip strings for the other controls on the form.
	
	Settings
	
	| Control
		ToolTip String |
		|---|---|
		| btnNext | Next photo |
		| txtPhotoFile | Image file containing photo |
		| txtCaption | Short caption for photo |
		| dateTimeTaken | When photo was taken |
		| cmbxPhotographer | Person who took photo |
		| txtNotes | Details about this photo |
		
		Note: You can assign tool tips to `Label` controls as well. Since the user cannot normally interact with such controls, it is typically not appropriate to do so.
			Visual Studio .NET generates the code required for each tool tip in the `InitializeComponent` method.
			
			``
			private void InitializeComponent()
			{
			    . . .
			    this.toolTipPhotos.SetToolTip(
			        this.btnNext, "Next photo");
			    . . .
			    this.toolTipPhotos.SetToolTip(
			        this.txtNotes,
			        "Details about this photo");
			    . . .
			}
			``

That's all it takes. Visual Studio .NET generates the code as is shown in the table. Of course, you can define tool tips explicitly in your code using the `SetToolTip` method without using Visual Studio. The steps used here simply demonstrate the support provided by the development environment.

Compile and run the program to make sure your tool tips work. Open an album and display the `PhotoEditDlg` dialog for a photo. Place the mouse over a control and watch the tool tip appear. As you look at the tool tips we just defined, note the following features:

- There is a short pause, about half a second, before the tool tip text appears, and then it disappears after about 5 seconds. These intervals are controlled by the `InitialDelay` and `AutoPopDelay` properties.

- Display a tool tip, then move the mouse to another control and note how the tool tip for the second control appears almost immediately. This secondary delay defaults to 100 milliseconds, and is specified by the `ReshowDelay` property.

- The tool tips for the Next and Prev buttons do not appear when these buttons are inactive. The behavior for inactive controls is determined by the `ShowAlways` property.

TRY IT! Create a `ToolTip` object for the `AlbumEditDlg` form and set tool tip text for the nonlabel controls in this form. Note that you can set tool tips for `Panel` and `GroupBox` objects, although this may confuse users and is probably not a good idea for this form.

That's pretty much all you need to know about tool tips. You may wonder if you can create balloon-style or custom drawn tool tips. Right now the answer is no, at least within the `ToolTip` class. We might see this type of support in a future release of the framework, or you can build a custom control for this purpose yourself.

More .NET The `HelpProvider` class is a component that provides popup help using a mechanism similar to the `ToolTip` class. The `HelpProvider` class provides a `SetHelpString` method for this purpose, in a manner similar to the `SetToolTip` method for the `ToolTip` component. You can see this by dragging a `HelpProvider` component onto a form and modifying the `HelpString` entry that appears in the Properties window. This string will appear when the user hits the F1 key while the control has the focus.

The `Form` class also provides a related `HelpButton` property. When the `MinimizeBox` and `MaximizeBox` properties for a form are `false`, setting the `HelpButton` property to `true` will cause a Help button to appear in the title bar. Clicking on this button and then on a control displays the popup help string assigned to that control.

It is also worth noting that the `HelpProvider` class supports more sophisticated help for an application. In particular, this class can specify a link into an HTML file where help text on specific elements of a form is available. Consult the online documentation for more information on this feature.

13.5 RECAP

This completes chapter 13 as well as part 2 of the book. We've come a long way from figure 1.1 on page 4, and hopefully have learned how to create Windows applications with a large variety of controls and behaviors.

In this chapter we looked at the `ToolBar` and `ToolTip` classes. We created a toolbar in our MyPhotos application, and used the four different styles of toolbar buttons supported by .NET. We also saw how to dynamically change the image displayed on a button.

We then created some tool tips for our `PhotoEditDlg` form. We associated a `ToolTip` instance with our form, and saw how to assign tool tips to the various controls contained within this form.

Along the way we examined the `ImageList` class as a way to store and manage a collection of `Image` objects on behalf of a control or other object. We again looked at the resource file generated by Visual Studio .NET to contain the images assigned to such a list, and we created an image list for use within our `ToolBar` control.

In addition, we pointed out how `Component` objects such as `ImageList` and `ToolTip` instances are disposed of when created within Visual Studio. Such objects are contained within the form's `components` member to ensure they can be tidied up when the `Dispose` method is invoked.

I would encourage you to experiment with the controls and features discussed here and in earlier chapters in this book. The foundation presented so far is critical to developing and understanding Windows Forms applications, and will come in handy as we discuss the concepts presented in part 3.

Advanced Windows Forms

If you have actually read this book from the beginning, then I applaud your fortitude and welcome you to the third and final part of this book. For those readers who have jumped directly to this page, I would encourage you to actually read the earlier chapters, as they build a foundation for much of the discussion that will occur in this part of the book. Of course, if you are browsing this book with the idea of buying it, then feel free to look around.

In part 3 we look at what might be considered advanced topics. If you have a firm, or at least decent, grasp of the material from part 2 of this book, then this section should be quite understandable.

Chapter 14 kicks off our discussion with the topic of "List views." This chapter creates a new MyAlbumExplorer application incorporating a `ListView` control, and demonstrates various means of displaying and interacting with objects in this control.

Chapter 15 on "Tree views" extends the MyAlbumExplorer application to support a standard explorer-style interface. The `Splitter` and `TreeView` controls are discussed, and various interactions between the `ListView` and `TreeView` controls in the MyAlbumExplorer application are examined.

Chapter 16 turns to the topic of "Multiple document interfaces." This chapter discusses the support provided by the .NET Framework for multiple document interface, or MDI, applications in Windows Forms. Here we return to our MyPhotos application from part 2 and convert it into an MDI application, using our `MainForm` class as the child window.

The topic of "Data binding" is taken up in chapter 17. This discusses complex data binding by way of the `DataGrid` control, and simple binding of data to Windows Forms controls in general. This chapter will illustrate how to provide transactional updates within a class and automatically invoke these updates from a bound control. A new MyAlbumData application is constructed over the course of this chapter.

Chapter 18 is called "Odds and ends .NET," and completes our discussion with a review of various topics that should be of further interest. These include printing, Windows Forms timers, drag and drop, and ActiveX controls. An example for each topic is provided using the MyPhotos MDI application built in chapter 16.

Following this last chapter are four appendices with some additional information on C#, an overview of .NET namespaces, a class hierarchy chart of the Windows Forms namespace, and resources for additional information on C# and the .NET Framework.

List views

14.1 The nature of list views 440

14.2 The ListView class 443

14.3 ListView columns 453

14.4 Selection and editing 464

14.5 Item activation 472

14.6 Recap 483

To kick off the advanced section of the book, we take a detailed look at the List-View class. This class is used by applications such as Windows Explorer to present a collection of items in list form. We will examine this class in detail, including the following topics:

- Various styles supported by the ListView class.

- Members of the ListView class.

- Defining list view columns in Visual Studio and programmatically.

- Selecting and editing items in the list.

- Activating list view items.

- Dynamically switching the contents of a list view.

We will start from scratch here and build a new application called MyAlbumEx-plorer. In this chapter we will display both albums and photographs in the main window. The next chapter will add support for a TreeView control to this application to create a window much like the Windows Explorer application utilizes for file system objects.

439

14.1 THE NATURE OF LIST VIEWS

In many ways, a list view is a more glamorous version of a list box. Other than the fact that they are both controls, there is no relation from a class hierarchy perspective, but conceptually both present a scrollable list to the user. The `ListBox` class stores a collection of `object` instances, while the `ListView` class contains a collection of `ListViewItem` instances, which in turn contains a collection of `ListViewSub-Item` objects.

Another difference is how their contents are displayed. The `ListBox` control displays a string associated with each object by default, and supports an owner-drawn style to display other formats. The `ListView` control displays its items in one of four views represented by the `View` enumeration, as described by .NET Table 14.1. When the `Details` view is displayed, the collection of subitems appears in a configured set of `ColumnHeader` objects associated with the control.

.NET Table 14.1	View enumeration	
The `View` enumeration specifies the different ways the contents of a ListView control can appear. This enumeration is part of the `System.Windows.Forms` namespace. The following table provides an example obtained from the Windows Explorer application.		
	LargeIcon	Each item appears as a large icon with a label below it. By default, items can be dragged around and placed at any location within the control. 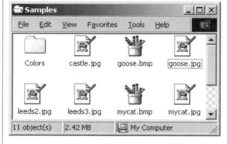
Enumeration Values	SmallIcon	Each item appears as a small icon with a label at the right. By default, items can be dragged and placed at any location in the control. 

.NET Table 14.1	View enumeration	
Enumeration Values	List	Items are arranged as small icons, in columns with no headers, and with the labels on the right. 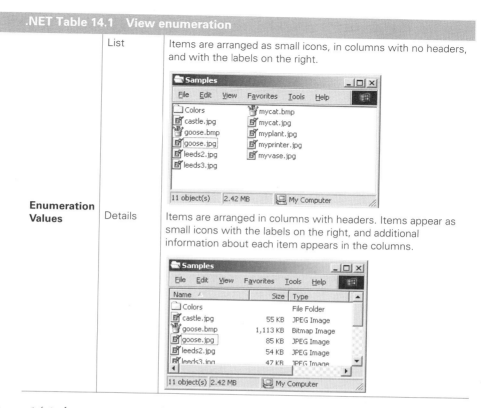
	Details	Items are arranged in columns with headers. Items appear as small icons with the labels on the right, and additional information about each item appears in the columns.

Figure 14.1 shows a `Form` with a `ListView` control displayed in the `Details` view mode. This figure illustrates various features and classes used by this control. We will look at these in detail as we progress through the chapter.

An icon taken from an **ImageList** instance is associated with each item. ①

The primary text associated with each item is called the item *label*. ②

The **ListViewItem** class represents a single item in the list. ③

Multiple instances of the **ListViewSubItem** class represent additional information associated with each item. ④

The **ColumnHeader** class represents a single column for the list. ⑤

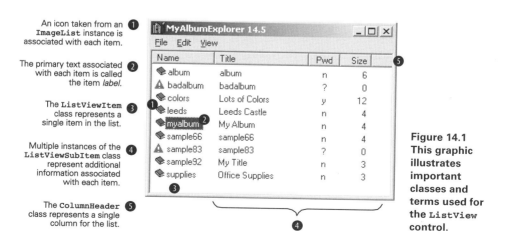

Figure 14.1 This graphic illustrates important classes and terms used for the `ListView` control.

The `ListView` class is a control that displays a collection of labeled items as a list in one of four different views. Typically an icon is displayed for each item in the collection to provide a graphical indication of the nature or purpose of the item. Items can be displayed with large icons, small icons, in a list format, or in a detailed list format. The detailed list permits additional information about each item to appear in columns within the control. This class is part of the `System.Windows.Forms` namespace, and inherits from the `Control` class. See .NET Table 4.1 on page 104 for a list of members inherited by this class.

Public Properties	Activation	Gets or sets how an item is activated, and whether the font changes as the mouse passes over the item.
	CheckBoxes	Gets or sets whether a check box is displayed next to each item. Default is `false`.
	Columns	Gets the collection of `ColumnHeader` components associated with the control.
	HeaderStyle	Gets or sets the column header style for the control. Default is `ColumnHeaderStyle.Clickable`.
	Items	Gets the collection of items in the list.
	LabelEdit	Gets or sets whether the user can edit item labels in the list. Default is `false`.
	LargeImageList	Gets or sets the `ImageList` for the `LargeIcon` view.
	ListViewItemSorter	Gets or sets an `IComparer` interface to use when sorting items in the list.
	MultiSelect	Gets or sets whether multiple items in the list may be selected at the same time. Default is `false`.
	SelectedItems	Gets the collection of items selected in the list.
	SmallImageList	Gets or sets the `ImageList` instance for the views other than the `LargeIcon` view.
	Sorting	Gets or sets how items in the list are sorted, if at all.
	StateImageList	Gets or sets the `ImageList` list for state icons.
	View	Gets or sets the current `View` enumeration value for the list. Default is `LargeIcon`.
Public Methods	Clear	Removes all items and columns from the list view control.
	EnsureVisible	Ensures a given item is visible, scrolling it into view if necessary.
Public Events	AfterLabelEdit	Occurs after an item label has been edited.
	ColumnClick	Occurs when the user clicks a column header in the `Details` view.
	ItemActivate	Occurs when an item is activated. How this occurs depends on the `Activation` property.
	ItemDrag	Occurs when a user begins dragging an item in the list.
	SelectedIndex-Changed	Occurs when the selection state of an item changes.

14.2   THE LISTVIEW CLASS

This section begins our examination of list views by creating our new application and displaying a list view control within its main window. An overview of the ListView class appears in .NET Table 14.2.

Our initial application is shown in figure 14.2. This window displays the default, or Large Icons, view. Creating this application will require three separate tasks. First we will create the new project, then add the Menu components and ListView control required, and finally populate the ListView with the available set of albums.

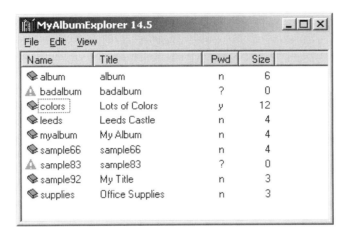

Figure 14.2
MyAlbumExplorer will use a book graphic for individual albums. Note how a separate icon is used when an album cannot be opened.

14.2.1   CREATING THE MYALBUMEXPLORER PROJECT

We discussed the steps for creating a new project in Visual Studio in chapter 2 and again in chapter 10. Since we have already seen this a couple of times, the following table will gloss over many of the details and just hit the highlights. We will also set an icon for our Form and application, as we discussed at the end of chapter 12.

CREATE THE MYALBUMEXPLORER PROJECT		
	Action	**Result**
1	Create a new Windows Application project called "MyAlbumExplorer."	
2	Rename the Form1.cs file and `Form1` class name to MainForm.cs and `MainForm`, respectively.	
3	Add the project MyPhotoAlbum to the solution.	
4	Reference this project within the MyAlbumExplorer project.	
5	In the MainForm.cs code window, override the `OnLoad` method to display the version number in the title bar.	```protected override void OnLoad(EventArgs e)
{
// Assign title bar
Version v = new Version(Application.
ProductVersion);
this.Text = String.Format(
"MyAlbumExplorer {0:#}.{1:#}",
v.Major, v.Minor);
}```

This creates a solution for our new application. We will also establish an icon for the Form as well as the generated application file. This uses the term *common image directory*, which as you'll recall is our shorthand for the graphics files provided with Visual Studio .NET. By default, these can be found in "C:\Program Files\Microsoft Visual Studio .NET\Common7\Graphics."

Set the version number of the MyAlbumExplorer application to 14.2.

DEFINE ICONS FOR THE FORM AND APPLICATION		
	Action	**Result**
6	In the MainForm.cs [Design] window, set the `Icon` property for the `Form` to use the icon file "icons/Writing/BOOKS04.ICO" in the common image directory.	BOOKS04.ICO
7	Delete the existing "App.ico" icon file for the MyAlbumExplorer project.	

	Action	Result
8	Set the Application Icon setting for the MyAlbumExplorer project to use the BOOKS04.ICO icon as well. **How-to** Right-click on the project name in Solution Explorer and select the Properties item to display the appropriate dialog.	The icon is presented to the Windows operating system to represent the application.

With these tasks out of the way, we are ready to add a `ListView` control to our form.

14.2.2 CREATING A LIST VIEW

This section will drop some menu objects and a list view control onto our form so we can examine and manipulate these controls in Visual Studio .NET. These steps will also create some menus we will use as we move through the chapter.

	Action	Result
	ADD A MENU AND LIST VIEW TO OUR FORM	
1	Add a `MainMenu` object to the form in the MainForm.cs [Design] window.	
2	Create the following top-level menus. **Settings** 	Menu	Property	Value
File	(Name)	menuFile
	Text	&File
Edit	(Name)	menuEdit
	Text	&Edit
View	(Name)	menuView
	Text	&View		This graphic is the result of steps 2 and 3.

	Action	Result
3	Create four menus underneath the View menu.	**Note:** The View menus allow the user to alter how the `ListView` appears. To match the style used by Windows Explorer, we set the `RadioCheck` property to `true` so that a small circle is used as the check mark.

Settings

Menu	Property	Value
Large Icons	(Name)	menuLargeIcons
	Checked	True
	RadioCheck	True
	Text	Lar&ge Icons
Small Icons	(Name)	menuSmallIcons
	RadioCheck	True
	Text	S&mall Icons
List	(Name)	menuList
	RadioCheck	True
	Text	&List
Details	(Name)	menuDetails
	RadioCheck	True

	Action	Result
4	Add an Exit menu underneath the File menu, along with an appropriate `Click` event handler to close the form.	

```
private void menuExit_Click
    (object sender, System.EventArgs e)
{
    Close();
}
```

Settings

Property	Value
(Name)	menuExit
Text	E&xit

	Action	Result
5	Establish appropriate `Size` and `Text` properties for the `MainForm` form.	

Settings

Property	Value
Size	400, 300
Text	MyAlbumExplorer

	Action	Result
6	Place a `ListView` control onto the form. **How-to** Use the tool box as you would for any other control. **Settings** | Property	Value
---	---
(Name)	listViewMain
Dock	Fill		 ![MyAlbumExplorer window with File, Edit, View menus and empty list area]

Since we already know how to manipulate menu objects, we may as well set up the appropriate event handlers here as well. We will need a `Popup` event handler for the View menu to make sure the appropriate menu item is checked, and a `Click` menu for each item to assign the `ListView.View` property to the corresponding value. We could try to do something fancy here to limit the amount of code we needed to write. Instead, we will simply code this up directly and save our fancy tricks for later.

	Action	Result
	ADD EVENT HANDLERS FOR THE VIEW MENU	
	Action	**Result**

7	Add a `Popup` event handler for the View menu.	```private void menuView_Popup```
		``` (object sender, System.EventArgs e)```
		```{```

8	Implement this handler to check the appropriate entry based on the `View` property of the `ListView` control.	```View v = listViewMain.View;```
		```menuLargeIcons.Checked = (v == View.LargeIcon);```
		```menuSmallIcons.Checked = (v == View.SmallIcon);```
		```menuList.Checked = (v == View.List);```
		```menuDetails.Checked = (v == View.Details);```
		```}```

	Action	Result
9	Add Click event handlers for each of the four menus in the View menu. **Note:** These handlers set the View property value in the listViewMain control, which alters how the contents of the control appear to the user.	```cs private void menuLargeIcons_Click (object sender, System.EventArgs e) { listViewMain.View = View.LargeIcon; } private void menuSmallIcons_Click(. . .) { listViewMain.View = View.SmallIcon; } private void menuList_Click(. . .) { listViewMain.View = View.List; } private void menuDetails_Click(. . .) { listViewMain.View = View.Details; } ```

Your program will work just fine here. It doesn't do very much, but it does work. Our final step for this section is to populate the list control with the available albums.

14.2.3 Populating a ListView

Our final task here is to populate the ListView control. As we said earlier in the chapter, a ListView control contains a collection of ListViewItem objects. As indicated in .NET Table 14.3, the ListViewItem object inherits directly from the System.Object class. All of the painting and other management of list items are performed by the ListView class itself. This painting behavior is consistent with other container controls we have seen such as the StatusBar control containing StatusBarPanel objects, and the ListBox control containing a set of object instances.

Our use of the ListViewItem object here will be fairly modest. We will get more complicated later in the chapter. For now, we simply wish to create an item for each album with the file name as the label and an appropriate image icon assigned. This requires that we create an ImageList for both the small and large icons to display in the view, and populate the Items property for the list with a ListViewItem for each album.

The ListViewItem class is an object that can be displayed within a ListView control. It is part of the System.Windows.Forms namespace, and supports the IClonable and ISerializable interfaces.

Public Constructors	ListViewItem	Initializes a new ListViewItem instance.
		
		Overloads
		`ListViewItem(string label);`
		`ListViewItem(string[] labelAndSubitems);`
		`ListViewItem(string label, int imageIndex);`
		`ListViewItem(ListViewItem item,`
		`            ListViewSubItem[] subitems,`
		`            int imageIndex);`

Public Properties	Bounds	Gets the bounding rectangle of the item, including any displayed subitems.
	Focused	Gets or sets whether the item has the focus within the containing view. Defaults to false.
	Font	Gets or sets the Font for the item. If null, the containing ListView uses its font for this purpose.
	ForeColor	Gets or sets the foreground Color for the item.
	ImageIndex	Gets or sets the index used to retrieve the icon for this item.
	Index	Gets the index corresponding to the current position of the item within the containing ListView.
	ListView	Gets the ListView control that contains this item.
	Selected	Gets or sets whether the item is currently selected in the containing view.
	StateImageIndex	Gets or sets the index for the state icon for this item.
	SubItems	Gets the collection of list view subitems assigned to this item. Note that this includes the item label as the first element in this collection.
	Tag	Gets or sets the object associated with this item.
	Text	Gets or sets the text string for this item. This is the item label.
Public Methods	BeginEdit	Initiates an edit of this item's label.
	EnsureVisible	Ensures a given item is visible, scrolling the containing view as necessary.
	Remove	Removes the item from the collection of ListViewItem objects in the containing view.

We will begin with the `ImageList` components.

	CREATE THE IMAGE LISTS FOR THE VIEW	
	Action	**Result**
1	In the MainForm.cs [Design] window, add two new `ImageList` objects to the form. **Settings**<table><tr><th>List</th><th>Property</th><th>Value</th></tr><tr><td>List 1</td><td>(Name)</td><td>imageListLarge</td></tr><tr><td></td><td>Size</td><td>32. 32</td></tr><tr><td>List 2</td><td>(Name)</td><td>imageListSmall</td></tr><tr><td></td><td>Size</td><td>16, 16</td></tr></table>	The objects appear in the component tray area below the form. **Note:** The first list will contain the large icons for the `View.LargeIcon` display mode, and the second the small icons for all other modes. Since the icons provided in the common image area define both image types, each list will use the same set of files. The `Size` property defines the actual image to use by each list.
2	Define the images from the common image area required for the `imageListLarge` object. **How-to** Use the Image Collection Editor, as discussed in chapter 13. **Settings**<table><tr><th>Image</th><th>File</th></tr><tr><td>0</td><td>icons/Misc/FACE01.ico</td></tr><tr><td>1</td><td>icons/Writing/BOOK01A.ico</td></tr><tr><td>2</td><td>icons/Misc/MISC02.ico</td></tr><tr><td>3</td><td>icons/Misc/FACE02.ico</td></tr><tr><td>4</td><td>icons/Writing/BOOK02.ico</td></tr><tr><td>5</td><td>icons/Writing/BOOKS04.ico</td></tr></table>	The icons are stored in the image list and available to the application. **Note:** The first icon will be used for `Photograph` objects later in this chapter. The next two are for a "good" and "bad" album, respectively. The final three will be used in chapter 15 when discussing the `TreeView` class.
3	Similarly, define the same set of images for the `imageListSmall` object. **Note:** You might be tempted to create this image list by making a copy of the `imageListLarge` object and then applying the settings from step 1. While this works, the small images are scaled from the larger size stored in the `imageListLarge` object, resulting in poorer quality icons.	The same set of icons, albeit in different sizes, is now available from both image lists.
4	Assign the two image lists to the corresponding property in the `ListView` control. **Settings**<table><tr><th>Property</th><th>Value</th></tr><tr><td>LargeImageList</td><td>imageListLarge</td></tr><tr><td>SmallImageList</td><td>imageListSmall</td></tr></table>	Images from each list can now be displayed for items in the `ListView` control.

The code generated by these changes is similar to examples we have seen before. The images are stored in a .resx file for the `MainForm` object, and loaded into the application using the `ResourceManager` class.

Now that we have the image lists defined, the form containing a `ListView` control, and the View menu primed and ready, we have nothing to do but add our photo albums to the list. We do this in the `OnLoad` method, which is called just before the `Form` displays the first time. We could instead add these items in the `MainForm` constructor, but the `OnLoad` method is preferred for such actions to ensure that the `Form` is fully initialized.

Let's see how this code looks.

	ADD EACH ALBUM TO THE VIEW	
	Action	**Result**
5	In the MainForm.cs source code window, indicate that this file will use members of the `System.IO` and the `Manning.MyPhotoAlbum` namespaces.	```using System.IO;
using Manning.MyPhotoAlbum;```
6	Add a set of constant fields for the image list indices required. **Note** Using constants in this manner is a good idea in case our values ever change in the future.	```private const int PhotoIndex = 0;
private const int AlbumIndex = 1;
private const int ErrorIndex = 2;```
7	Modify the `OnLoad` method to load the default set of albums through a private method.	```protected override void OnLoad(EventArgs e)
{
. . .
LoadAlbumData(PhotoAlbum.DefaultDir);
}```
8	Create a private `OpenAlbum` method to open an album.	```private PhotoAlbum OpenAlbum(string fileName)
{
    PhotoAlbum album = new PhotoAlbum();

    try
    {
        album.Open(fileName);
    }
    catch (Exception)
    {
        return null;
    }

    return album;
}``` |

	Action	Result
9	Implement the `LoadAlbumData` method by iterating over the set of album files in the given album directory. **Note:** Accepting the directory from which to load the albums may come in useful if we ever want to support multiple directories.	```private void LoadAlbumData(string dir)
{
string[] albumFiles
= Directory.GetFiles(dir, "*.abm");
foreach (string s in albumFiles)
{```
10	Try to open the album file.	```// See if we can open this album
PhotoAlbum album = OpenAlbum(s);``` **Note:** Of course, if the album requires a password, then the user must enter it here, which is not the best user interface. See the TRY IT! paragraph later in this section for a discussion on an alternative approach.
11	Initialize a new `ListViewItem` based on whether the album was opened successfully.	```// Create a new list view item
ListViewItem item = new ListViewItem();

item.Text
    = Path.GetFileNameWithoutExtension(s);
if (album != null)
    item.ImageIndex = MainForm.AlbumIndex;
else
    item.ImageIndex = MainForm.ErrorIndex;``` |
| 12 | Add the new item to the `ListView` control. | ```   listViewMain.Items.Add(item);
    }
}``` |

This creates a list item for each album found, using the base file name as the text for the album. If an album fails to open, then an error image is assigned as its icon. If any of your albums happen to have a nonempty password set, then the `PhotoAlbum` class will prompt you for this password before opening the album.

As you progress through this chapter, you will note that the album password is required repeatedly as the album is opened, which is not of course the nicest interface one could ask for. We could fix this by only requiring the password in the `Photo-Album` class when the user wants to examine the photos or modify the album settings. We will not actually do this, but we could.

Compile and run this program to see our new list view at work. Also alter the display setting using the items in the View menu. Assuming you have some album files in the album directory, you should find that the Large Icons, Small Icons, and List menus work just fine. Curiously, the `Details` setting displays nothing at all.

This is because the `Details` view requires a set of columns to be assigned to the form. So far we have not done this, so we will make it our next topic.

TRY IT! You may have noticed that our interface is not very friendly for albums that happen to contain a password. Since each album is opened in the `OnLoad` method, before the `MainForm` window is displayed, any passwords required must be entered before the user even sees the application window.

As an alternative approach, modify the `PhotoAlbum` class to provide a static `GetInfo` method, and use this new method in the `Main-Form.OpenAlbum` method of our application. This method should simply return the required statistics for a given album and ignore any password required. While this alters the meaning of the existing password mechanism slightly, it does not provide access to the photographs contained in the album.

In your implementation of the `GetInfo` method, return a new `Album-Info` structure that provides access to the statistics for the album. This structure can use the same property names as the `PhotoAlbum` class. In order to accommodate changes made in the remainder of this chapter, you should implement properties to provide the title of the album, whether or not a password is required, and the number of photographs stored in the album. Make certain you close the album regardless of whether or not an exception occurs.

14.3 LISTVIEW COLUMNS

The MyAlbumExplorer application displays three out of four possible `View` settings just fine. Not the best percentage we could hope for, so let's see what it takes to add a `Details` view to our application. This is the only view that displays the collection of subitems associated with each item. The subitems display in columns to the right of the item label, as shown in figure 14.3.

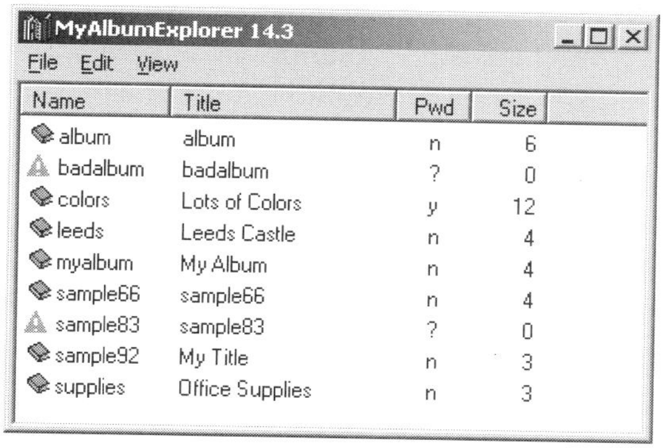

Figure 14.3
The size of a column in the Details view can be changed by clicking on the line at the end of the column.

The columns in a list view are contained in the control's `Columns` property. This property contains a collection of `ColumnHeader` components. The order of objects in this collection reflects the order in which columns are displayed in the control. As a result, the order of subitems in each `ListViewItem` object must match the order of objects contained in the `Columns` collection. An overview of the `ColumnHeader` class is given in .NET Table 14.4. Note that the contents of the `Columns` property are cleared whenever the `Clear` method is called on the associated `ListView` control.

In order to fill in the `Details` view for our list control, we will first create the columns for the list, and then add the required subitems to each item as we populate the list. This section will finish with a discussion of how sorting can be performed in the `Details` view.

.NET Table 14.4   ColumnHeader class

The `ColumnHeader` class represents a single column in a `ListView` control. These columns appear when the `View` property for the control is set to `Details`, and they display the subitems associated with each item in the view. The `ColumnHeader` class is part of the `System.Windows.Forms` namespace. It is derived from the `System.ComponentModel.Component` class, and supports the `IClonable` interface.

Public Properties	Index	Gets the location of the component within the containing `ListView` control's `Columns` collection.
	ListView	Gets the list view control containing this column header.
	Text	Gets or sets the text to display in the column header.
	TextAlign	Gets or sets the horizontal alignment of both the text in the header and the subitems displayed in the column.
	Width	Gets or sets the width of the header in pixels.
Public Methods	Clone	Creates an identical copy of the column header. This new header is not contained in any list view control.

14.3.1   CREATING THE COLUMNS

We will create four columns in our application. Each column will represent a setting associated with our `PhotoAlbum` object. In this section, we will create our columns in the Forms Designer Window, and allow Visual Studio to generate them as part of the `InitializeComponent` method. Since columns are cleared whenever the list view is cleared, in many cases it is better to create the `ColumnHeader` objects programmatically. This also permits alternate columns to be used for different types of items displayed in the list. We will see this later in the chapter when we display both `Photograph` and `PhotoAlbum` objects in our list.

The following table summarizes the columns for our application, providing the variable name we will use and the text to appear at the top of the column. A description of the contents of each column is given as well.

Columns for displaying the albums

ColumnHeader	Text	Description
columnName	Name	The base name of the album file.
columnTitle	Title	Value of the `Title` property.
columnPassword	Pwd	Whether the album requires a password.
columnSize	Size	Number of `Photograph` objects in the album.

So let's see how this is done. The following steps create these four columns and initialize their settings.

Set the version number of the MyAlbumExplorer application to 14.3.

<table>
<tr><th colspan="4">CREATE THE COLUMNS HEADERS FOR THE LIST</th></tr>
<tr><td></td><td colspan="2" align="center">Action</td><td align="center">Result</td></tr>
</table>

	Action		Result
1	In the MainForm.cs [Design] window, display the ColumnHeader Collection Editor for the `ListView` control. **How-to** Click the ... button associated with the `Columns` property item in the Properties window.		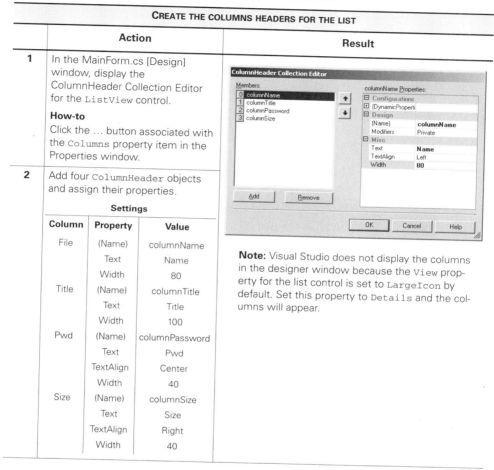
2	Add four `ColumnHeader` objects and assign their properties.		**Note:** Visual Studio does not display the columns in the designer window because the `View` property for the list control is set to `LargeIcon` by default. Set this property to `Details` and the columns will appear.

Settings

Column	Property	Value
File	(Name)	columnName
	Text	Name
	Width	80
Title	(Name)	columnTitle
	Text	Title
	Width	100
Pwd	(Name)	columnPassword
	Text	Pwd
	TextAlign	Center
	Width	40
Size	(Name)	columnSize
	Text	Size
	TextAlign	Right
	Width	40

A quick excerpt of the `InitializeComponent` method follows. As the code generated here is similar to other collections we have created in earlier chapters, we will not discuss this code any further.

```
private void InitializeComponent()
{
  . . .
  this.columnTitle = new System.Windows.Forms.ColumnHeader();
  this.columnSize = new System.Windows.Forms.ColumnHeader();
  . . .
  //
  // columnTitle
```

```
    //
    this.columnTitle.Text = "Title";
    this.columnTitle.Width = 100;
    //
    // columnSize
    //
    this.columnSize.Text = "Size";
    this.columnSize.TextAlign
            = System.Windows.Forms.HorizontalAlignment.Center;
    this.columnSize.Width = 40;
    . . .
    //
    // listViewMain
    //
    this.listViewMain.Columns.AddRange(
            new System.Windows.Forms.ColumnHeader[] {
                                    this.columnName,
                                    this.columnTitle,
                                    this.columnPassword,
                                    this.columnSize});

    . . .
}
```

Note that the order in which the ColumnHeader objects are added to the Columns collection is significant here as this determines the order in which the columns appear in the control. You can alter the order of a column in the ColumnHeader Collection Editor dialog using the up and down arrow buttons.

Feel free to run the application if you wish. You should now see the albums appear in the first column. The next section will populate these columns with the properties of each album.

14.3.2   POPULATING THE COLUMNS

The columns in a Details listing contain both the item label and the text associated with each subitem. The first column always contains the item label, and the subsequent columns contain the contents of the list item's SubItems property. The SubItems property contains a collection of ListViewSubItem objects. The ListViewSub-Item class is only valid within the ListViewItem class, so the fully qualified class name within the Windows Forms namespace is ListViewItem.ListViewSubItem.

This class is typically created implicitly while initializing an existing ListView-Item object or ListView control. A summary of this object appears in .NET Table 14.5.

The `ListViewSubItem` class is an object that represents a property or other value associated with a `ListViewItem` object. A `ListViewSubItem` appears in a `ListView` control when the control's `View` property is set to `Details` and a column is configured for the subitem. The set of `ListViewSubItem` objects associated with an item is defined by the `SubItems` property in the `ListViewItem` object.

This class is often written as `ListViewItem.ListViewSubItem`. It is defined within the `ListViewItem` class and is therefore part of the `System.Windows.Forms` namespace.

Public Constructors	ListViewSubItem	Initializes a new `ListViewSubItem` instance.
		
		Overloads
		`ListViewItem.ListViewSubItem(`
		`    ListViewItem owner,`
		`    string text);`
		`ListViewItem.ListViewSubItem(`
		`    ListViewItem owner,`
		`    string text,`
		`    Color foreColor,`
		`    Color backColor,`
		`    Font font);`

Public Properties	BackColor	Gets or sets the background `Color` for this subitem. If `null`, or if the `UserItemStyleForSubitems` property for the containing `ListViewItem` is `true`, then the background color of this subitem is identical to the `Color` used for the item.
	Font	Gets or sets the `Font` for this subitem, with the identical caveat as that given for the `BackColor` property.
	ForeColor	Gets or sets the foreground `Color` for this subitem, with the identical caveat as that given for the `BackColor` property.
	Text	The text string for this subitem.

There are a number of methods provided by the framework for adding subitems to items and items to list views. Some of the constructors available are shown here, and you can look through the online documentation to examine these and also the `Add` method overloads provided for each collection object. In our code we will use a fairly straightforward method to expose the individual steps along the way. In your own applications you can use the methods employed here or whatever other means works best for your situation.

Since the columns and items are already defined for our control, the only change required is to update the `LoadAlbumData` method to add the required subitems. The following steps outline the actions required to add the three required subitems, namely the password flag, the album size, and the album file name.

ADD THE SUBITEMS FOR EACH ITEM IN THE LIST		
	Action	**Result**
| 1 | Locate the `LoadAlbumData` method in the MainForm.cs source code window. | ```csharp
private void LoadAlbumData(string dir)
{
    . . .
``` |
| 2 | When the album is opened successfully, create the three subitems using the `PhotoAlbum` object. | ```csharp
foreach (string s in albumFiles)
{
    . . .
    ListViewItem item = new ListViewItem();

    item.Text
        = Path.GetFileNameWithoutExtension(s);
    if (album != null)
    {
        item.ImageIndex = MainForm.AlbumIndex;

        // Add the subitems
        item.SubItems.Add(album.Title);
        bool hasPwd = (album.Password != null)
            && (album.Password.Length > 0);
        item.SubItems.Add(hasPwd ? "y" : "n");
        item.SubItems.Add(album.Count.ToString());
    }
``` |
| 3 | When the album fails to load, set the subitems to appropriate defaults. | ```csharp
    else
    {
        item.ImageIndex = MainForm.ErrorIndex;
        item.SubItems.Add(item.Text);
        item.SubItems.Add("?");
        item.SubItems.Add("0");
    }
``` |
| 4 | In either case, add the item to the list view. | ```csharp
    listViewMain.Items.Add(item);
    }
}
``` |

Compile and run your code to ensure that it works. When you look at the `Details` view, note how the width of each column can be adjusted by clicking on the vertical line between two columns and dragging it to the left or right.

Congratulations, you have just completed your first list view! Your life may never be the same. Before you go off and celebrate, there is one other topic related to columns that is worth some discussion.

14.3.3 SORTING A COLUMN

It is typical in applications such as Windows Explorer to sort the contents of a `List-View` control column whenever a column title is clicked. The first time the title is clicked, the items are sorted based on the column's contents in *ascending* order, or a to z order for strings; and a second click sorts in *descending*, or z to a, order. Whether to support this behavior in your applications depends on the nature of the application and the user environment for which it is targeted. Many Windows users expect such behavior, and may find it odd if an application does not support this feature. In this section we look at how to support this feature in Windows Forms applications, using our MyAlbumExplorer application as an example.

The `ListView` class provides three members of particular importance when you wish to support sorting in the `Details` view.

- The `Sorting` property defines how the items are initially sorted. This is a `SortOrder` enumeration value, one of `None` for no sorting, `Ascending`, or `Descending`. This defaults to `None`, which is why our application currently displays the items in random order.
- The `ColumnClick` event occurs when a column is clicked. This is used to modify the control's sorting behavior as appropriate for the selected column. Event handlers for this event receive a `ColumnClickEventArgs` parameter that contains a `Column` property indicating the column header clicked by the user.
- The `ListViewItemSorter` property defines the `IComparer` interface used to compare two `ListViewItem` objects for the list. An overview of the `IComparer` interface is given in .NET Table 14.6.

We will use each of these members to define the sorting behavior for our application. We will define a class supporting the `IComparer` interface first, and then use this class to implement a `ColumnClick` event handler.

.NET Table 14.6   IComparer interface

The `IComparer` interface is an interface for comparing two objects, and is part of the `Systems.Collections` namespace. This namespace also provides two implementations of this interface for comparing `string` objects. The `Comparer` class supports case-sensitive comparisons, while the `CaseInsensitiveComparer` class supports case-insensitive comparisons. Both of these classes provide a `Default` property that returns an initialized instance of the class.

Public Methods	Compare	Returns an integer value indicating the equality relationship between two `object` instances. The value returned is less than zero, zero, or greater than zero, corresponding to whether the first `object` is less than, equal to, or greater than the second, respectively.

For a `ListView` object, the comparison interface must accept two `ListViewItem` objects and return an appropriate value depending on the current column and sorting order. The `ListView` object itself defines the current sorting order based on the `Sorting` property value. We will need to keep track of the current column as part of our `IComparer` implementation.

We will begin by implementing a comparison class within our `MainForm` definition. We will use the rather noncreative name `MyListViewComparer` for this class.

To avoid hard-coding integer values into our code, the following steps also define constants for the column indices.

	DEFINE A COMPARER CLASS FOR THE LIST VIEW	
	Action	**Result**

1	In the MainForm.cs source code window, define four constants for each of the columns in our ListView control.	`private const int AlbumNameColumn = 0;`
		`private const int AlbumTitleColumn = 1;`
		`private const int AlbumPwdColumn = 2;`
		`private const int AlbumSizeColumn = 3;`

2	Define the MyListViewComparer class within the MainForm class definition.	`private class MyListViewComparer : IComparer`
		`{`
		`    // Associate a ListView with the class`
		`    // Track the current sorting column`
		`    // Compare method implementation`
		`}`

3	Associate a ListView object with this class via the constructor.	`// Associate a ListView with the class`
		`private ListView _listView;`
		`public MyListViewComparer(ListView lv)`
		`{`
		`    _listView = lv;`
		`}`

4	Also define a ListView property to retrieve this setting.	`public ListView ListView`
		`{`
		`    get { return _listView; }`
		`}`

5	Allow the current sorting column to be specified via a SortColumn property.	`// Track the current sorting column`
		`private int _sortColumn = 0;`
		`public int SortColumn`
		`{`
		`    get { return _sortColumn; }`
		`    set { _sortColumn = value; }`
		`}`

6	Define the Compare method required by the IComparer interface.	`// Compare method implementation`
		`public int Compare(object a, object b)`
		`{`

7	In this method, convert the two objects into list view items.	`// Throws exception if not list items`
		`ListViewItem item1 = (ListViewItem)a;`
		`ListViewItem item2 = (ListViewItem)b;`

8	Swap the two items if the current sorting order is descending.
	
	Note: We could handle the sort order as part of each comparison, but swapping the items up front seems easier.
		`// Account for current sorting order`
		`if (ListView.Sorting`
		`        == SortOrder.Descending)`
		`{`
		`    ListViewItem tmp = item1;`
		`    item1 = item2;`
		`    item2 = tmp;`
		`}`

	Action	Result
9	Handle the case where the current view is not `Details`. **Note:** The comparer is called whenever the items must be sorted, regardless of the current view. Note how we use the default `Comparer` instance provided by the `CaseInsensitiveComparer` class.	```csharp\n// Handle nonDetails case\nif (ListView.View != View.Details)\n{\n return CaseInsensitiveComparer.Default.\n Compare(item1.Text, item2.Text);\n}\n```
10	For the `Details` view, use a separate method to compare the two items.	```csharp\n return CompareAlbums(item1, item2);\n}\n```
11	For the `CompareAlbums` method, the following steps are required. a. Find the subitem instances corresponding to each item. b. Return the appropriate result based on the current column.	```csharp\npublic int CompareAlbums\n (ListViewItem item1, ListViewItem item2)\n{\n // Find the subitem instances\n ListViewItem.ListViewSubItem sub1\n = item1.SubItems[SortColumn];\n ListViewItem.ListViewSubItem sub2\n = item2.SubItems[SortColumn];\n\n // Return value is based on sort column\n switch (SortColumn)\n {\n```
12	When one of the three string columns is selected, use the default `Comparer` to compare the two strings.	```csharp\n case MainForm.AlbumNameColumn:\n case MainForm.AlbumTitleColumn:\n case MainForm.AlbumPwdColumn:\n {\n return\n CaseInsensitiveComparer.\n Default.Compare(\n sub1.Text, sub2.Text);\n }\n```
13	When the Size column is selected: a. Convert the strings to integer values. b. Return the appropriate result. **Note:** The `ToInt32` method used here will throw an exception if the given string cannot be converted to an integer.	```csharp\n case MainForm.AlbumSizeColumn:\n {\n // Compare using integer values.\n int x1 = Convert.ToInt32(sub1.Text);\n int x2 = Convert.ToInt32(sub2.Text);\n\n if (x1 < x2)\n return -1;\n else if (x1 == x2)\n return 0;\n else\n return 1;\n }\n```
14	For any other column value, throw an exception indicating the column was not recognized.	```csharp\n default:\n throw new IndexOutOfRangeException(\n "unrecognized column index");\n }\n}\n```

This code defines a comparison class for our `ListView` control. The next step is to hook this into our actual form. This requires that we create an instance of the `MyListViewComparer` class and assign it as the comparer for our list. Let's do this first, and then we can handle the `ColumnClick` event to adjust the comparison settings. This continues our previous steps.

	ASSIGN COMPARER TO THE LIST VIEW CONTROL	
	Action	**Result**
15	Define a private variable to hold the comparer class for the form.	`private MyListViewComparer _comparer;`

16	Create and assign this comparer to the view in the `OnLoad` method. **Note:** This is done at the beginning of this method to ensure the comparer exists during control initialization.	`protected override void OnLoad(EventArgs e)`
		`{`
		`    // Define the list view comparer`
		`    _comparer = new`
		`        MyListViewComparer(listViewMain);`
		`    listViewMain.ListViewItemSorter = _comparer;`
		`    listViewMain.Sorting = SortOrder.Ascending;`
		`    . . .`
		`}`

We now have a comparison class assigned to our view. The `ListView` control will automatically call this class's `Compare` method whenever it must sort the contents of the view. This occurs each time the `Sorting` property is set to a new value other than `None`.

We can take advantage of this in our `ColumnClick` handler to ensure that the list is updated whenever a column is clicked. As we indicated earlier, `ColumnClick` event handlers receive a `ColumnClickEventArgs` class as the event parameter. This class defines a `Column` property containing the index of the selected column in the corresponding list view.

Let's define this handler to complete our implementation of column sorting.

	HANDLE THE COLUMNCLICK EVENT	
	Action	**Result**

17	Handle the `ColumnClick` event for the `listViewMain` control.	`private void listViewMain_ColumnClick`
		`    (object sender, System.Windows.`
		`        Forms.ColumnClickEventArgs e)`
		`{`

18	Reset the sorting order for the control.	`SortOrder prevOrder = listViewMain.Sorting;` `listViewMain.Sorting = SortOrder.None;`

19	If the current column was clicked, then invert the existing sort order.	`if (e.Column == _comparer.SortColumn)`
		`{`
		`    // Switch the sorting order`
		`    if (prevOrder == SortOrder.Ascending)`
		`        listViewMain.Sorting = SortOrder.Descending;`
		`    else`
		`        listViewMain.Sorting = SortOrder.Ascending;`
		`}`

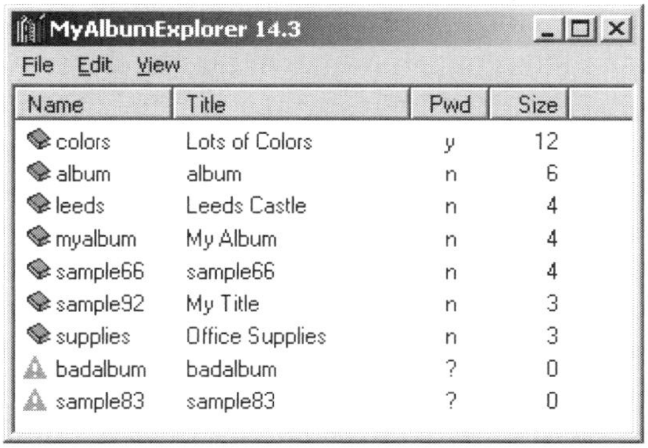

	Action	Result
| **20** | Otherwise, sort the control based on the newly selected column. | ```csharp
else
{
    // Define new sort column and reset order
    _comparer.SortColumn = e.Column;
    listViewMain.Sorting = SortOrder.Ascending;
}
}
``` |

Twenty steps in one section. That might be a record. Note how we reset the sort order to `None` at the beginning of the handler. This ensures that the framework will re-sort the contents when we set the actual sort order a few lines later. Without this reset, the control will not invoke the comparer if the sort order is not a new value, such as when two different columns are clicked one after another.

Compile and run to verify that this sorting works as advertised. Make sure you click the `Size` column to perform integer-based sorting. An example of such a sort in descending order is shown in figure 14.4.

Figure 14.4
In this graphic, the ListView control in the application is sorted by the Size column.

Alternate sorting mechanisms are possible here as well. Later in the chapter, we will see how to sort date and time values in the control.

TRY IT! The `AllowColumnReorder` property indicates that the user may rearrange the columns by clicking and dragging them with the mouse. Set this property to `true` to see how this works. What happens when you sort a column after reordering the columns? Note that the `ColumnClick` event does not occur during a drag, even though the user must click and then release the column header.

This completes our initial discussion of items and subitems in the list view control. The remaining sections examine some of the more common events normally used with this control.
```

14.4 SELECTION AND EDITING

So far we have created a `ListView` control in our application and supported column sorting. In this section we'll look at some of the events used to interact with specific items in the list. Specifically, we will look at adding the following features:

- Viewing the properties associated with a selected item in the list.
- Editing the label of an item in our list.
- Displaying the `Photograph` objects in the album when the user double-clicks on an item.

The first two topics are covered in this section. The last topic is related to item activation, which is the subject of section 14.5.

14.4.1 SUPPORTING ITEM SELECTION

Like the `ListBox` control, a list view can support single item or multiple item selection. The `MultiSelect` property is a boolean property that indicates which type of selection to support. We looked at multiple selection within list boxes in chapter 10, so we will stick with single selection in this chapter.

The `SelectedIndices` property holds the collection of indices corresponding to the selected items in the list. These index values refer to the position of the items within the collection represented by the `Items` property. The `SelectedItems` property holds the collection of selected items directly.

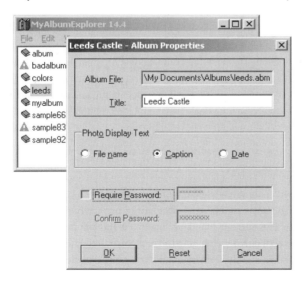

**Figure 14.5
The properties window
displayed for the
leeds.abm album.**

To make use of the selected item, we will create a menu item to display the properties associated with the selected album, as shown in figure 14.5. The `Click` event handler for this menu will open the selected album, display the properties dialog for this album, and update both the album and the `ListView` control with any changes made by the user.

The following steps explain how to add both the menu and the `Click` handler.

Set the version number of the MyAlbumExplorer application to 14.4.

	ADD A MENU TO DISPLAY ALBUM PROPERTIES	
	Action	**Result**
1	In the MainForm.cs [Design] window, add a Properties menu under the Edit menu. **Settings** **Property** / **Value** (Name) / menuProperties Text / &Properties...	
| **2** | Add a `Click` event handler for this menu to display the property dialog for the selected album, if any. <br><br> **Note:** We separate the display logic into a separate `DisplayAlbumProperties` method in case we ever want to call it from other portions of our application. | ```csharp
private void menuProperties_Click
    (object sender, System.EventArgs e)
{
  if (listViewMain.SelectedItems.Count <= 0)
    return;

  ListViewItem item
      = listViewMain.SelectedItems[0];
  DisplayAlbumProperties(item);
}
``` |
| **3** | In order to locate the album file name in our new method, record the album file name in the `Tag` property associated with each list item in the `LoadAlbumData` method. | ```csharp
private void LoadAlbumData(string dir)
{
  . . .
  foreach (string s in albumFiles)
  {
    . . .
    if (album != null)
    {
      item.Tag = album.FileName;
      item.ImageIndex = MainForm.AlbumIndex;
      . . .
``` |
| **4** | Add the `DisplayAlbumProperties` method to display the album dialog. | ```csharp
private void DisplayAlbumProperties
    (ListViewItem item)
{
``` |
| **5** | Implement this method by obtaining the file name for the selected album. | ```csharp
string fileName = item.Tag as string;
``` |
| **6** | Try to open the album corresponding to this file name. | ```csharp
PhotoAlbum album = null;
if (fileName != null)
  album = this.OpenAlbum(fileName);
``` |
```

	Action	**Result**
7	Display an error message if the album could not be opened. **Note:** Here and throughout the remainder of the book, we use the simplest form of the `Mes-sageBox` dialog. Feel free to use an alternate form if you prefer. See chapter 8 for detailed information on the `MessageBox` class.	```csharp\nif (album == null)\n{\n MessageBox.Show("The properties for "\n + "this album cannot be displayed.");\n return;\n}\n```
8	Display the `AlbumEditDlg` if the album is opened successfully.	```csharp\nusing (AlbumEditDlg dlg\n = new AlbumEditDlg(album))\n{\n```
9	If any changes are made by the user, save these changes into the album file. Catch any errors that occur.	```csharp\nif (dlg.ShowDialog() == DialogResult.OK)\n{\n // Save changes made by the user\n try\n {\n album.Save();\n }\n catch (Exception)\n {\n MessageBox.Show("Unable to save "\n + "changes to album.");\n return;\n }\n```
10	Also update any subitem text that might be affected by the user's changes.	```csharp\n // Update subitem settings\n item.SubItems[MainForm.\n AlbumTitleColumn].Text\n = album.Title;\n\n bool hasPwd = (album.Password != null)\n && (album.Password.Length > 0);\n item.SubItems[MainForm.\n AlbumPwdColumn].Text\n = (hasPwd ? "y" : "n");\n }\n}\n```
11	Dispose of the album at the end of the method.	```csharp\n album.Dispose();\n}\n```

We employ the `using` statement to ensure that our dialog is properly disposed of at the end of the handler. Also note how multiple exceptional handling blocks are used to catch errors that occur. You may wonder if it is expensive to perform such operations, especially if you are familiar with exception-handling mechanisms in languages like C and C++ where it indeed can be an expensive proposition to call `try` multiple times. In C#, the exception handling is built into the language and the compiler, so checking for exceptions as we do here is not much more expensive than an `if` statement. The expense comes if an exception actually occurs, since the compiler must then construct the Exception object, unravel the call stack and clean up any objects as required, plus locate the appropriate catch block for the particular exception.

The fact that exception clean up can impact a program's performance is one more reason to ensure that you throw exceptions only for truly exceptional conditions. Common problems or situations should be handled through the use of an error code. As a case in point, this is one reason why file-related read and write methods in the .NET Framework do not raise an exception when the end of a file is reached.

Back to our code, this discussion tells us that our use of try and catch here should not affect our performance very much since we do not normally expect an exception to occur other than when opening an invalid album. We could improve the performance if we kept track of the invalid albums during the OnLoad method, since then we would not need to re-open these albums again here. We will not actually do this here, but it was worth a mention.

The remainder of the previous code is fairly self-explanatory. One other point worth mentioning is our use of the Tag property. This works well in our Display-AlbumProperties method since all we need to keep track of is the album's file name. It is also possible here to assign a PhotoAlbum instance to the Tag property rather than a string instance, although this requires extra memory and other resources to maintain the album for each item in memory.

An alternative approach often used to track more complex relationships is to derive a new class from the ListViewItem class. For our application, an excerpt of such a class might look something like the code shown in listing 14.1. Since this class is a ListViewItem object, instances of it can be assigned to and manipulated within the ListView control. Whenever the PhotoAlbum object for an album is required, a list view item can be downcast to the PhotoAlbumListItem class, where the Album property and other members may be used to manipulate the album.

Listing 14.1 Example deriving a new class from ListViewItem (not our approach)

```
public class PhotoAlbumListItem : ListViewItem, IDisposable
{
  private string _fileName;
  private PhotoAlbum _album;

  PhotoAlbumListItem(string file)
  {
    _fileName = file;
    _album = null;
  }

  public void Dispose()
  {
    // Dispose implementation
    . . .
  }

  public PhotoAlbum Album
```

```
    {
      get
      {
        if (_album == null)
        {
          _album = new PhotoAlbum();
          _album.Open(_fileName);
        }

        return _album;
      }
    }

    // Other methods as required
    . . .
  }
```

For our purposes the use of a simple string value in the Tag property was sufficient to display the album's properties dialog. Another feature worth supporting here is the ability to edit item labels.

14.4.2   SUPPORTING LABEL EDITS

Editing an item label in place is one of the advantages the ListView class has over ListBox objects. In our application it would be nice if the user could edit the album name in order to rename an album file. This section will show how to support this feature.

Label editing is disabled by default, and turned on by setting the LabelEdit property to true. An actual edit of an item is initiated by the BeginEdit method of the ListViewItem class. The corresponding ListView control receives two events during the editing process. The BeforeLabelEdit event occurs before the edit process begins, while the AfterLabelEdit event occurs when the user completes the edit by pressing the Enter key or clicking outside of the edit area. Event handlers for both events receive the LabelEditEventArgs class as their event handler. See .NET Table 14.7 for an overview of this class.

We will allow an item to be edited in two ways. The first way is through a Name menu under the top-level Edit menu, and the second way is by selecting an item and pressing the F2 key. This matches the keyboard shortcut supported by Windows Explorer, so it seems appropriate here.

In a production environment, we would probably handle both events in our application. In the BeginLabelEdit event handler we would make sure the album is valid and can be successfully opened. This provides some assurance that the edit will be successful before the user begins typing. The AfterLabelEdit event handler would update the album with a new title and store the album to disk. It would also update the album file on disk with the change.

.NET Table 14.7   LabelEditEventArgs class

The `LabelEditEventArgs` class represents the event arguments received by `BeforeLabelEdit` and `AfterLabelEdit` event handlers for the `ListView` class. This class is part of the `System.Windows.Forms` namespace, and inherits from the `System.EventArgs` class.

Public Properties	CancelEdit	Gets or sets whether the edit operation should be cancelled. This property can be set both before and after the item is edited.
	Item	Gets the zero-based index into the list view's `Items` collection of the `ListViewItem` to be edited.
	Label	Gets the new text to assign to the label of the indicated item.

Since we are not in a production environment, we will take the easy way out and only handle the `AfterLabelEdit` event. This means a user may edit an album only to find that he or she cannot save his changes, which is not the best interface from a usability perspective.

The code changes required are given in the following steps:

	INITIATE LABEL EDITING	
	Action	**Result**
1	In the MainForm.cs [Design] window, set the `LabelEdit` property of the `ListView` control to `true`.	Item labels in the list view may now be edited.
2	Add a Name menu to the top of the Edit menu. **Settings** **Property** / **Value** (Name) / menuEditLabel Text / &Name	

3	Add a `Click` event handler for this menu.	```private void menuEditLabel_Click```
		 ``` (object sender, System.EventArgs e)```
		 ```{```

4	Within this handler, if an item is selected, edit the item.	``` if (listViewMain.SelectedItems.Count == 1)```
		 ``` listViewMain.SelectedItems[0].BeginEdit();```
		 ```}```
		
		 Note: This code only edits the label if a single item is selected. While we do not permit multiple items to be selected in our ListView control, this code establishes an appropriate behavior in case such selection is ever permitted in the future.

5	Add a `KeyDown` event handler for the ListView control.	```private void listViewMain_KeyDown```
		 ``` (object sender, System.Windows.```
		 ``` Forms.KeyEventArgs e)```
		 ```{```

	Action	Result
6	If the F2 key is pressed and an item is selected, edit the item.	```if (e.KeyCode == Keys.F2)
{
if (listViewMain.SelectedItems.Count == 1)
{
listViewMain.SelectedItems[0].
BeginEdit();
e.Handled = true;
}
}
}```

That's all it takes to begin an edit. The actual work of interacting with the user is handled by the framework. When the user is finished, we can pick up the result in an `AfterLabelEdit` event handler. There is also a `BeforeLabelEdit` event that is useful for selectively permitting an edit or altering an item before the edit begins. For our purposes, the `AfterLabelEdit` event will suffice.

PROCESS A LABEL EDIT		
	Action	**Result**
7	Add an `AfterLabelEdit` event handler for the `ListView` control.	```private void listViewMain_AfterLabelEdit
(object sender, System.Windows.
Forms.LabelEditEventArgs e)
{```
8	If the user cancelled the edit, then we are finished. **Note:** For example, if the user presses the Esc key during editing, this handler is invoked with a `null` label.	```if (e.Label == null)
{
// Edit cancelled by the user
e.CancelEdit = true;
return;
}```
9	In this handler, locate the item to be edited.	```ListViewItem item = listViewMain.Items[e.Item];```
10	Update the album name, and cancel the edit if an error occurs. **Note:** Once again we separate the logic to operate on our album into a separate method.	```if (UpdateAlbumName(e.Label, item) == false)
e.CancelEdit = true;
}```

	Action	Result
11	Add the `UpdateAlbumName` method to update the title of the album. **How-to** a. Retrieve the file name from the `Tag` property for the item. b. Rename the file using a private method that returns the new name. c. Inform the user if the file could not be renamed. d. Otherwise, update the `Tag` property with the new name.	```csharp\nprivate bool UpdateAlbumName\n (string newName, ListViewItem item)\n{\n string fileName = item.Tag as string;\n string newFileName\n = RenameFile(fileName, newName, ".abm");\n if (newFileName == null)\n {\n MessageBox.Show(\n "Unable to rename album to this name.");\n return false;\n }\n\n // Update Tag property\n item.Tag = newFileName;\n return true;\n}\n```
12	Implement the `RenameFile` method to construct the new name for the file. **How-to** a. Use the `GetDirectoryName` method to retrieve the directory for the file. b. Use the `ChangeExtension` method to ensure the file has the correct extension.	```csharp\nprivate string RenameFile\n (string origFile, string newBase, string ext)\n{\n string fileName = Path.\n GetDirectoryName(origFile) + "\\" + newBase;\n string newFile = Path.ChangeExtension(fileName,\n ext);\n```
13	Rename the file using the `Move` method in the `File` class.	```csharp\ntry\n{\n File.Move(origFile, newFile);\n return newFile;\n}\n```
14	Return `null` if an error occurs.	```csharp\ncatch (Exception)\n{\n // An error occurred\n return null;\n}\n}\n```

This code uses some methods from the `Path` and `File` classes to manipulate the file name strings and rename the album file. Our application now supports displaying album properties and editing of album labels. The next topic of discussion is item activation.

14.5 ITEM ACTIVATION

As you might expect, item activation is the means by which an item is displayed or otherwise activated by the control. Normally, activation is just a fancy way to say double-click. In our `ListBox` class in chapter 10, we activated an item in the list by handling the `DoubleClick` event and displaying the properties dialog associated with the item. Such behavior is activation.

The reason for the fancy term is that the `ListView` class allows activation other than a double-click to be supported. The `Activation` property determines the type of activation supported, based on the `ItemActivation` enumeration. The possible values for this enumeration are shown in .NET Table 14.8. Note that the `OneClick` style is similar to an HTML link in a Web browser. In our program, we will stick with the standard activation.

.NET Table 14.8   ItemActivation enumeration

The `ItemActivation` enumeration specifies the type of activation supported by a control. This enumeration is part of the `System.Windows.Forms` namespace.

Enumeration Values	OneClick	A single click activates an item. The cursor appears as a hand pointer, and the item text changes color as the mouse pointer passes over the item.
	Standard	A double-click activates an item.
	TwoClick	A double-click activates an item, plus the item text changes color as the mouse pointer passes over the item.

Regardless of how items are activated, an `ItemActivate` event occurs whenever an item is activated. The event handler for this event receives a standard `System.EventArgs` parameter, so the activated item is obtained from the `SelectedItems` collection.

The activation behavior for our MyAlbumExplorer application will display the `Photographs` in the selected album. This is a rather complicated change, since the columns and list item behavior must now accommodate the display of both albums and photos here. The fact that we were careful to separate much of the album logic into individual methods along the way will help us keep our code straight. Figure 14.6 shows our application with photographs displayed in the `ListView` control. These photographs are sorted by the date each photo was taken. The icon used here might not be your first choice for a photograph icon, but it will suffice for our purposes. If you find another icon you prefer, or are feeling creative, you can use an alternate icon in your application.

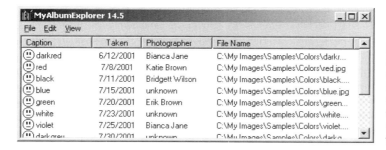

Figure 14.6
In this detailed view of Photographs, note how three dots automatically appear when the text length exceeds the width of the column.

14.5.1 HANDLING ITEM ACTIVATION

The ultimate goal here is to display either the list of albums or the list of photos in an album within our `ListView` control. To do this, we must keep track of whether albums or photographs are currently shown in the view, and whether the `PhotoAlbum` object corresponds to the view when photographs are displayed. The following steps create private fields in our `Form` to track this information, and also implement an event handler for the `ItemActivate` event. Once these are available, we will look at the additional steps required to fully support activation.

Set the version number of the MyAlbumExplorer application to 14.5.

	HANDLE THE ITEMACTIVATE EVENT FOR THE LIST VIEW	
	Action	**Result**
1	Add private fields to track the current `ListView` control contents in the MainForm.cs code window.	`private bool _albumsShown = true;` `private PhotoAlbum _album = null;`

2	Add an `ItemActivate` event handler to the `ListView` control.	`private void listViewMain_ItemActivate`
		`    (object sender, System.EventArgs e)`
		`{`

3	If albums are currently shown and an item is selected, then open the album corresponding to the selected item.	`  if (_albumsShown &&`
		`      listViewMain.SelectedItems.Count > 0)`
		`  {`
		`    ListViewItem item`
		`      = listViewMain.SelectedItems[0];`
		`    string fileName = item.Tag as string;`
		
		`    // Open the album for this item`
		`    PhotoAlbum album = null;`
		`    if (fileName != null)`
		`      album = OpenAlbum(fileName);`
		`    if (album == null)`
		`    {`
		`      MessageBox.Show("The photographs for "`
		`        + "this album cannot be displayed.");`
		`      return;`
		`    }`

4	If the album loads successfully, load the album's photographs into the list view.	`    // Switch to a photograph view`
		`    LoadPhotoData(album);`
		`  }`
		`}`

Of course, we need to implement the `LoadPhotoData` method that appears in this code. This method should set up the view to display photographs, including an appropriate set of columns, and reset the list of items to hold the set of photographs. Once this is done, there is also the support we created for our albums that must now be implemented for photographs. To help us keep our facts straight, let's make a list of the tasks we need to perform here.

- Define new columns for displaying photographs.
- Populate the `ListView` control with the photographs in the album.
- Support column sorting.
- Display the photo properties dialog.
- Support item editing on photographs.
- Allow the user to select the desired view, albums or photos.

We will cover each of these topics in a separate section, in the same order as shown here.

14.5.2 **DEFINING NEW COLUMNS**

As you'll recall, we defined the list of columns for our control using the Column-Header Collection Editor dialog in Visual Studio .NET. Now that we need to display different columns depending on what is displayed, this method no longer makes sense. Instead, we will create the columns programmatically in the `LoadAlbumData` method. Our new `LoadPhotoData` method we have yet to implement will define the columns for displaying photographs.

The easiest way to add columns to a `ListView` control programmatically is through the `Columns` property. The following steps remove the columns we created in Visual Studio and will add them via the `LoadAlbumData` method.

CREATE THE ALBUM COLUMNS PROGRAMMATICALLY		
	Action	**Result**
1	In the MainForm.cs [Design] window, remove the four columns currently defined for the `Columns` property. **How-to** Use the ColumnHeader Collection Editor dialog.	**Note:** This is not strictly required since we clear the contents of the list, including the column definitions, as part of the next step. Reducing unnecessary clutter in your code is always a good idea, so performing this step makes sense.
2	Modify the `LoadAlbumData` method to initially clear the existing contents of the control.	```private void LoadAlbumData(string dir) { listViewMain.Clear();```

	Action	Result
| 3 | Reset the fields that track the current album. | ```
_albumsShown = true;
if (_album != null)
{
    _album.Dispose();
    _album = null;
}
``` |
| 4 | Define the columns for the control before the album items are loaded.<br><br>**How-to**<br>Use the Add method available through the Columns property for the control. | ```
// Define the columns
listViewMain.Columns.Add("Name",
    80, HorizontalAlignment.Left);
listViewMain.Columns.Add("Title",
    100, HorizontalAlignment.Left);
listViewMain.Columns.Add("Pwd",
    40, HorizontalAlignment.Center);
listViewMain.Columns.Add("Size",
    40, HorizontalAlignment.Right);

// Load the albums into the control
    . . .
}
``` |

The Columns property refers to a ColumnHeaderCollection object. This collection class includes an Add method that creates a new column for the control. One version of this method simply accepts a ColumnHeader class instance. Our code uses a slightly more convenient form, with the following signature:

```
void Add(string columnText, int width, HorizontalAlignment align);
```

We can use this same method to add columns when photographs are displayed. The following table summarizes the columns we will use for this purpose.

Columns for displaying photographs

Column	Text	Description
0	Caption	The caption for this photo.
1	Taken	The date the photograph was taken.
2	Photographer	The photographer for this photo.
3	File Name	The fully qualified image file name.

The following table defines constants for our new albums as well as the beginnings of our LoadPhotoData implementation. This table continues our previous steps.

	Action	Result
	CREATE THE PHOTO COLUMNS PROGRAMMATICALLY	
	Action	Result
| 5 | In the MainForm.cs code window, create constants to hold the positions of the columns when photographs are displayed. | ```
private const int PhotoCaptionColumn = 0;
private const int PhotoDateTakenColumn = 1;
private const int PhotoPhotographerColumn = 2;
private const int PhotoFileNameColumn = 3;
``` |
```

	Action	Result
6	Add a private `LoadPhotoData` method.	`private void LoadPhotoData(PhotoAlbum album)` `{`

7	To implement this method, clear the list and set the album fields.	```listViewMain.Clear();```
		```if (_album != null && album != _album)```
		``` _album.Dispose();```
		```_albumsShown = false;```
		```_album = album;```
		
		Note: Disposing and assigning the `_album` field as shown is not strictly required here. This will come in useful in chapter 15 when we call this method with an album other than the default `_album` used in this chapter.

8	Define the columns required for displaying photographs.	```// Define the columns```
		```listViewMain.Columns.Add("Caption",```
		``` 100, HorizontalAlignment.Left);```
		```listViewMain.Columns.Add("Taken",```
		``` 70, HorizontalAlignment.Center);```
		```listViewMain.Columns.Add("Photographer",```
		``` 100, HorizontalAlignment.Left);```
		```listViewMain.Columns.Add("File Name",```
		``` 200, HorizontalAlignment.Left);```
		```}```

This code defines the four columns required to display photographs. We are now ready to populate the list view with the photos from a selected album.

14.5.3 POPULATING THE LISTVIEW

This section completes the implementation of the `LoadPhotoData` method by creating the `ListViewItem` objects for the control. The following steps add an item to our control for each `Photograph` in the album, and define the subitems associated with each item.

In the course of implementing support for photographs, we will need the `Photograph` object itself. We had a similar requirement for `PhotoAlbum` objects, and were able to use the file name setting to load the album into memory. While the file name is available for our photos as well, our `PhotoAlbum` class does not provide a good mechanism for locating a `Photograph` in an album based on the file name.

The most convenient means for locating a specific photograph is based on the index. What we need, then, is a way to look up the index. This value will be stored in the `Tag` property for our list view item, in a manner similar to how we used this property for photo albums.

Of course, an alternate technique here would be to derive a new class from the `ListView` class as we discussed at the end of section 14.4. The `Tag` property is fine for our purposes. In your application, you can use whichever technique seems appropriate for your current and expected requirements.

ADD THE PHOTOS IN AN ALBUM TO THE LIST		
	Action	**Result**

1	Modify the `LoadPhotoData` method to simply return if the given `album` is `null` or empty.	`private void LoadPhotoData(PhotoAlbum album)`
		`{`
		`    . . .`
		`    // Handle null or empty album`
		`    if (album == null || album.Count == 0)`
		`        return;`

2	Iterate over the photographs in the album.
	
	How-to
	Use a `for` loop to permit access to the index values.
		`    // Load the photo items`
		`    for (int i = 0; i < album.Count; i++)`
		`    {`

3	Create a new `ListViewItem` for each photo.	`        Photograph photo = album[i];` `        ListViewItem item = new ListViewItem();`

4	Assign the caption as the item label, and the image list index to our small photograph image.	`        item.Text = photo.Caption;`
		`        item.Tag = i;`
		`        item.ImageIndex = MainForm.PhotoIndex;`

5	Add the subitem values.
	
	How-to
	a. Use the short date format for the Taken column.
	b. Also place the photo's index value in a hidden subitem.
		`        // Add the subitems`
		`        item.SubItems.Add(photo.`
		`                DateTaken.ToShortDateString());`
		`        item.SubItems.Add(photo.Photographer);`
		`        item.SubItems.Add(photo.FileName);`

6	Add the new item to the control.	`        listViewMain.Items.Add(item);`
		`    }`
		`}`

This code initializes the control with the contents of the open album. Note in particular how we define the `Tag` property to hold the integer index. Since the `Tag` property holds an `object` instance, this line boxes the integer value in order to store it as a reference type. Boxing was mentioned in chapter 5, and is discussed in detail in appendix A.

You can compile and run this code if you like. Double-click on an album to activate it and display the contained photographs. Most of the support for photographs is still missing, so you'll find it rather easy to cause an error.

The remainder of this section implements the support required for both albums and photographs to coexist in our `ListView` control. We begin with column sorting.

14.5.4 SORTING A COLUMN (AGAIN)

Our users will want to sort the columns for both the album and photograph display, so we need to make some changes in our `MyListViewComparer` class to enable this support. Of key importance is the ability to tell which type of object we are comparing. When comparing photos, we also need to know the `PhotoAlbum` they come from. We can handle both requirements through a private album field. When the album is `null`, we are comparing `PhotoAlbum` objects. When an album is assigned, we are comparing `Photograph` instances.

Let's add this field and update our `Compare` method to make use of this value.

	IDENTIFY THE TYPE OF OBJECT TO COMPARE	
	Action	**Result**

1	Locate the `MyListViewComparer` class defined in the MainForm.cs source file.	<pre>private class MyListViewComparer
		        : IComparer
		{
		    . . .</pre>

2	Add a `PhotoAlbum` field and corresponding property.	<pre>PhotoAlbum _album = null;
		public PhotoAlbum CurrentAlbum
		{
		    get { return _album; }
		    set { _album = value; }
		}</pre>

3	Use this property to identify which object to compare in the `Compare` method.
	
	Note: Since the label for both types of items is a string, the existing code for the non-`Details` case will work for both objects.
		<pre>public int Compare(object a, object b)
		{
		    . . .
		    // Handle the nonDetails case
		    if (ListView.View != View.Details)
		    {
		        return CaseInsensitiveComparer.
		            Default.Compare(
		                item1.Text, item2.Text);
		    }
		
		    if (CurrentAlbum == null)
		        return CompareAlbums(item1, item2);
		    else
		        return ComparePhotos(item1, item2);
		    }
		}</pre>

Now all we have to do is implement the `ComparePhotos` method to compare two `Photograph` items. Much of this will be similar to the `CompareAlbums` method. The one difference is when we need to compare items using the Taken column. This column holds a date value, so a string comparison is not appropriate. It turns out the `DateTime` structure provides a `Compare` method for just this purpose.

We can use this method in the `ComparePhotos` method to our comparer class.

	IMPLEMENT METHOD TO COMPARE TWO PHOTO ITEMS	
	Action	**Result**

4	Add a new `ComparePhotos` method to the `MyListView-Comparer` class.	```csharp
		public int ComparePhotos
		  (ListViewItem item1, ListViewItem item2)
		{
		  ListViewItem.ListViewSubItem sub1;
		  ListViewItem.ListViewSubItem sub2;
		
		  switch (SortColumn)
		  {
		``

5	For the columns containing text strings, use the default comparer provided by the `CaseInsensitiveComparer` class.	```csharp
		case MainForm.PhotoCaptionColumn:
		case MainForm.PhotoPhotographerColumn:
		case MainForm.PhotoFileNameColumn:
		  sub1 = item1.SubItems[SortColumn];
		  sub2 = item2.SubItems[SortColumn];
		  return CaseInsensitiveComparer.
		     Default.Compare(sub1.Text,
		                     sub2.Text);
		``

6	For the Taken column, determine the index into the album for each photo.	```csharp
		case MainForm.PhotoDateTakenColumn:
		  // Find the indices into the album
		  int index1 = (int)item1.Tag;
		  int index2 = (int)item2.Tag;
		``

7	Then determine the corresponding `DateTime` value for each photo.	```csharp
		  // Look up the dates for each photo
		  DateTime date1
		     = CurrentAlbum[index1].DateTaken;
		  DateTime date2
		     = CurrentAlbum[index2].DateTaken;
		``

8	Use the `Compare` method provided by the `DateTime` structure to calculate the result.	```csharp
		  return DateTime.Compare(date1, date2);
		``

9	Throw an exception if an unrecognized column is provided.	```csharp
		default:
		  throw new IndexOutOfRangeException(
		     "unrecognized column index");
		  }
		}
		``

The last change required for column sorting is to update the `CurrentAlbum` property for our comparer field whenever the contents of the `ListView` control are refreshed. This ensures that our `Compare` implementation performs the proper comparison based on the contents of the control.

	UPDATE THE CURRENTALBUM PROPERTY WHEN REQUIRED	
	Action	**Result**

10	Update the `LoadPhotoData` method to assign the current album to the comparer.	```csharp
		private void LoadPhotoData(PhotoAlbum album)
		{
		  . . .
		  _albumsShown = false;
		  _album = album;
		  _comparer.CurrentAlbum = _album;
		  . . .
		}
		``

	Action	Result
11	Update the `LoadAlbumData` method to assign a `null` album to the comparer.	```private void LoadAlbumData(string dir)\n{\n listViewMain.Clear();\n _comparer.CurrentAlbum = null;\n . . .\n}```

Our application can now sort both photographs and albums. Once again you can compile and run the program if you are careful not to use any photograph functionality we have not yet implemented. Our next task is the Properties dialog.

14.5.5 UPDATING THE PROPERTIES MENU

You may think we are moving through this code rather quickly, and you would be right. While these changes are required as a result of our defined item activation behavior, there are not a lot of new concepts to cover. This is especially true here. As a result, we will simply run through the steps in the following table and then move on to our final topic of editing the item label.

		UPDATE THE CLICK HANDLER FOR THE PROPERTIES MENU	
	Action	Result
1	In the MainForm.cs code window, update the `Click` event handler for the Properties menu to call a new `DisplayPhotoProperties` method when photographs are shown in the control.	```private void menuProperties_Click\n (object sender, System.EventArgs e)\n{\n if (listViewMain.SelectedItems.Count <= 0)\n return;\n\n ListViewItem item\n = listViewMain.SelectedItems[0];\n if (this._albumsShown)\n DisplayAlbumProperties(item);\n else\n DisplayPhotoProperties(item);\n}```
2	Add the new `DisplayPhotoProperties` method.	```private void DisplayPhotoProperties\n (ListViewItem item)\n{```
3	Determine the index of the selected photo in the current album. **Note:** While the `is` keyword works fine with integer types, the `as` keyword can only be used with reference types.	```if (!(item.Tag is int))\n return;\n\n int index = (int)item.Tag;```
4	Assign the current position in the album to this index.	```_album.CurrentPosition = index;```

	Action	Result
5	Display the properties dialog for the photo.	```using (PhotoEditDlg dlg\n = new PhotoEditDlg(_album))\n{\n if (dlg.ShowDialog() == DialogResult.OK)\n {```
6	If any changes were made in the dialog, save the entire album to disk. **Note:** As you'll recall, we permit multiple photographs to be modified in the dialog. As a result, the entire album must be saved and reloaded into the control to pick up any changes.	```// Save any changes made\ntry\n{\n _album.Save(_album.FileName);\n}\ncatch (Exception)\n{\n MessageBox.Show("Unable to save "\n + "changes to photos in album.");\n}```
7	Reload the entire album into the control to pick up the new changes.	```// Update the list with any new settings\nLoadPhotoData(_album);\n }\n }\n}```

14.5.6 UPDATING LABEL EDITING

Updating the label for our photographs again does not use any new constructs, so we will hurry through this code as well. As you'll recall, the caption for each photograph is displayed as the item label. We should note that the menuEditLabel_Click handler does not require any changes, since this simply initiates the edit. The After-LabelEdit event handler is where the new value is processed.

	Action	Result
	UPDATE THE AFTERLABELEDIT EVENT HANDLER	
	Action	Result
1	In the MainForm.cs code window, modify the After-LabelEdit event handler to call a new UpdatePhotoCaption method to process an edit when photographs are displayed.	```private void listViewMain_AfterLabelEdit\n (object sender, System.Windows.\n Forms.LabelEditEventArgs e)\n{\n if (e.Label == null)\n {\n // Edit cancelled by the user\n e.CancelEdit = true;\n return;\n }\n\n ListViewItem item =\n listViewMain.Items[e.Item];\n\n if (this._albumsShown)\n e.CancelEdit = !UpdateAlbumName(e.Label,\n item);\n else\n e.CancelEdit = !UpdatePhotoCaption(e.Label,\n item);\n}```

	Action	Result
2	Add the `UpdatePhotoCaption` method to the `MainForm` class.	```private bool UpdatePhotoCaption (string caption, ListViewItem item) {```
3	Make sure the new caption is not empty.	```if (caption.Length == 0 || !(item.Tag is int)) { MessageBox.Show("Invalid caption value."); return false; }```
4	Determine the index for this photograph.	```int index = (int)item.Tag;```
5	Set the photograph's caption to the new value.	```_album[index].Caption = caption;```
6	Save the album to store the new value.	```try { _album.Save(_album.FileName); } catch (Exception) { MessageBox.Show("Unable to save new " + "caption to album file."); } return true; }```

One further change we can make here is to alter the text displayed in the corresponding menu item. This will provide visual feedback to the user on which property they are actually changing, especially when the `Details` view is not displayed.

	Action	Result
	MODIFY THE TEXT DISPLAYED IN THE EDIT LABEL MENU	
7	In the MainForm.cs [Design] window, add a `Popup` event handler for the `menuEditLabel` menu.	```private void menuEdit_Popup (object sender, System.EventArgs e) {```
8	Enable the contained menus only if a single item is selected in the view.	```menuEditLabel.Enabled = (listViewMain.SelectedItems.Count == 1); menuProperties.Enabled = (listViewMain.SelectedItems.Count == 1);```
9	Set the menu's text to "Name" or "Caption" depending on which type of object is displayed in the list.	```if (this._albumsShown) menuEditLabel.Text = "&Name"; else menuEditLabel.Text = "&Caption"; }```

REDISPLAYING THE ALBUMS

As a final change, we need to give our user the opportunity to redisplay the album view. We may as well provide a menu to display the photo view as well, as an alternative to double-clicking on the album.

	ALLOW USER SELECTION OF THE KIND OF OBJECT TO DISPLAY	
	Action	**Result**
1	In the MainForm.cs [Design] window, add three menu items to the bottom of the View menu.	

Settings

Menu	Property	Value
separator	Text	-
Albums	(Name)	menuAlbums
	Text	&Albums
Photos	(Name)	menuPhotos
	Text	&Photos

| 2 | Add a `Click` handler for the Albums menu. | ```csharp
private void menuAlbums_Click
    (object sender, System.EventArgs e)
{
    // Display albums in the list
    if (!_albumsShown)
    {
        LoadAlbumData(PhotoAlbum.DefaultDir);
    }
}
``` |
| 3 | Add a `Click` handler for the Photos menu.<br><br>**Note:** This is the same as activating an album item. | ```csharp
private void menuPhotos_Click
    (object sender, System.EventArgs e)
{
    // Activate the selected album
    listViewMain_ItemActivate(sender, e);
}
``` |
| 4 | Update the `Popup` handler for the View menu to enable or disable the Photos menu as appropriate. | ```csharp
private void menuView_Popup
    (object sender, System.EventArgs e)
{
    View v = listViewMain.View;
    . . .
    if (_albumsShown && listViewMain.
            SelectedItems.Count > 0)
        menuPhotos.Enabled = true;
    else
        menuPhotos.Enabled = false;
}
``` |

14.6   RECAP

This completes our discussion of the `ListView` class. In this chapter we discussed list views in detail, and created a new MyAlbumExplorer interface to display the collection of albums available in our default album directory. We supported all four possible views available in a `ListView` control, and provided support for column
```

sorting, item selection, and label editing. We finished by implementing this same support for the photos in an album, so that our application can display albums or photographs in the control.

Along the way we looked at a number of classes provided to support this control, most notably the `ListViewItem`, `ListViewItem.ListViewSubItem`, and `ColumnHeader` classes. We also examined the `IComparer` interface as a way to define how two objects should be compared, and implemented a class supporting this interface in order to sort the columns in our detailed view of the list.

The next chapter looks at a close cousin to the `ListView` class, namely the `TreeView` control.

CHAPTER 15

Tree views

15.1 Tree view basics 486
15.2 The TreeView class 486
15.3 Dynamic tree nodes 497

15.4 Node selection 505
15.5 Fun with tree views 513
15.6 Recap 524

In the previous chapter we created the MyAlbumExplorer application incorporating a `ListView` control. This program presents the default set of photo albums available and the collection of photographs contained within these albums.

In this chapter we extend this program to include a `TreeView` control in order to present a more traditional explorer-style interface. Specific topics we will cover in this chapter include the following:

- Exploring the `TreeView` class.
- Using the `Splitter` control to divide a container.
- Populating a tree with the `TreeNode` class, both in Visual Studio and programmatically.
- Selecting nodes in a tree.
- Editing the labels for a tree.
- Integrating a `ListView` and `TreeView` control into an application.

As we did for list views, we begin this chapter with a general discussion of tree views and a discussion of the terms and classes used for this control.

15.1   TREE VIEW BASICS

The `TreeView` class is a close cousin of the `ListView` class. List views display a collection as a list, while tree views display collections as a tree. Each item in a tree view is called a *tree node*, or just a *node*. Tree nodes can contain additional nodes, called *child nodes*, to arbitrary levels in order to represent a hierarchy of objects in a single control. Various elements of a `TreeView` control are illustrated in figure 15.1.

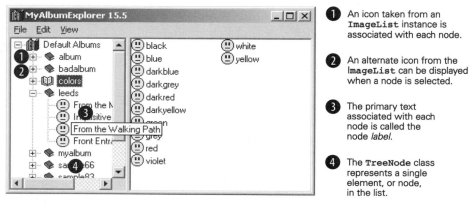

① An icon taken from an **ImageList** instance is associated with each node.

② An alternate icon from the **ImageList** can be displayed when a node is selected.

③ The primary text associated with each node is called the node *label*.

④ The **TreeNode** class represents a single element, or node, in the list.

Figure 15.1   **The TreeView control automatically shows the entire label in a tool tip style format when the mouse hovers over a node, as was done for the "From the Walking Path" entry in this figure.**

The explorer-style interface shown in the figure and used by other applications such as Windows Explorer is a common use of the `TreeView` and `ListView` classes. In this chapter we build such an interface by extending the MyAlbumExplorer project constructed in chapter 14.

15.2   THE TREEVIEW CLASS

The `TreeView` class is summarized in.NET Table 15.1. Like the `ListView` class, this class inherits directly from the `Control` class, and provides an extensive list of members for manipulating the objects displayed by the tree.

The TreeView class represents a control that displays a collection of labeled items as a tree-style hierarchy. Typically an icon is displayed for each item in the collection to provide a graphical indication of the nature or purpose of the item. Items in the tree are referred to as *nodes*, and each node is represented by a TreeNode class instance. This class is part of the System.Windows.Forms namespace, and inherits from the Control class. See .NET Table 4.1 on page 104 for a list of members inherited by this class.

Public Properties	CheckBoxes	Gets or sets whether check boxes are displayed next to each node in the tree. The default is false.
	HideSelection	Gets or sets whether a selected node remains highlighted even when the control does not have focus.
	ImageIndex	Gets or sets an index into the tree's image list of the default image to display by a tree node.
	ImageList	Gets or sets an ImageList to associate with this control.
	LabelEdit	Gets or sets whether node labels can be edited.
	Nodes	Gets the collection of TreeNode objects assigned to the control.
	PathSeparator	Gets or sets the delimiter used for a tree node path, and in particular the TreeNode.FullPath property.
	SelectedNode	Gets or sets the selected tree node.
	ShowPlusMinus	Gets or sets whether to indicate the expansion state of parent tree nodes by drawing a plus '+' or minus '-' sign next to each node. The default is true.
	Sorted	Gets or sets whether the tree nodes are sorted alphabetically based on their label text.
	TopNode	Gets the tree node currently displayed at the top of the tree view control.
Public Methods	CollapseAll	Collapses all the tree nodes so that no child nodes are visible.
	GetNodeAt	Retrieves the tree node at the specified location in pixels within the control.
	GetNodeCount	Returns the number of top-level nodes in the tree, or the total number of nodes in the entire tree.
Public Events	AfterExpand	Occurs after a tree node is expanded.
	AfterLabelEdit	Occurs after a tree node label is edited.
	BeforeCollapse	Occurs before a tree node is collapsed.
	BeforeSelect	Occurs before a tree node is selected.
	ItemDrag	Occurs when an item is dragged in the tree view.

A TreeView object is created much like any other control in Visual Studio .NET: you simply drag the control onto the form. In our MyAlbumExplorer application, we already have a ListView on our form, so it looks like all we need to add is a tree view in order to support the interface shown in figure 15.2.

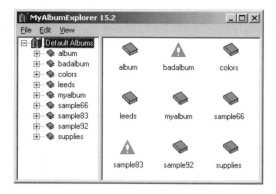

Figure 15.2
A traditional explorer-style interface displaying photo albums.

15.2.1 CREATING A TREE VIEW

There is, in fact, an issue here with how a tree view and list view are arranged on the form. The gray vertical bar in the middle of our interface is a special control called a *splitter* to separate the two controls. We will talk about splitters in a moment. First, let's add a TreeView to our form and see what happens.

Set the version number for the MyAlbumExplorer application to 15.2.

CREATING A TREE VIEW CONTROL		
	Action	**Result**
1	In the MainForm.cs [Design] window, drag a TreeView control onto the form and set its properties. **Settings** **Property** | **Value** (Name) | treeViewMain Dock | Left	
2	Bring the list view to the top of the z-order. **How-to:** Right-click the List-View control and select the Bring to Front option.	
3	Set the HideSelection property in both the ListView and the TreeView to false.	**Note:** This will highlight the selected object in both controls even when these controls do not have the focus.

So far, so good. We have a `TreeView` on the left and a `ListView` on the right. If you run this program, you will see the interface shown in figure 15.3. The tree control is on the left, and the list view on the right. We have not added any nodes to our tree yet, but the photo albums from the default album directory appear in the list view as was discussed in chapter 14. Note here that the `ListView` must be brought to the top of the z-order in step 2 to ensure it is not obscured by the `TreeView` control.

TRY IT!   Send the `ListView` control to the bottom of the z-order using the Send to Back menu item. Run the application to see what happens. Because the controls are placed on the form starting at the bottom of the z-order, the `ListView` in this case fills the entire client window. The `TreeView` is then docked to the left of the form. When the `ListView` is at the top, the `TreeView` is docked first, and then the `ListView` fills the remaining area.

You will note that if you resize the form in figure 15.3, the size of the tree view does not change. In addition, the line between the two controls cannot be dragged as is the case in other explorer-style programs such as Windows Explorer.

We can enable this behavior by adding a `Splitter` control to our form. We will do this next, after which we will look at populating our tree with some items.

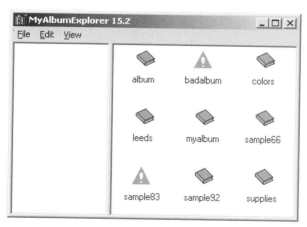

Figure 15.3
The ListView control here works as before, just within a smaller area.

15.2.2   USING THE SPLITTER CLASS

As a short aside to our discussion on tree views, the `Splitter` class is useful for dividing all or part of a form or other container into two resizable sections. While some readers may not consider a splitter control to be an advanced concept, it fits nicely into our discussion of the MyAlbumExplorer application, so this is where it goes.

Typically a splitter provides separate areas for two collection or container controls, normally one of the `ListBox`, `ListView`, `TreeView`, or `Panel` controls. An overview of the `Splitter` class is given in .NET Table 15.2.

A splitter can appear horizontally or vertically. When docked to the top or bottom of a container, it is a *horizontal splitter*; when docked to the left or right, it is a *vertical splitter.* We will create a vertical splitter in our MyAlbumExplorer application, and then discuss how to turn this into a horizontal splitter.

.NET Table 15.2 Splitter class		
The Splitter class represents a control that divides a container into two sections. Each section contains a docked control, and the splitter permits the user to resize each section at runtime. This class is part of the System.Windows.Forms namespace, and inherits from the Control class. See .NET Table 4.1 on page 104 for a list of members inherited by this class.		
Public Properties	BorderStyle	Gets or sets the border style for the control.
	Cursor (overridden from Control)	Gets or sets the cursor for the control. A horizontal splitter uses the HSplit cursor by default, while a vertical splitter uses the VSplit cursor by default.
	Dock (overridden from Control)	Gets or sets the docking style. A splitter must be docked to one side of its container. This setting determines the orientation, either vertical or horizontal, of the splitter. The None and Fill values are not permitted. The position of the splitter in the z-order determines the location of the splitter within its container.
	MinExtra	Gets or sets the minimum size for the remainder of the container, which is occupied by the subsequent control in the docking order.
	MinSize	Gets or sets the minimum size for the target of the splitter, which is the previous control in the docking order.
	SplitPosition	Gets or sets the position of the splitter, in pixels.
Public Events	SplitterMoved	Occurs when the splitter has moved.
	SplitterMoving	Occurs when the splitter is moving.

The steps to create a vertical splitter are detailed in the following table.

	Action	**Result**
	ADD A SPLITTER CONTROL	
1	In the MainForm.cs [Design] window, drag a Splitter object onto the form.	
2	Set the MinExtra property for the splitter to 100.	**Note:** This ensures that the large icons in our ListView will always be visible.
3	Move the ListView control to the front of the z-order.	The window looks much the same as before. The difference occurs when the application is executed.

Compile the application to see the splitter in action. Figure 15.4 shows our window with the splitter dragged far to the right. The MinExtra property setting ensures that the items in the ListView cannot be obscured by dragging the splitter all the way to the right side of the window. The ListView can still disappear when the form is resized, which we will fix in a moment.

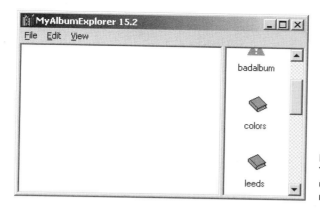

Figure 15.4
The splitter control permits the user to resize the display areas as required for the specific contents.

Before we make some additional changes to our application, let's talk briefly about how the splitter is positioned. Here is an excerpt of the `InitializeComponent` method generated by Visual Studio .NET for our form.

```
private void InitializeComponent()
{
    . . .
    this.listViewMain.Dock = System.Windows.Forms.DockStyle.Fill;
    . . .
    this.treeViewMain.Dock = System.Windows.Forms.DockStyle.Left;
    this.treeViewMain.Size = new System.Drawing.Size(100, 253);
    . . .
    //
    // splitter1
    //
    this.splitter1.Location = new System.Drawing.Point(100, 0);
    this.splitter1.MinExtra = 100;
    this.splitter1.Size = new System.Drawing.Size(3, 253);
    . . .
    //
    // MainForm
    //
    this.ClientSize = new System.Drawing.Size(392, 253);
    this.Controls.AddRange(new System.Windows.Forms.Control[] {
                                this.listViewMain,
                                this.splitter1,
                                this.treeViewMain});
    . . .
}
```

In the `AddRange` call made within this code, note how the `Splitter` control "splits" the `Control` array added to the `Controls` property for the form. This establishes the proper z-order for the form so that the controls appear properly. We can change this to a vertical splitter by changing the `Dock` property for both the `Splitter` and the `TreeView` controls to `DockStyle.Top`. Visual Studio .NET automatically adjusts the `Size` property for each control to accommodate the horizontal orientation.

While this is not part of our final application, these changes are shown in the following code. The corresponding application window appears in figure 15.5.

```
private void InitializeComponent()
{
  // Changes to configure the application with a horizontal splitter
  //      ( not part of our final application )
  . . .
  this.listViewMain.Dock = System.Windows.Forms.DockStyle.Fill;
  . . .
  this.treeViewMain.Dock = System.Windows.Forms.DockStyle.Top;
  this.treeViewMain.Size = new System.Drawing.Size(392, 100);
  . . .
  //
  // splitter1
  //
  this.splitter1.Dock = System.Windows.Forms.DockStyle.Top;
  this.splitter1.Location = new System.Drawing.Point(100, 0);
  this.splitter1.MinExtra = 100;
  this.splitter1.Size = new System.Drawing.Size(392, 3);
  . . .
}
```

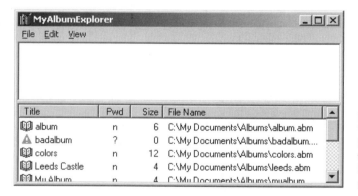

Figure 15.5
This figure displays a horizontal splitter between a tree view and list view control (not our approach).

If you make these changes in your code, make certain you undo them before continuing, as we would like to have a vertical splitter in our final application. Let's get back to our `TreeView` object and add some nodes to this control.

15.2.3   USING THE TREENODE CLASS

Now that the list and tree views on our form are separated by a splitter control, we will get back to the tree view itself. Tree views contain nodes, which may contain other nodes, which may contain still other nodes, and so forth. Each node in the tree is represented by a `TreeNode` object. This class is summarized in .NET Table 15.3. In the Windows Explorer application, for example, each directory is represented as a tree node, and may contain other directories or files.

CHAPTER 15   TREE VIEWS

The TreeNode class represents a marshal by reference object that acts as an element, or a *node*, within a TreeView control. A TreeNode object can contain other nodes to represent a hierarchy of objects within a tree view. Contained nodes are called *child nodes*. A top-level node in a TreeView object is called a *root node* of the tree. Each TreeNode object can be contained by exactly one TreeView or TreeNode object. This class is part of the System.Windows.Forms namespace, and inherits from the System.MarshalByRefObject class.

Public Constructors	TreeNode	Initializes a new TreeNode instance.
		
		Overloads
		`TreeNode(string label);`
		`TreeNode(string label,`
		`     TreeNode[] childNodes);`
		`TreeNode(string label,`
		`          int imageIndex,`
		`          int selectedImageIndex);`

Public Properties	FirstNode	Gets the first child node contained by this node.
	ImageIndex	Gets or sets an index into the tree's image list of the default image to display for this node.
	Index	Gets the position of this node within the Nodes collection of the containing TreeView or TreeNode.
	IsEditing	Gets whether this node is currently being edited.
	IsExpanded	Gets whether the children of this node are currently displayed.
	IsSelected	Gets whether this node is currently selected.
	IsVisible	Gets whether this node is currently visible in the containing tree view.
	NextVisibleNode	Gets the first subsequent child, sibling, or other node visible in the containing tree view control.
	NodeFont	Gets or sets the Font used to display the label text for this node.
	Nodes	Gets the collection of TreeNode objects assigned to this node.
	Parent	Gets the TreeNode object containing this node, if any.
	PrevNode	Gets the previous tree node in the Nodes collection containing this node.
	SelectedImage-Index	Gets or sets an index into the tree's image list of the image to display by this node when the node is selected.
	Tag	Gets or sets an object to associate with this tree node.
	Text	Gets or sets the text displayed in the label for this node.
Public Methods	BeginEdit	Initiates an edit of this node's label.
	Collapse	Ensures that no children of this node are currently displayed.
	ExpandAll	Expands all tree nodes contained by this node.
	Toggle	Toggles the tree node between the expanded or collapsed state, based on the IsExpanded setting.

In our tree view for the MyAlbumExplorer application, we would like to represent each album as a node in the tree, with each album containing a node for each photograph in that album. Since albums can appear in any directory, we might also wish to indicate where a set of albums is located. We will do this by generating a tree structure similar to the one shown in figure 15.6. This tree was generated in Visual Studio to illustrate the hierarchy we will employ. The `ListView` control in this figure is totally unrelated to the contents of our tree. This is not what we ultimately want, but it is okay for now.

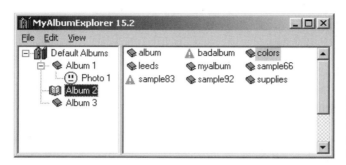

Figure 15.6
In the TreeView, note how the selected album employs a different icon than the unselected one

As an introduction to tree nodes, let's create the structure shown in figure 15.6 in Visual Studio .NET. The following table details the steps required.

	CREATE TREE NODES IN VISUAL STUDIO	
	Action	**Result**
1	In the MainForm.cs [Design] window, set the `ImageList` property of the tree view to use the existing `imageListSmall` component already associated with the form.	
2	Set default index values for nodes in the tree.	

Settings

Property	Value
ImageIndex	1
SelectedImageIndex	4

	Action	Result
3	Display the TreeNode Editor dialog box for the control. **How-to** Click the **...** button for the Nodes entry in the Properties window, as shown in the graphic for steps 1 and 2.	

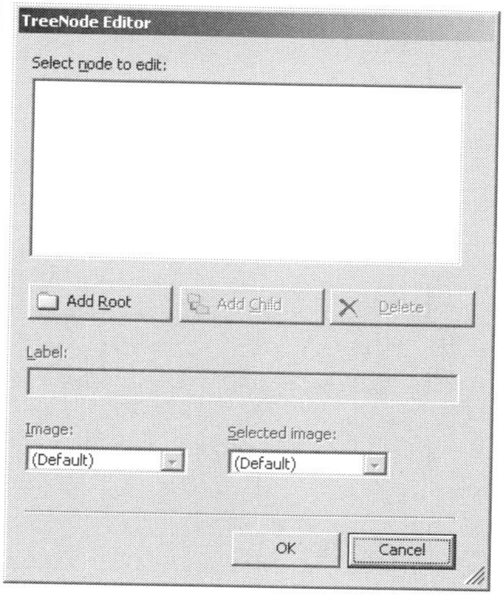

For step 4:

Action

Create a top-level node for the tree.

How-to
Click the Add Root button.

Settings

Property	Value
Label	Default Albums
Image	*books image*
Selected Image	*books image*

Result

A top-level Default Albums node appears in the TreeNode Editor. This node is shown in the graphic for step 6.

For step 5:

Action

Add three child nodes for the Default Albums node.

How-to
Add each node by clicking the Add Child button while the Default Albums node is selected.

Settings

Node	Property	Value
First	Label	Album 1
Second	Label	Album 2
Third	Label	Album 3

Result

Both nodes appear using the default indexes.

Note: When you select a node, notice how the selected image assigned to the node is displayed in the tree.

	Action	**Result**
6	Add a child node for the Album 1 node. **How-to** Click the Add Child button while the Album 1 node is selected. **Settings** **Property** / **Value** Label / Photo 1 Image / *The normal face image* Selected Image / *The smiley face image*	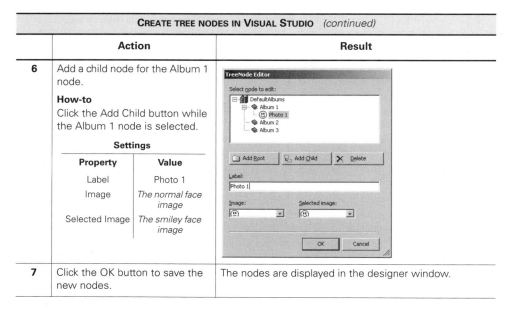
7	Click the OK button to save the new nodes.	The nodes are displayed in the designer window.

The new nodes appear in the designer window, and are present as we saw in figure 15.6. Run the program and note how the image changes when each node is selected. Also note the plus and minus signs that appear to indicate whether a node is expanded or collapsed.

Let's take a look at the code generated in the InitializeComponent method. The assignment of the Nodes property is shown, reformatted to be a bit more readable than the code that is generated by Visual Studio.

```
this.treeViewMain.Nodes.AddRange(new System.Windows.Forms.TreeNode[]
{
    new System.Windows.Forms.TreeNode("Default Albums", 5, 5,
                                    new System.Windows.Forms.TreeNode[]
    {
        new System.Windows.Forms.TreeNode("Album 1",
                                    new System.Windows.Forms.TreeNode[]
        {
            new System.Windows.Forms.TreeNode("Photo 1", 0, 3)
        }),
        new System.Windows.Forms.TreeNode("Album 2"),
        new System.Windows.Forms.TreeNode("Album 3")
    })
});
```

This code uses various forms of the TreeNode constructor to create the nodes in the tree. If you look carefully, you will realize that the Nodes property for the tree contains a single entry, our root Default Albums node. This root node is created to contain an array of three TreeNode objects, namely the Album 1, Album 2, and Album 3 nodes.

Of these, the first Album 1 node contains a single `TreeNode` object representing the Photo 1 node.

The point here is to see firsthand how `TreeNode` objects are created and appear on the form. In the next section we will create nodes for our actual albums and photographs programmatically. The TreeNode Editor we used here is useful for creating a fixed set of nodes, or for creating the top-level nodes for a tree. For example, in a program with a large number of application settings, you might organize these settings into a hierarchy and display them in a tree view. The user could then interact with the tree to modify the application's settings. In this case, the `TreeView.CheckBoxes` property might be useful to enable or disable each setting via a check box.

15.3 DYNAMIC TREE NODES

In this section we will look at programmatically creating and modifying the set of tree nodes associated with a tree view control. We have already decided to display a top-level "Default Albums" node, under which the albums in the default album directory will be displayed. Within each album the set of photos in the album will appear. The result should look something like figure 15.7. This section will focus on populating the tree view with the appropriate set of tree nodes. Section 15.4 will examine how to coordinate the contents of our `TreeView` and `ListView` controls.

To make this change, we will first create some index constants for use when accessing our image list. Once this is done, we will look at how to create the album nodes and photograph nodes in code.

Figure 15.7
A TreeView automatically displays horizontal and vertical scroll bars as required. Note that the contents of the TreeView and ListView controls are not yet synchronized.

15.3.1 ASSIGNING INDEX CONSTANTS

Before we talk about how to create this tree, recall that we created constants for the image indices in chapter 14. Figure 15.7 shows the closed book icon for each unselected album, and the open book icon for the selected "leeds" album. Let's create some constants for the remaining images in our `ImageList` objects so that we can use them in this section.

This is done with the following step.

Set the version number of the MyAlbumExplorer application to 15.3.

ASSIGN IMAGE INDEX CONSTANTS		
	Action	**Result**

1	In the MainForm.cs code window, update the image index constants to account for unselected and selected items.	`private const int PhotoIndex = 0;`
		`private const int AlbumIndex = 1;`
		`private const int ErrorIndex = 2;`
		`private const int SelectedPhotoIndex = 3;`
		`private const int SelectedAlbumIndex = 4;`
		`private const int AlbumDirectoryIndex = 5;`

With these constants in place, we are ready to discuss adding the actual albums to our tree.

15.3.2 CREATING THE ALBUM NODES

The proper way to add nodes to a tree depends somewhat on the size of a tree. For a small set of nodes, it makes sense to add the entire hierarchy of nodes at one time, and then allow the control to manage the nodes as they are expanded and collapsed by the user. For a large hierarchy, adding a huge number of nodes can use up a lot of memory. Imagine if the Windows Explorer program created a `TreeNode` object for every directory and file on your computer. This would be a lot of nodes on most computers.

Instead, applications typically add only the nodes a user initially requires, and then insert additional nodes based on the user's actions. This saves both time and memory, since less work is required to initialize the tree when the application starts, and memory is only allocated as new nodes are added to the tree.

In our application, the number of albums present could be few or many. We could create the entire hierarchy all at once as shown in listing 15.1. This requires that we open each album file and iterate through every photograph in every album. Since this could be expensive for a large number of albums, we will not use this method nor discuss this code in any detail. Hopefully, it is instructive to see how the entire hierarchy might be created in a single method.

Listing 15.1 Create the entire set of tree nodes required (not our approach)

```
private void InitTreeData()
{
  treeViewMain.BeginUpdate();
  treeViewMain.Nodes.Clear();

  // Create the top-level node
  TreeNode defaultRoot = new TreeNode("Default Albums",
      AlbumDirectoryIndex, AlbumDirectoryIndex);
  treeViewMain.Nodes.Add(defaultRoot);
```

```
// Create a node for each album file
foreach (string s in Directory.GetFiles(
                    PhotoAlbum.DefaultDir, "*.abm"))
{
  String baseName = Path.GetFileNameWithoutExtension(s);
  TreeNode albumNode = new TreeNode(baseName)
  defaultRoot.Nodes.Add(albumNode);

  // Open the album
  PhotoAlbum album = OpenAlbum(s);
  if (album == null)
  {
    // Bad album, so adjust the image index settings
    albumNode.ImageIndex = ErrorIndex;
    albumNode.SelectedImageIndex = ErrorIndex;
    continue;
  }

  // Create a node for each photo in this album
  foreach (Photograph p in album)
  {
    string text = album.GetDisplayText(p);
    TreeNode photoNode = new TreeNode(text,
        PhotoIndex, SelectedPhotoIndex);
    albumNode.Nodes.Add(photoNode);
  }

  album.Dispose();
}

treeViewMain.EndUpdate();
}
```

Instead, we will take an "as-needed" approach to our tree nodes. Initially we will create only the album nodes, and then add the photographs for an album only when the user expands that album's node.

To begin this process, we need to modify our OnLoad method to create the initial tree structure.

MODIFY THE ONLOAD METHOD		
	Action	**Result**
1	In the MainForm.cs code window, update the OnLoad method to initialize the tree view control before the form is displayed.	```protected override void OnLoad(EventArgs e)
{
    . . .

    // Initialize the tree and list controls
    InitTreeData();
    LoadAlbumData(PhotoAlbum.DefaultDir);
}``` |

The `InitTreeData` method will clear the nodes we created with the TreeNode Editor and add the top-level default node and set of albums from the default album directory. This table continues the steps from the previous table.

	ADD THE INITTREEDATA METHOD	
	Action	**Result**
2	Add an `InitTreeData` method to the MainForm.cs code window.	`private void InitTreeData()` `{`
3	To implement this method, first clear any existing nodes in the tree view control. **Note:** The `BeginUpdate` method should be used when adding multiple nodes to a `TreeView` control so that it will not repaint its window while the new nodes are added.	`treeViewMain.BeginUpdate();` `treeViewMain.Nodes.Clear();`

4	Create the top-level node for the tree.
	How-to
	a. Use the label "Default Albums."
	b. Set the image indices to use the album directory icon.
	c. Add the node as a root of the tree.
	d. Select this node by default.
		`// Create the top-level node`
		`TreeNode defaultRoot`
		`    = new TreeNode("Default Albums",`
		`                AlbumDirectoryIndex,`
		`                AlbumDirectoryIndex);`
		`defaultRoot.Tag = PhotoAlbum.DefaultDir;`
		`treeViewMain.Nodes.Add(defaultRoot);`
		`treeViewMain.SelectedNode = defaultRoot;`

5	Create a node for each album file in the default album directory.	`foreach (string s in Directory.GetFiles(`
		`        PhotoAlbum.DefaultDir, "*.abm"))`
		`{`

6	Create a new `TreeNode` for this album using the base file name as the label text for the node.	`// Create a node for this album`
		`String baseName = Path.`
		`    GetFileNameWithoutExtension(s);`
		`TreeNode albumNode`
		`    = new TreeNode(baseName,`

7	Create a child node in each album node with the label text "child."	`new TreeNode[] {`
		`new TreeNode("child")`
		`});`

8	Set the `Tag` property for the node to contain the album file path. **Note:** We will use the `Tag` property to identify the album related to a specified node when handling events for the `TreeView` control.	`albumNode.Tag = s;`
9	Add the new node to the collection of nodes under the default root node.	`defaultRoot.Nodes.Add(albumNode);` `}`
10	Allow the `TreeView` to repaint by calling the `EndUpdate` method.	`treeViewMain.EndUpdate();` `}`

This code uses a few tricks to ensure that our application will perform as expected. When a new album node is created, a single child node is added to ensure that the `TreeView` control will allow the node to be expanded.

```
TreeNode albumNode = new TreeNode(baseName,
    new TreeNode[] { new TreeNode("child") });
```

Without this child, the control would presume that our node has no children, and would not display a plus sign next to the album to permit the user to expand the node. We will make use of this in the next section, where we implement the expansion of an album node. This line simply ensures that the user can initiate this step.

We also assign the `Tag` property for each node to contain the file path corresponding to the node. For the root node, this path is the default album directory. For each album, this path is the fully qualified album file name.

```
. . .
defaultRoot.Tag = PhotoAlbum.DefaultDir;

foreach (string s in Directory.GetFiles(. . .)
{
  . . .
  albumNode.Tag = s;
  defaultRoot.Nodes.Add(albumNode);
}
```

This setting will permit us to identify the object corresponding to a given node while processing a user action on behalf of the tree view. Like other `Tag` properties we have seen for .NET, this property can be set to any `object` instance.

Notice as well that we use the default image index and selected image index for all album files. Since we do not open the corresponding `PhotoAlbum` during our initialization step, we have no way to know which albums can be opened and which will generate an error. We start by assuming that all albums can be opened, and will update the image index values if we discover any problems.

It is also worth noting that using the `Tag` property as we do in the previous code is not always a practical solution. Another common tactic, especially in more complex applications, is to derive a new class from the `TreeNode` class, and use this new class to populate the tree. This alternate approach can encapsulate node-specific functionality in the derived class, and can improve the maintenance and readability of the resulting code.

Compile and run your application to verify that the albums appear in the tree. Our next topic is the insertion of photographs when the user expands an album node.

15.3.3 CREATING THE PHOTOGRAPH NODES

So far our `TreeView` control displays the albums from the default album directory during start-up. We created a default child node within each album to permit the user to expand these nodes. The next step is to handle this expansion and replace the default child node with the set of photos in the album.

There are a number of ways tree nodes can be expanded and collapsed. These include the following:

- *From the mouse.* The user can double-click on a tree node to toggle between expand and collapse operations. When the ShowPlusMinus property is true, a click on a plus '+' sign will expand the node while a click on a minus '−' sign will collapse a node.

- *From the keyboard.* The user can press the right arrow key to expand the selected node in the tree, and the left arrow key to collapse the selected node.

- *From code.* The TreeNode class includes an Expand method to expand the node, a Collapse method to collapse the node, and a Toggle method to switch the node to the opposite of its current state. The TreeView class includes the ExpandAll and CollapseAll methods to expand or collapse all nodes in the tree.

In addition, the TreeNode.EnsureVisible method will expand nodes as required to have the node appear within the containing TreeView control.

Regardless of how a node is expanded or collapsed, the BeforeExpand, After-Expand, BeforeCollapse, and AfterCollapse events occur in the TreeView class for each node as it alters its state. The before events receive a TreeViewCancelEventArgs class instance as their event parameter, while the after events receive a TreeViewEventArgs class instance. The TreeViewCancelEventArgs class is summarized in .NET Table 15.4. The TreeViewEventArgs class provides the same two Action and Node properties shown in the table, but inherits from the System.EventArgs class rather than the CancelEventArgs class. The CancelEventArgs class is discussed in chapter 8.

.NET Table 15.4 TreeViewCancelEventArgs class

The TreeViewCancelEventArgs class is a CancelEventArgs object that contains event data for events in the TreeView class that occur before an operation takes place. The event handler receiving this class has the opportunity to cancel the operation by setting the inherited Cancel property to true. This class is part of the System.Windows.Forms namespace, and inherits from the System.ComponentModel.CancelEventArgs class.

Public Properties		
	Action	Gets the TreeViewAction enumeration member representing the action that caused this event to occur.
	Node	Gets the TreeNode object that is the target of the current operation.

Let's get back to our application and make use of some of these constructs. We would like to insert a set of nodes for the photos in an album whenever the album node is expanded. We can do this by handling the BeforeExpand event for our tree.

Before we actually do this, a utility method to open a PhotoAlbum using a given album node will turn out to be useful here and later on in the chapter. We will create this method first.

	CREATE AN OPENTREEALBUM METHOD	
	Action	**Result**

1	In the MainForm.cs code window, create a new OpenTreeAlbum method that accepts a TreeNode object and returns an album.	`private PhotoAlbum OpenTreeAlbum`
		`    (TreeNode node)`
		`{`

2	Begin this method by opening the album associated with the node. **How-to** Use the OpenAlbum method created in chapter 14.	`string s = node.Tag as string;` `PhotoAlbum album = OpenAlbum(s);`

3	Update the image index values for this node.
	
	How-to
	a. If the album cannot be opened, use the error icon for both images.
	b. Otherwise, use the standard album images.
		`if (album == null)`
		`{`
		`    // Unable to open album`
		`    node.ImageIndex = ErrorIndex;`
		`    node.SelectedImageIndex = ErrorIndex;`
		`}`
		`else`
		`{`
		`    // Album opened successfully`
		`    node.ImageIndex = AlbumIndex;`
		`    node.SelectedImageIndex`
		`        = SelectedAlbumIndex;`
		`}`

4	Return the result of the OpenAlbum call.	`    return album;` `}`

With this method in place, we can create a BeforeExpand event handler for our TreeView control. The following table continues the previous steps to create this handler.

	HANDLE THE BEFOREEXPAND EVENT	
	Action	**Result**

5	In the MainForm.cs [Design] window, add a BeforeExpand event handler for the TreeView control.	`private void treeViewMain_BeforeExpand`
		`    (object sender, System.Windows.`
		`        Forms.TreeViewCancelEventArgs e)`
		`{`
		`    TreeNode node = e.Node;`

	Action	Result

6	To implement this handler, see if the expanding node is an album.
	
	How-to
	a. Convert the `Tag` property for the node to a string.
	b. See if this string has an album file extension.
	c. If not, simply return.
		```string s = node.Tag as string;```
		```if (s == null```
		``` || (Path.GetExtension(s) != ".abm"))```
		```{```
		``` // Not an album node```
		``` return;```
		```}```

7	Clear the existing contents of the node.	```// Found an album node``` ```node.Nodes.Clear();```

8	Open the corresponding `PhotoAlbum` object for this node.	```using (PhotoAlbum album```
		``` = OpenTreeAlbum(node))```
		```{```
		
		Note: Recall that in chapter 5 we supported the `IDisposable` interface in our `PhotoAlbum` class, which allows us to employ the `using` statement here.

9	If the album could not be opened or is empty, then cancel the operation.	```// Cancel if null or empty album```
		```if (album == null || album.Count == 0)```
		```{```
		``` e.Cancel = true;```
		``` return;```
		```}```

10	Otherwise, enumerate through the `Photograph` objects in the album to update the contents of the album node.	```// Add a node for each photo in album```
		```treeViewMain.BeginUpdate();```
		```foreach (Photograph p in album)```
		```{```

11	Create a new `TreeNode` for this photo.
	
	Note: Set the default and selected image index for the node to use the appropriate photograph icon.
		```// Create a new node for this photo```
		```TreeNode newNode```
		``` = new TreeNode(```
		``` album.GetDisplayText(p),```
		``` MainForm.PhotoIndex,```
		``` MainForm.SelectedPhotoIndex);```

12	Assign the file path for the photo to the `Tag` property of the new node.	```newNode.Tag = p.FileName;```

13	Add the new node to the `Nodes` collection of the expanding tree node.	``` node.Nodes.Add(newNode);```
		```}```
		```treeViewMain.EndUpdate();```
		``` }```
		```}```

This code returns fairly quickly if the node does not represent an album. Before an album node is expanded, this code adjusts the node and its contents for one of three possible situations:

1 If the album cannot be opened, then the `ErrorIndex` constant is assigned to the `ImageIndex` and `SelectedImageIndex` properties via the `Open-`

`TreeAlbum` method. The `Nodes` collection is cleared and the expand operation is cancelled.

2 If the album is opened and found to be empty, then the `Nodes` collection is cleared and the expand operation is cancelled.

3 If the album is opened and found to be nonempty, then the existing `Nodes` collection is replaced with a collection of `TreeNode` objects based on the photographs in the album.

Note that we once again use the `Tag` property to hold the file path, this time for the `Photograph` object's file name. This will come in useful when we look at node selection in the next section.

Compile and run the program to exercise our new event handler. Try to reproduce each of these three possibilities to see the result. Also note how the icon for the photograph nodes differs when the node is selected.

TRY IT!   Handle the `AfterCollapse` event for the tree to clear the collection contained in an album node. This event handler should again use the `Tag` property for the node to determine if the node represents an album. When an album node is collapsed, call the `Clear` method on its `Nodes` collection and recreate the default "child" node so the album can be expanded later on.

Of course, a more complex tree hierarchy will require nodes at various levels of the tree to expand and collapse depending on their requirements. The code we created here is for a three-level tree, but can be extended to support more complicated structures. Once again it is worth mentioning that the use of the `Tag` property works well in our application since there are only three types of objects. For a more complex tree view, consider creating one or more new classes based on the `TreeNode` class.

So far we have not worried about synchronizing the contents of our `ListView` and `TreeView` controls. In the next section we finally take up this topic while discussing the selection of tree nodes.

15.4   NODE SELECTION

A node in a tree view is selected whenever the user clicks on the node with the mouse. In our application, the tree nodes correspond to albums and photographs that can be displayed in the `ListView` area of the form. Whenever a user selects a node, the contents of that node should be displayed in the list view.

Such behavior is typical of applications that employ a `TreeView` control. The nodes in the tree contain or refer to other data that is or can be displayed on the form. Whenever a new tree node is selected, the data displayed must be updated as well. For example, in Windows Explorer, the tree view contains directories,[1] while the list view

---

[1] It also contains disks, the desktop, the control panel, and other objects. For the purposes of our example, we can pretend that it contains only directories.

contains files contained in these directories. When the user selects a directory entry from the tree view, the contents of that directory are displayed in the list view of the window. The reverse is also true. When the user double-clicks on a directory in the list view, that directory is shown in the tree view and its contents are displayed in the list view.

In this section we will look at how to implement this behavior in our MyAlbumExplorer application. This will link up our `TreeView` and `ListView` controls so they work together and present a consistent interface to the user.

These changes come in two flavors. First there are changes to ensure that the `ListView` is properly updated when the `TreeView` changes. Next there are changes to ensure that the `TreeView` is properly updated when the `ListView` changes. All of these updates will be driven by the selection of a tree view node using the `SelectedNode` property of the `TreeView` control. Figure 15.8 shows our application with an album selected in the tree view and the corresponding collection of photographs displayed in the list view.

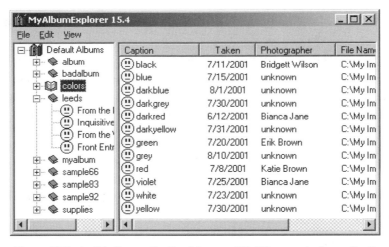

Figure 15.8   In this figure, the TreeView and ListView controls are finally coordinated.

We will begin these changes by updating our form when a node is selected in our `TreeView` control.

15.4.1   SUPPORTING NODE SELECTION

As we saw for the expand and collapse operations, there are two events associated with node selection. The `BeforeSelect` event occurs before the node is selected in the control, and receives a `TreeViewCancelEventArgs` instance containing the event data. The `AfterSelect` event occurs after the node has been selected, and receives a `TreeViewEventArgs` instance.

The `BeforeSelect` event is useful when you may wish to cancel a selection based on the state or other settings related to a given node. Since we have no need to do this here, we will use the `AfterSelect` event to update the `ListView` control based on the selected node. The following table summarizes the types of nodes in our tree, how to identify each type, and what the `ListView` control should contain for each type.

Contents of ListView for each type of TreeNode

TreeNode Type	How to identify this type	What to show in the ListView
Top-level node	The parent node is `null`.	The collection of albums.
Album node	The associated file has an album file extension.	The collection of photos in this album.
Photograph node	The node is not a top-level or an album node.	Nothing for now. Later we will draw the actual photograph associated with this node.

We can use this information to implement our event handler. The steps required are described by the following table.

Set the version number of the MyAlbumExplorer application to 15.4.

	IMPLEMENT A HANDLER FOR THE AFTERSELECT EVENT	
	Action	**Result**
1	In the MainForm.cs [Design] window, add an `AfterSelect` event handler for the `TreeView` control.	```private void treeViewMain_AfterSelect
(object sender, System.Windows.
Forms.TreeViewEventArgs e)
{```
2	Obtain the file name associated with the selected node.	``` TreeNode node = e.Node;
string fileName = node.Tag as string;```
3	If the file name string is `null`, throw an exception. **Note:** This should not happen, and indicates that something is wrong.	``` if (fileName == null)
throw new ApplicationException
("selected tree node has "
+ "invalid tag");```
4	If the node is a top-level node, display the albums associated with this node in the list view.	``` if (node.Parent == null)
{
// Top-level node
LoadAlbumData(fileName);
}```
5	If the node is an album node, display the photographs associated with the album in the list view.	``` else if (Path.GetExtension(fileName)
== ".abm")
{
// Album node selected
PhotoAlbum album
= OpenTreeAlbum(node);
LoadPhotoData(album);
}```
6	Otherwise, the node must be a photograph node.	``` else // must be a photograph
{
// Just clear the list for now.
listViewMain.Clear();
}
}```

As you can see, we take advantage of the `LoadAlbumData` and `LoadPhotoData` methods implemented in chapter 14. By encapsulating our load functionality in a method, we are able to reuse the methods here with no changes. Both of these methods are based on a file path from which to load the data, and we make use of this fact here to specify the appropriate data associated with the selected tree node. For a top-level node this is an album directory. For an album node this is an album file which is loaded as a new `PhotoAlbum` object. For a photograph node, this is the image file, although we do not make use of this fact here.

Astute readers will realize that there is some inefficiency here since we have separated the logic for updating our two views. For instance, when an album node is expanded and selected, we open the album to load the collection of photographs in the `treeViewMain_BeforeExpand` method, and then open the album again to update the contents of the `ListView` control from the `treeViewMain_After-Select` method. This is the result, in part, of how we have separated our discussion of the two controls. In a production program, you would likely want to merge these efforts to ensure that an album is only opened one time for each update.

One situation we will fix is the behavior of the `OnLoad` method. The method performs the following tasks:

1 The `InitTreeData` method is called, which does the following:

   a Creates and selects the top level node,

   b Creates tree nodes for each album in the default album directory.

2 As a result of selecting the top-level node, the `treeViewMain_After-Select` event handler is called, which does the following:

   a Calls `LoadAlbumData` to populate the `ListView` control.

3 Back in the `OnLoad` method, the `LoadAlbumData` method is called to initialize the `ListView` control.

Clearly the second call to `LoadAlbumData` is no longer required, so we can remove it from our program.

UPDATE THE ONLOAD METHOD		
	Action	**Result**
7	Modify the `OnLoad` method to only initialize the `TreeView` control.	```protected override void OnLoad(EventArgs e)
{
    . . .

    // Initialize the contents of the form
    InitTreeData();
}``` |

This completes the update of the list view as the contents of the tree view are modified. You can compile and run the application to verify that the `ListView` contents changes as different nodes are selected.

Our next topic is to update the contents of the `TreeView` control based on user interactions with the list view items.

15.4.2   REVISITING THE LIST VIEW

The contents of our `ListView` control can be modified directly by the user through the control itself and through the menu bar items. There are three actions a user can perform to alter the list contents:

1   Select the Albums menu item under the View menu. This invokes a `Click` event for the menu, and our `menuAlbums_Click` event handler.

2   Select the Photos menu item under the View menu, which can only be done when an item representing an album is selected in the list view. This invokes a `Click` event for the menu, and our `menuPhotos_Click` event handler.

3   Double-click on an item in order to activate it. This invokes the `ItemActivate` event, and our `listViewMain_ItemActivate` event handler.

We will handle each of these actions by selecting the appropriate node in our `TreeView` control. This permits the tree view to "be in charge" of ensuring that all controls on the form display the proper information based on the currently selected node. This is a good general mechanism that can be employed in any application.

Let's take a moment to consider what the behavior should be for each of these actions. These are summarized in the following table.

Result of user actions modifying the ListView control

Action	Result in TreeView	Result in ListView
Select the Albums menu item.	The top-level Default Albums node should be selected.	The collection of albums from the default album directory should be displayed.
Select the Photos menu item.	The tree node corresponding to the current album should be selected.	The collection of photographs for the current album should be displayed.
Double-click on an item in the list view.	The tree node corresponding to the activated item should be visible and selected.	The contents of the item should be displayed.

As you can see, all three actions should result in the selection of a node in the tree. This will cause the `AfterSelect` event to occur, which will invoke our `treeViewMain_AfterSelect` event handler. This handler will, in turn, cause the proper set of items to appear in the `ListView` control, as described in the previous table.

As a result, we simply need to modify the behavior for these three actions to select the proper tree node, and our existing code will do the rest. We will begin with our Albums menu item.

	Action	Result
1	Locate the `menuAlbums_Click` event handler in the MainForm.cs code window.	```private void menuAlbums_Click (object sender, System.EventArgs e) {```
2	Modify this handler to select the Default Albums tree node. **How-to** Set the `SelectedNode` property for the tree to the first node in the tree.	```// Select Default Albums node if (treeViewMain.Nodes.Count > 0) { treeViewMain.SelectedNode = treeViewMain.Nodes[0]; } }```

Since we initialize the tree with a top-level node, we know this will always exist and appear first in the tree view object's `Nodes` collection. We select this by assigning this node to the `SelectedNode` property of the tree.

For the Photos menu, you may recall that we created a `menuView_Popup` event handler that enables this menu only if an album is selected in the `ListView` control. The existing `menuPhotos_Click` event handler, shown in the following code, already activates the selected item. This behavior works just fine for our current application, so no changes are required to this handler.

```
private void menuPhotos_Click(object sender, System.EventArgs e)
{
  // Activate the selected album
  listViewMain_ItemActivate(sender, e);
}
```

The final event handler, the `listViewMain_ItemActivate` method, requires some discussion. Our existing handler, shown in the following code, only permits albums to be activated. This handler retrieves the selected item, opens the album file corresponding to the item, and calls `LoadPhotoData` to display the photographs in the album.

```
private void listViewMain_ItemActivate(object sender, EventArgs e)
{
  if (_albumsShown &&  listViewMain.SelectedItems.Count > 0)
  {
    ListViewItem item = listViewMain.SelectedItems[0];
    string fileName = item.Tag as string;

    // Open the album for this item
    PhotoAlbum album = null;
    if (fileName != null)
      album = OpenAlbum(fileName);
    if (album == null)
    {
      MessageBox.Show(
          "The photographs for this album cannot be displayed.");
```

```
      return;
    }

    // Switch to a photograph view
    LoadPhotoData(album);
  }
}
```

In our new code, we will permit any type of item to be activated. Albums will display the photos in the album, and photographs will display a blank list, which we will update shortly to display the actual image. Our logic to select the `TreeNode` corresponding to the item will go something like this:

```
private void listViewMain_ItemActivate(object sender, EventArgs e)
{
  if (listViewMain.SelectedItems.Count > 0)
  {
    // Find the file path for the selected item
    // Find the tree node with an identical path
    // Select the node to activate it
  }
}
```

We will need some assistance with the first two steps. As you may recall, we utilized the `Tag` property in chapter 14 to store the file name of album items and the index of photograph items. We can use this property to retrieve the path for either type item.

Our next step is to locate the node which matches a given file path. This is a little trickier than it seems, since the node may not yet exist. There are two critical observations we can make in order to properly implement this functionality:

- First, the node corresponding to the parent of the activated item will already be selected in the tree. We ensure that a node is selected at all times in our tree, so we can count on this fact to identify the `Nodes` collection containing our desired node.

- Second, the matching node may not actually exist. For example, if a user activates a photograph, a node for the photograph will only exist if the album node containing the photo has been expanded. As a result, we must expand the parent node before we search for a matching node to ensure that the node exists.

With these facts in mind, we are ready to implement a method to locate a node, which we will call `FindNode`.

IMPLEMENT A FINDNODE METHOD		
	Action	**Result**
| 3 | Create a new `FindNode` method. **Note:** This method accepts a file name and returns the matching `TreeNode` object, if any. This also accepts a boolean value indicating whether to expand the node. This feature will come in handy later in the chapter. | ```
private TreeNode FindNode
  (string fileName, bool expandNode)
{
``` |
| 4 | Make sure the selected node is not `null`. **Note:** This value should never be `null`, but it is always good to check. | ```
TreeNode node = treeViewMain.SelectedNode;
if (node == null)
   return null;
``` |
| 5 | If `expandNode` is `true`, make sure the contents of the selected node are loaded into the tree. | ```
// Ensure contents of node are available
if (expandNode)
   node.Expand();
``` |
| 6 | Find the node that matches the given string. **How-to** a. For each child of the selected node, find the file associated with the node. b. If a match is found, return it to the caller. | ```
// Search for a matching node
foreach (TreeNode n in node.Nodes)
{
   string nodePath = n.Tag as string;
   if (nodePath == fileName)
   {
      // Found it!
      return n;
   }
}
``` |
| 7 | If no match is found, return `null`. | ```
   }
   return null;
}
``` |

With these changes in place, we can revamp our `ItemActivate` handler to select the corresponding tree node.

REIMPLEMENT THE ITEMACTIVATE EVENT HANDLER		
	Action	**Result**
| 8 | Replace the `ItemActivate` event handler in the MainForm.cs code window. | ```
private void listViewMain_ItemActivate
  (object sender, System.EventArgs e)
{
``` |

	Action	Result
9	If an item is selected, locate the file name associated with this item. **How-to** a. If albums are displayed, the `Tag` property contains the album path. b. If photographs are displayed, the `Tag` property contains the index of this photo in the album.	```if (listViewMain.SelectedItems.Count > 0)\n{\n // Find the file path for selected item\n string fileName = null;\n ListViewItem item\n = listViewMain.SelectedItems[0];\n if (_albumsShown)\n {\n // Get the file for this album\n fileName = item.Tag as string;\n }\n else if (item.Tag is int)\n {\n // Use the index of the photograph\n int index = (int)item.Tag;\n fileName = _album[index].FileName;\n }```
10	If no file name is present, the item cannot be activated.	```if (fileName == null)\n{\n MessageBox.Show("This item cannot "\n + "be opened.");\n return;\n}```
11	If a file name is found, locate the `TreeNode` corresponding to this item.	```// Find tree node with identical path\nTreeNode node\n = FindNode(fileName, true);```
12	If the node is found, a. Make sure the node is visible. b. Select the node.	```if (node != null)\n{\n // Select the node to activate it.\n node.EnsureVisible();\n treeViewMain.SelectedNode = node;\n}\n }\n}```

Our two view controls are now totally in sync with each other. The appropriate tree node is always selected, and as a result the contents of the list view are updated as required.

15.5 FUN WITH TREE VIEWS

There are a few loose ends to tie up in our application. In this section we look at additional uses for a tree view class in order to complete the functionality required in the MyAlbumExplorer application. This section is to demonstrate various features and functionality, rather than explain additional Windows Forms concepts. As a result, this section will be short on discussion and simply present the code required to make the described changes.

There are three changes we will make here:

1 Display the image associated with a selected photograph node.
2 Permit the label text for a node to be edited.
3 Display the album or photo property dialog associated with a node.

We will discuss these topics in the order they appear in this list.

15.5.1 DISPLAYING THE PHOTOGRAPH

Our first topic is displaying the photograph when a photograph node is selected in the tree view. You might think that we could draw directly on the `ListView` control. In fact, the `ListView` class does not permit the `Paint` event to be handled by an instance of the class. So an alternate approach is required.

Instead, we will use a `PictureBox` control for this purpose. Since the `Picture-Box` control does not support a proper aspect ratio for its contained image, we will handle the `Paint` event and draw the image manually. This is shown in figure 15.9. When a list of albums or photographs is displayed, we will hide the picture box control. Conversely, when a photograph is displayed, we will hide the list view control.

Figure 15.9
Normally a PictureBox control appears with standard control colors. Since this PictureBox appears in place of a ListView control, we will use standard window colors instead.

The following table details the steps necessary to add this feature to our interface.

Set the version number of the MyAlbumExplorer application to 15.4.

DISPLAY PHOTOGRAPH IN A PICTUREBOX CONTROL	
Action	**Result**
1 In the MainForm.cs [Design] window, add a `PictureBox` control to the area where the `ListView` control is already located. **Settings** **Property** — **Value** (Name) — pictureBoxMain BackColor — Window (under the System tab) BorderStyle — Fixed3D Dock — Fill Visible — False	*(Properties panel showing pictureBoxMain System.Windows, AccessibleRole Default, Anchor Top, Left, BackColor Window, BackgroundImag (none), BorderStyle Fixed3D, ContextMenu (none), Cursor Default, Dock Fill, Enabled True)*

	Action	Result
| 2 | In the MainForm.cs code window, add a new `DisplayPhoto` method.<br><br>**Note:** We will use the `Tag` property for the `PictureBox` control to hold the photo to display, if any.<br><br>**How-to**<br>a. If the given node is `null`, hide the picture box and display the `ListView` control.<br>b. If a node was given, ensure the `PhotoAlbum` containing the photo is open.<br>c. Assign the `Photograph` to display to the `PictureBox.Tag` property.<br>d. Make the `PictureBox` visible. | ```csharp
private void DisplayPhoto(TreeNode node)
{
  if (node == null)
  {
    pictureBoxMain.Visible = false;
    listViewMain.Visible = true;
    return;
  }

  // Parent of photo node is album node
  string file = node.Parent.Tag as string;
  if (_album == null
      || (_album.FileName != file))
  {
    if (_album != null)
      _album.Dispose();

    _album = OpenTreeAlbum(node.Parent);
  }

  if (_album != null)
  {
    // Proper PhotoAlbum is now open
    pictureBoxMain.Tag = _album[node.Index];
    pictureBoxMain.Invalidate();
    pictureBoxMain.Visible = true;
    listViewMain.Visible = false;
  }
}
``` |
| 3 | Create a `Pen` object in the `MainForm` class for drawing a border around a photo. | ```csharp
private static Pen borderPen
    = new Pen(SystemColors.WindowFrame);
``` |
| 4 | Add a `Paint` event handler for the PictureBox control to draw the assigned `Photograph` in the `PictureBox` client area with the proper aspect ratio.<br><br>**How-to**<br>a. Retrieve the `Photograph` object stored in the picture box.<br>b. If a photograph is not found, simply clear the client area.<br>c. Otherwise, use the `ScaleToFit` method to determine the proper drawing rectangle.<br>d. Draw the assigned image into this rectangle.<br>e. Draw a border around the image using the `Pen` object created in the previous step. | ```csharp
private void pictureBoxMain_Paint
    (object sender, System.Windows.
        Forms.PaintEventArgs e)
{
  Photograph photo
    = pictureBoxMain.Tag as Photograph;

  if (photo == null)
  {
    // Something is wrong, give up
    e.Graphics.Clear(pictureBoxMain.
                        BackColor);
    return;
  }

  // Paint the photograph
  Rectangle rect = photo.ScaleToFit(
        pictureBoxMain.ClientRectangle);
  e.Graphics.DrawImage(photo.Image, rect);
  e.Graphics.DrawRectangle(borderPen, rect);
}
``` |

FUN WITH TREE VIEWS
```

	Action	Result
5	Update the `AfterSelect` event handler to use the new `DisplayPhoto` method to ensure the proper control is visible.	```private void treeViewMain_AfterSelect(. . .)
{
. . .
if (node.Parent == null)
{
// Bad tag or top-level node.
LoadAlbumData(fileName);
DisplayPhoto(null);
}
else if (Path.GetExtension(fileName) . . .)
{
// Album node selected
PhotoAlbum album = OpenTreeAlbum(. . .);
LoadPhotoData(album);
DisplayPhoto(null);
}
else // must be a photograph
{
// Clear the list and display the photo
listViewMain.Clear();
DisplayPhoto(node);
}
}```
6	Add a `Resize` event handler for the `PictureBox` control to force the control to redraw the entire image when it is resized.	```private void pictureBoxMain_Resize
(object sender, System.EventArgs e)
{
// Force the entire control to repaint
pictureBoxMain.Invalidate();
}```

As we mentioned at the start of this section, we will not spend much time discussing these changes, since they leverage concepts and features we have seen before. Let's move on to editing a tree node's label.

15.5.2   SUPPORTING LABEL EDITS

Tree nodes can be edited in a manner similar to list items. There is a `BeginEdit` method in the `TreeNode` class to initiate a label edit programmatically, and `BeforeLabelEdit` and `AfterLabelEdit` events in the `TreeView` class that occur before and after the user edits the label. Event handlers for these events receive the `NodeLabelEditEventArgs` class for the event parameter. This class is summarized in .NET Table 15.5, and is manipulated in much the same way as we saw for the `LabelEditEventArgs` class when handling label events for the `ListView` class.

.NET Table 15.5 NodeLabelEditEventArgs class

The NodeLabelEditEventArgs class represents the event data associated with the BeforeLabelEdit and AfterLabelEdit events in the TreeView class. This class is part of the System.Windows.Forms namespace, and inherits from the System.EventArgs class.

Public Properties	CancelEdit	Gets or sets whether the edit operation should be cancelled. This property can be set both before and after the node is edited.
	Label	Gets the new text to assign to the label of the indicated node.
	Node	Gets the TreeNode object being edited.

In our application, we will permit nodes to be edited using the menuEditLabel menu item, or by pressing the F2 key when a tree node is selected and the tree view has the focus. The following table details the steps required for this change:

	SUPPORT EDITING OF TREE NODE LABELS	
	Action	**Result**
1	Set the LabelEdit property for the TreeView control to true in the MainForm.cs [Design] window.	Tree node labels may now be edited.
2	Handle the KeyDown event for the TreeView control to initiate a label edit when the F2 key is pressed in the tree control.	```private void treeViewMain_KeyDown
(object sender, System.Windows.
Forms.KeyEventArgs e)
{
if (e.KeyCode == Keys.F2)
{
if (treeViewMain.SelectedNode != null)
{
treeViewMain.SelectedNode.BeginEdit();
e.Handled = true;
}
}
}```
3	Update the menuEdit_Popup event handler to use the text "Node" for the menuEditLabel menu when the TreeView has the focus. **How-to** Use the Focused property for the TreeView class.	```private void menuEdit_Popup
(object sender, System.EventArgs e)
{
if (treeViewMain.Focused)
{
menuEditLabel.Enabled
= (treeViewMain.SelectedNode != null);
menuEditLabel.Text = "&Node";
}
else // assume ListView has focus
{
menuEditLabel.Enabled
= (listViewMain.SelectedItems.Count > 0);
if (this._albumsShown)
menuEditLabel.Text = "&Name";
else
menuEditLabel.Text = "&Caption";
}
}```

	Action	Result
| **4** | Update the `menuEdit-Label_Click` event handler to edit the appropriate item based on the current focus. | ```csharp
private void menuEditLabel_Click
    (object sender, System.EventArgs e)
{
  if (treeViewMain.Focused)
  {
    if (treeViewMain.SelectedNode != null)
      treeViewMain.SelectedNode.BeginEdit();
  }
  else if (listViewMain.SelectedItems.Count > 0)
    listViewMain.SelectedItems[0].BeginEdit();
}
``` |
| **5** | Handle the `AfterLabelEdit` event for the `TreeView` control.<br><br>**How-to**<br>a. Cancel the edit if the new text is `null`.<br>b. Do nothing if the node is a root node.<br>c. For an album node, use the `UpdateAlbumName`.method.<br>d. For a photograph node, use the `UpdatePhotoCaption` method.<br><br>**Note:** We permit the user to edit the root node here to alter a top-level name in the tree, even though this change is discarded when the application exits. A more robust solution might be to prevent this from occurring, or to save the change in a configuration file. | ```csharp
private void treeViewMain_AfterLabelEdit
    (object sender, System.Windows.
        Forms.NodeLabelEditEventArgs e)
{
  if (e.Label == null)
  {
    // Edit cancelled by the user
    e.CancelEdit = true;
    return;
  }

  // No changes required for root node
  if (e.Node.Parent == null)
    return;

  string fileName = e.Node.Tag as string;
  if (Path.GetExtension(fileName) == ".abm")
    e.CancelEdit = !UpdateAlbumName(e.Label,
                                    e.Node);
  else
    e.CancelEdit = !UpdatePhotoCaption(e.Label,
                                       e.Node);
}
``` |
| **6** | Rewrite the `UpdateAlbum-Name` method to accommodate both list items and tree nodes.<br><br>**How-to**<br>a. Change the second parameter to an `object` rather than a `ListViewItem`.<br>b. Convert the given `object` to both a list item and a tree node.<br>c. Determine the file name for the appropriate object.<br>d. If the object is a list view item, also find the node corresponding to this item. | ```csharp
private bool UpdateAlbumName
    (string newName, object obj)
{
  ListViewItem item = obj as ListViewItem;
  TreeNode node = obj as TreeNode;

  // Determine the file name
  string fileName = null;
  if (item != null)
  {
    fileName = item.Tag as string;
    node = FindNode(fileName, false);
  }
  else if (node != null)
    fileName = node.Tag as string;
```<br><br>**Note:** Recall that the list view's `AfterLabelEdit` event handler from chapter 14 provides a `ListView-Item` object when calling this method. This invocation is still valid and is properly dealt with by this code. |
```

		Action	Result
7		Rename the file. **How-to** Use the `RenameFile` method from chapter 14.	```// Rename the file\nstring newFileName = null;\nif (fileName != null)\n{\n newFileName\n = RenameFile(fileName, newName, ".abm");\n}\n\nif (newFileName == null)\n{\n MessageBox.Show("Unable to rename album "\n + "to this name.");\n return false;\n}```
8		Update the `Tag` property for the appropriate object. **Note:** When the object is a list item, this updates the corresponding node as well.	```// Update the appropriate Tag property\nif (item != null)\n{\n item.Tag = newFileName;\n if (node != null)\n node.Text = newName;\n}\nelse if (node != null)\n node.Tag = newFileName;\n\nreturn true;\n}```
9		Rewrite the `UpdatePhoto-Caption` method to accommodate both list items and tree nodes. **How-to** a. Change the second parameter to an `object` rather than a `ListViewItem`. b. Convert the given `object` to both a list item and a tree node. c. Determine the album index for the appropriate object. d. If the object is a list view item, also find the node corresponding to this item.	```private bool UpdatePhotoCaption\n (string caption, object obj)\n{\n ListViewItem item = obj as ListViewItem;\n TreeNode node = obj as TreeNode;\n\n // Determine the album index\n int index = -1;\n if ((item != null) && (item.Tag is int))\n {\n index = (int)item.Tag;\n node = FindNode(_album[index].FileName,\n false);\n }\n else if (node != null)\n {\n index = node.Index;\n }```
10		Return `false` if the caption cannot be updated.	```if ((caption.Length == 0) || (index < 0))\n{\n MessageBox.Show("Invalid caption value.");\n return false;\n}```

	Action	Result
11	Update the photograph's caption, and save the changes to the album. **Note:** When the object is a list item, this updates the corresponding node as well.	```// Update caption\n_album[index].Caption = caption;\nif (item != null && node != null)\n{\n // Update node text as well\n node.Text = caption;\n}\n\n// Save the changes to the album\n. . .\n}```

Our program now permits editing of nodes in the TreeView and items in the List-View. Editing is initiated with the menuLabelEdit menu or the F2 key, and is based on which control currently has the focus.

In both update methods, note how the as keyword is used to convert the given object into both a TreeView and a ListView, as is shown in the following excerpt. The remainder of each method executes the appropriate statements based on which type of control is provided.

```
ListViewItem item = obj as ListViewItem;
TreeNode node = obj as TreeNode;
```

Also of note is our use of the FindNode method created earlier in the chapter as part of section 15.4.2. As you may recall, we included a parameter to this method that indicated whether to expand the selected node. We set this second parameter to false here to ensure that the contents of the tree view control are not altered.

Our final change is to support the display of our album and photograph property dialogs from the TreeView control.

15.5.3 UPDATING THE PROPERTIES MENU

In chapter 14 we created a Properties menu. We handled the Click event for this menu in a menuProperties_Click method, and created the DisplayAlbumProperties and DisplayPhotoProperties methods to display the two types of dialogs required. Here we would like to change the behavior of this menu to the following:

- When the TreeView has the focus, display the appropriate properties dialog if an album node or a photograph node is selected.
- When the ListView has the focus, display the appropriate properties dialog for the selected item.
- When the PictureBox has the focus, display the photograph properties dialog associated with the displayed image.

To make this change, we will modify our Display methods to accept either a List-ViewItem or a TreeNode object. The following table details the changes required.

	Action	Result
| **1** | In the MainForm.cs code window, update the `menuProperties_Click` event handler to accommodate the three controls that might have the focus.<br><br>**How-to**<br>a. For the `TreeView` control, ignore the parent node and call the appropriate `Proper-ties` method based on the node type.<br>b. For the `PictureBox` control, call the `DisplayPhoto-Properties` method on the selected photo node.<br>c. For the `ListView` control, the code is the same as in chapter 14. | ```cs
private void menuProperties_Click
  (object sender, System.EventArgs e)
{
  if (treeViewMain.Focused)
  {
    TreeNode node = treeViewMain.SelectedNode;
    string file = node.Tag as string;
    if (node == null || node.Parent == null
        || file == null)
      return;    // do nothing

    if (Path.GetExtension(file) == ".abm")
      DisplayAlbumProperties(node);
    else
      DisplayPhotoProperties(node);
  }
  else if (pictureBoxMain.Focused)
  {
    // Display photograph for this image
    TreeNode node = treeViewMain.SelectedNode;
    if (node != null)
      DisplayPhotoProperties(node);
  }
  else
    if (listViewMain.SelectedItems.Count > 0)
  {
    ListViewItem item
        = listViewMain.SelectedItems[0];
    if (this._albumsShown)
      DisplayAlbumProperties(item);
    else
      DisplayPhotoProperties(item);
  }
}
``` |
| **2** | Rewrite the `DisplayAlbum-Properties` method to accept an `object` instance.<br><br>**How-to**<br>a. Convert the given `object` to a `ListViewItem` and a `TreeNode` instance.<br>b. Open the `PhotoAlbum` using whichever object is not `null`.<br>c. If the album could not be opened, display an error message. | ```cs
private void DisplayAlbumProperties
    (object obj)
{
  ListViewItem item = obj as ListViewItem;
  TreeNode node = obj  as TreeNode;

  // Open the album as appropriate
  PhotoAlbum album = null;
  if (item != null)
  {
    string fileName = item.Tag as string;
    if (fileName != null)
      album = this.OpenAlbum(fileName);
  }
  else if (node != null)
  {
    album = OpenTreeAlbum(node);
  }

  if (album == null)
    . . .   // as in chapter 14
``` |

	Action	Result
| 3 | When displaying the album edit dialog, only update the list item settings if the given item is a list view item.<br><br>**Note:** If the given item is a tree node, then photographs are displayed in the list view, and these settings should not be updated. | ```csharp
using (AlbumEditDlg dlg
        = new AlbumEditDlg(album))
{
  if (dlg.ShowDialog() == DialogResult.OK)
  {
    // Save changes made by the user
    . . .
    // Update item settings
    if (item != null)
    {
      item.SubItems[MainForm.
                AlbumTitleColumn].Text
        = album.Title;

      bool hasPwd = (album.Password != null)
        && (album.Password.Length > 0);
      item.SubItems[MainForm.
                AlbumPwdColumn].Text
        = (hasPwd ? "y" : "n");
    }
  }
}

album.Dispose();
``` |
| 4 | Modify the `DisplayPhotoProperties` method to accept an `object` instance.<br><br>**How-to**<br>This is similar, at least in spirit, to the `DisplayAlbumProperties` method. | ```csharp
private void DisplayPhotoProperties
    (object obj)
{
  ListViewItem item = obj as ListViewItem;
  TreeNode node = obj as TreeNode;

  int index = 0;
  if (item != null && (item.Tag is int))
  {
    index = item.Tag;
  }
  else if (node != null)
  {
    index = node.Index;
  }

  _album.CurrentPosition = index;
``` |

	Action	Result

5	After displaying the dialog, update the list or node with any modified photograph settings.
	
	Note: Recall that our photo edit dialog permits all photographs in an album to be updated. As a result, when the photographs are shown in the tree node, the label for each related node must be updated as well. This is true regardless of the type `object` given.
		<pre>using (PhotoEditDlg dlg
		          = new PhotoEditDlg(_album))
		{
		  if (dlg.ShowDialog() == DialogResult.OK)
		  {
		    // Save any changes made
		    . . .
		    // Update controls with new settings
		    TreeNode baseNode = null;
		    if (item != null)
		    {
		      LoadPhotoData(_album);
		      baseNode = treeViewMain.SelectedNode;
		    }
		    else if (node != null)
		    {
		      baseNode = node.Parent;
		    }
		
		    if (baseNode != null)
		    {
		      // Update all child labels
		      foreach (TreeNode n in baseNode.Nodes)
		      {
		        n.Text = _album[n.Index].Caption;
		      }
		    }
		  }
		}</pre>

As you can see, the display methods use the `as` keyword to convert a given `object` into both a `ListViewItem` and a `TreeNode` instance. Whichever instance is non-`null` indicates how to display the property dialog.

TRY IT! As a further change to our `TreeView` control, add a context menu to this control to perform the following tasks.

1 An "Add Directory" menu item that permits a new album directory to be added to the tree. This should prompt for a directory name and add a top-level node to the tree for each album discovered in that directory.

2 A "Properties" menu item that displays the properties dialog for the nearest node. This should select the nearby node, and then call the `PerformClick` method for the `menuProperties` menu.

3 A "Delete" menu item that deletes a node from the tree. This should delete the album file from the file system or the `Photograph` from the containing album for the given node. You should prompt the user to make sure they really wish to do this.

You will need to use the `GetNodeAt` method to locate the `TreeNode` instance at a given pixel position, so that the action applies to the specific tree node located at the current mouse position.

You could also implement these items within the `ListView` control as well. This completes our discussion on the `TreeView` class. Before we move on, let's do a quick recap of what we covered in this chapter.

15.6   RECAP

In this chapter we extended the MyAlbumExplorer project built in chapter 14 to add a `TreeView` control. We divided our main window using the `Splitter` class in order to create a classic explorer window such as that used in the Windows operating system for browsing the file system.

A tree view contains a hierarchy of `TreeNode` objects, and we created a tree displaying our album files and the photos in each album. We discussed common operations within a tree view such as expand, collapse, selection, and label editing. During the course of the chapter, the `ListView` and `TreeView` controls were integrated to display a common interface, with changes to one control reflected in the other control. We also added a `PictureBox` control in order to display the image associated with a selected photograph node in the tree.

The explorer interface we saw in these last two chapters is one of three kinds of standard Windows interfaces. In part 2 of this book we built what is called a single document interface. In the next chapter we will look at another kind of interface, namely the multiple document interface.

C H A P T E R   1 6

Multiple document interfaces

16.1 Interface styles 526
16.2 MDI forms 530
16.3 Merged menus 535

16.4 MDI children 543
16.5 MDI child window management 557
16.6 Recap 563

The `ListView` and `TreeView` classes discussed in chapters 14 and 15 present a collection of objects within a single list or tree control. These are especially useful when creating an explorer-style interface such as our MyAlbumExplorer application, or the common Windows Explorer application. Another kind of interface is the multiple document interface, also called an MDI (normally pronounced *em-dee-eye*).

An MDI application presents a collection of forms within a single application window. We will discuss MDI applications through the following discussion areas:

- Understanding various interface styles.
- Creating an MDI container window.
- Converting an SDI application into an MDI application.
- Using MDI-related class members of various controls.
- Merging two menus into a single merged menu.
- Managing menus and forms in an MDI application.

These topics will be covered as we progress through the chapter, beginning with the concept of interface styles.

16.1 INTERFACE STYLES

Before we discuss exactly how multiple document interfaces are created, let's take a step back and consider the various types of application interfaces used for Windows applications. Most Windows applications fall into one of three interface categories:

- Single document interfaces.
- Explorer interfaces.
- Multiple document interfaces.

We will discuss each type of interface separately.

16.1.1 SINGLE DOCUMENT INTERFACES

A single document interface, also called an SDI, is an interface that displays a single document or other encapsulated data within a single form. Our MyPhotos application, as shown in figure 16.1, is a good example of this style, in which a single photo album is displayed. The user can look at multiple photo albums only by examining one after another. The contents of two albums cannot be compared unless two copies of the program are running.

In the Windows operation system, the Notepad and WordPad applications provide additional examples of the SDI style.

Figure 16.1
Our single document interface displays one photo album at a time.

16.1.2 EXPLORER INTERFACES

The MyAlbumExplorer application built in chapters 14 and 15 is an example of an explorer interface, and can be seen in figure 16.2. In this style, a hierarchy of information is presented to the user. Normally a `TreeView` control displays this hierarchy, typically on the left, with details on the selected node provided in a `ListView` control. Sometimes the `TreeView` control can be hidden, and sometimes it is always present. Alternate information may appear on the list side of the window as well, such as the photographic image we displayed in chapter 15 for a selected photograph in the MyAlbumExplorer application.

In Windows, of course, the Windows Explorer application is another example of this style.

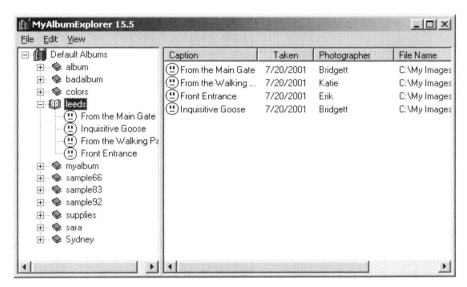

Figure 16.2   Our explorer interface presents the collection of photo albums in list form.

16.1.3   MULTIPLE DOCUMENT INTERFACES

A multiple document interface (MDI) allows multiple views of one or more documents or other encapsulated data to be displayed at the same type. This permits alternate views of the same data, or separate presentations of the same style of data, within a single window. For example, a stock market MDI application might present different historical or graphical views of a single portfolio, each as a separate window. Alternately, such an application might present multiple portfolios, each as its own window within a containing application window.

In the original conception of this style, a single window acted as a container for other windows, where each contained window displayed a specific instance or view of a type of data. More recently, well-known MDI applications such as Microsoft Word and Excel have taken the approach of displaying all of their windows directly on the desktop, each within a separate application window, while still preserving an MDI look and feel from the menu bar and other parts of the interface. This relatively new style, the Multiple Single Document Interface, or MSDI, is consistent with the manner in which Web browsers have typically worked. While an MSDI interface can be created in Visual Studio.NET, it is not necessarily an easy task.

Also note that Visual Studio .NET, while providing an MDI-like interface, uses more of a `TabControl` look and feel for the set of displayed windows, or what might be called a Multiple Tabbed Documents Interface, or MTDI. In this style, multiple sets of windows are displayed as horizontal or vertical groups of tabs. Both the MSDI and MTDI approaches can be created using the .NET Framework as an alternative to the traditional MDI interface, although there is not really any direct support for these newer interfaces. As a result, implementing such interfaces requires much more effort from the developer.

For our purposes, a traditional MDI application provides the means to discuss and demonstrate the manner in which the .NET Framework supports such applications. We will convert the existing MyPhotos application into the MDI application shown in figure 16.3. As you can see, this application will incorporate the `Form` classes we have created in part 2 of this book.

Figure 16.3   Our multiple document interface, created in this chapter, displays a selected set of photo albums within a single window.

The reuse of our existing classes is possible because of the manner in which the `Form` class in general and MDI support in particular is integrated into the Windows Forms hierarchy. As we discussed in chapter 7, a `Form` object is a `Control` instance that happens to display an application window. For MDI applications, `Form` controls are contained by a parent `Form`. Of course, the contained forms can be resized and moved within their container, and can still display menus, toolbars, status bars, and other controls. As we shall see, the relationship between MDI parent and child forms is different than the relationship between control containers and controls.

CHAPTER 16   MULTIPLE DOCUMENT INTERFACES

16.1.4   SUPPORT IN WINDOWS FORMS

To provide some insight and perhaps some perspective on MDI applications, the following table lists a number of class members specific to the implementation of MDI applications in the .NET Framework. Of course, these members can be used for other purposes, and additional properties, methods, and events are certainly used in MDI applications. These events highlight many of the MDI-specific tasks that are often performed in this style interface. The table provides a short description of each member and a reference to the section in this chapter where more information on each item may be found.

Class members often used in MDI applications

Class	Member type	Member name	Description	See section
Form	Properties	ActiveMdiChild	Gets the MDI child window that is currently active.	16.4.1
		IsMdiChild	Gets whether the form is an MDI child.	16.3.2
		IsMdiContainer	Gets whether the form is an MDI container form.	16.2.1
		MdiChildren	Gets the set of MDI children contained by this form as an array of `Form` objects.	16.4.3
		MdiParent	Gets or sets the MDI container for this form. If set, then this form is an MDI child form.	16.2.2
		MergedMenu	Gets the `MainMenu` object representing the current merged menu for an MDI container form.	16.3
	Methods	LayoutMdi	Arranges the MDI children within this form using a given layout style.	16.5.1
	Events	MdiChildActivate	Occurs when an MDI child form is activated or deactivated within an MDI application. Note that MDI children do not receive the `Activated` and `Deactivate` events.	16.4.4
Menu	Properties	MdiListItem	Gets the `MenuItem` object contained by this menu that displays a list of MDI child forms for the associated form object.	16.5.2
	Methods	MergeMenu	Merges the `MenuItem` objects in a given menu with those contained by this menu.	16.3
MenuItem	Properties	MdiList	Gets or sets whether this menu should be populated with a list of MDI child forms contained by the associated form.	16.5.2
		MergeOrder	Gets or sets the relative position of this menu item when it is merged with another menu.	16.3.2
		MergeType	Gets or sets how this menu should be merged with other menus. The default is `MergeType.Add`.	16.3.1

Also note that the behaviors of desktop-related actions within an MDI child form are modified. For example, the Minimize and Maximize buttons on the title bar work within the parent window, rather than on the desktop itself.

In the rest of this chapter we will enhance our MyPhotos application to support a multiple document interface. We begin with the MDI container form.

16.2   *MDI FORMS*

So let's convert our existing MyPhotos application into an MDI application. This initial work is not as difficult as you might think. Generally, we need one `Form` to act as the top-level container, and the ability to create other forms as children within this container. Here, we will do this via the following tasks:

1 Create a new parent form for the application to act as the MDI container.

2 Add a menu bar and New menu item to create MDI child forms.

3 Define a new `Main` method in the parent as the entry point for the application.

Of course, there will be other work to perform to clean up the behavior of our application. These steps will get us going, and subsequent sections will deal with other required changes. Figure 16.4 shows how our application will look by the end of this section. Note in particular the two File menus. We will address this issue in the next section while discussing Merged Menus.

Figure 16.4   Note the two File menus for this window. The menus from both our ParentForm and MainForm classes appear separately on the menu bar. We will address this in section 16.3.

16.2.1 CREATING AN MDI CONTAINER FORM

The creation of an MDI container form is much like the creation of any other form. Such a form is often referred to as a parent form, since it acts as the parent for one or more MDI child forms. The following table details the steps required for this task.

Set the version number of the MyPhotos application to 16.2.

	CREATE A NEW FORM AS AN MDI CONTAINER	
	Action	**Result**
1	In the Solution Explorer window, add a new Windows Form to the application called `ParentForm`.	The new file appears in the Solution Explorer window and the ParentForm.cs [Design] window is displayed.
2	Set the icon property for the form to the "icons/Writing/ BOOKS04.ICO" file in the common image directory.	
3	Set the `IsMdiContainer` property to `true`. **Note:** This establishes the form as an MDI container form.	
4	Set the `Size` property to 600×400 pixels.	

As you can see, the contents of the window appear in a darker color and includes a 3-D border to indicate that this form is now an MDI container. This color is the `System.AppWorkspace` color, which is typically a darker version of the `System.Control` color. This background is a hidden `MdiClient` control, and cannot be manipulated in code as it is not exposed by the `Form` class. This background contains the MDI child forms, and is always last in the z-order. As a result, any controls added to the form will appear above this background, and therefore in front of any MDI children. Typically, controls added to an MDI container are docked to one edge of the parent form.

The code generated for our `ParentForm` class is much like other forms we have seen in this book. The `InitializeComponent` method generated by Visual Studio .NET is as follows:

```
private void InitializeComponent()
{
  //
  // ParentForm
  //
  this.AutoScaleBaseSize = new System.Drawing.Size(5, 13);
  this.ClientSize = new System.Drawing.Size(592, 373);
```

```
        this.IsMdiContainer = true;
        this.Name = "ParentForm";
        this.Text = "ParentForm";
    }
```

With the parent form created, we can turn our attention to the child form.

16.2.2 CREATING AN MDI CHILD FORM

With our MDI container in place, we can add the infrastructure required for generating MDI child forms. This will consist of a menu bar and a New menu item. Fortunately, we already have our MainForm class available to act as the child form.

The following table shows how to create a child form in our application. As part of this task, we will add an Exit menu as well.

ADD ABILITY TO CREATE CHILD FORMS	
Action	**Result**
1 Add a MainMenu object to the ParentForm class in the ParentForm.cs [Design] window.	
2 Add a top-level File menu containing the three menu items as shown. **Settings** 	Menu	Property	Value
---	---	---
File	(Name)	menuFile
	Text	&File
New	(Name)	menuNew
	Shortcut	CtrlN
	Text	&New
separator		
Exit	(Name)	menuExit
	Text	E&xit		

3 Add a Click event handler for the Exit menu to close the form.	`private void menuExit_Click`
	`   (object sender, System.EventArgs e)`
	`{`
	`   Close();`
	`}`

4 Add a Click event handler for the New menu.	`private void menuNew_Click`
	`   (object sender, System.EventArgs e)`
	`{`

	Action	Result

5	Within this handler, create a `MainForm` object as an MDI child form.
	
	How-to
	a. Create a new `MainForm` object.
	b. Define this form as an MDI child by setting the current form as its MDI parent.
	c. Display the child form using the `Show` method.
		```MainForm newChild = new MainForm();```
		```newChild.MdiParent = this;```
		```newChild.Show();```
		```}```

That's all it takes to create a child form. You have almost created your first MDI application.

If you compile and run the application, you will note that the MyPhotos application runs exactly as before. This is because the `MainForm.Main` method is still the entry point for the application, and it displays the `MainForm` object using the `Application.Run` method. To fix this, we need to display the `ParentForm` class in the entry point for the application. This is our next subject.

16.2.3 ADDING A NEW ENTRY POINT

One quite simple means to fix our entry point would be to modify the `Main` method in the `MainForm` class directly. The new code would look as follows, with the change highlighted in bold:

```
public class MainForm : System.Windows.Forms.Form
{
  . . .
  [STAThread]
  static void Main()
  {
    Application.Run(new ParentForm());
  }
  . . .
}
```

While this code would do exactly what we want, a drawback of this change is that we could no longer compile the application as the single document interface we created in chapter 13. To preserve this ability, we will instead create a `Main` method as part of the `ParentForm` class, and modify the project to use this new method as the entry point.

The following table creates a new entry point within the `ParentForm` class.

CREATE AN ENTRY POINT IN THE PARENT FORM		
	Action	**Result**
1	Create a `Main` method in the ParentForm.cs code window to serve as the entry point for our MDI application. **Note:** If you compile the application after this step, you will get an error indicating that the program defines more than one entry point.	```\n/// <summary>\n/// Entry point for MDI application.\n/// </summary>\n[STAThread]\nstatic void Main()\n{\n Application.Run(new ParentForm());\n}\n```
2	Set the Startup Object for the MyPhotos project to the `MyPhotos.ParentForm` class. **How-to** a. Display the Property Pages dialog for the project. b. Click the down arrow associated with the Startup Object entry. c. Select the `MyPhotos.Parent-Form` class.	

The application is now ready. The startup object specified here is used by the C# compiler to establish the entry point for the application, and is only required if there are multiple `Main` methods in your project. On the command-line, the C# compiler accepts the /main switch to specify the class containing the `Main` method to use as the application's entry point.

Run the application to verify that the `ParentForm` window appears and the New menu can be used to create `MainForm` objects as child windows. If you explore this new application, you will find some rather peculiar behavior for some of the controls. We will discuss and address these issues throughout the remainder of this chapter.

TRY IT! Of course, the MyPhotos Property Pages dialog used in step 2 can also be used to set the Startup Object to the `MyPhotos.MainForm` class. When this is done, the application displays the familiar single document interface created in part 2 of this book. Make this change and run the application to observe this behavior.

Among the odd features you may notice in the MDI version of this application is the menu bar. In particular, there are two File menus when a `MainForm` window is displayed. Adjusting this behavior is our next topic.

16.3 MERGED MENUS

By definition, an MDI application permits multiple windows to be displayed. Each child window may be the same or different, and each may display different information about one or more objects. It would be nice if the menu items for the application could be customized depending on which child window is displayed. Exactly how to do this is the subject of this section.

As an example, consider a car-buying application that permits users to search for, display, and purchase used cars. As an MDI application, this might display a photograph of the car in one window, standard features and warranty information in another window, and optional packages and pricing information in a third window. Clearly the set of menus and the contents of each menu should differ depending on which style window is currently active. For instance, menus for the photograph window might permit different colors to be viewed or different parts of the vehicle to be shown. These concepts make no sense for the other windows, and should not be accessible when these windows are active.

While our application is not quite so ambitious, we do have the problem of our File menu, since both the `ParentForm` and the `MainForm` class contain this item. Once we make the two File menus merge, we also have to deal with the contents of these menus, to ensure the items appear in an appropriate order.

The `Menu` class provides a `MergeMenu` method for merging two menus together. This method accepts a `Menu` object and merges it with the calling `Menu` object. The `MenuItem` class provides additional overrides of this method to merge `MenuItem` objects and to copy a menu item so that it may be merged with other menus. This latter method has the advantage of not affecting the existing `MenuItem` object.

In MDI applications, an MDI container form automatically merges the menu for the active child form with the `MainMenu` object stored in its `Menu` property. The `Form.MergedMenu` property contains the result of this merge, and can be used to access or modify the merged menu directly. The `Form.Menu` property always contains the original menu assigned to the form.

Since this merging occurs automatically for MDI applications, this section will focus on how menus are merged together, and make the appropriate changes in our MDI application to merge the two File menus together. First we will discuss the various ways to merge two menus, followed by the mechanism for establishing the order of merged menu items.

16.3.1 ASSIGNING MERGE TYPES

As mentioned at the start of this chapter, the `MenuItem` class contains two properties that control exactly how two menus are merged together. This section will discuss the `MergeType` property that controls how the menus are merged. Later we will look at the `MergeOrder` property that controls the final position of a merged item.

The `MergeType` property gets or sets a `MenuMerge` enumeration value specifying how this menu should be merged with other menus. An overview of this enumeration appears in .NET Table 16.1. The default setting for the `MergeType` property is `MenuMerge.Add`. This default adds each item separately, and is the cause of the two File menus in our current application.

.NET Table 16.1 MenuMerge enumeration		
The `MenuMerge` enumeration specifies various types of behavior for a `MenuItem` object when it is merged with another menu. This enumeration is used by the `MergeType` property in the `MenuItem` class, and is part of the `System.Windows.Forms` namespace.		
Enumeration Values	Add	The item is added to the collection of `MenuItem` objects in the merged menu.
	MergeItems	All `MenuItem` objects contained by the item are merged with those contained by the menu at the same position in the merged menu.
	Remove	The item is not included in the merged menu.
	Replace	The item replaces an existing `MenuItem` object at the same position in the merged menu.

This explains why our existing application has two File menus. Since the `MergeType` property defaults to `Add`, the menus are simply added to the collection separately.

We can fix this by modifying the `MergeType` property for these menus.

Set the version number of the MyPhotos application to 16.3.

	MERGE THE PARENT AND CHILD FILE MENUS	
	Action	**Result**
1	In the MainForm.cs [Design] window, set the `MergeType` property of the File menu item to `MergeItems`.	The two File menus in the parent and child form will now merge into a single menu in the application, the result of which is shown in this graphic. The menu items exhibit the default merge behavior, which is `Add`.
2	Similarly, set the `MergeType` property to `MergeItems` for the File menu in the ParentForm.cs [Design] window. **Note:** The `MergeType` property must be set for both File menu objects to merge the two menus together.	

Compile and run the application, and open a client form in the parent window to see the merged menu as shown in the table. The two menus are merged, but their contents are not exactly in an acceptable order. This is because each of the `MenuItem` objects within their respective File menus use the default `MergeType` property, which is `Add`. As a result, each menu item is simply added to the end of the list. The items from the parent form appear first, followed by the items from the child form.

We can fix this, of course, but first a brief aside.

TRY IT! Modify the `MergeType` property for either File menu so that one menu uses the `MergeItems` member value and the other the `Add` value. Run the application to verify that the menus no longer merge.

Also rename the File menu in the `ParentForm` class to use the name "Fickle." Run the application and see which name is shown in the application. You will find that the name in the MDI child is preferred over the name in the parent. This is a consequence of how the menus are merged, and can be utilized to rename a menu in the parent form when a specific kind of child is displayed.

Back in our application, we have two problems with the merged File menu. The first is that we have two versions of the New and Exit menus, and the second is that the order of the merged menu is a bit of a mess.

We will address these two problems together as part of a discussion on the `Merge-Order` property.

16.3.2   ASSIGNING MERGE ORDER

So far we have merged our two File menus into a single menu. The next step is to clean up the contents of this menu. This involves setting the appropriate `MergeType` for each menu, and using the `MergeOrder` property to establish the order of these items within the merged menu. The `MergeOrder` property contains the zero-based position where the menu should appear within the merged menu. If multiple items are assigned the same order, they appear one after another in the merged menu. This is the case in our existing code, where all menus in the File menu use the default `MergeOrder` value of zero.

Before we start making changes to our existing menus, let's step back and consider what a reasonable File menu should contain for our MDI application. Such a menu is described by the following table, which shows the menu name, its position, a short description, and some implementation notes.

Contents of the merged File menu in our MDI application

Menu name	Position	Description	Implementation Notes
New	0	Opens a new album in a new MDI child window.	Same as existing New menu in the `ParentForm` class.
Open	1	Opens an existing album file in a new MDI child window.	This should be processed by the `ParentForm` class in order to create the new child window.

Contents of the merged File menu in our MDI application *(continued)*

Menu name	Position	Description	Implementation Notes
Close	2	Closes the active MDI child window.	Similar to the Exit menu in the `MainForm` class.
separator	3		
Save	4	Saves the album in the active MDI child window.	Same as existing Save menu in the `MainForm` class
Save As	5	Saves the album in the active MDI child window under a new name.	Same as existing Save As menu in the `MainForm` class.
separator	6		
Exit	7	Closes all child windows as well as the MDI container form.	Same as existing Exit menu in the `ParentForm` class.

This details how the merged menu should look. There is still the question of the menu structure in the `ParentForm` and `MainForm` classes. Based on the previous table, we can establish how the File menu should appear for each `Form` class. The following table details the contents of each menu, and describes its behavior in the merged menu object.

Individual File menu for our MDI parent and child classes

Class	Menu	Implementation notes
ParentForm	New	This menu should behave as it already does, and replace the New menu in the child form.
	Open	This is a new menu to open an existing album in a new window.
	separator	This menu should not exist when the menus are merged.
	Exit	This menu should behave as it already does, and appear at position 7 when the menus are merged.
MainForm	New	Should not be present in the merged menu for our MDI application.
	Open	Should not be present in the merged menu.
	separator	Should become the first separator at position 3 in the merged menu.
	Save	As currently exists, at position 4 in the merged menu.
	Save As	As currently exists, at position 5 in the merged menu.
	separator	Should become the second separator at position 6 in the merged menu.
	Exit	Should become the Close menu at position 2 in the merged menu.

We are now ready to update our menus based on these tables. Our first change will simply update the menus so that they appear as described within the application.

Once this is done, we will look at implementing any changes required to support these menus.

The following table details the steps required:

ASSIGN THE TYPE AND ORDER FOR OUR FILE MENUS	
Action	**Result**

1   In the ParentForm.cs [Design] window, add an Open menu to the File menu just after the existing New menu.

Settings	
Property	**Value**
(Name)	menuOpen
Shortcut	CtrlO
Text	&Open

2   Update the merge settings for the items in the File menu.

Settings		
Menu	**MergeType**	**MergeOrder**
New	Replace	0
Open	Replace	1
separator	Remove	0
Exit	Add	7

3   In the File menu for the MainForm.cs [Design] window, update the merge settings for the items in this menu.

Settings		
Menu	**MergeType**	**MergeOrder**
New	Remove	0
Open	Remove	1
separator	Add	3
Save	Add	4
Save As	Add	5
separator	Add	6
Exit	Add	2

The key points here are the fact that the New and Open menus in the `ParentForm` class replace those in the `MainForm` class, and the merge order for each menu must match the desired position we discussed earlier. One other interesting point is the reuse of the Exit menu in the `MainForm` class for the Close menu in the merged menu. This makes sense, although we still need to rename the menu text to read

"Close" rather than "Exit." We will do this in a way that continues to preserve the SDI application from part 2.

	Action	Result
	CHANGE THE EXIT MENU TEXT WHEN RUNNING AS AN MDI CHILD FORM	
4	Override the `OnLoad` method in the MainForm.cs code window.	`protected override void OnLoad(EventArgs e)` `{`

5	If the form is an MDI child window, then modify the Exit menu to appear as a Close menu.
	
	How-to
	Use the `IsMdiChild` property.
		`    if (IsMdiChild)`
		`        menuExit.Text = "&Close";`
		
		`    base.OnLoad(e);`
		`}`

This change ensures that the Exit menu displays "Close" when the `MainForm` object is created as an MDI child window. Otherwise, the default setting of "Exit" will be used.

Compile and run the application to verify that our changes produce the appropriate menu structure. Create a new MDI child window and display the File menu. Your application should appear as in figure 16.5. Note how all the menus are now in the desired order, including the separator menus. Also note that the Exit menu from the `MainForm` class is reincarnated as the Close menu in the MDI application.

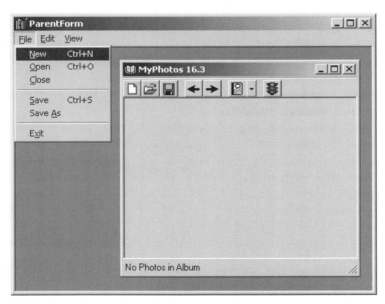

Figure 16.5   The merged File menu here gives no indication that different menu items are processed in different classes.

Of course, the Open menu is not yet implemented for our `ParentForm` class. Also note that the `Toolbar` control in our child window still provides access to the now hidden New and Open menus in the `MainForm` class.

We will deal with our toolbar shortly. First, let's discuss our new Open menu.

16.3.3 OPENING A CHILD FORM

The Open menu in the parent form should work much like the now hidden Open menu for the `MainForm` class. The handler for this menu should display an `Open-FileDialog` and create a new child window containing the selected album. To create the `MainForm` instance, we will create a new constructor that accepts an album file name with which to initialize the window.

The code required here is nothing new to us, so let's get to it.

	IMPLEMENT HANDLER FOR OPEN MENU IN PARENT FORM	
	ACTION	**RESULT**
1	Add a using statement for our library at the start of the ParentForm.cs code window.	`using Manning.MyPhotoAlbum;`

2	Add a `Click` handler for the Open menu in the ParentForm.cs [Design] window.	`private void menuOpen_Click`
		`  (object sender, System.EventArgs e)`
		`{`

3	Implement this handler to display an `OpenFile-Dialog` instance from which to select an album.	`// Allow user to select a new album`
		`using (OpenFileDialog dlg = new OpenFileDialog())`
		`{`
		`  dlg.Title = "Open Album";`
		`  dlg.Filter = "abm files (*.abm)|"`
		`    + "*.abm|All files (*.*)|*.*";`
		`  dlg.InitialDirectory = PhotoAlbum.DefaultDir;`
		`  dlg.RestoreDirectory = true;`
		
		`  if (dlg.ShowDialog() == DialogResult.OK)`
		`  {`

4	If an album is selected, try to open the file in a new window.
	How-to
	Use a not-yet-implemented constructor that accepts an album file.
		`    try`
		`    {`
		`      // Open new child window for the album`
		`      MainForm form = new MainForm(dlg.FileName);`
		`      form.MdiParent = this;`
		`      form.Show();`
		`    }`

	ACTION	RESULT

5	If an error occurs creating the child window, display an error message to the user.	```csharp
		catch (Exception ex)
		{
		  MessageBox.Show(this,
		    "Unable to open file " + dlg.FileName
		    + "\n (" + ex.Message + ")",
		    "Open Album Error",
		    MessageBoxButtons.OK,
		    MessageBoxIcon.Error);
		    }
		   }
		  }
		 }
		``

The code displays an open file dialog and creates a child window using the selected album file. This code requires a new constructor for the `MainForm` class, namely one that accepts the file name of a photo album.

In this new constructor, we would like to make use of the constructor code already present in the existing constructor. We can do this in C# by simply invoking the default constructor with the `this` keyword. The following table illustrates this syntax, and the changes required for our new constructor.

	CREATE A **MAINFORM** CONSTRUCTOR THAT ACCEPTS AN ALBUM FILE	
	Action	**Result**

6	In the MainForm.cs file, create a new constructor that accepts the name of an album file.	```csharp
		public MainForm(string albumFile)
		``

7	Invoke the default constructor within our new constructor.	```csharp
		  : this()
		{
		``

8	Within the constructor, create a `PhotoAlbum` for the given file.
	
	Note: If a file cannot be opened as an album, this will throw an exception.
		``csharp
		_album = new PhotoAlbum();
		_album.Open(albumFile);
		SetTitleBar();
		}
		``

These changes permit the `ParentForm` class to create a new child window containing an open album. Compile and run the application to verify that this works as expected. The File menu from our two classes is now fully merged, and all menus are fully implemented.

As can be seen from this discussion, the ability to merge menus provides a powerful mechanism for controlling the menu bar in MDI applications. They permit the exact placement of menu items, and control over which class, the parent or child, will process each item. While we only merged a single menu here, you may find in your own MDI applications that multiple menus must be merged. The principles and methods for doing this are identical to those utilized here.

With our menus completed, the next item in the development of our MDI application is to tidy up other parts of the interface such as the toolbar and the pixel data dialog. This cleanup is our next topic.

16.4   MDI CHILDREN

Our MDI application is coming along nicely. So far we have a parent form that contains `MainForm` class instances as child forms. Each form displays a new or existing album, and the menu bars have been integrated to present a logical set of choices for the user. There are additional members of the `Form` class that are related to the creation of MDI applications. This section will examine a few of these members as we correct some issues with our MyPhotos MDI application.

If you have experimented with the MyPhotos interface created in the previous section, you may have found the following three issues that do not behave as you might expect.

- *The toolbar control.*   The toolbar on the child form gives access to the New and Open menu in the `MainForm` class, which we are trying not to expose in the MDI version of our application.

- *The pixel data form.*   This dialog appears separate from the MDI application, rather than as a child form within it. In addition, when multiple album windows are open, each window opens its own separate `PixelDlg` form, which can get rather confusing.

- *Opening multiple albums.*   If you open the same album twice, you end up with two windows both showing the same album. Aside from the errors that can occur from having two instances operate on different versions of the same album simultaneously, it seems a bit strange to permit two copies of the same file to open in the same parent window.

We will address each of these items separately, and make use of MDI-related members of the `Form` class as required.

16.4.1   REPLACING THE TOOLBAR

Our toolbar was designed to interact with the menu bar for our `MainForm` class, and not the merged menu in our MDI application. As a result, it is no longer appropriate for our purposes. As a simple solution to this problem, we will simply hide the toolbar when the `MainForm` object is an MDI child form. While we are at it, we can create a very simple toolbar in the `ParentForm` class to demonstrate such a control in an MDI application. Figure 16.6 shows our application after these changes have been made.

Figure 16.6   The toolbar here must locate the appropriate event handler for the active child form whenever a button is clicked.

This following table shows the changes required to hide the toolbar in the child window.

Set the version number of the MyPhotos application to 16.4.

	HIDE THE TOOLBAR IN OUR CHILD FORM	
	Action	**Result**
1	Locate the `OnLoad` method in the MainForm.cs code window.	`protected override void OnLoad(EventArgs e)` `{`

2	Update this method to hide the toolbar when this form is an MDI child form.	`    if (IsMdiChild)`
		`    {`
		`        menuExit.Text = "&Close";`
		`        toolBarMain.Visible = false;`
		`    }`
		
		`    base.OnLoad(e);`
		`}`

Not very exciting, but it does the job. A similar argument could be made for the status bar. In this case, since the status bar is still accurate and provides some useful information related to the displayed album, we will simply leave this control alone.

As for a `Toolbar` control in the parent form, we will create a simple control with five buttons to demonstrate how this is done. Our buttons will correspond to the New, Open, Save, Previous, and Next menu items in our merged menu. The one change from what we saw in chapter 13 when creating our original toolbar is that the Save, Previous, and Next buttons must operate on the active child form, rather than the parent form.

The `ActiveMdiChild` property in the `Form` class is used to identify the active child for a form. We will use this to implement our toolbar buttons in the parent form.

We will also use the C# `internal` keyword here to expose some of our `MenuItem` objects in the `MainForm` class to other classes in our assembly, and in particular to our `ParentForm` class. This keyword is an access modifier like `public` or `protected`, and permits any other class in the same assembly to have access to the class member.

Let's see how these constructs are used by creating the `Toolbar` control for our parent form. Since toolbars were discussed in chapter 13, we will simply highlight the required changes without too much detailed discussion.

	CREATE A TOOLBAR IN THE PARENT FORM	
	Action	**Result**
3	Add an `ImageList` called `imageListParent` to the `ParentForm` class in the ParentForm.cs [Design] window.	The image list appears in the component tray for the form.
4	Add the following images to the `Images` property of this list: • bitmaps/OffCtlBr/Small/Color/ NEW.BMP • bitmaps/OffCtlBr/Small/Color/ OPEN.BMP • bitmaps/OffCtlBr/Small/Color/ SAVE.BMP • icons/arrows/ARW08LT.ICO • icons/arrows/ARW08RT.ICO	
5	Add a `ToolBar` control to the `ParentForm` class. **Settings** | Property	Value | |---|---| | (Name) | toolBarParent | | ImageList | imageListParent | | TextAlign | Right |	

	Action	Result
6	Using the ToolBarButton Collections Editor, add six `ToolBarButton` objects to this toolbar.	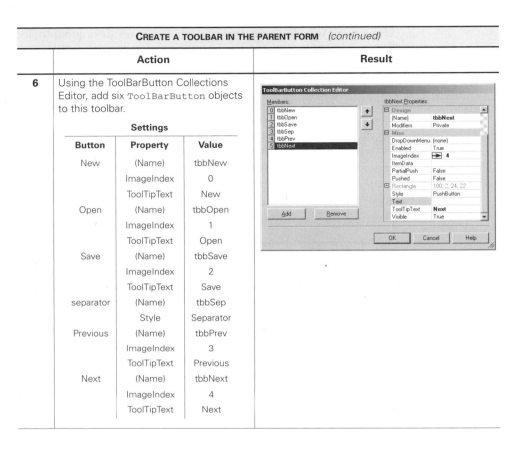

Settings

Button	Property	Value
New	(Name)	tbbNew
	ImageIndex	0
	ToolTipText	New
Open	(Name)	tbbOpen
	ImageIndex	1
	ToolTipText	Open
Save	(Name)	tbbSave
	ImageIndex	2
	ToolTipText	Save
separator	(Name)	tbbSep
	Style	Separator
Previous	(Name)	tbbPrev
	ImageIndex	3
	ToolTipText	Previous
Next	(Name)	tbbNext
	ImageIndex	4
	ToolTipText	Next

This adds the toolbar and toolbar buttons to the form. Next we need to add the code to handle the `ButtonClick` event for our toolbar. As you may recall from chapter 13, this event occurs when the user clicks one of the toolbar buttons.

HANDLE THE ButtonClick EVENT IN THE PARENT FORM

	Action	Result

7	In the `MainForm` class, add `internal` methods to click the `menuSave`, `menuPrevious`, and `menuNext` menu items.
	
	Note: We could alternately change the access for these objects from `private` to `internal`. This approach is a bit more robust.
		```internal void ClickSaveMenu()```
		```{```
		``` menuSave.PerformClick();```
		```}```
		
		```internal void ClickPreviousMenu()```
		```{```
		``` menuPrevious.PerformClick();```
		```}```
		
		```internal void ClickNextMenu()```
		```{```
		``` menuNext.PerformClick();```
		```}```

	Action	Result

8	In the `ParentForm` constructor, assign the `Tag` property for the New and Open buttons to the corresponding menu item.	<pre>public ParentForm()
		{
		    // Required for Designer support
		    InitializeComponent();
		
		    // Initialize toolbar buttons
		    tbbNew.Tag = menuNew;
		    tbbOpen.Tag = menuOpen;
		}</pre>

9	Also in the `ParentForm` class, add an event handler for the `ButtonClick` event in the toolbar.	<pre>private void toolBarParent_ButtonClick
		    (object sender, System.Windows.Forms.
		        ToolBarButtonClickEventArgs e)
		{</pre>

10	Implement this handler to invoke the corresponding menus for the New and Open buttons.	<pre> if (e.Button.Tag is MenuItem)
		    {
		        MenuItem mi = e.Button.Tag as MenuItem;
		        mi.PerformClick();
		        return;
		    }</pre>

11	For the other buttons, convert the active child form, if any, to a `MainForm` instance.	<pre> // Must be MDI child button
		    MainForm child
		        = ActiveMdiChild as MainForm;</pre>

12	If the active child is a `MainForm` object, then click the menu item corresponding to the selected button.	<pre> if (child != null)
		    {
		        if (e.Button == tbbSave)
		            child.ClickSaveMenu();
		        else if (e.Button == tbbPrev)
		            child.ClickPreviousMenu();
		        else if (e.Button == tbbNext)
		            child.ClickNextMenu();
		    }
		}</pre>

This code invokes the menus in the `ParentForm` class for the New and Open buttons, and the appropriate menu in the active `MainForm` object, if any, otherwise. Note the use of the `internal` keyword for the new methods in the `MainForm` class. This permits these members to be accessed from within the MyPhotos.exe assembly only, in this case from the `ParentForm` class.

Compile and run the code to verify that your toolbar works property. Make sure the buttons perform as expected when no child window is present, and when the active child does and does not contain any photographs in its album.

> **TRY IT!** Add a new button to the parent form similar to the `tbbImages` button in our `MainForm` toolbar. This will require a `DropDownButton` style of toolbar button, and a new internal method in `MainForm` to assign the display mode for the form.

With our toolbar complete, our next task is to handle the `PixelDlg` form.

16.4.2 DISPLAYING PIXEL DATA

The `PixelDlg` form is another area where the behavior in our MDI application is not quite as desired. Right now each child has a separate pixel dialog, and these dialogs are separate from the parent form. To integrate this feature with our MDI application, it would be nice if a single `PixelDlg` was used for all album windows, and if this dialog was an MDI child form as well. We would also like to preserve our ability to run the MyPhotos application as an SDI where only a single album is displayed at a time.

This section will make the changes in our code required by these features, the result of which appears in figure 16.7. These changes will involve the following tasks:

- Create a global `PixelDlg` instance that can be shared by all `MainForm` instances.
- Provide a means to display this dialog as an MDI child form.
- Access this global instance from the `MainForm` class instances.
- Ensure this dialog is always associated with any active `MainForm` window.

Figure 16.7 The PixelDlg form in this figure is partially obscured to prove that it really is a child form in our MDI application, rather than the modeless dialog originally created in chapter 8.

This may seem like a daunting task for a single section. In fact, our application is well-prepared for these changes. Pulling out my soap box for a moment, the real test of an architecture is not its ability to work as designed, but rather its ability to perform tasks for which it was not designed. The coding techniques we have used throughout the book are useful in any application to accommodate future requirements. These techniques include frequent encapsulation of tasks into separate methods; sketching a user interface design or enumerating the steps required before writing any code; and building reusable libraries and methods where possible.

As a result, our code has some advantages for new changes such as this in that we have consistently tried to use good coding practices and not duplicate our tasks in multiple places. While perhaps not always successful, I believe we have done a reasonable job.

In the PixelDlg form, for example, we were careful to only update this form in the UpdatePixelData method of the MainForm class. Similarly, the only location where the PixelDlg form is created right now is in the Click event handler for the menuPixelData object. Such organization occasionally requires a little extra work, or in our case a few more pages, but this effort often pays off as the code is maintained and updated in the future.

Stepping off my soap box and returning to the topic at hand, we will make our changes in the order shown in the previous list, beginning with a global PixelDlg instance. For this we will provide a static property in the PixelDlg class that returns a shared form.

	CREATE A SHARED PIXELDLG INSTANCE	
	Action	**Result**
1	In the PixelDlg.cs code window, create static members to hold the shared instance and an MDI parent form, if any.	`static private Form _mdiForm = null;` `static private PixelDlg _globalDlg;`
2	Create an internal property to assign and retrieve an MDI container form.	```static internal Form GlobalMdiParent` `{` ` get { return _mdiForm; }` ` set { _mdiForm = value; }` `}```
3	Create a public property to retrieve the shared form. **How-to** If the current _globalDlg value is invalid, then create a new instance of the Form.	```static public PixelDlg GlobalDialog` `{` ` get` ` {` ` if (_globalDlg == null` ` || _globalDlg.IsDisposed)` ` {` ` _globalDlg = new PixelDlg();` ` _globalDlg.MdiParent = GlobalMdiParent;` ` }` ` return _globalDlg;` ` }` `}```

The GlobalDialog property provides the mechanism by which all child MainForm instances can access the same PixelDlg form. Recall that our PixelDlg form is disposed whenever the user clicks the Close button. For this reason, this property recreates the dialog whenever it is `null` or disposed.

The `GlobalMdiParent` property provides a method for turning this global dialog into an MDI child form. We can use this property in our `ParentForm` class to establish the MDI container for our global dialog.

SET THE MDI PARENT FOR THE GLOBAL PIXELDLG FORM		
	Action	**Result**
4	In the ParentForm.cs code window, override the `OnLoad` method to assign this form as the MDI parent for the global `PixelDlg` form.	```protected override void OnLoad(EventArgs e)\n{\n PixelDlg.GlobalMdiParent = this;\n\n base.OnLoad(e);\n}```

This ensures that whenever a new global dialog is created, the `ParentForm` object is assigned as the MDI parent. With this in place, we are ready to access the global dialog from the `MainForm` class. As mentioned earlier, right now the dialog is created only in the `menuPixelData_Click` method, so this is the only place we need to call our new property.

ACCESS THE GLOBAL PIXELDLG FROM THE MAINFORM CLASS		
	Action	**Result**
5	Locate the `menuPixelData_Click` method in the MainForm.cs code window.	```private void menuPixelData_Click\n (object sender, System.EventArgs e)\n{```
6	Modify the creation of the `PixelDlg` form to use the new `GlobalDialog` property.	```if (_dlgPixel == null\n || _dlgPixel.IsDisposed)\n{\n _dlgPixel = PixelDlg.GlobalDialog;\n}\n\n_nPixelDlgIndex = _album.CurrentPosition;\nPoint p = pnlPhoto.PointToClient(\n Form.MousePosition);\nUpdatePixelData(p.X, p.Y);\nAssignPixelToggle(true);\n\n_dlgPixel.Show();\n}```

This change simply retrieves the global dialog rather than creating a new instance. You can compile and run this if you like. You will see that our code works fine for a single MDI child window. When a second window is added, the `PixelDlg` form is not associated with this window, and no longer works.

There are a couple ways to fix this problem. We will do so by observing that all mouse movement in each window is processed by the pnlPhoto_MouseMove event handler. This method in turn calls the UpdatePixelData method, as does all other updates to the dialog. As a result, we can associate an existing PixelDlg form with a new window by assigning the dialog at the start of our update method.

The following steps make this change in our application.

	Action	Result
	ENSURE AN EXISTING PIXELDLG FORM IS ASSIGNED TO NEW CHILD INSTANCES	
	Action	**Result**

7	Locate the UpdatePixelData method.	`protected void UpdatePixelData(int xPos,`
		`                               int yPos)`
		`{`

8	Assign the _dlgPixel field at the beginning of the method.	`    if (IsMdiChild)`
		`        _dlgPixel = PixelDlg.GlobalDialog;`
		`    . . .`
		`}`

This now guarantees that a child form will pick up the global PixelDlg form as needed. Of course, this change also causes the dialog to be created even when it is not used. Such a change might not be appropriate in a large application with multiple utility forms such as our pixel dialog. For our purposes, it is okay.

Compile and run the program to verify that our new code works. Also realize that these changes are consistent with our non-MDI application. When a single MainForm instance is present, it will now use the global PixelDlg instance to create the dialog, and all code will work as we originally intended in chapter 8. You can test this by modifying the MyPhotos project settings to use the MainForm.Main method as the entry point.

The PixelDlg form is now integrated into our MDI application. The next task is to ensure that we do not open multiple windows for the same album file.

16.4.3   OPENING AN ALBUM TWICE

In our current code for the Open menu, the user selects an album and a new child window is created to contain this album. This is fine as long as the selected album has not been previously opened by the user. In the case where a MainForm window already exists for the selected album, it would be more appropriate to simply display the existing window at the top of the z-order.

This can be done by searching through the list of child windows for one that displays the selected album. The MdiChildren property in the Form class retrieves the collection of child forms assigned to an MDI container form. This property can be treated like any other array to search for a matching form.

This property is useful whenever a specific form is desired, as we do here. It can also be used to see if any child forms are present in an MDI application and to obtain the number of MDI child forms, although checking the ActiveMdiChild property is typically a more efficient mechanism for the former task.

When implementing this change, we should keep in mind the fact that forms other than our `MainForm` class might be contained by this array. The following steps detail a solution for this change with this fact in mind.

	HANDLE AN ATTEMPT TO OPEN A DISPLAYED ALBUM	
	Action	**Result**
| 1 | In the MainForm.cs code window, add a new `AlbumFile` property to retrieve the file name of the displayed album. | ```csharp
public string AlbumFile
{
  get { return _album.FileName; }
}
``` |
| 2 | Locate the `menuOpen_Click` event handler in the ParentForm.cs code window. | ```csharp
private void menuOpen_Click
  (object sender, System.EventArgs e)
{
``` |
| 3 | Before opening a new `MainForm` window, search through the set of existing child forms. | ```csharp
    . . .
  if (dlg.ShowDialog() == DialogResult.OK)
  {
    try
    {
      // See if album is already open
      foreach (Form f in MdiChildren)
      {
``` |
| 4 | If a `MainForm` instance is found, see if it displays the selected album. | ```csharp
        if (f is MainForm)
        {
          MainForm mf = (MainForm) f;
          if (mf.AlbumFile == dlg.FileName)
          {
``` |
| 5 | If a match is found, bring the existing album to the front of the application window.<br><br>**How-to**<br>a. If the form is minimized, return it to a normal state.<br>b. Display the form at the front of the MDI window. | ```csharp
            if (mf.WindowState
                == FormWindowState.Minimized)
            {
              mf.WindowState
                = FormWindowState.Normal;
            }
            mf.BringToFront();
            return;
          }
        }
      }
``` |
| 6 | If no matching window is found, the existing code will create a new `MainForm` object for the album. | ```csharp
      // Open new child window for album
      MainForm form
        = new MainForm(dlg.FileName);
      . . .
  }
``` |

This code uses some properties we have not seen before. When a matching child `Form` is found, the `WindowState` property is used to assign or retrieve the current display state of the MDI child form within its container. For a top-level form, this affects the display state on the desktop. The `WindowState` property takes its values from the `FormWindowState` enumeration, summarized in .NET Table 16.2. In the previous table, we check to see if the MDI child is minimized, and if so return it to a `Normal` state.

The `FormWindowState` enumeration specifies the possible display states for a `Form` on the desktop or within an MDI application. This enumeration is part of the `System.Win-dows.Forms` namespace.

Enumeration Values	Maximized	The form is maximized so that it fills the entire possible display area, either the entire desktop or the entire display window when the form is an MDI child form.
	Minimized	The form is minimized and is listed in the task bar or at the base of the MDI container form.
	Normal	The form appears in its normal state. By default, the form is visible and not maximized. If a maximized `Form` is minimized, then setting the `Form` to `Normal` will return the form to a maximized state.

We also use the `BringToFront` method to display the form at the top of the z-order within the MDI container. This method is part of the `Control` class and can be used to adjust the z-order position of any Windows Forms control within its container. There is also a corresponding `SendToBack` method to place a control at the bottom of the z-order.

Run the application to verify this feature works. Try minimizing or maximizing the form before opening the same album to verify that the proper behavior occurs. Also verify that when a new album is selected, a new MDI child form appears as before.

This completes the three tasks we set out at the start of section 16.4. We have added a toolbar to our parent form and hidden the toolbar in the child, turned the `PixelDlg` form into an MDI child when running as an MDI application, and ensured that an album can only be opened within a single MDI child form.

As a final change, and to create a slightly more polished application, let's make one more addition here to place the current album in the title bar.

16.4.4   UPDATING THE TITLE BAR

An MDI application should normally update its title bar to reflect the contents of the currently active child form. This provides good feedback to your users, especially when the application is minimized and only appears in the task bar. In our case, we will also include the version number on the title bar as is our custom. The result of this change is shown in figure 16.8.

We could like to update the title bar whenever a new form is activated within the MDI container. There is an event for just this purpose, namely the `MdiChildActi-vate` event. This event occurs whenever an MDI child form is closed or becomes the active form within the container.

Figure 16.8 The title bar for our MDI application must handle the various types of child forms the application can display.

We should also point out that MDI child forms do not receive the `Activated` or `Deactivate` events. As a result, when converting from a single document interface into a multiple document interface, any tasks performed in these events must now be handled via another mechanism. Often the `MdiChildActivate` event can handle the work previously done in these events. Another option is to use the focus-related events, such as the `Enter` or `Leave` event. We will look at the activation events in our `MainForm` window in a moment.

Let's implement an `MdiChildActivate` event handler to update the title bar for our application.

	UPDATE TITLE BAR IN THE PARENT FORM	
	Action	**Result**

1	In the ParentForm.cs code window, override the protected `OnMdiChildActivate` method.	`protected override void OnMdiChildActivate`
		`    (System.EventArgs e)`
		`{`

2	Implement this method to set the title bar for the MDI application.	`  SetTitleBar();`
		`  base.OnMdiChildActivate(e);`
		`}`

3	In the MainForm.cs code window, add an `AlbumTitle` property to retrieve the title of the currently displayed album.	`public string AlbumTitle`
		`{`
		`  get { return _album.Title; }`
		`}`

	Action	Result

4	Back in the ParentForm.cs code window, implement the SetTitleBar method to retrieve the version number for the application.	<pre>protected void SetTitleBar()
		{
		    Version ver
		        = new Version(Application.ProductVersion);</pre>

5	If the active child is a MainForm object, include the album title in the title bar.
	
	How-to
	
	Cast the active child to a MainForm object in order to retrieve the current album title.
		<pre>string titleBar
		    = "{0} - MyPhotos MDI {1:#}.{2:#}";
		
		if (ActiveMdiChild is MainForm)
		{
		    string albumTitle
		        = ((MainForm)ActiveMdiChild).AlbumTitle;
		    this.Text = String.Format(titleBar,
		        albumTitle, ver.Major, ver.Minor);
		}</pre>

6	If the active child is a PixelDlg object, display the string "Pixel Data" in the title bar.	<pre>else if (ActiveMdiChild is PixelDlg)
		{
		    this.Text = String.Format(titleBar,
		        "Pixel Data", ver.Major, ver.Minor);
		}</pre>

7	Otherwise, just display the version number in the title bar.	<pre>else
		{
		    this.Text = String.Format(
		        "MyPhotos MDI {0:#}.{1:#}",
		        ver.Major, ver.Minor);
		    }
		}</pre>

8	Also set the title bar in the OnLoad method.
	
	Note: This sets the title bar as the application begins, before any child windows are displayed.
		<pre>protected override void OnLoad(EventArgs e)
		{
		    PixelDlg.GlobalMdiParent = this;
		    SetTitleBar();
		
		    base.OnLoad(e);
		}</pre>

The text to appear in the title bar depends on which type of window is currently active. When no window, or an unrecognized window, is active, then the title bar simply includes the version number. The MdiChildActivate event gives no indication of the activating child, so we use the ActiveMdiChild property to retrieve the active Form. We separate the title bar logic into a separate member SetTitle-Bar, which allows us to call this method from the OnLoad method as well as our event handler.

Compile and run the application to verify that these changes work as expected. The title bar for both parent and child forms is rather similar. Feel free to modify one or the other to make the title bars more unique. If you do this, make sure you consider the behavior of the MainForm class as both an SDI and MDI application.

16.4.5 REVISITING THE ACTIVATION EVENTS

Before we leave this section, there is one more additional change required in our program. Take a look at the following OnActivated and OnDeactivate methods from the MainForm class. As we mentioned previously, these events are not received by MDI child forms, so our existing methods will never be called.

```
protected override void OnDeactivate(EventArgs e)
{
  if (ctrlKeyHeld)
    ReleaseControlKey();

  base.OnDeactivate(e);
}

protected override void OnActivated(EventArgs e)
{
  // Update toggle toolbar button if required
  if (this._dlgPixel == null || _dlgPixel.IsDisposed)
    AssignPixelToggle(false);
  else
    AssignPixelToggle(_dlgPixel.Visible);

  base.OnActivated(e);
}
```

As you may recall, we overrode the OnDeactivate method in earlier chapters to note that the Ctrl key should be released when the Form is no longer the active application on the desktop. We overrode the OnActivated method as part of the implementation for a toggle toolbar button tied to the PixelDlg form for the window. The deactivate logic is still required, since the Ctrl key is still a part of our MDI application. The pixel toggle button is not included in our current MDI application, so the activation logic is not required here.

For the Ctrl key logic, we can duplicate the deactivation logic in an OnLeave method. This method, you may recall, is invoked when a control, in this case our form, loses focus. A standalone window, such as our SDI application, does not receive this event, so this addition has no effect on our SDI program.

	ENSURE THE CTRL KEY IS RELEASED WHEN AN MDI CHILD FORM LOSES FOCUS	
	Action	**Result**
1	In the MainForm.cs code window, override the OnLeave method to duplicate the logic from the OnDeactivate method for the MDI application.	```protected override void OnLeave(EventArgs e)
{
  if (IsMdiChild && ctrlKeyHeld)
    ReleaseControlKey();

  base.OnLeave(e);
}``` |

With this change, our MDI application is ready. Compile and run the application and try to find an error.[1]

TRY IT! We have been careful to use the `IsMdiChild` property in all our changes to the MainForm.cs source file to ensure that the application can run as a single document interface or a multiple document interface. Test this out by modifying the Startup Object in the properties for the MyPhotos project to use the `MainForm.Main` method. Recompile the application and verify that it now runs as an SDI application. Change it back to an MDI application by setting the Startup Object to `ParentForm.Main`.

Our final change in this chapter will be the addition of layout management for our MDI child forms.

16.5 MDI CHILD WINDOW MANAGEMENT

Ultimately, an MDI application is simply a collection of `Forms` displayed in a parent window. The .NET Framework provides some assistance in managing these forms within this parent. In this section we will discuss child form layout and how to show the active forms in a menu. The `Form` class contains a `LayoutMdi` method for the former, while the `MenuItem` class contains an `MdiList` property for the latter. A new top-level Window menu, as shown in figure 16.9, will make use of these constructs.

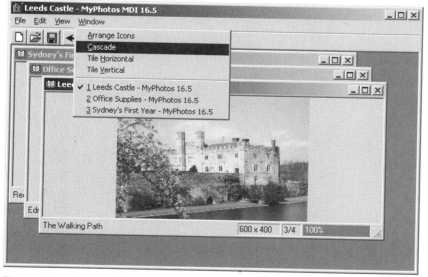

Figure 16.9 The new Window menu for our application will support options related to managing child forms within the parent window.

---

[1] Of course, if you do find an error here or elsewhere in the book, please send me an email so the correction can be posted online and the error corrected in the next edition.

We will begin with the automatic layout of MDI child forms.

16.5.1 ARRANGING MDI FORMS

In an MDI application, as well as on the Windows desktop, a number of windows are created and strewn about in various locations. It would be nice if our application permitted automatic organization of the windows at the user's request. This would allow the user to immediately see all open windows and select the desired one.

Such support is provided by the `LayoutMdi` method of the `Form` class. This method accepts an enumeration value specifying the type of layout to apply to the MDI container, as shown by the following signature:

```
public void LayoutMdi( MdiLayout layoutValue );
```

This method is called from the MDI container form, in our case the `ParentForm` class. The `MdiLayout` enumeration is summarized in .NET Table 16.3. To demonstrate how this is used, we will create a new `Windows` menu containing options for each of the main layout options. An illustration of each option is shown in the table.

.NET Table 16.3 MdiLayout enumeration		
The `MdiLayout` enumeration specifies the possible layout options for a set of MDI child forms. This is used in the `LayoutMdi` method of the `Form` class to automatically display a set of forms with the given layout mode. This class is part of the `System.Windows.Forms` namespace. The following table illustrates each layout style with a set of three child forms.		
Enumeration Values	ArrangeIcons	The icons or minimized forms are arranged within the client window. Note that this has no effect on child forms that are not minimized.

Enumeration Values	Cascade	The child forms are displayed on top of each other in step fashion so that only the title bar of the hidden forms is visible.

	TileHorizontal	The client area is divided horizontally into equal sections and each open window is displayed in a section.

	TileVertical	The client area is divided vertically into equal sections and each open window is displayed in a section.

In your application, you can choose to support some or all of these options. The various layout styles are useful for quickly seeing the entire set of open windows in an MDI application, and typically appear in a Windows menu located on the MDI parent form. Since our application is nothing if not typical, we will do exactly this. The following table details the required steps.

Set the version number of the MyPhotos application to 16.5.

ADD LAYOUT MENUS TO THE PARENT FORM	
Action	**Result**

<table>
<tr><td>1</td><td>In the ParentForm.cs [Design] window, add a new top-level Windows menu to the form.

 Settings
<table><tr><td>Property</td><td>Value</td></tr><tr><td>(Name)</td><td>menuWindows</td></tr><tr><td>MergeOrder</td><td>3</td></tr><tr><td>Text</td><td>&Window</td></tr></table></td><td></td></tr>
<tr><td>2</td><td>Add a menu item for each of the layout styles.

 Settings
<table><tr><td>Menu</td><td>Property</td><td>Value</td></tr><tr><td>Arrange</td><td>(Name)</td><td>menuArrange</td></tr><tr><td></td><td>Text</td><td>&Arrange Icons</td></tr><tr><td>Cascade</td><td>(Name)</td><td>menuCascade</td></tr><tr><td></td><td>Text</td><td>&Cascade</td></tr><tr><td>Horizontal</td><td>(Name)</td><td>menuTileHorizontal</td></tr><tr><td></td><td>Text</td><td>Tile &Horizontal</td></tr><tr><td>Vertical</td><td>(Name)</td><td>menuTileVertical</td></tr><tr><td></td><td>Text</td><td>Tile &Vertical</td></tr></table></td><td></td></tr>
</table>

	Action	Result
| 3 | Add a `Click` event handler for each menu that calls the `LayoutMdi` method with the corresponding `MdiLayout` enumeration value. | ```csharp
private void menuArrange_Click
    (object sender, System.EventArgs e)
{
    LayoutMdi(MdiLayout.ArrangeIcons);
}

private void menuCascade_Click
    (object sender, System.EventArgs e)
{
    LayoutMdi(MdiLayout.Cascade);
}

private void menuTileHorizontal_Click
    (object sender, System.EventArgs e)
{
    LayoutMdi(MdiLayout.TileHorizontal);
}

private void menuTileVertical_Click
    (object sender, System.EventArgs e)
{
    LayoutMdi(MdiLayout.TileVertical);
}
``` |

This change permits the user to automatically arrange the open windows in the selected style. Compile and run the application, open a few windows, and verify that these changes work as advertised.

The other topic related to our Windows menu is that of the `MdiList` property.

16.5.2 CREATING AN MDI CHILD LIST

It is common in MDI applications to provide a list of open windows as part of the Window menu. This permits the user to quickly jump to an open window at the click of the mouse. The .NET folks at Microsoft were kind enough to provide a quick way to do this through the `MdiList` property of the `MenuItem` class.

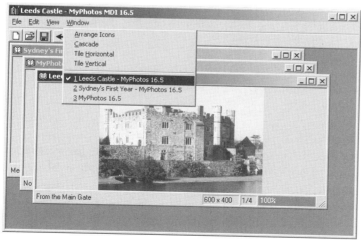

Figure 16.10
In the list of child forms, note how the active child form is automatically checked by the framework.
```

When this property is set to `true` on a top-level menu within an MDI application, the list of child forms is automatically added to the menu. Figure 16.10 shows an example of this behavior for the Window menu in our `ParentForm` class. The list of forms appears below any existing menu items, with a separator added just before the list.

Up to nine forms are displayed, with a "More Windows..." menu added if more than nine child forms exist. This additional menu is added by the .NET Framework, and will display a dialog showing the list of all child forms. An example of this "More Windows..." dialog is shown in figure 16.11. Note that even our `PixelDlg` form appears in this window.

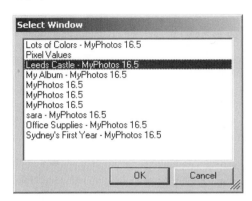

Figure 16.11
The Select Window dialog displays all active windows in the application.

We can add this feature to our application simply by setting the `MdiList` property for the Window menu.

ENABLE A LIST OF CHILD WINDOWS TO APPEAR		
	Action	**Result**
1	In the ParentForm.cs [Design] window, set the `MdiList` property of the Window menu to `true`.	The MDI child windows will be automatically inserted when the contents of this menu are displayed.

That's all it takes. Compile, run, and see it in action.

The related property `MdiListItem` exists in the `Menu` class, and can be used to identify the `MenuItem` instance that displays the list of child forms within a `Main-Menu` instance. We have not used this property in our application.

Before we leave the topic of child form layout, it is also worth mentioning that child forms can be positioned manually using the standard members of the `Control` class such as the `Top`, `Width`, `Size`, and `Location` properties.

This completes our MDI application for the moment. As is our custom, a short recap of our accomplishments here will round out the chapter.

16.6 RECAP

In this chapter we converted the single document interface, or SDI, application created in part 2 of the book into a multiple document interface, or MDI, application. This amazing feat was done through the creation of a new parent form window and by using members of the `Form` class and other Windows Forms constructs.

We began by creating the `ParentForm` class to serve as our MDI container form, and used the existing `MainForm` object as our child form. We examined the `Merge-Order` and `MergeType` properties of the `MenuItem` class to merge the menus of our parent and child forms into a single menu bar. We created a toolbar on our parent form and integrated the `PixelDlg` form into the application as well.

From MDI applications we move to the topic of data binding.

C H A P T E R   1 7

Data binding

17.1 Data grids 565
17.2 Data grid customization 573
17.3 Editable objects 580
17.4 Simple data binding 586
17.5 Recap 602

Data binding is a means for associating Windows Forms controls with one or more data sources. We saw a little of this concept in chapter 10 for list controls such as the `List-Box` and `ComboBox` classes. These controls provide the `DataSource` and `DataMember` properties for binding the list displayed by the control to a specific source of data.

   In this chapter we will explore data binding in more detail. While we will keep the discussion focused on Windows Forms classes, many of the examples and discussions carry over to databases and the `System.Data` namespace where classes such as `DataSet` and `DataTable` are found.

   The application in this section will be similar in spirit to the MyAlbumEditor application created in chapters 10 and 11. A `ComboBox` control will display a list of available albums, and the photographs in the selected album will appear on the remainder of the form. Our new application will be called MyAlbumData and is shown in figure 17.1.

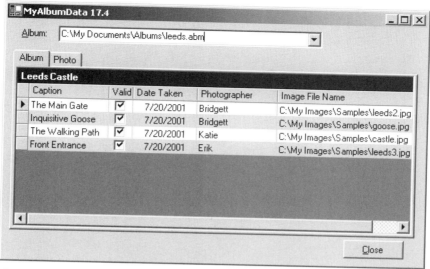

Figure 17.1   Our new application will include a tab control with a data grid on one tab page and a set of data-bound controls on a second tab page.

We begin with the `DataGrid` control, which displays a data source in tabular format. We will look at this class in some detail, and discuss the concept of simple data binding later in the chapter.

17.1   DATA GRIDS

A data grid is just that: a grid in which data is displayed. The `DataGrid` class encapsulates this concept, allowing various collections of data to be displayed and manipulated by a user. The concept of data binding is central to the `DataGrid` class, as data is typically displayed in the control by binding an existing database table or collection class to the data grid object.

As shown in figure 17.1, the `DataGrid` class displays data as a set of rows and columns. The grid in general represents a specific collection of data, and this case represents a `PhotoAlbum` instance. Each row, in turn, represents a specific item in the overall collection, and each column represents a specific field that can be assigned to each item. In our application, each row will represent a `Photograph` object, and each column a possible property of a photograph.

There are a number of terms related to `DataGrid` controls. A summary of these is shown in figure 17.2 as they relate to our application. An overview of the `DataGrid` class is provided in .NET Table 17.1.

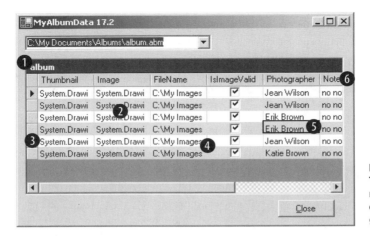

Figure 17.2
This chapter will discuss many of the terms and classes related to data grids.

❶ Caption

Displays a short string describing the table.

❷ DataGridTableStyle class

Used to customize the appearance and behavior of tables.

DataGridColumnStyle class

Used to customize the order, appearance and behavior of columns. The framework supports text and boolean columns by default.

❸ Row Header

The area in front of a row. The small triangle indicates the current item.

❹ Grid Lines

The color and style of lines are configurable.

❺ Cell

Refers to an individual value within the grid.

❻ Column Header

Shows the name of each column.

The `ListView` class discussed in chapter 14 can also be used to present a table of information. The Windows Forms namespace provides explicit classes to represent the rows and columns in a list view. As you may recall, each item, or row, in the list is represented by the `ListViewItem` class instance, and each column by a `ListViewSubItem` instance and is presented based on a `ColumnHeader` instance.

As illustrated by figure 17.2, the `DataGrid` class takes a somewhat different approach. The contents of the grid are contained in a single collection, such as an array, a photo album, or a database table. Classes exist to configure the style in which the provided data is displayed, including colors, column ordering, and other properties. We will discuss the details of these style classes later in the chapter.

The `DataGrid` class represents a control that displays a collection of data as a grid of rows and columns. The data displayed and the style in which it is presented is fully configurable. This class is part of the `System.Windows.Forms` namespace, and inherits from the `Control` class. See .NET Table 4.1 on page 104 for a list of members inherited by this class.

Public Properties	AllowNavigation	Gets or sets whether navigation is permitted.
	AlternatingBackColor	Gets or sets the background color to use on every other row in the grid to create a ledger-like appearance.
	CaptionText	Gets or sets the text to appear in the caption area.
	CaptionVisible	Gets or sets whether the caption is visible. Other properties related to this and other grid areas are also provided.
	CurrentCell	Gets or sets a `DataGridCell` structure representing the cell in the grid that has the focus.
	CurrentRowIndex	Gets or sets the index of the selected row.
	DataMember	Gets or sets which list in the assigned data source should be displayed in the grid.
	DataSource	Gets or sets the source of data for the grid.
	Item	Gets or sets the value of a cell. This property is the C# indexer for this class.
	ReadOnly	Gets or sets whether the grid is in read-only mode.
	RowHeaderWidth	Gets or sets the width of row headers in pixels.
	TableStyles	Gets the collection of `DataGridTableStyle` objects specifying display styles for various tables that may be displayed by the grid.
Public Methods	BeginEdit	Attempts to begin an edit on the grid.
	HitTest	Returns location information within the grid of a specified point on the screen. This works much like the `HitTest` method in the `MonthCalendar` class.
	SetDataBinding	Assigns the `DataSource` and `DataMember` properties to the given values at run time.
	Unselect	Deselects a specified row.
Public Events	CurrentCellChanged	Occurs when the current cell has changed.
	DataSourceChanged	Occurs when a new data source is assigned.
	Navigate	Occurs when the user navigates to a new table.
	Scroll	Occurs when the user scrolls the data grid.

17.1.1 CREATING THE MYALBUMDATA PROJECT

While the `DataGrid` class includes numerous members for customizing the appearance and behavior of the control, it is possible to create a very simple grid with only a few lines of code. We will begin with such an application, and enhance it over the course of the chapter.

The following table lays out the creation and initial layout of our new application.

	CREATE THE MYALBUMDATA PROJECT	
	Action	**Result**
1	Create a new project and solution in Visual Studio .NET called "MyAlbumData."	The new solution is shown in the Solution Explorer window, with the default Form1.cs [Design] window displayed.
2	Rename the Form1.cs file and related class file to our standard `MainForm` class and assign some initial settings for this form.	

Settings

Property	Value
(Name)	MainForm
Size	450, 300
Text	MyAlbumData

3	Drag a `Label`, `ComboBox`, `DataGrid`, and `Button` control onto the form. Arrange these controls as shown in the graphic.	

Settings

Control	Property	Value
Label	Text	&Album
ComboBox	(Name)	cmbxAlbum
	Anchor	Top, Left, Right
DataGrid	(Name)	gridPhotoAlbum
	Anchor	Top, Bottom, Left, Right
Button	(Name)	btnClose
	Anchor	Bottom, Right
	Text	&Close

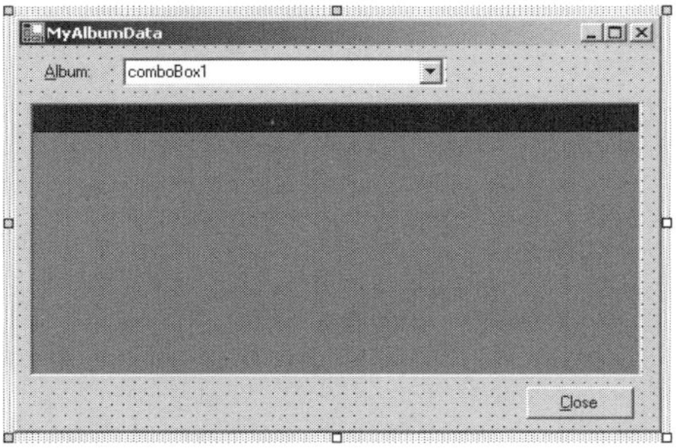

4	Create a `Click` event handler for the Close button to shut down the application.	```private void btnClose_Click
(object sender, System.EventArgs e)
{
Close();
}```

With our initial window in place, we are ready to display some album data in the window.

17.1.2 DISPLAYING DATA IN A DATA GRID

Our main window in the MyAlbumData application contains a combo box and a data grid. Our `ComboBox` control will contain a list of the albums located in the default album directory, while our `DataGrid` control will display the contents of the selected album. This section will make the changes required for this behavior. Section 17.2 will look at customizing the information displayed by the grid.

Fortunately, our existing MyPhotoAlbum project can do most of the work here. The changes required are detailed in the following steps.

Set the version number of the MyAlbumData application to 17.1.

DISPLAY ALBUM DATA IN THE MYPHOTOALBUM APPLICATION		
	Action	**Result**
1	In the Solution Explorer window, add the MyPhotoAlbum project to the solution and reference it from the MyAlbumData project.	
2	At the top of the MainForm.cs code window, add a `using` statement for the new project and the `System.IO` namespace.	`using System.IO;` `using Manning.MyPhotoAlbum;`
3	Define a private `PhotoAlbum` field within the `MainForm` class.	`private PhotoAlbum _album;`

	Action	Result
4	Override the `OnLoad` method to: a. Add the version number to the title bar. b. Initialize the photo album. c. Set the album file names to appear in the `ComboBox` control. **Note:** The assignment of the `DataSource` property here is an example of data binding. In this case, we are binding the collection of objects for the `ComboBox` control to an array of directory strings.	```csharp\nprotected override void OnLoad(EventArgs e)\n{\n Version ver\n = new Version(Application.ProductVersion);\n Text = String.Format(\n "MyAlbumData {0:#}.{1:#}",\n ver.Major, ver.Minor);\n\n _album = new PhotoAlbum();\n\n cmbxAlbum.DataSource = Directory.GetFiles(\n PhotoAlbum.DefaultDir, "*.abm");\n}\n```
5	Handle the `SelectedIndex-Changed` event for the `ComboBox` object.	```csharp\nprivate void cmbxAlbum_SelectedIndexChanged\n (object sender, System.EventArgs e)\n{\n```
6	In this handler, retrieve the string selected in the combo box and dispose of any existing album.	```csharp\nstring albumFile\n = cmbxAlbum.SelectedItem.ToString();\n\nif (_album != null)\n _album.Dispose();\n```
7	Open the selected album file.	```csharp\n_album.Clear();\ntry\n{\n _album.Open(albumFile);\n```
8	If the album opens successfully, assign the album title as the caption text for the `DataGrid` control.	```csharp\n gridPhotoAlbum.CaptionText = _album.Title;\n}\n```
9	If the album cannot be opened, clear the album and assign an error message as the caption text.	```csharp\ncatch (Exception)\n{\n _album.Clear();\n gridPhotoAlbum.CaptionText\n = "Unable to open album";\n}\n```
10	Bind the contents of the resulting album to appear in the `DataGrid` control.	```csharp\ngridPhotoAlbum.SetDataBinding(null, null);\ngridPhotoAlbum.SetDataBinding(_album, null);\n}\n``` **Note:** Since the value of the `_album` field does not actually change, we force the data grid to reload the album data by binding it to `null` and then rebinding to our `PhotoAlbum` instance. We will do this a bit more elegantly later in the chapter.

This code opens the selected album and assigns the title of the album to appear in the caption area of the data grid. The collection of photographs in the album is bound to the contents of the data grid. The result is shown in figure 17.3.

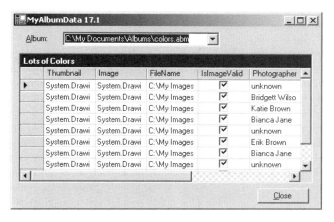

Figure 17.3
The DataGrid control supports two types of entries by default. Boolean values, such as the IsImageValid property, appear as check boxes. All other properties display the result of their ToString property as a text entry.

The caption area at the top of the control is assigned using the `CaptionText` property. In the figure, the title of the colors.abm album is "Lots of Colors" as is shown in the caption. The data source for the grid is assigned using the `SetDataBinding` method. This method has the following signature:

```
public void SetDataBinding(object dataSource, string dataMember);
```

The `dataSource` parameter is assigned to the `DataSource` property of the control, while the `dataMember` parameter is assigned to the `DataMember` property. In our application, the control recognizes our `PhotoAlbum` object as an `IList` interface containing a collection of `Photograph` objects. This is performed internally using the `GetType` method available on all `object` instances.

The properties of the `Photograph` object are determined internally using the members of the `System.Reflection` namespace. These properties are then used as the columns in the grid, and each `Photograph` in the album is presented as a row in the grid.

We will not discuss the `System.Reflection` namespace in detail here. This namespace permits .NET objects such as the `DataGrid` control to determine the type of object and members of that type at runtime. In this way our data grid can understand how the `PhotoAlbum` object is organized, and automatically create an appropriate grid structure.

Since the order of columns in the grid corresponds to the internal order of properties in the `PhotoAlbum` class, your columns might be ordered differently than is shown in figure 17.3. Also note that properties which only provide a `get` access method are treated as read-only, while properties with both a `get` and `set` access method are modifiable. As a result the Image and IsImageValid columns in our grid are read-only, while the Photographer and Notes columns can be modified. We will look at how to update the class with these changes shortly.

Back to our `SetDataBinding` method, there are a number of different classes that can serve as a source of data, depending on the type of C# interfaces they support. A summary of data sources for the `DataGrid` class is given in the following table.

Data sources for the data grid control

Interface	Usage	Notes
`IList`	A homogenous collection of objects. The first item in the list determines the type. The first property in that type is displayed as the only column when bound to a data grid.	This includes any simple array in C#, and all classes based on the `Array` object.
typed `IList`	A typed collection, such as our `PhotoAlbum` class. The type returned by the `Item` property is used as the assigned type, and all properties in this type can be displayed in a data grid. These can be bound to a data grid only at run time.	Most notably, classes derived from `CollectionBase`, such as our `PhotoAlbum` class. Other classes with an indexer of a fixed type will also work here.
`IList` and `IComponent`	With both interfaces available, the class may appear in Visual Studio .NET in the component tray and be bound to a data grid at design time.	Integrating a collection class with Visual Studio .NET is beyond the scope of this book. A control can be added to the Toolbox using the Customize entry in the Toolbox window's popup menu. This often requires members of the `System.Windows.Forms.Design` namespace to properly interact with the Windows Forms Designer and Property windows.
`IBindingList`	This interface permits two-way notification of changes, both from the control to the class and from the class to the control.	The `DataView` class in the `System.Data` namespace implements this interface, allowing a data grid to update its contents when the underlying database is modified.
`IEditableObject`	Classes implementing this interface are permitted to roll back, in a transaction-oriented manner,[a] changes made to an object.	The `DataRowView` class is a customized view of a row that supports transactional changes to the elements of the row.
`IDataErrorInfo`	Objects can offer custom error information that controls can bind to.	The `DataRowView` class supports this interface as well in order to provide appropriate feedback in a `DataGrid` control when an error occurs.

[a.] The term *transaction* indicates that a series of steps either fully completes or appears to never have happened. For example, when transferring money between bank accounts, you must debit the first account and then credit the second account. By making such a transfer transactional, you ensure that the first account is never debited without guaranteeing that the second account is also credited. Aborting an operation part-way through the required steps is said to *roll back*, or *undo*, the operation.

For our purposes, we will continue to use the typed `IList` interface supported by our `PhotoAlbum` class. Later in the chapter we will add support for the `IEditableObject` interface in order to properly save modifications made in our data grid.

The next section discusses various ways of customizing what appears in the grid.

17.2   DATA GRID CUSTOMIZATION

One of the obvious drawbacks of letting .NET do all the work in laying out the contents of a data grid is that we have no control over the selection and order of columns to appear in the grid. In this section we will look at how to customize the contents of a data grid for a particular data source using table and column styles. This will enable us to build the application shown in figure 17.4.

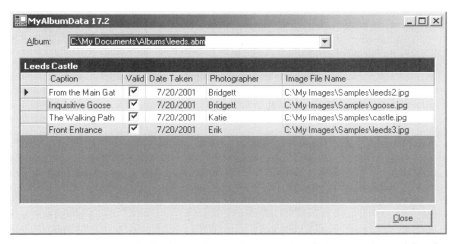

Figure 17.4   This data grid displays only certain properties of photographs, and the size and content of each column are somewhat customized compared with the application in the previous section.

In our current application we display a single kind of table, namely one based on the `PhotoAlbum` class. In general, the data displayed in a data grid may vary depending on the actions of the user. For example, just as our `ListView` control in chapter 14 displayed both albums and photographs, we could create an `AlbumCollection` class derived from `CollectionBase` to contain the set of albums located in a given directory. We could then use this class to display both album files and the contents of albums in our data grid.

More commonly, a data grid is filled with information from a database, which includes one or more tables. An employee database at a company might have one table containing department information, another table containing the employees assigned to each department, and another containing the projects each employee is assigned to. A single data grid could display all three types of tables based on a set of options, and it would be nice to customize the appearance of each type of table.

The `TableStyles` property in the `DataGrid` class supports this notion of configuring the appearance of multiple tables. This property contains a collection of `DataGridTableStyle` objects, each of which describes the configuration for a table that might be displayed by the grid. The `DataGridTableStyle` class, in turn, provides a `GridColumnStyles` property that contains a collection of `DataGridColumnStyle` objects. We will discuss each of these classes separately.

17.2.1 CUSTOMIZING TABLE STYLES

The `DataGridTableStyle` class permits a custom style for a specific type of table to be defined. Many of the members of this class are duplicates of similar members in the `DataGrid` class. The members of the active table style always override the default settings for the data grid. A summary of this class appears in .NET Table 17.2.

.NET Table 17.2 DataGridTableStyle class		
The `DataGridTableStyle` class represents the style in which to display a particular table that can appear in a `DataGrid` control. It configures not only the general properties for the table but also the individual columns that should appear in the table. This class is part of the `System.Windows.Forms` namespace, and inherits from the `System.ComponentModel.Component` class.		
Public Properties	AllowSorting	Gets or sets whether sorting is allowed on the grid when this `DataGridTableStyle` is used.
	AlternatingBack-Color	Gets or sets the background color for alternating rows in the grid when this `DataGridTableStyle` is used.
	DataGrid	Gets or sets the DataGrid control containing this style.
	GridColumn-Styles	Gets or sets the collection of `DataGridColumnStyle` objects to use for the grid when this style is used.
	LinkColor	Gets or sets the color of link text to use in the grid when this style is used.
	MappingName	Gets or sets the name used to associate this table style with a specific data source. For a data source based on an `IList` interface, the name of the list is specified, as in `myList.GetType().Name`. For a data source based on a `DataSet` instance, a valid table name in the data set should be specified.
	ReadOnly	Gets or sets whether columns can be edited in the grid when this style is used.
	RowHeader-Width	Gets or sets the width of row headers in the grid when this style is used.
Public Methods	BeginEdit	Requests an edit operation on a row in the grid.
	EndEdit	Requests an end to an edit operation in the grid.
	ResetBackColor	Resets the `BackColor` property to its default value. A number of other reset methods exist with a similar purpose.
Public Events	AllowSorting-Changed	Occurs when the AllowSorting property value changes. A number of other changed events exist with a similar purpose.

There are two keys to understanding the `DataGridTableStyle` class. The first is the `MappingName` property. When a new source of data is assigned to a `DataGrid` control, the list of table styles is examined to locate a style whose `MappingName` setting matches the name of the table. If one is found, then that style is used to display the grid. If no match is found, then the default settings for the grid control are used. It is an error to assign identical mapping names to multiple styles within the same data grid.

The second key to understanding this class is the `GridColumnStyles` property. This property is a collection of `DataGridColumnStyle` objects and specifies the selection and order of columns to display in the grid. If the `GridColumnStyles` property is `null`, then the default set of columns is displayed.

We can use the `DataGridTableStyle` class to modify the appearance of our `DataGrid` control when a `PhotoAlbum` is displayed. We will make the very simple change of providing an alternating background color for the table. The steps required are presented in the following table.

Set the version number of the MyAlbumData application to 17.2

	PROVIDE A CUSTOM TABLE STYLE WHEN A PHOTOALBUM IS DISPLAYED	
	Action	**Result**
1	In the MainForm.cs code window, create a table style instance in the `OnLoad` method. **Note:** A table style can also be created in the [Design] window by clicking on the **...** button in the `TableStyles` property. Here we elect to create the table style by hand.	```protected override void OnLoad(EventArgs e)\n{\n . . .\n // Table style for PhotoAlbum data source\n DataGridTableStyle albumStyle\n = new DataGridTableStyle();```
2	Configure the new style for a `PhotoAlbum` table with an alternating background color of `LightGray`.	```albumStyle.MappingName = "PhotoAlbum";\nalbumStyle.AlternatingBackColor\n = Color.LightGray;\nalbumStyle.RowHeaderWidth = 15;```
3	Assign the new style to the existing `DataGrid` control.	```// Assign the table style to the data grid\ngridPhotoAlbum.TableStyles.Add(albumStyle);\n}```

This very simple change causes the application to display as is shown in figure 17.5. Of course, the `AlternatingBackColor` and `RowHeaderWidth` properties are available in the `DataGrid` class and can be set explicitly for this class. Assigning them in a table style uses these properties only when a matching table name is displayed, in this case a `PhotoAlbum` object.

Note that our choice of light gray may not work very well with some user's desktop colors. You can use an alternate color if you prefer, or a system color such as `System-Colors.ControlLight`. In your own applications, make sure you carefully select color choices for settings such as this, and use system settings where possible. Hard-coding a specific color such as we do here is not typically recommended, since different users may configure their desktops to appear using different sets of conflicting colors.

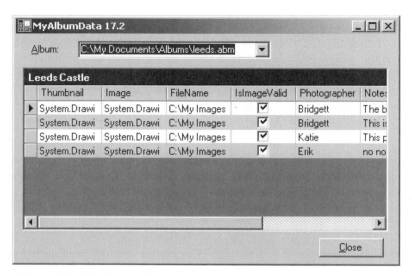

Figure 17.5 This figure shows an alternating background color of light gray to present a ledger-like appearance.

Note that the assignment of the `MappingName` is critical here. Using a name other than `PhotoAlbum` would have no effect on our table since the name of the table would not match the mapping name of the table style.

Of course, our table still uses the default set of columns since we have not yet assigned any column styles to the `GridColumnStyles` property. Customizing the columns in our table is our next topic.

17.2.2   CUSTOMIZING COLUMN STYLES

Now that we know how to customize the properties of a table, let's look at how to customize the columns that appear in the table. The `DataGridColumnStyle` class is used for this purpose, and is summarized in .NET Table 17.3. This is an abstract class from which various types of columns are derived. The .NET Framework currently provides classes to represent boolean and text columns, namely the `Data-GridBoolColumn` and `DataGridTextBoxColumn` classes.

The DataGridColumnStyle class represents a specific column that should appear when a specific style table is displayed in a DataGrid control. This object is typically contained within a DataGridTableStyle object, and indicates the position and style for the corresponding column when a table of the specified type is displayed. This class is part of the System.Windows.Forms namespace, and inherits from the System.ComponentModel.Component class.

A DataGridColumnStyle object cannot be instantiated, as this is an abstract class. The DataGridBoolColumn and DataGridTextBoxColumn classes derived from this class are used to represent a column of boolean or textual values, respectively. Custom column styles derived from this class may also be created.

Public Properties	Alignment	Gets or sets the alignment of data within the column.
	DataGridTableStyle	Gets the table style containing this column style.
	HeaderText	Gets or sets the header text for this column when the associated table style is used.
	MappingName	Gets or sets the name used to associate this column style with a specific data value in an associated data source. For an IList data source, a valid property name in the list should be specified. For a DataSet data source, a valid column name in the associated table should be provided.
	NullText	Gets or sets the text that is displayed when the column contains a null reference.
	PropertyDescriptor	Gets or sets the PropertyDescriptor object containing attributes of the data displayed by this column style.
	ReadOnly	Gets or sets whether to treat the column as read-only.
	Width	Gets or sets the width in pixels for this column.
Public Methods	ResetHeaderText	Resets the HeaderText property to its default value, which is a null reference.
Public Events	AlignmentChanged	Occurs when the Alignment property for the column style changes.
	FontChanged	Occurs when the column's font changes. A number of other changed events exist with a similar purpose.

The order in which columns are assigned to a table style determines the order in which they will appear in the data grid. We will use this feature to extend the table style we created for our form to display only a subset of the available columns.

The code to make this change is detailed in the following table. Note that this code uses the DataGridBoolColumn and DataGridTextBoxColumn classes. We will discuss these classes in more detail in a moment.

	CUSTOMIZE THE COLUMNS TO APPEAR IN THE DATA GRID	
	Action	**Result**
1	Locate the `OnLoad` method in the MainForm.cs code window.	```protected override void OnLoad(EventArgs e)
{
. . .```
2	Create a column style for the `Caption` property. **How-to** Use the `DataGridTextBoxCol-umn` class and assign the `MappingName` to match the `Caption` property name.	```// Table style for PhotoAlbum data source
    . . .

// Column styles for PhotoAlbum source
DataGridColumnStyle captionCol
    = new DataGridTextBoxColumn();
captionCol.MappingName = "Caption";
captionCol.HeaderText = "Caption";
captionCol.Width = 100;``` |
| 3 | Create column styles for the `IsImageValid`, `DateTaken`, `Photographer`, and `FileName` properties as well.

How-to
Use the class specified for each property in the following table.

Column Style Classes
<table><tr><th>Property</th><th>Class</th></tr><tr><td>IsImageValid</td><td>BoolColumn</td></tr><tr><td>DateTaken</td><td>TextBoxColumn</td></tr><tr><td>Photographer</td><td>TextBoxColumn</td></tr><tr><td>FileName</td><td>TextBoxColumn</td></tr></table> | ```DataGridColumnStyle validCol
    = new DataGridBoolColumn();
validCol.MappingName = "IsImageValid";
validCol.HeaderText = "Valid?";
validCol.ReadOnly = true;
validCol.Width = 30;

DataGridTextBoxColumn dateCol
    = new DataGridTextBoxColumn();
dateCol.MappingName = "DateTaken";
dateCol.HeaderText = "Date Taken";
dateCol.Alignment
    = HorizontalAlignment.Center;
dateCol.Format = "d";
dateCol.Width = 80;

DataGridColumnStyle photographerCol
    = new DataGridTextBoxColumn();
photographerCol.MappingName ="Photographer";
photographerCol.HeaderText = "Photographer";
photographerCol.Width = 100;

DataGridColumnStyle fileNameCol
    = new DataGridTextBoxColumn();
fileNameCol.MappingName = "FileName";
fileNameCol.HeaderText = "Image File Name";
fileNameCol.ReadOnly = true;
fileNameCol.Width = 200;``` |
| 4 | Add the new column styles to the `GridColumnStyles` property of the existing table style object.

How-to
Use the `AddRange` method to add all column styles at once. | ```// Add the column styles to the table style
albumStyle.GridColumnStyles.AddRange(
    new DataGridColumnStyle[] {
        captionCol,
        validCol,
        dateCol,
        photographerCol,
        fileNameCol
    });

// Assign the table style to the data grid
gridPhotoAlbum.TableStyles.Add(albumStyle);
}``` |

This adds the new column styles to the existing table style object. When a data source of type `PhotoAlbum` is displayed, the new styles specify which columns should appear and how they should look. For example, the column style based on the `IsImageValid` property is as follows:

```
DataGridColumnStyle validCol = new DataGridBoolColumn();
validCol.MappingName = "IsImageValid";
validCol.HeaderText = "Valid?";
validCol.ReadOnly = true;
validCol.Width = 30;
```

This column will appear as read-only with a width of 30 pixels. The column header is modified to use the string `"Valid?"` rather than the property name. This column is our only column based on the `DataGridBoolColumn` class. This class appears as a check box, which is checked only if the corresponding value is `true`. In fact, the displayed check box is a three-state check box in order to support a `null` state in addition to `true` and `false`.

The remaining column styles are all based on the `DataGridTextBoxColumn` class. A summary of this class appears in .NET Table 17.4. Of particular note is the date column, which uses the `Format` property in this class to display the date value as a short date string. The `Alignment` property from the base class is also assigned for this column in order to center the displayed date.

```
DataGridTextBoxColumn dateCol = new DataGridTextBoxColumn();
dateCol.MappingName = "DateTaken";
dateCol.HeaderText = "Date Taken";
dataCol.Alignment = HorizontalAlignment.Center;
dateCol.Format = "d";
dateCol.Width = 80;
```

Compile and run the application to see your code in action. The application should appear as in figure 17.4 at the start of this section.

.NET Table 17.4   DataGridTextBoxColumn class

The `DataGridTextBoxColumn` class represents a data grid column style for string data. This class *hosts*, or manages within a cell of the `DataGrid` control, a `TextBox` instance to support editing of string values within the table. This class is part of the `System.Windows.Forms` namespace, and inherits from the `DataGridColumnStyle` class. See .NET Table 17.3 for a list of members inherited from this class.

Public Properties	Format	Gets or sets a string specifying how text should be formatted within the cell.
	FormatInfo	Gets or sets an `IFormatProvider` interface that is used to interpret the `Format` setting.
	TextBox	Gets the `TextBox` object hosted by this column style. This object is an instance of the `DataGridTextBox` class, which is derived from `TextBox`.

The `DataGridBoolColumn` class has an alternate set of properties appropriate for boolean columns. Check out the .NET documentation for detailed information on this class.

TRY IT!   Modify the `MappingName` setting for the table style to use a name other than the `"PhotoAlbum"` string. Verify that the `DataGrid` displays the album data in the default format shown in section 17.1.

If you are feeling ambitious, create the `AlbumCollection` class mentioned earlier in the chapter. This class should derive from the `CollectionBase` class and encapsulate a set of `PhotoAlbum` objects. You can copy much of the code from the `PhotoAlbum` class implementation by modifying the use of `Photograph` to use `PhotoAlbum` instead. The default constructor should use the `PhotoAlbum.DefaultDir` value. You can also add a constructor that accepts a directory name. Modify the MyAlbumData application to use this class to display a collection of `PhotoAlbum` objects. Create a second `DataGridTableStyle` object to configure how an `AlbumCollection` object should look as opposed to our style for the `PhotoAlbum` object. Add this new style to the `TableStyles` property for the grid, and verify that the correct table style displays based on the type of data source assigned to the control.

As we mentioned earlier, some of our columns are configured as read-only while some of them can be edited. You can see this in the existing application by clicking on an editable cell and modifying its contents. Unfortunately, changing the contents of a cell has no effect at the moment since we are not saving the modified values in our album file. Saving such changes properly requires the use of the `IEditableObject` interface, which is our next topic.

17.3   *EDITABLE OBJECTS*

So far we have bound a `PhotoAlbum` object to our `DataGrid` control and customized the table and columns that appear in the grid. At the moment, any changes made by the user to the `PhotoAlbum` object are discarded when the displayed album changes or the application exits. This is not really desirable, so let's discuss how to properly save changes made to the grid.

There are three areas for discussion here. The first is the way in which data grids support editing of their contents. The second is how to enable such support in the `Photograph` objects displayed by our table. The third is how to actually save the data into an album file once such editing is possible. We will discuss each topic separately.

17.3.1   THE IEDITABLEOBJECT INTERFACE

The editing of rows in a grid is handled by the `DataGrid` control directly using the discovered properties associated with our `PhotoAlbum` object. When the user changes a caption, the `Caption` property is called automatically by the grid to update the corresponding `Photograph` object with the new value. Similarly, when the photographer is changed, the `Photographer` property is called. The control even handles the `DateTaken` property gracefully so that an invalid date value is never assigned to the object.

The problem is that our updated `Photograph` objects are never saved in the corresponding album file. A quick and easy solution would be to forcibly save the album whenever a new album is selected. For example, the `SelectedIndexChanged` event handler could be altered as follows, with the modified lines in bold.

```
private void cmbxAlbum_SelectedIndexChanged
  (object sender, System.EventArgs e)
{
  string albumFile = cmbxAlbum.SelectedItem.ToString();

  // Forcibly save previous album - not our approach
  if (_album != null)
  {
    _album.Save();
    _album.Dispose();
  }

  _album.Clear();
  try
  . . .
}
```

This would ensure that the album is always saved, even if the user does not wish to save the changes. Not the best solution, although it does work. A better solution would only save the album if it has been modified, and give the user an opportunity to elect not to save the changes. In order to do this we must know when a `Photograph` has been changed, and then use this information when a new album is selected.

Implementing this change requires the `IEditableObject` interface, summarized in .NET Table 17.5. This interface defines a mechanism for modifying an object in a transactional manner, so that either all changes to an object are made or none of the changes are made. This is especially important in databases, where the fields of a row may be dependent on one another, or in multi-user environments, where different users may wish to update the same object at the same time. For example, in a customer order database, you would not want to modify the shipping method without also updating the shipping costs. The `IEditableObject` interface is used to ensure that this happens.

As an example, the `DataRowView` class in the `System.Data` namespace supports the `IEditableObject` interface to ensure transactional update to the rows in a database. We are not building a database here, but we would like to update the `PhotoAlbum` object in a consistent manner. The `IEditableObject` interface provides a way for us to do this over the course of this section.

The IEditableObject interface represents an interface for performing transactional operations on an object. This interface is used by various .NET classes such as the Windows Forms DataGrid control to allow an object to track and enforce transactional behavior. This interface is part of the System.ComponentModel namespace.

Public Methods	BeginEdit	Initiates an edit operation on an object.
	CancelEdit	Discards any changes made since the last edit operation began, including any new objects added to the list with the IBindingList.AddNew method.
	EndEdit	Finalizes an edit operation. Any changes made since the last edit operation began are made permanent in the object, including any new objects added with the IBindingList.AddNew method.

17.3.2   SUPPORTING THE IEDITABLEOBJECT INTERFACE

Looking at the Photograph class, there are four modifiable properties. These are the Caption, Photographer, DateTaken, and Notes properties. As a result, these are the properties we need to consider in our IEditableObject implementation. The following table summarizes the implementation of the required methods:

Implementation of IEditableObject methods for the Photograph class

Method	Implementation notes
BeginEdit	Should record the existing values of the modifiable properties and place the photo in an editing state.
CancelEdit	Should reinstate the recorded values from BeginEdit, and place the photo in a nonediting state.
EndEdit	Should discard the recorded values from BeginEdit, note if the photo has been changed, and place the photo in a nonediting state.

Our implementation will not be something you would present at a computer science convention. In particular, a Photograph object can be modified without using our edit methods, which kind of defeats the whole purpose of the interface. The code presented here is intended to illustrate the behavior of these methods and indicate how they are used by the DataGrid control.

With this excuse in mind, let's see how to support the editable object interface for our Photograph class.

Set the version number of the MyPhotoAlbum library to 17.3.

	SUPPORT THE IEDITABLEOBJECT INTERFACE IN THE PHOTOGRAPH CLASS	
	Action	**Result**
1	In the Photograph.cs code window, indicate that we will use members of the System.ComponentModel namespace.	`using System.ComponentModel;`
2	Add IEditableObject to the list of supported interfaces for this class.	```public class Photograph : IDisposable, IEditableObject { . . . ```
3	Add internal fields to track when the object is in an editable state or has been modified.	```private bool _modified; private bool _editing;```
4	Initialize these fields in the constructor.	```public Photograph(string fileName) { . . . _modified = false; _editing = false; }```
5	Reset these values when the photograph is saved into a StreamWriter object.	```public void Write(StreamWriter sw) { . . . _modified = false; _editing = false; }```
6	Add internal fields to record the existing values of the four modifiable properties.	```private string _editCaption; private string _editPhotographer; private DateTime _editDateTaken; private string _editNotes;```
7	Implement the BeginEdit method. **How-to** If editing is not already enabled, record the current values and enable editing. **Note:** Ideally, we would permit nesting of these calls. In this example we will avoid this additional complexity.	```public void BeginEdit() { if (!_editing) { _editCaption = Caption; _editDateTaken = DateTaken; _editPhotographer = Photographer; _editNotes = Notes; _editing = true; } }```
8	Implement the CancelEdit method. **How-to** If editing is enabled, restore the recorded values and disable editing.	```public void CancelEdit() { if (_editing) { Caption = _editCaption; Photographer = _editPhotographer; DateTaken = _editDateTaken; Notes = _editNotes; _editing = false; } }```

EDITABLE OBJECTS

	Action	Result

9	Implement the EndEdit method.
	
	How-to
	If editing is enabled, record whether the data has been modified and disable editing.
		``csharp
		public void EndEdit()
		{
		  if (_editing)
		  {
		    _modified |= ((Caption != _editCaption)
		      || (Photographer != _editPhotographer)
		      || (DateTaken != _editDateTaken)
		      || (Notes != _editNotes));
		    _editing = false;
		  }
		}```

10	Also add a HasEdits property to report whether the object has been modified.	```csharp
		public bool HasEdits
		{
		  get { return _modified; }
		}```

The IEditableObject interface is now fully implemented. Another useful change in our library is the ability to identify if a PhotoAlbum, and not just a Photograph, has been modified. We can do this by continuing the previous steps to add a HasEdits method in the PhotoAlbum class.

ADD A HASEDITS PROPERTY TO THE PHOTOALBUM CLASS		
	Action	Result

11	In the PhotoAlbum.cs code window, Implement a HasEdits method in this class.
	
	How-to
	Use the Photograph.HasEdits method to determine the appropriate result.
		``csharp
		public bool HasEdits
		{
		  get
		  {
		    foreach (Photograph p in this)
		    {
		      if (p.HasEdits)
		        return true;
		    }
		
		    // No edits found
		    return false;
		  }
		}```

The MyPhotoAlbum library is ready to go. Make sure the library compiles with no errors. The next step is to make use of these changes in our MyAlbumData application. This is taken up in the next section.

17.3.3 USING EDITABLE OBJECTS

Typically, you do not actually use the editable object methods directly. These are used internally by Windows Forms as required for the task at hand. In this case, our Data-Grid control automatically recognizes that our PhotoAlbum object supports this interface, and calls BeginEdit whenever a user initiates a change to a row in the grid. If a user cancels an edit by pressing the Esc key, then CancelEdit is called. When the

CHAPTER 17 DATA BINDING

user finishes an edit by pressing the Enter key or selecting an alternate row, the EndEdit method is invoked. The EndEdit method makes the changes to the object permanent within the object itself.

In most applications, there is an operation or class that coordinates the in-memory version of an object with the permanent version of an object. In our application, the in-memory version is our PhotoAlbum class, while the permanent version is our album file. The Save method updates the album file with the version in memory, while the Open method fills the in-memory version with the recorded version in the album file.

This is true in the System.Data namespace as well. While we have avoided discussing this namespace in any real depth, it is useful to understand how the classes in this namespace relate to our discussion. The abstract DataAdaptor class is the coordinator between the in-memory version of the database, typically a DataSet instance, and the permanent version is an external database. The DataAdaptor class provides a Fill method to populate a DataSet with the external values, and an Update method to save modifications in the DataSet into the external database.

For our purposes, we have provided the HasEdits method in our in-memory objects in order to identify whether any changes must be saved into the album file. We can do this in the SelectedIndexChanged event handler before the new album is bound to our data grid.

The following table details the steps required to save our PhotoAlbum instance into its associated album file:

Set the version number of the MyAlbumData application to 17.3.

SAVE A MODIFIED ALBUM		
	Action	**Result**
1	In the MainForm.cs window, create a new SaveChanges method to store any changes to the displayed album into the album file. **How-to** a. If the album has been modified, prompt the user to see if he or she wishes to save the changes. b. If yes, then save the album in the existing album file.	```private void SaveChanges()
{
if (_album.HasEdits)
{
DialogResult result = MessageBox.Show(
"Do you wish to save your changes "
+ "to the album \'" + _album.Title
+ "\'?",
"Save Changes?",
MessageBoxButtons.YesNo,
MessageBoxIcon.Question);
if (result == DialogResult.Yes)
_album.Save();
}
}```

	Action	Result

2	Use this new method when the user selects a new album in the `ComboBox` control.	```csharp
		private void cmbxAlbum_SelectedIndexChanged
		  (object sender, System.EventArgs e)
		{
		  string albumFile
		    = cmbxAlbum.SelectedItem.ToString();
		
		  if (_album != null)
		  {
		    SaveChanges();
		    _album.Dispose();
		  }
		
		  _album.Clear();
		  try
		  . . .
		}```

3	Also make sure any changes are saved when the application exits.	```csharp
		protected override void OnClosing
		  (CancelEventArgs e)
		{
		  SaveChanges();
		  base.OnClosing(e);
		}```

With these modifications, our edits are now saved. Compile and run to verify that the application works as advertised.

More .NET Additional information on the `DataGrid` control is available in the .NET documentation and in various sample programs freely available on the Internet. One such example is the CdrCatalog program built by Andrew Skowronski that is available at http://cdrcatalog.sourceforge.net/. This program manages offline media, such as a collection of recordable compact discs, and makes use of a number of Windows Forms classes in addition to the `DataGrid` control. The data source used by this application is a `DataSet` object loaded from a local XML file.

17.4 SIMPLE DATA BINDING

Binding data to a data grid is referred to as *complex data binding*, since multiple values are bound to a single control. Complex data binding also refers to binding objects to a list control, such as a list box or combo box. For example, if we had actually implemented the `AlbumCollection` class I keep mentioning to contain an array of `PhotoAlbum` objects, then the line to assign the `DataSource` for our combo box could instead be written as:

```csharp
cmbxAlbum.DataSource = myAlbumCollection;
cmbxAlbum.DataMember = "FileName";
```

This would display the collection of `PhotoAlbum` objects in the `myAlbumCollection` variable in the `cmbxAlbum` combo box, using the `FileName` property as the name to display. The result would be the same as that which currently appears in our application. This type of binding to a list control can also be done with database objects, such as binding the entries in a `ListBox` control to the set of customer names found in one column of a database table.

Simple data binding is used for binding single property values to a specific data source. This type of binding is supported by the `Control` class directly, and is therefore inherited by and available in all controls in Windows Forms. The concepts and techniques for so-called simple data binding are fairly identical to those we have already discussed for the `DataGrid` control.

In this section we will alter our application to permit some simple data binding to a photo album. We will see how to perform simple binding; update bound controls dynamically, including the image associated with a photograph; and save changes to bound controls.

17.4.1 ALTERING THE MYALBUMDATA APPLICATION

Before we get into the details of exactly how simple data binding is performed, let's whip through some changes to our MyAlbumData application in preparation for this discussion. The change we will make is to place our existing `DataGrid` control within a `TabPage` object, and add a new tab to display the `Photograph` information for an album one photo at a time. Figure 17.6 shows the modified application we will build throughout this and the next few sections.

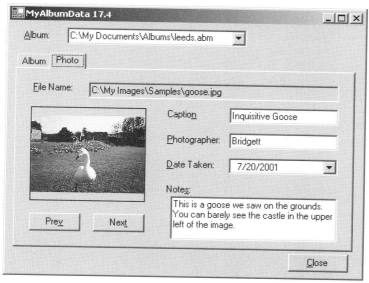

Figure 17.6   These controls on the Photo tab are bound to their corresponding values in a Photograph object.

In this section we will simply move our existing `DataGrid` control into an Album tab, and create a Photo tab containing the controls shown in the figure. The following steps implement this change.

Set the version number of the MyAlbumData application to 17.4.

	CREATE THE CONTROLS WITHIN A TAB CONTROL OBJECT	
	Action	**Result**
1	In the MainForm.cs [Design] window, alter the `Size` property for the form to be 450×350.	
2	Move the existing `DataGrid` control to exist within a tab page.	

How-to

a. Create a tab control containing two tab pages.

b. Set their properties as shown.

c. Move the data grid into the Album tab page, and set its `Dock` property to `Fill`.

Settings

Control	Property	Value
TabControl	(Name)	tcMain
	Anchor	Top, Bottom, Left, Right
TabPage (Album)	(Name)	tabAlbum
	Text	Album
TabPage (Photo)	(Name)	tabPhoto
	Text	Photo

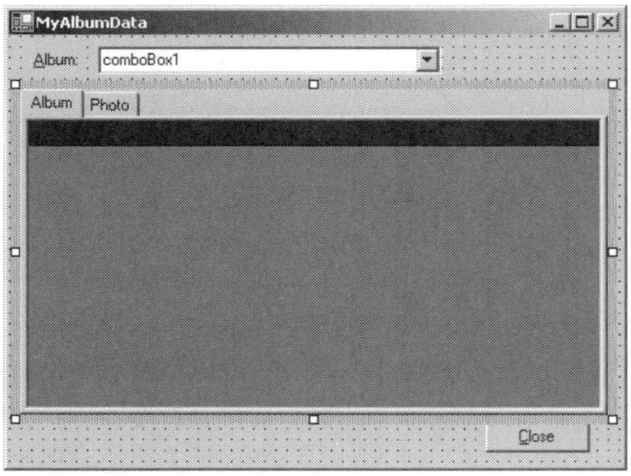

	Action	Result
3	Create and position the controls for the Photo tab page as shown in the graphic.	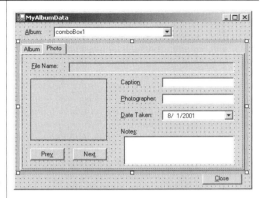

Note: In the rather long Settings table here, the `Label` controls are not shown. For these controls, use the default name, the text shown in the graphic, and the same `Anchor` property as the related control.

Also note that all `TextBox` controls should have their Text property set to an empty string.

Note: When assigning the `Anchor` property, you may find it easier to first create and position the controls and then use the following technique:

a. Select a group of related controls by dragging the mouse over a region of the form.

b. Assign the `Anchor` property for all controls at once.

Settings

Control	Property	Value
FileName	(Name)	txtFileName
	ReadOnly	True
PictureBox	(Name)	pboxPhoto
	Anchor	Top, Bottom, Left, Right
	BorderStyle	FixedSingle
Prev	(Name)	btnPrev
	Anchor	Bottom, Left
	Text	Pre&v
Next	(Name)	btnNext
	Anchor	Bottom, Right
	Text	Nex&t
Caption	(Name)	txtCaption
	Anchor	Top, Right
Photo-grapher	(Name)	txtPhoto-grapher
	Anchor	Top, Right
Date Taken	(Name)	dtpDateTaken
	Anchor	Top, Right
	Format	Short
Notes	(Name)	txtNotes
	Anchor	Top, Bottom, Right
	Multiline	True

	Action	Result
4	Assign the tab order for the controls within the Photo tab page as is shown in the graphic.	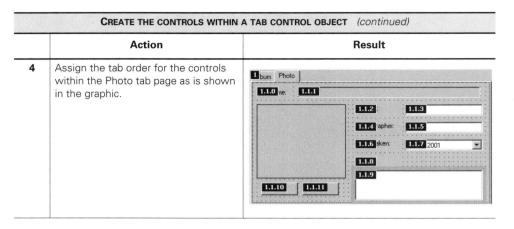

That took a bit of work. As we mentioned earlier in the book, you can reduce the amount of time spent drawing forms in Visual Studio by sketching out your controls on paper before using Visual Studio. While not illustrated in these pages, I really did sketch the Photo tab page by hand before creating this page in Visual Studio .NET.

With our controls defined, we are ready for our data binding discussion.

17.4.2 PERFORMING SIMPLE BINDING

The binding of controls to data involves four distinct roles, each with a corresponding class. These correspond to the work performed by the .NET Framework on behalf of bound controls, namely tracking which data has been bound to which control, managing a bound data source, tracking specific bindings to a control, and managing the actual bindings. A summary of these roles, along with the Windows Forms class and property related to these roles, is outlined in the following table:

Roles required for simple data binding

Role	Class	Accessing from Control class
Tacking bound data	BindingContext	`BindingContext` property

Managing a bound data source	BindingManagerBase	Index into `BindingContext` collection:
		`BindingContext[ source ]`
		`BindingContext[ source, member ]`

Managing bindings	ControlBindingsCollection	`DataBindings` property
Tracking a binding	Binding	Index into `DataBindings` collection: `DataBindings[ property ]`

We will discuss these classes and properties in more detail as we build our example. As a brief explanation, the `BindingContext` class manages a collection of `Binding-ManagerBase` objects. While any control can create an instance of this class in its `BindingContext` property, the `Form` class creates one automatically to serve as the default container for all data bound to the form. In our case, we will simply use the default `BindingContext` for our form, and not discuss this class in too much detail.

A single `BindingManagerBase` object exists for each bound data object. In our case, with a single `PhotoAlbum` object bound to our controls, our application will have a single `BindingManagerBase` created. For an object with multiple members, such as a database with multiple tables, a `BindingManagerBase` will exist for each member bound to a control.

A `ControlBindingsCollection` object contains the collection of actual bindings created for a control. The `DataBindings` property in the `Control` class contains the collection of these binding objects.

Each binding object is a `Binding` class instance. The `Binding` class permits any property of any control to be bound to any column or property of a data source. We will see this in our application shortly.

Let's discuss the previous table from the bottom up, beginning with the `Binding` class. Typically, it is not necessary to access this class directly. Even so, it is likely useful to see the properties that make up each individual binding, so a summary of this class appears in .NET Table 17.6. Note that the possible data sources for simple data binding correspond to those shown earlier in the chapter for the `DataGrid` control.

As you can see, this class is fairly generic, and permits any property to be bound to pretty much anything. The `Format` and `Parse` events can even be used to specify exactly how this binding will take place when converting between the data source and the control's property.

If you are thoroughly confused at this point, don't fret. We will lay this out step by step for our application, which should aid your understanding. Let's start with a summary of exactly what should be bound to what. The following table shows our controls, the property in each control that we would like to bind, and the member of the `Photograph` object within our `PhotoAlbum` data source that can provide this value.

Details of our initial data binding approach

Control name	Control property to bind	Photograph property for binding source
txtFileName	Text	FileName
txtCaption	Text	Caption
dtpDateTaken	Value	DateTaken
txtNotes	Text	Notes
pboxPhoto	Image	Image

The `Binding` class represents a simple data binding between a data source entry and a Windows Form control. The `Binding` instances defined for a control are contained by the `DataBindings` property of that control. This class is part of the `System.Windows.Forms` namespace.

Public Constructor	Binding	Create a new `Binding` instance. This has the following signature:
		
		`Binding(string propertyName,`
		`        object dataSource,`
		`        string dataMember);`

Public Properties	BindingManagerBase	Gets the `BindingManagerBase` class instance for the data source used by this binding.
	BindingMemberInfo	Gets the `BindingMemberInfo` structure containing information about the data member used by this binding. This value is created using the `dataMember` value passed to the `Binding` constructor. For a database source, this indicates the table and column that should be bound. For an `IList` source, this indicates the property member in the contained object that should be bound.
	Control	Gets the control that is the subject of this binding.
	DataSource	Gets the data source used by this binding, taken from the corresponding value passed to the `Binding` constructor.
	IsBinding	Gets whether this binding is currently active.
	PropertyName	Gets or sets the property name of the control that is the subject of this binding. This is taken from the corresponding value passed to the `Binding` constructor.
Public Events	Format	Occurs when the value from the data source must be processed, or formatted, and assigned to the bound property in the control.
	Parse	Occurs when the value from the control must be processed, or parsed, and assigned to the appropriate entry in the data source.

So let's do this. We already have a `PhotoAlbum` field in our `MainForm` class, so we can bind these controls in our `OnLoad` method, as shown in the following table.

	Action	Result
1	Locate the `OnLoad` override in the MainForm.cs code window.	```protected override void OnLoad(EventArgs e)``` `{` `. . .`

2	Assign data bindings to the controls on the Photo tab page.
	
	Note: Of critical importance here is the fact that we use the same `PhotoAlbum` instance throughout the life of our application. Since we bind these controls as the main form is loaded, the value of our album cannot change unless we also rebind the controls to the new value.
		```// Bind data for the Photo tab``` `txtFileName.DataBindings.`
		`   Add("Text", _album, "FileName");`
		`txtCaption.DataBindings.`
		`   Add("Text", _album, "Caption");`
		`txtPhotographer.DataBindings.`
		`   Add("Text", _album, "Photographer");`
		`dtpDateTaken.DataBindings.`
		`   Add("Value", _album, "DateTaken");`
		
		`txtNotes.DataBindings.`
		`   Add("Text", _album, "Notes");`
		`pboxPhoto.DataBindings.`
		`   Add("Image", _album, "Image");`
		`}`

The controls are now bound to the appropriate properties of the `Photograph` objects contained by the `PhotoAlbum` instance. Take, for example, the `DateTimePicker` control. We bind the `Value` property of this control to the `DateTaken` property of the active `Photograph` object in the `_album` collection with the following code:

```
dtpDateTaken.DataBindings.Add("Value", _album, "DateTaken");
```

The `DataBindings` collection supports the standard `Add` method to place a `Binding` object in the list. We could have created the `Binding` object explicitly with the following code:

```
Binding theBind = new Binding("Value", _album, "DateTaken");
dtpDateTaken.DataBindings.Add(theBind);
```

Instead, since we do not need the `Binding` instance here, we used an override for the `Add` method that accepts the constructor parameters for this object explicitly.

Note that the `Photograph.DateTaken` property is a `DateTime` value, which happens to match the type of the `DateTimePicker.Value` property. In fact the type of all our bindings, including the `Image` property for the `PictureBox` control, matches the bound property in the `Photograph` object. The .NET Framework will attempt to convert between the binding value and the bound value, but in our case conversion is not necessary. As we mentioned earlier, the `Format` and `Parse` events can be used to specify the conversion explicitly.

It is worth mentioning once again that any property of a control can be bound. For example, we could add a `MatteColor` property to our `Photograph` object, and bind the background color, the `BackColor` property, of the `PictureBox` or even the `TabPage` itself to this color. We will not do this here, and I should probably caution you not to get too carried away with such features both in your data and in your applications. In some situations, such as a picture frame ordering interface, this type of feature could be very useful.

This code will compile and run and show a result similar to figure 17.7. Some work is still required to update the controls when the album changes or the Next or Prev button is pressed, and the `PictureBox` control has a size mode of `Normal` so that only the upper left corner of the image is shown. We will address these issues as we go along.

Before we do, it is also worth mentioning here that Visual Studio .NET provides direct graphical support for data binding when using a database or other class that supports both the `IList` and `IComponent` interfaces. In particular, the values from a database can be bound to a control during design time using the (DataBindings) setting in the Properties window. This is beyond the scope of this book, but worth keeping in mind as you develop more complex applications.

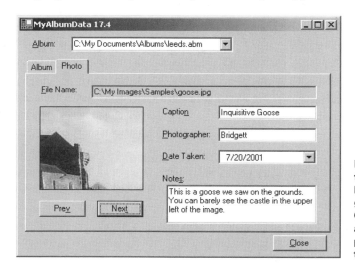

Figure 17.7 In this version, the controls automatically bind to the active Photograph selected in the Data-Grid control. Note that only a portion of the image appears in the PictureBox control here.

17.4.3 UPDATING DATA BOUND CONTROLS

With our controls bound, our next task is to properly update them as the selected album changes. We also need to hook up the Next and Prev buttons so that they display the next or previous photo from the current album. Doing this requires the `BindingManagerBase` class.

A summary of this class appears in .NET Table 17.7. An instance of this class is created for each data source active in an application, and stored in a `BindingContext` instance associated with a `Control` object. Normally, the `BindingContext` created for the `Form` object is used, although a `BindingContext` can be attached to any `Control`. For example, a `BindingContext` can be created for a `GroupBox`, `Panel`, or other parent control to contain the data sources for all controls within the container.

As indicated in the table, the BindingManagerBase class is an abstract class. When a control is bound, the framework automatically creates the appropriate subclass of this object. A CurrencyManager instance is created for objects that support the IList interface, while a PropertyManager is created for single-value objects.

Two of the more commonly used members of the BindingManagerBase class are the Current and Position properties. The Current property retrieves the object currently used to bind controls, while the Position property manages the index of this object. In our application, this means that the Current property retrieves the Photograph currently displayed by our controls, while the Position property is used to assign or retrieve the index of the current Photograph object.

.NET Table 17.7   BindingManagerBase class

The BindingManagerBase class represents a data source bound to one or more controls within a Windows Forms control. This class enables synchronization of all controls with a property bound to the associated data source. This class is part of the System.Windows.Forms namespace.

This class is abstract and cannot be instantiated. The CurrencyManager class is used for all data sources that support the IList interface, while the PropertyManager class is used for all single-value data sources. Also note that most of the members listed here are abstract as well, and must be overridden by a derived class.

Public Properties	Bindings	Gets the collection of bindings managed by this object.
	Count	Gets the number of rows managed by this object.
	Current	Gets the current, or active, list item in the associated data source.
	Position	Gets or sets the position, or index, of the item to consider active in the associated data source.
Public Methods	AddNew	Adds a new item of the appropriate type to the associated data source.
	CancelCurrentEdit	Cancels the current edit, if any, of the associated data source.
	EndCurrentEdit	Completes the current edit, if any, of the associated data source.
	GetItemProperties	Retrieves the collection of PropertyDescriptor objects from the associated data source.
	RemoveAt	Deletes the item at the specified index from the associated data source.
	ResumeBinding	Resumes data binding for the data source.
	SuspendBinding	Suspends data binding for the data source.
Public Events	CurrentChanged	Occurs when the the Current property changes.
	PositionChanged	Occurs when the the Position property changes.

We can make immediate use of the `Position` property to implement the Next and Prev buttons for our application.

	HANDLE THE CLICK EVENTS FOR THE NEXT AND PREV BUTTONS	
	Action	**Result**
1	Create a new `EnablePhotoButtons` method to enable or disable the Next and Prev buttons as required based on a given `BindingManagerBase` object.	```private void EnablePhotoButtons (BindingManagerBase bm) { btnNext.Enabled = (bm.Position < _album.Count - 1); btnPrev.Enabled = (bm.Position > 0); }```
2	Add a `Click` event handler for the Next button in the Photo tab page control of the MainForm window.	```private void btnNext_Click (object sender, System.EventArgs e) {```
3	Retrieve the `BindingManagerBase` object associated with the `_album` data source.	``` BindingManagerBase bm = BindingContext[_album];```
4	If the object was retrieved and the `Position` is not at the maximum value, increment the current position.	``` if ((bm != null) && (bm.Position < bm.Count - 1)) { bm.Position ++; }```
5	Call the `EnablePhotoButtons` method at the end of this handler.	``` EnablePhotoButtons(bm); }```
6	Handle the `Click` event for the Prev button in a similar fashion.	```private void btnPrev_Click (object sender, System.EventArgs e) { BindingManagerBase bm = BindingContext[_album]; if ((bm != null) && (bm.Position > 0)) bm.Position --; EnablePhotoButtons(bm); }```

This change allows the user to move forward and backward within the selected album. The controls automatically update whenever the `Position` property is altered. If you compile and run the current code, you will find that the controls still do not update properly when the selected album changes. For this we will need some additional code.

If you look back at .NET Table 17.7 on the `BindingManagerBase` class, you will see that there is no method to update, or refresh, the controls bound to the associated data source. This is because some binding managers, notably the `PropertyManager`, have no need for this functionality. The refresh behavior is only required when a data source contains multiple instances. In this case, the binding manager is a `CurrencyManager` class instance. A summary of this class appears in .NET Table 17.8.

The `CurrencyManager` class represents a binding manager that is associated with a data source supporting the `IList` interface. This class is part of the `System.Windows.Forms` namespace, and inherits from the `BindingManagerBase` class. See .NET Table 17.7 for the members inherited from the base class.

Public Methods	Refresh	Forces a repopulation of all bound controls for a data source that does not support notification when the underlying data changes.
Public Events	ItemChanged	Occurs when an item in the associated data source is altered. This event will only occur if the associated data source supports two-way notification, such as the support provided by the `IBindingList` interface.

From the table, it appears that the `Refresh` method is the solution we need. This method updates the bound controls with the underlying data. For classes that support the `IBindingList` interface, most notably the database-related objects, this method is not generally needed since the `ItemChanged` event will occur whenever the database object itself is modified. Do not confuse the `ItemChanged` event with the `PositionChanged` event, which occurs when a new item, or row, in the associated list is selected; or with the `CurrentChanged` event, which occurs when the control's bound property is altered.

For our purposes, the default behavior that occurs when the `Position` or `Current` properties change will suffice. Since we do not support the `IBindingList` interface, we need to call the `Refresh` method directly when our `PhotoAlbum` is altered internally. In our current interface, this occurs each time a new album file is selected in the Album combo box control.

The following table continues our prior steps to alter our `SelectedIndexChanged` event handler to invoke the `Refresh` method.

	UPDATE THE SELECTEDINDEXCHANGED EVENT HANDLER	
	Action	**Result**
| 7 | Move the `DataGrid.SetDataBinding` call from the `SelectedIndexChanged` event handler to the end of the `OnLoad` method. | ```
protected override void OnLoad(EventArgs e)
{
    . . .
    gridPhotoAlbum.SetDataBinding(_album,
null);
}
```<br><br>**Note:** At the start of the chapter, we had to clear the binding and then rebind to the album each time the album changed. This is no longer required. |
```

	Action	Result
8	At the end of the `Selected-IndexChanged` event handler, add a single empty `Photograph` object to the cleared `PhotoAlbum` instance when the album is empty.	```csharp private void cmbxAlbum_SelectedIndexChanged (object sender, System.EventArgs e) { . . . // Required to prevent binding exception if (_album.Count == 0) _album.Add(new Photograph("")); ``` **Note:** Our bound controls required that at least one object be present in the collection. Otherwise, the subsequent lines will throw an exception. A more elegant solution might be to unbind the controls and disable the tab control in this case.
9	Add code to the end of the method to retrieve the `CurrencyManager` object used to manage the `_album` data source. **How-to** Retrieve the `BindingManager-Base` for this data source from the `Form` and convert it to a `CurrencyManager` object.	```csharp // Refresh the Photo tab controls BindingManagerBase bm = this.BindingContext[_album]; CurrencyManager cm = bm as CurrencyManager; ```
10	If the `CurrencyManager` was located, refresh the bound controls.	```csharp if (cm != null) cm.Refresh(); ```
11	Also call `EnablePhotoButtons` to enable or display the Next and Prev buttons as required.	```csharp EnablePhotoButtons(bm); } ```

The controls in the Photo tab now update properly in all cases. You can compile and run this to experience the magic. Note how the index into the album, based on the `Position` property, is preserved when you change albums. If the second item in an album is shown and a new album is selected, the second item in the new album is selected. What happens when the number of photos in the current album is more than the number in a newly selected album?

TRY IT!   We have not discussed the data binding for list controls very much here. As a way to see this in action, replace the `txtPhotographer` control with a combo box called `cmbxPhotographer`. Use data binding to automatically fill this list with the `Photographer` entries from the current album. This should be done in the `OnLoad` method and should look like the following:

```csharp
cmbxPhotographer.DataSource = _album;
cmbxPhotographer.DataMember = "Photographer";
```

As you will see if you compile this change, all photographers assigned to the album are listed, even if they occur multiple times. Even so, this is a good example of how to populate a list quickly with values from a data source.

To provide a more robust implementation, implement a `GetPhotographers` method in the `PhotoAlbum` class that returns an array of unique photographer strings in the album. This array can then be set as the `DataSource` for the combo box. Be careful here, as you will need to update this setting in the `SaveChanges` method to accommodate any changes made to the list.

As already mentioned, when binding to a database, the `IBindingList` interface will ensure that the bound properties and the database object stay in sync. When either object is modified, the other is automatically updated.

One issue that remains in our current application is the display of our image in the `PictureBox` control. We will address this topic next.

17.4.4 DISPLAYING THE IMAGE

While our application is working quite well, there is the small matter of our `PictureBox` control. As a simple solution, we could modify the `SizeMode` property of our `PictureBox` control to use the `StretchImage` value. This would stretch our image to fit the window, but would not preserve the aspect ratio of our images.

A better solution, as we know very well, is to scale the image to preserve the aspect ratio within the window. We can do this if we paint the image ourselves rather than provide a value for the `Image` property. The `Paint` event for the `PictureBox` control can be used to perform this painting, although we still need to know which image to paint. For this, we will use the `Tag` property to keep track of the current image.

Of course, as we mentioned earlier in the book, it would be nice to build a "PhotoBox" control that did this automatically. Such a control would extend the Windows Forms `PictureBox` control to scale an image as we do in the subsequent table. Coding this by hand is not much extra work, so we did this explicitly here. A short discussion on how to build such a "PhotoBox" control is given at the end of section 18.2.

The following steps are required to scale the image within the `pboxPhoto` control.

	MODIFY THE PICTUREBOX CONTROL TO DISPLAY A SCALED IMAGE	
	Action	**Result**
1	In the `OnLoad` method of the MainForm.cs code window, replace the binding of the `Image` property in the `pboxPhoto` control to use the `Tag` property instead.	```protected override void OnLoad(EventArgs e)
{
    . . .
    txtNotes.DataBindings.Add(
        "Text", _album, "Notes");
    pboxPhoto.DataBindings.Add(
        "Tag", _album, "Image");

    gridPhotoAlbum.SetDataBinding(_album, null);
}``` |

	Action	Result
2	Invalidate the `PictureBox` control in the `EnablePhotoButtons` method.	```csharp private void EnablePhotoButtons (BindingManagerBase bm) { btnNext.Enabled = (bm.Position < _album.Count - 1); btnPrev.Enabled = (bm.Position > 0); // Force image to repaint pboxPhoto.Invalidate(); } ```
3	Add a handler for the `Paint` event for the `PictureBox` control.	```csharp private void pboxPhoto_Paint (object sender, System.Windows.Forms.PaintEventArgs e) { ```
4	Convert the `Tag` property to a `Bitmap` object.	```csharp Bitmap image = pboxPhoto.Tag as Bitmap; ```
5	If no image is present, clear the graphics area.	```csharp if (image == null) { // No image, just clear the graphics e.Graphics.Clear(SystemColors.Control); return; } ```
6	Retrieve the current `Photograph` object from the binding manager. **How-to** Use the `Current` property of the binding manager object.	```csharp // Load the current photo BindingManagerBase bm = BindingContext[_album]; Photograph photo = bm.Current as Photograph; ```
7	If for some reason the current `Photograph` is not found, simply draw the image in the client rectangle.	```csharp Rectangle r = pboxPhoto.ClientRectangle; if (photo == null) { // Something is wrong, just draw the image e.Graphics.DrawImage(image, r); } ```
8	If the photo is found, draw the image in the scaled rectangle.	```csharp else { // Paint the image with proper aspect ratio e.Graphics.DrawImage(image, photo.ScaleToFit(r)); } } ```

The photograph is now scaled and displayed within our `PictureBox` control. Note how we used the entire client rectangle rather than the rectangle provided in the `Graphics` object to ensure that the entire control area is redrawn.

It is worth noting here that binding to the `Tag` property is not strictly required. Since we access the current `Photograph` object here, we could simply load the associated image correctly. There may be a slight performance advantage here in having the image already available in the `Tag` property, so we selected the approach shown in the table.

If you compile and run this application, make sure you note how the form resizes. In particular, notice how we set the Anchor properties in this example to maximize the area allocated for the image and notes controls.

Our final topic is to ensure that any changes we make to the controls in the Photo tab are reflected in the album file.

17.4.5   SAVING CHANGES TO BOUND CONTROLS

Changes made to bound controls are saved much like we saw for the DataGrid control earlier in the chapter. When an object supports the IEditableObject interface, the BeginEdit method is called whenever a bound property is assigned a new value, and the EndEdit method is called when the user is done making changes to the current item.

If you experiment with our interface, you will find that the program usually but not always offers to save the most recent changes. The problem occurs when you edit a couple of values for a Photograph and then click the Close button. In this case, the EndEdit call is never made since the framework believes the edit is still active for the displayed item. As a result, the PhotoAlbum.HasEdits property will return the value false, and the changes are not saved.

We can fix this by forcing the current edit to end when we exit the program.

	FINISH ANY ACTIVE EDIT WHEN THE PROGRAM EXITS	
	Action	**Result**

1	Locate the OnClosing override in the MainForm.cs code window.	`protected override void OnClosing`
		`    (CancelEventArgs e)`
		`{`

2	Retrieve the binding manager for the _album data source.	`// Complete any in-progress edits`
		`BindingManagerBase bm`
		`    = BindingContext[_album];`

3	Call the EndCurrentEdit method to complete any outstanding edits.	`if (bm != null)`
		`    bm.EndCurrentEdit();`
		
		`SaveChanges();`
		`base.OnClosing(e);`
		`}`

This change ensures that any modifications made to the current item are taken into account when the application is closed. Note that there is also an EndEdit method in the DataGrid class, which performs similar functionality on the data grid control. Our approach is more general, and applies to all edits on any control related to the given binding manager.

Compile and run the application and make sure this works correctly. Figure 17.8 shows the application with the message dialog for saving a change displayed.

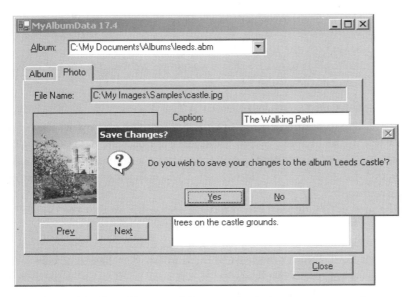

Figure 17.8 The Save Changes dialog permits the user to save any changes made to the individual controls.

This completes our discussion on data binding. We end with the usual summary of our accomplishments.

17.5 RECAP

In this chapter we investigated the concept of data binding and constructed a new MyAlbumData application. We began with the `DataGrid` class and saw how to create and fill a data grid, and how to customize the contents and appearance of the grid for a specific type of data.

We then looked at the `IEditableObject` interface as a way to support transactional updates to bound data. We implemented this interface in our `Photograph` class in order to track and save any changes made by a user.

Binding to data grids is referred to as complex data binding. We also examined simple data binding, used to bind a single property of a control to a value in a data source. We created a `TabPage` object in our application to hold a set of controls related to a `Photograph` object, and bound properties of our controls to the active `Photograph` in a `PhotoAlbum` collection. We finished our chapter by examining the update and storage of data sources as the user interacts with the application in general and the bound controls in particular.

While the examples here did not use the `System.Data` namespace, the binding of data grids and controls to database objects was discussed along the way in order to provide some insight into how such binding might be performed.

C H A P T E R   1 8

Odds and ends .NET

18.1 Printing 604
18.2 Timers 611
18.3 Drag and drop 618
18.4 ActiveX controls 625
18.5 Recap 635

In this last chapter of the book, it seems appropriate to mention a number of different topics worthy of further exploration. This chapter presents various concepts that might be of interest to you as you build and deploy Windows Forms applications. Since the details of each topic could easily fill all or most of a chapter, we will instead show a rather quick example for each subject. These examples should point you in the right direction as you expand your knowledge of .NET in general and Windows Forms in particular.

We will take a quick look at four different topics:

• Printing, including page setup and print preview.

• Windows Forms Timers, including stopping and restarting a timer.

• Drag and drop, both into and out of Windows Forms applications.

• Hosting ActiveX controls, by way of hosting a web browser control.

For no particular reason, these topics are presented in the same order as they are listed. We begin with printing from Windows Forms applications.

18.1 PRINTING

Printing in Windows Forms is supported by the `System.Drawing.Printing` namespace in addition to Windows Forms constructs. In this section we add printing support to the MyPhotos MDI application built in chapter 16. The main classes required are as follows:

Printing related classes

Class	Description
PrintDocument	A reusable component that is used to send output to the printer. The `PrintPage` event occurs when print data should be sent to the printer device.
PrintDialog	A common dialog that offers options related to printing.
PrintPreviewDialog	A form that contains a `PrintPreviewControl` object for presenting how a document will look when it is printed on a specific printer device.
PageSetupDialog	A common dialog that permits a user to alter the page settings associated with a print document.

Our example will use each of these four classes in order to support printing of an individual photograph. Figure 18.1 shows the print preview dialog for one of our images.

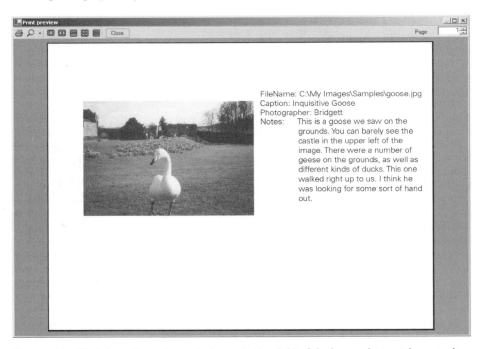

Figure 18.1   Note how the text here is drawn to the right of the image. Long strings, such as the Notes text, are formatted to fit within the available page margins

While this may not be the prettiest image printing application, it does demonstrate some important principles, such as using the page margins and text wrapping. We will present the changes in two parts, one for each of our `ParentForm` and `MainForm` objects.

18.1.1 USING THE PRINT CLASSES

The parent form will make direct use of the print classes previously mentioned, contain the menu items for printing, and maintain the required `PrintDocument` object. Placing the print document on the parent form ensures that any changes made to the page margins or other document settings are seen by all child forms in the application.

The following tables detail the changes required on the parent form.

Set the version number for the MyPhotos application to 18.1.

MODIFY PARENT FORM TO SUPPORT PRINT MENUS	
Action	**Result**
1 In the ParentForm.cs [Design] window, add three menus and a separator to the File menu.	

Settings		
Menu	**Property**	**Value**
separator	MergeOrder	6
Page Setup	(Name)	menuPageSetup
	MergeOrder'	7
	Text	Page Set&up…
Print Preview	(Name)	menuPrintPreview
	MergeOrder	7
	Text	Print Pre&view
Print	(Name)	menuPrint
	MergeOrder	7
	Shortcut	CtrlP
	Text	&Print…

2 Also drag a `PrintDocument` object onto the form.	

Settings	
Property	**Value**
(Name)	printDoc
DocumentName	Image Document

The object appears in the component tray of the designer window.

These menus provides the necessary user interface support. Next we hook up our three print menus in the `ParentForm` class.

	Action	**Result**
	HANDLE PRINT RELATED MENUS IN PARENT FORM	
3	Add a `Click` event handler for the Page Setup menu to display a `PageSetupDialog` window for the form's print document.	```private void menuPageSetup_Click (object sender, System.EventArgs e) { PageSetupDialog dlg = new PageSetupDialog(); dlg.Document = printDoc; dlg.ShowDialog(); }```
4	Add a Click event handler for the Print Preview menu to display a `PrintPreviewDialog` window for the form's print document. **Note:** The `PrintPreviewDialog` window displays the document to be printed within a `PrintPreview-Control` object contained within the preview window.	```private void menuPrintPreview_Click (object sender, System.EventArgs e) { PrintPreviewDialog dlg = new PrintPreviewDialog(); dlg.Document = printDoc; dlg.ShowDialog(); }```
5	Add a `Click` event handler for the Print menu to display a `PrintDialog` window for the form's print document. **Note:** The common print dialog allows the user to select standard settings such as which printer to use and the number of copies to make. If the user clicks the OK button, then we invoke the `Print` method in the `PrintDocument` class to initiate the actual print operation.	```private void menuPrint_Click (object sender, System.EventArgs e) { PrintDialog dlg = new PrintDialog(); dlg.Document = printDoc; if (dlg.ShowDialog() == DialogResult.OK) { printDoc.Print(); } }```
6	Handle the `PrintPage` event for the `PrintDocument` object on the parent form. **Note:** This event occurs for each page to be printed. The `BeginPrint` and `EndPrint` events occur at the start and end of the entire print operation, respectively.	```private void printDoc_PrintPage (object sender, System.Drawing. Printing.PrintPageEventArgs e) {```
7	In this handler: a. If the active child is a `MainForm` object, call the yet-to-be-written `PrintCurrentImage` method on this object. b. Otherwise, cancel the print operation.	``` MainForm f = ActiveMdiChild as MainForm; if (f != null) f.PrintCurrentImage(e); else e.Cancel = true; }```

These event handlers establish the required printing support for the parent form. The printing logic for the child form is presented next.

18.1.2 DRAWING A PRINT PAGE

With our user interface logic in place, we are ready to implement the printing of a page. This is done using the `PrintPageEventArgs` parameter provided to the `PrintPage` event handler. This class is summarized in .NET Table 18.1.

	.NET Table 18.1 PrintPageEventArgs class	
	The `PrintPageEventArgs` class represents an event argument containing information required for printing pages to a printer. This class is part of the `System.Drawing.Printing` namespace, and inherits from the `System.EventArgs` class.	
Public Properties	Cancel	Gets or sets whether the print job should be cancelled.
	Graphics	Gets the `Graphics` object on which to paint the page to print.
	HasMorePages	Gets or sets whether an additional page should be printed after the current one.
	MarginBounds	Gets the printable area of a page, which is the rectangle within the margins of the page.
	PageBounds	Gets the page area, which is the rectangle representing the entire page.
	PageSettings	Gets the `PageSettings` object representing the settings for the current page.

We will implement a `PrintCurrentImage` method in the `MainForm` class to make use of this parameter. Internally, this will draw the photograph using the provided `Graphics` object, and use an internal `PrintTextString` method to draw the individual properties for the photograph.

	IMPLEMENT THE PRINTCURRENTIMAGE METHOD	
	Action	**Result**
1	In the MainForm.cs code window, indicate that we will use members of the `System.Drawing.Printing` namespace.	`using System.Drawing.Printing;`

2	Add a `PrintCurrentImage` method that accepts a `PrintPageEventArgs` object as a parameter.	`public void PrintCurrentImage`
		`  (PrintPageEventArgs e)`
		`{`

	Action	Result
| **3** | If there is no current photo, then abort the print operation. | ```csharp
Photograph photo = _album.CurrentPhoto;
if (photo == null)
{
   // nothing to print, so abort
   e.Cancel = true;
   return;
}
``` |
| **4** | Otherwise, create some shortcuts for the margins of the page and the Graphics object. | ```csharp
// Establish some useful shortcuts
float leftMargin = e.MarginBounds.Left;
float rightMargin = e.MarginBounds.Right;
float topMargin = e.MarginBounds.Top;
float bottomMargin
   = e.MarginBounds.Bottom;
float printableWidth = e.MarginBounds.Width;
float printableHeight
   = e.MarginBounds.Height;
Graphics g = e.Graphics;
``` |
| **5** | Create a Font object:<br><br>a. Use 11 point Times New Roman.<br>b. Use the GetHeight method to determine the height of each line of text.<br>c. Use the MeasureString method to determine the size of a space. | ```csharp
Font printFont
   = new Font("Times New Roman", 11);
float fontHeight = printFont.GetHeight(g);
float spaceWidth = g.MeasureString(" ",
                   printFont).Width;
``` |
| **6** | Determine the correct length so that the image can be drawn into a box which is 75% of the shortest side of the page.<br><br>**Note:** This logic accounts for both landscape and portrait page orientation. The xPos and yPos variables represent where the first line of text should be drawn. | ```csharp
// Draw image in box 75% of shortest side
float imageBoxLength;
float xPos = leftMargin;
float yPos = topMargin + fontHeight;
if (printableWidth < printableHeight)
{
   imageBoxLength = printableWidth * 75/100;
   yPos += imageBoxLength;
}
else
{
   imageBoxLength = printableHeight * 75/100;
   xPos += imageBoxLength + spaceWidth;
}
``` |
| **7** | Draw the image into a box of the determined size. | ```csharp
// Draw image at start of the page
Rectangle imageBox
   = new Rectangle((int)leftMargin + 1,
              (int)topMargin + 1,
              (int)imageBoxLength,
              (int)imageBoxLength);
g.DrawImage(photo.Image,
        photo.ScaleToFit(imageBox));
``` |
| **8** | Determine the RectangleF object where all text should be drawn. | ```csharp
// Determine rectangle for text
RectangleF printArea
   = new RectangleF(xPos, yPos,
           rightMargin - xPos,
           bottomMargin - yPos);
``` |

	Action	Result

9	Print the file name, caption, photographer, and notes properties for the photograph onto the page.
	
	How-to
	Use the yet-to-be-written PrintTextString method.
		``
		PrintTextString(g, printFont,
		    "FileName:", photo.FileName,
		    ref printArea);
		PrintTextString(g, printFont,
		    "Caption:", photo.Caption,
		    ref printArea);
		PrintTextString(g, printFont,
		    "Photographer:", photo.Photographer,
		    ref printArea);
		PrintTextString(g, printFont,
		    "Notes:", photo.Notes,
		    ref printArea);
		}
		``

The `PrintTextString` method is implemented by the subsequent steps. Note that our implementation prints the given string across multiple lines if necessary by drawing each word in the text string separately. Also note that the `printArea` variable is passed by reference. This is required in order to modify the printable area for text strings in the `PrintTextString` method. Since the `RectangleF` structure is a value type, it is normally passed by value.

	IMPLEMENT THE PRINTTEXTSTRING METHOD	
	Action	**Result**

10	Add a PrintTextString method to the MainForm.cs code window.	```
		protected void PrintTextString(
		    Graphics g,
		    Font printFont,
		    string name,
		    string text,
		    ref RectangleF printArea)
		{
		``

11	Create some local variables for the margins of the printable area.	```
		// Establish some useful shortcuts
		float leftMargin = printArea.Left;
		float rightMargin = printArea.Right;
		float topMargin = printArea.Top;
		float bottomMargin = printArea.Bottom;
		``

12	Also determine the height of the font and the coordinates where the text should be drawn.	```
		float fontHeight = printFont.GetHeight(g);
		float xPos = printArea.Left;
		float yPos = topMargin + fontHeight;
		``

13	Find the width of a space and the name for the text string.	```
		float spaceWidth = g.MeasureString(" ",
		    printFont).Width;
		float nameWidth
		    = g.MeasureString(name, printFont).Width;
		``

14	If this name does not fit in the printable area, then abort the operation.	```
		if (!printArea.Contains(xPos + nameWidth,
		                         yPos))
		{
		  // Does not fit, so abort
		  return;
		}
		``

	Action	Result
15	Otherwise, draw the name on the page and adjust the left margin to occur after this string.	```g.DrawString(name, printFont,\n Brushes.Black, new PointF(xPos, yPos));\nleftMargin += nameWidth + spaceWidth;\nxPos = leftMargin;```
16	Divide the text string into individual words, and iterate over these words.	```// Draw text, use multi-lines if necessary\nstring[] words\n = text.Split(" \r\t\n\0".ToCharArray());\nforeach (string word in words)\n{```
17	Determine the width of the next word.	```float wordWidth = g.MeasureString(\n word, printFont).Width;\nif (wordWidth == 0.0)\n continue;```
18	If the size of this word takes it past the right margin, then adjust the drawing coordinates to start a new line.	```if (xPos + wordWidth > rightMargin)\n{\n // Start a new line\n xPos = leftMargin;\n yPos += fontHeight;\n if (yPos > bottomMargin)\n {\n // no more page, abort foreach loop\n break;\n }\n}```
19	Draw this word at the current position, and adjust the x coordinate appropriately.	```g.DrawString(word, printFont,\n Brushes.Black,\n new PointF(xPos, yPos));\nxPos += wordWidth;\n}```
20	When finished drawing the text, adjust the printable area to exclude the area just drawn.	```// Adjust print area based on drawn text\nprintArea.Y = yPos;\nprintArea.Height = bottomMargin - yPos;\n}```

When you test this code, make sure it works properly when printing with both landscape and portrait orientation. The page setup dialog can be used to alter the orientation, as well as the margins on the page. For further information on printing, or for details on the classes or methods used here, consult the .NET Framework online documentation.

18.2   TIMERS

We will look at Windows Forms timers next. A *timer* is an object that raises an event after a configurable period of time has elapsed. There are, in fact, three Timer classes provided by the .NET Framework. There is one in the System.Threading namespace for use among multiple threads; one in the System.Timers namespace for server-based recurring tasks; and one in the System.Windows.Forms namespace that is optimized for the single-threaded processing environment used to handle events in a Form object.

Here we will concern ourselves with the Windows Forms timer. This timer object is normally associated and configured within a form. For our example, we will create a small slide show form that

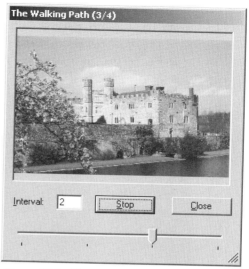

Figure 18.2   The slide show uses a TrackBar control to track the current position within the album.

will flip through each photo in an album. Our new window is shown in figure 18.2, and will be accessible from a new menu item in the View menu of our MyPhotos MDI application. A quick summary of the Timer class we will use is given in .NET Table 18.2.

.NET Table 18.2   Timer class

The Windows Forms Timer class represents a timer component that raises events at user-defined intervals. This timer is optimized for use in Windows Forms applications and is expected to occur within the processing thread for a Form object. This class is part of the System.Windows.Forms namespace, and inherits from the System.Component-Model.Component class.

Public Properties	Enabled	Gets or sets whether the time is currently active.
	Interval	Gets or sets the time in milliseconds between timer ticks.
Public Methods	Start	Starts the timer. This is equivalent to setting the Enabled property to true.
	Stop	Stops the timer. This is equivalent to setting the Enabled property to false.
Public Events	Tick	Occurs when the timer is enabled and the specified interval has elapsed.

Our discussion is divided into the user interface portion and the code portion.

18.2.1 CREATING A SLIDE SHOW FORM

We begin our discussion with the design of the new form. This form will use a control we have not previously discussed, namely the `TrackBar` control. A summary of this control is given in .NET Table 18.3.

.NET Table 18.3 TrackBar class		
The `TrackBar` class represents a control that supports tracking of an integer value through a scrolling interface. The control may appear horizontally or vertically. This class is part of the `System.Windows.Forms` namespace, and inherits from the `Control` class.		
Public Properties	AutoSize	Gets or sets whether the control should automatically resize based on its current settings.
	LargeChange	Gets or sets the amount added or subtracted from the `Value` property for a large scroll in the control. The default is five (5).
	Maximum	Gets or sets the maximum value for this track bar. The default is ten (10).
	Minimum	Gets or sets the minimum value for this track bar. The default is zero (0).
	Orientation	Gets or sets the `Orientation` enumeration value for the display orientation of the control.
	SmallChange	Gets or sets the amount added or subtracted from the `Value` property for a small scroll in the control. The default is one (1).
	TickFrequency	Gets or sets the delta between tick marks drawn on the control. The default is one (1).
	TickStyle	Gets or sets how the tick marks are displayed on the control.
	Value	Gets or sets the numeric value of the current position of the slider in the control.
Public Methods	SetRange	Sets the minimum and maximum values for the control.
Public Events	ValueChanged	Occurs when the `Value` property of the control is modified, either by movement of the slider or assignment in code.

The following table details the steps for drawing the user interface for the `Slide-ShowForm` class, including the `TrackBar` control:

Set the version number of the MyPhotos application to 18.2.

		CREATE THE SLIDE SHOW FORM	
	Action		**Result**
1	Add a new `Form` class file to the MyPhotos project called SlideShowForm.cs.		The new file is shown in the Solution Explorer window, and the form in the Windows Forms Designer window.

Settings

Property	Value
ControlBox	False
MaximizeBox	False
MinimizeBox	False
ShowInTaskbar	False
Size	300, 340
StartPosition	CenterParent

2	Place a `PictureBox` object at the top of the form.	This is shown in the graphic for the following step.

Settings

Property	Value
(Name)	pboxSlide
Anchor	Top, Bottom, Left, Right
BorderStyle	Fixed3D

3	Place a `Label`, `TextBox`, and two `Button` controls below the picture box. Position these as shown in the graphic.

Settings

Control	Property	Value
Label	Text	&Interval
	Anchor	Bottom, Left
TextBox	(Name)	txtInterval
	Anchor	Bottom, Left
Button 1	Text	2
	(Name)	btnStop
	Anchor	Bottom, Right
	Text	&Stop
Button 2	(Name)	btnClose
	Anchor	Bottom, Right
	Text	&Close

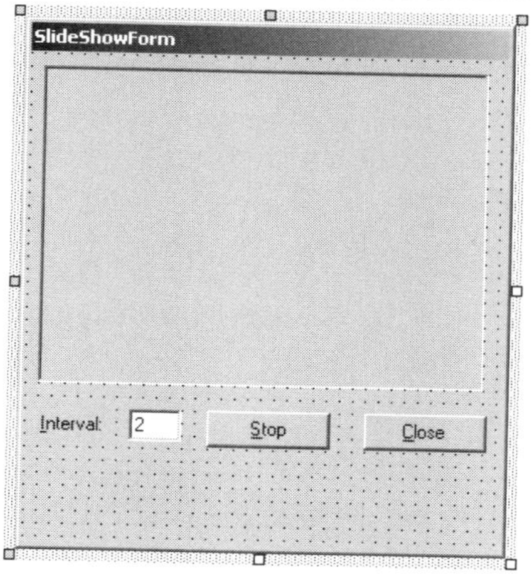

	Action	Result
4	Place a `TrackBar` control at the base of the form. **Settings** | Property	Value
---	---
(Name)	trackSlide
Anchor	Bottom, Left, Right		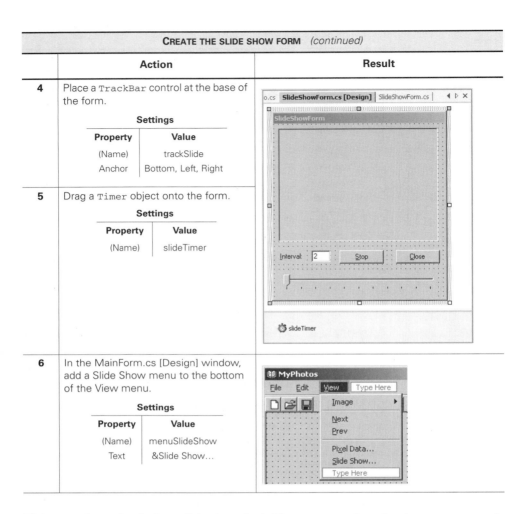
5	Drag a `Timer` object onto the form. **Settings** | Property	Value
---	---
(Name)	slideTimer		
6	In the MainForm.cs [Design] window, add a Slide Show menu to the bottom of the View menu. **Settings** | Property	Value
---	---
(Name)	menuSlideShow
Text	&Slide Show…		

This completes the design of the interface. The next step is to hook up our controls in the code.

More .NET The `ProgressBar` class represents a control that permits the progress of an event or procedure to be displayed. This class is related to the `TrackBar` class in that it contains `Minimum`, `Maximum`, and `Value` properties to manage the current appearance of the control. You can check out this class in the .NET documentation.

I opted to use a track bar in our example because of its support for user adjustment of the current position via the `Scroll` event. This feature is not available in the `ProgressBar` class as it is not really intended to interact directly with the user.

18.2.2   IMPLEMENTING THE SLIDE SHOW BEHAVIOR

Our user interface is ready to go. The following table details the steps required to implement this form to present a slide show to the user:

IMPLEMENT THE SLIDE SHOW BEHAVIOR		
	Action	**Result**
1	In the SlideShowForm.cs code window, Indicate that we will use the MyPhotoAlbum library in this file.	```using Manning.MyPhotoAlbum;```
2	Create two private fields in the class to hold the album and the current display position.	```private PhotoAlbum _album;``` ```private int _albumPos;```

3	Modify the constructor to accept a `PhotoAlbum` object and initialize these private fields.	```public SlideShowForm(PhotoAlbum album)```
		```{```
		  ```// Required for Form Designer support```
		  ```InitializeComponent();```
		
		  ```// Other initialization```
		  ```_album = album;```
		  ```_albumPos = 0;```
		```}```

4	Implement a `SetInterval` method to calculate the timer interval based on the value in the text box control.
	
	Note: Since we do not prevent our text box from containing letters, we need to catch the possible exception here.
		```protected void SetInterval()```
		```{```
		  ```int interval = 0;```
		  ```try```
		  ```{```
		    ```interval```
		      ```= Convert.ToInt32(txtInterval.Text);```
		  ```}```
		  ```catch```
		  ```{```
		    ```// Reset interval value```
		    ```txtInterval.Text = "2";```
		    ```interval = 2;```
		  ```}```
		
		  ```slideTimer.Interval = interval * 1000;```
		```}```

5	Override the `OnLoad` method to:
	a. Set the timer interval.
	b. Enable the timer.
	c. Set the minimum and maximum value for the track bar based on the number of photos in the album.
		```protected override void OnLoad(EventArgs e)```
		```{```
		  ```SetInterval();```
		  ```slideTimer.Enabled = true;```
		
		  ```trackSlide.Minimum = 0;```
		  ```trackSlide.Maximum = _album.Count - 1;```
		  ```base.OnLoad(e);```
		```}```

	Action	Result
6	Add a `Paint` event handler for the `PictureBox` control to do the following: a. If the current position is out of range, simply return. b. Load the current `Photograph`. c. Display the caption in the title bar. d. Preserve the aspect ratio when drawing the image into the window.	```csharp\nprivate void pboxSlide_Paint\n (object sender,\n System.Windows.Forms.PaintEventArgs e)\n{\n if (_albumPos >= _album.Count)\n return;\n\n Photograph photo = _album[_albumPos];\n if (photo != null)\n {\n this.Text\n = String.Format("{0} ({1:#}/{2:#})",\n photo.Caption,\n _albumPos + 1, _album.Count);\n e.Graphics.DrawImage(photo.Image,\n photo.ScaleToFit(\n pboxSlide.ClientRectangle));\n }\n else\n e.Graphics.Clear(SystemColors.Control);\n}\n```
7	Add a `Tick` event handler for the `slideTimer` component. **How-to** This is the default event for this component, so simply double-click the timer in the component tray.	```csharp\nprivate void slideTimer_Tick\n (object sender, System.EventArgs e)\n{\n```
8	In this handler, increment the current album position.	```csharp\n_albumPos ++;\n```
9	If the position is passed the end of the album, reset the slide show as follows: a. Modify the Stop button text to be Start. b. Reset the track bar value to zero. c. Invalidate the picture box to draw the initial photograph. d. Disable the timer.	```csharp\nif (_albumPos > _album.Count)\n{\n btnStop.Text = "&Start";\n _albumPos = 0;\n trackSlide.Value = 0;\n pboxSlide.Invalidate();\n slideTimer.Enabled = false;\n}\n```
10	If the position is at the end of the album, set the title bar to indicate the slide show is finished.	```csharp\nelse if (_albumPos == _album.Count)\n{\n this.Text = "Finished";\n}\n```
11	Otherwise, for a valid album index: a. Invalidate the picture box to draw the next image. b. Set the track bar value to the current position.	```csharp\nelse\n{\n pboxSlide.Invalidate();\n trackSlide.Value = _albumPos;\n}\n```
12	Reassign the interval value to pick up any changes made by the user.	```csharp\n// Reset the interval\nSetInterval();\n}\n```

	Action	Result
| 13 | Add a `Click` event handler for the Close button to close the form. | ```csharp
private void btnClose_Click
    (object sender, System.EventArgs e)
{
    this.Close();
}
``` |
| 14 | Add a `Click` event handler for the Stop button. | ```csharp
private void btnStop_Click
    (object sender, System.EventArgs e)
{
``` |
| 15 | If the current `Text` value is Stop, stop the timer and set the button text to Resume.<br><br>**Note:** While our Stop button has three different display strings, we preserve the keyboard access key of Alt+S in all three values. | ```csharp
if (btnStop.Text == "&Stop")
{
    // Stop
    slideTimer.Stop();
    btnStop.Text = "Re&sume";
}
``` |
| 16 | For other text values, start the timer and set the button text to Stop. | ```csharp
else
{
    // Resume or Start
    slideTimer.Start();
    btnStop.Text = "&Stop";
}
}
``` |
| 17 | Add a `Scroll` event handler for the `TrackBar` control.<br><br>**Note:** This is the default event for the track bar control, and occurs when the user manually adjusts the slider position. | ```csharp
private void trackSlide_Scroll
    (object sender, System.EventArgs e)
{
``` |
| 18 | In this handler:<br><br>a. Set the album position to the new value.<br>b. Invalidate the picture box to draw the selected photo. | ```csharp
_albumPos = trackSlide.Value;
pboxSlide.Invalidate();
}
``` |
| 19 | Add a `Resize` event handler for the `PictureBox` control to invalidate the control and redraw the image. | ```csharp
private void pboxSlide_Resize
    (object sender, System.EventArgs e)
{
    pboxSlide.Invalidate();
}
``` |
| 20 | Back in the `MainForm` class, add a `Click` event handler for the Slide Show menu to create and display a `SlideShowForm` dialog. | ```csharp
private void menuSlideShow_Click
    (object sender, System.EventArgs e)
{
    using (SlideShowForm f
            = new SlideShowForm(_album))
    {
        // Display slide show as modal dialog
        f.ShowDialog();
    }
}
``` |

The slide show form is now fully integrated into our main application. Compile and run to see this window. Load an album and select the Slide Show menu to display the new dialog.

TRY IT! Throughout the book we have used the photo album and photograph abstractions we constructed in chapter 5 to represent and display images. In the MyPhotos application we display photographs in a `Panel` control, while in our other applications we use a `PictureBox` control. In both cases we were forced to override the `Paint` event in order to draw a photograph with the proper aspect ratio. It would be nice to have a control that provided this functionality directly.

Try creating a new `PhotoBox` class based on the Windows Forms `PictureBox` control that adds a new `SizeMode` setting called `ScaleImage` to the control. When set to this value, this new control should display the entire image with the proper aspect ratio within the control, just as we have done throughout the book. You can replace the existing `Picture-Box.SizeMode` property using a new set of enumeration values by defining the property in the following manner. You will also need to override the `OnPaint` and `OnResize` methods to properly draw an image within the new control.

```
private PhotoBoxSizeMode _sizeMode;
public new PhotoBoxSizeMode SizeMode
{
  get { return _sizeMode; }
  set { _sizeMode = value; }
}
```

Use your new control in place of the `PictureBox` control in the `Slide-ShowForm` window. My implementation of this control is available on the book's web site. Also included on the site are the instructions for making this new control, referred to as a *custom control*, available in the Toolbox window of Visual Studio .NET.

18.3 DRAG AND DROP

Continuing with our whirlwind tour of topics, let's take a quick look at *drag and drop*. This refers to dragging an object from one location to another, and can occur within an application or between applications. Typically, a drag and drop operation is begun by clicking an object with the mouse pointer, holding down the mouse button while moving, or dragging, the object to a new location; and dropping the object at the new location by releasing the mouse button.

This topic can get fairly complicated, so we will show a rather basic example supporting the following types of drag and drop operations.

• Dragging a file from the Windows file system into a `PhotoAlbum` in a `Main-Form` window.

- Dragging a photograph file from the `MainForm` window to an external Windows location.
- Dragging the photograph caption from the `MainForm` window to a text editor.
- Dragging a photograph file from one `PhotoAlbum` to another within the MyPhotos MDI application.

The Windows Forms `Control` class provides direct support for drag and drop operations. The following table summarizes these members.

Members of the Control class related to drag and drop

Public Properties	AllowDrop	Gets or sets whether the control will permit drag and drop operations within its boundaries. The default is `false`.
Public Methods	DoDragDrop	Initiates a drag and drop operation from within this control. Typically, this is called from a `MouseDown` event handler.
Public Events	DragDrop	Occurs when the user completes a drag and drop operation within this control.
	DragEnter	Occurs when an object is dragged into the control's boundaries.
	DragLeave	Occurs when an object formerly dragged into the control is dragged out of the control's boundaries.
	DragOver	Occurs when an object within the control is moved within the control's boundaries.

At a high level, a drag and drop operation performs the following steps. These steps are illustrated by the code in the subsequent sections. Note that the source and target of the operation may be within the same application or in separate applications.

1. A source control initiates drag and drop, typically within a `MouseDown` event handler, using the `DoDragDrop` method. One or more data objects and associated formats are provided as part of invoking this method.

2. The user drags the object to a target control that has its `AllowDrop` property set to `true`.

3. As the mouse enters the target control, the `DragEnter` event occurs to permit the target to identify whether the data can be recognized by this control. This permits the operating system to display an appropriate mouse cursor for the user.

4. If so, then the `DragOver` event occurs as the user moves the drag and drop object within the control.

5. If the object is dragged out of the control, the `DragLeave` event occurs.

6. If the user releases the object within the target control, then the `DragDrop` event occurs to permit the control to receive the data.

7. The result of the operation is returned by the `DoDragDrop` method in the original source control.

We will divide our example into two sections. First, we will begin a drag and drop operation from within the `PictureBox` control of our `MainForm` class. Next, we will receive external drag and drop operations within this same control.

18.3.1 INITIATING DRAG AND DROP

The key to beginning a drag and drop operation is the `DoDragDrop` method. This method defines the data for the operation and the kind of operation permitted.

```
public DragDropEffects DoDragDrop(object data,
                                  DragDropEffects allowedEffects);
```

While the `data` parameter can be any data, the `DataObject` class provides a standard mechanism for safely transferring data between applications. The `DragDrop-Effects` enumeration permits different types of drag and drop operations to be supported. For example, the `Move`, `Copy`, and `Link` values permit an object to be moved, copied, or linked from the original data source to the drop target.

The `DoDragDrop` method does not return until the drag and drop operation is completed. The return value indicates what effect was performed by the operation. The `QueryContinueDrag` event in the `Control` class can be used to keep tabs on the operation. This event occurs periodically during drag and drop and can be used to cancel the operation or to modify the application window as required.

In our application, we will simply begin the operation and let the .NET Framework take care of the rest. We will provide two types of data formats using the `DataObject` class. The first will be the `FileDrop` format recognized by the Windows file system and applications such as Microsoft Paint. The second will be the `Text` format recognized by most word processors.

The following table details the changes required.

Set the version number of the MyPhotos application to 18.3.

	BEGIN A DRAG AND DROP OPERATION	
	Action	**Result**

1	Locate the `MouseDown` event handler for the `Panel` control in the MainForm.cs code window.	`private void pnlPhoto_MouseDown`
		`    (object sender,`
		`        System.Windows.Forms.MouseEventArgs e)`
		`    {`

2	If the Ctrl key is not held down, then retrieve the current photograph for the album.	`if (ctrlKeyHeld)`
		`{`
		`    . . .`
		`}`
		`else`
		`{`
		`    // Initiate drag and drop for this image`
		`    Photograph photo = _album.CurrentPhoto;`

	Action	Result

3	If this `Photograph` is found, create a `FileDrop` data format for dragging the photograph to a new location.
	
	How-to
	a. Construct a `DataObject` instance to hold the data formats.
	
	b. Construct a `string` array to hold the associated file.
	
	c. Associate the string array with the `FileDrop` format for the data.
		```if (photo != null)```
		```{```
		``` // Create object for encapsulating data```
		``` DataObject data = new DataObject();```
		
		``` // Construct string array for FileDrop```
		``` string[] fileArray = new string[1];```
		``` fileArray[0] = photo.FileName;```
		``` data.SetData(DataFormats.FileDrop,```
		``` fileArray);```
		
		Note: The `DataFormats` class encapsulates various data formats that can be used by drag and drop operations. The `FileDrop` format used here requires a `string` array as the data type. This permits multiple files to be provided at once.

4	Also assign a Text format using the `Caption` property of the photograph as the associated data.	``` // Use the caption for the text format```
		``` data.SetData(DataFormats.Text,```
		``` photo.Caption);```

5	Call the `DoDragDrop` method with the constructed data object to initiate a drag and drop `Copy` operation.	``` // Initiate drag and drop```
		``` pnlPhoto.DoDragDrop(data,```
		``` DragDropEffects.Copy);```
		``` }```
		``` }```
		```}```

This code begins a drag and drop operation that can be received by any other application running on the computer. Other applications look at the provided data formats to identify whether they can accept the dragged data. We will look at how to do this in Windows Forms in a moment.

Of course, for applications that can receive multiple formats, the result they receive depends on which format they prefer. Most word processing applications look for the `Text` format first, and will therefore receive the `Caption` property of our photo, rather than the associated file object.

Compile and run the application. Display an album and click on the image. Hold the mouse and drag it to a new location to perform a drag and drop operation. Figure 18.3 shows the result of dragging one of our favorite images from the MyPhotos application into a Microsoft Paint application. The Paint application opens the given file and displays a copy of the image in its main window. Also try dragging an image into WordPad or some other word processor to see how the caption string appears.

Figure 18.3 The FileDrop format used here to drag an image into Microsoft Paint is a common method for transferring files between applications.

This completes our example for initiating a drag and drop operation. The next topic is to handle drag and drop operations within the `MainForm` window.

18.3.2 RECEIVING DRAG AND DROP

Regardless of where a drag and drop operation originates, an application can elect to handle the incoming data. The `DragEnter` and `DragDrop` events are used to receive such operations. Event handlers for both of these events receive a `DragEventArgs` object as their event parameter. A summary of this object appears in .NET Table 18.4.

The DragEventArgs class represents the event arguments required for drag and drop events, namely the DragEnter, DragOver, and DragDrop events in the Control class. This class is part of the System.Windows.Forms namespace, and inherits from the System.EventArgs class.

	AllowedEffect	Gets which drag and drop operations are permitted by the source of the drag event.
	Data	Gets the IDataObject interface that holds the data and data formats associated with the event.
Public Properties	Effect	Gets or sets the DragDropEffects enumeration values indicating which drag and drop operations are permitted in the target of the drag event.
	KeyState	Gets the current state of the Shift, Ctrl, and Alt keyboard keys.
	X	Gets the x-coordinate of the current mouse pointer position.
	Y	Gets the y-coordinate of the current mouse pointer position.

For our example, we will recognize the FileDrop format in the MainForm window to receive files dragged from the file system or from other MainForm windows.

The steps required are detailed in the following table:

	HANDLE DRAG AND DROP IN THE MAINFORM WINDOW	
	Action	**Result**
1	In the MainForm.cs [Design] window, set the AllowDrop property on the Panel control to true.	Drop operations are now permitted in the panel control.
2	Add a DragEnter event handler for the panel.	```private void pnlPhoto_DragEnter (object sender, System.Windows.Forms.DragEventArgs e) {```
3	If the data associated with the event supports the FileDrop data format, then indicate that this control will support the Copy drag and drop effect. **How-to** Use the GetDataPresent method from the IDataObject interface.	``` if (e.Data.GetDataPresent(DataFormats.FileDrop)) e.Effect = DragDropEffects.Copy;```

	Action	Result
| 4 | Otherwise, indicate that the current drag and drop data is not accepted by this control. | ```
else
    e.Effect = DragDropEffects.None;
}
``` |
| 5 | Add a `DragDrop` event handler for the panel. | ```
private void pnlPhoto_DragDrop
    (object sender,
     System.Windows.Forms.DragEventArgs e)
{
``` |
| 6 | In this handler:<br><br>a. Retrieve the data in `FileDrop` format associated with the event.<br>b. Convert this data to an `Array` instance.<br>c. For each `object` in the array, convert the `object` to a `string`. | ```
object obj = e.Data.GetData(
                 DataFormats.FileDrop);
Array files = obj as Array;

int index = -1;
foreach (object o in files)
{
    string s = o as string;
``` |
| 7 | If a string is found, then:<br><br>a. Create a new `Photograph` object using this string.<br>b. See if the `Photograph` is already in the current album.<br>c. If not, then add the new photo to the album.<br><br>**Note:** Recall that the `Photograph` object will simply display a bad image bitmap if an invalid or non-image file name is provided. | ```
if (s != null)
{
    Photograph photo
        = new Photograph(s);

    // Add the file (if not present)
    index = _album.IndexOf(photo);
    if (index < 0)
    {
        index = _album.Add(photo);
        _bAlbumChanged = true;
    }
}
}
``` |
| 8 | If a `Photograph` was found in the `foreach` loop, then<br><br>a. Adjust the current album position to the discovered index.<br>b. Invalidate the form to redraw the window. | ```
if (index >= 0)
{
    // Show the last image added
    _album.CurrentPosition = index;
    Invalidate();
}
}
``` |

This completes our handling of drag and drop. Compile and run the program to see this in action. Display two different albums in separate `MainForm` windows. You should be able to perform the following drag and drop operations to obtain the described results:

- Find a new image file in Windows Explorer. Drag this file into one of the album windows. The image is added to the album and displayed in the window.

- Find an image file in Windows Explorer that is already in an album. Drag this file into the album. The existing `Photograph` object is displayed in the window.
```

- Highlight a set of files in Windows Explorer. Drag these files into one of the album windows. Each file is added to the window if not already present. The last file added is displayed in the window.
- Click on an image displayed in one album window and drag it to a second album window. The image is added to the second album, or displayed if it is already present.

This completes our drag and drop example. We should also mention that the List-View and TreeView classes support per-item dragging via the ItemDrag event. The ItemDrag event occurs when the user begins dragging an item in the list or tree. Typically, the event handler for the ItemDrag event calls the DoDragDrop method as we did in this section, with the object associated with a specific list item or tree node as the source of the operation. For example, we could modify our MyAlbumExplorer interface to permit photographs to be reordered within the ListView control, or dragged into a new album in the TreeView control.

18.4 ACTIVEX CONTROLS

Our final section will look at how to include an ActiveX control, more specifically the Microsoft Web Browser control, within a Windows Forms application. We will avoid a detailed discussion of ActiveX in general and the Web Browser control in particular, and instead allow the example to speak for itself.

Our example will host a browser control within an About Box dialog for our MyPhotos application. This may seem slightly unorthodox, but should create an interesting example while still presenting the topic at hand.

The foundation of ActiveX support in Windows Forms is the AxHost control. This abstract class is, quite simply, a control that hosts, or displays, an ActiveX control as a full-featured Windows Forms control. The class is based on the Windows Forms Control class so that the standard properties, methods, and events we have discussed throughout the book are available in hosted controls. The .NET framework provides an ActiveX Control Importer tool to generate an AxHost interface for a specific ActiveX control. We will discuss this tool in a moment.

In our application, we will create an AboutBox form to display information about the application. As shown in figure 18.4, this Form will include a LinkLabel object that will link to the web site for this book.

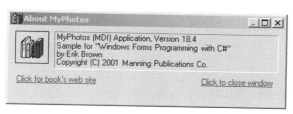

Figure 18.4
This form uses a Label control to display the application Icon, and LinkLabel controls to initiate user actions.

We could just as easily use `Button` controls rather than link labels. Since we have not used `LinkLabel` objects in a previous example, this is a good opportunity to do so here. When the user clicks the "Click to close window" label, the window will close as we have seen with a Close button in previous examples. When the user clicks the "Click for book's web site" label, a hidden panel will appear and display the web site for the book you are reading. This is shown in figure 18.5. Note in this figure that the title bar of the form reflects the current web page title, and the link label text now allows the user to hide the web browser. Of course, connecting to the web site presumes you have an active connection to the Internet available.

Figure 18.5 In the embedded web page in this window, the user can follow any links displayed and perform other standard browser actions in the window.

We will divide our discussion into three sections. First we will create the form required; then we will wrap the Web Browser control in an `AxHost` control, and finally we will use this new control to display the web page as in figure 18.5.

18.4.1 CREATING THE ABOUT BOX

Our first task is to create the new `Form` class for our new About box. The steps required are as follows:

Set the version number of the MyPhotos application to 18.4.

	DESIGN THE ABOUT BOX FORM	
	Action	**Result**
1	Add a new `Form` class file to the MyPhotos project called AboutBox.cs.	
2	Assign the following settings to the form.	

Settings (step 2)

Property	Value
MinimizeBox	False
ShowInTaskbar	False
Size	400,144
StartPosition	CenterParent
Text	About MyPhotos

| **3** | Drag an `ImageList` onto the form and set the following properties: | |

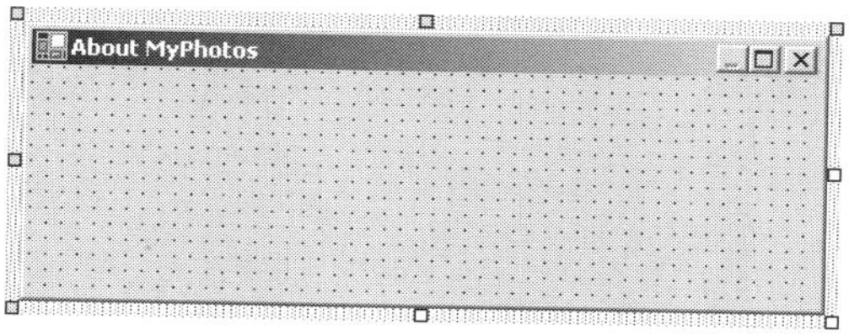

Settings (step 3)

Property	Value
(Name)	imageIcons
ImageSize	32, 32

4	Add the following icons from the common image directory to the `Images` collection for this list.
	• icons/Writing/BOOK02.ICO
	• icons/Writing/BOOKS04.ICO

<table>
<tr><th colspan="3">DESIGN THE ABOUT BOX FORM (continued)</th></tr>
<tr><th></th><th>Action</th><th>Result</th></tr>
<tr><td>5</td><td>Add the four labels, namely two <code>Label</code> controls and two <code>LinkLabel</code> controls, to the form. Size and position them as shown in the graphic.
Settings
<table>
<tr><th>Control</th><th>Property</th><th>Value</th></tr>
<tr><td>Icon Label</td><td>(Name)</td><td>lblIcon</td></tr>
<tr><td></td><td>BorderStyle</td><td>FixedSingle</td></tr>
<tr><td></td><td>ImageList</td><td>imageIcons</td></tr>
<tr><td></td><td>ImageIndex</td><td>0</td></tr>
<tr><td></td><td>Text</td><td></td></tr>
<tr><td>Text Label</td><td>(Name)</td><td>lblAboutText</td></tr>
<tr><td></td><td>Anchor</td><td>Top, Left, Right</td></tr>
<tr><td></td><td>BorderStyle</td><td>Fixed3D</td></tr>
<tr><td></td><td>Text</td><td>MyPhotos</td></tr>
<tr><td>Site Link</td><td>(Name)</td><td>linkWebSite</td></tr>
<tr><td></td><td>Text</td><td>Click for book's web site</td></tr>
<tr><td>Close Link</td><td>(Name)</td><td>linkClose</td></tr>
<tr><td></td><td>Anchor</td><td>Top, Right</td></tr>
<tr><td></td><td>Text</td><td>Click to close window</td></tr>
<tr><td></td><td>TextAlign</td><td>TopRight</td></tr>
</table></td><td>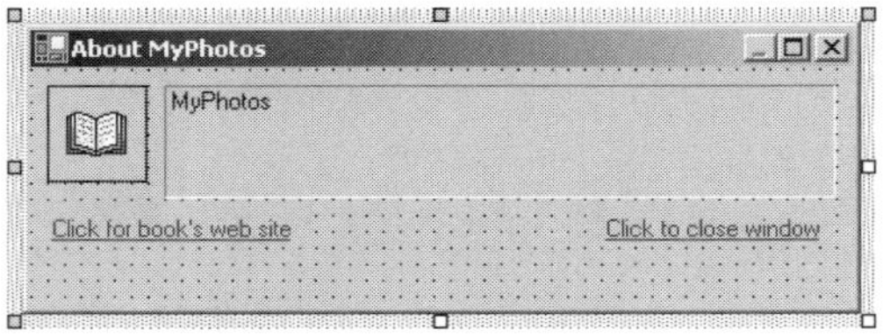
</td></tr>
<tr><td>6</td><td>Also add a hidden <code>Panel</code> control to the base of the form.
Settings
<table>
<tr><th>Property</th><th>Value</th></tr>
<tr><td>(Name)</td><td>pnlWebSite</td></tr>
<tr><td>Anchor</td><td>Top, Bottom, Left, Right</td></tr>
<tr><td>BorderStyle</td><td>Fixed3D</td></tr>
<tr><td>Visible</td><td>False</td></tr>
</table></td><td>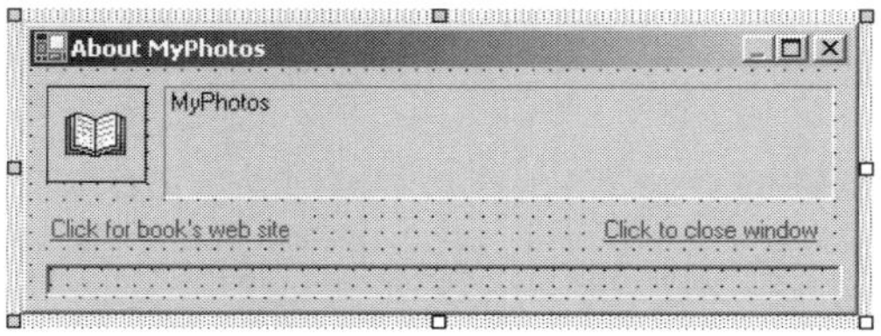

Note: The panel is visible in Visual Studio even though it will be hidden when the form is actually displayed.</td></tr>
</table>

This completes the design of our `AboutBox` form. We will also need a menu in the `ParentForm` class to display this form.

	Action	Result
7	In the ParentForm.cs [Design] window, add a new top-level Help menu.	

<table>
<tr><td colspan="2" align="center">Settings</td></tr>
<tr><td>Property</td><td>Value</td></tr>
<tr><td>(Name)</td><td>menuHelp</td></tr>
<tr><td>MergeOrder</td><td>9</td></tr>
<tr><td>Text</td><td>&Help</td></tr>
</table>

	Action	Result
8	Add a single About MyPhotos menu item under this new menu.	

<table>
<tr><td colspan="2" align="center">Settings</td></tr>
<tr><td>Property</td><td>Value</td></tr>
<tr><td>(Name)</td><td>menuAbout</td></tr>
<tr><td>Text</td><td>&About MyPhotos...</td></tr>
</table>

Our design is ready to go. Our next topic is the generation of wrapper classes for ActiveX controls.

18.4.2 WRAPPING THE WEB BROWSER CONTROL

As we mentioned earlier, the .NET Framework provides a tool for creating a derived AxHost class from an existing ActiveX control. This section will use this tool to wrap the standard browser control for use in our application.

The Windows Forms ActiveX Control Importer program is called "aximp" and is available as part of the Visual Studio .NET product. This program is run on the command line and accepts an ActiveX control library.

```
C:\> aximp source-file
```

The *source-file* here is the DLL or OCX file containing the ActiveX control. For our purposes, the Web Browser control is located in the file shdocvw.dll in the Windows "system32" directory. An AxHost based class can be created with the following steps:

CREATE WRAPPER CLASS FOR WEB BROWSER CONTROL		
	Action	**Result**
1	Display a Visual Studio .NET Command Prompt. **How-to** This is available from the Start menu in the Microsoft Visual Studio .NET folder, under the Visual Studio .NET Tools heading.	

2	Create a suitable directory for holding the generated wrapper class.
	
	`cd Windows Forms\Projects`
	`mkdir WebBrowser`
	
	Note: This example uses the directory "C:\Windows Forms\Projects\WebBrowser" for this purpose. You should use an appropriate directory for your application.	

3	Change the current directory to be this new directory. `cd WebBrowser`	

4	Generate the wrapper class by executing the following command:
	
	`aximp`
	`c:\winnt\system32\shdocvw.dll`
	
	Note: Depending on your operating system, you may need to replace "`c:\winnt`" in this command with the appropriate Windows directory.
		Two new assemblies are generated in the current directory. These are:
		
		`aximp c:\winnt\`
		`   system32\shdocvw.dll`

The two generated files work together to present the ActiveX control as a Windows Forms control in the .NET environment. The first file AxShDocVw.dll, is named by prepending "Ax" to the given source file name. This file encapsulates the Windows Forms proxy class for the control, derived from the AxHost class. Each object from the original library is defined under a namespace identical to the assembly name, in this case the AxShDocVw namespace.

The second file ShDocVw.dll, named identical to the given source file name, contains the common language runtime proxy for the COM types from the source library. This file is used implicitly by the Windows Forms control defined in the first file.

With a wrapper for our Web Browser control defined, we are ready to implement the internals of our About box.

18.4.3 USING THE WEB BROWSER CONTROL

So far we have defined a user interface and created a wrapper class for the Web Browser ActiveX control. In this section we will implement the `AboutBox` form to work as described earlier.

The following table begins this process by describing the changes required for our standard Windows Forms controls.

	HANDLE THE STANDARD CONTROLS	
	Action	**Result**
1	In the AboutBox.cs code window, create two constants for the two types of icons in our image list.	`protected const int SDI_ICON = 0;` `protected const int MDI_ICON = 1;`
| 2 | Implement an `IsMdiApplication` property to define whether the active form is a MDI application.<br><br>**How-to**<br>a. In the `get` accessor, return whether the current image index in the `lblIcon` control is the MDI icon.<br>b. In the `set` accessor, assign the `ImageIndex` for the `lblIcon` control based on the assigned `value` setting. | ```csharp
public bool IsMdiApplication
{
    get { return (lblIcon.ImageIndex
                     == MDI_ICON); }
    set
    {
        if (value)
            lblIcon.ImageIndex = MDI_ICON;
        else
            lblIcon.ImageIndex = SDI_ICON;
    }
}
``` |
| 3 | Implement an `AboutText` property to get or set the `Text` property for the `lblAboutText` control. | ```csharp
public string AboutText
{
    get { return lblAboutText.Text; }
    set { lblAboutText.Text = value; }
}
``` |
| 4 | In the `ParentForm` class, add a `Click` handler for the About MyPhotos menu to create an `AboutBox` instance and assign its settings.<br><br>**How-to**<br>a. Set `IsMdiApplication` to true.<br>b. Set the `AboutText` property to an appropriate string.<br>c. Set the `Owner` property to the current `Form`.<br>d. Set the dialog's `Icon` to use the current form's icon.<br>e. Show the dialog. | ```csharp
private void menuAbout_Click
    (object sender, System.EventArgs e)
{
    AboutBox dlg = new AboutBox();
    dlg.IsMdiApplication = true;

    Version ver = new
        Version(Application.ProductVersion);
    dlg.AboutText
        = String.Format("MyPhotos (MDI) "
        + "Application, Version {0:#}.{1:#} "
        + "\nSample for /"Windows Forms "
        + "Programming with C#\"\nby "
        + "Erik Brown \nCopyright (C) 2001 "
        + "Manning Publications Co.",
        ver.Major, ver.Minor);
    dlg.Owner = this;
    dlg.Icon = this.Icon;

    dlg.Show();
}
``` |
```

	Action	Result

5	Back in the `AboutBox` class, add a `LinkClicked` handler for the `linkClose` link label control to close the form.
	
	How-to
	This is the default event for link labels, so simply double-click the link control in the design window.
		```private void linkClose_LinkClicked```
		 ``` (object sender, System.Windows.Forms.```
		 ``` LinkLabelLinkClickedEventArgs e)```
		 ```{```
		 ``` Close();```
		 ```}```

These changes configure the controls with the appropriate information and behavior. Note that the `LinkClicked` event handler receives a `LinkLabelLinkClicked-EventArgs` object as its event parameter. The `LinkLabel` class provides a `Links` property that defines one or more links, as a collection of `LinkLabel.Link` objects, within the single link label control. The `LinkLabelLinkClickedEvent-Args` object specifies the link that was clicked by the user.

In our application, our labels use the entire text string as a link. Let's continue the previous steps and handle the `linkWebSite` control to see how to bring up a Web Browser.

	HANDLE THE linkWEBSITE CONTROL	
	Action	**Result**
6	Add a reference to the generated AxSHDocVW.dll assembly in the MyPhotos project. **How-to** In the Add Reference dialog, click the Browse... button to locate and select the generated assembly.	
7	In the AboutBox.cs code window, indicate that we will use this library in our code.	```using AxSHDocVw;```

	Action	**Result**

8	Define the following fields in our `AboutBox` class:
	
	a. A browser field representing a `WebBrowser` control.
	
	b. A constant `string` containing the web site we will display.
		```private AxWebBrowser browser;```
		 ```private const string startPage```
		 ``` = "www.manning.com/eebrown";```
		
		Note: The `AxWebBrowser` class here is based on Microsoft's SHDocVw.dll library from the Windows directory. We will not cover the contents of this library in detail, as it is beyond the scope of our current discussion. Look up the *WebBrowser Control* index entry in the online documentation provided with Visual Studio .NET for more information on this class.

9	Add a `LinkLabel` event handler for the `linkWebSite` control.	```private void linkWebSite_LinkClicked```
		 ``` (object sender, System.Windows.Forms.```
		 ``` LinkLabelLinkClickedEventArgs e)```
		 ```{```

10	If the `browser` control already exists, then shut down the web site and hide the `Panel` object.
	
	Note: This code resets the dialog to its original state.
		```if (browser != null)```
		 ```{```
		 ``` // Shut down existing browser```
		 ``` pnlWebSite.Visible = false;```
		 ``` browser.Dispose();```
		 ``` browser = null;```
		
		 ``` // Reset dialog settings```
		 ``` linkWebSite.Text```
		 ``` = "Click for book's web site";```
		 ``` this.Size = new Size(400, 140);```
		 ``` this.Text = "About MyPhotos";```
		 ```}```

11	If the `browser` control does not exist, then create the browser and define some initial settings.
	
	How-to
	
	a. Create a new `AxWebBrowser` control.
	
	b. Set its `Dock` property to `Fill`.
	
	c. Add a `TitleChange` event handler.
	
	d. Add a `HandleCreated` event handler.
		```else```
		 ```{```
		 ``` // Create web browser object```
		 ``` browser = new AxWebBrowser();```
		 ``` browser.Dock = DockStyle.Fill;```
		
		 ``` browser.TitleChange += new```
		 ``` DWebBrowserEvents2_TitleChangeEventHandler```
		 ``` (this.browser_TitleChange);```
		 ``` browser.HandleCreated += new```
		 ``` EventHandler(this.browser_HandleCreated);```
		
		Note: The `HandleCreated` event is inherited from the `Control` class and uses the familiar mechanism. The `TitleChange` event is part of the `WebBrowser` control, and is part of the `AxSHDocVw` namespace.
		Details on the `DWebBrowserEvents2` interface and the `TitleChange` event are included with the online documentation for Visual Studio .NET.

12	Make the `Panel` control on the form visible and add the `browser` control to appear within this panel.	``` // Show panel containing new browser```
		 ``` pnlWebSite.SuspendLayout();```
		 ``` pnlWebSite.Visible = true;```
		 ``` pnlWebSite.Controls.Add(browser);```
		 ``` pnlWebSite.ResumeLayout();```

	Action	Result
13	Modify the text displayed for the `linkWebSite` control and enlarge the `Form` to be 600x400 pixels.	```csharp linkWebSite.Text = "Click to hide web page"; this.Size = new Size(600, 400); } } ```
14	Create the handler for the `TitleChange` event to display the new document title in the title bar of the `AboutBox` form.	```csharp private void browser_TitleChange (object sender, DWebBrowserEvents2_TitleChangeEvent e) { this.Text = e.text; } ```
15	Add a `DisplayPage` method to navigate to a given URL. **How-to** a. Create `object` instances to represent the reference parameters. b. Display the wait cursor. c. Use the `Navigate` method to display the given URL. d. Finally, reset the current cursor. **Note:** The `Navigate` method is discussed in the online documentation. The four `param` objects are required here to match the signature of the `Navigate` method as defined by the ActiveX Control Importer (aximp.exe). A future version of the importer may permit these settings to be `null`.	```csharp protected void DisplayPage(string url) { // These are required because the importer // assumes these are in/out parameters // and defines them as passed by reference. object param2 = 0; object param3 = ""; object param4 = ""; object param5 = ""; try { Cursor.Current = Cursors.WaitCursor; browser.Navigate(url, ref param2, ref param3, ref param4, ref param5); } finally { Cursor.Current = Cursors.Default; } } ```
16	Create the handler for the `HandleCreated` event to display the start page. **How-to** a. Display the starting page using the `DisplayPage` method. b. Remove the `HandleCreated` handler.	```csharp public void browser_HandleCreated (object sender, EventArgs evArgs) { // The WebBrowser has been created // Display the starting page DisplayPage(startPage); // Remove this handler browser.HandleCreated -= new EventHandler(this.browser_HandleCreated); } ```

This completes our implementation. Compile and run to view the `AboutBox` dialog in all its glory. You will notice that when viewing the web page within our application, the user cannot navigate to an arbitrary web address. This is very different than using a Web Browser such as Internet Explorer, where the user has more control over which pages are displayed.

This completes our example wrapping the Web Browser ActiveX control as a Windows Forms control. It also completes this chapter as well as the book.

In keeping with tradition, we provide a final recap of the topics covered in this chapter.

18.5 RECAP

This chapter presented an overview of various topics in Windows Forms application development. Each topic was discussed very briefly, and we demonstrated each feature with an example that extended the MyPhotos MDI application built in chapter 16.

The specific topics covered included printing from an application, using Windows Forms timers, dragging and dropping objects into and out of an application, and hosting an ActiveX control within a Windows Forms program. On the final topic, we illustrated this feature by embedding a Web Browser control within an `AboutBox` form displayed by our application.

Along the way we also illustrated some classes not previously discussed, notably the `TrackBar` and `LinkLabel` controls. More details on these as well as the other topics in this chapter are available in the online documentation for the .NET Framework.

If you have read this book from cover to cover, then congratulations. Regardless of how you came to this sentence, the appendices include some reference material on C# and .NET namespaces, as well as class hierarchy charts for the Windows Forms namespace.

Good luck with your programming endeavors. May your code always compile and applications never fail.

APPENDIX A

C# primer

A.1   C# programs 638
A.2   Types 639
A.3   Language elements 654
A.4   Special features 667

This appendix provides an introduction and reference to the C# programming language. If you are looking for a detailed description of C#, there are a number of resources listed in the bibliography that provide this kind of coverage. If you are familiar with object-oriented programming or with C-based languages such as C++ or Java, then this appendix will get you started and serve as a quick reference for terms and keywords you encounter in this book and elsewhere.

You will also discover that many of the terms and keywords presented here are discussed in detail in the text. A reference to one or more of these locations is provided for many of the topics shown here. These are also indexed at the back of the book.

This appendix will approach C# in a somewhat formal manner. We will discuss the following topics:

- The organization of a C# program.

- The types and type members available in the language.

- The formal elements of the language, including built-in types, operators, and keywords.

- Special features of C#, such as arrays and automated documentation.

637

A.1 *C# PROGRAMS*

A C# program consists of a collection of *source files* where each source file is an ordered sequence of Unicode characters. Typically, each source file corresponds to a single file in the file system. A program is *compiled* into a set of computer instructions known as an *assembly*. The .NET Framework interprets or otherwise executes an assembly to perform the instructions given in the original program.

A.1.1 ASSEMBLIES

Assemblies are containers for types, and are used to package and deploy compiled C# programs. An assembly may contain one or more types, the instructions to implement these types, and references to other assemblies. While not strictly required, an assembly is normally a single file in a file system. For example, the System.Windows.Forms.dll file is the assembly for the `System.Windows.Forms` namespace.

There are two kinds of assemblies: *Applications* and *libraries*. An application is an assembly that has a *main entry point* and usually has a ".exe" extension. Applications are used to perform a specific task or tasks on behalf of a computer user. The main entry point of an application is the initial instruction to execute in the program.

A library is an assembly that does not have a main entry point and usually has a ".dll" extension. Libraries are used to encapsulate one or more types for use when building other assemblies.

A.1.2 NAMESPACES

Logically, the source files in a C# program contain a collection of *namespaces*. Each namespace defines a scope, or *declaration space*, in which a set of zero or more *type declarations* and zero or more nested namespaces are defined. The possible type declarations are classes, structures, interfaces, enumerations, and delegates. Each type declaration is assigned a *name* that is unique within its declaration space, in this case within the defined namespace. It is an error for two type declarations to have the same name within the same namespace.

All type declarations are assigned to a namespace. If a specific namespace is not specified, then the type is assigned to the *default namespace*, also called the *global namespace*.

A namespace is declared in the following manner:[1]

```
namespace <name>
{
  <nested-namespaces>opt
  <type-declarations>
}
```

---

[1]   We use the convention here and in other syntax examples where items in angle brackets < > are filled-in by the programmer. An optional item will include an "opt" subscript following the item.

APPENDIX A   C# PRIMER

The <name> for a namespace can be a single identifier, or a series of identifiers separated by periods. Nested namespaces are declared in the same way as non-nested namespaces. The various kinds of type declarations each have their own syntax, and are described next.

A.2 TYPES

All types are classified as either a *value type* or a *reference type*. These correspond to whether the type stores the actual data, or value, for the type, or whether the type simply stores a reference to the actual data.

Value types include simple built-in types such as int and char, enumerations, and structures. A value type contains its data. For example, an int type assigned to the number 5 stores this number directly. Thus, two different value types contain separate copies of the data and, therefore, modifying one of these types has no affect on the other. Value types include the built-in types, structures, and enumerations.

Reference types, on the other hand, contain a reference to their data. Examples include the string type and all Windows Forms controls. A string type assigned to the string "Hello" stores a reference to a section of memory where the characters "Hello" are actually stored. The area of memory reserved for reference types is called the *heap*, and is managed internally by the .NET Framework. Thus, two different reference types can point to the same physical data. As a result, the modification of one reference type can affect another reference type. Reference types include classes, interfaces, delegates, and arrays.

The following table illustrates the difference between these two kinds of types.

Comparison of value and reference types

	Value type	Reference type
Declaration	```struct ValInt { public int vData; }```	```class RefInt { public int rData; }```
Usage	```ValInt v1, v2; v1.vData = 5; v2 = v1; v1.vData = 7```	```RefInt r1, r2; r1.rData = 5; r2 = r1; r1.rData = 7;```
Result	Value of v2.vData is still 5.	Value of r2.rData is now 7.

In the value type column of the above table, the assignment of v2 = v1 copies the contents of v1 into v2. As a result, changing the value of v1.vData has no effect on the value stored by v2. In the reference column, the assignment of r2 = r1 causes both objects to refer to the same data. Here, changing the value of r1.rData also affects the value seen by r2. Note that all value types in the .NET Framework implicitly inherit from the System.ValueType class. This class overrides the methods inherited from the System.Object class with more appropriate implementations for value types.

Back to the topic at hand, a type is specified with a type declaration as part of a namespace, or within the default namespace. The possible type declarations are classes, structures, interfaces, enumerations, and delegates.

A.2.1 CLASSES

A *class* is a reference type that defines a new data abstraction. Each class is composed of one or more *members* that define the contents, operations, and behavior permitted by instances of the class.

A class is declared using the class keyword in the following manner:

```
<modifiers>opt class <identifier> : <base>opt <interfaces>opt
{
    <class-members>
}
```

where

- <modifiers> is optional, and is an accessibility level as defined in the subsequent table or one of the keywords new, abstract, or sealed. If unspecified, a class is assigned the default accessibility level of the containing declarative scope. Multiple complementary modifiers may be specified.

- <identifier> is the unique name to assign to the class.

- <base> is optional, and defines a single base class for the new class.

- <interfaces> is optional, and specifies one or more interface types which this class supports. If both <base> and <interfaces> are omitted, then the colon ':' is also omitted.

- <class-members> are the members of the class. The possible members of a class are constants, fields, methods, properties, events, indexers, operators, constructors, and nested type declarations. Nested type declarations are simply other types defined to exist within the declarative scope defined by the class. The other kinds of members are discussed in the subsequent sections.

Every member of a class, and in fact every member of any type, has a defined *accessibility* associated with it. The accessibility of a member controls which regions of a program may make use of that member. The five levels of accessibility are shown in the following table:

Accessibility levels for C# types

Accessibility level	Meaning
public	Any type in any assembly can access the member.
protected	Any derived type in any assembly can access the member.

Accessibility levels for C# types *(continued)*

Accessibility level	Meaning
internal	Any type in the same assembly can access the member.
protected internal	Any derived type in the same assembly can access the member.
private	Only the containing type can access the member.

These accessibility levels are used to declare nested types as well as other members. The default accessibility level of top-level types is `internal`. Within a class declaration, the default accessibility level is `private`. The default value of a class instance is `null`.

The various kinds of class members other than nested types are described in the following sections.

Constants

A *constant* is an unchangeable value that can be computed at compile time. A constant is declared using the const keyword in the following manner:

```
<modifiers>opt const <type> <constant-name> = <value> ;
```

where

- `<modifiers>` is optional, and must be either an accessibility level or the `new` keyword. If unspecified, a constant is assigned the default accessibility level of the containing declarative scope. Multiple complementary modifiers may be specified.

- `<type>` is any value type.

- `<constant-name>` is the unique name for the constant.

- `<value>` is the fixed value to assign to the constant.

A few examples of constant declarations are given below.

```
const int DaysPerYear = 365;

// The constant value here is calculated by the compiler.
const double AlmostPi = 22.0 / 7.0;

// A constant taken from a public enumeration.
public enum Weekday = { Sun, Mon, Tue, Wed, Thu, Fri, Sat };
protected const Weekday FirstDayOfWeek = Sun;
```

Fields

A *field* is a variable value that can be modified at run time. A field is declared in the following manner:

```
<modifiers>opt <type> <field-name> = <initial-value> ;
```

where

- `<modifiers>` is optional, and must be either an accessibility level or one of the keywords new, readonly, static, or volatile. If unspecified, a field is assigned the default accessibility level of the containing declarative scope. Multiple complementary modifiers may be specified.

- `<type>` is any valid type.

- `<field-name>` is the unique name for the field.

- `<initial-value>` is the value to initially assign to the field. This value may be modified by the program at runtime.

A few examples of field declarations are given below.

```
public readonly string _defaultDir = @"C:\My Documents\Albums";
private PhotoAlbum _album;

// Possible fields in a Fraction class
public class Fraction
{
  private long _num;
  private long _den;
  . . .
}
```

Methods

A *method* is a member that implements an operation or action that can be performed by a class or other object. For example, in a Fraction class, a method could be used to add two fractions together or compute the inverse of a fraction. A method may return a result, and can optionally accept one or more parameters that are used to perform the implemented action. A method is declared in the following manner:

```
<modifiers>opt <return-type> <member-name> ( <parameters>opt )
{
  <statements>opt
}
```

where

- `<modifiers>` is optional, and must be either an accessibility level or one of the keywords new, static, virtual, sealed, override, abstract, or extern. If unspecified, a method is assigned the default accessibility level of the containing declarative scope. Multiple complementary modifiers may be specified.

- `<return-type>` is either a valid type or the void keyword. When a type is specified, the return keyword is used to return an instance of this type as the result of the method.

- `<member-name>` is the unique name for the method.

- `<parameters>` is optional. When specified, each parameter provides a type and an identifier, with possible modifiers `out` and `ref`. The `params` keyword may be used as the final parameter to indicate an array of values of a given type.
- `<statements>` is optional and specifies one or more statements specifying the computer instructions for performing the defined action.

A few examples of method declarations that might be provided as part of a `Fraction` class are given as follows:

```
// public method
public void Add(Fraction b)
{
  this._den = this._den * b._den;
  this._num = (this._num * b._den) + (b._num * this._den);
}

// protected method with ref parameter
protected void Invert(ref Fraction a)
{
  Fraction f = new Fraction(a._den, a._num);
  a = f;
}

// static method with return type and params parameter
public static Fraction AddMultiple(params Fractions[] fracts)
{
  Fraction a = new Fraction(1, 1);
  foreach (Fraction f in fracts)
  {
    a.Add(f);
  }

  return a;
}
```

Properties

A *property* is a member that provides access to a characteristic of a class or other object. For example, in a `Fraction` class, a property might provide the numerator of the fraction, or the floating-point value of the fraction. A property provides *accessors* that specify the operations to perform when its value is read or written. A property may support both read and write accessors, called `get` and `set` respectively, or be read-only or write-only. A property is declared in the following manner:

```
<modifiers>opt <type> <member-name>
{
  <property-accessors>
}
```

where

- `<modifiers>` is optional, and must be either an accessibility level or one of the keywords new, static, virtual, sealed, override, abstract, or extern. If unspecified, a property is assigned the default accessibility level of the containing declarative scope. Multiple complementary modifiers may be specified.
- `<type>` is the type for the property.
- `<member-name>` is the unique name for the property.
- `<property-accessors>` is one or both of the get and set accessor. Each accessor consists of its accessor type, either get or set, and the block of statements defining the programming instructions for this accessor. In the get accessor, the type of the property must be returned using the return keyword. In the set accessor, an implicit parameter called value is used to represent the instance of the specified type provided by the caller.

Note that properties are declared much like methods, except that properties do not use parentheses and cannot have explicit parameters. A few examples of property declarations that might be used within a Fraction class are given below.

```
public long Numerator
{
  get { return this._num; }
  set { this._num = value; }
}

public long Denominator
{
  get { return this._den; }
  set
  {
    if (value == 0)
      throw new DivideByZeroException("Denominator cannot be zero");

    this._den = value;
  }
}

// a read-only property
protected double Value
{
  get { return ((double)this._num / (double)this._den); }
}
```

Events

An *event* is a member that enables a class or other object to provide notifications. An instance of a class can associate one or more methods, known as *event handlers*, with specific events in order to receive such notifications. An event is declared using the event keyword. Like properties, an event can declare *accessors* to specify how event handlers are added to or removed from the event. Such accessors are optional, resulting in the following forms for an event declaration:

```
<modifiers>opt event <delegate-type> <member-name> ;

<modifiers>opt event <delegate-type> <member-name>
{
  <event-accessors>
}
```

where

- `<modifiers>` is optional, and must be an accessibility level or one of the keywords new, `static`, `virtual`, `sealed`, `override`, `abstract`, or `extern`. If unspecified, a property is assigned the default accessibility level of the containing declarative scope. Multiple complementary modifiers may be specified.
- `<delegate-type>` is the delegate on which this event is based.
- `<member-name>` is the unique name for the property.
- `<event-accessors>`, when specified, must provide both the `add` and `remove` accessor. These accessors define how a method is added to and removed from the event. In both accessors, an implicit parameter called `value` is used to represent the specified method.

Outside of the type where an event is defined, only the += and −= operators are permitted in order to add and remove methods, respectively. Methods are added to events as delegate instances based on the delegate type for the event. The following code shows how a `DivideByZero` event might be implemented within a `Fraction` class:

```
// public class for event data
public class DivideByZeroArgs
{
  . . .
}

public delegate void DivideByZeroHandler(object sender,
                                         DivideByZeroArgs e);

public class Fraction
{
  . . .
  // Declare the DivideByZero event for this class
  public event DivideByZeroHandler DivideByZero;

  // Declare a method to invoke the event
  public virtual void OnDivideByZero(DivideByZeroArgs e)
  {
    if (DivideByZero == null)
    {
      // No handlers, so raise exception
      throw new DivideByZeroException("Divide by zero");
    }
    else
      DivideByZero(this, e);  // call event handlers
  }
```

```
// Declare property that can invoke event
public long Denominator
{
  get { return this._den; }
  set
  {
    if (value == 0)
    {
      DivideByZeroArgs args = new DivideByZeroArgs(..);
      OnDivideByZero(this, args);
      // Do something based on event handler
    }
    else
      this._den = value;
  }
}
```

Indexers

An *indexer* is a member that enables an object to be treated as an array. Elements in the "array" are referenced using square brackets. An indexer employs the this keyword as part of its declaration, which typically appears as follows:

```
<modifiers>opt <type> this [ <parameters> ]
{
  <accessors>
}
```

where

- <modifiers> is optional, and must be an accessibility level or one of the keywords new, virtual, sealed, override, or abstract. If unspecified, an indexer is assigned the default accessibility level of the containing declarative scope. Multiple complementary modifiers may be specified.

- <type> is the type returned by this indexer. This typically corresponds to the type of objects contained by the containing class.

- <parameters> are the parameters for the indexer. The format corresponds to that of a method, except that at least one parameter is required for an indexer, and ref and out parameters are not permitted.

- <property-accessors> provide the block of statements associated with reading and writing indexer elements. These are identical to the accessors used for properties.

The following code shows a PartsOfOne class that provides the fractions between 0 and 1, inclusive, that divide an object into an equal number of parts. An indexer is used to return the nth Fraction object. For example, PartsOfOne(3) will return the fractions for zero (as 0 over 3), one-third, two-thirds, and one (as 3 over 3).

```
public class PartsOfOne
```

```
{
  private ulong _parts;

  PartsOfOne(ulong parts)
  {
    _parts = parts;
  }

  // Indexer to return nth part as a Fraction between 0 and 1
  public Fraction this[ulong n]
  {
    if (n < 0 || n > _parts)
      throw new IndexOutOfRangeException();

    return new Fraction(n, _parts);
  }
}
```

Operators

An *operator* is a member that defines the meaning of an expression operator as applied to an instance of an object. There are three types of operators. A *unary operator* applies to a single type, a *binary operator* applies to two types, and a *conversion operator* converts an object from one type to another. The corresponding three operator types all use the `operator` keyword, and are formatted as follows:

```
<modifiers> <type> operator <unary-op> (<parameter>)
{
  <statements>
}

<modifiers> <type> operator <binary-op> (<parameter>, <parameter>)
{
  <statements>
}

<modifiers> <conv-kind> operator <type> (<parameter>)
{
  <statements>
}
```

where

- `<modifiers>` must be one of the keywords `public`, `static`, or `extern`.
- `<type>` is the type returned by the operator.
- `<unary-op>` is a unary operator: `+ - ! ~ ++ -- true false`
- `<binary-op>` is a binary operator: `+ - * / % & | ^ << >> == != > < >= <=`
- `<conv-kind>` is the kind of conversion, either `implicit` or `explicit`. An implicit conversion is invoked automatically by the compiler, such as from `int` to `long`. An explicit conversion requires an explicit cast, such as from `int` to `byte`.

- `<parameter>` is a type and identifier to accept in the conversion.
- `<statements>` is the block of statements associated with the operator. This block must return a value of the specified type.

The following code shows an example of unary, binary, and conversion operator declaration for a `Fraction` class.

```
// Unary operator for the negative operation
public Fraction operator -(Fraction a)
{
  return new Fraction(-a.Numerator, a.Denominator);
}

// Binary operator for the addition operation
public Fraction operator +(Fraction a, Fraction b)
{
  int den = a.Denominator * b.Denominator;
  int num = (a.Numerator * b.Denominator)
          + (b.Numerator * a.Denominator);
  return new Fraction(num, den);
}

// Explicit conversion from Fraction to double
static explicit operator double(Fraction a)
{
  return ((double)a.Numerator / (double)a.Denominator);
}
```

Constructor

A *constructor* is a member that initializes a class or an instance of a class or other object. There are two types of constructors. A *static constructor* performs one-time initialization for an object, while an *instance constructor* initializes a specific instance of an object. Static constructors cannot be invoked explicitly and are executed at most once in a program after any static fields have been initialized and before any static class members are referenced or instances of the class created. Instance constructors are executed as an object is created. The *default constructor* for a class is an instance constructor with no parameters, and is created automatically if no instance constructors for a class are provided.

Constructors are declared as follows, with static constructors declared using the `static` keyword:

```
static <identifier>()
{
  <statements>
}

<modifiers> <identifier> (<parameters>opt) <initializer>opt
{
  <statements>
}
```

where

- `<identifier>` is the name of the type for which the constructor is defined.
- `<modifiers>` is optional, and must be an accessibility level or the keyword `extern`. If unspecified, a constructor is assigned the default accessibility level of the containing declarative scope. Multiple complementary modifiers may be specified.
- `<parameters>` is optional, and specifies one or more parameters for the constructor. These are identical to method parameters.
- `<initializer>` is optional, and specifies another instance constructor to invoke before this instance constructor is executed. This has the form `base(<args>)` or `this(<args>)`, where `<args>` specifies zero or more arguments for the constructor to invoke. The `base` keyword form invokes an instance constructor in the base class, while the `this` keyword form invokes another instance constructor in the same object.
- `<statements>` is the block of statements associated with the constructor.

The following code shows some examples of constructors as might be provided for a `Fraction` class:

```
public class Fraction
{
  private static readonly int Unit;

  // This a lame example of a static constructor
  static Fraction()
  {
    Unit = 1;
  }

  private long _num;
  private long _den;

  // Instance constructors
  public Fraction(long top, long bottom)
  {
    _num = top;
    _den = bottom;
  }

  public Fraction(long number) : this(number, 1)
  {
  }
  . . .
}
```

Destructor

A *destructor* is a member that implements the actions required to destroy an instance of a class. The destructor for a class may be invoked any time after the instance is no longer accessible by any code. Any destructors for inherited classes are invoked at this time as well. A destructor is declared as follows:

```
~ <identifier>()
{
  <statements>
}
```

where

- <identifier> is the name of the class for which the destructor is defined.
- <statements> is the block of statements associated with the destructor.

In many, if not most, situations, a destructor is not required. When a Dispose method is required to clean up non-memory resources, a destructor should normally be provided to call the Dispose method in the event a program fails to do so explicitly.

For a Fraction class, a destructor is most likely not required. However, in order to give an example, a destructor for this class might be concocted as follows:

```
public class Fraction
{
  private long _num;
  private long _den;
  . . .

  // Destructor (not the best example)
  ~Fraction()
  {
    _num = 0;
    _den = 1;
  }
}
```

A.2.2   STRUCTURES

A *structure* is a value type that defines a new data abstraction. Structures are very similar to classes, except that classes are allocated on the heap while structures are allocated in place, either on the stack or within the type that declares them. Structures also cannot be inherited, nor can they inherit from other classes. The default value of a structure instance is the value obtained by setting each value type member to its default value and all reference types to null.

A structure is declared using the struct keyword with the following form:

```
<modifiers>opt struct <identifier> : <interfaces>opt
{
  <struct-members>
}
```

where

- `<modifiers>` is optional, and must be an accessibility level or the keyword new. If unspecified, a structure is assigned the default accessibility level of the containing declarative scope. Multiple complementary modifiers may be specified.
- `<identifier>` is the unique name to assign to the structure.
- `<interfaces>` is optional, and specifies one or more interface types which this structure supports. If `<interfaces>` is omitted, then the colon ':' is also omitted.
- `<struct-members>` are the members of the structure. Structures contain the same kinds of members as classes, namely constants, fields, methods, properties, events, indexers, operators, constructors, and nested type declarations. The meaning and purpose of these members is identical to that previously described for classes. One difference is that a default constructor for structures is provided automatically, and cannot be explicitly specified. If not specified, a struct member is assigned the private accessibility level.

Structures are appropriate for short-lived or small objects where local allocation is beneficial. The Fraction class used in examples throughout this appendix might be a good candidate for a structure. Here is an example of a PageRef structure that stores a range of page numbers:

```
public struct PageRef
{
    private int _startPage;
    private int _endPage;

    // Declarations of members to manipulate pages
}
```

A.2.3 INTERFACES

An *interface* is a reference type that defines a contract consisting of a set of members. A class or structure supports an interface by specifying the interface in its specification and adhering to the defined contract. This is done by providing implementations of each interface member within the class or structure. An instance of an interface type cannot be explicitly declared, although an instance of a class or structure may be cast to an interface type.

An interface is declared using the interface keyword in the following manner:

```
<modifiers>opt interface <identifier> : <interfaces>opt
{
    <interface-members>
}
```

where

- `<modifiers>` is optional, and must be an accessibility level or the keyword new. If unspecified, an interface is assigned the default accessibility level of the containing declarative scope. Multiple complementary modifiers may be specified.

- `<identifier>` is the unique name to assign to the interface. By convention, all interface identifiers begin with a capital I.

- `<interfaces>` is optional, and specifies one or more interface types which must also be supported in order for a class or structure to support this interface. If `<interfaces>` are omitted, then the colon ':' is also omitted.

- `<interface-members>` are the members required in order to support this interface. The possible members of an interface are methods, properties, events, and indexers. The declarations of these members mimic the declaration shown for classes, except that an implementation is not provided nor is an accessibility level defined. All interface members are considered to be publicly accessible.

Here is an example of an `IBookDisplay` interface that might be provided to indicate how a book is displayed in a Windows Forms `Panel` control:

```
interface IBookDisplay
{
  // Interface properties must indicate which accessors to support
  int ReadingRate
  {
    get;
    set;
  }

  void BeginDisplay(Panel displayPanel);
  void NextPage();
  void EndDisplay();

  Page this[int pageNum];
}

// Class that supports the IBookDisplay interface
public class PhotoAlbum : CollectionBase, IBookDisplay
{
  // Implementation of IBookDisplay
  // interface and other members
}
```

A.2.4 ENUMERATIONS

An *enumeration* is a value type that defines a related group of symbolic constants, and is quite similar to enumeration types in C. The default value of an enumeration instance is the value obtained by casting the number zero (0) to the enumeration type. All enumeration types implicitly inherit from the `System.Enum` class in the .NET Framework. This class provides a standard set of methods that may be used when manipulating enumerations.

An enumeration is declared using the enum keyword in the following manner:

```
<modifiers>opt enum <identifier> : <int-type>opt
{
  <enum-members>
}
```

where

- <modifiers> is optional, and must be an accessibility level or the keyword new. If unspecified, an enumeration is assigned the default accessibility level of the containing declarative scope. Multiple complementary modifiers may be specified.
- <identifier> is the unique name to assign to the enumeration.
- <int-type> is optional, and specifies a built-in integer type to represent the declared enumeration values. This integer type is one of byte, sbyte, short, ushort, int, uint, long, or ulong. If an <int-type> is not specified, the colon is omitted and the int type is used. Note that the possible values for an enumeration are not limited to its explicitly declared members. Any valid value of the underlying type is a valid value for the enumeration type.
- <enum-members> are the members of this enumeration. Each member is written as <identifier> or as <identifier> = <int-value>. Multiple members are separated by commas ',' and each member has an assigned constant integer value. The default assigned value for the first member is zero, and the default value for subsequent members is one greater than the value assigned to the previous member.

Here are a few examples of enumerations:

```
// Days of week (values 0 to 6)
enum DaysOfWeek1 = { Sun, Mon, Tue, Wed, Thu, Fri, Sat }

// Days of week as unsigned short types (values 1 to 7)
enum DaysOfWeek2 : ushort = { Sunday = 1, Monday, Tuesday,
                              Wednesday, Thursday, Friday, Saturday }

// Multiples of 10 enumeration
enum TensTable =
{
  Ten = 10, Twenty = 20, Thirty = 30, Forty = 40, Fifty = 50,
  Sixty = 60, Seventy = 70, Eighty = 80, Ninety = 90
}
```

A.2.5   DELEGATES

A *delegate* is a reference type that encapsulates one or more methods. A delegate is created with a defined method signature, and any method in any class or structure that adheres to this defined signature may be assigned to the delegate. Each method assigned to a delegate is referred to as a *callable entity*.

In the .NET Framework, a delegate is a class implicitly derived from the System.Delegate class. Note that an instance of a delegate, since it is implicitly a class, has a default value of null.

Delegates are declared and used somewhat like function pointers in C++, except that delegates encapsulate both an object instance and a method. This encapsulation of the object as well as the method permits delegates to refer to both static and instance methods. The declaration of a delegate requires the `delegate` keyword employed in the following manner:

<modifiers>_{opt} delegate <return-type> <identifier> (<parameters>_{opt})

where

- `<modifiers>` is optional, and must be an accessibility level or the keyword new. If unspecified, a delegate is assigned the default accessibility level of the containing declarative scope. Multiple complementary modifiers may be specified.

- `<return-type>` is the return type for the delegate.

- `<identifier>` is the unique name to assign to the delegate.

- `<parameters>` is optional, and indicates the parameters for the delegate. Delegate parameters are specified in the same manner as method parameters for a method within a class or structure.

A few examples of delegates are given below. Delegates are also used to create events in the Events discussion on page 644. A detailed example using a delegate appears in section 9.2.1 on page 272.

```
protected delegate int FindIndex(string name);
public delegate void EventHandler(object sender, EventArgs e);
public delegate Photograph ReadDelegate(StreamReader sr);
```

A.3 LANGUAGE ELEMENTS

This section presents the built-in types, operators, and keywords of C# in tabular form. The tables present a brief description of each item. The following aspects of the C# language are presented:

- Built-in types

- Operators

- Keywords

A.3.1 BUILT-IN TYPES

The following table summarizes the types built into C#. These types, as well as all user-defined types in C#, implicitly inherit from the `object` class, which also appears in this table. The table provides a short description of each type, along with each type's default value and the class used to represent the type in the .NET Framework. Within C# source files written for the framework, the type and the .NET class are interchangeable.

C# built-in types

Type	Description	Default value	.NET class
bool	A boolean value	`false`	System.Boolean
byte	An unsigned 8-bit integer	`(byte)0`	System.Byte

Type	Description	Default value	.NET class
char	A 16-bit Unicode character	`'\0'`	System.Char
decimal	A 128-bit decimal value	`0.0m`	System.Decimal
double	A 64-bit floating point value	`0.0d`	System.Double
float	A 32-bit floating point value	`0.0f`	System.Single
int	A 32-bit integer	`0`	System.Int32
long	A 64-bit integer	`0L`	System.Int64
object	Any object. The ultimate base class of any type.	`null`	System.Object
sbyte	An 8-bit integer	`(sbyte)0`	System.SByte
short	A 16-bit integer	`0`	System.Int16
string	A reference type of a collection of char types	`null`	System.String
uint	An unsigned 32-bit integer	`0u`	System.UInt32
ulong	An unsigned 64-bit integer	`(ulong)0`	System.UInt64
ushort	An unsigned 32-bit integer	`(ushort)0`	System.UInt16

A.3.2 OPERATORS

Many of the operators in C# are taken from C++ and have identical meanings. The following table summarizes the operators available as they relate to the built-in types. Most of these operators may be overridden for user-defined types. Keyword operators such as `true`, `new`, and `is` are not shown in this table. These are summarized in the table of keywords given in the next section.

C# operators

Category	Operators	Examples

Arithmetic	`+ - * / %`	`int num = -12;`
		`int age = days / 365;`
		`int onesPlace = number % 10;`

Logical (boolean and bitwise)	`&	^ ! ~ && ||`	`bool isTrue = ! false;` `int choices = gates & openSet;`
String concatenation	`+`	`string hi = "Hello " + "World!";`
Increment, decrement	`++ --`	`index ++;`
Shift	`<< >>`	`long kilobyte = 1 << 10;`
Relational	`== != > < <= >=`	`bool isDigit = (x >= 0) && (x < 10);`
Assignment	`= += -= *= /= %= &=` `|= ^= <<= >>=`	`int byFives += 5;`
Member access	`.`	`return myString.ToLower();`

Category	Operators	Examples
Indexing	[]	`Photograph first = _album[0];`
Cast	()	`short num = (short)7;` `Photograph photo = (Photograph) obj;`
Conditional	?:	`int size` `  = (list == null) ? 0 : list.Count;`
Delegates	+ - += -=	`photo.Display += new` `    DisplayHandler(photo_Display);`
Indirection and Address (in unsafe code only)	* -> {} &	`int num = 11;` `int* pnum = &num;`

A.3.3 KEYWORDS

This section presents a complete list of all keywords used by C#, along with a description and example of each keyword. These keywords are reserved words that have special meanings to the C# compiler, and should not normally be used as identifiers in your programs. To use a reserved keyword as an identifier, prefix the string with an at-sign '@' character. For example, while `class` is a reserved keyword, `@class` is a valid identifier.

Some of these keywords are discussed in detail in section A.2 beginning on page 639. Many of these keywords also appear elsewhere in the book. Sometimes a detailed discussion is provided, and sometimes the keyword just occurs as part of the presented code. The "See also" column in the following table provides a reference to these sections where appropriate:

C# keywords

Keyword	Description	Example	See also

abstract	Indicates that a class cannot be instantiated and is intended as a base for other classes.	`// Define an abstract class`
		`public abstract class Person`
		`{`
		`    // Define abstract members`
		`    public abstract string Address;`
		`    public abstract Point GetHomeCoord();`
		`    . . .`
		`}`
			sealed;
			Menu class in .NET Table 3.1, page 72

	Within an abstract class, indicates that a property or method has no implementation and must be overridden in a derived class.		sealed
as	Converts an expression to a given type. On an error, returns the value `null`.	`object obj = lstPhotos.SelectedItem;` `Photograph photo = obj as Photograph;`	is; example in section 9.3.4, page 300

APPENDIX A C# PRIMER

C# keywords *(continued)*

Keyword	Description	Example	See also
base	Represents the base class from within a derived class.	*See example for* `override` *keyword*.	example in section 5.3.3, page 148
bool	Denotes a boolean type, with possible values `true` and `false`.	`bool result = photo.IsValidImage();` `bool isExample = true;`	true; false; discussion in section 3.4.1, page 89

break	Terminates the enclosing loop or conditional construct. Execution resumes after the terminated construct.	`foreach (Photograph p in _album)`
		`{`
		`   if (p == myPhoto)`
		`     break;`
		`}`
			case;
			examples in section 6.7.1, page 190 and section 18.1.2, page 607

byte	Denotes an unsigned 8-bit integer value, with values 0 to 255.	`char c = 'y';` `byte b = Convert.ToByte(c);`	
case	Identifies a possible expression within a `switch` statement.	*See example for* `switch` *keyword*.	default; switch; discussion in section 6.7.1, page 190 and section 9.2.1, page 272
catch	Identifies a type of exception to handle in a try-catch statement.	*See example for* `try` *keyword*.	try; finally throw; section 2.3.2 on page 58
char	Denotes a Unicode 16-bit character value.	`char response = ReadResponse();` `char yes = 'y', no = 'n';`	

checked	Performs integer overflow checking on the given statement. If an overflow occurs, an exception is raised. By default, all integer expressions are checked.	`try`
		`{`
		`   y = checked(a/b + c);`
		`}`
		`catch (System.OverflowException e)`
		`{`
		`   . . .`
		`}`
			unchecked;

class	Defines a new data abstraction, or data type, along with a set of members that interact with this type. Classes are represented as reference types. A class can inherit from at most one other class and from multiple interfaces.	*See examples for* `const` *and* `override` *keywords*.	struct; chapter 5 on Reusable Libraries, section 5.1, page 127

Keyword	Description	Example	See also
const	Indicates that a field or variable cannot be modified. The value for a constant must be assigned as part of the declaration.	```public class BookReference { // Must be assigned here protected int timeout = 30; protected const string defaultURL = "www.manning.com/eebrown"; // Assigned here or in constructor public readonly string bookURL; BookReference(string name, string url) { if (url == null) bookURL = defaultURL; else bookURL = url; . . . } }```	readonly; example in section 6.6.1, page 182
continue	Passes control to the next iteration of the enclosing loop.	```for (int x = 0; x < Contractors.Count; x++) { if (Contractors[x].IsSalaried) continue; // Determine hourly pay }```	example in section 15.3.2, page 498, listing 15.1
decimal	Denotes a decimal number with up to roughly 28 significant digits. Stored as a 128-bit data value. Use the suffix m or M to denote a numeric value as a `decimal` type.	```decimal circumference; decimal radius = 7m; decimal pi = 3.1415; circumference = 2m * pi * radius;```	
delegate	Defines a reference type that encapsulates a method with a specific signature.	```// Define the ReadDelegate delegate public delegate Photograph ReadDelegate(StreamReader sr);```	discussion in section 1.3.1, page 20; example in section 9.2.1, page 272
default	In a switch block, identifies the statement to execute if none of the given constant expressions match the given expression.	*See example for* `switch` *keyword.*	case; switch; discussion in section 6.7.1, page 190 and section 9.2.1, page 272
do	Executes a statement or block one or more times until a specified `while` expression evaluates to `false`.	```do { name = reader.ReadLine(); if (name != null) // Make use of the name } while (name != null);```	while; example in section 6.7.1, page 190

Keyword	Description	Example	See also

double	Denotes a 64-bit floating point value. By default, all non-integral numbers are treated as values of this type. Use the d or D suffix to denote a numeric value as a `double` type.	```double circumference;```
		```double radius = 7d;```
		```double pi = 3.1415;```
		```circumference = 2d * pi * radius;```
			float;

else	In an `if` statement, the statement to execute if the expression returns `false`.	*See example for* `if` *keyword.*	if; examples throughout text
enum	Denotes an enumeration, or enumerated type, consisting of a defined set of constants each assigned a value from a given integral type.	```enum WeekDays= { Sun, Mon, Tue, Wed,``` ``` Thu, Fri, Say };```	example in section 7.2.2, page 199

event	Defines a handler abstraction in which to define a set of methods that should be invoked when a specific incident, or event, occurs. Methods are added or removed to an event with the += and -= operators.	```class Photograph```
		```{```
		``` public event ReadDelegate LoadPhoto;```
		``` . . .```
		```}```
			delegate; section 1.3.1, page 20 and section 3.3, page 85

explicit	Declares that a type conversion must be invoked with a cast. Omitting the cast results in a compile-time error.	```public static explicit```
		``` operator Photograph(string s)```
		```{```
		``` // code to convert from string```
		```}```
			implicit;

extern	Modifies a class member declaration to indicate that the member is implemented outside the current class file.	```class Photograph```
		```{```
		``` public extern void Draw(Graphics g);```
		``` . . .```
		```}```	

false	As an operator in user-defined types, defines the meaning of "false" for instances of that type.	```public static bool```
		``` operator false(MyType x)```
		```{```
		``` // Return whether MyType is "false"```
		```}```
			true;

	As a literal, the boolean value of false.	```bool isChapter = false;```	true; discussion in section 3.4.2, page 93
finally	Indicates a block of code that executes regardless of whether an exception occurs in the preceding `try` block.	*See example for* `try` *keyword.*	catch; try; throw; example in section 6.6.1, page 182

Keyword	Description	Example	See also
fixed	In unsafe code, prevents relocation of a variable by the garbage collector.	```// In unsafe code, pin current photo`` `fixed (Photograph photo = CurrentPhoto)` `{` `   // Perform unsafe operations` `}` `// CurrentPhoto no longer pinned`	unsafe
float	Denotes a 32-bit floating point value. Use the f or F suffix to denote a numeric value as a `float` type.	`float circumference;` `float radius = 7f;` `float pi = 3.1415f;` `circumference = 2f * pi * radius;`	double
for	Executes a statement or block repeatedly as long as a given expression evaluates to `true`.	`public bool FindPhoto(string name,` `                        out int index)` `{` `  for (int x = 0; x < this.Count; x++)` `  {` `    if (this[x].Name == name)` `    {` `      index = x;  // assign out param` `      return true;` `    }` `  }` `` `  return false;` `}`	foreach; example in section 10.2.2, page 328
foreach	Executes a statement or block using every element in an array or collection, if any.	`foreach (Photograph p in CurrentAlbum)` `{` `  // Do something with each Photograph` `}`	for; in; example in section 3.4.2, page 93 and section 5.1.1, page 128
goto	Transfers program control directly to a labeled statement. **Note:** The use of this keyword is generally discouraged. In a `switch` statement, transfers control to a given case label or to the default label.	`do` `{` `  // Do something` `  if (unable to continue)` `    goto CleanUp;` `` `  // Do something else` `} while ( some expression );` `` `CleanUp:` `  f.Close();` `` `switch (version)` `{` `  case 67:` `    photo = Photograph.ReadVer67(s);` `    goto default;` `` `  case 77:` `    // Version 77 specific tasks` `    goto case 67;` `` `  default:` `    Photograph.ReadGlobalData(s);` `    Break;` `}`	

Keyword	Description	Example	See also

if	A control statement in which a statement is executed only if a given expression evaluates to `true`.	```if (_album.Count > 0)```
		``` DisplayPhotos(_album);```
		```else```
		``` statusBar.Text = "Album is empty";```
			else; examples throughout book

implicit	Declares that a type conversion should be invoked automatically by the compiler as required.	```public static implicit```
		``` operator Photograph(Bitmap img)```
		```{```
		``` // code to convert from Bitmap```
		```}```
			explicit

in	In a `foreach` block, separates the identifier from the expression.	*See example for* `foreach` *keyword.*	foreach

int	Denotes a 32-bit integer value. Integer values are treated as `int` by default. Note that there is no implicit conversion from floating point values to `int`.	```int apprxCircum```
		```int radius = 7;```
		```int pi = 31415;```
		```apprxCircum = 2 * pi * radius / 10000);```
			long; short

interface	Defines a new data abstraction, or data type, in which all members are implicitly abstract. A class or structure can inherit from multiple interfaces.	```interface IBookDisplay```
		```{```
		``` // Declaration of interface members```
		```}```
			class; struct; section 5.1 on page 127

internal	Access modifier for types and type members that indicates the identifier is only accessible by objects within the same assembly.	*See example for* `public` *keyword.*	public; protected; private; see section 16.4.1, page 543

is	Identifies whether a given expression can be converted, or cast, to a given type.	```object obj = lstPhotos.SelectedItem;```
		```if (obj is Photograph)```
		```{```
		``` Photograph photo = (Photograph) obj;```
		``` . . .```
		```}```
			as; discussion in section 3.4.1, page 89

lock	Marks a statement block as a critical section, ensuring that only one thread can execute the statement block at a time.	```public void SortPhotos(bool ascending)```
		```{```
		``` lock (this)```
		``` {```
		``` . . .```
		``` }```
		```}```	

long	Denotes a 64-bit integer value. Use the `L` suffix to denote an integer value as a `long` type. The `l` suffix may also be used, but is easily confused with the number 1 and is not recommended.	```long apprxCircum```
		```long radius = (long)7;```
		```long pi = (long) 314159265;```
		```apprxCircum```
		``` = 2L * pi * radius / 100000000L);```
			int; short

Keyword	Description	Example	See also
namespace	Declares a scope for organizing code and naming types and members. If no namespace is defined, an object is part of the unnamed, or global, namespace.	```namespace MyPhotoAlbum { class PhotoAlbum : CollectionBase { . . . } }```	example in section 5.2.1, page 134; step in section 9.1.1, page 265
new	As an operator, creates an object and invokes its constructor. Value types are created in place, while reference types are created on the heap.	```int index = new int(); string s; Photograph photo = new Photograph(s); s = new string();```	discussion on page section 1.1.3, page 9
	As a modifier, explicitly hides a member inherited from a derived class. This is typically used to give a new meaning or purpose to an identifier.	```public MainForm : Form { . . . protected new void OnLoad(EventArgs e) { . . . } }```	override; discussion in section 5.4.2, page 154
null	Literal that represents an uninitialized state, often referred to as a null reference. This is the default value for all reference types.	```Photograph photo = _album.CurrentPhoto; if (photo != null) { // Do something with photograph }```	examples throughout text
object	The base class of all types in C#. Any value of any type can be assigned to variables of type `object`.	```object o1 = 7; object o2 = new string("hear me roar!"); object o3 = _album.CurrentPhoto;```	.NET Table 5.3 on page 155
operator	Declares the behavior of an operator when used with a specific type, such as a class or structure. Three kinds of operators are supported: unary operators, binary operators, and conversion operators.	```public static Complex operator -(Complex x) { return new Complex(-x.Real, -x.Imgn); } public static Complex operator +(Complex x, Complex y) { return new Complex(x.Real + y.Real, x.Imgn + y.Imgn); }```	explicit; implicit
out	Indicates that any changes made to a method parameter should be reflected in the variable when control returns to the caller. A variable used as an `out` method parameter may be uninitialized.	*See example for `for` keyword.*	ref; params

Keyword	Description	Example	See also
| override | Explicitly replaces a member inherited from a derived class. This is typically used to provide a more appropriate implementation of an inherited member in the current type. | ```csharp
public class CollectionBase
{
  . . .
  public virtual void Clear()
  {
    // Base implementation of Clear
  }
}

public class PhotoAlbum : CollectionBase
{
  . . .
  public override void Clear()
  {
    // Override implementation of Clear
    base.Clear();
  }

  public static void Main()
  {
    CollectionBase c = new PhotoAlbum();

    // invokes PhotoAlbum.Clear
    c.Clear();
  }
}
``` | new; discussion in section 5.4.2, page 154 |
| params | Indicates that a method will receive a set of parameters. This can occur only once and at the end of the list of parameters. | ```csharp
public void AddRange
    (params Photograph[] photos)
{
  foreach (Photograph p in photos)
  {
    _album.Add(p);
  }
}
``` | out; ref |
| private | Access modifier for types and type members that indicates the object or member is accessible only to the type in which it is defined. | ```csharp
public class PhotoAlbum : CollectionBase
{
  // only available within this class
  private int _defaultPhotoIndex;

  // Only available in this assembly
  internal bool IsDisplayed
  {
    . . .
  }

  // available to any derived class
  protected void TurnPage()
  {
    . . .
  }

  // available to any type
  public Photogram CurrentPhoto
  {
    . . .
  }
}
``` | internal; section 1.2.2, page 16 and section 9.1.1, page 265 |
```

Keyword	Description	Example	See also
protected	Access modifier for types and type members that indicates the object or member is only accessible by the containing type or by types derived from the containing type.		section 1.2.2, page 16 and section 9.1.1, page 265
public	Access modifier for types and type members that indicates the object or member is accessible by any type.		section 1.2.2, page 16 and section 9.1.1, page 265
readonly	Indicates that a field cannot be assigned except in the declaration of the field or the constructor of the containing type.	*See example for* `const` *keyword.*	const
ref	Indicates that any changes made to a method parameter should be reflected in the variable when control returns to the caller. Unlike the `out` keyword, a variable used as a `ref` method parameter must be initialized.	```// Locate photo after given index
public bool FindPhotoAfter
(string name, ref int index)
{
. . .
}```	out; params; section 18.1.2, page 607
return	Terminates execution of the containing method and passes control and the result of the method back to the caller.	*See example for* `for` *keyword.*	examples throughout text
sbyte	Denotes a signed 8-bit integer value from −128 to 127. An explicit cast is required to convert an integer value to a `sbyte` type.	```sbyte sb = 'y';
sbyte sb = (sbyte)5; e```	byte
sealed	Indicates that a class cannot be inherited. A `sealed` class cannot also be `abstract`. Note that `struct` types are implicitly `sealed`.	```public sealed class
SecurePerson : Person
{
. . .
}```	sealed; Application class on page 12
short	Denotes a 16-bit integer value from −32,768 to 32,768. An explicit cast is required to convert an integer value to a `short` type.	```short apprxCircum
short radius = (short)7;
short pi = (short) 314;
apprxCircum
= (short)(2 * pi * radius / 100);```	int; long
sizeof	Determines the size in bytes of a value type.	```int size1 = sizeof(long);
int size2 = sizeof(Rectangle);
int size3 = sizeof(Complex);```	

Keyword	Description	Example	See also
stackalloc	In unsafe code, allocates a block of memory on the stack and returns a pointer to this block. This memory is not subject to garbage collection and is valid only within the method in which it is defined.	```csharp\npublic unsafe void QuickSort()\n{\n Photograph* photos\n = stackalloc Photograph[Count];\n\n // Sort album contents\n // using local memory\n}\n```	unsafe
static	Declares a member that is associated with the type itself rather than with each instance of that type.	```csharp\nprivate string _defaultDir\n = @"C:\My Documents\Albums";\npublic static string DefaultAlbumDir\n{\n get { return _defaultDir; }\n set { _defaultDir = value; }\n}\n```	example in section 5.4.1, page 151
string	Object representing a set of Unicode characters. While string is a reference type, the equality operators == and != are defined to compare values rather than references.	```csharp\nstring s = null;\nstring defaultAlbum = "myAlbum";\nstring _defaultDir\n = @"C:\My Documents\Albums";\n```	discussion in section 5.4.2, page 154
struct	Defines a new data abstraction, or data type, along with a set of members that interact with this type. Structures are represented as value types, and are implicitly sealed.	```csharp\nstruct Complex\n{\n double real;\n double imaginary;\n}\n```	class; discussion in section 1.1.3, page 9
switch	Executes one of a given set of statements based on the constant value of a given expression. If a match for the current value is not found, then a default statement can optionally be executed.	```csharp\nswitch (version)\n{\n case 67:\n photo = Photograph.ReadVer67(s);\n break;\n . . .\n\n default:\n throw ApplicationException(\n "Unrecognized album version");\n}\n```	case; default; discussion in section 6.7.1, page 190 and section 9.2.1, page 272
this	Represents the current instance for which a method is called. Static member functions cannot employ the this keyword.	*See example for* for *keyword.*	example in section 1.1.2, page 8
throw	Raises a new exception, or re-raises a caught exception.	*See example for* switch *keyword.*	try; catch; section 2.3.2, page 58)

Keyword	Description	Example	See also
true	As in operator in user-defined types, defines the meaning of "true" for instances of that type.	```public static bool operator true(MyType x) { // Return whether MyType is "true" } ```	false
	As a literal, the boolean value of true.	```bool isAppendix = true;```	false; discussion in section 3.4.2, page 93
try	Begins a block in which exceptions may be handled, depending on the attached catch clauses.	```// Open a file FileStream fs = new FileStream(...); try { // Do something with open file } catch (IOException ex) { // Handle caught exception } finally { fs.Close(); // ensure file closure } ```	catch finally throw section 2.3.2, page 58
typeof	Obtains the System.Type object for a given type. Use the Object.GetType method to obtain the type instance for an expression.	```Type t = typeof(Photograph);```	code in section 10.5.3, page 348
uint	Denotes an unsigned 32-bit integer value. Use the u or U suffix to denote an integer value as a uint type.	```uint apprxCircum uint radius = 7u, pi = 314159; apprxCircum = 2u * pi * radius / 100000u; ```	ulong; ushor
ulong	Denotes an unsigned 64-bit integer value. When using the L suffix to denote a long integer or the U suffix to denote an unsigned integer, the value is considered ulong if it is beyond the range of the long or uint type, respectively.	```ulong apprxCircum ulong radius = 7L; ulong pi = 31415926535 apprxCircum = 2 * pi * radius / 10000000000L); ```	ulong; ushort
unchecked	Suppresses integer overflow checking on the given statement. If an overflow occurs, the result is truncated. By default, all integer expressions are checked.	```long bigPrime = 9876543211; long notSoBigNum = unchecked(bigPrime * bigPrime); ```	checked

Keyword	Description	Example	See also
unsafe	Indicates an unmanaged region of code, in which pointers are permitted and normal runtime verification is disabled.	*See example for* `stackalloc` *keyword.*	

ushort	Denotes an unsigned 16-bit integer value. A cast is required to convert an `int` or `uint` value to `ushort`.	```ushort apprxCircum```
		```ushort radius = (ushort)7;```
		```ushort pi = (ushort)314;```
		```apprxCircum = (ushort)2```
		``` * pi * radius / (ushort)100;```
			uint;
			ulong

using	As a directive, indicates a namespace from which types do not have to be fully qualified.
	    Alternatively, indicates a shortcut, or alias, for a given class or namespace name.
		```using System.Windows.Forms;```
		```using App = Application;```
		```public void Main()```
		```{```
		``` Form f = new MainForm();```
		``` App.Run(f);```
		```}```
			section 1.2.1 on page 15

	As a statement, defines a scope for a given expression or type. At the end of this scope, the given object is disposed.	```using (OpenFileDialog dlg```
		``` = new OpenFileDialog())```
		```{```
		``` // Do something with dlg```
		```}```
			discussion in section 8.2.1, page 233

virtual	Declares that a method or property member may be overridden in a derived class. At runtime, the override of a type member is always invoked.	*See example for* `override` *keyword.*	override; section 9.1.1, page 265

volatile	Indicates that a field may be modified in a program at any time, such as by the operating system or in another thread.	```// Read/Write x anew for each line.```
		```volatile double x = 70.0;```
		```int num = x;```
		```x = x * Sqrt(x);```	

void	Indicates that a method does not return a value.	*See examples for* `override` *and* `protected` *keywords.*	examples throughout text

while	As a statement, executes a statement or block of statements until a given expression is `false`.	```Photograph p = _album.FirstPhoto;```
		```while (p != null)```
		```{```
		``` // Do something with Photograph```
		``` p = _album.NextPhoto;```
		```}```
			for;
			foreach

	In a `do-while` loop, specifies the condition that will terminate the loop.	*See example for* `do` *keyword.*	do;

A.4   SPECIAL FEATURES

This section presents some noteworthy features of the C# language. These topics did not fit in previous sections of this appendix, but are important concepts for programming in the language. The topics covered are exceptions, arrays, the Main entry point, boxing, and documentation.

Readers more familiar with C# will recognize certain features omitted from this discussion and the book in general. These include attributes, reflection, and the preprocessor. These features, while important, were considered beyond the scope of this book, and are not required in many Windows Forms applications. A brief discussion of attributes is provided in chapter 2 as part of a discussion on the AssemblyInfo.cs file.

A.4.1 EXCEPTIONS

An *exception* is a type of error. Exceptions provide a uniform type-safe mechanism for handling system level and application level error conditions. In the .NET Framework, all exceptions inherit from the `System.Exception` class. Even system-level errors such as divide-by-zero and `null` references have well-defined exception classes.

If a program or block of code ignores exceptions, then exceptions are considered *unhandled*. By default, an unhandled exception immediately stops execution of a program.[2] This ensures that code which ignores exceptions does not continue processing when an error occurs. Code that does not ignore exceptions is said to *handle* exceptions, and must indicate the specific set of exception classes that are handled by the code. An exception is said to be *handled* or *caught* if a block of code can continue processing after an exception occurs. Code which generates an exception is said to *throw* the exception.

The `try` keyword is used to indicate a block of code that handles exceptions. The `catch` keyword indicates which exceptions to explicitly handle. The `finally` keyword is used to indicate code that should be executed regardless of whether an exception occurs.

Code that handles one or more exceptions in this manner uses the following format:

```
try
  <try-block>
<catch-blocks>opt
<finally-block>opt
```

where

- `<try-block>` is the set of statements, enclosed in braces, that should handle exceptions.

- `<catch-blocks>` is optional, and consists of one or more *catch blocks* as defined below.

---

[2] Well, most of the time. If an unhandled exception occurs during the execution of a static constructor, then a `TypeInitializationException` is thrown rather than the program exiting. In this case, the original exception is included as the *inner exception* of the new exception.

- `<finally-block>` is optional, and consists of the `finally` keyword followed by the set of statements, enclosed in braces, that should execute whether or not an exception occurs.

The format of a `try` block allows for one or more catch blocks, also called *catch clauses*, to define which exceptions to process. These are specified with the `catch` keyword in the following manner:

```
catch <exception>opt
    <catch-block>
```

where

- `<exception>` is optional, and indicates the exception this `catch` clause will handle. This must be a class enclosed in parenthesis with an optional identifier that the block will use to reference this exception. If no class is provided, then all exceptions are handled by the clause.

- `<catch-block>` is the set of statements, enclosed in braces, that handles the given exception.

For example, one use for exceptions is to handle unexpected conversion errors, such as converting a string to an integer. The following side-by-side code contrasts two ways of doing this:

``
// A string theString requires conversion
int version = 0;
try
{
  version = Convert.ToInt32(theString);
}
catch
{
  version = 0;
}
``
	``
	// A string theString requires conversion
	int version = 0;
	try
	{
	  version = Convert.ToInt32(theString);
	}
	catch (FormatException)
	{
	  version = 0;
	}
	``

If any exception occurs while converting the string to an `int`, then the `catch` clause will set `version` to 0. For example, if the `theString` variable is `null`, an `ArgumentException` will occur, and `version` will still be set to 0.	The `catch` clause will set `version` to 0 only if a `FormatException` exception occurs while converting the `string` to an `int`. Any other exception is unhandled and will exit the program if not handled by a previous method.

When an exception occurs in a program that satisfies more than one `catch` block within the same `try` block, the first matching block is executed. For this reason, the more distinct exceptions should appear first in the list of catch blocks. As an example, consider the `IOException` class, which is thrown when an unexpected I/O error occurs. This class derives from the `Exception` class. The following code shows how an exception block might be written to handle exceptions that might occur while reading a file:

```
// Open some file system object
FileStream f = new FileStream(...);
```

```
try
{
  //Code that makes use of FileStream object
}
catch (IOException ioex)
{
   // Code that handles an IOException
   // This code can use the "ioex" variable to reference the exception
}
catch (Exception ex)
{
   // Code that handles any other exception
}
```

Additional examples of exceptions appear throughout the book, beginning in section 2.3.2 on page 58.

A.4.2 ARRAYS

An *array* is a data structure consisting of a collection of variables, all of the same type. Arrays are built into C# and may be one-dimensional or many-dimensional. Each dimension of an array has an associated integral length. Arrays are treated as reference types. In the .NET Framework, the System.Array class serves as the base class for all array objects. More information on the Array and related ArrayList class can be found in chapter 5.

A standard array for any type is constructed using square brackets in the following manner:

<type> [<dimension>$_{opt}$]

where

- <type> is the non-array type for the array. A non-array type is any type that is not an array.

- <dimension> is zero or more commas ',' indicating the dimensions of the array.

Note that multiple square brackets may be specified to have variable length array elements. An example of this is shown below. To reference a value in an array, square brackets are again used, with an integer expression from zero (0) to one less than the length of the array. If an array index is outside of the valid range of the array, an IndexOutOfRangeException object is thrown as an exception.

Some examples of arrays and additional comments on the use of arrays are given below. Note that the Length property from the System.Array class determines the number of elements in an array, and the foreach keyword can be used on all arrays to enumerate the elements of the array.

```
// an uninitialized array defaults to null
int[] a;
```

```
// This array contains 4 int values, which default to 0
// Here, the valid indexes are b[0], b[1], b[2], b[3]
int[] b = new int[4];

// An array can be initialized directly or with the new keyword
// evens.Length will return 6
// foreach (int p in primes) iterates through the elements in primes
int[] evens = { 2, 4, 6, 8, 10, 12 };
int[] primes = new int[] {2, 3, 5, 7, 11, 101, 9876543211 };

// This example shows a 2 by 2 string array
// Here, names[0,0] = "Katie" and names[1,1] = "Bianca"
string[,] names = { { "Katie", "Sydney" }, { "Edmund", "Bianca"} };

// This example shows an array of arrays.
// Here, x[0] is an int array of length three with values 1, 2, 3.
// Also, x[1][1] = 12 and x[2][4] = 25.
// Attempting to reference x[3] or x[1][2] will throw an exception
int[][] x = { { 1, 2, 3 }, { 11, 12 }, { 21, 22, 23, 24, 25} };
```

A.4.3 MAIN

A program has to start somewhere. In C and C++ programs, the global procedure main is the defined entry point for the program. This starting point is referred to as the *entry point* for the program.

In C#, a class must define a static method called Main to serve as the entry point. The method must have one of the following signatures.

```
static void Main()
static void Main(string[] args)
static int Main()
static int Main(string[] args)
```

A program will return a value if the Main method returns a value. A program can receive command-line arguments by specifying an array of string objects as the only parameter to the Main method.

If two or more classes in a program contain a Main method, then the /main switch must be used with the C# compiler to specify which method to consider the entry point for the program.

A.4.4 BOXING

By definition, the object class is a reference type. However, it also serves as the ultimate base class for all types, including the built-in types. As a result, value types such as int and bool can be used wherever an object instance is required. For example, the ArrayList class represents a dynamically-sized array, and includes an Add method to add an object to the array. This method is declared as follows:

```
public virtual int Add(object value);
```

Within the `Add` method, a reference type is expected. So what happens when a value type is passed into this method? Clearly, an explicit mechanism for treating value types as a reference type is required.

This mechanism is called *boxing*. Boxing implicitly copies the data in a value type into an `object` instance allocated on the heap. For example:

```
// Boxing of an integer constant
object obj = 123;

// Boxing of an int type.
ArrayList list = new ArrayList();
int x = 32768;
list.Add(x);
```

A boxed value is converted back into a value type through a process called *unboxing*. Conceptually, boxing and unboxing happens automatically and the programmer can remain blissfully unaware of this concept. Boxed values can be treated as their unboxed equivalents. For example:

```
int n = 5;
object obj = 123;
if (obj is int)
  n = (int) obj;
```

These statements are perfectly legal, and result in the value of 123 for the variable n. The reason boxing is important is because of the performance implications involved. The boxing and unboxing of values takes time, and this can seriously impact the performance of an application.

Note in particular that boxing occurs when a structure, which is a value type, is cast to an interface, which is a reference type. For this reason, care should be taken when creating structures that support one or more interfaces. In such a situation, the performance implications of boxing might warrant using a class instead of a structure.

A.4.5 DOCUMENTATION

A final topic worth mentioning in this appendix is that of automated documentation. C# supports a set of XML-style tags that can be used in comments and extracted by the compiler. Such comments must begin with a triple-slash (`///`) and can occur before the declaration of most types and type members.

The C# compiler supports the `/doc` switch to generate the XML documentation file. Details on this process and the resulting output are available in the .NET documentation.

The following table provides a summary of the tags that are currently recognized by the compiler. An example using the `<summary>` tag appears in section 5.2.1 on page 134.

C# documentation tags

Tag	Purpose
<c>	Specifies text that should be marked as code.
<code>	Specifies multiple lines that should be marked as code.
<example>	Documents an example of a type or method.
<exception>	Specifies documentation for an exception class.
<include>	Includes an external file to include in the documentation.
<list>	Specifies a list of items within another tag. This supports bulleted lists, numbered lists, and tables.
<para>	Starts a new paragraph within another tag.
<param>	Documents a parameter within a method or other construct.
<paramref>	Specifies text that should be marked as a parameter.
<permission>	Documents the accessibility level of a member.
<remarks>	Documents general comments about a type or type member.
<returns>	Documents the return value of a method.
<see>	Specifies a link in running text to another member or field accessible from the current file.
<seealso>	Specifies a link in a See Also section to another member of field accessible form the current file.
<summary>	Documents a short description of the member or type.
<value>	Documents a short description of a property.

.*NET* namespaces

B.1   System.Collections 675
B.2   System.ComponentModel 675
B.3   System.Data 675
B.4   System.Drawing 675
B.5   System.Globalization 676
B.6   System.IO 676
B.7   System.Net 676

B.8   System.Reflection 677
B.9   System.Resources 677
B.10 System.Security 678
B.11 System.Threading 678
B.12 System.Web 679
B.13 System.Windows.Forms 679
B.14 System.XML 679

This appendix provides an overview of some of the System namespaces provided by Microsoft in the .NET Framework, and discusses their relationship to Windows Forms applications. For a complete list of namespaces in .NET, see the *.NET Framework Class Library* documentation.

The System namespace contains the commonly-used types[1] required by .NET programs and libraries, as well as services such as data type conversion, environment management, and mathematical operations. In particular, most of the classes mentioned in Appendix A that implement core functionality such as the built-in types, enumerations, and delegates are included in this namespace. Members of this namespace are discussed throughout the book as they are used in the sample programs.

---

[1]   The word *type* is used in the C# sense here, as defined in Appendix A. More generally, a type can be a class, structure, interface, enumeration, or a delegate. By definition, a namespace defines one or more types.

The remainder of this appendix discusses specific namespaces under the `System` umbrella. Each section discusses a separate namespace, with the sections arranged in alphabetical order.

For additional information on these and other namespaces in .NET, see the resources listed in Appendix D and in the bibliography. For some sample applications along with a discussion of many of these namespaces, see the book *Microsoft .NET for Programmers* by Fergal Grimes, available from Manning Publications.

B.1   SYSTEM.COLLECTIONS

The `System.Collections` namespace defines various types required to manipulate collections of objects, including lists, queues, stacks, hash tables, and dictionaries. An exception is the `Array` class, which is part of the `System` namespace, since this class provides core functionality defined by the C# language.

Members of this namespace are discussed throughout the book, and in particular in chapter 5, where the `PhotoAlbum` class is built as a collection of `Photograph` objects.

B.2   SYSTEM.COMPONENTMODEL

This namespace defines various types that define the runtime and design-time behavior of components and controls. In particular, this class defines the `Component` and `Container` classes and their corresponding interfaces.

The `Component` class is introduced in chapter 3 as the base class for much of the functionality in the Windows Forms namespace. Members of this namespace are also critical for data binding support, which is discussed in chapter 17.

B.3   SYSTEM.DATA

The `System.Data` namespace defines classes and other types that constitute the ADO.NET architecture. This architecture enables the manipulation and management of data from multiple data sources, including both local and remote databases and connected or disconnected interaction.

Although this namespace is not discussed in detail in the book, chapter 17 provides some details on using databases with the data binding interface supported by Windows Forms, and in particular with the `Windows.Forms.DataGrid` control.

See the bibliography for references to additional information on this namespace, and in particular the book *ADO.NET Programming* by Arlen Feldman, available from Manning Publications.

B.4   SYSTEM.DRAWING

This namespace defines basic functionality in the GDI, or graphical device interface, architecture. This includes the `Graphics` class for drawing to a device, as well as the

Pen class for drawing lines and curves and the Brush class used to fill the interiors of shapes. It also includes the Point, Size, Rectangle and other structures used for positioning and sizing Windows Forms controls within a container.

The System.Drawing.Design namespace provides design-time support for user interface logic and drawing. The UITypeEditor class in this namespace can be used to provide a graphical editor for a type, including types used with Windows Forms controls.

An overview of the System.Drawing namespace is provided in .NET Table 4.6 on page 124. Members of this namespace are used in chapter 4 to draw a rectangle into an owner-drawn StatusBar control; in chapter 7 and elsewhere to paint an image; and in chapter 10 to draw both an image and text into an owner-drawn ListBox control.

B.5   SYSTEM.GLOBALIZATION

The System.Globalization namespace defines locale-related information such as the formatting of dates, times, currency, and numbers.

A number of Windows Forms controls include some sort of formatting property that can be used to specify formatting information. Chapter 11 discusses the Data-TimeFormatInfo class defined in this namespace, and the MonthCalendar control that relies on the calendar information maintained by classes within this namespace. Chapter 17 also introduces the Format event in the Windows.Forms.Binding class that can be used to specify how bound data should be formatted for a particular data binding.

B.6   SYSTEM.IO

This namespace defines types for performing synchronous and asynchronous reading and writing of data streams and files. It also defines types for interacting with the file system, such as the Directory, File, and Path classes.

The FileStream, StreamReader, and StreamWriter classes are introduced in chapter 6 in order to read and write album files from the MyPhotos application. Members for interacting with the file system are discussed here as well.

For detailed information on this namespace, consult the references listed in Appendix D and the bibliography.

B.7   SYSTEM.NET

The System.Net namespace defines types for common Internet protocols such as HTTP and local file management, including the abstract WebRequest and WebRe-sponse classes. The related System.Net.Sockets namespace defines a managed implementation of the Windows Sockets interface.

These interfaces can be very useful in Windows Forms applications for interacting with remote servers and services, and for building custom communication interfaces between one or more applications. In Windows Forms applications, it is common to create a specific thread responsible for external communication of this kind, rather than performing such communication as part of a user interface thread. See the discussion on the `System.Threading` namespace later in this appendix for more information on threading.

Since the programs in this book are designed to be standalone applications, neither of these interfaces is discussed in the book.

B.8   SYSTEM.REFLECTION

This namespace defines a managed view of loaded types and their members, including classes and their methods, properties, and events. It supports the ability to dynamically create new types and invoke existing types and their members. For example, the classes in this namespace can be used to query the classes in an assembly and invoke specific properties and methods within that assembly.

Windows Forms controls use this namespace internally to query and interact with various types of objects. A brief exercise at the end of chapter 10 discusses how the `ListBox` control uses reflection to determine the value of the `DisplayMember` setting in this control, and illustrates how to invoke a property by name using the `PropertyInfo` class. Reflection is also briefly discussed in chapter 17.

B.9   SYSTEM.RESOURCES

The `System.Resources` namespace defines types that permit programs to create, store, and manage resources used by an application. Resources can be stored in a loaded assembly or in a satellite assembly that is external to the application. In particular, this namespace is used to manage culture-specific resources for an application, and is used for localization of applications.

Localization is the process of building an interface that can be used in multiple cultures and languages. Typically, it involves placing strings, images, and other culture-specific resources into a resource file, and loading such resources dynamically at runtime. This resource file can then be *translated* into another language or based on another culture to generate alternate resource files. These alternate resource files can then be used with the same program assembly to execute the program in the corresponding language or culture.

For example, while the applications in this book were written for a U.S. English user, we might want to support users that understand Canadian French, or Mexican Spanish. Placing our original strings and other constructs in a separate resource file would allow us to do just this.

If you are interested in writing an application targeted at multiple cultures, it is worth your time to understand this process before you begin. It can be quite difficult to localize an existing program, rather than building in such support from the start.

While the book does not discuss localization in particular, a brief discussion of resources can be found while discussing the storage of images in chapter 12 and again in chapter 13. The .NET documentation provides some sample programs that illustrate localization, as do many of the resources provided later in the book.

B.10 SYSTEM.SECURITY

This namespace defines the common language runtime security system, including security permissions for code and assemblies. The SecurityManager class in this namespace is the main access point for classes interacting with the security system.

This namespace is beyond the scope of the book, and aside from a brief mention in chapter 9, it is not really discussed. See the resources listed in appendix D and the bibliography for more information, and in particular look at *.NET Security* by Tom Cabanski, which is available from Manning Publications.

B.11 SYSTEM.THREADING

The System.Threading namespace defines the types that enable multithreaded programming, including the Thread class and synchronization primitives such as the Monitor and Mutex classes. A *thread* is a sequence of execution corresponding to a defined set of computer instructions. All C# programs in .NET begin with a Main method, running in what is called the *main thread*. This main thread may create, or *spawn*, additional threads as required. Each thread performs a defined task or set of tasks. At a basic level, multiple threads simply permit a program to do multiple things at once.

Generally speaking, threads are either *interface threads* or *worker threads*. An interface thread is a thread that interacts with the user in some fashion. The main thread in a Windows Forms program is typically an interface thread, and the Application.Run method introduced in chapter 1 is used to start a message loop on this thread which receives operating system messages and converts them into .NET events that invoke event handlers registered with the program.

A worker thread is a thread that performs some kind of analysis or other work on behalf of a program, and typically is hidden from a user. For example, a worker thread might receive stock price information from a remote server that a user interface thread displays in a ListView control.

Threads are created using the Thread class, with a ThreadStart delegate specifying the method or other program code that should be executed within the thread. The trick with multithreaded programming isn't the ability to have multiple threads; it is the synchronization, or co-existence, of these threads that causes difficulties. For this reason, synchronization constructs such as *locking* have evolved to control the interaction between multiple threads, and to make sure that different threads do not access the same portion of memory, databases, or other shared data at the same time.

As we focused on the Windows Forms namespace in this book, our examples did not include multiple threads of control. For a detailed discussion of how threads are used in .NET applications, including Windows-based programs, see *.NET Multithreading* by Alan Dennis, available from Manning Publications.

B.12   SYSTEM.WEB

This namespace defines types and additional namespaces for interacting with Web browsers and servers over the Internet. It contains the `System.Web.Services` namespace used when building Web services, and the `System.Web.UI` namespace for building user interfaces in Web applications.

As this book is all about building Windows-based applications, it does not discuss these namespaces. See the references listed in appendix D and the bibliography for more information on building Web applications and services.

B.13   SYSTEM.WINDOWS.FORMS

The `System.Windows.Forms` namespace defines types for building Windows-based applications. The `Control` class in this namespace is the basis for the user interface objects defined here.

The related `System.Windows.Forms.Design` namespace is used to provide design-time support for Windows Forms controls, most notably for integrating custom controls into Visual Studio .NET. The design namespace permits custom controls to define their behavior in the Toolbox and Properties windows, and manage their appearance when displayed in the Windows Forms Designer window.

The Windows Forms namespace is, of course, the topic of this book. While some basic custom controls are built in the book by defining a new class from an existing control, a discussion of design-time integration of such controls is beyond the scope of the book.

B.14   SYSTEM.XML

This namespace defines types in support of various Extensible Markup Language, or XML, standards, including XML 1.0 and XSD schemas. The XML standards were based on an older Standards Generalized Markup Language, or SGML, originally developed as a generalized solution for formatting documentation. Pure SGML proved a bit problematic for communication over networks, most notably the Internet, so XML was designed as a restricted form of SGML to overcome these difficulties.

XML is a great way to specify data in a generalized manner for use with the `DataSet` class in the `System.Data` namespace, and for interacting with remote applications and databases. For a detailed discussion of XML, see *Complete .NET XML* by Peter Waldschmidt, available from Manning Publications.

Visual index

C.1 Objects 682

C.2 Marshal by reference objects 683

C.3 Components 684

C.4 Common dialogs 685

C.5 Controls (part 1) 686

C.6 Controls (part 2) 687

C.7 Event data 688

C.8 Enumerations 688

This appendix presents a visual index of the Windows Forms classes covered in this book, as well as other .NET classes discussed in the text. These are organized as a set of class hierarchies in order to fit neatly on these pages. The following figure shows a diagram of the sections in this appendix.

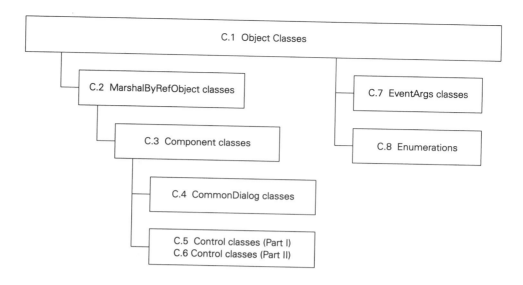

The figures and tables on subsequent pages have the following features:

- Classes in the Windows Forms namespace are gray.
- Classes from other namespaces are white.
- Classes presented or discussed in the book provide the corresponding table or section and page number.

The complete set of all Windows Forms classes derived from the `MarshalByRef-Object`, `Component`, and `Control` classes are provided. For more information on other classes and namespaces in the .NET Framework, consult the online documentation.

C.1 OBJECTS

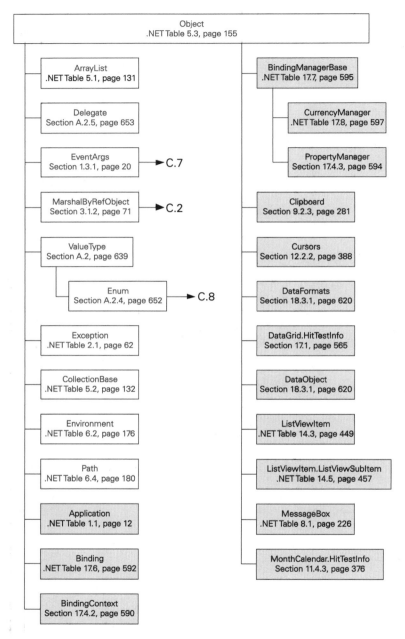

Figure C.1 The Object class is the base class of all types in the .NET Framework. This figure shows the classes derived from the System.Object class that appear in the book.

C.2   MARSHAL BY REFERENCE OBJECTS

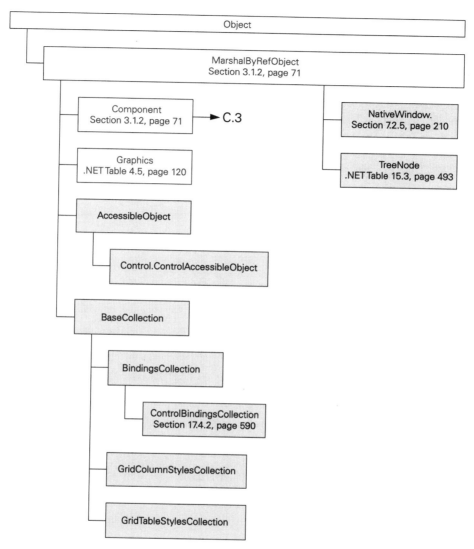

Figure C.2   The MarshalByRefObject class represents an object that is marshaled by reference. This figure shows the complete set of Windows Forms classes derived from the System.MarshalByRefObject class.

C.3 COMPONENTS

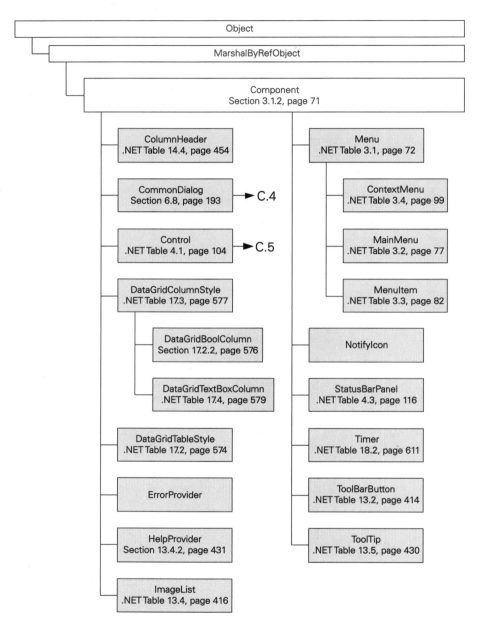

Figure C.3 The Component class represents an object that is marshaled by reference and can exist within a container. This figure shows the complete set of Windows Forms classes derived from the System.ComponentModel.Component class.

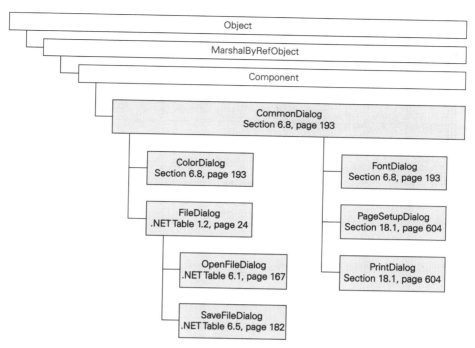

Figure C.4 **The CommonDialog class represents a component that provides a standard interface for common functionality required by Windows Forms applications. This figure shows the complete set of Windows Forms classes derived from the System.Windows.Forms.CommonDialog class.**

C.5 CONTROLS (PART 1)

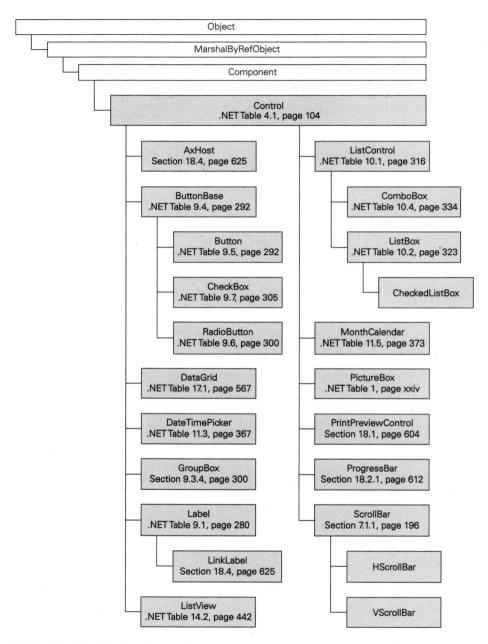

Figure C.5   The Windows Forms Control class represents a component with a visual representation on the Windows desktop. This and the following figure show the complete set of Windows Forms classes derived from the System.Windows.Forms.Control class.

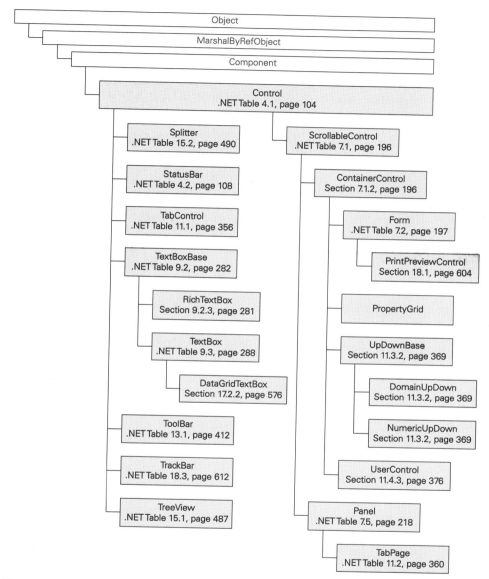

Figure C.6   The Windows Forms Control class represents a component with a visual representation on the Windows desktop. This and the preceding figure show the complete set of Windows Forms classes derived from the System.Windows.Forms.Control class.

C.7 EVENT DATA

This table shows the Windows Forms classes derived from the `System.EventArgs` class that are covered in the book. The complete list of Windows Forms event classes is available in the .NET documentation. This table simply serves as a quick index to those that are represented in the text.

EventArgs class	Covered in
CancelEventArgs	Section 8.2.2, page 235
ColumnClickEventArgs	Section 14.3.3, page 458
DragEventArgs	.NET Table 18.4, page 623
DrawItemEventArgs	.NET Table 4.4, page 119
KeyEventArgs	.NET Table 12.2, page 386
KeyPressEventArgs	.NET Table 12.1, page 384
LabelEditEventArgs	.NET Table 14.7, page 469
LinkLabelLinkClickedEventArgs	Section 18.4.1, page 626
MeasureItemEventArgs	.NET Table 10.7, page 346
MouseEventArgs	.NET Table 12.3, page 389
NodeLabelEditEventArgs	.NET Table 15.5, page 517
PaintEventArgs	.NET Table 7.3, page 205
PrintPageEventArgs	.NET Table 18.1, page 607
QueryContinueDragEventArgs	Section 18.3.1, page 620
StatusBarDrawItemEventArgs	Section 4.4.1, page 118
ToolBarButtonClickEventArgs	Section 13.3.1, page 420
TreeViewCancelEventArgs	.NET Table 15.4, page 502
TreeViewEventArgs	Section 15.3.3, page 501

C.8 ENUMERATIONS

This table shows the enumerations defined in the Windows Forms namespace that are covered in the book. The complete list of Windows Forms enumerations is available in the .NET documentation. This table simply serves as a quick index to those that are represented in the text.

Enumeration	Covered in
AnchorStyles	.NET Table 1.3, page 30
BorderStyle	Section 2.2.3, page 48
CheckState	Section 9.3.5, page 304
ColumnHeaderStyle	Section 14.2, page 443

Enumeration *(continued)*	Covered in *(continued)*
ComboBoxStyle	.NET Table 10.5, page 336
ControlStyles	.NET Table 7.4, page 210
DateTimePickerFormat	.NET Table 11.4, page 369
DialogResult	.NET Table 8.2, page 230
DockStyle	.NET Table 1.4, page 32
DragDropEffects	Section 18.3.1, page 620
DrawItemState	Section 10.5.3, page 348
DrawMode	.NET Table 10.6, page 346
FlatStyle	Section 9.2.2, page 277
FormBorderStyle	Section 8.3.3, page 240
FormWindowState	.NET Table 16.2, page 553
ItemActivation	.NET Table 14.8, page 472
Keys	Section 12.1.2, page 386
MdiLayout	.NET Table 16.3, page 558
MenuMerge	.NET Table 16.1, page 536
MessageBoxButtons	.NET Table 8.1, page 226
MessageBoxDefaultButton	.NET Table 8.1, page 226
MessageBoxIcon	.NET Table 8.1, page 226
MessageBoxOptions	.NET Table 8.1, page 226
MonthCalendar.HitArea	.NET Table 11.6, page 381
MouseButtons	Section 12.2.1, page 388
Orientation	Section 18.2.1, page 612
PictureBoxSizeMode	Section 3.4.1, page 89
SelectionMode	.NET Table 10.3, page 328
Shortcut	Section 3.2.3, page 79
SortOrder	Section 14.3.3, page 458
StatusBarPanelAutoSize	Section 4.3.1, page 111
StatusBarPanelBorderStyle	Section 4.3.1, page 111
StatusBarPanelStyle	Section 4.3.1, page 111
TabAlignment	Section 11.2.2, page 363
ToolBarButtonStyle	.NET Table 13.3, page 415
TreeViewAction	Section 15.3.3, page 501
View	.NET Table 14.1, page 440

For more information

This appendix lists additional sources of information about the .NET Framework. The Internet sites listed here were valid as of January 1, 2002. The sites are listed without prejudice. You can make your own judgment on which ones most closely match your needs.

Internet resources

csharp.superexpert.com
msdn.microsoft.com (Microsoft Developer Network)
www.4guysfromrolla.com
www.codeproject.com
www.csharpfree.com
www.csharphelp.com
www.csharpindex.com
www.csharp-station.com
www.cshrp.net
www.c-sharpcenter.com
www.c-sharpcorner.com

www.dotnet247.com
www.dotnetjunkies.com
www.dotnetwire.com
www.devasp.net
www.devdex.com
www.gotdotnet.com
www.mastercsharp.com
www.pune-csharp.com
www.vscodeswap.com

Magazines

Dr. Dobbs Journal: www.ddj.com
MSDN Magazine: msdn.microsoft.com/msdnmag
.NET Magazine: www.thedotnetmag.com
.NET Programmer's Journal: www.sys-con.com/dotnet
Visual Studio Magazine: www.vcdj.com
Web Services Journal: www.wsj2.com
XML Magazine: www.xmlmag.com

Newsgroups

The following newsgroups are available from the news.microsoft.com server:

microsoft.public.dotnet.framework.sdk
microsoft.public.dotnet.framework.windowsforms
microsoft.public.dotnet.languages.csharp

bibliography

Microsoft .NET Framework

Archor, Tom. *Inside C#*, Redmond, WA: Microsoft Press, 2001.

Cabanski, Tom. *.NET Security*. Greenwich, CT: Manning Publications Co., 2002.

Conrad, James, et al. *Introducing .NET*. Birmingham, UK: Wrox Press, 2001.

Dennis, Alan. *.NET Multithreading*, Greenwich, CT: Manning Publications Co., 2002

Feldman, Arlen. *ADO.NET Programming*, Greenwich, CT: Manning Publications Co., 2002

Grimes, Fergal. *Microsoft .NET for Programmers*, Greenwich, CT: Manning Publications Co., 2001.

Gunnerson, Eric. *A Programmer's Introduction to C#, Second Edition*, Berkeley, CA: Apress, 2001.

Liberty, Jesse. *Programming C#*, Sebastopol, CA: O'Reilly & Associates, 2001.

Robinson, Simon, et al. *Professional C#*. Birmingham, UK: Wrox Press, 2001.

Troelsen, Andrew. *C# and the .NET Platform*, Berkeley, CA: Apress, 2001

Waldschmidt, Peter. *Complete .NET XML*, Greenwhich, CT: Manning Publications Co., 2002

Related languages and environments

Flanagan, David. *Java in a Nutshell, Second Edition*, Sebastopol, CA: O'Reilly & Associates, 1997.

Kernighan, Brian W. and Ritchie, Dennis M. *The C Programming Language, Second Edition*, Prentice Hall, 1988.

Liskov, B., Atkinson, et al. *CLU Reference Manual*, Harrisonburg, VA: Springer-Verlag, 1984.

Prosise, Jeff. *Programming Windows 95 with MFC*, Redmond, WA: Microsoft Press, 1996.

Robinson, Matthew and Vorobiev, Pavel. *Swing*, Greenwich, CT: Manning Publications Co., 2000.

Stroustrup, Bjarne. *The C++ Programming Language, Third Edition*, Reading, Mass: Addison-Wesley, 1977.

Software development and user interface design

Brooks, Jr., Frederick P. *The Mythical Man-Month, Anniversary Edition*, Reading, MA: Addison-Wesley, 1995.

Kelly, Tom. *The Art of Innovation: Lessons in Creativity from IDEO, America's Leading Design Firm*, NewYork, NY: Doubleday, 2001.

Norman, Donald. *The Design of Everyday Things*, New York, NY: Doubleday, 1990.

Schneiderman, Ben. *Designing the User Interface, Third Edition*, Reading, Mass: Addison-Wesley, 1997.

index

Symbols

#region directive 42
& character
   for access keys 17, 77
(Name) property 50
* character
   in version string 44
+ (plus sign)
   strings 228
.NET Framework xxxi
.resources files 404
.resx files 405
\n character 228
/addmodule switch 139
/doc switch 42
/main switch 11, 536
/out switch 139
/r switch 20
/reference switch 5
/target switch 138
<c> tag 675
<code> tag 675
<example> tag 675
<exception> tag 675
<include> tag 675
<list> tag 675
<para> tag 675
<param> tag 675
<paramref> tag 675
<permission> tag 675
<remarks> tag 675

<returns> tag 675
<see> tag 675
<seealso> tag 675
<summary> tag 57, 675
   adding in Visual Studio 90
<value> tag 675
? conditional operator 259
@ character
   identifiers 658
   strings 177
| operator 30

A

AbbreviatedDayNames
   property 371
AbbreviatedMonthNames
   property 371
Abort value 230
AboutBox form 628
abstract class 71
   comparison with
     interface 128
abstract keyword 24, 658
AcceptButton property 197
   example 248
   for dialog box 241
AcceptsReturn property 288
   example (TextBox) 283
AcceptsTab property 282
AcceptsTabChanged event 282

access keys 17, 77, 281
access methods 143
accessibility level 642
accessors 645
Action property 504
Action-Result tables
   description of xxv
Activate method 197
ActivateControl method 197
Activated event 556
activation
   in ListView 474
Activation property 444
Active property 431
ActiveControl property 196
ActiveForm property 197
ActiveMdiChild property
   example 549
ActiveX Control Importer
   tool 631
ActiveX controls
   hosting 627
Add method
   in ArrayList class 131
   in Forms.Collection class 18
   in IList interface 129
Add value 538
AddAnnuallyBoldedDate
   method 374
AddExtension property 24
AddMessageFilter method 12

AddNew method 584
   in BindingManagerBase
      class 597
AddRange method 131
   example (for Controls) 53
AfterExpand event 489
AfterLabelEdit event
   in ListView class 444, 470
   in TreeView class 489
alias, with using keyword 15
Alignment property
   example (DataGridText-
      BoxColumn) 581
   example (TabControl) 366
   in DataGridColumnStyle
      class 579
   in StatusBarPanel class 116
   in TabControl class 357,
      363, 367
AlignmentChanged event 579
AllowColumnReorder
   property 465
AllowDrop property 104, 621
   example (Panel) 625
AllowedEffect property 625
AllowNavigation property 569
AllowSorting property
   in DataGridTableStyle
      class 576
AllowSortingChanged event 576
Alt property 387
Alt value 387
AlternatingBackColor property
   example 577
   in DataGrid class 569
   in DataGridTableStyle
      class 576
AMDesignator property 371
ampersand character 17
Anchor property 29, 104
   example (Button) 266
   example (GroupBox) 318
   example (TabControl) 366
   example (within TabPage) 591
   in Panel class 215

relationship to Dock 31
   values 30
Anchor property. *See also* Dock
   property 30
anchored menu 70
AnchorStyles enumeration 30,
   63
   values 30
AnnuallyBoldedDates
   property 374
App.ico file 409
Appearance property
   in CheckBox class 305
   in RadioButton class 300
   in TabControl class 357, 363
   in ToolBar class 413
AppearanceChanged event 300
AppendText method 282
Application class 12
   members 12
   ProductVersion property 45
   Run method 11
application data
   global 12
   user 12
ApplicationData value 177
ApplicationExit event 12
applications 640
AppWorkspace color 533
ArrangeIcons value 560
Array class 130–131, 672
ArrayList class 130–131
   members 131
arrays 672
as keyword 304, 658
ascending order 460
Ascending value 461
aspect ratio 28
assemblies 5, 640
   attributes 44
   version conventions 44
AssemblyCompanyAttribute
   class 44
AssemblyCopyrightAttribute
   class 44

AssemblyDescriptionAttribute
   class 44
AssemblyInfo.cs file 43
AssemblyProductAttribute
   class 44
AssemblyTitleAttribute class 44
AssemblyVersionAttribute
   class 44
asterisk (*)
   in version string 44
Attribute class 43
attributes 43, 670
   in AssemblyInfo.cs 44
AutoCheck property
   in CheckBox class 305
   in RadioButton class 300
AutomaticDelay property 431
AutoPopDelay property 431
AutoScroll property 196, 213
   example 214
AutoScrollMargin property 196
AutoScrollMinSize
   property 196, 213
   example 215
AutoScrollPosition
   property 196, 213
   example 215
AutoSize property
   in Label class 280
   in StatusBarPanel class 116
   in TackBar class 614
   in ToolBar class 413
AutoSizeChanged event 280
AxHost class 627
aximp.exe 631

B

B method 260
BackColor property
   in Control class 104
   in ListViewSubItem
      class 459
base keyword 149, 659
BaseEditDlg form 265

BeforeCollapse event 489
BeforeExpand event
   example 505
BeforeLabelEdit event
   in ListView class 470
BeforeSelect event 489
BeginEdit method
   in DataGrid class 569
   in DataGridTableStyle
      class 576
   in IEditableObject
      interface 584
   in ListViewItem class 451,
      470
   in TreeNode class 495
BeginInit method 114
   in StatusBarPanel class 116
BeginPrint event 608
BeginUpdate method
   example (ListBox) 327
   in ComboBox class 335
   in ListBox class 324
binary operator 649
Binding class 592, 594
   members 594
Binding constructor 594
BindingContext class 592
BindingContext property 592
BindingManagerBase class 592,
   597
   Current property 602
   EndCurrentEdit method 603
   members 597
   Position property 598
BindingManagerBase
   property 594
BindingMemberInfo
   property 594
BindingMemberInfo
   structure 594
Bindings property 597
Bitmap class
   custom drawing 152
   drawing by hand 153
   file formats supported 168

GetPixel method 260
   performance implications 127
Bitmap Editor window 400
bitmaps, common files for 406
BoldedDates property 374
bool keyword 659
bool type 95, 656
Boolean class 656
BorderStyle enumeration 51, 280
BorderStyle property
   example (Label) 254
   example (Panel) 216
   for dialog box 241
   in Label class 280
   in Panel class 218
   in PictureBox class xxvi
   in Splitter class 492
   in StatusBarPanel class 116
Bottom property 17
Bottom value
   in AnchorStyles
      enumeration 30
   in DockStyle
      enumeration 32
   in TabAlignment
      enumeration 367
Bounds property
   in DrawItemEventArgs
      class 119
   in ListViewItem class 451
boxing 185, 674
break keyword 659
BringToFront method 104
   example 555
Brush class 120, 124
Brushes class 120, 122
   SlateGray property 122
Built-in types 656
Button class 291–292
   DialogResult property 249
   members 292
Button property
   in MouseEventArgs class 390
   in ToolBarButtonClickEvent-
      Args class 423

Button1 value 226
Button2 value 226
Button3 value 226
ButtonBase class 292
   Image property 394
   ImageAlign property 394
   members 292
ButtonClick event 423
ButtonClick property 413
ButtonDropDown event 427
ButtonDropDown property 413
Buttons property 413
ButtonSize property 413
Byte class 656
byte keyword 659
byte type 656

C

c documentation tag 675
C language xxx
C# compiler 5, 138
   /addmodule switch 139
   /doc switch 42
   /main switch 11, 536
   /out switch 139
   /r switch 20
   /reference switch 5
   /target switch 138
   executables 139
   libraries 139
   modules 139
   output type 138
C# files
   extension 5
C# language
   #region directive 42
   @ prefix 658
   abstract keyword 24
   as keyword 304
   base keyword 149
   boolean type (bool) 95
   built-in types 656
   case keyword 191
   delegate keyword 22, 275

C# language *(continued)*
  documentation lines 42
  documentation tags 675
  event keyword 170
  exceptions 60
  foreach loop 95
  foreach, implementing 129
  inheritance 128, 133
  internal keyword 268, 547
  is keyword 92
  keywords 658
  namespace keyword 6
  new keyword 9
  object class 154
  override keyword 155
  private keyword 268
  properties 17
  protected keyword 268
  public keyword 268
  sealed keyword 12
  source files 133
  strings 177
  switch keyword 191
  throw keyword 190
  using keyword 15, 234
C++ destructor 251
C++ language xxx
CalendarBackground value 382
CalendarFont property 368
CalendarForeColor
  property 368
callable entity 655
Cancel property 236
  in PrintPageEventArgs
    class 609
Cancel value 230
CancelButton property
  example 249
  for dialog box 241
CancelCurrentEdit method 597
CancelEdit method 584
CancelEdit property 471
  in NodeLabelEditEventArgs
    class 519
CancelEventArgs class 236, 309

Cancel property 236
CanUndo property 282
Capacity property 131
CaptionDlg class 242
CaptionText property 569
  example 572
Cascade value 561
case keyword 191, 659
case label, fall through 211
CaseInsensitiveComparer
  class 461, 463
catch 59
catch blocks 61
catch keyword 659
CausesValidation property 309
CDialog class 194, 251
CFrameWnd class 194
ChangeExtension method 180
  example 473
Char class 289, 657
char keyword 659
char type 657
CharacterCasing property 288
check box buttons 291
CheckAlign property 300
CheckBox class 291, 305
  example 306
  members 305
CheckBoxes property
  in ListView class 444
  in TreeView class 489
checked keyword 659
Checked property
  example (MenuItem) 94
  in CheckBox class 305
  in DateTimePicker class 368
  in MenuItem class 82
  in RadioButton class 300
Checked value 305
CheckedChanged event
  in CheckBox class 305
  in RadioButton class 300
CheckFileExists property 24
CheckState enumeration 305
CheckState property 305

CheckStateChanged event 305
class hierarchy 71
class keyword 659
classes 6, 642
  indexers 148
Clear method
  example (Graphics) 205
  in ArrayList class 131
  in CollectionBase class 132
  in ListView class 444
ClearSelected method 324
  example 332
Click event
  in Control class 104
  in MenuItem class 82
Clickable value 444
Clicks property 390
ClientRectangle property 104
  for Forms 17
Clipboard 282
Clipboard class 282
ClipRectangle property 205
Clone method
  in ColumnHeader class 456
CloneMenu method
  example (MenuItem) 100
  in MainMenu class 77
  in MenuItem class 82
Close method 197, 233
  in Form class 88
  relationship to Dispose 233
  vs. Application.Exit
    method 88
CloseUp event 368
Closing event 197, 235
code documentation tag 675
code, Web Page
  documentation 42
Collapse method 495, 504
CollapseAll method 489, 504
CollectionBase class 130, 133
  members 132
  OnClear method 149
  OnRemoveComplete
    method 150

Color structure 120, 193
  B method 260
  G method 260
  R method 260
  RGB values 260
ColorDepth property 417
ColorDialog class 193
Colors window 401
Column property 461
ColumnClick event 444, 461
ColumnClickEventArgs
  class 461
  example 464
ColumnHeader class
  displaying in Visual
    Studio 457
  members 456
ColumnHeaderCollection
  class 477
ColumnHeaderStyle
  enumeration 444
Columns property 444, 455,
  476
COM 128
ComboBox class 335
  comparison with ListBox 334
  FindString method 344
  members 335
  SelectedItem property 342
  Text property 342
ComboBoxStyle
  enumeration 337
  values 337
common dialogs 193
common image directory 406
CommonAppDataRegistry
  property 12
CommonDialog class 24, 193
Compare method 461
Comparer class 461
compiled 640
compiling .NET programs 5
complex data binding 588
Component class 72, 114
component tray 76, 99

components xxxii, 73
components field
  disposing of 420
const keyword 660
constants 643
constructors 8, 650
  instance 650
  invoking existing
    constructor 544
  static 650
ContainerControl
  class 195–196
  ActivateControl method 197
  ActiveControl property 196
containers xxxii
Contains method 129, 131
ContentAlignment
  enumeration 404
Contents value
  in StatusBarPanelAutoSize
    enumeration 115
context menu 70
ContextMenu class 73, 97–99
  members 99
ContextMenu property 97, 99,
  104, 290
  example (PictureBox) 98
continue keyword 660
control
  forcing Paint event 93
Control class 53, 103, 105
  AllowDrop property 625
  BindingContext
    property 592
  BringToFront method 555
  ContextMenu property 99
  ControlCollection class 18
  DataBindings property 593,
    595
  DoDragDrop method 622
  drag and drop 621
  DragDrop event 624
  DragEnter event 624
  Focus method 307
  GetStyle method 210

  members 104
  OnPaint method 170
  QueryContinueDrag
    event 622
  SendToBack method 555
  SetStyle method 210
Control property 205, 387, 594
  in Splitter class 492
Control value 387, 391
Control.ControlCollection
  class 18
ControlBindingsCollection
  class 592
ControlBox property 29, 197
  and icons 409
ControlCollection class 18
ControlKey value 391
controls xxxii
  anchoring 29
  associating data with 304
  class heirarchy 103
  cutting and pasting 365
  enter and leave events 309
  events related to focus 309
  in MDI applications 533
  setting focus to 309
Controls property 18, 104
  example (Form) 18
Controls, docking 31
ControlStyles enumeration 210
  values 210
conversion operator 649
Convert class
  ToInt32 method 463
Cookies value 177
Copy method 282
CopyTo method 129, 131
  implementation 146
Count property 129, 131
  in BindingManagerBase
    class 597
  in CollectionBase clas 132
CreateDirectories method 178
CreatePrompt property 182
csc. See C# compiler 5

CStatic class 244, 280
Ctrl key
    multiple selection 173
culture-specific resource 404
CurrencyManager class 597,
    599
    members 599
Current property 129, 597
    example 602
CurrentCell property 569
CurrentCellChanged event 569
CurrentChanged event 597
CurrentCulture property 12
CurrentDirectory property 176
CurrentRowIndex property 569
Cursor class, in controls 104
Cursor property 104, 393
cursors
    common files for 406
    modifying defaults 393
Cursors class 393
custom controls 381, 620
custom date-time formats 371
custom menu class 378
Custom value 370
CustomFormat property 368,
    371
CView class 194

D

d suffix 661
data binding 321
    data sources 574
data collections
    classes 129
    interfaces 129
Data property 625
DataAdaptor class 587
    Fill method 587
    Update method 587
DataBindings property 592
    example 595
DataFormats class 623
    FileDrop field 623
    Text field 623

DataGrid class 569
    CaptionText property 572
    members 569
    SetDataBinding method 573
    sources of data 574
    TableStyles property 576
DataGrid property 576
DataGrid.HitTestInfo class 569
DataGridBoolColumn class 581
DataGridCell structure 569
DataGridColumnStyle class 579
    members 579
DataGridTableStyle class 576
    example 577
    members 576
DataGridTableStyle
    property 579
DataGridTextBox class 581
DataGridTextBoxColumn
    class 581
    members 581
DataMember property
    in DataGrid class 569
DataObject class 622
DataRowView class 574, 583
DataSource property
    in Binding class 594
    in DataGrid class 569
    in ListControl class 316
DataSourceChanged event
    in ListControl class 316
DataView class 130, 574
date and time, customizing 371
Date property 378
Date value 382
date values, customizing 371
DateChanged event 374
dates
    comparing 480
    formating 371
DateSelected event 374
DateSeparator property 371
DateTime structure 273
    Compare method 480
    Date property 378

DateTimeFormatInfo class 371
DateTimePicker class 368
    CustomFormat property 371
    Format property 370
    members 368
DateTimePickerFormat
    enumeration 370
    members 370
DayNames property 371
DayOfWeek value 382
days of the week
    specifying 371
DCE 128
Deactivate event 197, 556
Decimal class 657
decimal keyword 660
decimal type 657
declaration space 640
default constructor 650
    in structures 653
default keyword 660
default namespace 640
Default property 461
default value
    for built-in types 656
DefaultItemHeight field 323
delegate
    example 276
Delegate class 655
delegate keyword 22, 275, 660
delegates 22, 655
delete
    in C++ 10
Delta property 390
descending order 460
Descending value 461
DesktopBounds property 29
DestopLocation property 29
destructors 651
Details value 443
detents 390
deterministic scope 234
device contexts 124
dialog boxes
    hiding 262

dialog boxes (continued)
modal 225
nonmodal 225
properties required 240
DialogResult
enumeration 23–24, 226, 230
members 230
DialogResult property 197, 249, 292
Directory class 178
CreateDirectories method 178
GetFiles method 336
DirectorySeparatorChar field 180
DisplayMember property
in ListControl class 316
DisplayMemberChanged event
in ListControl class 316
DisplayMode enumeration 200
DisplayRectangle property 104
in Panel class 218
Dispose method 23, 42, 72, 158
components field 420
relationship to Close 233
Disposed event 72
Divider property 413
DLL 128
do keyword 660
Dock property 31, 104
default value 108
example
(MonthCalendar) 375
example (PictureBox) 76
example (TreeView) 490
in Panel class 215
in Splitter class 492
in StatusBar class 108
relationship to Anchor 31
values 31
Dock property. See also Anchor property 31
DockPadding property 196
DockStyle enumeration 31–32
values 32

documentation 42
documentation tags 675
DoDragDrop method 621–622
DomainUpDown class 372
Double class 657
double keyword 661
double type 657
DoubleBuffer value 210
DoubleClick event 390
example (ListBox) 325
drag and drop 620
Control members 621
steps to perform 621
DragDrop event 621, 624
DragDropEffects
enumeration 622, 625
DragEnter event 621, 624
DragEventArgs class 625
members 625
DragLeave event 621
DragOver event 621
Draw event 417
DrawBackground method 119
DrawFocusRectangle method 119
DrawImage method 205
Drawing namespace 120
types 120
drawing, selected text 351
DrawItem event 108, 118
and Paint event 205
example 121
in ComboBox class 335
in ListBox class 324
in MenuItem class 82
in TabControl class 357
DrawItemEventArgs
class 118–119
members 119
DrawItemState
enumeration 119
DrawLine method
example 152
DrawMode enumeration 347
values 347

DrawMode property 323, 335
example (ListBox) 346
in TabControl class 357
DrawRectangle method 120
DropDown event 335
in DateTimePicker class 368
dropdown menus
tool bars, customizing 427
DropDown value 337
DropDownArrows
property 413, 426
DropDownButton value 416
DropDownStyle property 335
DropDownWidth property 335
DroppedDown property 335
Dynamic Link Library. See DLL 128

E

Effect property 625
else keyword 661
Empty property 181
Enabled property
example (MenuItem) 94
in Control class 104
in MenuItem class 82
in Panel class 218
in Timer class 613
in ToolBarButton class 415
EndCurrentEdit method 597
example 603
EndEdit method
in DataGridTableStyle class 576
in IEditableObject interface 584
EndInit method 114
in StatusBarPanel class 116
EndPrint event 608
EnsureVisible method 444, 451, 504
Enter event 309
Enter key
in TextBox class 283

entry point 11, 640, 673
Enum class 654
enum keyword 661
enumerated type
    cast from integer 201
enumerations 654
    as flags 63
Environment class 175
    members 176
    SpecialFolder
      enumeration 177
Equals method 155
event delegates
    naming conventions 170
event handlers 21, 646
    adding in Visual Studio 55
    calling from constructor 211
    naming convention 55
event keyword 170, 661
EventArgs class
    Empty property 181
EventHandler delegate 22
events 21, 646
    multiple handlers 22
example documentation tag 675
Exception class 60, 62, 670
    members 62
    Message property 61
exception documentation
    tag 675
exception handling 58
    performance
      considerations 469
exceptions 59, 670
    alternatives to 58
    finally block 185
    in static constructors 670
Exit method 12, 176
ExitCode property 176
ExitThread method 12
Expand method 504
ExpandAll method 495, 504
explicit keyword 649, 661
extern keyword 661

F

f suffix 662
false keyword 661
Favorites value 177
fields 16, 643
FIFO queue 130
File class
    Move method 473
file extensions
    C# 5
    projects 38
    solutions 38
FileAccess enumeration 184
FileDialog class 23–24
    members 24
FileDrop field 623
FileMode enumeration 184
FileName property 24
    in OpenFileDialog 25
FileNames property 24
FileOK event 24
files, renaming 46
FileShare enumeration 184
FileStream class 184
Fill method 587
Fill value 32
FillRectangle method 120
    example 122
Filter property 24
    example
      (OpenFileDialog) 23
finally block 185
finally keyword 661
FindString method 324, 344
FirstNode property 495
fixed keyword 662
FixedHeight value 210
FixedSingle value 253
FixedWidth value 210
FlagsAttribute attribute 63
FlatStyle enumeration 280
FlatStyle property 292
    in Label class 280
flicker, preventing 212, 327
float keyword 662

float type 657
flyby text 105, 108
    implementing 109
focus events 309
Focus method 307
Focused property
    example 519
    in ListViewItem class 451
Font class 120
    example 610
    GetHeight method 610
Font property
    in DrawItemEventArgs
      class 119
    in ListViewItem class 451
    in ListViewSubItem
      class 459
FontChanged event 579
FontDialog class 193
for keyword 662
foreach keyword 95, 662
foreach statement
    supporting in classes 129
ForeColor property
    in DrawItemEventArgs
      class 119
    in ListViewItem class 451
    in ListViewSubItem
      class 459
Form class 7, 198
    ActiveMdiChild
      property 549
    adding to a project 242
    as dialog box 240
    BindingContext
      property 592
    class hierarchy 195
    ClientRectangle property 17
    Close method 88, 233
    desktop properties 29
    displaying a Form 12
    exiting 12
    Height property 17
    HelpButton property 435
    Hide method 233, 262

Form class *(continued)*
  Icon property 406
  IsMdiChild property 542
  keyboard events, receiving 386
  LayoutMdi method 560
  MdiChildActivate event 555
  MdiChildren property 553
  members 197
  Menu property 76
  MenuComplete event 109
  MenuStart event 109
  MergedMenu property 537
  MinimumSize property 28
  MousePosition property 258
  OnClosing method 235
  OnKeyPress method 386
  OnLeave method 558
  OnMouseMove method 261
  Owner property 258
  Show method 233, 257
  ShowDialog method 251
  Visible property 262
  Width property 17
  WindowState property 554
Form controls
  centering 17
  resizing 26
form inheritance 264
Format event 594
Format method
  example (String) 117
Format property 370
  in DataGridTextBoxColumn
    class 581
  in DateTimePicker class 368
FormatChanged event
  in DateTimePicker class 368
FormatInfo property 581
FormBorderStyle
  enumeration 241
FormBorderStyle property 29
  FixedSingle value,
    example 253
Forms Designer. *See* Windows
  Forms Designer 48

FormWindowState
  enumeration 555
  values 555
forward declarations 100
FromImage method 153
fully qualified name 7, 15

G

G method 260
garbage collection 10
GDI+ 118, 124
get accessor 645
get keyword 143
GetBaseException method 62
GetCommandLineArgs
  method 176
GetContextMenu method 72
GetDataPresent method 625
GetDirectoryName method 180
  example 473
GetDisplayRange method 374
GetEnumerator method 129,
  132
GetEnvironmentVariable
  method 176
GetExtension method 180
GetFileName method 180
GetFileNameWithoutExtension
  method 180
GetFiles method
  example 336
GetFolderPath method 176
GetForm method 77
GetFullPath method 180
GetHashCode method 155
  reason to override 156
GetHeight method,
  example 610
GetItemProperties method 597
GetItemText method 316
GetLogicalDrives method 176
GetMainMenu method 72
GetNextControl method 104
GetNodeAt method 489
GetNodeCount method 489

GetObject method 405
GetPathRoot method 180
GetPixel method 260
GetSelected method 324
  example 328
GetStyle method 210
GetTabRect method 357
GetTempFileName method 180
GetToolTip method 431
GetType method 155
global namespace 640
GotFocus event 309
goto keyword 662
Graphics class 120, 123
  Clear method 205
  DrawImage method 205
  drawing a Bitmap 152
  FromImage method 153
  MeasureString method,
    example 349
  members 124
Graphics property 205
  in DrawItemEventArgs
    class 119
  in MeasureItemEventArgs
    class 347
  in PrintPageEventArgs
    class 609
GraphicsUnit enumeration 124
GridColumnStyles property 576
  example 580
GroupBox class 215, 300
  compared to Panel 301
  example 301, 318
  tab order behavior 302

H

Handle property 72
  in ImageList class 417
HandleCreated property
  in ImageList class 417
Handled property 288
  in KeyEventArgs class 387
  in KeyPressEventArgs
    class 385

HasExtension method 180
Hashtable class 130
HasMorePages property 609
header files 133
HeaderStyle property
    in ListView class 444
HeaderText property 579
heap 10, 641
Height property 17
    for Forms 17
HelpButton property 435
    for dialog box 241
HelpLink property 62
HelpProvider class 435
    SetHelpString method 435
HelpRequested event 24, 241
Hide method 233
HideSelection property 489
Highlight property
    example 351
HighlightText property
    example 351
HightlightText property 119
HitArea enumeration 382
    values 382
HitArea property 380
HitTest method
    example
        (MonthCalendar) 378
    in DataGrid class 569
    in MonthCalendar class 374
HitTestInfo class 380
    HitArea values 382
    in DataGrid class 569
    in MonthCalendar class 380
    Time property 380
    Time values 382
HorizontalAlignment
    enumeration 116
hot tracking 359
HotTrack property 357
hours
    specifying 371
HScroll property 196

I

IBinding interface
    AddNew method 584
IBindingList interface 574
ICloneable interface 128
ICollection interface 129
    CopyTo method 129, 146
    Count property 129
    implementing 146
    SyncRoot property 129
IComparer interface 444, 461
    default comparer 463
    members 461
IComponent interface 72–73,
    574
Icon class 406
Icon Editor window 409
Icon property 29, 197, 406
icons
    common files for 406
    editing 409
IDataErrorInfo interface 574
IDataObject interface 625
    GetDataPresent method 625
IDE 34
identifiers
    @ prefix 658
IDictionary interface 176
IDisposable interface 73, 158
    members 158
Idle event 12
IEditableObject interface 574,
    584
    members 584
IEnumerable interface 129
    GetEnumerator method 129
IEnumerator interface 129
    Current property 129
    MoveNext method 129
    Reset method 129
IExtenderProvider interface 431
if keyword 663
IFormatProvider interface 581

Ignore value 230
IList interface 129
    Add method 129
    as data source 574
    Contains method 129
    data binding 321
    implementing 147
    Item property 129
    RemoveAt method 129
Image class 25, 120, 417
Image Collection Editor dialog
    box 418
Image Editor toolbar 401
Image property 292, 394
    example 404
    example (PictureBox) 25
    in Label class 280
    in PictureBox class xxvi
ImageAlign property 292, 394
    example 404
ImageIndex property 280, 292,
    418
    in ListViewItem class 451
    in TabPage class 361
    in ToolBarButton class 415
    in TreeNode class 495
    in TreeView class 489
ImageList class 417
    disposing of 420
    members 417
ImageList property 292, 418
    example (ToolBar) 422
    in Label class 280
    in TabControl class 357
    in ToolBar class 413
    in TreeView class 489
ImageListStream class 417, 420
Images property 417
ImageSize property 417
    in ToolBar class 413
ImageStream property 417
IMessageFilter interface 12
implicit keyword 649, 663
in keyword 663

include documentation tag 675
Index property 81, 347
  in ColumnHeader class 456
  in DrawItemEventArgs
    class 119
  in ListViewItem class 451
  in MenuItem class 82
  in TreeNode class 495
indexers 148, 648
IndexFromPoint method 324
IndexOf method 131
Information value 226
inheritance 6
Inheritance Picker dialog
  box 270
InitialDelay property 431
InitialDirectory property 24
InitializeComponent
  method 245
InnerException property 62
InnerList property 132
instance constructors 650
int keyword 663
Int type 657
Int16 class 657
Int32 class 657
Int64 class 657
integer type
  cast to enumeration 201
interactive development environment (IDE) 34
interface keyword 663
interfaces 128, 653
  collection related 129
  comparison with abstract
    class 128
  data binding 574
  supporting from a class 145
Intermediate value 305
internal keyword 268, 547, 663
Internal modifier 268
internationalization 12
Interval property 613
Invalidate method 93, 104
InvalidCastException class 93

InvalidOperationException
  class 305
InvalidPathChars field 180
IOException class 61, 190, 228
is keyword 92, 663
  compared with as
    keyword 92
IsBinding property 594
IsDigit method 289
IsEditing property 495
IsExpanded property 495
IsInputChar method 387
IsInputKey method 387
IsLetter method 289
IsMdiChild property 197
  example 542
IsParent property 72
IsSelected property 495
IsVisible property 495
Item property 129, 471
  in DataGrid class 569
ItemActivate event 444, 474
ItemActivation
  enumeration 474
  members 474
ItemChanged event 599
ItemDrag event 627
  in ListView class 444
  in TreeView class 489
ItemHeight property 323
  in MeasureItemEventArgs
    class 347
Items property 323
  in ComboBox class 335
  in ListView class 444
ItemSize property 357
ItemWidth property
  in MeasureItemEventArgs
    class 347

K

keyboard events
  sequence of 288
keyboard shortcuts
  enumeration 81

for Add New Item dialog 400
KeyChar property 288, 385
KeyCode property 387
KeyData property 387
KeyDown event 288, 385
KeyEventArgs class 387
  members 387
KeyPress event 104, 288, 385
KeyPressEventArgs class 288,
  385
  members 385
KeyPreview property 386
Keys enumeration 387
  Ctrl key 391
KeyState property 625
KeyUp event 288, 385
KeyValue property 387

L

L suffix 663
Label class 280
  AutoSize property 283
  BorderStyle property 254
  compared to read-only text
    box 281
  example 244
  image example 630
  members 280
  tab order behavior 280
Label property 471
  in NodeLabelEditEventArgs
    class 519
LabelEdit property 444, 470
  in TreeView class 489
LabelEditEventArgs class 471
  members 471
LargeChange property 614
LargeIcon value 442
LargeImageList property 444
LayoutMdi method 560
Leave event 309
Left property 17
Left value
  in AnchorStyles
    enumeration 30

Left value *(continued)*
  in DockStyle
    enumeration 32
  in TabAlignment
    enumeration 367
libraries 640
Life, the universe, and
  everything 42
LIFO queue 130
Lines property 282
Link class 634
LinkClicked event, example 634
LinkColor property 576
LinkLabel class 281, 628
  example 630
  Link class 634
  LinkClicked event 634
  Links property 634
LinkLabel.Link class 634
LinkLabelLinkClickedEvent-
  Args class 634
Links property 634
list documentation tag 675
List property 132
List value 443
ListBox class 323
  ClearSelected method 332
  comparison with
    ComboBox 334
  contrasted with ListView 442
  DrawMode property 346
  GetSelected method 328
  members 323
  preventing flickering 327
  SelectedIndices property 332
  SelectedItems property 332
  SetSelected method 332
ListBox.SelectedIndexCollection
  class 332
ListControl class 316
  members 316
ListView class 444
  AfterLabelEdit event 470
  BeforeLabelEdit event 470
  ColumnClick event 461

columns in Visual Studio 457
Columns property 455, 476
contrasted with ListBox 442
display styles 442
item definition 451
ItemActivate event 474
LabelEdit property 470
ListViewItemSorter
  property 461
members 444
MultiSelect property 466
SelectedIndices property 466
SelectedItems property 466
Sorting property 461
View property 450
ListView property 451
  in ColumnHeader class 456
ListViewItem class 442, 451
  BeginEdit method 470
  constructors 451
  members 451
  subitems 459
ListViewItem.ListViewSubItem
  class 459
ListViewItemSorter
  property 444, 461
ListViewSubItem class 442, 459
  constructors 459
  members 459
Load event 197
locale. *See*
  internationalization 12
localization 405, 679
Location property 104
lock keyword 663
long keyword 663
long type 657
Long value 370
LostFocus event 309

M

m suffix 660
MachineName property 176
Main function 11
main menu 70

Main method 673
MainMenu class 73, 77
  members 77
makefiles 138
MappingName property
  example (DataGridTable-
    Style) 577
  for DataSet data source 576,
    579
  for IList data source 576, 579
  in DataGridColumnStyle
    class 579
  in DataGridTableStyle
    class 576
MarginBounds property 609
MarshalByRefComponent
  class 72
MarshalByRefObject class 72
marshaling 73
MaxDate property 368, 374
MaxDropDown property
  example 341
MaxDropDownItems
  property 335
MaximizeBox property 29, 197
  for dialog box 241
Maximized value 555
MaximizedBounds property 29
Maximum property
  in TrackBar class 614
MaximumSize property 29, 197
MaxLength property 282, 335
MaxSelectionCount property 374
MDI child forms
  and other controls 533
MdiChildActivate event 555
MdiChildren property 553
MdiClient class 533
MdiLayout enumeration 560
  values 560
MdiList property 565
MdiListItem property 72, 565
MeasureItem event 82
  example 348
  in ListBox class 324

MeasureItemEventArgs
class 347
members 347
MeasureString method 349
members 8, 642
Menu 71
menu bars 70
Menu class 72–73
class hierarchy 72
MdiListItem property 565
members 72
MergeMenu method 537
Popup event 88
Menu property 76, 197
menu separator 74
MenuComplete event 109
MenuItem class 73, 82
CloneMenu method 100
Index property 81
MdiList property 565
members 82
MergeOrder property 539
MergeType property 538
merging menus 537
RadioCheck property 448
Select event 109
Tag property, lack of 378
MenuItemCollection class 72
MenuItems property 72
MenuMerge enumeration 538
values 538
menus
access keys 77
context menus 97
duplicating 100
inserting menu bar item 164
providing help text 109
submenus. *See* MenuItems
property 72
MenuStart event 109
MergedMenu property 537
MergeItems value 538
MergeMenu method 72, 82,
537
MergeOrder property 82, 539

MergeType property 538
Message property
example 61
MessageBox class 225–226
members 226
newline in text 228
MessageBoxButtons
enumeration 226
MessageBoxDefaultButton
enumeration 226
values 226
MessageBoxIcon
enumeration 226
values 226
MessageBoxOptions
enumeration 226
metafiles
common files for 406
MethodBase class 62
methods 8, 644
MFC, group boxes 215
Microsoft Development
Environment 37
MiddleCenter value 404
MinDate property 368
MinExtra property 492
MinimizeBox property 29
for dialog box 241
Minimized value 555
Minimum property
in TrackBar class 614
MinimumSize property 28–29
MinSize property 492
minutes, specifying 371
MinWidth property 116
mnemonics 281
modal dialog box 225
Dispose method 234
Modal property 197
modeless dialog boxes 225
modeless dialog. *See* nonmodal
dialog 257
Modifiers property 267, 387
values 267
MonthCalendar class 374

HitArea enumeration 382
HitTest method 378
members 374
MonthCalendar.HitArea
enumeration 382
MonthCalendar.HitTestInfo
class 380
HitArea values 382
Time values 382
MonthNames property 371
months, specifying 371
mouse pointers 393
MouseButtons
enumeration 390
MouseDown event 377, 389
MouseEnter event 389
MouseEventArgs class 261, 390
members 390
MouseHover event 389
MouseLeave event 389
MouseMove event 261, 389
MousePosition property 258
MouseUp event 104, 389
MouseWheel event 389
Move method, example 473
MoveNext method 129
Muliline property 282
MultiColumn property 323
MultiExtended value 329
Multiline property 357, 363
MultilineChanged event 282
MultiSelect property
in ListView class 444, 466
Multiselect property 167
MultiSimple value 329
multithreading 680
MyListViewComparer class 461
MyPhotos application 35

N

Name property 50
example 53
namespace keyword 6, 664
namespaces xxi, 640

namespaces *(continued)*
  naming convention 136
  setting default 265
naming conventions
  controls in Visual Studio 49
  event delegates 170
  event handlers 55
  namespaces 136
  properties 143
NativeWindow class 210
Navigate event 569
new keyword 9, 664
  as modifier 155
New Project dialog box 37
NextMonthButton value 382
NextMonthDate value 382
NextVisibleNode property 495
No value 230
Node property 504
  in NodeLabelEditEventArgs
    class 519
NodeFont property 495
NodeLabelEditEventArgs
  class 519
  members 519
nodes 488–489
Nodes property 489, 495
NoMatches field 323
None value 387
  in AnchorStyles
    enumeration 30
  in DialogResult
    enumeration 230
  in DockStyle
    enumeration 32
  in SelectionMode
    enumeration 329
  in SortOrder
    enumeration 461
  in StatusBarPanelAutoSize
    enumeration 115
  in StatusBarPanelBorderStyle
    enumeration 115
nonmodal dialog boxes 225, 252
  displaying 257

Normal value
  in DrawMode
    enumeration 347
  in FormWindowState
    enumeration 555
Nowhere value 382
null keyword 664
NullText property 579
NumericUpDown class 372

O

Object class 72, 154, 657
  inheritance from 134
  members 155
object class 154
  vs. Object class 154
object keyword 664
object type 657
objects
  equality 155
OK value 230
  in MessageBox class 226
OKCancel value 226
OnClear method 132
  example (PhotoAlbum) 149
OnClosing method 235
  example 236, 269
One value 329
OneClick value 474
OnInsert method 132
OnKeyDown method 387
  example 388
OnKeyPress method
  example 386
OnLeave method
  example 558
OnLoad method
  example 572
OnMenuComplete method 110
OnMouseMove method 261
OnPaint method 170
OnRemoveComplete method
  example (PhotoAlbum) 150

OnwerDraw value
  in StatusBarPanelStyle
    enumeration 115
OpenFile method 167, 182
  example
    (OpenFileDialog) 25
OpenFileDialog class 23–24,
  167
  FileName property 25
  Filter property 23
  members 167
  OpenFile method 25
  ShowDialog method 23
  Title property 23
OperatingSystem class 176
operator keyword 664
operators 649
option button 291
Orientation enumeration 614
Orientation property 614
OSVersion property 176
out keyword 664
OutOfMemoryException
  class 61
override 129
override keyword 155, 665
OverwritePrompt property 182
Owner property
  example 258, 633
OwnerDraw property 82
OwnerDrawFixed value 347
owner-drawn list 345
owner-drawn objects
  events for 118
OwnerDrawVariable value 347

P

PageBounds property 609
PageSettings class 609
PageSettings property 609
PageSetupDialog class 193, 606
  example 608
Paint event 104, 118, 170
  and DrawItem event 205
  example 220

PaintDialog class 193
PaintEventArgs class 170,
  204–205
  members 205
PaintEventHandler delegate 170
painting 170
Panel class 215–216
  BorderStyle property 216
  ClientRectangle
    property 218
  compared to GroupBox 301
  example 217
  members 218
  Paint event, example 220
  PointToClient method 258
Panel property 108, 119
PanelClick event 108
para documentation tag 675
param documentation tag 675
paramref documentation
  tag 675
params keyword 665
Parent property
  in Control class 104
  in MenuItem class 82
  in StatusBarPanel class 116
  in ToolBarButton class 415
  in TreeNode class 495
Parse event 594
PartialPush property 415
PasswordChar property 288
  example 297, 306
Paste method 282
Path class 180
  ChangeExtension
    method 473
  GetDirectoryName
    method 473
  GetFileNameWithoutExten-
    sion method 179
  members 180
PathSeparator field 180
PathSeparator property 489
Pen class 120, 124, 153
  example 152

Red property 153
PerformClick method 292
  in MenuItem class 82
  in RadioButton class 300
PerformSelect method 82
permission documentation
  tag 675
Personal value 177
PhotoAlbum class 127
  Save method 182
PhotoBox class 620
Photograph class 127, 141
  ScaleToFit method 207
PictureBox class xxvi
  customizing 620
  Image property 25
  members xxvi
  Paint event, example 517
  SizeMode property 25
PictureBoxSizeMode
  enumeration 90
PMDesignator property 371
Point structure 120
PointF structure 120
PointToClient method 104,
  258
Popup event 82, 88
  example 94
  in ContextMenu class 99
popup menu 70
Position property 597
  example 598
PositionChanged event 597
PreferredHeight property
  in Label class 280
PreferredWidth property
  in Label class 280
preprocessor 670
PrevMonthButton value 382
PrevMonthDate value 382
PrevNode property 495
Print method
  example 608
PrintDialog class 606
  example 608

PrintDocument class 606
  Print method 608
  PrintPage event 608
PrintPage event 606
  example 608
PrintPageEventArgs class 609,
  690
  members 609
PrintPreviewControl class 606
PrintPreviewDialog class 606
  example 608
private inheritance 133
private keyword 268, 665
Private value 268
ProductName property 12
ProductVersion property 12
  example 45
ProgressBar class 616
projects 38
  creating 37
  file extension 38
  setting default
    namespace 265
properties 17, 645
  constructing 143
  editing in Visual Studio 50
  naming convention 143
Properties window 50
  features 87
  graphic 87
PropertyDescriptor class 597
PropertyDescriptor
  property 579
PropertyInfo class 352
PropertyManager class 597
PropertyName property 594
protected inheritance 133
protected internal keyword 268
protected keyword 268, 666
Protected modifier 268
public keyword 268, 666
Public modifier 268
push buttons 291
PushButton value 416
Pushed property 415

Q

QueryContinueDrag event 622
question mark (?)
   as conditional operator 259
Question value 226
Queue class 130

R

R method 260
radio buttons 291
RadioButton class 291, 300
   members 300
   tab order behavior 302
   Tag property 301
RadioCheck property 82
   example 448
Raised value
   in StatusBarPanelBorderStyle
     enumeration 115
readonly keyword 666
ReadOnly property 569
   in DataGridColumnStyle
     class 579
   in DataGridTableStyle
     class 576
   in TextBoxBase class 282
ReadOnlyChecked
   property 167
RecreateHandle event 417
Rectangle class 207
Rectangle property 415
Rectangle structure 120
redrawing a control 93
ref keyword 666
reference types 9, 641
ReferenceEquals method 155
reflection 670
Refresh method 599
Region class 120, 124
RegistryKey class 12
remarks documentation tag 675
Remove method
   in ArrayList class 131
   in ListViewItem class 451

Remove value 538
RemoveAll method 431
RemoveAt method 129
   example 169
   in ArrayList class 131
   in BindingManagerBase
     class 597
   in CollectionBase class 132
RemoveBoldedDate
   method 374
renaming files 46
Replace dialog box 47
Replace value 538
Reset method 24, 129
ResetBackColor method 576
ResetHeaderText method 579
resgen.exe compiler 404
ReshowDelay property 431
ResizeRedraw value 210
resources, compiling 404
ResourcesManager class 405
RestoreDirectory property 24
ResumeBinding method 597
ResumeLayout method
   example (Form) 53
Retry value 230
Return key. *See* Enter key 283
return keyword 666
returns documentation tag 675
RGB 252
RichTextBox class 282
Right property 17
Right value
   in AnchorStyles
     enumeration 30
   in DockStyle
     enumeration 32
   in TabAlignment
     enumeration 367
   in ToolBarTextAlign
     enumeration 414
RightToLeft property
   in ContextMenu class 99
   in MainMenu class 77
RowCount property 357

RowHeaderWidth
   property 569, 576
   example 577
Run method 12
   example 11

S

SaveFileDialog class 24, 182
   members 182
saving files, conventions 186
SByte class 657
sbyte keyword 666
sbyte type 657
Scale to fit
   graphic 206
ScaleToFit method 206
Scroll event 569
ScrollableControl class 195–196
ScrollBar class 196
ScrollBars property 288
ScrollChange property 374
ScrollToCaret method 282
sealed keyword 12, 666
seconds
   specifying 371
see documentation tag 675
seealso documentation tag 675
Select event 82, 109
Select method
   in TextBoxBase class 282
Selectable value 210
SelectAll method
   in ComboBox class 335
   in TextBoxBase class 282
Selected property
   in ListViewItem class 451
SelectedImageIndex property
   in TreeNode class 495
SelectedIndex property
   in ListControl class 316
   in TabControl class 357
SelectedIndexChanged event
   in ListBox class 324
   in ListView class 444
   in TabControl class 357

SelectedIndices property 323, 332

SelectedItem property 323, 342
   in ComboBox class 335

SelectedItems property 323, 466
   in ListBox class 332
   in ListView class 444

SelectedNode property 489
   example 512

SelectedStart property 282

SelectedTab property 357

SelectedText property
   in ComboBox class 335
   in TextBoxBase class 282

SelectedValue property 316

SelectionChangeCommitted
   event
   in ComboBox class 335

SelectionLength property
   example (ComboBox) 343

SelectionMode enumeration
   values 329

SelectionMode property 323

SelectionRange property 374

SelectionStart property
   example (ComboBox) 343
   in MonthCalendar class 374

SendTo value 177

SendToBack method 104, 555

Separator value 416

set accessor 645

set keyword 143

SetAutoScrollMargin
   method 196

SetDataBinding method 569, 573

SetDate method 374

SetHelpLink method 62

SetHelpString method 435

SetRange method 614

SetSelected method 324

SetStyle methods 210

SetToolTip method 431

Shared Library. *See* DLL 128

Shift key, multiple selection 173

Shift property 387

Shift value 387

short keyword 666

short type 657

Short value 370

Shortcut enumeration 81

shortcut menu 70

Shortcut property 82
   example 81

Show method 233, 257
   in ContextMenu class 99
   in MessageBox class 226

ShowAlways property 431

ShowCheckBox property 368

ShowDialog method 24, 197, 251
   example
   (OpenFileDialog) 23

ShowHelp property 24

ShowInTaskBar property 29, 197
   for dialog box 241

ShowPanels property 108

ShowPlusMinus property 489

ShowReadOnly property 167

ShowShortcut property 82
   example 85

ShowToday property 374

ShowTodayCircle property 374

ShowToolTips property 357, 413

ShowUpDown property 368

Simple data binding 589

Simple value 337

Single class 657

Size property, for dialog box 241

Size structure 28, 120

SizeF structure 120

SizeMode property
   example (PictureBox) 25
   in PictureBox class xxvi
   in TabControl class 357

SizeModeChanged event xxvi

sizeof keyword 666

SizingGrip property 108

SmallChange property 614

SmallIcon value 442

SmallImageList property 444

SmoothingMode
   enumeration 124

Solution Explorer
   viewing source code 40

Solution Explorer window 38

solutions 38
   file extension 38

Sort method 131

Sorted property 323
   in ComboBox class 335
   in TreeView class 489

SortedList class 130

sorting
   ListView columns 460

Sorting property 461
   in ListView class 444

SortOrder enumeration 461

source code
   documentation 42

source files 640

Source property 62

SourceControl property 99

SpecialFolder enumeration 177
   members 177

SplitPosition property 492

Splitter class 492
   members 492

SplitterMoved event 492

Spring value
   in StatusBarPanelAutoSize
   enumeration 115

Stack class 130

stackalloc keyword 667

StackTrace property 62

standard error 184

standard in 184

standard out 184

Standard value 474

StandardClick value 210

StandardDoubleClick value 210

Start property 613

StartMenu value 177

StartPosition property 197
  for dialog box 241
startup project 135
StartupPath property 12
State property 119
StateImageIndex property
  in ListViewItem class 451
StateImageList property 444
static constructors 650
static keyword 667
status bar panels 105
StatusBar class 109
  class heirarchy 103
  Dock Property 108
  example 106
  flyby text 108
  members 108
  owner-drawn panels 115
  TabStop property 107
StatusBarDrawItemEventArgs
  class 119
StatusBarPanel class 116
  AutoSize property,
    values 114
  BorderStyle property,
    values 115
  displaying 108
  example 111
  members 116
  Style property, values 115
  Text property, example 116
  Width property 115
StatusBarPanel Collection Editor
  dialog box 112
StatusBarPanelAutoSize
  enumeration 114
StatusBarPanelBorderStyle
  enumeration 115
StatusBarPanelCollection
  class 108
StatusBarPanelStyle
  enumeration 115
Stop property 613
StreamWriter class 184
StretchToFit value 204

String class 657
  comparison 156
  Equals override 156
  Format method 117
  ToLower method 156
string class vs. String class 154
string keyword 667
string type 657
StringCollection class 130
strings
  @ notation 177
  construction with +
    operator 228
  ignoring escape
    sequences 177
  measuring graphical size 124
strongly typed 132
struct keyword 9, 667
structures 652
  performance
    considerations 674
Style property
  in StatusBarPanel class 116
  in ToolBarButton class 415
SubItems property 451
summary documentation tag 675
Sunken value
  in StatusBarPanelBorderStyle
    enumeration 115
SuspendBinding method 597
SuspendLayout method
  example (Form) 52
switch keyword 191, 667
switch statement
  with enumeration type 201
SyncRoot property 129
System
  AppWorkspace color. 533
system menu 235
System namespace
  classes, for C# types 656
System.Array class 672
System.Attribute class 43
System.Collections
  namespace 677

System.ComponentModel
  namespace 677
System.Data namespace 574,
  677
System.Delegate class 655
System.Drawing namespace 29,
  118, 121, 203, 677
  types 120
System.Drawing.Design
  namespace 678
System.Enum class 654
System.Exception class 60, 670
System.Globalization
  namespace 678
System.IO namespace 178, 678
System.Net namespace 678
System.Net.Sockets
  namespace 678
System.Object class. See Object
  class 72
System.Reflection
  namespace 43, 352, 573, 679
System.Resources
  namespace 405, 679
System.Security namespace 680
System.Threading
  namespace 680
System.ValueType class 641
System.Web namespace 681
System.Web.Services
  namespace 681
System.Web.UI namespace 681
System.Windows.Forms
  namespace xxi, 681
System.Windows.Forms
  namespace. See Windows
  Forms namespace 682
System.Windows.Forms.Design
  namespace 381, 574, 681
System.XML namespace 186,
  681
SystemColors class 120, 205
  Control property 205
Systems.Collections
  namespace 461

T

tab strip 357
TabAlignment enumeration 367
TabControl class 357
    Alignment property 367
    class hierarchy 356
    members 357
TabCount property 357
TabIndex property 104
    example 53
Tabindex property 49
table styles
    mapping names 576
tables
    action-result format xxv
TableStyles property 569, 576
TabPage class 361
    class hierarchy 356
    creating by hand 361
    creating in Visual Studio 366
    members 361
TabPage Collection Editor dialog
    box 366
TabStop property 104
    in StatusBar class 107–108
Tag property 301, 423, 503
    example
        (ToolBarButton) 423
    example (TreeNode) 502
    in ListViewItem class 451
    in ToolBarButton class 415
    in TreeNode class 495
TagPages property 357
TargetSite property 62
templates 147
Text field 623
Text property 342
    example (StatusBar) 109
    for status bars 108
    in ColumnHeader class 456
    in Control class 104
    in ListViewItem class 451
    in ListViewSubItem
        class 459
    in MenuItem class 82

    in StatusBarPanel class 116
    in ToolBarButton class 415
    in TreeNode class 495
    menu separator 81
Text value 115
TextAlign property 288
    example (Button) 404
    example (ToolBar) 414
    in ColumnHeader class 456
    in Label class 280
    in ToolBar class 413
TextAlignChanged event 288
    in Label class 280
TextBox class 282, 288
    AcceptsReturn property 283
    ContextMenu property 290
    DataBindings property 595
    example 244
    members 288
    Multiline property,
        example 283
    PasswordChar property 297
TextBox property 581
TextBoxBase class 282
    members 282
TextChanged event
    example 290
    example (ComboBox) 342
TextRenderingHint
    enumeration 124
TextWriter class 185
    WriteLine method 185
this keyword 8, 667
Thread class 680
ThreadException class 12
ThreadException event 12
ThreadExit event 12
threading 680
three-state check boxes 305
ThreeState property 305
throw 59
throw keyword 190, 667
thumbnail 345
tick 273
Tick property 613

TickCount property 176
TickFrequency property 614
TickStyle property 614
TileHorizontal value 561
TileVertical value 561
Time property 380
Time value 370
time values, customizing 371
Timer class 613
    members 613
timers 613
times
    comparing 480
    formatting 371
TimeSeparator property 371
TimeSpan structure 273
Title property 24
    example (OpenFileDialog) 23
TitleBackground value 382
TitleMonth value 382
TitleYear value 382
TodayDate property 374
TodayLink value 382
toggle button 291
Toggle method 495, 504
ToggleButton value 416
ToInt32 method
    example 463
ToLower method 156
tool bar
    separator 416
ToolBar class 413
    Dock property 414
    members 413
ToolBarButton class 413, 415
    custom dropdown menu 427
    members 415
    PushButton style 422
    Separator style 424
    Tag property 423
ToolBarButtonClickEventArgs
    class 423, 427
ToolBarButtonStyle
    enumeration 416
    members 416

ToolBarTextAlign
  enumeration 414
Toolbox window 48
  locking in place 243
  sorting alphabetically 243
ToolTip class 432
  members 431
  SetToolTip method 434
ToolTipText property 431
  in StatusBarPanel class 116
  in TabPage class 361
  in ToolBarButton class 415
Top property 17
Top value
  in AnchorStyles
    enumeration 30
  in DockStyle
    enumeration 32
  in TabAlignment
    enumeration 367
TopIndex property 323
TopNode property 489
ToString method
  in Exception class 62
  in Object class 155
TrackBar class 614
  example 616
  members 614
transaction 574
transparency 406
TransparentColor property 417
TreeNode class 495
  Collapse method 504
  collapsing nodes 504
  constructors 495
  EnsureVisible method 504
  Expand method 504
  expanding nodes 504
  members 495
  Tag property 503
  Toggle method 504
TreeNode Editor dialog box 497
TreeView class 489
  BeforeExpand event 505
  CollapseAll method 504

ExpandAll method 504
Focused property 519
GetNodeAt method 525
members 489
SelectedNode property 512
TreeViewAction
  enumeration 504
TreeViewCancelEventArgs
  class 504
  members 504
TreeViewEventArgs class 504
TrimToSize method 131
true keyword 668
try keyword 668
try-catch blocks 61
TwoClick value 474
type declarations 640
TypeInitializationException
  class 670
typeof keyword 668
type-safe 22

U

u suffix 668
uint keyword 668
uint type 657
UInt16 class 657
UInt32 class 657
UInt64 class 657
UITypeEditor class 678
ulong keyword 668
ulong type 657
unary operator 649
unchecked keyword 668
Unchecked value 305
Underneath value 414
Undo method 282
unsafe keyword 669
Unselect method 569
Update method 587
UpdatePixelData method 259
UpDownBase class 372
UseMnemonic property 280
UserAppDataRegistry
  property 12

UserControl class 381
UserMouse value 210
UserName property 176
UserPaint value 210
ushort keyword 669
ushort type 657
using keyword 669
  and Dispose method 234
  as directive 15
  as statement 234
using statement
  example 506

V

Validated event 307, 309
  example 307
  example (ComboBox) 342
value documentation tag 675
Value property
  example
    (DateTimePicker) 369
  in DateTimePicker class 368
  in TrackBar class 614
value types 9, 641
  assignment 28
ValueChanged event
  in DateTimePicker class 368
  in TrackBar class 614
ValueMember property 316
ValueType class 641
Version class 46
version number 6
  modifying 45
versions
  conventions 44
  examples 44
  generating build number 44
  generating revision
    number 44
  retrieving 12
vertical bar 30
videos, common files for 406
View enumeration 443
  values 442

View property 444
    example 450
virtual keyword 669
Visible property
    in Control class 104
    in MenuItem class 82
    in Panel class 218
    in ToolBarButton class 415
Visual Studio .NET 34
    and data binding 596
    building documentation 42
    components field 420
    controls, transferring between
        containers 365
    creating a class library 134
    event handlers, adding 55
    integrating custom
        controls 620
    projects, compiling 39
    projects, properties 265
    projects, running 39
    Properties window 50
    references 137
    renaming files 46
    statement completion 56
    window location, altering 50
Visual Studio .NET Command
    Prompt 5
Visual Studio .NET *See also* Solu-
    tion Explorer 40
Visual Studio .NET. *See also*
    Windows Forms Designer 75
void keyword 669
volatile keyword 669
VS .NET. *See* Visual Studio
    .NET 34
VScroll property 196

W

Warning value 226
weekdays
    specifying 371
WeekNumbers value 382
while keyword 669
Width property 17
    for Forms 17
    in ColumnHeader class 456
    in DataGridColumnStyle
        class 579
    in StatusBarPanel 115
    in StatusBarPanel class 116
Win32 API xxx
window handles 124
Window property
    example 352
Windows Desktop 29
Windows Forms Designer 39,
    42
    adding controls 48
    altering z-order 107
    Bring to Front 107
    menu, adding 76
    removing controls 75
    Send to Back 107
    setting control properties 48
Windows Forms namespace xxi,
    682
    common dialogs 687
    components 687
    controls 688–689
    enumerations 690
    event data 690
    marshal by ref objects 686
    objects 684
    types 682
WindowState property 197, 554
WindowText property 119
    example 352

WM_ERASEBKGND
    message 210
WM_MOUSEDOWN
    message 210
WM_MOUSEMOVE
    message 210
WM_MOUSEUP message 210
WM_PAINT message 210
WordWrap property 282
WorkingSet property 176
Wrappable property 413
WriteLine method 185

X

X property
    in DragEventArgs class 625
    in MouseEventArgs class 390
XML 186, 681
XmlReader class 186

Y

Y property
    in DragEventArgs class 625
    in MouseEventArgs class 390
years
    specifying 371
Yes value 230
YesNo value 226
YesNoCancel value 226

Z

z-order 18
    changing for a control 104
    example 32
    example
        (MyAlbumExplorer) 490
    modifying 555

Windows Forms controls (part 1)

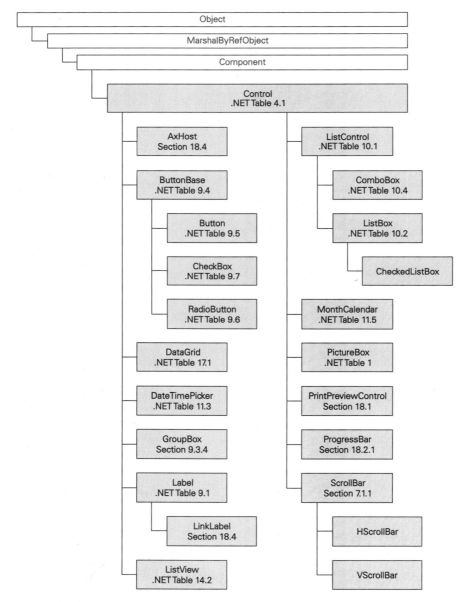

The Windows Forms Control class represents a component with a visual representation on the Windows desktop. This and the following figure show the complete set of Windows Forms classes derived from the System.Windows.Forms.Control class.